THE EXPANSION OF CHRISTIANITY

SUPPLEMENTS TO

VIGILIAE CHRISTIANAE

Formerly Philosophia Patrum

TEXTS AND STUDIES OF EARLY CHRISTIAN LIFE
AND LANGUAGE

EDITORS

J. DEN BOEFT — J. VAN OORT — W.L. PETERSEN
D.T. RUNIA — C. SCHOLTEN — J.C.M. VAN WINDEN

VOLUME LXIX

THE EXPANSION OF CHRISTIANITY

A GAZETTEER OF ITS FIRST THREE CENTURIES

BY

RODERIC L. MULLEN

BRILL
LEIDEN · BOSTON
2004

This book is printed on acid-free paper.

Library of Congress Cataloging-in-Publication Data

Mullen, Roderic L.
   The expansion of Christianity : a gazetteer of its first three centuries / Roderic L. Mullen.
      p. cm. — (Supplements to Vigiliae Christianae, ISSN 0920-623X ; v. 69)
   Includes bibliographical references and index.
   ISBN 90-04-13135-3 (alk. paper)
   1. Church history—Primitive and early church, ca. 30-600. I. Title. II. Series.

BR165.M96 2003
270.1—dc22

2003065171

ISSN   0920-623X
ISBN   90 04 13135 3

PRINTED IN THE NETHERLANDS

For Anya

CONTENTS

PART THREE

CHRISTIAN COMMUNITIES IN AFRICA BEFORE 325 C.E.

PREFACE

This work began some seven years ago as a rainy-day project born out of a fascination with data on the early spread of Christianity. From checking some of the evidence cited for the more far-flung sites, such as Volubilis, Aksum, Rewardashir, and Valarshapat, I progressed to a more systematic assembling of the material. None of the early but possible sites just named are in Europe, nor are they anywhere near the areas that many historians would consider to be the heartland of Christianity. Many people in our century consider Christianity to be a "Western" religion. Indeed, this is the case even with some Christians who have lived their entire lives in Asia. Yet it should never be forgotten that Christianity had its beginnings in Asia among the followers of a crucified Middle-Eastern Jew from Nazareth by the name of Jesus. Biblical scholars have long noted that the native language of Jesus and his followers was Aramaic, and many early Christian works survive in the closely related Syriac language. Even when they were translated into Greek within the first generation of Christianity, the ideas of early Christianity seemed to cultured individuals of classical antiquity, speaking Greek and Latin, to be the work of an Eastern cult. In the introduction, I will survey some of the factors that led this "Eastern cult" to become one of the dominant religions of the late ancient world, but I reserve the major part of my efforts for documenting the geographical spread of the new faith.

When I first started the process of documentation, I doubted whether such a project could be completed outside of the great libraries of Europe. I was more than pleasantly surprised to discover that the book could have been finished easily without leaving the United States. More than ninety percent of the works I needed were available in the libraries of my two *almae matres*, Duke University and the University of North Carolina at Chapel Hill. A score or so of works were retrieved from other libraries in the Southeastern United States, and another dozen perhaps from the Library of Congress and elsewhere. A special debt of thanks goes to Mrs. Becky Hall and her colleagues at Currituck County Library for finding a copy of Raymond Thouvenot's article on Volubilis from 1939. My relocation to the

United Kingdom to take up text-critical work in 2001 necessitated
a brief delay in the research as I became accustomed to new libraries,
particularly those at the University of Birmingham, and double-
checked references. I have also made use of the Bodleian and related
libraries at Oxford and of the British Library.

It remains for me to thank colleagues who have been helpful, perhaps without realizing it, along the way. My colleagues in the
Department of Theology at the University of Birmingham have been
more than patient with my requests for books and information, especially David Parker, David Taylor, David Thomas, and Werner
Ustorf. Carol Bebawi has read the text of the manuscript and has
graciously allowed me to use her computer to print the entire manuscript more than once. Nathan Samwini and Catherine Smith helped
to check the maps. Colleagues from elsewhere who have offered suggestions, information, insights, or resources include John Oates, Eric
Meyers, Hans Martin Schencke, Joshua Sosin, Hosam El-Tawil, Peter
van Minnen, Johannes Karavidopoulos, Klaus Wachtel, and an anonymous reader for Brill. Thanks also go to Mrs. F. E. Derksen-Janssens
for drawing the maps from my sketches. These and many others are
responsible for making this book a better one. Any remaining short-
comings and errors in the work are, of course, my own. It would
be appreciated if readers who are aware of solid evidence for
Christianity before 325 in communities not listed here would forward the appropriate references to the author.

—Birmingham, England
27 September 2003

INTRODUCTION

The title of the present work is a conscious reflection of the debt owed to Adolf Harnack's *Mission und Ausbreitung des Christentums*, whose fourth edition appeared in 1924. Some eight decades after Harnack's work, it seems worthwhile to survey again the evidence for the diffusion of Christianity in its first three centuries. The material in the present study covers much the same ground as that discussed by Harnack in the fourth part of his survey and focuses on the data available for specific sites. The effective cut-off date for the study is the Council of Nicaea in 325, the first of the great ecumenical councils. There are two main reasons for choosing this date. First, the data relating to the period before 325 are widely scattered and deserving of collection. Second, the documentation for the period after 325, when the danger of persecution had passed in the Roman world, is much more easily accessible. It seems right, then, to adopt the date of the first ecumenical council as the ending date for the period studied in this present work.

Numerous recent writers in English and other languages have discussed the background to and the factors affecting the spread of Christianity in general (see the list on page 5 below), material covered by Harnack in the first three sections of his work. Yet few recent writers have chosen to concentrate on verifying and documenting the primary sources for the gradual diffusion of Christian communities in the ancient world. Perhaps scholars of early Christianity have considered the material to be too widely scattered for any useful survey of the evidence to be made, or perhaps they have simply found the assembly of geographical data to be an uninteresting task, or have believed that the assemblage of evidence made eighty years ago could not be bettered. Several scholars have devoted their research to a single region, or even to a group of regions in the ancient world, but, so far as I know, none since Harnack have covered the ancient world in its entirety. The various atlases of Christianity often devote a few maps to the earliest period of Christianity, but the documentation for many of the sites on those maps often refers one back to Harnack or to the standard lists of signatories to early church councils.

Widely informed though he was, Harnack was not infallible. In an era when the community of scholars was smaller, when there was far less secondary material to contend with, and when bibliographic references were not necessarily expected to be as thorough as today, he could often assume that a rather general reference would lead his readers to the correct documentation. Thus one sometimes finds a site mentioned as Christian because "martyrs" were known there. We are surely entitled to ask, "which martyrs, and when?" Harnack was sometimes overly generous in his interpretation of the evidence as well; for example, few scholars working in Syriac would estimate the historical value of the *Chronicle of Arbela* to be as high as Harnack thought. While he generally avoided giving credence to sites that were uncertainly attested before 325, one finds the occasional slip in his maps, as when he marks as Christian a site called "Parembole" far to the South in upper Egypt. A study of the evidence in fact shows that the "Parembole" under consideration was almost certainly near Lake Mareotis. Likewise, Persia is not represented by a map of its own.

The above comments are not meant to detract from the value of his work overall, but rather to point out that Harnack's scholarship was foundational and not the last word on the subject of the expansion of the Christian *oikoumene*. In the eight decades since Harnack's work was published, newer critical editions of many primary sources have appeared, new inscriptions have been uncovered, new excavations have been made, and new interpretations have sometimes been given to old data. The bibliography at the end of the present work is intended to be as comprehensive as possible for primary evidence and should lead the reader to the pertinent sources for each site listed. A wealth of secondary literature could have been cited, but it has been considered more important to concentrate first of all on documentation and to let the synthesis of material be the focus of later research.

Evidence. Broadly speaking, there are three types of evidence for the early spread of Christianity: literary, inscriptional, and archaeological. Literary evidence is the most helpful for our period, for Christianity developed a literary culture in its first century. The development of a recognizably distinct material culture took at least two centuries longer. The books of the New Testament canon are of primary importance for documenting the early diffusion of the religion in

Asia and Europe, but are practically silent on Christianity in Africa. Only the *Bezae Codex*, and then only in Acts, purports to give any evidence at all for a site on the continent of Africa; *viz*, Alexandria in Egypt. Other early Christian writers down to the Fifth Century provide evidence for various sites, but Eusebius is the first, after Luke, whose systematic study of early Christian history has survived intact. One highly important group of documents is the lists of those bishops and others who attended the earliest councils. The earliest surviving such list would seem to be the *Sententiae Episcoporum numero 87*, associated with Cyprian of Carthage in the middle of the Third Century. Within Egypt, finds of early literary and documentary papyri are an important and unique source. The documentary papyri are particularly interesting as they provide a window into the daily lives of the early Christians. We may judge from them that the sobriquet "Christian" was a useful one for identification and had a variety of connotations for ordinary Egyptians. Finally, one must mention martyr accounts, some of which are early, but others of which are quite late. The martyrological and hagiographical literature has been studied extensively by numerous scholars over the decades. Some indication has generally been given in this *Gazetteer* about which accounts have been thought by scholars to contain solid information and which are of less certain value.

Inscriptional evidence plays an important role in documenting the early spread of Christianity. Yet Christian inscriptions are not known until the last decades of the Second Century when the Abercius inscription, *ca*.180, provides evidence for the provinces of Asia and Mesopotamia. To be useful for the purposes of the present work, an inscription must be datable with reasonable certainty to 325 or before or at least provide reasonably solid information for that period. In addition, the inscriptions should be fairly plainly Christian; thus whole groups of inscriptions that have one or two words of possibly Christian character such as a specific age at death, sometimes taken as a sign of Christianity, are excluded. Early Christian inscriptions are found in most provinces of the Roman Empire, but are most useful in North Africa and in the Province of Asia. The North African inscriptions often relate to the developing veneration of the local saints. For Asia, they allow us to see something of the character of everyday Christianity much as the papyri do for Egypt. Those who have published the "Christians for Christians," inscriptions of the upper Tembris valley have thus concluded that the inscriptions represent members of a reasonably well-off rural population confident about their faith. On occasion, non-Christian inscriptions, such as the *Kartir Inscription* in Persia, provide evidence for the presence of Christians. A particularly useful tool for locating clearly datable inscriptions has been *ICE*. As *SEG* and *AÉ* take some years to assemble and publish, it was only possible to survey the inscriptions in *SEG* through 1998 and *AÉ* through 1999. Such other publications since 1998 as have come to the author's attention have of course been included here when they have some bearing on possible Christian presence at a site.

Archaeological evidence for early Christianity is often problematic for reasons of dating and interpretation. The earliest known church building to have survived, at Dura Europos in Mesopotamia, is known to us only because it was buried in an attempt to defend the city in the mid-Third Century. The data from the site have been studied extensively by others, but, taking into account the relative wealth and tastes of the various congregations, it is striking how much the architectural and artistic style used by the Christians has in common with the local Jewish synagogue and the local Mithraeum. Other evidence for Christian buildings before 300 is highly uncertain, and it is only in the Fourth Century that we begin to have clear evidence of buildings designed for Christian use. In Bethlehem and elsewhere one may still see material evidence of the favor shown by the Emperor Constantine to Christian communities. For some areas, especially on the Italian peninsula and in Hispania, early Christian sarcophagi are important clues to the existence of Christian communities. Again, such large carved objects speak of increasing numbers of wealthy Christians. Early inscribed crosses, seemingly concentrated in the regions surrounding the Black Sea, are rare; one of the most notable dates to 304 and comes from Pantikapaion/Bosphorus. A much more common motif in early Christian art is the Good Shepherd, found in the church at Dura Europos, in the catacombs of Rome, and elsewhere. Small finds such as jewelry and the like are of sporadic importance and are difficult to interpret, in part because of the possibility that they may have been moved from their place of manufacture or use. Nevertheless, small finds do allow some tentative conclusions with regard to Christian presence in Dacia Traiana and Mauretania Tingitana when they are found with sufficient frequency or in a known context.

The expansion of Christianity. I have deliberately refrained from a detailed discussion of the ground covered in the first three sections of Harnack's *Mission und Ausbreitung.* The factors that allowed for or impeded the spread of Christianity generally have been discussed in great detail and with keen perception by other authors, and to enter at length into that discussion would be to diverge from the present task. Nevertheless, as a means of providing some context for the list of sites, many of the factors involved as discussed by others have been set forth in summary fashion below. In addition, attention has been drawn to sites listed in the *Gazetteer* when they seem especially illuminating on a particular point. As with each of the subsequent chapters on particular regions or provinces, this section is headed with a list of those authors whose works are used in the analysis. Further information will be found in the full bibliographic entries toward the end of the volume.

BACKGROUND TO AND FACTORS AFFECTING THE SPREAD OF CHRISTIANITY

Bibliography
De Bhaldraithe
Dodds
Fox
Goodman
Kreider
Labriolle
MacMullen
Meeks
Nock
Stark
Theissen
Wilken
Wischmeyer

The contribution of socio-political settings. As noted in the preface, the Jewish roots of Christianity must never be forgotten. Especially in the first two centuries, Jewish scriptures and social networks provided one of the primary contexts within which Christian ideas could spread. It is perhaps deceptive to focus attention on Paul in a discussion of early Christian mission activity. On the one hand, Paul is the only missionary about whom we have a substantial body of information, both from his own pen and the pens of others. On the

other hand, the very fact of Paul's singularity may skew any conclusions that are drawn from his work. Apart from Paul, there does
not seem to have been an organized Christian mission to spread the
good news of/about Jesus the Christ. Theissen, 39–55, notes the
early importance of wandering charismatic teachers to the Jesus
movement, but as far as can be determined there is no historical
evidence for an overarching or centralized organization behind their
work. It might be suggested, though, that the fact that many of
Paul's letters were preserved in the canon of the New Testament
indicates that the letters had some important and generalizable value
to Christians of the first three centuries.

If it is permissible, then, to derive any general principles from
Acts and the letters of Paul, it is worthy of note that virtually all of
Paul's work began within the Jewish congregations of various cities
and spread outward to embrace gentiles. To judge from his letters,
Paul could assume wide familiarity on the part of his readers with
concepts drawn from the Septuagint. Whether Paul regularly consulted the Hebrew Bible (later known as the "Old Testament" to
Christians) rather than the Greek translation found in the Septuagint
is open to doubt. Yet the solutions offered by Jesus to questions
related to the Hebrew Bible's treatment of issues such as fasting,
diet, and family arrangements, seem to have caused surprise, even
shock, among those first, Jewish, followers of Jesus. Those issues did
not disappear with the crucifixion of Jesus and the subsequent Easter
event. It should come as no surprise then that Paul and other early
Christians had to consider the impact of those and other issues on
their lives in the generations immediately following the ministry of
Jesus. What were tensions among Jews during the ministry of Jesus
became, over the course of the following century, tensions between
Jews and adherents of the daughter faith as Christianity slowly became
distinct from Judaism. Those tensions are evident not only in the
Gospels, Acts, and the Pauline corpus, but in other parts of the New
Testament as well.

In the Second Century, Justin Martyr's *Dialogue with Trypho* shows
that Jews were still important partners in dialogue as Christianity
tried to work out its relation to its parent faith. The strength of the
bond between the two faiths may be seen in part in Christianity's
retention of the Hebrew Bible, albeit in the Greek translation of the
Septuagint, in its life and worship. Much of the discussion in Justin's
Dialogue revolves around the interpretation of Justin's and Trypho's

common scriptural heritage. At about the same time, Marcion's attempt to reject the Jewish elements within Christianity was ultimately a failure, and Stark, 56 & 63, takes that failure as an important sign of the continuing strength of Jewish elements within Christianity. One of the arguments used by Tertullian in his *Adversus Marcionem* is that Marcion was inconsistent in rejecting some, but not all, of the Jewish elements found in Paul's writings. Exceedingly interesting with regard to Marcion's relation to Judaism is the fact that Marcionite Christians referred to their own places of worship as synagogues, as we learn from an early Fourth-Century inscription at Lebaba in Syria. Was the term "synagogue" used among Marcionites simply to mean place of assembly, or was it used in an attempt to deny the legitimacy of the word's use by Jews, or was it perhaps the reflection of a deeper link with the parent faith that even Marcionites could not entirely reject? The continuing appeal of Judaism among Christians is evident even down into the late Fourth Century, as John Chrysostom's invective against it shows.

Within the Roman world, public religious life has often been portrayed as stultified. Yet Fox, 200–258, and others have shown that traditional Greco-Roman piety continued to be vital, even with the influx of beliefs from Eastern mystery religions such as the Isis cult. Wilken, 48–68, would likewise emphasize the continuing strength of traditional Roman piety toward various deities. Stark, 201–202, on the other hand, points to a "creeping monotheism," especially among the cultured elites, accompanied by the social and political disruptions of the Third Century. It should noted that most of the systematic attempts at stamping out Christianity in the Roman Empire date from this era. Stark also notes, 129–62, that the transience and disruption of the times allowed for a certain openness to new religious influences. One might at this point illustrate the notion of religious openness by reference to the idea of "status inconsistency" as put forward by Meeks, 52–72. That is, people may be open to a new religious influence if it helps to remove status inconsistency, *e.g.* a difference between relatively high income and relatively low prestige. Fox, 319, is perhaps too simplistic in suggesting that early Christianity often dealt with power issues not by resolving differences but by attempting to sidestep them altogether. To the contrary, Labriolle, 288, shows that the pagan critic Porphyry recognized the subversive power of Jesus' parables.

From a geographic point of view, one might note also that the developed system of transportation within the Roman world aided the spread of Christianity immensely; for example, along the River Rhone and along the Danube frontier. The Rhone was an important trade route between the Mediterranean littoral and the interior of Gaul. The Danube served as a key supply line for the legions stationed along the Northern frontier of the empire. Within Hispania, it is in the Romanized province of Baetica that we find the highest concentration of Christian communities.

In the Parthian Empire religious attitudes seem to have been more relaxed. Indeed the Parthian political system generally was decentralized and depended on the cooperation of many different societal elements and princes. At the same time communication and travel were relatively easy, as we learn from the land route set forth in the *Parthian Stations* of Isidore of Charax. The *Periplus Maris Erythraei* shows that the sea routes between Roman Egypt and the coastal towns of the Parthian empire and beyond were also well known. The decentralized approach of the ruling powers proved to be the chief weakness of the empire, allowing the Sassanian Persians to gain control during the Third Century. With the rise of the Sassanians came a conscious attempt to revive distinctly Persian values and styles. The portrayal of the monarchs on the coinage changed drastically. The Persian revival was evident also in the religious sphere, *e.g.*, in the *Kartir Inscription*, set up by the chief magus of the empire to advertise his attempt to promote strict adherence to the Zoroastrian faith. Kartir thus took pride in his own efforts to eradicate Christianity and a fair number of other minority religions within the Sassanian Empire. Yet it was not until well into the Fourth Century that systematic attempts to persecute those Christians who lived within the Sassanian empire began.

Issues of class and social status. The social milieu within which Christianity spread was as complex as that of ancient Middle Eastern and Mediterranean society itself. Scholars have singled out several groups that seem to have constituted key elements within the matrix from which early Christians came. Fox, 272–77, notes the importance of Jewish communities and of traders, allowing the spread of Christianity across wide distances and across political frontiers such as the divide between the Roman and the Persian realms. These Jewish communities may well have formed a cross-section of the social strata of their day. As suggested above, one could indeed argue that the work of Paul presupposes a basic familiarity with the content and method of argument in the Septuagint on the part of his readers and hearers.

MacMullen, 38, and Fox, 301, note the importance that early Christians attached to the lower classes. Theissen, 39–53, provides a detailed study of these predominantly rural disciples, many of them wandering apostles and teachers who were truly on the fringes of acceptable society. Yet Meeks, 54–72, notes that the earliest settled Christian communities were a cross section of the population and drew people from many backgrounds. As is evident from the *Didache*, there was a mutually beneficial relationship between the settled communities and the wandering charismatic teachers. The settled communities provided sustenance, while the wandering teachers provided a word of prophecy in the name of Jesus the Christ and no doubt a challenge to the settled lifestyle as well. Fox, 281 & 288, distinguishing the idea of rural presence from the idea of rural mission, suggests that both Christians and Manichees focused their work on the towns rather than on the countryside. If the evidence relating to the upper Tembris valley in Asia is taken into account, though, it may be unwise to conclude that the countryside was largely devoid of Christians. Stark, 19, 39, & 46, is specific in pointing to the religiously discontented, the relatively deprived, and religious seekers from privileged backgrounds as the natural audience for the Christian message. Obviously, such persons could be found in rural areas as well as in cities and towns. One suspects that the surviving evidence is skewed toward urban areas simply by virtue of the greater density of population to be found there.

At all strata of the Christian movement, women were especially important as transmitters of Christian faith and practice; see MacMullen, 39, Fox, 351–74, and Stark, 95–128. This is clear from Paul's dealings with Lydia at Philippi all the way through to the Emperor Constantine's accedence to his mother's advice on the building of churches in Palestine. The martyrdom of Candida at the Persian court in Gundeshapur or Seleucia-Ctesiphon in the latter part of the Third Century suggests that Christian women could be a similarly influential (and perhaps even threatening) presence in the Persian realm as well. Among the Montanist Christians of Pepouza and elsewhere the role of women as prophets was greatly esteemed. The martyrdom of Perpetua and Felicitas at Carthage shows both the honor in which Christian women were held and the danger to which they could be exposed. The account of the martyrdom is especially

important because part of the story of her imprisonment may well
be based on Perpetua's own writings, which would be one of the
few surviving written works from the hand of an early Christian
woman. Much of the surviving work of Tertullian, also at Carthage,
is devoted to the proper role and example of Christian women.

On the basis of Matthew 8:5–15, Luke 7:1–10, and Acts 10:1–48,
one should note also the early importance of the army as one of
the groups within which Christianity spread, though military service
was not without its difficulties for practicing Christians; see De
Bhaldraithe, 166–75. The difficulties stemmed as much from the idea
that soldiers might have to participate in sacrificial offerings to the
Emperor as from the problems of a career that might involve vio-
lently shedding human blood. Meeks, 63, reminds us too of the
importance of contacts and social networks within "Caesar's household," essentially the civil service of the Roman empire.

External factors in favor of Christianity. Harnack and others have advanced
several possible factors that enhanced the spread of Christianity.
Among external factors not having to do with the content of Christian
faith itself, one might suggest that some Christian concepts, such as
the high moral precepts of Christianity and the idea of life after
death, were not out of keeping with the teachings of some pagan
philosophies such as Stoicism and Platonism; see Nock, 215–32. Some
of the similarities were in fact close enough to be turned against
Christianity, as when Celsus argued that Christianity was a deformed
and debased version of Platonism; see Labriolle, 118.

Another external factor was the universality of the Christian message across divides of gender, class, and race. Certain occupations,
such as the military professions, as noted above, did cause difficulties
if believers were not careful about how they carried out their work,
but there was nothing in the essence of any person that would have
rendered him or her unfit to be a Christian. Unlike Mithraism, for
example, which was restricted to men, Christianity was open to the
entire population. Without doubt, Christianity enhanced the status
of the women whose talents it utilized; see Dodds, 134, and Stark,
95–128. Paul's writings are quite clear on the notion that one's social
class or monetary holdings simply did not matter within earliest
Christianity. Marcion was no doubt quite surprised when the church
at Rome returned the enormous sum of money that he had given
them in hope of being allowed to teach there. Similarly, having

crossed the divide between Aramaic and Greek even before Paul began writing, and having embraced the notion that the good news of/about Jesus was meant for people of every nation and race, the Christians were not hesitant to translate their scriptures into other languages such as Syriac or Latin or Coptic for the benefit of those who did not know Greek.

Though Christianity was open to all, it was also an exclusive religion in that it demanded complete adherence. What might seem at first like a paradox, being both universalist and exclusivist at the same time, proved to be an immense asset in the spread of the new faith. While it would welcome people from any gender, class, or race, Christianity expected complete adherence from those who chose to follow the new faith. The new faith thus gained strength from the fact that the faithful were not allowed to divide their loyalties between Christianity and other religions; see MacMullen, 28, and Stark 203–204. In its straightforward universality, Christianity distinguished itself from the ambivalent attitude of its Jewish parent toward converts; see Goodman, 105. At the same time, like Judaism, it was distinct from most other religions in the Greco-Roman and Persian worlds in expecting undivided loyalty from its believers. The work of catechesis, teaching the essentials of the Christian faith, whether done by Origen at Alexandria in the Third Century or by Cyril of Jerusalem in the middle of the Fourth Century, helped to make sure that Christians had the mental resources to remain firm in their choice of faith.

Nothing pointed out the cost of Christian exclusivism more than the stories of the Christian martyrs, whose deaths were certainly an aid to impressing the seriousness of the Christian faith on outsiders and in helping to insure that "free riders," i.e. nominal Christians, were not a serious problem in Christianity before the edict of Milan in 313; see Stark, 174–76. It is an interesting fact that the rise of organized asceticism, promoting a rigorous and disciplined lifestyle for those who chose to follow it, did not get underway until after the outwardly visible dangers to Christianity had passed from the scene in the Roman world.

Among other external factors in favor of the spread of Christianity, one might also list the liberation of social relationships that it engendered and the crucial importance of new social networks which promoted a sense of belonging; see Dodds, 136–38, and Stark, 16. Stark in fact suggests that it is when a person's in-group relationships overbalance her or his out-group relationships that the individual is most likely to convert to the faith of the in-group. While his analysis might appear rather mechanistic on the surface, it does seem reasonable to suggest that the more Christian acquaintances one had, the more likely one was to be exposed to Christianity and to be open to Christian teaching. Social networks, whether of family, or neighborhood, or profession, were certainly one of the means by which Christianity spread in its first centuries, even as is true today. Within those networks, Christianity was able to provide concrete help in times of sickness and a means of sharing stories of divine power, as Wischmeyer, 132–35, notes.

Internal factors in favor of Christianity. Internal factors touching the mind and heart were also at work in the spread of Christianity. Some, such as Justin Martyr, saw Christianity in part as the satisfactory end to an intellectual quest; see MacMullen, 32–33. For him the journey was explainable in more-or-less philosophical terms. Yet one should not overlook the power of worship in the spread of any religion, and Justin is the first to give an outline of a typical service of Christian worship. In his *Apology I*, he was careful to present for the emperor a picture of what took place when Christians gathered in prayer. As we see from the Book of Acts and from the lives of individuals such as Gregory Thaumaturgus, the demonstration of divine power in miracles and healings made an impact, not only on those immediately affected, but also on those who heard about the events at second hand. Christian teaching about the real but mysterious powers of life and death also played an important role in the spread and development of the new religion; see Dodds, 134–35, MacMullen, 26–27, and Fox, 326. The numerous prayers, rituals, and spells recorded in *PGM* suggest that the major preoccupations of life, what some would call "ultimate questions," have not changed greatly in the past two millennia, though the methods of dealing with them may have. To the extent that Christians could provide a more powerful and satisfying answer to those questions than could people of other religions, they were successful in getting their message across. Indeed, the earliest written Christian document to have been collected into the New Testament, Paul's first letter to the Thessalonians, is meant to give an answer to just such a question of life and death.

A Christian stress on divine revelation, coupled with moral rigor, would have played especially well among those influenced by

Montanism in the Second and Third Centuries; see Dodds, 63–68. During the same period, the Ebionite Christians, Christians of Jewish background, were seeking to live a rigorous life in the regions of Palestine, Syria Phoenice, Syria, and Arabia. Devoted to an ascetic lifestyle perhaps out of reverence for the dietary regulations inherited from Judaism, they were later seen as heretics by such writers as Epiphanius in his *Panarion*. Rigorism during and after the persecutions was also a hallmark of the Donatist sects, for whom the possession of Christian fortitude was an important virtue.

The images of Jesus as savior, of forgiveness and regeneration from sin, and of renewal of life as set forth in the writings that came to comprise the New Testament also played a great part in attracting people to Christianity; see Nock, 209–210, Fox, 312–314, and Stark, 172. Time and again these images are lifted up by the writers of the gospels and epistles of the New Testament as crucial to an understanding of the new faith and its relation to the God whom Jesus the Christ proclaimed. Along with the notion of renewal would have come a stress on virtue, compassion, and mercy, no doubt traceable to the parables of Jesus himself; see Stark, 212.

Conversion was, and is, a complex and multi-dimensional phenomenon, involving the transformation of a person's worldview and the resocialization of the individual; see Kreider, 4–14. We should note, though, that the process did not always work in one direction, from paganism to Christianity; the most notable example of a move in the opposite direction is Peregrinus, the religious seeker whose life was satirized by Lucian. The histories of the Christian communities of Egypt and North Africa are particularly instructive regarding those who lapsed from the faith in times of persecution as well as those who were able to rejoin their local congregations. Some of the most valuable material in this regard is preserved by Optatus of Milev. At a later period, we might note the Emperor Julian, who reacted strongly against the Christianity favored by his uncle Constantine.

Factors opposing Christianity. Several factors worked against the spread of Christianity, at least within the Roman Empire. First of all, as noted above, Christians could be accused of deforming traditional religious beliefs; see Labriolle, 118. The idea that Christianity was a second-hand religion, and a counterfeit one at that, would have turned away many who thought of religion as a means of bolstering their own sense of worth and purpose. Likewise, several pagan commentators considered Christianity to be based on unthinking gullibility rather than reasoned faith; see Dodds, 116–33. The accusation occurs often enough for it to have been current in the thoughts of ordinary people as well as in the minds of cultured writers. In a similar vein, Christianity could be seen as uncultured, aloof, and as an outright attack on the state; see Labriolle, 117 & 128. The notion of Christians as aloof, contrary, and secretive, even when they might be harmless, goes back at least as far as the letters of Pliny the Younger. Porphyry could see resurrection of the body and an abundance of other Christian beliefs as worthy of ridicule; see Labriolle, 270–88. Certainly the materialist and chiliastic understanding of the next life as found in writers as late as Victorinus of Pettau, *ca.*300, would have been difficult for educated Greeks and Romans to accept. Indeed, in the works of Justin Martyr and the other apologists, we can see Christian writers trying their best to make Christianity intellectually palatable. Origen faced a problem similar in kind but different in orientation in the Third Century when, in his *Commentary on John* he tried to rescue the Gospel of John from internal Christian misrepresentation propounded by Gnostic teachers such as Heracleon, Valentinus, and Basilides.

As another factor detrimental to Christianity, one should note the heavy social stigma that would adhere to practitioners of what cultured Greeks and Romans such as Pliny and Tacitus would consider to be a "superstition;" see Wilken, 48–50. For Pliny and Tacitus, a "superstition" would have been outside the familiar religions of the day and would have been particularly attractive to those unthinkingly gullible persons mentioned in the paragraph above. Within the Greco-Roman sphere, superstition would have been regarded as dangerous because it detracted from the usual worship of those deities who were seen as essential to the state. To be considered dangerous and to be excluded from much of the daily life of one's community might have been too high a price for some who were attracted to Christianity; see Kreider, 15–17. The fact that Christians were not only ostracized, but often persecuted, would have been a serious deterrent to anyone considering the Christian way. It is not our purpose here to document the continuing strength of paganism right through until the middle of the Fourth Century or to note every instance of opposition to Christianity, yet the presence of Christian martyrs in a given place is a sure sign of public or official hostility toward the faith.

The spread of Christianity very briefly outlined. Scholars have often been puzzled by the seemingly unbelievable rate of growth in the number of Christians; see MacMullen, 32–33. Apart from Paul and the wandering teachers studied by Theissen, there does not appear to have been any early developed sense of mission that might account for such rapid growth; see Nock, 193–211. Yet Stark, 5–13, suggests that with only about one thousand adherents in *ca*.40 C.E., an average annual growth rate of just 3.42 percent would easily put Christians at just over half the population of the Roman Empire by *ca*.350. That rate of growth was not unknown among some new religious groups in the Nineteenth and Twentieth Centuries. What would seem to be very slow growth at first would build over time until the number of new converts seemed amazing. As Fox, 269, points out, Origen, in the first half of the Third Century, admitted that even in his day Christians were still only a small part of the population. It is perhaps the case, then, that the spread of Christianity can be described by some such mathematical model of growth as outlined by Stark, with the numbers becoming very large only during the course of the Third Century.

The first 150 years of Christianity, with the development of the role of bishops, seem to have been a time of internal organization; see Fox, 493–545. The letters of Ignatius of Antioch were preoccupied with making sure that ecclesiastical authority did not break down at Antioch, even as he was taken, perhaps a bit too willingly, to be martyred at Rome. Dodds, 121, and Fox, 334, suggest that it was only at about the time of Origen that Christianity became intellectually acceptable to the masses. Indeed, at that time the heirs of the Severan imperial dynasty and some of their successors may have made an attempt to incorporate Christianity, or at least the figure of Christ, into their belief system; see the material noted below with regard to Emesa and Philippopolis in Syria. In the middle of the Third Century, and again toward its end, there was serious official hostility toward Christianity when practitioners of the new religion were seen by the imperial authorities as a threat to the state; Eusebius structures much of his *Ecclesiastical History* around those times of danger to the church. The danger of persecution in fact seems to have brought out the strength of Christianity's internal coherence and dedication at a time when the rate of growth had perhaps begun to taper off; see Kreider, 22. Thus paradoxically the imperial attempts to stamp out Christianity may have provided martyrs as attractive examples of faith and have served as an important impetus to growth.

The aftermath of the various persecutions led to a different sort of difficulty as rigorists such as the Novatians and Donatists wished to deal severely with believers who had lapsed while others wished to be more generous and lenient; see Fox, 556. The problem proved to be a delicate one, with opinions very firmly held on both sides. On the one hand Christians were confronted with the command of Jesus to be forgiving, as those within the mainstream church insisted. On the other hand, from the rigorist point of view, to be overly generous would seem to devalue the sacrifice of the Christian martyrs and perhaps of Christ himself. Particularly acute were the cases involving clergy, those who had been lifted up as leaders of the church, who had lapsed under persecution. The difficulties were unresolved even more than a century later when Augustine was still having to deal with troublesome Donatists.

After the peace of the church in 313, some who desired a more disciplined life began to turn toward ascetic practices as noted above. Some of these practices, such as a limited diet and dedicated celibacy, already had a long history among some individuals in Syria and Egypt; see De Bhaldraithe, 156–61. Vegetarianism, for example, seems to have been a hallmark of the Ebionite Christians of Palestine and Syria who were concerned about the dietary regulations of their Jewish forefathers. So too, individuals such as Paul, the hermit whose life is recounted by Jerome, and Antony, whose life is reported by Athanasius, began to take up a solitary and reclusive way of life at about the year 300 C.E. It is only around 325 and thereafter that there is solid evidence of organized and collective asceticism with the likes of Pachomius of Tabennesi and the hermits who began to gather near Nitria in Egypt.

One might judge that the imperial favor shown by Constantine to Christians within the Roman empire placed Christians in the Sassanian Persian empire in a contrastingly precarious position *vis-à-vis* their rulers. Certainly Constantine's building projects in Palestine, his benefactions to the church at Rome, and his grants of immunities from various kinds of public service to the clergy were a great boon to the church. When the Persians saw the imperial favor of their Roman adversaries bestowed upon Christians, it was only natural for them to look with suspicion on Christians in Persia. Already the prominence of individual Christians, such as we find recounted in the story of Candida noted above, had provoked the jealousy of some within the Persian court. Toward the end of Constantine's reign, this suspicion broke into open hostility and persecution directed against the martyrs of Persia.

Principles of organization and presentation. As noted at the outset, the purpose of the present volume is to document the geographical expansion of Christian communities down to *ca.*325 C.E. The documentation within each section is divided into two, sometimes three, parts. First of all, for each region or province there is a brief general discussion of pertinent material. The catalogue of specific documentable sites from before 325 then follows; these will also be found recorded on the maps at the end of the volume. Finally in each section there is a list of possibly early Christian sites, often those documented in the second or third quarter of the Fourth Century. This group of possible sites is not recorded on the maps. The combined information for each entry should give readers sufficient information to make a reasoned judgment and to engage in further research and analysis on those Christian sites that are certainly or possibly documentable to before 325. On the maps at the end of the volume, a question mark before or after a place-name indicates only that the location of the place itself is uncertain, not that the presence of Christians in the named community is uncertain.

A few brief notes to the reader: when the name "Harnack" appears in the following chapters without further documentation, it refers to the 1924 German edition of Harnack's *Mission und Ausbreitung.* Except in relation to Britain, reference to "Turner" indicates C. H. Turner, *Ecclesiae occidentalis monumenta iuris antiquissima.*

No single system for the transliteration of ancient names into modern dress is likely to satisfy all readers. The various atlases and other sources used are not always consistent in their spelling of geographical names. The spelling given in Talbert has usually been followed unless there is a more localized atlas or similar source.

The more familiar personal names generally appear in their English forms; thus "Martin" rather than "Martinus." Greek personal names commonly, but not always, appear in their English or Latinized forms; so, for example; "Macarius" rather than "Makarios."

PART ONE

CHRISTIAN COMMUNITIES IN ASIA BEFORE 325 C.E.

PALESTINE

Bibliography
ABD
Abu 'l-Fath
Appold
Athanasius, *Apologia contra Arianos*
Atlas
Avi-Yonah, *Gazetteer*
Avi-Yonah, *Holy Land*
Avi-Yonah, *Jews*
Bagatti, *Church from the Circumcision*
Bagatti, *Church from the Gentiles*
Barhadbešabba
Bauckham
BHG
Clement of Alexandria, *Stromata*
pseudo-Clement, *Recognitiones*
CPG
DHGE
Ecclesiastes Rabbah
Egeria
Epiphanius, *De Mensuris et Ponderibus*
Epiphanius, *De XII Gemmis*
Epiphanius, *Panarion*
Eusebius, *Chronicle*
Eusebius, *Demonstratio*
Eusebius, *Ecclesiastical History*
Eusebius, *Martyrs of Palestine*
Eusebius, *Onomasticon*
Eusebius, *Vita Constantini*
Finegan
Freyne
Gelzer
Goranson
Hoglund & Meyers
Itinerarium Burdigalense
Jerome, *Chronicle*

Jerome, *Epistulae*
Jerome, *In Hieremiam Prophetam*
Jerome, *Onomasticon*
Jerome, *De viris inlustribus*
Jerome, *Vita S. Hilarionis*
Josephus, *Antiquities*
Josephus, *Vita*
Justin Martyr, *Apology I*
Justin Martyr, *Dialogue with Trypho*
Lehmann & Holum
Lüdemann
Mark the Deacon, *Vie de Porphyre*
Meyers & Strange
NEAEHL
OEANE
Origen, *Commentary on John*
Origen, *Contra Celsum*
Pritz
Protevangelium Jacobi
Robinson, *Bauer*
SEG
Simon
Socrates
Sozomen
Strange, Groh, & Longstaff
Talbert
Tertullian, *Adversus Iudaeos*
Thomsen
TIRJP
Vita Sancti Epiphanii
White

General

Palestine. Jesus began his ministry in Roman Palestine, chiefly in the region of Galilee, and within a clearly Jewish context. The fact that Jewish influence continued to be formative in the development of Christianity is clear not only from the books that came to make up the New Testament canon, but also from the several groups, such as the Ebionites, who continued to value the Jewish elements within Christianity. Within Roman Palestine the Ebionites were active in several sites. What is more, in the religious capital of the region,

Jeusalem itself, the names of the leaders of the Jerusalem church continued to be Jewish until at least the Bar Kochba War.

The evidence for Jerusalem does not dominate the records of the province though. In the case of Palestine, unlike other regions in which one city seems to predominate in ecclesial affairs, influence was divided between two centers, Jerusalem and Caesarea. From the Second Century until the Council of Nicaea, in fact, Caesarea was the more prominent of the two cities in ecclesiastical matters. Many of the Christian communities in Palestine were represented by their bishops at Nicaea in 325. Shortly after our period, Athanasius, *Apologia contra Arianos*, 37.1, notes the presence of bishops from Palestine at the Council of Serdica in 343 as well.

Specific Sites

Anaea. (South of Hebron.) The ascetic Apselamus from Anaea was martyred at Caesarea *ca.*308; see Eusebius, *Martyrs of Palestine*, 10.2, & *Onomasticon*, 26.9 & 26.14. Bagatti, *Church from the Circumcision*, 16. Avi-Yonah, *Gazetteer*, 28 & 105. *TIRJP*, 62. *Atlas*, 5. Talbert, map 70.

Ascalon. Ares, Promus, and Elias from Egypt were martyred there *ca.*308; see Eusebius, *Martyrs of Palestine*, 10.1. Bishop Longinus was at the Council of Nicaea; see Gelzer, lx. *TIRJP*, 68–70. *Atlas*, 5. Talbert, map 70.

Azotus/Ashdod. Acts 8:40 reports that Philip worked briefly in Azotus. Bishop Silvanus was at the Council of Nicaea; see Gelzer, lxi. *TIRJP*, 72. *Atlas*, 5. Talbert, map 70.

Bethabara. (just West of the Jordan River.) Origen, *Commentary on John*, 6.40 [204–207] (24), refers to the place. Eusebius, *Onomasticon*, 58.18, knows the location as a place where Christians came for sacred ablutions in his day. Avi-Yonah, *Gazetteer*, 36 & 112. *TIRJP*, 78–79. Talbert, map 50.

Bethlehem. Justin Martyr, *Dialogue with Trypho*, 78.5–6, mentions the tradition that Jesus was born in a cave in Bethlehem. However, Justin does not explicitly mention any contemporary Christians there. The cave tradition is also mentioned in *Protevangelium Jacobi*, 18.1 & 21.3. Tertullian, *Adversus Iudaeos*, 13.3, says that there were no Jews remaining in Bethlehem in his day. Origen, *Contra Celsum*, 1.51, indicates that in his day even "the enemies of the faith" in the surrounding area spoke of the traditional cave of Jesus' birth. By implication it would seem that there were also people *of the faith* in Bethlehem in Origen's day. Construction of the present church building there began in 326; see *NEAEHL*, 1:203–210. Jerome, *Epistulae*, 58.2, mentions the church. *TIRJP*, 83. *Atlas*, 5. Talbert, map 70.

Bethsaida. One of the towns in which Jesus worked, see Mark 6:45 & 8:22, and Luke 9:10. According to the Q tradition, Bethsaida was one of the towns over which Jesus pronounced woes; see Matt. 11:21 and Luke 10:13. The apostle Philip was a native of the town, as were perhaps Peter and Andrew as well; see John 1:44 & 12:21. Mark Appold, 229–42, writes that the several New Testament references to Bethsaida suggest intensive Christian mission activity around Bethsaida in the First Century. Through 1998 at least, no Christian inscriptions of Roman or Byzantine date have been found. *TIRJP*, 85. Talbert, map 69.

Betoaenea/Batanaea. (East of Caesarea.) Eubulus and Adrianus from Batanaea near Caesarea were martyred *ca.*310; see Eusebius, *Martyrs of Palestine*, 11.29. *Onomasticon*, 30.5 & 52.24. Avi-Yonah, *Gazetteer*, 37 & 108, calls the site Beth Anath I. *TIRJP*, 88, identifies it tentatively as Beth Yannai. Talbert, map 69.

Caesarea Maritima. Acts 8:40 reports the Philip worked there briefly. Acts 10 records Peter's initial work in Caesarea at the behest of the centurion Cornelius. At Acts 21:16, it is stated that the early disciple Mnason of Cyprus had his home in Caesarea. Origen settled at Caesarea in the mid-Third Century and on one occasion preached against Elkesites there; see Eusebius, *Ecclesiastical History*, 6.38.1.

Eusebius, *Ecclesiastical History*, 7.15.1, mentions the martyr Macrinus during the reign of Valerius. Procopius, the first martyr of the Diocletianic persecution, died at Caesarea on 7 ides June, 303; see Eusebius, *Martyrs of Palestine*, introduction & 1.1. Numerous others, including Eusebius's own teacher Pamphilus, were martyred; see *Martyrs of Palestine*, 1.5, 2.1, 7.4–7, 8.8, & 11.1–27. At 10.2, Eusebius notes that a Marcionite bishop named Asclepius died along with the rest. It is thus apparent that imperial authorities at the time made slight distinction between mainstream and heterodox Christians. Bishop Eusebius himself was at the Council of Nicaea; see Gelzer, lx, and Barhadbešabba, 6 (p. 209). Lehmann & Holum, #129–14 & #197–243, are Christian inscriptions from the Fourth/Seventh Centuries, but cannot be more closely dated. *TIRJP*, 94–96. *Atlas*, 5. Talbert, map 69.

Capernaum. The name of the town appears a dozen times in the Gospels as a place where Jesus worked. He also healed Peter's mother-in-law and many others who lived there; see Mark 1:29–34 and parallels. Capernaum is also one of the towns recorded in the Q tradition as having been the object of one of Jesus' woe pronouncements; see Matthew 11:23 & Luke 10:15.

It is apparently Egeria, *[Appendix ad Itenerarium Egeriae]*, II.V.2., *apud* Peter the Deacon (text 98, trans., 194–96) who indicates that the church at Capernaum was built on the site of Peter's house. Rabbinic traditions preserved in *Ecclesiastes Rabbah*, 1.8.4 & 7.26.3, speak of "minim" (i.e. heretics) at Capernaum. The first of these references seems clearly to refer to Jewish Christians. At the same time, Epiphanius, *Panarion*, 30.11.9–10, writing of the work of "Count Joseph," who built a church there, suggests that there had been no gentiles in the town prior to the Fourth Century.

An early Christian place of worship, popularly known as "Peter's House" has in fact been excavated at Capernaum. According to the excavators, the place of worship seems to have been originally a domestic structure that was converted to ecclesiastical use *ca.*100; see Virgilio Corbo, "Capernaum," in *ABD*, 1:866–69. See also *NEAEHL* 1:291–96. Meyers & Strange, 128–30, give provisional acceptance to the reports. White, 2:152–59, strikes a cautionary note and indicates that nothing in the archaeological evidence requires a Christian use of the structure before the Fourth Century. *TIRJP*, 97. Talbert, map 69.

Chorazin. The town appears in the Q tradition as one of the places that resisted Jesus' message and thus received one of his woes; see Matthew 11:21 and Luke 10:13. Following the line of reasoning laid out with respect to Bethsaida by Appold, 229–42, it seems that Chorazin too must have been the object of much Christian activity in the First Century for the tradition to have been remembered. Yet the town appears only in the Q tradition and is completely absent from later Christian records. Eusebius, *Onomasticon*, 174.23, records it as deserted. Nevertheless, remains of a large synagogue of late Roman date have been found; see *TIRJP*, 103. Talbert, map 69.

Cochaba. (probably the Kaukab to the North-Northwest of Sepphoris; Avi-Yonah's "Cochaba I." A less likely site would be Kokhav ha-Yarden/Belvoir. For details, see Avi Yonah, *Gazetteer*, 50 & 106, and *TIRJP*, 105. Bagatti, *Church from the Circumcision*, 21. *NEAEHL*, 1:182–86.) Julius Africanus, *apud* Eusebius, *Ecclesiastical History*, 1.7.14, apparently has this place in mind when he speaks of Christian relatives of Jesus (the "desposunoi") from Cochaba advertising their genealogy in the land. See Bauckham, 61–66, esp. 64.

Eleutheropolis. (modern Beth Gubrin.) Zebinus, a native of Eleutheropolis, was martyred *ca.*308; see Eusebius, *Martyrs of Palestine*, 9.5. The schismatic Bishop Melitius of Lykopolis in Egypt ordained several clergy at Eleutheropolis between the time of Diocletian's persecution and the Council of Nicaea; see Epiphanius, *Panarion*, 68.3.8. Bishop Maximus represented Eleutheropolis at the Council of Nicaea; see Gelzer, lxi. Avi-Yonah, *Gazetteer*, 38 & 111. *TIRJP*, 118. *Atlas*, 5. Talbert, map 70.

Gadara. (in the Decapolis.) Bishop Sabinus was at the Council of Nicaea; see Gelzer, lx. Avi-Yonah, *Gazetteer*, 58 & 109. *Atlas*, 5. Talbert, map 69.

Gaza. Philip was reported to have been on the road from Jerusalem to Gaza when he met the Ethiopian eunuch; see Acts 8:26. Paul, Timotheus, Agapius, Thecla, and Alexander were among the martyrs of 303–304; see Eusebius, *Martyrs of Palestine*; 3.1 & 3.3. Silvanus, described as "bishop of the churches around Gaza," was forced to work in the mines at Phaeno before he was beheaded; see Eusebius, *Ecclesiastical History*, 8.13.5, and *Martyrs of Palestine*, 7.3 & 13.4. A Christian woman from the same region is mentioned at *Martyrs of Palestine*, 8.8. The schismatic Bishop Miletius of Lykopolis ordained several clergy at Gaza between the time of Diocletian's persecution and the Council of Nicaea; see Epiphanius, *Panarion*, 68.3.8. Bishop Asclepas was at the Council of Nicaea; see Gelzer, lxi. Sozomen, 7.15.11, notes strong pagan resistance at Gaza and Raphia in the latter part of Fourth Century. Mark the Deacon, *Vie de Porphyre*, 19 (*BHG*, #1570), notes that even as late as the end of the Fourth Century, Gaza itself was said to have only 280 Christians. *DHGE*, 20:154–160. *TIRJP*, 129–31. *Atlas*, 5. Talbert, map 70.

Hebron. Epiphanius, *Panarion*, 40.1.3–7, says the archontic heresy was propagated by a certain hermit Peter in the village of Kephar Baricha, 3 roman miles East of Hebron. Epiphanius further notes that Peter had settled in Kefar Baricha after being deposed from the presbyterate by Bishop Aetius (presumably of Lydda) early in the Fourth Century. It seems likely then that Christians would have been active in the town of Hebron. Eusebius, *Onomasticon*, 6.8, notes the tomb of Abraham there, and at 112.18 mentions the town again. *TIRJP*, 141. Talbert, map 70.

Jamnia. (Yavneh.) A certain Paul from Jamnia was martyred at Caesarea *ca*.309–310; Eusebius, *Martyrs of Palestine*, 11.5. Bishop Macrinus was at the Council of Nicaea; see Gelzer, lx. Avi-Yonah, *Gazetteer*, 67 & 110. *TIRJP*, 149–50. *Atlas*, 5. Talbert, map 70.

Jericho. Bishop Januarius was at the Council of Nicaea; see Gelzer, lxi. *TIRJP*, 143–44. *Atlas*, 5.

Jerusalem. (Roman Aelia Capitolina.) Many of the resurrection narratives of the gospels are set in Jerusalem; see Matthew 28:1–10, Mark 16:1–8, Luke 24:1–12 & 34, and John 20:1–29. Compare I Corinthians 15:3–9.

Acts 1:12–8:1, 9:26–30, 11:1–12:25, 15:1–35, 16:4, (possibly 18:22), 19:21, 20:16, 21:15–23:22 report activities related to the church there. For Paul's perspective on his relations with the Jerusalem church, see Romans, 15:28, II Corinthians 1:15–16 & 9:1–15, and Galatians 1:13–2:14. Eusebius, *Ecclesiastical History*, 2.23.1–24, passes on Hegesippus's account of the martyrdom of James the brother of Jesus. Compare Josephus, *Antiquities*, 2.200 (2.9.1).

Eusebius, 4.5.1–4, lists the bishops down to the time of the Emperor Hadrian, *i.e.* the time of the Second Jewish War. Nearly all bear Jewish names. They are: James the brother of Jesus, Simeon, Justus, Zaccheus, Tobias, Benjamin, John, Matthias, Philip, Seneca, Justus II, Levi, Ephres, Joseph, and Judas.

Following the reign of Hadrian, there were fifteen bishops of gentile origin: Marcus, Cassian, Publius, Maximus, Julianus, Gaius, Symmachus, Gaius II, Julianus II, Kapiton, Maximus II, Antoninus, Valentius, Dochlianus, and Narcissus: see Eusebius, *Ecclesiastical History*, 5.12.1–2; Eusebius, *Chronicle*, anno Abrahae 2200; Jerome, *Chronicle*, year corresponding to 185 C.E. According to Eusebius, *Ecclesiastical History*, 5.22.1, the last of these was still serving as bishop in year ten of Emperor Commodus.

Narcissus retired to an unknown location and was followed as bishop by Dius, Germanion, and Gordius, before returning to office. Finally Narcissus was joined by Alexander, a native of Cappadocia, as his coadjutor; see Eusebius, 6.8.7–6.11.6. Small portions of Alexander's writings are preserved in Eusebius; see *CPG*, 1:1698–1701. Alexander was followed as bishop by Mazabanes, who is mentioned by Dionysius of Alexandria; see Eusebius, 6.39.2–4, 7.5.1, and 7.14.1. The next three bishops were Hymenaeus, Zabdas, and Hermo; see Eusebius, 7.14.1, and 7.32.29.

A certain Vales of Aelia was martyred at Caesarea *ca.*309–310; see Eusebius, *Martyrs of Palestine*, 11.4. The schismatic Bishop Miletius of Lykopolis ordained several clergy at Aelia between the time of Diocletian's persecution and the Council of Nicaea; see Epiphanius, *Panarion*, 68.3.8. Macarius succeeded Hermo as bishop of Jerusalem/ Aelia in 313; see Jerome, *Chronicle*, year corresponding to 313 C.E. Macarius was also at the Council of Nicaea; see Gelzer, lx. *Atlas*, 5. Robinson, *Bauer*, 84–87. Talbert, map 70.

Jethira. (in the Daroma.) Eusebius, *Onomasticon*, 88.3, 108.2, & 110.18, describes the town as completely Christian. Bagatti, *Church from the Circumcision*, 16. Avi-Yonah, *Gazetteer*, 70 & 105. *TIRJP*, 151–52. Talbert, map 70.

Joppa. Acts 9:36–43 indicates that there were at least two Christian households, those of Tabitha and of Simon the tanner, in Joppa in Peter's day. *TIRJP*, 152–53. *Atlas*, 5. Talbert, map 70.

Kapitolias. (Beth Reshah, North of Abila in the Decapolis.) Bishop Antiochus was at the Council of Nicaea; see Gelzer, lxi. Bowersock, 91. Thomsen, 77. Avi-Yonah, *Gazetteer*, 47 & 107. *Atlas*, 5. Talbert, map 69.

Kefar Baricha. (three roman miles East of Hebron.) Epiphanius, *Panarion*, 40.1.3–7, mentions the "Archontic" heresy as being prop-agated by a certain hermit there named Peter. Peter had tried several sects and had been deposed from the presbyterate by Bishop Aetius (presumably of Lydda) in the early Fourth Century before coming to Kefar Baricha. Avi-Yonah, *Gazetteer*, 46 & 111. *TIRJP*, 98. Talbert, map 70.

Kefar Sakniah. (probably classical Asochis, modern Tel Badawiya; see Strange, Groh, & Longstaff, in *IEJ* 44 (1994): 216–27 & 45 (1995): 171–87.) Jacob the "min" from Kefar Sakniah (or Kefar Soma) spoke a word of heresy in the name of Jesus during a visit to Sepphoris; *q.v.* Goranson, 341. Avi-Yonah, *Gazetteer*, 33. *TIRJP*, 70. Talbert, map 69.

Lydda/Diospolis. (modern Lod.) Acts 9:32–35 mentions "the saints living in Lydda." Bishop Aetius was at the Council of Nicaea; see

Gelzer, lxi. Avi-Yonah, *Gazetteer*, 75 & 110. *TIRJP*, 171. *Atlas*, 5. Talbert, map 70.

Maiumas/Constantia Neapolis. (modern el-Mineh, on the coast a few km West of Gaza.) Hilarion settled just South of Maiumas *ca.*306; see Jerome, *Vita S. Hilarionis*, 3, for the fact and *ODCC*, 769, for the date. Sozomen, 2.5.7 & 5.3.6, indicates that Constantine changed the name of the town to Constantia because almost its entire population had become Christian. The context of Sozomen's remark suggests that this took place shortly after the Council of Nicaea, and it would be fair to assume a substantial Christian population before that date. At 7.28.6, Sozomen mentions Zeno, who was bishop in the late Fourth Century. Eusebius, *Vita Constantini*, 4.37–38, mentions the rivalry between this place and Gaza. Avi-Yonah, *Gazetteer*, 77 & 110. *TIRJP*, 175. Talbert, map 70.

Maximianopolis/Legio. (modern Lejjun, East of Caesarea.) Bishop Paul was listed among the bishops of Palestine at the Council of Nicaea, indicating that this is the correct site for Bishop Paul rather than the Maximianopolis in Trachonitis; see Gelzer, lxi. Harnack, 649. Avi-Yonah, *Gazetteer*, 74 & 108. Avi-Yonah, *Holy Land*, 141–42. *TIRJP*, 170. *Atlas*, 5. Talbert, map 69.

Nazareth. Julius Africanus, *apud.* Eusebius, *Ecclesiastical History*, 1.7.14 & 3.30, notes that believing relatives (desposunoi) of Jesus had carefully kept the genealogy of the family there. Hegesippus, *apud.* Eusebius, *Ecclesiastical History*, 3.20.1–7, mentions descendants of Jesus' brother Jude. For the martyrdom of a native of Nazareth named Conon in the Third Century, see Musurillo, xxxii–xxxiii & 186–93, with reservations. Bauckham, 121–24. See also Meyers & Strange, 131–35, for potentially Christian artifacts. The comment in Epiphanius, *Panarion*, 30.11.9–10, that there were no gentiles in the town prior to the Fourth Century, if accurate, would not, of course, rule out the presence of Christians of Jewish background. Pritz, 11, 32–33, 54–55, & 95. Finegan, 43–62. *NEAEHL*, 3:1103–06. *OEANE*, 4:113–14. *TIRJP*, 194. Talbert, map 69.

Neapolis. (Biblical Shechem; modern Nablus.) Justin Martyr, who became a Christian later in life, was a native of Neapolis; see Jerome, *De viris inlustribus*, 23. Bishop Germanus was at the Council of Nicaea; see Gelzer, lx. The Samaritans relate an interesting tradition that Germanus allowed the Samaritan high priest Aqbon's son to be circumcised and thus gained the great respect of the Samaritan community; see Abu 'l-Fath, text, 163–64; translation, 209–11. Origen, *Contra Celsum*, 2.31, notes that the prohibition of Samaritan circumcision was in effect in his day. *TIRJP*, 194–95. *Atlas*, 5. Talbert, map 69.

Nicopolis/Emmaus. (modern Imwas.) Bishop Peter was at the Council of Nicaea; see Gelzer, lx. Avi-Yonah, *Gazetteer*, 55 & 111. *TIRJP*, 119–20. *Atlas*, 5. Talbert, map 70.

Pella. (in the Decapolis; modern Tabaqat Fahil.) At least some members of the Christian community at Jerusalem are reported to have fled there during the First Jewish War *ca*.70: see Eusebius, *Ecclesiastical History*, 3.5.3–4; Epiphanius, *Panarion*, 30.2.7–8; and Epiphanius, *De Mensuris et Ponderibus*, 15. Lüdemann, 161–73, argues that the tradition was a source of pride for the Christians at Pella. Bowersock, 91. *NEAEHL*, 3:1174–80. Avi-Yonah, *Gazetteer*, 86 & 109. *Atlas*, 5. Talbert, map 69.

Peraea. (region just East of the Jordan; see Bowersock, 92.) The gnostic sect of the "Peratikoi" mentioned by Clement of Alexandria may have been located there since Clement says they were named for their location; see *Stromata*, 7.17.108.2. Compare also Epiphanius, *Panarion*, 29.7.8 & 53.1.1. Jerome, *Epistle* 112.13, says that Ebionite Christians inhabited the regions to the East in his day. Talbert, map 71.

Scythopolis. (Beth Shean.) Ennathas, a virgin from Scythopolis, was martyred at Caesarea *ca*.308; see Eusebius, *Martyrs of Palestine*, 9.6. Bishop Patrophilus was at the Council of Nicaea; see Gelzer, lxi. Epiphanius claims that in his own day the town was predominantly Arian and that Count Joseph was the only orthodox Christian there; see *Panarion*, 30.5.5. *TIRJP*, 223–25. *Atlas*, 5. Talbert, map 69.

Sebaste/Samaria. There were apparently two bishops in the area. Bishop Gaianus of "Sebaste," and Bishop Marinus of "Sebastenus" were both at the Council of Nicaea; see Gelzer, lx. *TIRJP*, 220–21. *Atlas*, 5. Talbert, map 69.

Sepphoris / Diocaesarea. A rabbinic tradition preserved in *Tosefta, Hullin*, II.24; in *Babylonian Talmud, Abodah Zarah*, 16b–17a; and also in *Ecclesiastes Rabbah*, 1.8.3 (trans. 26–28), relates that a rabbi of the First Century conversed at Sepphoris with one of the "minim" from Kefar Sakniah (or Kefar Soma, see *Tosefta, Hullin*, II.22) who spoke a word in the name of Jesus of Nazareth. Goldstein, 39–51, indicates that this is one of the few secure early references to Jesus in rabbinic tradition. Simon, 183–84, concurs, as does Freyne, 67–73.

Epiphanius, *Panarion*, 30.11.9–10, probably exaggerating, claims that there were no gentiles at Sepphoris in the Fourth Century. Jewish ritual baths are known to be present, but archaeological evidence also shows substantial non-Jewish influence there; see Hoglund & Meyers, 42, also Freyne, 67–73. *TIRJP*, 227–28. Talbert, map 69.

Sharon region. Acts 9:35 mentions residents of the Sharon who came to believe as a result of Peter's preaching.

Terebinthus/Mamre. (just North of Hebron. Avi-Yonah, *Holy Land*, 119, 161, 163, 218. Avi-Yonah, *Gazetteer*, 99–100 & 111.) Eusebius, *Demonstratio*, 5.9.7, mentions the place as a venerated site, though he does not specify that Christians were the ones doing the venerating. Eusebius, *Vita Constantini*, 3.51–53, records Constantine's order that a church be built there to help stamp out pagan rites, indicating that Constantine had received word of the rites from his mother-in-law. Sozomen, 2.4.6–8, elaborates by stating that Constantine's mother in-law Eutropia had gone to Terebinthus to pray and that Constantine built the church there as a pure place of worship following her visit. Thus it is also possible that the place was a Christian place of prayer before 325. The church there is mentioned by the Bordeaux pilgrim; see *Itinerarium Burdigalense*, 599.3–4 (text, 20). Jerome, *In Hieremiam Prophetam*, on 31:15, (VI.18.6), mentions the location as a venerated gathering place. *TIRJP*, 177–78.

Zabulon. (either the town of Chabulon/Cabul to the Southeast of Acco, or the Biblical territory of Zebulon.) Josephus, *Vita*, 213–14, describes one of his actions in the First Jewish War as having taken place "in the land of Galilee in the district of Chabulon." Bishop Heliodorus was at the Council of Nicaea; see Gelzer, lxi. *ABD*, 1:797. Avi-Yonah, *Gazetteer*, 48 & 106. *TIRJP*, 102–103.

Possible Sites
Bethany? (modern el-Azariya, just East of Jerusalem.) Eusebius, *Onomasticon*, 58.15, notes a monument shown there in his day, which could suggest a place of Christian veneration. Jerome's revision of Eusebius, *Onomasticon*, 59.16, indicates that there was a church building there by the end of the Fourth Century. Avi-Yonah, *Gazetteer*, 37. *TIRJP*, 80.

Bethsura? (modern Beth Zur.) Eusebius, *Onomasticon*, 52.1, notes that the site of Philip's baptism of the Ethiopian eunuch was shown there in his day. Avi-Yonah, *Gazetteer*, 42. *TIRJP*, 88. Talbert, map 70.

Beth Zedek/Besanduke? (to the South-Southwest of Eleutheropolis.) Sozomen, 6.32.3, records that Epiphanius was born there. The date would be *ca*.315–320; see *EEC*. The tradition recorded in *Vita Sancti Epiphanii*, 1–2, indicates that his parents were Jewish, although Harnack, 649, thinks they were Christians. Jerome, *Epistle*, 82.8, says that Epiphanius's monastery was nearby. Avi-Yonah, *Gazetteer*, 42 & 110. *TIRJP*, 87.

Bitolium/Bethelea? (to the Northeast of Gaza.) Writing *ca*.443, Sozomen, 5.15.14–15, records that his own grandfather, along with a certain Alaphion, was one of the first Christians in Bitolium. Although Sozomen notes that Alaphion had been converted under the influence of the ascetic Hilarion, it hardly seems likely that Sozomen's own grandfather could have been converted before 325. Sozomen, 7.28.5, mentions Bishop Ajax of Bitolium in the Fourth Century. Avi-Yonah, *Gazetteer*, 43 & 110. *TIRJP*, 81–82. Compare Talbert, map 70, "Bitylion."

Capparetaea? (about 2 km East-Northeast of Antipatris.) Justin Martyr, *Apology I*, 26.4, says that this was the hometown of Menander, a disciple of Simon Magus. Is it possible that Justin, a native of Neapolis, knew of heterodox Christians there in the Second Century? Epiphanius, *Panarion*, 22.1.1–2, gives the name of the place as "χάβραι." Thomsen, 77. Harnack, 648. *TIRJP*, 100.

Gitthon/Gitta? (about 10 km Northwest of Samaria/Sebaste, and 8km Southeast of Caesarea.) Justin Martyr, *Apology I*, 26.2, identifies this as the hometown of Simon Magus. See also pseudo-Clement, *Recognitiones*, 2.7.1, and Epiphanius, *De XII Gemmis*, text, 42; trans. 137–38. Assuming that later tradition is correct in identifying Simon Magus as a Christian heretic rather than simply a magician, it might be possible to suggest that some heterodox Christians were know to be from there in the Second Century. Thomsen, 50 & 53. Harnack, 648. *TIRJP*, 135.

Raphia? (on the border with Egypt.) Sozomen, 7.15.11, notes strong pagan resistance to Christianity at Gaza and Raphia in the latter part of the Fourth Century. Harnack, 633, 640, & 645. Talbert, map 70.

Sychar/Askar? (near Neapolis.) John 4:5 reports that Jesus met the Samaritan woman there, though the town does not play any other role in the writings of the New Testament period. Eusebius, *Onomasticon*, 164.1, mentions the site. Jerome, *Onomasticon*, 165.3, says there was a church there in his day. Avi-Yonah, *Gazetteer*, 98 & 108. *TIRJP*, 238.

Thabatha? (about five roman miles South of Gaza according to Jerome, *Vita S. Hilarionis*, 2.) The Christian ascetic Hilarion was born there of pagan parents in the late Third Century. *TIRJP*, 246.

Tiberias? See Epiphanius, *Panarion*, 30.4.1–30.12.9, on the work of Count Joseph of Tiberias in the mid-Fourth Century. At 30.4.5, Epiphanius mentions an unnamed bishop of Tiberias, who was said to have baptized the Jewish patriarch Hillel II on his deathbed. At 30.12–1–9, Epiphanius affirms that Joseph was later able to build a church at Tiberias with imperial permission. Avi-Yonah, *Jews*, 166–69, doubts the existence of the unnamed bishop, and much more that he could have baptized the Jewish patriarch. *TIRJP*, 249–50. Talbert, map 69.

Wadi Haggag? (in the Sinai.) *SEG* 26 (1976): #1697, is one of several inscriptions proposed by A. Negev as possibly monotheistic or Jewish from *ca.*300. Yet further study suggests that the inscription could be pagan or Christian, and perhaps from a considerably later date; see *SEG* 27 (1976–77): #1024; *SEG* 39 (1989): #1635; and *SEG* 42 (1992): #1470. *SEG* 26 (1976): #1695 & 1696, may include the word "χάριν." *TIRJP*, 257. Talbert, maps 76 & 101.

SYRIA PHOENICE

Bibliography
AASS
AB
Atlas
Avi-Yonah, *Gazetteer*
Avi-Yonah, *Holy Land*
Bagatti. *Church from the Gentiles*
Bauckham
BHG

Canivert
Chehab, "Découvertes"
Chehab, "Une nécropole"
pseudo-Clement. *Homilies*
Delehaye, "Hagiographie Napolitaine"
DHGE
EEC
EnECh
Eusebius, *Ecclesiastical History*
Eusebius, *Martyrs of Palestine*
Eusebius, *Vita Constantini*
Gelzer
Harnack
Harnack, *Marcion*
Jidejian, *Byblos*
Jidejian, *Sidon*
Jidejian, *Tyre*
Lassus
Liber Pontificalis
Liebeschuetz
Menologium Sirletianum
Millar
OCD
ODCC
OEANE
OGIS
Scriptores historiae Augustae
SEC
Shahid
Socrates
Sourdel
Stoneman
Talbert
Tchalencko, *Villages antiques*
Theodoret, *Ecclesiastical History*
Thomsen
Trimingham
Waddington
White

General

Syria Phoenice. The Southern portion of the original Province of Syria was cleaved off in 295 to form the Province of Syria Phoenice; see Millar, 121–23. Aside from the imperial policy of "divide and rule," there is perhaps some justification for the name Syria Phoenice when it is remembered that Mark 7:26 speaks of Jesus being approached by a "Syrophoenician" woman. This survey includes all cities in the Southern portion of the original province, even those that were transferred to Arabia in 295. Acts 11:19 mentions Christian evangelists in Phoenicia. Eusebius, *Martyrs of Palestine*, 13.2, mentions that several Christians from Palestine were exiled to Lebanon during the eighth year of the Diocletianic persecutions. Eusebius, *Vita Constantini*, 3.55.2–3, reports a pagan temple at Aphaca being destroyed in the time of Constantine. Further general information may be gleaned from *DHGE*, 3:1158–1339.

Specific Sites

Alassos. (exact location unknown; see Harnack, map IV.) Bishop Thadoneus was at the Council of Nicaea; see Gelzer, lxi.

Berytus. (modern Beirut.) Eusebius, *Martyrs of Palestine*, 4.2–3, records that a certain Apphianus was martyred under Maximinus. Theodoret, *Ecclesiastical History*, 1.5.1–6, notes that Arius counted Bishop Gregorius as a potential supporter before the Council of Nicaea. In fact, Gregorius became one of the orthodox signatories at Nicaea; see Gelzer, lxi. Jerome, *Epistle*, 108.8, mentions Berytus as the starting point of Paula's journey to the Holy Land. Theodoret, *Ecclesiastical History*, 4.22.10, records that a certain Magnus burned the church in the time of Julian. For the general background, see *DHGE*, 8:1300–1340. *Atlas*, 5. Talbert, map 69.

Bosana. (Busan in the Hauran, which was part of the original Province of Syria until 295 when Auranitis/Hauran was transferred to the Province of Arabia.) The martyr Inos is mentioned in an undated inscription; see Waddington, #2249. *DHGE*, 3:1171. Trimmingham, 65. Talbert, map 69.

Byblos. (Biblical Gebel, modern Jubayl.) The virgin Aquilina was martyred there on 13 June sometime during the reign of Diocletian; see *SEC*, 13 June, and *Menologium Sirletianum*, 13 June. See also *AASS*, Junii 3, 165–66 (*BHG*, #163). Delahaye, "Hagiographie Napolitaine,"

24–25. On the pagan background, see Jidejian, *Byblos*, 119–30, and Millar, 274–79. *Atlas*, 5. Talbert, map 68.

Damascus. Acts 9:2 records that Paul went to Damascus to arrest Christians there, and Acts 9:10–22 reports that he was sheltered by those same Christians. Paul himself, in II Corinthians 11:36, tells how he escaped from the agents of Aretas at Damascus. Galatians 1:17 records his subsequent return after a sojourn in Arabia. Eusebius, *Ecclesiastical History*, 9.5.2, reports slanders against Christians at Damascus under the Emperor Maximinus. Bishop Magnus was at the Council of Nicaea; see Gelzer, lxi. *Atlas*, 5. *EnECh*, 218. Talbert, map 69.

Dionysias. (modern Suweida in the Hauran, which was part of the Province of Syria until 295 when Auranitis/Hauran was transferred to the Province of Arabia.) Bishop Severus was at the Council of Nicaea; see Gelzer, lxi. Avi-Yonah, *Gazetteer*, 52 & 105. Avi-Yonah, *Holy Land*, 172–73. *OEANE*, 5:111–14. *Atlas*, 5. Talbert, map 69.

Emesa. (modern Homs.) According to *Liber Pontificalis*, 12, "Anicetus," Pope Anicetus was a native of "Umisa" in Syria. The Emperor Elagabalus was hereditary priest of the local deity. It is reported that his cousin and successor Alexander Severus, a native of Arca Caesarea in Syria Phoenice, kept a statue of Christ among other deities, see *Scriptores historiae Augustae*, Severus Alexander, 29.2. Eusebius, *Ecclesiastical History*, 6.28.1, indicates that many members of Alexander Severus's household were Christians. In *Ecclesiastical History*, 8.13.3–4 & 9.6.1, Eusebius also records that Bishop Silvanus, who had charge of the churches around Emesa, and several others were martyred there during the Diocletianic persecutions. Bishop Anatolius of Emesa was at the Council of Nicaea; see Gelzer, lxi. *OEANE*, 3:89–90. *Atlas*, 5. Talbert, map 68.

Heliopolis/Baalbek. For the important pagan temples, see *OEANE*, 1:347–48. A martyr Lucianus is recorded in *Martyrologium Syriacum*, 6 June. According to Eusebius, *Vita Constantini*, 3.58, the Emperor provided funds for building the church there; see also Socrates, 1.18.7. Talbert, map 69.

Khoba. (a few km Southwest of Damascus; see Thomsen, 116, & Bauckham, 63–64.) Eusebius, *Onomasticon*, 172.2, distinguishes two villages of this name near Damascus. The one to the North of Damascus was mentioned in Genesis 14:15. At the other village of the same name to the Southwest of Damascus, Eusebius knew of the presence of Jewish Christians (specifically Ebionites). Possibly a duplicate of Kochaba, although Bauckham, 63–64, thinks they are distinct from each other and from the Kochaba in Palestine. Compare *Atlas*, 5, which opts for the site just North of Damascus as the Ebionite site.

Kochaba. (in Batanaea; modern Kaukab. The place name is a common one.) Epiphanius, *Panarion*, 30.2.8, knew of this place in Batanaea as a center of Ebionite Christian activity. Thomsen, 82. Harnack, 635. Avi-Yonah records the site as Cochaba II; see *Gazetteer*, 50 & 107. Possibly a duplicate of Khoba, although Bauckham, 63–65, thinks they are distinct from each other and from the Kochaba/ Cochaba in Palestine. Talbert, map 69.

Lebaba. (modern Deir-Ali, just outside Damascus.) An inscription records the presence of a Marcionite "Synagogue," see Waddington, #2558. Harnack, *Marcion*, 341–44*. White, 2:140 = *OGIS*, 608. *Atlas*, 5. Talbert, map 69.

Orthosia. (modern Khan ard-Artusi.) Mentioned as a place supposed to have been visited by Clement of Rome and in which earlier preaching had been done; see pseudo-Clement, *Homilies*, 12.1.1. The passage suggests the presence of a continuing Christian community. *Atlas*, 5. Talbert, map 68.

Palmyra. (modern Tudmur.) For a summary of the pagan background, see Stoneman, 70–76. Bishop Marinus was at the Council of Nicaea; see Gelzer lxi. *Atlas*, 5. Talbert, map 68.

Paneas. (Caesarea Philippi, modern Banyas.) According to Mark 8:27 & Matthew 16:13, Jesus and his disciples visited the place. Eusebius, *Ecclesiastical History*, 7.18.1, localizes the healing of the woman with an issue of blood at this place, although the account in Mark 5:25–34 and parallels seems to place the incident near the Sea of Galilee. Eusebius, *Ecclesiastical History*, 7.17.1, records the tradition that the Christian prayers of a certain senator Astyrius confounded a pagan sacrifice at Paneas, apparently during the time between the persecutions of Valerian and Diocletian. Bishop Philocalus was at the Council of Nicaea; see Gelzer, lxi. *Atlas*, 5. Talbert, map 69.

Ptolemais. (modern Acco.) Acts 21:7 mentions the presence of Christians there. Bishop Clarus, apparently a contemporary of Irenaeus, and others in council composed a letter on the date of Easter; see

Eusebius, *Ecclesiastical History*, 5.25.1. Bishop Aeneas was at the Council of Nicaea; see Gelzer, lxi. *Atlas*, 5. Talbert, map 69.

Sidon. Mark 7:31 records the tradition that Jesus journeyed through the region of Tyre and Sidon. Acts 27:3 reports the presence of Christians there. Eusebius, *Ecclesiastical History*, 8.13.3, records the martyrdom of the presbyter Zenobius there under Diocletian. Bishop Theodorus was as the Council of Nicaea; see Gelzer lxi. On the Mithraeum and other pagan sites there, see Jidejian, 79–93. *Atlas*, 5. Talbert, map 69.

Tripolis. (modern Tarabulus.) Eusebius, *Martyrs of Palestine*, 3.3, mentions the martyr Dionysius. Theodoret, *Ecclesiastical History*, 1.5.1–6, records that Bishop Hellanicus was an adversary of Arius before the Council of Nicaea. Indeed, Gelzer, lxi, shows that Hellanicus was one of the signatories at the Council of Nicaea. *Atlas*, 5. Tripolis, map 68.

Tyre. Mark 7:31 records the tradition that Jesus journeyed through the region of Tyre and Sidon. Acts 21:3–4 reports the existence of Christians there. Bishop Cassius, apparently a contemporary of Irenaeus, along with others in council composed a letter on the date of Easter; see Eusebius, *Ecclesiastical History*, 5.25.1. In the middle of the Third Century, Dionysius of Alexandria mentioned Bishop Marianus of Tyre and his predecessor Alexander; see Eusebius, *Ecclesiastical History*, 7.5.1. Porphyry, the learned opponent of Christianity, was probably a native of Tyre; see *OCD*, 1226–27. Eusebius also records, 7.32.2–4, that his contemporary Dorotheus, a presbyter of Antioch, was given charge of the imperial dye-works at Tyre. Jerome, *De viris inlustribus*, 83, was probably mistaken in saying that Methodius lived at Tyre for a time; see *ODCC*, 1080. Chehab, "Une nécropole," 2:157–61, and "Découvertes", 405–405, refers to a necropolis at Tyre with a sarcophagus that may date back as early as the Third Century.

Eusebius, 8.7.1–8.8.1 & 8.13.3, mentions the martyrdom of Bishop Tyrannion and several others at Tyre under Diocletian. At 9.7.3–14 he records the edict of Maximinus Daia against the Christians as published at Tyre; a copy of it survives from Arycanda in the Dioecesis of Asia. Eusebius, *Martyrs of Palestine*, 5.1, speaks of the martyr Ulpianus, and 7.1 speaks of the martyr Theodosia. At *Ecclesiastical History*, 10.1.2 & 10.4.1, Eusebius dedicates his work to Bishop Paulinus of Tyre and writes of a pangyric on the church that he (Eusebius) delivered before Paulinus. Theodoret, *Ecclesiastical History*, 1.5.2 & 1.5.5, indicates that Arius counted Paulinus as a potential supporter before the Council of Nicaea. Bishop Zenon was at the Council of Nicaea; see Gelzer, lxi. Jidejian, *Tyre*, 94–113. *Atlas*, 5. Talbert, map 69.

Possible Sites

Antarados? (modern Tartous.) According to one Greek manuscript and the Coptic tradition, the city may have been represented at the Council of Nicaea by Bishop Zenodorus; see Gelzer, lxx, 72, & 82–83. *DHGE*, 3:511–512. *Atlas*, 5. Talbert, map 68.

Arados? (modern Rouad.) The tradition reported in pseudo-Clement, *Homilies*, 12.12.1, mentions a brief visit by Peter, but does not suggest the presence of a continuing Christian community. *DHGE*, 3:1345–46. *Atlas*, 5. Talbert, map 68.

Paltos? (modern Arab el-Moulk.) Mentioned later as a place supposed to have been visited by Clement of Rome; see pseudo-Clement, *Homilies*, 13.1.3. But was there a continuing Christian community in the town? *Atlas*, 5. Talbert, map 68.

Philippopolis? (modern Shubba, in Trachonitis.) Presumably the hometown of the Emperor Philip the Arab (244–249). The question of Philip's Christian sympathies has been much discussed: see Trimingham, 58–60; Shahid, 65–93; *EEC*, 2:910; and the article "Iulius Philippus, Marcus" in *OCD*, 786. Eusebius, *Ecclesiastical History*, 6.34.1–6.39.1, records the tradition that Philip, being a Christian, had once been required to do penance before worshiping at the paschal vigil. Eusebius, 6.36.3, also reports that he had seen correspondence between Origen and Philip and also between Origen and Philip's wife. He further records that the Decianic persecution took place out of envy toward Philip. Could there have been Christians at Philip's hometown in the Third Century? Avi-Yonah, *Gazetteer*, 88 & 105. Talbert, map 69.

Thelseai? One Greek manuscript and the Coptic tradition indicate the possibility that a Bishop Ballaos represented the city at the Council of Nicaea; see Gelzer, lxx, 72, & 82–83. Talbert, map 69.

SYRIA PROPER

Bibliography
Athanasius, *De synodis*
Atlas
Baccache
Brown & Meier
Canivert
Chronicle of Seert
CIL
pseudo-Clement, *Epistula*
pseudo-Clement, *Homilies*
CPG
DACL
Downey
Dussaud
EEC
Epiphaniu, *Panarion*
Eusebius, *Chronicle*
Eusebius, *Ecclesiastical History*
Eusebius, *Vita Constantini*
Fedalto
Gelzer
Harnack, *Chronologie*
Harnack
Hilary, *De synodis*
Hippolytus, *Refutatio*
IGLS
Ignatius of Antioch
Irenaeus
Jerome, *Chronicle*
Jerome, *De viris inlustribus*
Joannou
Julian, *Epistles*
Labourt
Lassus
Le Quien
Liebeschuetz
Martyrologium Hieronymianum
Meeks & Wilken

OCD
OEANE
Peeters, "Demetrianus"
Pitra
Robinson, *Bauer*
Schoedel
SEG
Shahid
Socrates
Sozomen
Talbert
Tchalencko, *Églises*
Tchalencko, *Villages*
Theodoret, *Ecclesiastical History*
Theodoret, *Epistles*
Trimingham
Turner
Wallace-Hadrill
Wellesz
White

General

Syria. In 72/73, the cities of the region of Commagene became a federation within the province of Syria when Commagene was annexed formally to Rome; see *OCD*, 373. Two chorepiscopoi from Syria, Phaladus and Seleucus, were at the Council of Nicaea; see Gelzer, lxi. Harnack, 675, shows that pseudo-Clement, *Epistula* (compare *CPG*, 1:6), indicates the important presence of Christian women even in small communities.

Specific Sites

Antioch. (modern Antakya in Turkey.) Acts 6:5 records that one of the early deacons in Jerusalem was Nicolaus a proselyte from Antioch. In Acts 11:19–30 Luke records that the Gospel was brought to Antioch by unknown Christians from Jerusalem who had been natives of Cyprus and Cyrene. At the same place he notes that the designation "Christians" was first used at Antioch at about the time Barnabas and Paul were there. Visits to Antioch by Barnabas, Paul, and others are recorded at Acts 13:1, 14:21, 26, and 18:22. It was Barnabas and Paul who journeyed from Antioch up to Jerusalem to defend the mission to the gentiles; see Acts 15:22–35. Galatians 2:11 records Peter's altercation with Paul at Antioch over the mission to the gentiles. The church there is also mentioned at II Timothy 3:11. Eusebius, *Ecclesiastical History*, 3.36.2, counts Peter as the apostolic founder of the church at Antioch. At 3.4.6, he claims Luke as a native of the city. He lists Evodius as Peter's successor; see 3.22.1. Trimingham, 47, suggests that the name Evodius may represent the Aramean name "'Awad." Brown & Meier, 22–27, suggest that Matthew may have been written in the neighborhood of Antioch.

Eusebius, *Ecclesiastical History*, 3.36.1–3, considers Ignatius of Antioch to be the second successor of Peter at Antioch. The letters of Ignatius are justly famous and give important insights into the factionalism in the church at Antioch; see Schoedel. According to Eusebius, 4.20.1, Bishops Heron, Cornelius, Eros, and Theophilus were respectively third, fourth, fifth, and sixth in succession to the apostles. Theophilus was in place by year eight of the Emperor Marcus Aurelius (i.e. 168); see also Jerome, *De viris inlustribus*, 25. Eusebius mentions the writings of Theophilus at 4.24.1. Bishop Maximinus appears at 4.24.1 & 5.19.1. At about this time, Irenaeus, 1.24.1, mentions the gnostic Saturninus.

At *Ecclesiastical History*, 5.19.1, 5.22.1 & 6.11.5–6.13.1, Eusebius mentions the writings of Bishop Serapion, who, according to Jerome, *De viris inlustribus*, 41, was ordained bishop in year 11 of Commodus. At the same point in his work, Eusebius also discusses a letter from Dionysius of Alexandria (delivered by the hand of Clement of Alexandria when he was still a presbyter) concerning Serapion's successor Asclepiades. Asclepiades also appears at 6.21.2. Eusebius, 6.21.2 & 6.23.3, mentions Bishop Philetus as a contemporary of the Emperor Alexander Severus. According to Jerome, *De viris inlustribus*, 64, the presbyter Geminus was an important writer at about this time. At 6.23.3 & 6.29.4, Eusebius writes of Bishop Zebennus who took office as a contemporary of Emperor Gordian III.

Bishop Babylas and his death in the Decianic persecutions are mentioned at Eusebius, *Ecclesiastical History*, 6.29.4 & 6.39.4. His successor Fabian appears at 6.39.4. Fabian received letters from Dionysius of Alexandria (see 6.41.1 & 6.44.1) and from Rome (see 6.43.3) warning him about the Novatianist schism. Dionysius also mentioned Fabian's successor Demetrianus; see Eusebius, 6.46.1–4. Labourt, 19, and others following the *Chronicle of Seert*, 221, have suggested that Demetrianus may have been deported to Persia. See also Peeters, "Demetrianus," 288–314.

The council of 268 pertaining to the dispute provoked by the doctrines of Demetrianus's successor Paul of Samosata as Bishop of Antioch is discussed at Eusebius, *Ecclesiastical History*, 7.27.1–7.30.19. Paul's opponent Malchion the rhetorician appears at 7.29.2; see also Jerome, *De viris inlustribus*, 71. Eusebius, *Ecclesiastical History*, 7.30.19, mentions the Emperor Aurelian's unusual step of intervening to solve property issues related to the dispute. See also Athanasius, *De synodis*, 43.1–4, and Hilary, *De synodis*, 86. For further discussion of this and other councils, see Wallace-Hadrill, 69–76; *EnECh*, 48–49 & 618; and *ODCC*, 78.

Paul's successor Domnus is named at Eusebius, *Ecclesiastical History*, 7.30.18 & 7.32.2. An inscription from 276 is known; see *IGLS*, 2: #393. Bishops Cyril and Tyrannus followed him to the time of the Diocletianic persecutions; see 7.32.2–4 where Eusebius also speaks of the learned presbyter Dorotheus. The teacher Lucian is mentioned at Theodoret, *Ecclesiastical History*, 1.4.36, and by Jerome, *De viris inlustribus*, 77. Various martyrs, including Lucian, appear in Eusebius at 8.12–3–5 & 8.13.2. *Martyrologium Hieronymianum*, 15 kal. Mar., 13 kal. Apr., 12 kal. Sept., and 4 id. Dec., mentions martyrs. Eusebius mentions other disturbances at 9.2.1.

Theodoret, *Ecclesiastical History*, 1.2.3 & 5.40.4, mentions Bishop Vitalius. Bishop Vitalius was at the Councils of Ancyra and Neocaesarea; see Turner, 2:32, 50–53. He was followed by Bishop Philogonius; see Theodoret, *Ecclesiastical History*, 1.2.3; 1.4.62; 1.5.6; and 5.40.4, and compare *CPG* 2: 4319, for Chrysostom's sermon on the life of Philogonius. Bishop Eustathius was at the Council of Nicaea; see Gelzer, lxi, and compare Theodoret, *Ecclesiastical History*, 5.40.4. For Canon 6 of Nicaea, regarding the ranking of churches; see Joannou, 29. Harnack, 671, mentions an inscription from 331. For bibliography on the Council of Antioch in 330, see *CPG*, 4: #8535–8536.

Socrates, 6.8.1, Sozomen, 8.8.1, and Theodoret, 2.24.9, all mention the popularity of antiphonal singing at Antioch in the middle of the Fourth Century; see also Wellesz, 54–55. Socrates projects the development back to the time of Ignatius, but Theodoret indicates that it was popularized by Flavian (later Bishop of Antioch) and Diodore (later Bishop of Tarsus). Downey, 163–379. Meeks & Wilken, 13–25. For the episcopal list, see *EEC*, 1:66–70; also Eusebius, *Chronicle*; Jerome, *Chronicle*; and Harnack, *Chronologie, passim*. Robinson, *Bauer*, 87–91. Also *OEANE*, 1:144–45. *Atlas*, 5. Talbert, map 67.

Apamea. (*CIL*, 3, Suppl. #6687, links Quirinius, the legate of Syria under Augustus, with Apamea during part of his career. Compare Luke 2:2.) Hippolytus, *Refutatio*, 9.13.1–5, mentions Elkasites there. Bishop Alphaeus of Apamea was at the Council of Nicaea; see Gelzer, lxi. *Atlas*, 5. Talbert, map 68.

Arbokadama. (site unidentified. Perhaps a name like Harba Qadm is meant; see Harnack, 673.) Bishop Pegasius was at the Council of Nicaea; see Gelzer, lxi.

Areth(o)usa. Bishop Eustathius was at the Council of Nicaea; see Gelzer, lxi. A presbyter George of Arethusa is mentioned by Eusebius, *Vita Constantini*, 3.62. Compare Sozomen, 2.19.6. *Atlas*, 5. Talbert, map 68.

Balanea. Bishop Euphrateus was at the Council of Nicaea; see Gelzer, lxi. The town is also mentioned in pseudo-Clement, *Homilies*, 13.1.1–3. *Atlas*, 5. Talbert, map 68.

Beroia. (Aleppo/Halab.) Epiphanius, *Panarion*, 29.7.7, mentions a group of Nazoreans at Beroia, indicating that they had been there for a long time. Jerome, *De viris inlustribus*, 3, says that he had seen one of their gospel books there. Emperor Julian's paganizing program was cordially received there; see Julian, *Epistle*, 58, "to Libanius." See *OEANE*, 1:63–65. *Atlas*, 5. Talbert, map 67.

Cyrrhus. Bishop Siricius was at the Council of Nicaea; see Gelzer, lxi. Theodoret, *Epistle* 113, notes that there were about 800 parishes under the guidance of the Bishop of Cyrrhus in his day. In *Epistles*, 81, 82, 113, & 146, he refers to problems with Marcionite and other heretics in his diocese. Le Quien, 2:929–34. *DHGE*, 13:1186–87. *Atlas*, 5. Fedalto, 2:785. Talbert, map 67.

Doliche. (in the federation of Commagene.) Bishop Archelaeus was at the Council of Nicaea; see Gelzer, lxi. *Atlas*, 5. Talbert, map 67.

Epiphaneia. (modern Hama.) Bishop Maniceius was at the Council of Nicaea; see Gelzer, lxi. *OEANE* 2:466–68. *Atlas*, 5. Talbert, map 68.

Gabala. (on the coast.) Bishop Zoilus was at the Council of Nicaea; see Gelzer, lxi. Socrates, 6.11.2–3, notes that even in the mid-Fourth Century, Severian of Gabala spoke Greek with a heavy Syriac accent. *Atlas*, 5. Talbert, map 68.

Gabboula. (some distance East of Antioch.) Bishop Bassones was at the Council of Nicaea; see Gelzer, lxi. *Atlas*, 5. Talbert, map 67.

Germanikeia. (In the federation of Commagene; see *OCD*, 373.) Bishop Salamanus was at the Council of Nicaea; see Gelzer, lxi. Compare Theodoret, *Ecclesiastical History*, 2.25.1. *Atlas*, 5. Talbert, map 67.

Gindaros. Bishop Peter was at the Council of Nicaea; see Gelzer, lxi. *Atlas*, 5. Talbert, map 67.

Hierapolis. (Mabbug/Bambyke.) Bishop Philoxenus was at the Council of Nicaea; see Gelzer, lxi. *SEG* 32 (1982): #1456, from *ca*.321, contains the possibly Christian word "χάριν." *Atlas*, 5. Talbert, map 67.

Laodicea. (probably the one on the sea, not the one near Emesa; see Harnack, 673.) Bishops of the city are mentioned from the time of Dionysius of Alexandria onward. Dionysius corresponded with Thelymidres; see Eusebius, *Ecclesiastical History*, 6.46.2. Thelymidres's successor was Heiodorus, who took office shortly after the death of the Emperor Decius; see 7.5.1. Other bishops were Socrates, Eusebius (a native of Alexandria who came to Syria initially concerning the dispute over Paul of Samosata), Anatolius (also a native of Alexandria and remembered for his writings on the date of Easter), Stephen (the last bishop prior to the Diocletianic persecutions) and Theodotus; see 7.32.5–23. Bishop Theodotus was at the Council of Nicaea; see Gelzer, lxi. *Atlas*, 5. Talbert, map 68.

Larissa. Bishop Gerontius was at the Council of Nicaea; see Gelzer, lxi. *Atlas*, 5. Talbert, map 68.

Margarita. (location uncertain; see Harnack, 673. Talbert, map 67, records a town named "Magzartha" between Beroia and Antioch.) *Martyrologium Hieronymianum*, 2 id. Aug., lists the martyrdom of Macarius and Julianus.

Neocaesarea. (on the Euphrates, some distance downriver from Zeugma.) Theodoret, *Ecclesiastical History*, 1.7.5, mentions the location and notes the sufferings of Bishop Paul. Paul was later at the Council of Nicaea; see Gelzer, lxi. *Atlas*, 5. Talbert, map 68; compare Harnack, 631.

Perre. (Perrhe, in the federation of Commagene; see *OCD*, 373.) Bishop Johannes is listed among the bishops of Mesopotamia at Nicaea; see Gelzer, lxi. One suspects that the name of this Bishop

John of Perre has been co-opted to provide a name for the unnamed bishop from Persia mentioned in Eusebius, *Vita Constantini*, 3.7.1 & 4.43.3. The Syriac traditions thus present a Bishop "Johanan d'Beit Parsai;" see Gelzer, 102–103 & 126–27. Talbert, map 67.

Qirqbize. (just South of Imma [Yeni Shehir], and just Northeast of Qalbloze, about 40 km East of Antioch.) Remains of a church dating to the first third of the Fourth Century have been found. The church was apparently planned as an addition to a large domestic structure. See Tchalencko, *Villages*, 1:325–32, 2: plates III & XC, and also Tchalencko, *Églises*, 151–56. White, 2:135–40. Compare Talbert, map 67.

Raphaneai. (modern Rafniye.) Bishop Basianus was at the Council of Nicaea; see Gelzer, lxi. *Atlas*, 5. Talbert, map 68.

Samosata. (modern Samsat. In Commagene, on the West bank of the Euphrates, upstream from Zeugma.) Paul, the heterodox bishop of Antioch, was originally from Samosata; see Eusebius, *Ecclesiastical History*, 7.27.1. Bishop Piperius was at the Council of Nicaea; see Gelzer, lxi. Julian, *Epistle* 41, "to the citizens of Bostra," mentions persecution of heretics there under Constantius. See also *OEANE*, 4:476–77. *Atlas*, 5. Talbert, map 67.

Seleukeia (Pieria). Bishop Zenobius was at the Council of Nicaea; see Gelzer, lxi. Harnack, 670 & 672. *Atlas*, 5. Talbert, map 67.

Zeugma/Seleucia on the Euphrates. (on the West bank of the Euphrates.) Bishop Bassus was at the Council of Nicaea; see Gelzer, lxi. *SEG* 26 (1976/77): #1617, a monotheistic and possibly Christian inscription from 325, speaks of "εἷς θεὸς ὁ δύναη τὰ πάντα." *Atlas*, 5. Talbert, map 67.

Possible Sites
Alcheon? Perhaps a village near Antioch from which Paul of Samosata's opponent Malchion came; see Pitra, 3:600. Alcheon may perhaps be a corruption of Malchion's own name; see Harnack, 666 & 671. Compare Eusebius, *Ecclesiastical History*, 7.29.1–2.

Aprocavictu? (in the region of Apamea. Harnack, 673, suggests Capra-Awith near Bara, following Moritz.) One manuscript tradition of the *Martyrologium Hieronymianum* mentions martyrs there on 3 non. Sept.

Dana (North)? (near Antioch.) *IGLS*, 2: #491, records a tomb consecration inscription from 324, evidently with the name Martha, that is possibly, but not necessarily, Christian. *DACL*, 4.1:218–20, discusses remains of a church at the Dana between Antioch and Beroia (Aleppo). Dussaud, 202, 221, 239, 343, and carte X. Compare Talbert, map 67.

Joueikhat? (in the Alawite Mountains, apparently near Baetocece/ Baitokaike [modern Hosn Soleiman]. West of the Orontes and North of the Boquee.) An inscription beginning "εἷς θεὸς μόνος," now in secondary use in the wall of a church, dates to 287/88 and is certainly monotheistic, possibly Christian; see *IGLS*, 7:4042, and map at end. Dussaud, 200, and carte VIII. Compare Talbert, map 68.

ARABIA

Bibliography
ABD
Abul-Faraj al-Isbahani
Athanasius, *Apologia contra Arianos*
Atlas
Avi-Yonah, *Gazetteer*
Avi-Yonah, *Holy Land*
BHG
Bowersock
Brunnow & Domaszewski
Chronicle of Arbela
Cyril of Scythopolis
DACL
DHGE
Dihle
Epiphanius, *Panarion*
Eusebius, *Ecclesiastical History*
Eusebius, *Commentary on Isaiah*
Eusebius, *Martyrs of Palestine*
Eusebius, *Onomasticon*
Eusebius, *Vita Constantini*
Fedalto

Gabrieli
Gelzer
Harnack
Hippolytus, *Refutatio*
Horovitz
'Ibn-Ishaq
IGLS
Jerome, *Epistulae*
Martyrologium Hieronymianum
Millar
Mingana
Moffett
Mombritius
Nau, "Étude"
OEANE
Origen, *Homilies on Luke*
Parker
Philostorgius
Rufinus, *Ecclesiastical History*
Sartre
SEG
Shahid
Sozomen
Talbert
Thomsen
Trimingham

General

Arabia. Paul relates that after his conversion he went away into "Arabia" before returning to Damascus; see Galatians 1:15–17. Damascus may have been briefly under control of the Nabateans, since Paul indicates that the Nabatean King Aretas was able to garrison the city; see II Corinthians 11:32–33; see Bowersock, 67–69. Paul need not have gone far into Arabia proper in any case to get away from the region of Damascus. Trimingham, 42, suggests that there may have been some followers of Christianity in Arabia already to assist Paul.

When the Nabatean kingdom was absorbed into the Roman Empire in 106 C.E. it became the Province of Arabia. At the same time the Decapolis was dissolved and the cities of Philadelphia, Adraa, and Gerasa came under control of the new province; see Trimingham, 50, and Bowersock, 90–109, esp. 90–92. Hippolytus, *Refutatio*, 8.3, 8.11.2–12.1, 8.15.1–3, 10.17.1, 10.17.5 mentions the heretic Monoimus of Arabia without giving sufficient detail to localize him. Jerome, *Epistulae*, 33.4, indicates that Origen had the support of bishops in Arabia when Demetrius of Alexandria condemned him. Dionysius of Alexandria, *ca.*255, indicates the presence of Christians in Arabia; see Eusebius, *Ecclesiastical History*, 7.5.2. Eusebius, *Ecclesiastical History*, 8.12.1, and *Vita Constantini*, 2.53, both indicate martyrs in Arabia under Diocletian. The regions of Batanaea and Auranitis (both in the Hauran) were transferred from Syria to Arabia in 295; see Avi-Yonah, *Holy Land*, 180. Athanasius, *Apologia contra Arianos*, 37.1, notes the presence of bishops from Arabia at the Council of Serdica in 343. For possibly Christian inscriptions of later or uncertain date, see *IGLS* 21, #105 &106. There is no evidence for Christianity in the part of Western Arabia South of Aila until much later; see Trimingham, 251–67. *DHGE*, 3:1158–1339. Harnack, 697, would seem to be mistaken in suggesting the Third-Century presence of Christians in Qatar (Beit Qatraye) on the basis of *Chronicle of Arbela*, text 31, trans. 51.

Specific Sites

Adra(h)a. (modern Dar‘a.) Epiphanius, *Panarion*, 30.18.1, mentions the place to note that "Ebion" had taught in the region beyond it. Bishop Arabio of Adraha was a signatory to the letter of the Synod of Seleucia in 358; see Epiphanius, *Panarion*, 73.26.8. Harnack, 635–36. Talbert, map 69.

Aila. (Biblical Ezion-Geber; modern Aqaba. The city was transferred from Arabia to Palestina Salutaris *ca.*295; see Avi-Yonah, *Gazetteer*, 27 & 105.) S. Thomas Parker has recently discovered what may be the remains of a church dating to *ca.*300; see Parker, 182. Bishop Peter was at the Council of Nicaea; see Gelzer, lxi. For somewhat later inscriptions from Aila, see *IGLS* 21, #154–56. *Atlas*, 5. Talbert, map 76.

Beretane. (perhaps in Batanaia.) Bishop Sopatrus was at the Council of Nicaea; Gelzer, lxi. Harnack, 702.

Bostra/Bosra. (Biblical Bosor. Capital of the Nabatean kingdom.) Bishop Beryllus of Bostra was a contemporary of Origen. Because of Beryllus's suspect teachings, Origen was asked to make a presentation on Christian doctrine to the governor of Arabia; see Eusebius,

Ecclesiastical History, 6.20.2 & 6.33.1–3. Eusebius says Beryllus taught that Christ did not preexist in any form and that he did not have a divinity of his own. Eusebius also indicates that Christians in Bostra did not believe that the soul lived on after death, but that it died for a while to be raised at the general resurrection; Eusebius, *Ecclesiastical History*, 6.33.1–3 & 6.37.1. Eusebius, *Onomasticon*, 46.8. Beryllus's successor was Maximus, a contemporary of Dionysius of Alexandria; see Eusebius, *Ecclesiatical History*, 7.28.1. For the possibility that a Bishop Hippolytus intervened between the time of Beryllus and of Maximus, see Sartre, 102–103; compare Harnack 102–3.

The martyr Therenus (whom Trimingham, 65, dates to the time of Diocletian) is said to have suffered at Bostra; see Mombritius, 2:598–99 (*BHL*, 8129). Yet the tradition relating Therenus to Bostra in Arabia may be a mistake by a Latin-writing scribe for Bouthrotos in Epirus; see *BHG*, #1798z & #1799. *DHGE*, 3:1171.

Bishop Nichomachus represented Bostra at the Council of Nicaea; see Gelzer, lxi. Sartre, 99–104. See *OEANE*, 1:350–53. *Atlas*, 5. Talbert, map 69.

Esbon. (Heshbon.) Eusebius, *Onomasticon*, 84.4. Bishop Gennadius was at the Council of Nicaea; Gelzer, lxi. Avi-Yonah, *Gazetteer*, 65 & 112. *Atlas*, 5. Talbert, map 71.

Gerasa. (modern Jerash.) Epiphanius, *Panarion*, 51.30.2, mentions a shrine of the martyrs there. At *Panarion*, 73.26.8, Bishop Exersius is mentioned in the Synodal letter of the Council of Seleucia. Talbert, map 69.

Idumaea. (Considered as part of Arabia until *ca.*295, but then transferred to the new Province of Palestina Salutaris; Avi-Yonah, *Holy Land*, 12 & 125.) Origen, *Homilies on Luke*, 12.6, (trans. 50), mentions apparently Christian proselytes there. Bowersock, 141–43. Talbert, map 70.

Keriathaim. (Southwest of Madaba.) Eusebius, *Onomasticon*, 112.14–17, says the village is Christian. Avi-Yonah, *Gazetteer*, 47 & 112.

Petra. (part of the Nabatean kingdom and thus originally part of the Province of Arabia, but became part of the Province of Palestina Salutaris in 295.) Eusebius, *Commentary on Isaiah*, 42:11–12, (pp. 272–3) notes churches in the vicinity of Petra. Epiphanius, *Panarion*, 73.26.8, shows that Bishop Germanus was at the Synod of Seleucia in 359. Likewise, Epiphanius, *Panarion*, 51.22.11, knows of pagans/hellenists there. Sozomen, 7.15.11, mentions opposition to pagans under Arcadius here and at Areopolis. For some Fifth-Century inscriptions, see *IGLS*, 21: #75–76. Avi-Yonah, *Holy Land*, 125. Bowersock, 141–43. *ABD*, 4:970–73. Talbert, map 71.

Phaino. (originally part of the Province of Arabia, but apparently counted as part of Palestina Salutaris by the time of Eusebius; see Bowersock, 143.) Eusebius, *Ecclesiatical History*, 8.13.5, knows of Bishop Sylvanus of Gaza as well as Bishops Paulus and Nilus from Egypt who were martyred at the mines at Phaino. Likewise, his *Martyrs of Palestine*, 7.2, 8.1 & 13.1, mentions the martyrs there; see also the second rescension, text 49–50, trans. 46. *Atlas*, 5. Talbert, map 71.

Philadelphia. (modern Amman.) *Martyrologium Hieronymianum*, kal. Aug., mentions the martyr Sidonus. Bishop Kyrion was at the Council of Nicaea; Gelzer, lxi. *Atlas*, 5. Talbert, map 71.

Sodom. (probably near the Southern end of the Dead Sea.) Bishop Severus was at the Council of Nicaea; Gelzer, lxi. The area was originally part of the Province of Arabia but became part of Palestina Salutaris after 295; Avi-Yonah, *Holy Land*, 121 & 125.

South Arabia. Eusebius, *Ecclesiastical History*, 5.10.1–4, mentions that Pantaenus made a journey to "India," and found there Christians who used a Hebrew book of Matthew and owed their traditions to Bartholomew. Given the sometimes confusing references to "India" in ancient geographers, this reference by itself is inconclusive, and modern scholars are divided as to whether it relates to the Indian subcontinent or to South Arabia; Moffett, 37–38, and Dihle, 309, favor the subcontinent, while Harnack, 698, and Mingana, 449, favor South Arabia. Rufinus, *Ecclesiastical History*, 10.9, also associates the work of Bartholomew with "hither India, adjoining Ethiopia," that is, apparently South Arabia. Philostorgius, 3.4–5, gives an account of the journeys *ca.*356 of Theophilus "the Indian," a native of Dibus, which seems to point clearly in the direction of South Arabia. Trimingham, 291, followed by Dihle, 308, identifies Dibus with the island of Socotra (Sanskrit, *Dvipa Sukhadara*). Philostorgius, 2.6, first repeats the tradition that the residents of "inner India" claimed to have been evangelized by Bartholomew. He then relates this tradition to the later work of Theophilus, noting that "these Indians are now called Homeritae instead of their old name of Sabeans." (Mention of Sabeans points clearly to South Arabia and would seem to show that Eusebius's account is meant to connect with that area.) Dihle, 308–309, is probably right in translating "Homeritae" as "Himyarites." Philostorgius, 3.4–5, then reports that Theophilus converted the prince of the Sabeans and built three churches, one near the Roman emporium at Adane (i.e. modern Aden) before going on to "the other India." 'Ibn-Ishaq, text 972, trans. 653, also knows the tradition linking Bartholomew with Arabia. The history attributed to John of Ephesus records a later tradition that the Himyarites were converted by a slave girl *ca*.305, but this seems to be dependent on a statement of Socrates with respect to the church in Caucasian Iberia; see Nau, "Étude," 55. Trimingham, 293, correctly says that the accounts of Theophilus show no early evidence of work among indigenous Christians in South Arabia. Instead it appears likely that the work of Theophilus concentrated on providing for the needs of Christian traders. *DHGE*, 3:1233–1253.

Zoara. (South of the Dead Sea.) Eusebius, *Onomasticon*, 42.1. Eusebius, *Martyrs of Palestine*, second rescension, text 49–50, trans. 46, mentions that prisoners from Phaino stopped at Zoara. Bowersock, 90. The town was part of the Province of Arabia, but transferred to Palestina Salutaris after 295; see Avi-Yonah, *Gazetteer*, 104–105, and *Holy Land*, 121 & 125. Talbert, map 71.

Possible Sites

Areopolis? (Ariel Rabba/er-Rabbah/Rabbath Moab, East of the Dead Sea.) Sozomen, 7.15.11, refers to opposition to pagans at Areopolis and at Petra under the Emperor Arcadius, so it is just possible that Areopolis had been traditionally linked with Petra even before that date. Eusebius, *Onomasticon*, 124.15–17. Thomsen, 25. Harnack, 702. *DHGE*, 3:1647. Avi-Yonah, *Holy Land*, 116–17. Avi-Yonah, *Gazetteer*, 90 & 105. Fedalto, 2:1041. Talbert, map 71.

Bacatha? (Southwest of Philadelphia; see Avi-Yonah, *Gazetteer*, 34 & 112.) Epiphanius, *Panarion*, 58.1.2, mentions "Valesian" heretics of unknown date. Cyril of Scythopolis, *Bios to hosiou patros hemon Saba*, 73, mentions Bishop Barachos of Bacatha as a contemporary of Sabas in the Fifth Century.

Central Arabia? Abu al-Faraj al-Isbahani, 2:95–96, contains a genealogy of the pre-Islamic Arabic poet Adi ibn Zayd ibn Hammad ibn Zayd ibn Ayyub ibn Mahruf of the clan Imru al-Qays and tribe of Tammim from the region of Yamama. The genealogy of the clan as a whole would go back to the early years of the Fourth Century. In the account of the family, it is explicitly stated that Adi's great-great-grandfather, Ayyub ibn Mahruf, as well as Ayyub's father, mother, and family, were Christian. According to the account by Abu al-Faraj al-Isbahani, Ayyub fled from the Yamama region of central Arabia to Hira to escape from a feud, presumably near the end of the Fifth Century. Since the full genealogy of Adi's family named in the account would go back to the early years of the Fourth Century, Trimingham, 278–79, suggests that the account indicates the presence of Christians in Central Arabia by the middle of the Fourth Century. See also *DHGE*, 3:1222, 1228–32; Horovitz, 31–35; and Gabrieli, 1:196.

Madaba? *SEG* 39 (1989): #1663, is an inscription, much restored, from *ca.*219 connected to the dedication of a city gate and possibly mentioning bishops and presbyters. Yet the key words $\pi\rho\epsilon\sigma\beta(\epsilon\upsilon\tau\upsilon\hat{\upsilon})$ and $[\dot{\epsilon}\pi\iota\sigma]\kappa\upsilon\pi\epsilon\upsilon\acute{o}\nu\tau\omega\nu$ should perhaps be taken simply as references to local "elders" and "overseers." Talbert, map 71.

Migdala? (modern Medjdel esch-schor in Nabataea.) A possibly Christian inscription of the mid-Fourth Century with the words "$\chi\acute{a}\rho\iota\tau\alpha\varsigma$" and "$\theta\rho\acute{\epsilon}\pi\tau\alpha$" is listed in Waddington, #2031. Peek, #1974, would date it somewhat earlier.

Umm el-Jimal? (Southwest of Bostra.) Remains of a house and church dating to the Fourth Century have been found; see Lassus, 24–28; and White, 2:141–52. Talbert, map 69.

Zanaatha/Zadocatha? (modern Ain-Sadaka, 18 Roman miles South-Southeast of Petra.) A certain Maron of Zamathon appears only in one Greek list and in the Arabic list of those present at the Council of Nicaea; see Gelzer, 74 & 155. Harnack, 702, apparently identifies Zamathon with Zanaatha and, following Thomsen, 63, identifies the site as being near Petra. For a description of the site, see Brunnow & Domaszewski, 465–69. Compare Avi-Yonah, *Holy Land*, 121 & 125; also Bowersock, 141–43. Talbert, map 71.

(ROMAN) MESOPOTAMIA

Bibliography
AASS
Ammianus Marcellinus
Assemani, *Acta*
Atlas
Bardaisan
Barhadbešabba
Bauer
Baum & Winkler
Bedjan
BHL
BHO
Bratke
Burkitt, *Euphemia*
Buzandaran Patmut'iwnk', trans. Garsoian
Chabot
Chaumont
Chronicle of Arbela
Chronicle of Edessa
Chronicle of Seert
Cureton, *Ancient*
Cureton, *Spicilegium*
DHGE
Drijvers, "Facts and Problems"
Drijvers, "Jews and Christians"
Egeria
Elias of Nisibis
EnECh
Erbetta
Eusebius, *Ecclesiastical History*
Falla Castelfranchi
Fiey, *Jalons*
Fiey, *Nisibe*
Fuller & Fuller
Garsoian
Gelzer
Harnack
Hegemonius

Hoffmann
Howard, *Teaching of Addai*
Jerome, *De viris inlustribus*
Jerome, *Vita Malchi*
Julius Africanus
Kraeling
Labourt
LaGrange
Le Quien
Lipsius & Bonnet
Martyrologium Syriacum
Moffett
Nöldeke
OCD
Ortiz de Urbina
Photius, *Bibliotheca*
PS
Robinson, *Bauer*
Ross. *Roman Edessa*
Segal
Snyder
Talbert
Thee
Wallace-Hadrill
White

General

Mesopotamia. Dionysius of Alexandria knew of Christians in Mesopotamia; see Eusebius, *Ecclesiastical History*, 7.2.1. See also Fiey, *Jalons*, 46. For deportations by the Persian Emperor Shapor I in the Third Century, see entry for Parthia below.

Harnack, 687–89, would seem to be mistaken in listing Arzon, Gordyene, and Sophene on the basis of *Chronicle of Arbela*, 9 (text 31, trans. 51). Arzon does not certainly appear as a locale with a Christian presence until the Synod of Isaac in 410; see Chabot, text 34, trans. 272. Labourt, 13 & 50.

Dubious traditions of a martyr Febronia at "Sibapolis" during the time of Diocletian are found in Latin texts; see *AASS*, Junii, 7.13, nn.1–2 (compare *BHL*, #2843–44).

Specific Sites

Amida. (modern Diyarbakir. In the part of Armenian territory ceded
to Rome in 298 C.E. See *Buzandaran Patmut'iwnk'*, trans. Garsoian,
440, and map at end.) An offshoot of the Abgar legend, *Acta Thaddai*,
5–6, has Thaddeus preaching in a synagogue there and winning converts; see Lipsius & Bonnet 1:275–78; also Erbetta, 2:577–78. Ebedjesus
says that Bishop Simeon was at the Council of Nicaea; see Gelzer,
126–27. Compare Barhadbešabba, 6 (p. 209). Talbert, map 89.

Dura Europos. Excavations have revealed several frescoes and a
baptistry in the remains of a Christian church destroyed in defen-
sive measures against the Persian invasion of 256 C.E. This remains
the earliest clearly identifiable church building anywhere; see Kraeling,
1–233, plates I–XLVI, and plans I–VIII. *Atlas*, 4. White, 2:123–31.
Talbert, map 91.

Edessa. (modern Urfa. in the region of Osrhoene.) Bardaisan, who
considered himself to be a Christian but was counted as a heretic
by his enemies, was active there *ca.*200 C.E. Julius Africanus, *Kestoi*, 1.20,
records that Bardaisan was known as a skilled archer at the court
of King Abgar; see also Thee, 147–48. Bardaisan, 58–59, reports
that Abgar himself "came to believe," though he does not specify
the substance of that belief. Manicheans were also active there.

Eusebius, *Ecclesiastical History*, 5.23.4, makes mention of the churches
of Osrhoene being consulted at the time of the Easter controversy
just before 200 C.E. Little factual information can be gleaned from
the *Doctrina Addai*, but it is certain that Palut was leader of the orthodox party just before 200 C.E.; see Bauer, 17, and Howard, 94–107.
Bauer, 13–14, argued that the reference in the *Chronicle of Edessa*,
1(8), (text 145–47, trans., 86), to a church being destroyed by a flood
in 201 C.E. was an anachronistic interpolation, but White, 1:118
&2:102–3, believes that the building in question may have been a
renovated *domus ecclesia* type of church.

Two further bishops, Abeshelama and Barsamya, are known to have
followed Palut in the Third Century, although it is uncertain how
closely the latter should be tied to the Decianic persecutions; see
Martyrdom of Barsamya in Cureton, *Ancient*, text 71–72, trans. 71; *Chronicle
of Edessa*, 52; Bedjan, 1:95–130; and Bauer, 17. Shmona and Guria
were martyred *ca.*309; see the *Martyrdom of Shmona and Guria* in Burkitt,
text 3–25, trans. 30 & 90–110, also *Martyrologium Syriacum*, 15 Tishri.
Habib the deacon was martyred *ca.*310: see *Martyrdom of Habib the*

Deacon in Cureton, *Ancient Syriac*, text 72–76, trans. 72–85. See also Bedjan, 1:144–60; Burkitt, text 26–43, trans. 30 & 112–28; and *Martyrologium Syriacum*, 2 Ilul.

According to the *Chronicle of Edessa*, Kune was the Bishop in 313 when a new church was started and completed under his successor Bishop Sa'ad; see *Chronicle of Edessa*, 12 (text, 147–48; trans., 93), and White, 2:102–3. Bishop Aethilas (or Abselama) was at the Council of Nicaea in 325; see Gelzer, lxi, and Barhadbešabba, 6 (p. 209). Le Quien, 2:955–56. Segal, 62–109. Robinson, *Bauer*, 45–59. Ross, 104–109 & 127–38. Baum & Winkler, 8. *Atlas*, 5. *EnECh*, 263. Talbert, map 67.

Euphrates River and beyond. The Christian inscription of the traveler Abercius, *ca.*170–200, affirms that he found Christians in the region beyond the Euphrates; see Snyder, 139–40. Talbert, map 91.

Macedonopolis/Birtha. (just East of Zeugma. Birtha was the Semitic name according to the Syriac lists of participants at the Council of Nicaea; see Gelzer, 102–103 & 126–27.) Bishop Mareas represented the city at the Council of Nicaea. Gelzer, lxi. *Atlas*, 5. Talbert, map 67.

Nisibis. According to his memorial inscription *ca.*170–200, the Christian pilgrim Abercius found brethren at Nisibis; see Snyder, 139–40. *Martyrologium Syriacum* records the martyrdom of Hermas the soldier and his companions on the Friday after Easter and of unnamed martyrs on 21 Iyar. For Hermas, see also *Martyrdom of Shmona and Guria*, 5, in Burkitt, text 4, trans. 92. Bishop Babu was perhaps in place by 300/301; see Elias of Nisibis, text, 1:97; trans 1:47. The Christian ascetic Malchus was a native of the city; see Jerome, *Vita Malchi*, 3. Bishop Jacob, who may have been in place by 308, was certainly at the Council of Nicaea; see Elias of Nisibis, text, 1:98, trans., 1:47; Barhadbešabba, 6 (p. 209); and Gelzer, lxi. For a reference to Jacob's tomb, see Falla Castelfranchi, 1267–79. By 410, Nisibis was considered a part of the Church of the East; see Chabot, 285. Fiey, *Nisibe*, 19–26. Baum & Winkler, 8. *Atlas*, 5. Talbert, map 89.

Resaina. Bishop Antiochus was at the Council of Nicaea; see Gelzer, lxi. *Atlas*, 5. Talbert, map 89.

Possible Sites

Batnae/Batana? Egeria notes many martyria; see Egeria, 19.1 (text, 59, trans., 115–117). Talbert, map 67.

Beth Zabdai/Bezabde? (modern Hendek and environs.) Bishop Heliodorus and others were deported from there by Shapor II in 362; see *BHO*, #375; Assemani, *Acta*, 1:134–39; Bedjan, 2:316–24; and LaGrange, 104–108. For fighting in the region, see Ammianus Marcellinus, 20.7.1–17. Fiey, *Nisibe*, 163–73. Harnack, 685–87, apparently relying on the rather uncertain evidence of the *Chronicle of Arbela*, places Christians there a century earlier. Talbert, map 89.

Circesium? (modern al-Busaira; to the Northwest of Dura Europos.) Barhadbešabba, 6 (p. 209), mentions Bishop Nonnus of Circesium at the Council of Nicaea. His name is otherwise unattested. Talbert, map 91.

Goustra? (probably in Northeastern Mesopotamia; see Nöldeke, 32, and Bratke, 264–65.) Acccording to Barhadbešabba, 6 (p. 209), Bishop John was at the Council of Nicaea. Harnack, 691. Wallace-Hadrill, 166.

Haran? (classical Carrhae.) Hegemonius, *Acta Archelai*, 1.1, reports a tradition about Archelaus disputing with Mani in "Carcharis civitate Mesopotamiae." Fiey, *Assyrie*, 3:152–55, argues that the tradition should be assigned to Carrhae in Mesopotamia rather than to Kashkar in Assyria. Compare Photius, *Bibliotheca*, 85. Contrast, Jerome, *De viris inlustribus*, 72. Egeria, 20.1–5 (text, 62–63; trans., 117–21), notes many martyria, especially that of the monk and martyr Helpidus, though she says the town was largely pagan. *Atlas*, 5. Talbert, maps 67 & 89.

Maipherqat? (just Northeast of Amida.) Some Syriac manuscripts anachronistically place Bishop Marutha at the Council of Nicaea, see Gelzer, 102–103 & 126–127. See also Barhadbešabba, 6 (p. 209). Marutha lived a generation or two after the Council of Nicaea; see *EnECh*, 537. Wallace-Hadrill, 166. Compare Talbert, map 89.

Singara? (West of Mosul, near modern Beled.) Several captives, apparently with Christians among them, were taken *ca.*252 or 256 by Shapor I to Karka d-Leidan; see *Chronicle of Seert*, 221–22. According to Ebedjesus, Bishop Georgius of Singara was at the Council of Nicaea; see Gelzer, 126–27. The same information is found in Barhadbešabba, 6 (p. 209).

Traditions are also recorded of a martyr Abd el-Masih; see *BHO*, #3, and Bedjan, 1:173–201. According to later legends, a certain General Mu'ain of Singara was martyred at the same time in the

Fourth Century; see Wright, *Catalogue*, 3:1134–35, #960.67; Hoffmann, 28–33; *BHO*, #783; and Ortiz de Urbina, 198. Fiey, *Nisibe*, 15 & 50. Talbert, map 89.

Thannuris? (probably modern Tell Tuneinir, West of Singara.) Excavations at Tell Tuneinir have revealed evidence of an early Christian presence, perhaps dating as early as the Fourth Century; see Fuller & Fuller, 70. Talbert, map 89.

Assyria and Babylonia

Bibliography
AASS
Aphrahat
Assemani, *Acta*
Assemani, *Bibliotheca*
Atlas
Baarda
Bardaisan
Barhadbešabba
Bar-Hebraeus
Bauer
Baum & Winkler
Bedjan
BHO
Braun, *Ausgewählte*
Braun, "Briefwechsel"
Brightman
Brock, "A Martyr"
Chabot
Chaumont
Chronicle of Arbela
Chronicle of Seert
DHGE
EEC
Elias of Nisibis
Eusebius, *Praeparatio Evangelica*
Fedalto

Fiey, *Assyrie*
Fiey, "Diptyques"
Fiey, *Jalons*
Fiey, *Pour*
Fiey, "Vers"
Gelzer
Harnack
Hegemonius
Higgins
Hoffmann
Labourt
LaGrange
Martyrologium Syriacum
Moffett
Neusner
Ortiz de Urbina
Photius, *Bibliotheca*
Quaesten
Talbert
Wallace-Hadrill
Wiessner
Wigram

General

Assyria and Babylonia. During our period, this lower part of Meso-potamia belonged usually to the Parthian and Sassanian Empires of Persia. The region down to the Persian Gulf, known as the province of Assyria, was held briefly by the Romans during the reign of Trajan but was given back to the Parthian Empire upon his death. For relations between the Parthian Emperors and their Jewish subjects generally, see Neusner, 44–121. For the deportations by the Sassanian Persian Emperor Shapor I in the Third Century, see under Parthia below.

Specific Sites

Arbela. (modern Irbil. In the country of Adiabene [Syriac name "Hadyab,"].) The highly suspect *Chronicle of Arbela* claims that Christianity reached the area by 104 C.E.; see text 2–3, trans. 19–20. Yet until the Fourth Century, Christianity in Arbela is not documented by any other texts, including the *Nestorian Diptychs* published by Brightman and Fiey; see Brightman, 277, and Fiey, "Diptyques," 385. Fiey,

Assyrie, 1:41, notes the otherwise unattested Bishop Paqida from the *Chronicle*. For a positive judgment on the reliability of unconfirmed evidence from the *Chronicle of Arbela*, see Harnack, 683–89, and for a strongly negative assessment, see *EnECh*, 11 & 67.

Barhadbešabba, 6 (p. 209), claims that Bishop Addai of Arbela was at the Council of Nicaea. It is fairly certain that Bishop Yohanan of Arbela was martyred in 343 (see *BHO*, #500, and Bedjan 4:128–30), and that Bishop Abraham was martyred in 345 (see *BHO*, #12, and Bedjan 4:130–31). See also *Martyrologium Syriacum*.

Several other martyrs are noted in the region as well; see Fiey, *Jalons*, 89. For example, the youth Vahunam of Hadyab/Gazab was martyred in the Fourth Century: see Assemani, *Acta*, 1:99–100; Bedjan, 2:286–89; *AASS*, Novembris, 4:427–28. LaGrange, 82. *BHO*, #807. The large number of martyrs in mid-century makes it clear that a developed Christian community existed at Arbela by the early Fourth Century. Labourt, 73. *Atlas*, 5. Fedalto, 2:939–40. Talbert, map 89.

Beth Niqator. (probably to be equated with Awana on the Tigris about 75 km North of Seleucia-Ctesiphon.) Bishop Shapur was martyred there *ca*.340. See *BHO*, #1042. Assemani, *Acta*, 1:230. Bedjan, 2:39–51. *AASS*, Novembris, 4:429–32. LaGrange, 31–34. Braun, *Ausgewählte*, 1–4. Fiey, *Assyrie*, plate 2. Fiey, *Pour*, 65 & 139–40. Talbert, map 91.

Hatra. (just inside the borders of the Parthian Empire; *OEANE*, 2:484–85.) Bardaisan, 60–61, mentions Christians there. Quoted also in Eusebius, *Praeparatio Evangelica*, 6.10.46. For the civic history of the place, see *OCD*, 669. Talbert, map 91.

Karka d-Beth Seloq. (modern Kirkuk, ancient metropolis of the region of Beth Garmai.) The somewhat confused account of Christian origins in the *History of Karka d-Beth Seloq* (Bedjan, 2:512–15) projects the later ecclesiastical structure at Karka back into the Second Century and suggests that the first Christian in the town was a certain Joseph. According to the same source, the first Bishop was the legendary Tuqritos, who had fled from presecutions under Hadrian. An undefined herersy is said to have disturbed the church *ca*.261. Fiey, "Vers," 201, sees no reason to doubt the existence of Bishop Abdisho, mentioned in the *History* prior to the martyrs of the Fourth Century; see Bedjan, 2:513, and Hoffmann, 46.

The Bishop Aqballaha who, according to the apocryphal *Letters of*

Papa, #5 (see Braun, "Breifwechsel," 167–69), is said to have been one of those who opposed Papa at the Council of Seleucia in 325, may have been from Karka; compare Labourt, 21, and Chaumont, 140–41. Aqballaha seems to have been a popular name at Karka, but if this bishop really existed, he must be distinguished from the Aqballaha who was at the Synod of Mar Isaac in 410.

According to the early *S.S. Martyres Karka d'Beth Seloq*, bishops Yohannan, Shapor, and Isaac were martyred under King Shapor II: see Assemani, *Acta*, 1:99–101; Bedjan 2:286–89; and also *AASS*, Novembris, 4:427. Yohannan and Shapor also appear in the *Martyrologium Syriacum* and in Sozomen, 2.13.7; see also Labourt, 66.

Fiey, "Vers," 209–11, suggests that the Bishop Aqballaha who is mentioned in the *History* in the Fourth Century may not have been from the Fourth Century at all but was in fact the same person who attended the Synod of Mar Isaac in 410; compare Chabot, text 35, trans. 274. *Atlas*, 5. Talbert, map 91.

Karka d-Maishan. (just above the Persian Gulf, a few km East-Southeast of modern Basra.) According to the *Chronicle of Seert*, 236, Bishop Yohannan was one of those opposing Papa at the Council of Seleucia *ca.*325. Fiey, *Assyrie*, 3:273 & plate 2. Compare Talbert, map 93.

Kashkar. (across the river from modern Wasit.) *Chronicle of Seert*, 236, says Bishop Abdisho was one of those who opposed Papa bar Aggai *ca.*325. Bishop Paul was martyred in the 340s: see Assemani, *Acta*, 1:151; Sozomen, 2.13.7; and *Martyrologium Syriacum*. Hegemonius, 1.1, mentions a tradition of a disputation between bishop Archelaus and Mani that took place at "Carcharis civitate Mesopotamiae." Quaesten, 3:357, locates "Carcharis" at Kashcar. On the other hand, Fiey, *Assyrie*, 3:151–55, argues that traditions concerning Archelaus relate to Haran/Carrhae in Mesopotamia rather than to Kashcar. *Atlas*, 5. Talbert, maps 92 & 93.

Perat d-Maishan. (near modern Basra, see Fiey, *Assyrie*, 3:263–66 & plate 2. Talbert, map 93, suggests modern Maglub.) Bishop David was mentioned as one of those opposed to Papa at the Council of Seleucia *ca.*325; see *Chronicle of Seert*, 236. Indeed, Bar-Hebraeus, 10 (3:28), says that David had ordained Papa; see also Assemani, *Bibliotheca*, 2:397, and Fiey, 3:266. *Martyrologium Syriacum* lists martyr bishops Bulida, Bar-Abda, and Yohannan. For Bulida's martyrdom *ca.*340, see also Bedjan, 2:131, Braun, *Ausgewählte*, 5 & 21, and Sozomen, 2.13.7. LaBourt, 66. *Atlas*, 5. Fedalto, 2:936. *DHGE*, 6:1279–81.

Seleucia-Ctesiphon. (near modern Baghdad.) Shahlupa may have been the first bishop, but there is also the possibility that Demetrius of Antioch was carried there as a captive by Shapur I; see Labourt, 19–20. Chabot, text 47, trans. 291, does suggest at least two bishops prior to Papa. For a discussion of the possible names, see Chaumont, 42–47, quoting Elias of Nisibis, *Opus Chronologicum*, text 62*:44–45, trans. 63*:27.

The martyrdom of Candida under Vahram *ca.*276–93 may have taken place at Seleucia; see Brock, "A Martyr," 167–81.

The *Nestorian Diptychs* for Seleucia-Ctesiphon begin with Bishop Papa bar Aggai; see Brightman, 276, and Fiey, "Diptyques," 384. Yet Papa ran into serious opposition at the Council of Seleucia *ca.*325. For the account favorable to Papa, see Chabot, text 46–48, trans. 289–92. For the viewpoint of his opposition, see the *Acts of Miles* in Assemani, *Acta*, 1:72–73, and Bedjan, 2:266–68; trans. in Lagrange, 67–68. For the date of the Council, see Chaumont, 145–47, and *EEC*, 2:859–60. Higgins, 99, would date it some ten years earlier. For further comment on matters related to this council, see Baum & Winkler, 9–10.

LaBourt, 24–28, suggests that Aphrahat, *Demonstrationes* 10 & 14, may be descriptive of the problems at Seleucia-Ctesiphon. For the Tannatic Judaism of the capital at a slightly earlier period, see Neusner, 122–77. *Atlas*, 5. Talbert, map 91.

Shadhshapur. (Deir Mihraq/Rima, in Babylonia. Just East of the Tigris and North-Northeast of Basra.) According to the *Chronicle of Seert*, 236, Bishop Andreas was one of those who opposed Papa *ca.* 325. *DHGE*, 8:1238–39. Fiey, *Assyrie*, 3:277–79 and plate 2, describes it as later subject to the bishop of Perat d-Maishan. Fiey, *Pour*, 125–26. Wigram, map at front. Compare Talbert, map 93.

Shahrqart. (in the region of Karka d-Beth Seloq and Lasqom. Baum & Winkler, 31, place it on the Lesser Zab River to the North-Northeast of Kirkuk.) The city was listed as an early bishopric in the *History of Karka d-Beth Seloq*; see Bedjan, 2:513, and Fiey, "Vers," 200. Bishop Narses was martyred in 343/44; see Assemani, *Acta*, 97–99; Bedjan 2:284–86; and LaGrange, 80–83. *AASS*, Novembris, 4:425–27. See also *Martyrologium Syriacum*. Bishop Paulus was at the Synod of

Mar Isaac in 410 C.E.; see Chabot, text, 34; trans. 273. LaBourt, 73. Fiey, *Assyrie*, 3:130–33 and plate 2. Fiey, *Pour*, 131. Compare Talbert, map 91.

Possible Sites

Diodoris? (near Kashkar?) Hegemonius, 43(39).4–5, seems to refer to a Diodorus presbyter of Diodorus near "Carcharis," but Fiey, *Assyrie*, 3:152–54, thinks the Archelaus traditions relate to Carrhae in Mesopotamia rather than to Kashkar in Assyria.

Dura? (on the Tigris.) Barhadbešabba, 6 (p. 209), mentions a bishop Mara of Doura as being at the Council of Nicaea. As Dura on the Euphrates had been destroyed by the Persians in the previous century, it is apparently Dura on the Tigris that is meant. Bishop Mara is otherwise unattested at Nicaea. Talbert, map 91.

Harbeth Gelal? (on the Lesser Zab, but not otherwise identified.) The city was listed as an early bishopric in the *History of Karka d-Beth Seloq*; see Bedjan, 2:513, and Fiey, "Vers," 200. Indeed, a later and somewhat doubtful account names a bishop 'Abda in connection with the year 319; see Bedjan, 2:1–2 (*BHO*, #1106 = Ortiz de Urbina, 147), Hoffmann, 9–10, and Fiey, *Assyrie*, 3:136–38.

The city was the site of the martyrdom of the presbyter Papa of Helmin under Shapor II; see Assemani, *Acta*, 1:99–100; Bedjan 2:286–89, and *AASS*, Novembris, 4:427. LaGrange, 82. *BHO*, #807. Bishop Joseph was at the Synod of Mar Isaac in 410 C.E.; see Chabot, 273. Fedalto, 2:954.

Haura? (In the region of Beth Garmai.) Tatun and three others were martyred at a place called Haura: see Assemani, *Acta*, 1:101–102; Bedjan, 2:286–89; and *AASS*, Novembris, 4:429. LaGrange, 82. *BHO*, #807.

Helmin? (in the region of Beth Garmai.) Papa of Helmin was martyred at Harbeth Gelal under Shapor II; see Assemani, *Acta*, 1:99–100; Bedjan, 2:286–89, and *AASS*, Novembris, 4:427. LaGrange, 82. *BHO*, #807.

Henaita? (also Hnaitha or Honaita. In the country of Adiabene, near the Greater Zab; see Hoffmann, 216–22.) Mentioned under Bishops Habel and Hairan of Arbela in *Chronicle of Arbela*, text 19 & 31; trans. 39 & 51. The revered octogenarian Bishop Aqebshema is said to have been martyred in 378/79; see *BHO*, #22; Assemani, *Acta*, 1:182; Bedjan 2:351–96, esp. 362. LaGrange, 21. Braun, *Ausgewählte*, 116. Fiey, *Assyrie*, 1:208–11.

Hulsar? (In the region of Beth Garmai.) The Presbyter Isaac of Hulsar was martyred at Karka d-Beth Seloq in the Fourth Century: see Assemani, *Acta*, 1:99–100; Bedjan 2:286–89; and *AASS*, Novembris, 4:427. LaGrange, 82.

Lashqom? (modern Lashin; about 50 km South of Kirkuk.) The city was listed as an early bishopric in the *History of Karka d-Beth Seloq*; see Bedjan, 2:513, and Fiey, "Vers," 200. The martyrdom of the laypersons Sasan, Mari, Timai, and Zaruan occurred under Shapor II; see Assemani, *Acta*, 1:100–101; Bedjan, 2:286–89; and LaGrange, 82. Labourt, 21. *AASS*, Novembris 4:428. Bishop Bata was at the Synod of Mar Isaac in 410 C.E.; Chabot, text 34 & 36, trans. 273 & 274. Fiey, *Assyrie*, 3:54–60. *Atlas*, 5. Talbert, map 91.

Mar Mattai? (North of Mosul.) According to later but perhaps reliable tradition in a manuscript from 1364 C.E., Aphrahat is said to have been active at Mar Mattai in the middle of the Fourth Century: see Harnack, 691; the introduction by the editor of Aphrahat's *Demonstrationes*, xx & lxxiii–lxxiv, and Baarda, 1:5–6.

Ressonin? (or Ramonin? probably Northwest of Arbela, in the mountains of Adiabene.) *Chronicle of Arbela*, text 36, trans. 57, under the episcopate of "Shahlupa of Arbela," mentions the place. Bishop Aqballaha was at the Synod of Mar Isaac in 410 C.E.; see Chabot, text 34, trans. 273. Fiey, *Assyrie*, 1:208.

(Tell) Dara? (On the Greater Zab in the region of Adiabene.) Mentioned as an early bishopric in the later *History of Karka d-Beth Seloq*; see Bedjan, 2:513, and Fiey, "Vers," 513. The priest Jacob, his sister Maria, and a certain Mahdad were martyred there by beheading in 347; see *BHO*, #426; Assemani, *Acta*, 1:122; Bedjan, 2:307; and Braun, *Ausgewählte*, 105, 111. Wiessner, 199. Fiey, *Assyrie*, 1:218.

Tella Shallila? (unidentified locale.) The priest Jacob martyred at Tell Dara in 347 was from Tella Shallila. *BHO*, #426. Assemani, *Acta*, 1:122. Bedjan 2:307. Braun, *Ausgewählte*, 105. See also *Martyrologium Syriacum*. LaBourt, 75. Wiessner, 199. Fiey, *Assyrie*, 1:218.

PERSIA

Bibliography
AASS
Aphrahat
Assemani, *Acta*
Atlas
Bardaisan
Baum & Winkler
Bedjan
BHO
Braun, *Ausgewählte*
Brock, review of Wiessner
Brock, "A Martyr"
Brock & Harvey
Chabot
Chaumont
Chronicle of Seert
pseudo-Clement, *Recognitiones*
Eusebius, *Ecclesiastical History*
Eusebius, *Vita Constantini*
Fedalto
Fiey, "L'Élam"
Gelzer
Hoffmann
Kartir Inscription
Labourt
LaGrange
Le Quien
Martyrologium Syriacum
Mingana, "The Early Spread"
Moffett
Ortiz de Urbina
Peeters, "S. Demetrianus"
PS
Res gestae Divi Saporis
Talbert
Wiessner

General

Parthia. Mentioned by Bardaisan, text, 60–61, as a place inhabited by Christians. Origen, *Commentary on Genesis*, 3 (*apud* Eusebius, *Ecclesiastical History*, 3.1.1), reported a tradition that the apostle Thomas had worked in Parthia. See also pseudo-Clement, *Recognitiones*, 9.29.2. The *Res gestae Divi Saporis*, text 325–27, trans. 16, records that the Persian Emperor Shapor I deported numerous captives from the Roman Empire into Parthia *ca*.252 or 256. The same deportation is attested by *Chronicle of Seert*, 221. Some of these captives were likely to have been Christians; compare Harnack 697. For a discussion of the dating and events of Shapor's deportations, see Chaumont, 57 & 64.

Gilan? (classical name "Hyrcania," region to the Southwest of the Caspian Sea.) Mentioned by Bardaisan, 60–61, as a place inhabited by Christians, though this is unconfirmed. The martyrdom of "Milites Persae," relating to events of *ca*.350 mentions that some of the soldiers martyred were from Gilan; see Ortiz de Urbina, 196, referring to Bedjan 2:166–70. Chaumont, 135–36. Talbert, map 90.

Khuzistan? (classiacal Susiane.) The *Res gesta Divi Saporis*, text 325, trans. 16, mentions that Shapor I deported several people from the territory of the Roman empire to Khuzistan in the 250s. Some of them may have been Christians; see under Gundeshapur.

Persia? (perhaps intended to mean the region of Fars.) LaBourt, 16, suggests that Acts 2:9, with the mention of Persians, Elamites, and Mesopotamians, could be an indication of Christians within those regions as early as *ca*.80, though the region of Fars is unconfirmed for that early date. Persia is mentioned by Bardaisan, 60–61, as a place inhabited by Christians. See also *Res gestae Divi Saporis*, text 325–27, trans. 16, for Persiae/Fars as a region to which Sapor deported captives *ca*.252. Chaumont, 64. Eusebius, *Vita Constantini*, 3.7.1, reports the presence of an unnamed Persian bishop at the Council of Nicaea. (The bishop named John who was at the Council of Nicaea and who is sometimes associated with Persia was more likely to have been from Perre in Northern Syria; see Gelzer, lxi.) At 4.43.3, he reports the presence of a Persian Bishop at the dedication of the Church of the Holy Sepulchre in Jerusalem in 335; cf. also Mingana, 425–26. For the middle of the Fourth Century, Aphrahat is one of the principal sources for theology in the Parthian and Persian sphere. *Atlas*, 5.

Media? Mentioned by Bardaisan, 60–61, as a region inhabited by Christians, though this is unconfirmed.

Specific Sites

Gundeshapur. (Syriac name, Beth Lapat.) *Res gestae Divi Saporis*, text 325–27, trans 16, shows that Shapor I deported numerous captives from the Roman Empire into the region of Khuzistan/Susiane *ca*.252. *Chronicle of Seert*, 221, indicates that many of these captives were Christians who were sent to Gundeshapur; see also *AASS*, Novembris 4, 390. It is possible that Bishop Demetrianus of Antioch was among them; see LaBourt, 19–20, and Peeters, "S. Demetrianus," 292. Perhaps the martyr Candida who was put to death under Vahran (*ca*.276–93) at Gundeshapur or at Seleucia-Ctesiphon was from one of those captive families; see Brock, "A Martyr," 169.

Bishop Gadihab of Gundeshapur ordained Miles as Bishop of Susa before *ca*.325; see *Acta S. Miles* (Assemani, *Acta*, 1:69–70; Bedjan, 2:264; and LaGrange, 65–66). Gadihab was one of those in opposition to Papa at the Council of Seleucia *ca*.325 C.E.; see *Chronicle of Seert*, 236. Gadihab and Sabinus were also martyrs from Gundeshapur *ca*.340: see *Acta Mar Simeon bar Sabbai*, in Bedjan, 2:131–2 & 154; *PS* II.1, cols.831–32; Braun, *Ausgewählte*, 5 & 21; also Sozomen, 2.13.7.

The bishopric of Beth Lapat was mentioned by the Synod of Mar Isaac in 410 C.E; see Chabot, 272. Le Quien, 2:1181–86. Fedalto, 2:931–32. Chaumont, 124–26. Labourt, 21. Baum & Winkler, 9. *Atlas*, 5. Talbert, maps 92 & 93.

Persepolis. (near Istakhar.) The Third-Century *Kartir Inscription*, text 415; trans. 51, set up at Nasq-i-Rustum near Persepolis in the second half of the Third Century, exalts Kartir's efforts to stamp out Christianity in the Persian Empire. *Chronicle of Seert*, 222, makes mention of Istakhar in connection with Christians. Assemani, *Acta*, 1:93, records the martyrdom of Barshabia and his followers who were accosted by the Mobed of Istakhar *ca*.347; see also LaGrange, 78. These three pieces of evidence suggest that Christianity had an early and recognizable presence in the environs of Persepolis. LaBourt, 72. Baum & Winkler, 9. *Atlas*, 5. Talbert, map 94.

Susa. Bishop Miles of Susa was spokesman for those opposing Papa of Seleucia-Ctesiphon *ca*.325. For an account favorable to Miles and his side, see *Acta S. Miles* in Assemani, *Acta*, 1:72–73; Bedjan, 2:266–68; and LaGrange, 67–68. For an account favorable to Papa, see the record

of the Synod of Dadisho in 424 C.E. in Chabot, text 46–48, trans.,
289–92. See also *Chronicle of Seert*, 236, and Chaumont, 124–26, 140.

Miles was martyred *ca.*340, see *Acta S. Miles* in Assemani, *Acta*,
1:66–79; Bedjan, 2:260–75; *BHO*, #772; and LaGrange, 65–73.
Labourt, 21 & 71–72. Talbert, maps 92 & 93.

Possible Sites

Ardashir-khourra? (Firuzabad/Gor.) Harnack, 697, claims the place
as a possible early Christian site. Yet the earliest certain mention of
Christians there comes with the mention of Bishop Pharbokt at the
Synod of Dadisho in 424; see Chabot, text 44, trans. 287.

Bishapur? (near modern Kazerun; in Fars.) The Martyrdom of
Pusai indicates that he was descended from a family deported from
the Roman Empire by Shapor I *ca.*252 and settled in Bishapur; see
Bedjan 2:208–210, and Braun, *Ausgewählte*, 58–59. See also Chaumont,
73. Talbert, map 94.

Darabgird? (present Darab; Southeast of Persepolis.) The city was
represented by Bishop Yzedbozed at the Synod of Dadisho *ca.*424;
see Chabot, text 44; trans. 287. LaBourt, 120–21. Harnack, 697.
Atlas, 5. Talbert, map 3.

Hormizd Ardashir? (in Khuzistan; see Mingana, 491.) John, Bishop
of Hormizd Ardashir was martyred *ca.*340; see *Acta Mar Simeon bar
Sabbai* (Assemani, *Acta*, 1:41; Bedjan, 2:131 & 154; *PS* II.1, cols. 831–32;
and Braun, *Ausgewählte*, 5 & 21), also *Martyrologium Syriacum.* Represented
at the Synod of Mar Isaac in 410 C.E. by Bishop Yohanan; see
Chabot, text 34, trans. 272. Bishop Abda was martyred in 420; see
BHO, #6; Hoffmann, 34–35; Braun, *Ausgewählte*, 139–41; and Bedjan,
4:250–53. Labourt, 21. *Atlas*, 5. Talbert, map 93.

Hulwan? (East of the Diyala River, near modern Qasr-e Shirin in
modern Iran. possibly Biblical Halah, so Chabot, 672–73.) Bishop
Hurma was martyred there in the Fourth Century; see *Martyrologium
Syriacum.* Le Quien, 2:1247–48. Labourt, 21. Fiey, *Assyrie*, 3:13–14,
202, & Plate 1. Talbert, map 92.

Karka d-Leidan? (South of Susa and on the same river, in Khuzistan;
see Fiey, "L'Élam," 222.) Pusai was martyred there on 17 April 340;
see Bedjan, 2:208–232, *BHO*, #993, and Braun, *Ausgewählte*, 58–75.
Pusai's daughter Marta was also killed; see Bedjan, 2:233–41, *BHO*,

#698, and Braun, *Ausgewählte*, 76–82. Wiessner, 94–105. Talbert, map 93.

Mashkena? (in Fars.) The presbyter Longinus and the deacons Varan and Medin were martyred there in the Fourth Century; see *Martyrologium Syriacum*. See also *BHO*, #174, #175, and #176. The city was represented by Bishop Ardaq at the Synod of Dadisho in 424 C.E.; see Chabot, text 43, trans. 285. Labourt, 21. Harnack, 697.

Rewardashir? (in Fars. Syriac name, Beit Raziqaye; just Northwest of modern Bushire; see Mingana 438 & 493.) *Res gestae Divi Saporis*, text 325–27, trans. 16, indicates that Shapor deported numerous captives from the Roman Empire to the region of Fars *ca.*252. *Chronicle of Seert*, 222, claims that some of these captives were Christians who were sent to Rewardashir (Yaransahr), and that there were both Greek speaking and Syriac speaking congregations in the town.

Fedalto, 2:962, rather tentatively assigns the Bishop John of Persia who was said to have attended the Council of Nicaea to Rewardashir; contrast Gelzer, lxi, where this John is assigned to Perre. A certain Yaphan or Yabdin was martyred at Rewardashir in the Fourth Century; see *Martyrologium Syriacum*. Bishop Yazdad of Rewardashir is mentioned in the minutes of the Synod of Dadisho 424 C.E.; see Chabot, 285. Chaumont, 63. Labourt, 21. *Atlas*, 5. Talbert, map 94.

Shustar/Sostrate? (in Khuzistan.) *Chronicle of Seert*, 236, claims that Bishop Abraham of Sousterin was one of those who opposed Papa in the Council of Seleucia *ca.*325 C.E. The city was represented at the Synod of Mar Isaac in 410 C.E. by Bishop Abisho and Bishop Simeon Bardouq; see Chabot, text 34 & 36, trans. 272 & 275. See also Chaumont, 125 & 140. Talbert, map 93.

INDIA AND BACTRIA

Bibliography
Assemani, *Bibliotheca*
Bardaisan
Baum & Winkler
Bedjan
Chronicle of Seert

Cureton, *Ancient*
Dihle
Eusebius, *Ecclesiastical History*
Eusebius, *Praeparatio Evangelica*
Fedalto
Giamil
Girshman
Harnack
Isidore of Charax
Klijn, *Acts of Thomas*
Land
Lipsius & Bonnet
Mingana, "The Early Spread"
Moffett
Nau, "Deux"
Origen, *Commentary on Matthew*
Periplus Maris Erythraei
Pfister
Philostorgius
Schneemelcher
Talbert
Tisserant
Trimingham
Warmington
Wheeler
Wright, *Apocryphal Acts*

Specific Regions

India. Early sources for Christianity in India are remarkably scarce, and there is no ancient evidence for the traditions that Thomas reached South India. Yet the *Periplus Maris Erythraei* certainly shows that sea travel to South India and beyond would have been possible in the First Century C.E., and this is confirmed by Roman coins found at Akrimedu on the East coast of India; see Wheeler, 145–45. The *Acts of Thomas* (Wright, *Apocryphal Acts*, text, 1:172–333, trans., 2:146–298; Bedjan, 3:1–175; Lipsius & Bonnet, II.2:99–291; Schneemelcher, 339–411), with their mention of Thomas reaching "Andrapolis" then having an interview with King Gondophares, seemingly point to a Christian presence in Northwest India at the time the *Acts* were written in the early Third Century. Warmington, 83, thought that Andrapolis might refer to "some point on the West coast of India under Andhra control" and that references to Gondophares might point to land or sea journeys to the Indus. Yet according to Isidore of Charax, 8–9 & 34, writing at the turn of the eras, *Alex*andrapolis (modern Kandahar in Afghanistan) was the last station on one of the Parthian postal routes. Note that in the First Century C.E., Kandahar would have been on the border of Gondophares's domains; see Moffett, 30. Traditions related to the *Didascalia Apostolorum*, in the Third Century, also say that Judas Thomas was the person responsible for evangelizing India; see Cureton, *Ancient*, text 33, trans. 33.

The description of Pantaenus's presumed visit to "India" and his discovery of Christians there who attributed their traditions to Bartholomew and who used a Hebrew "Gospel of Matthew" (Eusebius, *Ecclesiastical History*, 5.10.1–4) seems to me to relate to South Arabia (*q.v.*) rather than to India.

Origen presents some negative evidence of the territory into which Christianity was not thought to have reached in his day: "*non ergo fertur praedicatum esse evangelium apud omnes Aethiopas, maxime apud eos, qui sunt ultra flumen; sed nec apud Seras nec apud Ariacin nec . . . audierunt Christianitatis sermonem.*" Trans., "For it has not been reported that the Gospel has been preached among all the Ethiopians, especially among those who are beyond the river, nor among the Seres, nor in Aricae has the tale of Christ been heard;" *Commentary on Matthew, Commentariorum series*, 39, on Matthew 24:9. The contrasting names here seem to suggest that Origen is mentioning lands at various points of the compass into which Chrisianity had not yet penetrated, so it seems likely that "Ethiopia" here refers to part of the Aksumite realm, while the word "Seres" refers to various peoples along the silk routes to China. According to Harnack, 536–37, "Ariacin" must refer to Ariake, a region on the West coast of India which *Periplus Maris Erythraei*, 76–77 & 197, localizes between the Gulf of Kutch and the Naranda River. The Indus estuaries of modern Sindh lie just West of Ariake, so if Origen was mentioning regions just beyond the Christian horizon, he may give here an indication that Christianity had reached the Indus valley but not beyond.

The later but often reliable *Chronicle of Seert*, 236 & 292, mentions Bishop David of Basra (i.e. Perat d-Maishan) undertaking a voyage to India and finding Christians there. David's dates are uncertain. Mingana, 450, would date the journey to 295–300 C.E., but a glance at David's contemporaries as listed in the *Chronicle* suggests that the journey could have taken place as late as 325.

Also, according to native tradition attested later, a certain bishop, sometimes called Joseph, is said to have been sent from Edessa to the Malabar region of India in 345: see *De Rebus quae Acciderunt Syris (in ripa Malabarica) Eorumque Historia* in Land, text, 1:24–27, trans. 1:124–25 & 181–82; Giamil, *Genuinae Relationes*, 578–79; and Mingana, 496. A similar tradition was edited in Nau, "Deux," text, 75; trans., 79. Baum & Winkler suggest that the *Hodoiporia apo Edem*, a work connected with the Alexander Romance, may contain Fourth-Century evidence for Christianity in India and Sri Lanka as well as other Eastern regions; even so, in its present form it cannot predate the establishment of Constantinople as the Eastern Roman capital; see Pfister, 353–55. For other traditions, see Assemani, *Bibliotheca*, 3.2:xxv–xxvii & ccccxli–ccccxliii. So too, the report of Philostorgius, 3.5, that Theophilus "the Indian" had found Christians in "the other India," *ca.*356 may relate to some spot on the Indian Subcontinent. Tisserant, 8–10 & 187. Trimingham, 290–91. Fedalto, 2:981. See also Baum & Winkler, 51–57.

It is safe to say that residents of Edessa, and perhaps of Alexandria, believed that Christianity had spread to some parts of ancient India by 325, but the details of that spread escape us.

Bactria/Kushan Kingdom? (Region to the Southeast of the Caspian Sea.) The Kushan people overran Bactria in the First Century C.E. and seized part of India from the successors of Gondophares; see Girshman, 260. The early Third-Century reference in Bardaisan, 60–61, to Christians among the "Kushan" people thus covers a large and indefinite region. By the middle of the Third Century, however, Shapor I of Persia had wrested control of Bactria away from the Kushan; see Girshman, 291–92. Hence Eusebius, in his *Praeparatio Evangelica*, 6.10.46, quoting the passage from Bardaisan, updates the reference to read "Bactrians." See also Chaumont, 136–37. Especially if Christianity reached the Indus valley from overland, it would be natural to believe, as Bardaisan did, that there were Christians in Kushan controlled Bactria.

Isauria, Cilicia, and Cyprus

Bibliography
AASS
ABD
Ammianus Marcellinus
Athanasius, *Apologia contra Arianos*
Athanasius, *De synodis*
Atlas
Basil of Caesarea, *Letters*
Bezae codex
BHG
BHL
Calder, "Some Monuments"
Dagron
DHGE
pseudo-Dionysius of Tel-Mahre
Epiphanius, *Panarion*
Eusebius, *Ecclesiastical History*
Eusebius, *Martyrs of Palestine*
Eusebius, *Vita Constantini*
Fedalto
Gelzer
Grégoire, "Saints jumeaux"
Grégoire, *Saints jumeaux*
Gregory of Nazianzus, *Carmina*
Hagel & Tomaschitz
Harnack
Ignatius
Jerome, *Epistulae*
Jerome, *De viris inlustribus*
Jones, *Cities*
Jones, *Later Roman Empire*
Kalendarium Carthaginiense
Laminger-Pascher, *Die Kaiserzeitlichen*
Le Quien
Lightfoot, *Apostolic Fathers*
Lipsius & Bonnet
MAMA
Mansi

Martyrologium Hieronymianum
Martyrologium Romanum
Methodius of Olympus, *De Resurrectione*
Nicephorus Callistus
Pauly-Wissowa
Philostorgius
Ramsay, A. M.
Ramsay, W. M. *Historical Geography*
Rufinus, *Ecclesiastical History*
Ruinart
Sayar, *Anazarbos*
SEC
Socrates
Sozomen
Talbert
Theodoret, *Ecclesiastical History*
TIB
Tomaschitz
Turner

General

Cilicia. The Province of Cilicia had close connections with Syria even in the First Century; see Acts 15:41, for example. It was attached to the Dioecesis of Oriens under Diocletian; see Jones, *Later Roman Empire*, 1460.

According to Acts 6:9, Jews, presumably including Saul/Paul, from Cilicia were present at the stoning of Stephen. In Galatians, 1:21, Paul refers to his early visit as a Christian to Cilicia. Ignatius, *Philadelphians*, 11, mentions the faithful service of the deacon Philo from Cilicia. Eusebius, *Martyrs of Palestine*, 10.1 & 11.6, mentions confessors from Cilicia being taken to the mines in Palestine during the Diocletianic persecutions. Bishop Eudaimon was chorepiskopos at the Council of Nicaea; see Gelzer, lxi. Philostorgius, 3.15, mentions Borborian gnostics in Cilicia in the middle of the Fourth Century. *TIB*, 5:85–86.

Cyprus. The early missionary Joseph, better known as Barnabas, was a Levite and a native of Cyprus; see Acts, 4:36. Likewise, Mnason of Cyprus was an early disciple settled in Caesarea in Palestine; see Acts 21:16. The *Bezae codex*, Acts 21:16, suggests that he may have become a Christian while still on Cyprus.

Isauria. Under Diocletian the province was attached to the Dioecesis of Oriens; see Jones, *Later Roman Empire*, 1460. Bishops Hesychius, Anatolius, Kuntos, Aquila, were chorepiskopoi in Isauria; see Gelzer, lxiii. Bishop Eusebius had charge of the *paroikoi*, "resident aliens" who lived in the Dioecesis of Isauria; see Gelzer, lxiii. The Province of Lacaonia was formed from parts of Pisidia, Isauria, and Galatia in 387; see Basil of Caesarea, *Letters*, 138. Basil of Caesarea, *Letters*, 190, commends Bishop Amphilocius of Iconium for his care of the churches in Isauria. *TIB*, 5:85.

Specific Sites

Adana. (in Cilicia.) Bishop Paulinus was at the Council of Nicaea; see Gelzer, lxi. He was possibly at the Council of Antioch *ca*.330; see Turner, 2:231 & 313–14, and compare Mansi, 2:1308. Jones, *Cities*, 540. *TIB*, 5:154. *Atlas*, 5. Talbert, map 66.

Aigaiai. (in Cilicia.) A martyr Thaleleus is mentioned under Numerian; see *SEC*, 20 May. *AASS*, Augustus 4:570–71 (*BHL*, #1829), records the martyrs Claudius and Asterius, supposedly in the time of Emperor Aurelian.

AASS, Octobris 13:259–63 (*BHG*, #1884) mentions a certain martyred Bishop Zenobius, if "Cilicia" may be read for "Lycia" as the editors suggest. *SEC*, 30 October, puts Zenobius in the time of Diocletian. The Ethiopian tradition puts Zenobius in the time of Claudius II; see *AASS*, Octobris 13:270. See also *DHGE*, 1:645–47, and *BS*, 12:1471–72.

Bishop Tarcondimantus was at the Council of Nicaea; see Gelzer, lxii. Tarcondimantus appears to have initially had Arian leanings; see Philostorgius, 1.8a. He was also at the Council of Antioch *ca*.330; see Turner, 231 & 312–13, and Mansi, 2:1308. Eusebius, *Vita Constantini*, 3.56.1–3, comments upon the destruction of the Temple of Asclepius at Aigaiai. The *Life and Miracles of Thecla*, miracle 9, mentions a certain Bishop Menodorus, who is otherwise unattested, in the late Fourth Century; see Dagron, 304–309 (*BHG*, #1718). *TIB*, 5:160–64. Harnack, 731. Jones, *Cities*, 540. Fedalto, 2:763. *Atlas*, 5. Talbert, map 67.

Alexandreia (ad Issum). (in Cilicia, near the border with Syria.) Pseudo-Dionysius of Tell Mahre, fol. 35r (text, 1:128, trans., 1:96), mentions Bishop Alexander of Alexandria minor *ca*.188. *SEC*, 3

September, mentions a Bishop Aristion. *SEC*, 12 September, mentions a Bishop Theodorus. *SEC*, 24 December, mentions Bishop Helenus in the time of the Emperor Commodus. The first certain bishop, Hesychius, was at the Council of Nicaea; see Gelzer, lxii. Hesychius was possibly at the Council of Antioch *ca*.330; see Turner, 2:231 & 314–15, and Mansi, 2:1308. Jones, *Cities*, 540. *DHGE*, 2:287–89. *TIB*, 5:170–72. Fedalto, 2:764. *Atlas*, 5. Talbert, map 67.

Anazarbos. (in Cilicia; modern Anazarva Kalesi.) The spurious *Letter of Maria of Cassabola to Ignatius*, 1, mentions a certain Bishop Marin; see Lightfoot, *Apostolic Fathers*, 2.3:137–38. This is perhaps a reflection of the martyr Marin of Anazarbus under Diocletian; see *AASS*, Augustus 2:347–48 (*BHG*, #1171); see also *Martyrologium Romanum*, 8 August. Compare *Martyrologium Hieronymianum*, 12 kal. Sept., and *Kalendarium Carthaginiense.*, 2 id. Aug.

One manuscript of *Martyrologium Hieronymianum*, 5 id. Oct., mentions the martyrs Tarachus, Andronicus, and Probus. See also *AASS*, Octobris 5:566–84 (*BHG*, #1574), which dates them to the time of Diocletian.

Bishop Athanasius of Anazarbos was an Arian sympathizer just prior to the Nicene Council; see Athanasius, *De synodis*, 17.1. For further details, see Philostorgius, 1.8a & 3.15. Theodoret, *Ecclesiastical History*, 1.5.1–6, preserves the letter of Arius that refers to Athanasius of Anazarbos as well as Theodoret's comments on the letter. Le Quien, 2:885–88. Harnack, 651 & 731. Jones, *Cities*, 540. *TIB*, 5:178–85. *DHGE*, 2:1504–06. Fedalto, 2:761. *Atlas*, 5. Talbert, map 67.

Antiocheia (epi Krago). (on the coast of Isauria.) Bishop Antoninus was at the Council of Nicaea; see Gelzer, lxiii. *TIB*, 5:191–93. *Atlas*, 5. Talbert, map 66.

Barata. (in Isauria; later Lacaonia.) Bishop Stephanus was at the Council of Nicaea; see Gelzer, lxiii. Jones, *Cities*, 534. *TIB*, 4:53, & 5:33–35. *Atlas*, 5. Talbert, map 66.

Derbe. (in the region of Lacaonia in the First Century; in the province Isauria in the time of Diocletian; later in the province Lacaonia. Perhaps modern Kerti Hüyük near Suduragi, just Northeast of Laranda.) Acts 14:6, 14:20, & 16.1 reports the work of Barnabas and Paul there, begun almost by accident after harassment by the residents of Iconium. Acts 20:4 mentions Gaius of Derbe. A. M. Ramsay, #34 (pp. 60–62), lists an inscription from the Fourth Century set up in memory of the martyr Paulus. See also Calder, "Some Monuments," 356. Jones, *Cities*, map following 28, also 132, 135–36, & 534. *ABD*, 2:144–45. Fedalto, 1:269. *TIB*, 5:32–33. *Atlas*, 5. Talbert, map 66.

Dorla. (in Isauria; modern Aydoğmuş. For the identification, see Talbert, map 66. Dorla has been identified as an alternative site for Isauropolis/Isaura Nova/Leontopolis; see Pauly-Wissowa, 9.2:2055–56, and *TIB*, 4:180–81. Talbert, map 66, notes the possibility but opts for Zengibar Kalesi as the site of Isaura Nova/Isauropolis. See also Jones, *Cities*, map following 28, also 137–38. Laminger-Pascher, *Die Kaiserzeitlichen*, 213–16.) A. M. Ramsay, #12 (=*MAMA*, 8: #117), records the Christian inscription of a certain Aurelia [or Septima] Domna, from the first half of the Third Century at Dorla. Similarly, A. M. Ramsay, #7 (=*MAMA*, 8:162; =Laminger-Pascher, *Die Kaiserzeitlichen*, #408), dates from the late Third Century, and A. M. Ramsay, #18 (=*MAMA*, 8: #120) dates to the early part of the Fourth Century. See also the early but not firmly dated inscriptions in Laminger-Pascher, *Die Kaiserzeitlichen*, # 409 (=*MAMA*, 8: #161; =A. M. Ramsay, #13); # 410; #411 (=*MAMA*, 8:164; =A. M. Ramsay, #14); and #412 (=*MAMA*, 8: #163).

At Emir Han, about 8km Southeast of Dorla, Laminger-Pascher, *Die Kaiserzeitlichen*, #10 (=*MAMA*, 8: #200) is an apparently Christian inscription from the end of the Third Century. Similarly, near Dinek, about 8km North of Dorla, Laminger Pascher, *Die Kaiserzeitlichen*, #368, is a Christian inscription of perhaps pre-Constantinian date. Other possibly Christian inscriptions of early date are Laminger-Pascher, *Die Kaiserzeitlichen*, # 304 (=*MAMA*, 8: #131) and #328 (=*MAMA*, 8: #119). *OCD*, 767–68.

Epiphaneia. (in Cilicia.) The confessor Amphion survived the persecution under the Emperor Maximinus; see Sozomen, 1.10.1. It was apparently the same Amphion who represented the church as Bishop of Epiphaneia at the Council of Ancyra in 314; see Turner, 2:51. His name also appears in the list of signatories to the Council of Neocaesarea *ca*.319; see Turner, 2:32 & 52–53. Bishop Amphion was also at the Council of Nicaea; see Gelzer, lxi. According to Ammainus Marcellinus, 22.11.3, Georgius, the rival of Athanasius in Egypt, was a native of Epiphania. *DHGE*, 15:633–34. *TIB*, 5:249–50. *Atlas*, 5. Talbert, map 67.

Flavias. (in Cilicia.) Later authors place Bishop Alexander of Jerusalem at Flavias earlier in his career; see Le Quien, 2:899–902, and *DHGE*,

2:178. This tradition is apparently a development of the one found in Eusebius, *Ecclesiastical History*, 6.8.7 & 11.2, and in Nicephorus Callistus, 5.10 (PG 145:1088) and 14.39 (PG 146:1189), which locates Alexander in Cappadocia. See also *DHGE*, 17:374–75.

Bishop Nicetas of Flavias was at the Council of Nicaea; see Gelzer, lxi. Nicetas may also have been at the Council of Antioch *ca*.330; see Turner, 2:231 & 312–13, and Mansi, 2:1308. Jones, *Cities*, 540. *TIB*, 5:378–79. Fedalto, 2:767. *Atlas*, 5. Talbert, map 67.

Homonada. (in Isauria, on the border with Pisidia; later in Lacaonia.) Bishop Cyril was at the Council of Nicaea; see Gelzer, lxiii. Harnack, 773 & 778. Pauly-Wissowa, 8.2:2265. Jones, *Cities*, 534. *TIB*, 5:35 & 86 as "Umanada". Ramsay, *Historical Geography*, 335 & 419. Talbert, map 65.

Ilistra. (in Isauria; later in Lacaonia. Modern Yollarbasi; formerly Ilisre.) Bishop Tiberius was at the Council of Nicaea; see Gelzer, lxiii. Jones, *Cities*, 534. *TIB*, 4:179 and 5:35 & 86. *Atlas*, 5. Talbert, map 66.

Isaura Palaia/Isaura Vetus. (Leontopolis/Metropolis, in Isauria in the time of Diocletian; later in Pisidia. Identified as Metropolis of Isauria on coins of the Third Century; see Pauly-Wissowa, 9.2:2055–56, which places Isaura Palaia at modern Zengibar Kalesi, as does *TIB*, 4:198–200. Talbert, map 66, places Isaura Palaia at modern Bozkir and says Leontopolis is to be identified with Isaura Nova.) Bishop Silvanus of Metropolis in Isauria was at the Council of Nicaea; see Gelzer, lxiii. Jones, *Cities*, map following 28, also 137–38. *Atlas*, 5. *OCD*, 767–68.

Kastabala. (ancient Hierapolis; in Cilicia.) The spurious *Letter of Maria of Cassabola to Ignatius* is apparently intended to place its author in Kastabala; see Lightfoot, *Apostolic Fathers*, 2.3:135–45. Bishop Moses was at the Council of Nicaea; see Gelzer, lxi. Moses was also at the Council of Antioch *ca*.330; see Turner, 2:231 & 314–15, and Mansi, 2:1308. Harnack, 731–31, suggests that Bishop Moses may have been of Jewish descent. Jones, *Cities*, 540. *TIB*, 5:293. *Atlas*, 5. Talbert, map 67.

Klaudiopolis. (in Isauria.) Bishop Aidesius was at the Council of Nicaea; see Gelzer, lxiii. Jones, *Cities*, 541. *TIB*, 5:307. *Atlas*, 5. Talbert, map 66.

Koropissos. (in Isauria, probably modern Alahan near Dağpazari.) Bishop Athenaeus was at the Council of Nicaea; see Gelzer, lxiii.

Harnack, 738. *DHGE*, 13:914. *TIB*, 5:35 & 313–14. *Atlas*, 5. Talbert, map 66.

Laranda. (in Isauria in the time of Diocletian; later in Lacaonia. Modern Karaman.) A letter from Alexander of Jerusalem and Theoctistus of Caesarea mentions that Bishop Neon invited a certain Euelpis to preach at Laranda; see Eusebius, *Ecclesiastical History*, 6.19.17–18. Bishop Paulus of Laranda was at the Council of Nicaea; see Gelzer, lxiii. Jones, *Cities*, 534. *TIB*, 5:35–36, 86, & 140. *Atlas*, 5. Talbert, map 66.

Mopsuestia. (in Cilicia.) Eusebius, *Ecclesiastical History*, 7.30.2, mentions a certain Theodorus as a bishop in Cilicia in the time of Paul of Samosata. Le Quien, 2:889, reports the supposition that this Theodorus may have been a bishop of Mopsuestia.

Bishop Macedonius was at the Council of Nicaea; see Gelzer, lxii. Macedonius may also have been at the Council of Antioch *ca.*330; see Turner, 2:231 & 312–13. Auxentius, a former associate of the Emperor Licinius, later became bishop of Mopsuestia; see Philostorgius, 5.2a. For early references to Theodore of Mopsuestia, bishop from the late Fourth Century, see Socrates, 6.3.4–5, and Sozomen, 8.2.7. Jones, *Cities*, 540. Fedalto, 2:770–71. *TIB*, 5:351–52. *Atlas*, 5. Talbert, map 67.

Neronias/Eirenopolis. (in Cilicia.) Bishop Narcissus was at the Council of Ancyra in 314; see Turner, 2:32 & 50. The name of Narcissus also appears in the list of signatories to the Council of Neocaesarea *ca.*319; see Turner, 2:32 & 52–53. He was also at the Council of Nicaea; see Gelzer, lxi. He may have been at the Council of Antioch *ca.*330; see Turner, 2:231 & 314–15, and Mansi, 2:1308. Narcissus was involved in the struggle against Athanasius of Alexandria; see Socrates, 2.18.1. He was later deposed for his Arian sympathies by the Council of Serdica in 343; see Athanasius, *Apologia contra Arianos*, 36.6 & 40.3; also Sozomen, 3.10.4 & 3.12.3. Harnack, 731–32. Jones, *Cities*, 540. *TIB*, 5:245–46. Fedalto, 2:765. *Atlas*, 5. Talbert, map 67.

Olba/Ourba. (in Isauria.) Aspects of the Martyrdom of Speusippus, Elasippus, and Melesippus (*BHG*, #1646) are associated with a village called Orba; see Grégoire, "Saints jumeaux," 474, and Grégoire, *Saints jumeaux*, 22–24. Harnack, 746. Jones, *Cities*, 541. *TIB*, 5:369–70. Fedalto, 2:871. The *Life and Miracles of Thecla*, miracle 24, makes an undatable reference to Olba; see Dagron 350–53 (*BHG*, #1718). *Atlas*, 5. Talbert, map 66.

Ouasada/Vasada. (in the province Isauria, later in Lacaonia; modern Bostandere.) Bishop Theodorus was at the Council of Nicaea; see Gelzer, lxiii. Ouasada/Vasada is apparently duplicated in the list for Pisidia. Jones, *Cities*, 137 & 534. At the Council of Antioch in 341, Ouasada was counted as part of Isauria; see Mansi, 2:1308, and *TIB*, 4:239. Talbert, map 65.

Paphos. (on Cyprus.) Acts 13:6–13 indicates that Barnabas and Paul preached there. Bishop Cyril was at the Council of Nicaea; see Gelzer, lxiv. *Atlas*, 5. Talbert, map 72.

Pompeiopolis. (in Cilicia.) A centurion in the martyr account of Tarachius, Andronicus, and Probus mentions Pompeiopolis as a site where Christians live; see *AASS*, Octobris 5:566 (*BHG*, #1574). Pauly-Wissowa, 21.2:2043–44. Harnack, 731. *TIB*, 5:381–82. *Atlas*, 5. Talbert, map 66.

Rhossos. (considered as part of Cilicia II by the Fifth Century when it was linked with Anazarbos. Yet both cities remained ecclesiastically subject to Antioch in Syria; see *TIB*, 5.1, 392.) Eusebius, *Ecclesiastical History*, 6.12.2, mentions Christians there *ca.*200 who were led astray by the *Gospel of Peter* and who had received a letter from Serapion of Antioch to set them straight. *Atlas*, 5. Talbert, map 67.

Salamis. (on Cyprus.) Acts 13:6 indicates that Barnabas and Paul preached in the synagogue there. Bishop Gelasius was at the Council of Nicaea; see Gelzer, lxiv. *Atlas*, 5. Talbert, map 72.

Seleucia Tracheia. (in Isauria; modern Selifke.) Bishop Agapius was at the Council of Nicaea; see Gelzer, lxiii. He may also have been at the Council of Antioch *ca.*330; see Turner, 2:231 & 314–15; and Mansi, 2:1308.

Gregory of Nazianzus, *Carmina*, 2.1.11.547 (PL 37:1067), mentions the cultus of Thecla there. For inscriptions from the Thecla complex of the Fourth Century at nearby Meryamlik, see *MAMA*, 2:x &43–44.

Harnack, 778. Jones, *Cities*, 541. *TIB*, 5:402. Seleucia was later the principal see of Isauria; see Fedalto, 2:861. *Atlas*, 5. Talbert, map 66.

Syedra. (in Isauria.) Bishop Nestor was at the Council of Nicaea; see Gelzer, lxiii. Early on, the city was counted as part of Western Cilicia (*i.e.* Isauria), but it was counted as part of Pisidia by the Fifth Century; see Jones, *Cities*, 213 & 536. Pauly-Wissowa, 4.A.1.1017–18. *TIB*, 5:33 & 35. *Atlas*, 5. Talbert, map 66.

Tarsus. (in Cilicia.) Acts, 9:11, 21:39 & 22:3 show that Tarsus was Paul's home town. Jerome, *Epistle* 121.10.3, comments on Paul's upbringing there. Epiphanius, *Panarion*, 30.25.4–6, also comments on Paul's origins from a Jewish family at Tarsus. Sozomen, 7.19.10, mentions a house reputed to be that of Paul, and also an apocryphal "Apocalypse of Paul," associated with the place.

Acts 9:30 reports that Christians from Palestine arranged for Paul to escape from Jerusalem to Tarsus. Acts 11:25 reports that Barnabas later went there to find Paul.

SEC, 30 June, reports the legend that Luke was the first bishop of Tarsus. Bishop Helenus was mentioned by Dionysius of Alexandria in his writings against the Novatians; see Eusebius, *Ecclesiastical History*, 6.46.3 & 7.5.4. Bishop Lupus was at the Council of Ancyra in 314; see Turner, 2:32 & 50–51. His name also appears on the list of signatories to the Council of Neocaesarea *ca.*319; see Turner 2:32 & 52–53. Bishop Theodorus was at the Council of Nicaea; see Gelzer, lxi. He may also have been at the Council of Antioch *ca.*330; see Turner 2:231, 313 & 315, and Mansi, 2:1308. Harnack, 730. *TIB*, 5:428–39. *Atlas*, 5. Talbert, map 66.

Tremithous. (on Cyprus.) Rufinus, *Ecclesiastical History*, 10.5, mentions Bishop Spyridion. Socrates, 1.8.12, 1.11.1 & 1.12.1–5, calls Spyridion a bishop of Cyprus and says he was present at the Council of Nicaea. Sozomen 1.11.1–11, locates Spyridion's see at Tremithous and notes that he had been a confessor during the Diocletianic persecutions. At 1.11.8–9, he also reports Spyridion's rebuke of Triphyllius of Ledroi. One Greek manuscript of the signatories to the Council of Nicaea records Spyridion's name; see Gelzer, lxx & 71. *Atlas*, 5. Talbert, map 72.

Possible Sites

Hamaxia? (in Isauria; modern Sinekkalesi.) Methodius of Olympus, *De Resurrectione*, 1.1.2, mentions a Christian interlocutor named Sistelius "Amaskeunitinia'." In the 1891 edition, xxxii–xxxiii, the editor Bonwetsch suggests that if a place name is intended, Hamaxia may be the place meant. See also the 1917 edition, xxxviii. Harnack, 778. Pauly-Wissowa, 7.2:2296. *TIB*, 5:115. Talbert, map 65.

Ledroi? (on Cyprus.) Bishop Triphyllius was rebuked for his high-flown rhetoric by Bishop Spyridion of Tremithous; see Sozomen, 1.11.8–9. Jerome, *De viris inlustribus*, 92, and *Epistulae*, 70.4, also mentions Triphyllius's work. Harnack, 677. Talbert, map 72.

Palaia(i)/Philaia? (in Isauria; modern Tahta Limani.) The Fifth-Century *Acts of Barnabas*, 11, mentions Palaia of Isauria as a place in Barnabas's ministry; see Lipsius & Bonnet, 2.2:296. *TIB*, 5:372. Talbert, map 66.

DIOECESIS OF ASIA

Bibliography
AASS
AB
ABD
Abicht & Reichelt
Achelis, *Das Christentum*
Acta Pauli
AÉ
Anderson
Apostolic Constitutions
Athanasius, *Apologia de fuga sua*
Atlas
Basil, *Letters*
BHG
BHL
BS
Calder, "Early Christian"
Calder, "Some Monuments"
Catalogue
CIJ
CIL
Cumont, "Les inscriptions"
DACL
Déléage
Delehaye, *Origines*
pseudo-Dionysius of Tell Mahre
pseudo-Dorotheus of Tyre
Drew-Bear
Drew-Bear & Nouar
Ehrhard
EnECh
Epiphanius, *Panarion*

Eusebius, *Ecclesiastical History*
Eusebius, *Martyrs of Palestine*
Fedalto
Ferrua
Franchi de' Cavalieri, *I martiri*
Franchi de' Cavalieri, *Note agiografiche*
Gelzer
Gibson
Grégoire, "Notes"
Grégoire, *Recueil*
Guralnick
Harnack
Hasluck
Haspels
Herrmann
Hilary, *Decretum*
Hippolytus, *Refutatio*
Horsley
IG
Ignatius
IGRR
Irenaeus, *Adversus haereses*
Jerome, *De viris inlustribus*
Johnson
Jones, *Cities*
Jones, *Later Roman Empire*
Kitzinger
Knopf & Krueger
Koester
Lactantius, *Divinae Institutiones*
Laminger-Pascher, *Beiträge*
Laminger-Pascher, *Die Kaiserzeitlichen*
Latyshev, *Menologii*
LeBas & Waddington
Leontius Scholasticus
Le Quien
Lightfoot, *Apostolic Fathers*
Lightfoot, *St. Paul's Epistles*
Lucian, *Satires*
MAMA

Martyrdom of Polycarp
Martyrologium Hieronymianum
Martyrologium Romanum
Martyrologium Syriacum
Melito
Mendel
Menologium Basilianum
Menologium Sirletianum
Michael the Syrian
Mitchell, *Anatolia*
Mitchell & Waelkens
Muratorian Canon
Musurillo
New Documents
Nicetas Paphlagonis
Nollé
OCD
ODCC
Pallas, "Investigations"
Paris
Pauly-Wissowa
Petzl
Philostorgius
Poljakov
Polycarp
Praedestinatus
Ramsay, "Cities"
Ramsay, *Cities*
Rehm, *Didyma*
Rehm, *Milet*
Robert
Robinson, *Bauer*
Ruinart
Şahin, *Arykanda*
Şahin, *Perge*
Schneemelcher
SEC
SEG
Simeon Metaphrastes, *Martyrium SS. Martyrum Leonis et Paregorii*
Snyder

Socrates
Sozomen
Tabbernee
Tabbernee, "Portals"
Talbert
TAM
Tertullian, *Adversus Marcionem*
Theophylact of Ohrid
TIB
Turner
Yamauchi

General

Asia. The dioecesis of Asia contained the Diocletianic provinces of Asia, Hellespontus, Insulae, Lydia, Caria, Pamphylia, Lycia, Phrygia I (later Pacatiana), Phrygia II (later Salutaris), and Pisidia; see Jones, *Later Roman Empire*, 2:1456–57; and Talbert, map 101. With respect to the division of Lycia and Pamphylia, see also Gelzer, lxiii. Lycaonia was created as a separate province out of part of Pisidia, Isauria, and Galatia late in the Fourth Century; see Basil, *Letters*, 138. For further details, see Mitchell, *Anatolia*, 155 & 158–63.

The *Acta Pauli* contains numerous legends relating to the work of Paul and his companions. The *Martyrs of Lyon*, 1, is addressed to the Christians of Asia and Phrygia; see Musurillo, 62. Irenaeus, *Adversus haereses*, 3.3.4, mentions his own connection with Polycarp of Smyrna.

On the wide ranging activity of Papylas, see the *Martyrdom of Carpus, Papylus, and Agathonike*, 32, in Musurillo, 26.

Note also Apollonius's mention of the renegade Bishop Alexander, without designation of his see, in Eusebius, *Ecclesiastical History*, 5.18.9. Socrates, 6.19.7, mentions the continuing presence of Novatians and Quartodecemians in Asia and Lydia in the Fifth Century. On Christian inscriptions generally, see *MAMA*, 10:xxxvi–xli.

The Cleveland marbles, Christian sculpture from *ca*.270–280, may have originated in Southern Asia Minor; see Kitzinger, 660–62. Several inscriptions now found at Afyon Karahisar were brought from elsewhere without any record being kept of their original provenance; see *MAMA*, 4:ix. For a copy of Maximin Daia's anti-Christian rescript of 312 found at Kusbaba (Colbasa); see *AÉ* 1988, #1046.

The martyrdom of Theogenes, somewhere in Hellespontus at about the time of Licinius, see *AB* 2(1883): 206–210 (*BHL*, #8106), and *AB*

17(1898): 121 (*BHL*, #8107), may in fact be connected with Apamaea Kibotos in Phrygia.

For a brief study of some of the issues facing the churches in Asia Minor, see Robinson, *Bauer*, 123–205.

Phrygia. (in general.) Philostorgius, 8.15, claims that the Roman writer Novatian was a native of Phrygia. Many of the inscriptions from Phrygia have been alleged to be Montanist, though it would be fairer to say that they represent an exceptionally self-confident Christian community; see Tabbernee, 8, 60, 139 & 143–44. Alexander the physician, a native of Phrygia, was martyred at Lyon in the late Second Century; see *Martyrs of Lyon*, 49, in Musurillo, 76; compare Eusebius, *Ecclesiastical History*, 5.1.49. Epiphanius, *Panarion*, 47.1.2, makes mention of encratites who were active in Phrygia and Pisidia. Basil, *Letters*, 188.1 & 5; & 236, gives the policy for dealing with encratites who seek to join the great church; see *EnECh*, 686. For the broad scope of church development, see *TIB*, 7:125–38. On Phrygia in general, see *DACL*, 14:758–806, *EnECh*, 686, and Haspels, 1:205–54. For the continued strength of pagan cults there, see Drew-Bear & Nouar, 1907–2044.

Specific Sites

Abeikta. (apparently in Phrygia I, perhaps modern Yalnizsaray.) Tabbernee, #47 (=Gibson, #3, =Johnson #2.11), found at Yalnizsaray and bearing the familiar "Christians for Christians" formula, is an inscription of Aurelius Eutychus for his family *ca.*295–310 C.E. *TIB*, 7:414.

Aizanoi. (in the province Phrygia I, modern Çavdarhisar; see Tabbernee, map 7.) *MAMA*, 7:xxxix, refers to an inscription from 179/80 C.E., found at nearby Çeltikci, with motifs that can possibly be interpreted as Christian, see Calder, "Early Christian," 33–35. Tabbernee, #53 (=Gibson, #16), records a possibly Christian inscription by Aurelius Marceianus, *ca.*304/305. Bishop Pisticus was at the Council of Nicaea; see Gelzer, lxiii. *Atlas*, 5. Talbert, map 62.

Akçaköy. (in Phrygia I, possibly ancient Kreura.) Tabbernee, #40 (=Gibson, #8), is a Christian inscription of Aurelia Domna for her family, *ca.*305–310. Tabbernee, 181, & map 11. *TIB*, 7:174.

Akmonia/Keramon Agora. (in Phrygia I; modern Ahat.) Jewish inscriptions would include *CIJ* #760 from 248/49, *CIJ* #770 from

243/44, and *MAMA* 6: #335a from 248–49. *MAMA*, 6: #325 is also a Jewish inscription from 255/56 C.E.

Tabbernee, #21 (=Gibson, #32), is an inscription of 253/54 C.E. by Aurelia Julia for her Christian family. Tabbernee, #22 (=Gibson, #33), is the epitaph of Hedia, a Christian, from *ca.*250–274.

Ramsay, *Cities*, #467–469 & note on p. 790 (=*IGRR*, 4, #607), records the activities of a pagan priestly family residing here and at Meiros and evidently opposed to Christianity *ca.*313/14. Harnack, 772. *Atlas*, 5. Talbert, map 62.

Alibey köy. (in Phrygia I, ancient name uncertain.) Tabbernee, #39 (=Gibson, #14, =Johnson, #2.4), is a Christian inscription of Aurelia Kyrilla for her family, *ca.*305–310. Tabbernee, map 11.

Altıntaş town. (in Phrygia I; ancient name uncertain.) Tabbernee, #27 (=Gibson, #22, =Johnson, #2.6), is a "Christians for Christians" inscription of Aurelia Ammeia for her family in 248/49 C.E. *MAMA*, 6: #238, is also Christian, but the editors do not supply a date. Pagan inscriptions are also known; see *SEG* 28 (1978), #1089, an inscription from 239/240. Harnack, 739. Talbert, map 62.

Amblada. (in the province Pisidia.) Bishop Patricius was at the Council of Nicaea; see Gelzer, lxiii. Philostorgius, 5.2, mentions that Constantius exiled Aetius there. *Atlas*, 5. Talbert, map 65.

Anaia. (in the province Asia.) Bishop Paul was at the Council of Nicaea; see Gelzer, lxii. *Atlas*, 5. Talbert, map 61.

Ancyra Sideras. (in the province Lydia.) Bishop Florentius was at the Council of Nicaea; see Gelzer, lxii. *Atlas*, 5. Delehaye, *Origines*, 154–55. Talbert, map 62.

Antioch/Colonia Caesarea. (in the province Pisidia.) The work of Paul and his companions is reported in Acts 13:14 & 13:49. *Acta Pauli*, 2.1–3.1, may refer to legends of Paul's work in Antioch of Pisidia.

The Bishop Acacius who was martyred under Decius may have been a chorepiscopus related to Antioch; see *AASS*, Martius 3:899–900 (*BHL*, #25). Harnack, 772, notes the clear distinction made in the martyr account between Montanist, *i.e.* "cataphrygian," and catholic teaching.

Le Quien, 1:1036–37, doubtfully identifies four early figures as bishops. Bishop Eudoxias appears in *SEC*, 23 June. Bishops Optatus, Anthemius, and Cyprianus appear in *AASS*, Septembris, 7:200–202.

Bishop Sergianus was certainly at the Council of Ancyra in 314;

see Turner, 2:32 & 50–51. *Atlas*, 5. Fedalto, 255. Mitchell & Waelkens, 11–12 & 201–18. Talbert, map 62.

Antiochia (ad Menandrum). (in the province Caria.) Bishop Eusebius was at the Council of Nicaea; see Gelzer, lxiii. Atlas, 5. Talbert, maps 61 & 65.

Apamea Kibotos/Kelainai. (in the province Phrygia I, near the border with Pisidia; modern Dinar.) Eusebius, *Ecclesiastical History*, 5.16.17, mentions Bishop Julian opposing early Montanists there.

Apamea seems to have had an influential Jewish population in the Third Century, for a coin of the city depicts Noah and his ark; see *Catalogue*, 101, #182. For an illustration, see Achelis, *Christentum*, 31. Harnack, 771.

MAMA, 6: #226, is an inscription with the Eumeneian formula from 250 C.E. *MAMA*, 6: #221, #222 & #231 are similar. Tabbernee, #19 (=*MAMA*, 6: #236; =Gibson, 38) is the Christian epitaph of Aurelius Proclus and his wife Meletine from *ca*.225–274. Tabbernee, #20 (=*MAMA*, 6: #235; =Gibson, 39; =Johnson, #2.18), is the Christian epitaph of Kapiton from the same date range. Tabbernee, #33 (=*MAMA*, 6: #234; =Gibson, 40), is the Christian epitaph of Aurelius Valens from *ca*.275–313. The epitaph of Aurelius Pancharius with the Eumeneian formula from 253/54 has been claimed as Christian (Cumont, "Les inscriptions," #209), but also as Jewish (Ramsay, *Cities*, #385; *CIJ*, #773).

Greek traditions of the martyrs Tryphon and Respicius under Decius are associated with the village of Sampsados near Apamea. See *AASS*, Novembris, 4:330 & 332 (*BHG*, #1856). Note also the paraphrase by Simeon Metaphrastes; *AASS*, Novembris, 4:345–46, and PG 114:1312–28 (*BHG*, #1857). See also *SEC*, 1 February. For the related Latin texts, see *AASS*, Novembris 4:360–61 (*BHL*, #8339); and *AASS*, Novembris 4:368, with Ruinart, 208–10 (*BHL*, #8337).

There seems to be some duplication regarding Apamea in the lists for the Council of Nicaea. Bishop Tarsicius of Apamea (listed in Pisidia) was recorded as being at the Council of Nicaea; see Gelzer, lxiii. At the same time a Bishop Paul of Apamea (listed in Phrygia) was also recorded as being at the Council; see Gelzer, lxiii. Perhaps Paul should be counted as a suffragan or coadjutor bishop. Harnack, 776. Jones, *Cities*, 42, 535, & map facing 28. *Atlas*, 5. *TIB*, 7:188–89. Fedalto, 1:258. Tabbernee, map 8. Talbert, map 65.

Aphrodisias. (in the province Caria.) *Martyrologium Syriacum*, 30 April, mentions the martyred presbyter Diodotus and the deacon Rhodopianus; compare *Martyrologium Hieronymianum*, 2 kal Maii. Delehaye, *Origines*, 146. Bishop Ammonius was at the Council of Nicaea; see Gelzer, lxiii. *Atlas*, 5. For further bibliography, see *SEG* 39 (1989): #1100. Talbert, map 65.

Apollonia/Sozopolis. (in the province Pisidia, formerly Phrygian territory; modern Uluborlu, near Senirkent.) Tabbernee, #34 (=Gibson, #44, =*MAMA*, 4:221), found at Senirkent, is an inscription of Aurelia Domna from *ca.*280 mentioning her Christian grandfather, Diogenes. MAMA, 4: #222, contains the inscription A-Ω and dates apparently to the Third Century. *MAMA*, 4: #220, contains a mention of presbyters and dates to the Third or perhaps the Fourth Century. *MAMA*, 4: #224, is from the Fourth Century. Jones, *Cities*, map following 28 & 139–41. *TIB*, 7:387–88. Talbert, map 65.

Apollonia Salbakes. (in the province Caria; modern Medet.) Bishop Eugenius was at the Council of Nicaea; see Gelzer, lxiii. *Atlas*, 5. Talbert, map 65.

Appia. (in the province Phrygia I; formerly Abiye; later Pinarcik (köy); now Pinarbasi. See Tabbernee, 179–80.) Tabbernee, #24 (=Anderson, #12; =Gibson, #2; =Johnson, #2.3), is a Christian inscription of Markion and others from *ca.*225–274. Tabbernee, #26 (=Anderson, # 13; =Gibson, #17), is the Christian epitaph of Tation from the same time frame. Tabbernee, #25 (=Anderson, #14; =Gibson, #1), is a Christian inscription by Aurelia Rophenia for her husband *ca.*225–274. *Martyrologium Hieronymianum*, 2 non. Mar., mentions martyrs who were taken from "Appia in Bithynia" to Nicomedia. The martyrology of Bede attempts to correct the place name to Apamaea. *Atlas*, 5. *MAMA*, 10:xxxvii. *TIB*, 7:189–90. Talbert, map 62.

Ardabau. (in Phrygia. Tabbernee, 17, discusses possible locations.) Eusebius, *Ecclesiastical History*, 5.16.7, reports that Montanus first prophesied in Ardabau. Harnack, 771. *TIB*, 7:190.

A(r)slanapa. (in Phrygia II, on the territory of Kotiaion; ancient name unknown.) Tabbernee, # 31 (=Gibson, #24, =*MAMA*, 10: #275), is the "Christians for Christians" epitaph of Kyrilla from the late-Third or early-Fourth Century. *TIB*, 7:152, 349, & 389.

Arykanda. (in Lycia, modern Aruf.) An inscription at Arycanda, dating to *ca.*312, contains a request of the people of Lycia and Pamphylia to the emperors to suppress Christianity, so it is likely that Christians were in the town; see *CIL*, 3, Suppl. 2.4, #12132 (=*TAM*, 2.3: #785). Compare Eusebius, *Ecclesiastical History*, 9.7.13. For further analysis, see *DACL*, 1:2835–43. Şahin, *Arykanda*, #310–15, lists Christian inscriptions of later date. Harnack, 776. *Atlas*, 5. Talbert, map 65.

Aspendos. (in the province Pamphylia.) Bishop Domnos was at the Council of Nicaea; see Gelzer, lxiii. *Atlas*, 5. Talbert, map 65.

Assos. (in the province Asia; later in Hellespontus.) Acts 20:14 records a brief stop by Paul and his companions. Yamauchi, 21–29. *ABD*, s.v. Jones, *Cities*, 526. Talbert, map 56.

Attalea. (in the province Pamphylia; see Jones, *Cities*, 536.) Paul and his companions made a brief stop there; see Acts 14:25. *AASS* Maiius 1, xvi–xvii (=*BHG*, #746) lists martyrs Hesperius, Zoe, and others under Hadrian; see also *SEC*, 2 May, and *Menologium Sirletianum*, 2 May. *Atlas*, 5. Talbert, map 65.

Aureli(an)opolis. (perhaps Tmolos in the province Lydia, just West of Sardis at modern Gökkaya according to Talbert, map 56. Harnack, map VI, and *Atlas*, 5, place Aurelianopolis just East of Sardis without noting a link with Tmolos.) Bishop Antiochus of Aurelianopolis was at the Council of Nicaea; see Gelzer, lxii. *Atlas*, 5. Pauly-Wissowa, 2:2431. Fedalto, 1:182, gives the alternate name of the site as Perikome/Perikomma.

Aykirikçi. (in Phrygia I, ancient name uncertain.) Tabbernee, #38 (=Gibson, #12), is a Christian inscription by Aurelia Appes for her family, *ca.*290–300. Note also Tabbernee, #60 (=Gibson, #29), #61 (=Gibson, #27), and #62 (=Gibson, #28, =Johnson, #2.7), which are Christian inscriptions from *ca.*325–374. *TIB*, 7:201.

Bagis. (in the province Lydia.) Bishop Pollion of "Baris" in Lydia was at the Council of Nicaea; see Gelzer, lxii. Harnack, 784, identifies the site as Bagis. Jones, *Cities*, 528. Talbert, map 62.

Baris. (in the province Pisidia.) Bishop Heraclius was at the Council of Nicaea; see Gelzer, lxiii. Harnack, 773 & 776. *Atlas*, 5. *TIB*, 7:206. Talbert, map 65.

Brouzos. (in the province Phrygia II, modern Kara-Sandykli.) Ramsay, *Cities*, #635, records a possibly Christian inscription from the late Third Century. Harnack, 772. *Atlas*, 5. *TIB*, 7:215. Talbert, map 62.

Chios. (island off the coast of Asia Minor.) Acts 20:15 records a brief stop by Paul and his companions. *AASS*, Maiius 3:62*–63* (*BHG*, #960), lists the martyr Isidoros under Decius. *SEC*, 13 July, mentions the martyr Myropes under Decius. For Myropes, see also Latyshev, *Menologii*, 2:171–73 (*BHG*, #2282). Delehaye, *Origenes*, 226–27. Harnack, 734 & 786. *Atlas*, 5. Talbert, map 56.

Cibyra. (in the region of Cibyratis in the province Caria.) Bishop Letodorus was at the Council of Nicaea; see Gelzer, lxiii. Ramsay, *Cities*, #432 bis, contains the name Epaphras, which Ramsay suggests may be Christian. Ramsay, *Cities*, #433, is likewise Christian but of uncertain date. Epiphanius, *Panarion*, 51.30.2, alludes to a miracle in which the waters of the local stream changed to wine each year. Harnack, 784. *Atlas*, 5. Talbert, map 65.

Colossae. (in Phrygia I.) The letter to the Colossians is part of the Pauline corpus. *Apostolic Constitutions*, 7.46.12, claims Philemon as the first bishop. Le Quien, 1:815, counts Epaphras of Colossians 1:7 & 4:12 as the first bishop and Philemon as the second. *ABD*, 2:533. Fedalto, 1:159. *Atlas*, 5. Talbert, map 65.

Conana. (in Pisidia, formerly Phrygian territory; modern Gönen, see Tabbernee, 2, and *TIB*, 7:311.) Eusebius, *Ecclesiastical History*, 5.16.17 & 5.18.12–13, mentions Bishop Zoticus of "the village Koumana" and Julian of Apamea as opposing early Montanists in their area. Jones, *Cities*, 142. According to Turner 1:78–79, and Fedalto, 241, there is a possibility that Bishop Cyril of Homonada in Isauria, who attended the Council of Nicaea, should be assigned to Conana instead; contrast Gelzer, lxiii. Conana is close to Apamea, but alternatively, Comama (modern Serefönü) may be the place intended by Eusebius. *Atlas*, 5. Compare Talbert, map 65.

Cos. (island in the Aegean.) Bishop Meliphron was at the Council of Nicaea; see Gelzer, lxiii. *Atlas*, 5. Talbert, map 61.

Cyzicus. (in the province Hellespontus.) Grégoire, *Recueil*, #8, lists an inscription from the late Third Century with the Eumeneian formula from nearby Yeni Keui. Martyr stories are known from the time of Maximian; see *BHL*, #2833. Bishop Theonas was at the

Council of Nicaea; see Gelzer, lxii. Socrates, 2.38.28 & 3.11.3, mentions a Novatianist church there in the time of the Emperor Julian. Jones, *Cities*, 527. *Atlas*, 5. Le Quien, 1:747–49. Fedalto, 1:138. Talbert, map 52.

Dorylaion. (in the province Phrygia II; near modern Eskişehir.) Bishop Athenodorus was at the Council of Nicaea; see Gelzer, lxiii. *Atlas*, 5. Tabbernee, #63, is an inscription from *ca.*325–374 mentioning the woman Mountane, "Christian and pneumatike," evidently a Montanist. The inscription includes a Latin cross, and also the symbol Π twice. Talbert, map 62.

Dumanli. (in Phrygia I; ancient name unknown.) Two inscriptions found at Dumanli, *MAMA*, 4: #356, from 258; and *MAMA*, 4: #357, from 273/74, both contain the Eumeneian formula. Harnack, 771, suggested Dumanli as the location for ancient Tymion, though that site has now been located near modern Susuzören; see Tabbernee, "Portals," 88. Compare *TIB*, 7:242–43 & 409. Compare Talbert, map 62.

Elaea. (in Asia; modern Kazikbağlari.) Bishop Orion of "Ilion" was at the Council of Nicaea; see Gelzer, lxii, where the name of the place is recorded as Ilion in Asia and is distinct from Ilion in Hellespontus. Turner, 1:64–65, gives a careful rendition of the Latin evidence. Harnack, 784, identifies this place as Ilion/Troas in Hellespontus. Fedalto, 122, conjectures Elaea, which is certainly in Asia. Talbert, map 56.

Ephesus. (in the province Asia.) Acts 18:19–20:17 records the work of Paul and his companions at Ephesus. The letter to the Ephesians is part of the Pauline corpus. The church at Ephesus and its members are also mentioned at I Corinthians 15:32 & 16:8, as well as at I Timothy 1:3, and II Timothy 1:18 & 4:12. Revelation 2:1–9 is addressed to Ephesus. *Apostolic Constitutions*, 7.46.7, claims that Timothy and John were the first bishops of Ephesus. Ignatius, *Ephesians*, 1.3 & 6.2, mentions the Bishop Onesimus of Ephesus warmly. Irenaeus, *Adversus haereses*, 3.3.4, reports the story that John and the heretic Cerinthus nearly met at Ephesus. Apollonius records the story that John also raised a dead man at Ephesus; see Eusebius, *Ecclesiastical History*, 5.18.14.

Hippolytus, *Refutatio*, 9.7.1 & 10.27.1, says that the modalist Noetus was from Smyrna. Epiphanius, *Panarion*, 57.1.1, however, claims that

Noetus was from Ephesus. Bishop Polycrates, in writing to Pope Victor in the late Second Century, says that John's remains were at Ephesus, as were the remains of one of Philip's daughters; see Eusebius, *Ecclesiastical History*, 3.31.3, 5.22.1 & 5.24.2–4. A certain bishop Isaac is mentioned; see *DHGE*, 15:558. Bishop Menophantus of Ephesus was at the Council of Nicaea; see Gelzer, lxii. *Martyrologium Romanum*, 30 April, mentions the martyr Maximus under Decius. See also *Menologium Sirletianum*, 30 April. For a recent study of the church there, see Koester, 119–40, and contrast, Robinson, *Bauer*, 93–121. *Atlas*, 5. For inscriptions illustrative of the background for Christianity in Ephesus, see Horsley, 105–68, For further bibliography, see *SEG* 46 (1996): #1449. Talbert, map 61.

Eukarpia. (in the province Phrygia II, modern Emirhisar; see Tabbernee, map 8.) Bishop Eugenius was at the Council of Nicaea; see Gelzer, lxiii. *TIB*, 7:250–51. *Atlas*, 5. Jones, *Cities*, 531. Talbert, map 62.

Eumeneia. (in the province Phrygia I, modern Işikli.) Bishop Polycrates, in writing to Pope Victor in the late Second Century, mentions Thraseas of Eumeneia, bishop and martyr, whose relics were kept at Smyrna; see Eusebius, *Ecclesiastical History*, 5.24.4. An anonymous anti-Montanist tract cited by Eusebius, 5.16.22, mentions both Montanist and orthodox martyrs, among them Gaius and Alexander, at Eumeneia. *Atlas*, 5. Delehaye, *Origines*, 158. Fedalto, 1:157. Jones, *Cities*, 530.

Tabbernee, #32 (=Gibson, #41), from *ca.*275–313, is an inscription mentioning Bishop Aurelius Glyconides. Ramsay, *Cities*, #372 (=*SEG* 6 (1932): #219) dates to 249. Johnson, #2.17 (=Ramsay, *Cities*, #374) is a Christian inscription from *ca.*270. Ramsay, *Cities*, #371 & #373 (=Cumont, "Les inscriptions," #135) are of similar date. *MAMA*, 4: #353 (=Ramsay, *Cities*, #447), from 253/54, contains the probably Christian word "kumeterion." Paris, 8:252, #20 (=Cumont, "Les inscriptions," #136), is the epitaph of Zenodotus from *ca.* 256.

MAMA, 4: #360 (=Ramsay, #377), is a Third-Century inscription containing the Eumeneian formula "whoever disturbs this tomb let it be with him and God." Similar is *SEG* 15 (1958): #811 from nearby Emircik and datable to 246. Inscriptions from nearby Sirikli with the Eumeneian formula or variants of it, and also with fish motif, include *MAMA*, 4: #354 (=Ramsay, *Cities*, #445) from 253; and *MAMA* 4: #355 (=Ramsay, *Cities*, #446) from *ca.*255. *MAMA*, 4: #356 from 258, and #357 from 273/74.

Possibly Christian inscriptions include the following: Drew-Bear 75,8 (=*SEG* 28(1978): #1126), and 109,48 (=*SEG* 28(1978): #1144), which have the Eumeneian formula and may be early Third Century. Ramsay, *Cities*, #373, from *ca.*324/25. Ramsay, *Cities*, #362 (=*SEG* 6(1932): #204) from *ca.*200–250, and #364 (=*SEG* 6(1932): #203 from *ca.*250. *SEG* 45(1995): #1743, =6(1932): #210, =26(1979–77): #1377, =29(1979): #1400 is an inscription of the Third Century. *TIB*, 7:251–52. Talbert, map 62.

Eymir. (in the province Phrygia I, ancient name uncertain.) Tabbernee, #50 (=Gibson, #19), is a "Christians for Christians" inscription of Aurelius Patrikis from *ca.*275–325. *TIB*, 7:253.

Gagai. (in Lycia.) Eusebius, *Martyrs of Palestine*, 4.2–5, mentions the martyr Apphianus from Gagai. Jones, *Cities*, 532. *Atlas*, 5. Talbert, map 65.

Gecek. (in Phrygia I; ancient name uncertain.) Tabbernee, #52 (=Gibson, #21), is the Christian epitaph of Aurelius Glycon from *ca.*300–325. *TIB*, 7:256–57.

Hadrianopolis. (in the province Pisidia.) Le Quien, 1:1049, mentions a Bishop Olympus. Bishop Telemachus was at the Council of Nicaea; see Gelzer, lxiii. Harnack, map VI, gives two possible locations for the Hadrianopolis represented by Telemachus. Talbert, map 65, likewise gives two possible locations for the town. *MAMA*, 10: map following xiv, seems to favor the more Southeasterly location.

Hierapolis. (in the province Phrygia I; modern Pamukkale.) Colossians 4:13 mentions Christians at Hierapolis. Eusebius, *Ecclesiastical History*, 3.31.2–3 & 5.24.2, mentions the relics of Philip and his daughters there. In a much later work, Nicetas Paphlagonis, *Oratio IX, In Laudem S. Philippi Apost.*, PL 105: 192, also makes reference to the apostle Philip being at Heirapolis. Le Quien, 1:833 mentions a Bishop Hieros. Eusebius, 3.36.2, mentions Bishop Papias as a contemporary of Ignatius and Polycarp. Eusebius, 3.39.1–17, discusses Papias's writings. At 3.39.4–9, he says that Papias knew Philip's daughter and also the presbyters Aristion and John. Eusebius, 4.26.1 & 5.19.1, mentions Apollinaris as an adversary of the Montanists in the time of Irenaeus. Fedalto, 1:158.

The Abercius inscription from *ca.*180 is commonly regarded as the earliest known Christian inscription; see Johnson, #2.15 (=Ramsay,

Cities, #657); also Snyder, 139–40. For a recent analysis, see *New Documents*, 6:177–81. For additional bibliography, see *SEG* 37 (1987): #1166. *AÉ* 1994, #1660, is an apparently Jewish inscription from the Third Century.

Tabbernee, #10 (=Gibson, #42) and #11 (=Gibson, 41), are Christian sarcophagi from *ca.*180–224 C.E. Ramsay, *Cities*, #404, is a Christian inscription of uncertain date. *Martyrologium Syriacum*, 25 October, mentions the martyrs Claudianus & Cyriacus. Delehaye, *Origines*, 158–59. Bishop Flaccus was at the Council of Nicaea; see Gelzer, lxiii. *Atlas*, 5. *TIB*, 7:268–72. Talbert, map 65.

Hierapolis. (in Phrygia II; modern Koçhisar, near Kelendres.) Johnson, #2.13 (=Ramsay, *Cities*, #656), is the epitaph of a Christian named Alexander from *ca.*216 found at the modern town of Kelendres and is based on the Abercius inscription. Ramsay, *Cities*, 679–83, initially believed Kelendres to be ancient Otrous, but on the basis of further exploration placed Otrous at modern Çorhisar. *TIB*, 7:272–79. Talbert, map 62.

Hierocaesarea. (ancient Hieracome, just South of Thyatira, in the province Lydia. Jones, *Cities*, 83 & 85.) Tabbernee, #13 (=Gibson, #37) is the sarcophagus of the Christians Gaius and Stratoneikiane from *ca.*180–224 C.E. Bishop Antiochus was at the Council of Nicaea; see Gelzer, lxii. Talbert, map 56.

Hypaipa. (in the province Asia; modern Datbey.) Jones, *Cities*, 78–79 & 526). Bishop Mithres was at the Council of Nicaea; see Gelzer, lxii. *Atlas*. 5. Talbert, map 56.

Iconium. (in the province Pisidia, later in Lycaonia; modern Konya.) The work of Paul and his companions is mentioned in Acts 13:51, 14:1, 14:19, and 14:21. *Acta Pauli*, 2.1–3.41, reports legends of activity by Paul, Onesiphorus, and Thecla in the vicinity of Iconium. *Martyrdom of Justin and companions*, recension B, 4.8, indicates that the martyr Hierax was from Iconium; see Musurillo, 50. Delehaye, *Origines*, 160–62.

Several legendary bishops are found in the literature. On the dubious authority of pseudo-Dorotheus of Tyre, 46, Le Quien, 1:1067, lists the Sossipater of Romans 16:21 as the first "bishop." See also *Menologium Sirletianum*, 29 April, and compare *BS*, 11:1318.

For Bishop Terentius, see *SEC*, 22 June; *Menologium Sirletianum*, 21 June & 30 October; and *BS*, 12:432–33. The martyr bishop Carnotas is found in *Menologium Sirletianum*, 12 September. Fedalto, 266.

Eusebius, *Ecclesiastical History*, 6.19.18, mentions a letter from Alexander of Jerusalem to Demetrius of Alexandria, in which Alexander noted that Bishop Celsus had invited a certain Paulinus to preach at Iconium. Eusebius, 7.7.5, is a letter of Dionysius of Alexandria in which he mentions a synod at Iconium. Eusebius, 7.28.1, contains a mention of Bishop Nicomas of Iconium as a contemporary of Dionysius of Alexandria. Bishop Petrus was at the Council of Ancyra in 314; see Turner, 1:32, 50–51. Bishop Eulalius was at the Council of Nicaea; see Gelzer, lxiii. *Atlas*, 5. Talbert, map 66.

Ilion/Troas. (in the province Hellespontus; modern Hisarlik.) The work of Paul and his companions at Troas is mentioned at Acts 16:8 & 11, also 20:5–6. Further mention of church members there is made at II Corinthians 2:12, and II Timothy, 4:13. Bishop Marinus of Ilion in Hellespontus was at the Council of Nicaea; see Gelzer, lxii. Turner, 1:64–65. Harnack, 784, conjectures Dascylion for this site, which would be East of Cyzicus; see Jones, *Cities*, 86–87 & map following p. 28. Fedalto, 1:149, identifies the bishop of Ilion in Hellespontus with this site and the bishop of Ilion in Asia with Elaia. *Atlas*, 5. Talbert, map 56.

Kadoi. (i.e. Cadi; modern Eski Gediz. In the region of Mysia. By the Byzantine era counted as part of Phrygia I; see Jones, *Cities*, 81 & 530.) Tabbernee, #57 (=Gibson, #30), is a Christian inscription of Auxanon for his parents, *ca.*275–325. For comment on this and similar inscriptions, see *MAMA*, 10:xxxvi–xxxviii. *TIB*, 7:285). Talbert, map 62.

Kalytos. (village near Antioch in Pisidia.) *SEC*, 28 September, records Alpheus and six other martyrs from Kalytos who suffered in Antioch of Pisidia during the Decianic persecutions. See also, *SEC*, 21 May & 22 November. *TIB*, 7:286.

Karaağaç. (just East of Appia in Phrygia; ancient name uncertain.) Tabbernee, #29 (=Gibson, #18) is a Christian inscription from *ca.*225–274. Tabbernee, #48 (=Gibson, #5), is a Christian inscription from *ca.*300–310. *TIB*, 7:288–89.

Karene/Carina. (in the province Asia.) A Christian woman from there is mentioned as a prisoner in the time of Decius in *Martyrdom of Poinius*, 11; see Musurillo, 150. Talbert, map 56.

Keçiller. (in Phrygia I; ancient name uncertain.) Tabbernee, #45 (=Gibson, #7), is a Christian inscription of Eutyches for his family, *ca.*275–325. *TIB*, 7:297.

Kotiaion. (in Phrygia II; near modern Kütahya.) Tabbernee, #54, from *ca.*250–300, is a possibly Christian inscription. *MAMA*, 10: #254, reading "οἶκος θεοῦ," is a Third-Century inscription from the nearby village of Çukurca. *SEG* 31 (1981): #1116 is a clearly Christian epitaph set up for the wife or daughter of an Aurelius Gaius during the tetrarchy. Similarly, Tabbernee, #64, #65, and #66, are possibly Christian inscriptions from *ca.*325–374. More certainly Christian is Tabbernee, #67 (see Gibson, 87), the epitaph of Domnus from *ca.* 325–375. The town had a Novatianist bishop in the middle of the Fourth Century; see Socrates, 4.28.18. *TIB*, 7:312–16. Talbert, map 62.

Kuyuçak. (apparently in Phrygia I, just Northeast of Zemmeana; ancient name uncertain.) Tabbernee, #28 (=Gibson, #23), is a "Christians for Christians" inscription from *ca.*225–274. *TIB*, 7:320.

Lampsacus. (in the province Hellespontus.) *Martyrologium Hieronymianum*, id. Maii, mentions martyrs Peter, Andrew, Paul, and Dionysia. *AASS*, Maii 3:450–51 (*BHL*, #6716), places them in the time of Decius. See also *SEC*, 15 & 18 May. For further comment, see *New Documents*, 3: 156.

AASS, Februarius, 2:38–43, is the acts of the Bishop Parthenius, whose father Christodoulus was deacon of the local church. The document shows Parthenius to have been a contemporary of Constantine. Compare *SEC*, 7 February. See also *BHG*, #1422, #1423, & #1423a. *BS*, 10:341–42. Jones, *Cities*, 527. Delehaye, *Origines*, 147. *Atlas*, 5. Talbert, map 51.

Laodicea. (on the Lycus River in the Diocletianic province Phrygia, earlier counted as part of Asia.) The church at Laodicea is mentioned in Colossians 2:1, also 4:13, 15–16. Revelation 3:14–22 is addressed to the church at Laodicea. According to the legend recorded in *Apostolic Constitutions*, 7.46.12, Archippus was the first bishop. For "bishop" Nymphas, see Le Quien, 1:791–92, and compare Colossians 4:15.

Tertullian, *Adversus Marcionem*, 5.17.1, says that the Marcionites knew Ephesians under the title "Laodiceans." *Muratorian Canon*, line 64, knows of a falsified letter to the Laodiceans. Perhaps this is the apocryphal letter surviving in Latin; see Lightfoot, 287–89, for the text. Schneemelcher, 2:42–46, dates this apocryphal letter broadly to somewhere in the Second through Fourth Centuries.

According to Eusebius, *Ecclesiastical History*, 4.26.3–4, Melito of Sardis, *Peri Pascha*, mentioned the martyr Sagaris. As the text reads, it is possible that Eusebius got his information about Melito on this point at second hand from Clement of Alexandria. The surviving text of Melito, *Peri Pascha*, makes no mention of Sagaris. Bishop Polycrates of Ephesus mentioned Sagaris, bishop and martyr of Laodicea, in a letter to Victor of Rome; see Eusebius, *Ecclesiastical History*, 5.24.5. Compare *AASS*, Octobris 3:261–62, and *Martyrologium Romanum*, 6 October.

Le Quien, 1:793–94, mentions the bishops Sisinnius and Eugenius as successors to Sagaris. Sissinius is found in *SEC*, 12 April & 8 October. For an inscription related to Eugenius, see *DACL*, 5.1:694–702.

SEG 34 (1984): #1353, and 37 (1987): #1240, mention the presbyter Ioulianos from nearby Kindaraz from before the Fourth Century.

The presbyter Artemon was martyred under Diocletian; see Abicht & Reichelt, 185–97 (*BHG*, #175). Compare *Martyrologium Sirletianum*, 8 October. Bishop Nounechius was at the Council of Ancyra in 314; see Turner, 1:32, 50–51. He was also at the Council of Nicaea; see Gelzer, lxiii. *Atlas*, 5. Fedalto, 150. *DACL*, 8.1:1321–23. *TIB*, 7:323–26. Talbert, map 65.

Laodikeia (Kata)kekaumene. (in the province Phrygia I; modern Ladik/Altinekin.) *MAMA*, 7: #82, is a Third-Century inscription with the teltale Christian name Kyriakos. *MAMA*, 7: #94, is a late Third-Century epitaph dedicated to Damas, builder of the local church. *MAMA*, 1: #154 (=Johnson, #2.12), #155, and #156, appear to be Christian inscriptions from the Third Century. *AÉ* 1997: #1479 (=*SEG* 47 (1997): #1826) is the epitaph of Traianus for his parents; based on the script it dates to the Third Century, though it may be later. Tabbernee, #56 (=*MAMA*, 1: #157) is the epitaph of the martyred pastor Gennadeios from *ca*.310–313. *MAMA*, 1: #158, dates from the late-Third or early-Fourth Century. Tabbernee, #69 (=*MAMA*, 1: # 170; =Johnson, #3.5), an inscription from *ca*.340, is the epitaph of the soldier Marcus Julius Eugenius, later bishop, who had suffered during the Diocletianic persecutions. See also Johnson, #2.9 (=*MAMA*, 1: #213) for the inscription of Aurelius Pappas. *AÉ* 1997, #1479, is a possibly Christian inscription from as early as the Third Century. For further discussion of Christian inscriptions, see *MAMA*, 1:xxii–xxiii. *Atlas*, 5. Jones, *Cities*, 127. *TIB*, 7:327–28. Talbert, map 63.

Limenai. (in the province Pisidia. Exact location uncertain, compare Talbert, map 65. *Atlas*, 5, puts it just East of Antioch in Pisidia.) Bishop Aranius was at the Council of Nicaea; see Gelzer, lxiii. *TIB*, 7:328–29.

Lyrbe. (in the province Pamphylia.) Bishop Zeuxios of "Suarbon" was at the Council of Nicaea; see Gelzer, lxiii. Turner, 1:72–73. Le Quien, 1:1009, conjectures Lyrbe. Pauly-Wissowa, 13.2:2498. Harnack, 777. Fedalto, 1:243. Talbert, map 65.

Lystra. (in the region of Lycaonia; in the Diocletianic province of Pisidia, later in the province of Lycaonia. Modern Zoldera near Hutunsaray, about 35 km South-Southeast of Iconium.) The church at Lystra and its people are mentioned in Acts 14:6, 8, 21, and 16:1–2. At 16:1 it is identified as the home of Timothy. Another brief mention occurs at II Timothy 3:11. Pseudo-Dorotheus of Tyre, 58, makes the Artemas mentioned in Titus 3:12 the first "bishop" of Lystra; compare Le Quien, 1:1075. Laminger-Pascher, *Die Kaiserzeitlichen*, #204, dates a Christian inscription from Hutunsaray to the end of the Third Century. Another possible early Christian inscription is Laminger-Pascher, *Die Kaiserzeitlichen*, #250 (=*MAMA*, 8: #64) from Çesme, about eight miles South. Jones, *Cities*, 134 & 534. Pauly-Wissowa, 13.2:2261–62 & 14.1:71–72. *ABD*, 4:426–27. Talbert, map 66. Fedalto, 271, suggests that Bishop Tiberius of Ilistra, who attended the Council of Nicaea, should be assigned to Lystra. *TIB*, 4:200. Talbert, map 66.

Magnesia. (on the Maeander river; part of the conventus of Miletus, in the Diocletianic province Asia. Jones, *Cities*, 78 & 526.) Ignatius, *Magnesians*, 2.1, mentions Bishop Damas, the presbyters Bassus and Apollonius, as well as the deacon Zotion. *Atlas*, 5. Talbert, map 61.

Magydos. (in the province Pamphylia.) The *Martyrdom of Conon* took place at Magydos under Decius; see Musurillo, 186–92. Bishop Aphrodisius was at the Council of Nicaea; see Gelzer, lxiii. *Atlas*, 5. Talbert, map 65.

Marcianopolis. (in Caria. Marcianopolis was either Kidrama or Bargylia; see Talbert, maps 65 & 61 respectively. Jones, *Cities*, 387 & 529. Fedalto, 1:196 seems to opt for Kidrama.) Bishop Pistus was at the Council of Nicaea; see Gelzer, lxiv. *DHGE*, 12:828.

Maximianopolis. (in the province Pamphylia.) Bishop Patricius was at the Council of Nicaea; see Gelzer, lxiii. *Atlas*, 5. Pauly-Wissowa, 14.2:2485 (#3). Fedalto, 1:251.

Metropolis. (in the province Pisidia; modern Tatarli.) Bishop Polycarp was at the Council of Nicaea; see Gelzer, lxiii. *Atlas*, 5. Jones, *Cities*, 535. *TIB*, 7:339–40. Talbert, map 62, coordinate E5.

Miletos. (in the Diocletianic province Caria.) Acts 20:17, records the stop of Paul and his companions there. A dedicatory inscription from the last quarter of the Third Century found in the baths at Miletos contains the distinctive Christian name Eucharia and the probably Christian name Macarius; see Rehm, *Milet*, 1.9: #339 (=Herrmann, 339b), and also Robert, 4:129 & 134. Bishop Eusebius was at the Council of Nicaea; see Gelzer, lxiii. Sozomen, 5.20.7, mentions relics of martyrs there destroyed by the Emperor Julian. Delehaye, *Origines*, 146. *Atlas*, 5. Jones, *Cities*, 517. Talbert, map 61.

Moxiane. (district in Phrygia I; modern Hodjalar.) An inscription from the middle of the Third Century is apparently Christian; see Ramsay, *Cities*, #651. Harnack, 772. Jones, *Cities*, 71. *TIB*, 7:233–34 & 383–84. Talbert, map 62.

Myra. (in the province Lycia.) Paul made a brief stop at Myra on his way to Rome as a prisoner; see Acts 27:5. *Acta Pauli*, 3.40–5.1 (*P. Heid.* ss. 28–35, pp. 17*–25*; Lipsius & Bonnet, 1:266; translation in Schneemelcher, 2:246–49), records a legend of a lengthy stay by Paul, apparently during his first missionary journey. Harnack, 776.

AASS, Novembris 2:225–26 (*BHG*, #2295) mentions the martyred bishop Nicander and the deacon Hermaeus. See also *SEC*, 4 November; and *Menologium Sirletianum*, 4 November. Nicander was perhaps followed by a certain Nicholas; see Le Quien, 1:967. Le Quien suggests two bishops with the name Nicholas, yet there does not seem to be any evidence to distinguish an earlier Nicholas from an immediately following bishop of the same name.

According to some manuscripts, Bishop Nicholas of Myra was at the Council of Nicaea; see Gelzer, lxv–lxix, 67 & 180–81, and compare *SEC*, 6 December, and *BS*, 9:923–24. *Atlas*, 5. Fedalto, 1:225. Talbert, map 65.

Nakoleia. (in Phrygia II; modern Sayitgazi.) Tabbernee, #55, is a tombstone from *ca.*275–325 bearing the symbol Π, possibly in reference to the Montanist designation "Pneumatikoi." The symbol Π is also found on a clearly Montanist inscription from Dorylaion, *q.v.* Jones, *Cities*, 531. Talbert, map 62.

Neapolis. (in the province Pisidia.) Bishop Hesychius was at the Council of Nicaea; see Gelzer, lxiii. *Atlas*, 5. *TIB*, 7:347. Talbert, map 65.

Nuhören. (apparently in Phrygia I; ancient name uncertain.) Tabbernee, #46 (=Gibson, #6), is a "Christians for Christians" inscription of Epitynchanus from *ca.*285–300. *TIB*, 7:349.

Olympus. (in the province Lycia.) Jerome, *De viris inlustribus*, 83, says that the Christian writer Methodius of Olympus died under Decius or Valerian. Talbert, map 65.

Otrous. (in Phrygia II; modern Yanik Ören; see Talbert, map 62.) The presbyter Zoticus of Otrous was an early opponent of Montanism; see Eusebius, *Ecclesiastical History*, 5.16.5 & 18.12–13, citing an earlier work. At Kilter, just to the East of Yanik Ören, an inscription has been found. Ramsay, "Cities," #21 (=Ramsay, *Cities*, #652; =Cumont, "Les inscriptions," #156), is the epitaph of Aurelia Asclepiodora from 260. See *TIB*, 7:309, for Kilter (modern Çevrepinar).

Panemoteichos. (in Pamphylia, though the Nicene list wrongly places it in Isauria; modern Bogazköy.) Bishop Faustus was at the Council of Nicaea; see Gelzer, lxiii. Pauly-Wissowa, 18.3:586. Jones, *Cities*, map following 28, also 144 & 536. Fedalto, 1:251–52. Talbert, map 65.

Panormus /Panderma. (ancient name uncertain; on the coast, just Southeast of Cyzicus.) Grégoire, *Recueil*, #7, records an inscription with the Eumeneian formula by Aurelius Chrestus for his wife from the end of the Third Century. Hasluck, 50–51, and maps at end. *Atlas*, 5.

Pappa/Tiberiupolis. (in the province Pisidia; modern Yunisler.) Bishop Academius was at the Council of Nicaea; see Gelzer, lxiii. See also Fedalto, 261, who suggests the alternative site Parlais (modern Barla), based on the Latin manuscripts cited in Turner, 1:70–71. Jones, *Cities*, 136–37 & 535. *TIB*, 7:355. *Atlas*, 5. Talbert, map 65.

Parium. (in the province Hellespontus.) According to Lucian of Samosata, *Passing of Peregrinus*, Peregrinus, the Cynic philosopher and sometime Christian, was a native of Parium; see Lucian, *Satires*, 5:16–17.

SEC, 3 January, mentions the bishop's son Theagenes as martyred at Parium under Licinius. See the *Passio S. Theagenis Graeca*, in Franchi de' Cavalieri, *Note agiografiche* 4 (Studi e Testi 24), 177–85 (*BHG*, #2416). See also *AASS*, Januarius 1:133–35 (*BHL*, #8107), and *Martyrologium Hieronymianum*, 3 non. Jan. *BS*, 3:1340. Delehaye, *Origines*, 147–48.

SEC, 22 & 23 November, and also 15, 16 & 17 March, mentions a commemoration of the martyr Menignus who was killed under Decius; see Latyshev, *Menologii*, 1:241–45 (*BHG*, #2270); see also Ehrhard, 845, #13 (*BHG*, #2271). *SEC*, 12 April, mentions commemoration of Bishop Basil, of uncertain date. See also *Menologium Sirletianum*, 12 April. Harnack, 783. Jones, *Cities*, 527. Talbert, map 52.

Patara. (in the province Lycia.) Acts 21:1 makes mention of a brief stop by Paul and his companions. According to Leontius Scholasticus, *De sectis*, 3.1, Methodius of Olympus was also Bishop of Patara, though this information seems to be uncertain; see *ODCC*, 1080.

The martyrs Paregorius and Leo are attributed to the Third Century; see Simeon Metaphrastes, *Martyrium SS. Martyrum Leonis et Paregorii* (PG 114: 1452–61, =*BHG*, #983). Compare *AASS*, Februarius 3:58–61.

Bishop Eudemus was at the Council of Nicaea; see Gelzer, lxiii. *Atlas*, 5. Talbert, map 65.

Patmos. (island off the coast of Asia Minor.) Revelation 1:9 indicates that John was on the island (presumably imprisoned) as a result of his testimony to Jesus. Irenaeus, *Adversus haereses*, 3.3.4, says that Polycarp of Smyrna was a disciple of the presbyter John. Talbert, map 61.

Pepouza. (probably near modern Karayakuplu; in Phrygia I; see Tabbernee, "Portals," 92–03. Other suggested locations are modern Üçkuyu or Karapinar, *qqv*. Ramsay, "Cities," 4:404–405, suggested Yanik Ören.) Eusebius, *Ecclesiastical History*, 5.18.2, records that the Montanists viewed Pepouza as the new Jerusalem. At 5.18.13, he records that Maximilla prophesied there. Jerome, *Epistle*, 41.3, says Pepouza was the Montanist headquarters. Pseudo-Dionysius of Tell Mahre, fol. 117r (text 2:125, trans., 2:94), reports the finding of the bones of Montanus in the year equivalent to 549/50 C.E. For English translation, see Tabbernee, #1. Tabbernee, #2, reports the account of Montanus's tombstone as found in Michael the Syrian, *Chronicle*, 9.33 (vol. 4:323–25).

Eusebius, *Ecclesiastical History*, 8.11.1, refers to a town destroyed during the persecutions in Phrygia. Lactantius, *Divinae Institutiones*, 5.11.10, writing of a church destroyed with its members inside, seems to refer to the same incident. Calder, "Some Monuments," 362–63, conjectures that the town referred to is Pepouza. *TIB*, 7:358–59. *Atlas*, 5.

Pergamum. (in the province Asia.) Revelation 2:12–17 is addressed to this church and mentions the martyr Antipas. *Apostolic Constitutions*, 7.46.9, claims that Gaius was the first bishop. The martyr Papylus was from Pergamum; see *Martyrdom of Carpus, Papylus, and Agathonike*, Greek recension, 1; in Musurillo, 22. See also, Eusebius, *Ecclesiastical History*, 4.15.48. Delehaye, *Origins*, 146–47.

Attalus of Pergamum was martyred at Lyon in Gaul; see *Martyrs of Lyon*, 17, in Musurillo, 66. See also Eusebius, *Ecclesiastical History*, 5.1.17. A Bishop Eusebius was there in 342/43; see Hilary, *Decretum*, A.IV.3.27. *Atlas*, 5. Jones, *Cities*, 526. Talbert, map 56.

Perge. (in the province Pamphylia.) The work of Paul and his companions is mentioned at Acts 13:13 & 14:25. The martyr Bishop Nestor is mentioned as having suffered under Decius; see Franchi de' Cavalieri, *Note agiografiche* 3 (Studi e Testi 22), 115–17 (*BHG*, #1328e). Compare *Menologium Basilianum*, 28 February & 1 March, which associates the deacon Tribimus with Bishop Nestor. See also *AASS* Februarius 3: 633–35 (*BHL*, #6068). *BS*, 9:825–27.

Bishop Epidaurus was at the Council of Ancyra in 314; see Turner 2:32, 50–51. Bishop Kallikles was at the Council of Nicaea; see Gelzer, lxiii. Şahin, *Perge*, does not appear to contain any certainly Christian inscriptions from our period. *Atlas*, 5. Talbert, map 65.

Philadelphia. (in the Diocletianic province Lydia; earlier counted as part of Asia.) Revelation 3:7–13 is addressed to the church at Philadelphia. *Apostolic Constitutions*, 7.46.9, claims that Demetrius was the first bishop. Ignatius, *Philadephians*, is addressed to this church. *Martyrdom of Polycarp*, 19.1, mentions martyrs from Philadelphia; see also Musurillo, 16. Bishop Hetoimasius was at the Council of Nicaea; see Gelzer, lxii. *Atlas*, 5. Fedalto 1:186. Talbert, map 56.

Philomelion. (in the province Pisidia.) The *Martyrdom of Polycarp* was addressed to Christians at Philomelium; see also Musurillo, 2. Jones, *Cities*, 535. *TIB*, 7:359–61. Talbert, map 62.

Poketos. (in Mysia.) *SEC*, 20 May & 18 December, records the martyr Eubiotus under Maximian. Compare *AASS*, Maii 4:311–327, and *BHG*, #1515. See also *BS*, 5:701–702. *Atlas*, 5.

Rhodes. (island off the coast of Asia Minor.) Le Quien, 1:923, lists two possible early bishops, Euphranon and Photinus. For Euphranon, see Praedestinatus, 24. Photinus is mentioned in connection with the *Acts of Clement*; see *AASS*, Januarius, 3:77 & 89. Bishop Euphrosunus was at the Council of Nicaea; see Gelzer, lxiii. *Atlas*, 5. Talbert, maps 60–61.

Samos. (off the coast of Ephesus.) Acts 20:15 records a brief visit by Paul and his companions. Talbert, map 61.

Sanaos. (in the province Phrygia I.) Bishop Flaccus was at the Council of Nicaea; see Gelzer, lxiii. *Atlas*, 5. Jones, *Cities*, 530. *TIB*, 7:371. Talbert, map 65.

Sardis. (in the Diocletianic province Lydia; earlier counted as part of the province Asia.) Revelation 3:1–6 is addressed to the church at Sardis. Le Quien, 1:859, on the basis of some Greek menologia, counts a certain Clemens as the first bishop; compare *SEC*, 22 April, note "Synaxaria selecta."

Bishop Melito is mentioned briefly in Eusebius, *Ecclesiastical History*, 4.13.8, 4.21.1, & 5.28.8. Eusebius, 4.26.1–14, is a fuller discussion of Melito's work. Not all of the fragments of Melito *Peri Pascha* mentioned by Eusebius are found in the surviving manuscript of Melito's work. At 5.24.5, Eusebius mentions the tomb of Melito. At 4.26.4 & 6.13.9, Eusebius records that Clement of Alexandria used Melito's work. See also Jerome, *De viris inlustribus*, 24.

Bishop Artemidorus was at the Council of Nicaea; see Gelzer, lxii. *Atlas*, 5. For a discussion of the large synagogue at Sardis, see Guralnick, 62–73. Talbert, map 56.

Sebaste/Dioscome. (in Phrygia I, modern Payamalani.) Tabbernee, #23 (=Gibson, #34), is the Christian epitaph of Paithus from *ca.*225–74. Contrast the identification in Johnson, #2.1. Another inscription, Johnson, 3.13 (=Ramsay, *Cities*, #449; =Cumont, "Les inscriptions," #161), with the Eumeneian formula, is the epitaph of Antonius Pollion from 255/56 C.E. LeBas & Waddington, #735 (=Cumont, "Les inscriptions," #160), is the epitaph of Dionysius with the Eumeneian formula from 353. Grégoire, "Notes," 59, records another early inscription from there. *Atlas*, 5. Talbert, map 62.

Seleucia Sidera. (in the province Pisidia.) *AASS*, Martius 3:472–73, mentions the legend of the First-Century martyr Artemon; see also

SEC, 24 March, *DHGE*, 4:799, and *BS*, 2:491. Bishop Eutychius was at the Council of Nicaea; see Gelzer, lxiii. *Atlas*, 5. Jones, *Cities*, 127. *TIB*, 7:378. Talbert, map 65, coordinate E2.

Seleukeia. (in the province Pamphylia.) Bishop Cuntianus was at the Council of Nicaea; see Gelzer, lxiii. *Atlas*, 5. Talbert, map 65, coordinate F4.

Side. (in the province Pamphylia.) Eustathius, bishop first of Beroea and then of Antioch in Syria, was a native of Side; see Jerome, *De viris inlustribus*, 85. Le Quien, 1:995–97, counts the martyr bishop Nestor as being from Side rather than from Perge. According to *SEC*, 24 August & p. 909, the Diocletianic martyr Severus was from Side.

According to some manuscripts, Bishop Epidaurus of Side was at the Council of Ancyra in 314; see Turner, 2:32. Turner, 2:50, puts Epidaurus at Perge, and Turner, 2:51, simply states that he was from Pisidia. Greek traditions represented in *SEC*, 28 February, and in *Menologium Basilianum*, 28 February, place Epidaurus at Perge.

Eustathius represented Antioch at the Council of Nicaea; see Gelzer, lxi. Athanasius, *Apologia de fuga sua*, 3.3, calls Eustathius a confessor. Harnack, 777, surmises that Eustathius must have suffered as a Christian during his youth at Side. See also *BS*, 5:296–98. Side was listed as a metropolis shortly after 325. *SEC*, 11 July, mentions the martyred presbyter Cindeus at the village of Talmenias near Side. The same tradition is recorded in *AASS* July 3:177–78. Nollé, *Side*, does not appear to have any certainly Christian inscriptions from our period, though #187 is an undated reference to the cultus of Conon of Nazareth. Fedalto 1:239. *Atlas*, 5. Talbert, map 65.

Silandos. (in the province Lydia.) Bishop Marcus of "Standos" was at the Council of Nicaea; see Gelzer, lxii. Harnack, 784, conjectures that "Standos" must be a corruption of "Silandos" or "Blaundus." *Atlas*, 5, opts for Silandos. Talbert, map 62.

Sillyon. (in Pamphylia.) *SEG* 38 (1988): #1440b is the Fourth Century epitaph of the martyred deacon Tribimus. See also *SEC*, 1 March, and *AASS*, Martius 1:127–28. His name is associated with that of Bishop Nestor of Perge; see *BHG*, #1328–1328e. Talbert, map 65.

Smyrna. (in the province Asia.) Revelation 2:8–11 is addressed to Smyrna. *Apostolic Constitutions*, 7.46.8, lists the first three bishops as Ariston, Strataias, and another Ariston. The *Life of Polycarp*, 2–3 (*BHG*, #1561), lists early bishops as Strataias and Bucolus; see Lightfoot, *Apostolic Fathers*, 2.3:433–34 (*BHG*, #1561). Le Quien, 1:740–41, cites the *Life of Pionius* as evidence for a Bishop Camrius. Harnack, 782, rightly questions the reliability of these lists without further documentation.

Ignatius, *Smyrnaeans*, is addressed to this church. Ignatius, *To Polycarp*, is addressed to its bishop; compare Eusebius, *Ecclesiastical History*, 3.26.5. The church at Smyrna addressed the *Martyrdom of Polycarp* to the church at Philomelium; see Musurillo, 2, and compare Eusebius, 4.15.3. Eusebius, *Ecclesiastical History*, 4.15.46, notes the presence of the Marcionite presbyter Metrodorus, a contemporary of Polycarp.

Irenaeus, *Adversus haereses*, 3.3.4, notes that in his youth he himself had met Polycarp. Irenaeus, *Letter to Florinus*, mentions meeting Florinus in Polycarp's household; see Eusebius, *Ecclesiastical History*, 5.20.5. Irenaeus, *Letter to Victor*, indicates that Polycarp had a hand in trying to settle the date of Easter in the time of Pope Anicetus; see Eusebius, *Ecclesiastical History*, 5.25.16–17.

The modalist Noetus was from Smyrna; see Hippolytus, *Refutatio*, 9.7.1 & 10.27.1. Epiphanius, *Panarion*, 57.1.1, however, claims that Noetus was from Ephesus.

According to the *Martyrdom of Pionius*, 4.2, Pionius was martyred under Decius; see Musurillo, 138. The apostate leader Euctemon is mentioned at 15.2 & 18.13–14; see Musurillo, 156 & 160. Le Quien, 1:741, counts Euctemon/Eudaemon as a bishop.

Eusebius, *Ecclesiastical History*, 5.24.4, mentions the tomb of bishop Thraseas of Eumeneia at Smyrna. Bishop Eutychius was at the Council of Nicaea: see Gelzer, lxii. Petzl, #547, is the epitaph of Lampadia and the deacon Pactolius; the editor compares it to a Third-Century inscription from Thessalonica, though the date of the Smyrna inscription itself does not seem to be firmly established. *Atlas*, 5. Fedalto, 1:133–34. Talbert, map 56.

Soa. (in the province Phrygia I; modern Altintaş köy.) Tabbernee, #53 (=Gibson, #20) is a "Christians for Christians" epitaph for Androneicus, *ca.*275–313. Jones, *Cities*, 69 & 530. *TIB*, 7:385–86. Talbert, map 62.

Stektorion. (in the province Phrygia II; modern Maghajil.) Ramsay, *Cities*, #654 (=Johnson, 2.14), is a Christian epitaph by the presbyter Aurelius Dionysius addressed "to all the brethren." This inscription, along with Ramsay, *Cities*, #655, dates to the latter part of the Third Century. Harnack, 772. *Atlas*, 5. *TIB*, 7:389. Talbert, map 62.

Sy(n)nada. (in the province Phrygia II; modern Şuhut.) Alexander of Jerusalem, in writing to Demetrius of Alexandria, mentions that Bishop Atticus of Synnada had invited a certain presbyter Theodorus to preach; see Eusebius, *Ecclesiastical History*, 6.19.18. Bishop Dionysius of Alexandria knew of synods at Synnada; see Eusebius, 7.7.5. Tabbernee, #35 (=Johnson, #4.2), is the ossuary of the martyr Trophimus from *ca.*275–300; see also Calder, 357–58, and Mendel, 342–48, #102. *Martyrologium Syriacum*, 30 June, 19 July, 13 August, and 20 September, lists martyrs there. Bishop Procopius was at the Council of Nicaea; see Gelzer, lxiii. *Atlas*, 5. Delehaye, *Origines*, 159.

As a cautionary note on regarding the Eumeneian formula as exclusively Christian, *MAMA*, 4: #91, contains the Eumeneian formula in a pagan context. Talbert, map 62.

Temenouthyrai. (in Phrygia I; modern Uşak.) Tabbernee, #3, is an inscription from *ca.*180–224 mentioning the Bishop Artemidorus and also Deigas who had commissioned the inscription out of church funds. Tabbernee #4 (=Johnson, #4.8), #5, #6, #7, and #8, are also Christian inscriptions from *ca.*180–224. Compare Gibson, 136.

Tabbernee, #36 (=Gibson, #36, =Johnson, #2.2), is an inscription from 278/279, of uncertain provenance, but the Christian family commemorated claimed to be from Temenouthyrai. Jones, *Cities*, 81 93, & 530. Talbert, map 62.

Teos. (in the province of Asia, Southwest of Smyrna.) The *Life of Polycarp*, 25 (*BHG*, #1561), mentions a Bishop Daphnus of Teos as a contemporary of Polycarp; see Lightfoot, *Apostolic Fathers*, 2.3:457 (*BHG*, #1561). *Atlas*, 5. Jones, *Cities*, 526. Talbert, map 56.

Termessos. (in the province Pamphylia.) Bishop Euresius was at the Council of Nicaea; see Gelzer, lxiii. Johnson, #2.10, is a possibly Christian inscription. *Atlas*, 5. Talbert, map 65.

Thera. (island in the Cyclades, administered as part of Asia.) *IG*, 12.3: #343–349, are inscriptions from *ca.*296–305 containing possibly Christian names; see also Déléage, 173–76. Other inscriptions are known using the word "ἄγγελος," possibly in the sense of protector of the tomb; see *IG*, 12.3, #933–74, and Ferrua, 160. They are perhaps datable to the early Fourth Century; see Pallas, "Investigations," 3. *Atlas*, 5. *OCD*, 417 & 1507. *EnECh*, 940. Talbert, map 61.

Therasia. (island near Thera in the Cyclades, administered as part of Asia.) Inscriptions are known using the word "ἄγγελος," possibly in the sense of protector of the tomb; see *IG*, 12.3, #1056–57, and Ferrua, 160. They are perhaps datable to the early Fourth Century; see Pallas, "Investigations," 3. *Atlas*, 5. *OCD*, 1507. *EnECh*, 940. Talbert, map 61.

Thyatira. (in the Diocletianic province Lydia; earlier counted as part of the province Asia.) Revelation 2:18–29 is addressed to the church at Thyatira. The martyr Carpus is placed at Thyatira; see *Martyrdom of Carpus, Papylus, and Agathonike* (Greek recension, 27, Latin recension, 1), in Musurillo, 26 & 28. Bishop Seras was at the Council of Nicaea; see Gelzer, lxii. *Atlas*, 5. Epiphanius, *Panarion*, 51.33.1–10, notes the presence of Alogoi and Montanists there. Talbert, map 56.

Traianoupolis. (Grimenothyrae in the province Phrygia I; modern Çarikköy.) Tabbernee, #9 (=Gibson, #35), is the Christian epitaph of Theodorus from *ca.*200–224. Le Bas and Waddington, #727 (=Cumont, "Les Inscriptions," #172; =Ramsay, *Cities*, #444), is an epitaph of Christians from 279. Harnack, 772, suggests that the Bishop Piso of Traianoupolis mentioned in the late *Acts of Acacius*, 5.11, may be from this Traianoupolis. For the *Acts of Acacius*, see Knopf & Krueger, 57–60; also *AASS*, Martius 3:899–900 (BHL, #25). *Atlas*, 5. *TIB*, 7:407. Talbert, map 62.

Tralles. (in the province Asia.) Ignatius, *Trallians*, 1.1, mentions the Bishop Polybius. Poljakov, #250, is an inscription from *ca.*284–305 containing the possibly Christian name Eucarpus. *Atlas*, 5. Talbert, map 61.

Tripolis. (in the province Lydia.) Bishop Agogius was at the Council of Nicaea; see Gelzer, lxii. *Atlas*, 5. Jones, *Cities*, 528. Talbert, map 65.

Tymion. (on the territory of Eumeneia in Phrygia I; probably near modern Susuzören; see Tabbernee, "Portals," 88. The inscriptional evidence now reported by Tabbernee corrects Harnack, 771, who suggested modern Dumanli, and Tabbernee, #17, where Üçkuyu was suggested.) Montanists considered Tymion and Pepouza to be their new Jerusalem; see Eusebius, *Ecclesiastical History*, 5.18.2. Compare *TIB*, 7:242–43 & 409. Compare Talbert, map 62.

Üçhüyük. (in Phrygia I; ancient name uncertain.) Tabbernee, #41 (=Gibson, #11), is a Christian inscription of Aurelia Kyrila from *ca.*305–310. *TIB*, 7:412.

Üçkuyu. (just South of Dumanli in Phrygia I). Tabbernee, #17 (=Gibson, #42), is the tombstone of Satoreinus with a Latin cross from 243 C.E. Tabbernee, #18, from is the tombstone of Alexandrus, also with a Latin cross, from *ca.*225–274. Compare the tombstone with cross from Pantikapaion, *q.v.*, *ca.*304. Tabbernee, "Portals," 91. Compare Talbert, map 62.

Upper Tembris Valley. (in Phrygia I.) Several Christian inscriptions whose exact provenance is unknown come from this region: Tabbernee, #30, from 260/261. Tabbernee, #42 (=Gibson, #10), from *ca.*290–300. Tabbernee, #43 (=Gibson, #9, =Johnson, #2.5, who suggests the provenance as Gediz), from *ca.*300–310. Tabbernee, #44 (=Gibson, #13), from *ca.*300–310. Tabbernee, #49, from *ca.*300–310. *SEG* 40 (1990): #1249 mentions a similar stone listed in an antiquities catalogue. Talbert, map 62.

Zingotos. (apparently in Phrygia I; modern Doğalar near Anasultan.) Tabbernee, #37 (=*MAMA*, 10: #217), is a Christian inscription of Aurelia Alexandria for her family, *ca.*285–90. *TIB*, 7:183. Talbert, map 62.

Possible Sites

Akoluk? (in Phrygia II; ancient name uncertain.) Tabbernee, #68 (=Haspels, #107), records an inscription of the Christian prophetess Nana from *ca.*325–75; see also *SEG* 43 (1993): #943a. The presence of Christianity there a bit later is confirmed by Tabbernee, #68.2 (=Haspels, #108). Tabbernee, map 11. *TIB*, 7:176–77.

Astypalaia? (in the South Aegean.) *IG* 12.3: #182 mentions a certain Theodoulus, possibly a Christian to judge from his name, *ca.*295–305 in a capitation list; see also Déléage, 190–94. Talbert, map 61.

Cakirsaz? (in Phrygia II; ancient name possibly Kassa; see Tabbernee, map 11.) Tabbernee, #59 (=Gibson, #25), is the Christian epitaph of Zosimus from *ca.*325–375. *TIB*, 7:385.

Çepni köy? (in Phrygia; about 5 km Northeast of modern Hocalar; see *TIB*, 7:275, and map at end, "Topographische Grundlage".) *SEG* 15 (1958): #801 is an inscription with the Eumeneian formula from *ca.*250–275.

Chairetopa? (exact location uncertain; in the province Phrygia I.) The Emperor Constantius II deposed Bishop Theodoulus; see Socrates, 2.40.43, and Philostorgius, 7.6. Jones, *Cities*, 530. *TIB*, 7:221.

Didyma? (in Caria.) Rehm, *Didyma*, #306, is an inscription of an oracle from *ca.*305 mentioning Christians, perhaps in relation to the Diocletianic persecutions. Christians were certainly known in the town, but it is unclear whether a Christian community was active there. Talbert, 61.

Gordos/Iulia Gordos? (in Lydia.) The Latin recension of the *Martyrdom of Carpus, Papylus, and Agathonike*, 1, says that Carpus was bishop of Gordos; see Musurillo, 28–29. Jones, *Cities*, map following p. 28. Talbert, map 56.

Hyrgaleis? (region in Phrygia I, around Lunda and Motella.) The inscriptions recorded by Ramsay, *Cities*, #402 & #403, are late or uncertain. Harnack, 772, however, claims them as evidence for early Christianity. Jones, *Cities*, 71–72. Talbert, map 62.

Kadi Oglu? (in Phrygia I; about 10 miles South-Southwest of Appia/ Pinarbaşi.) *MAMA*, 7:xl, xlvi & #377, is an inscription with a Latin cross, dating possibly to the pre-Nicene period.

Karapinar? (Southwest of Dumanli in Phrygia I). Tabbernee, #58 (=*MAMA*, 4: #320, =*SEG* 6(1932): #242), is a Christian inscription from the Fourth Century found at Karapinar on the territory of Bekilli. Tabernee, "Portals," 91. Compare Talbert, map 62.

Kolophon? (in Lydia.) Some traditions make Onesiphorus bishop of Kolophon; see *SEC*, 7 September. Yet accounts of Onesiphorus are tangled and are notoriously difficult to localize; see *BS*, 9:1177–80. Le Quien, 1:723–26, makes no mention of Onesiphorus in connection with Kolophon.

Pseudo-Dorotheus of Tyre, 52–53, makes the Sosthenes of I Corinthians 1:2 and the Tychichas of Titus 3:12 early bishops of Kolophon. Such traditions are again of doubtful historical utility; see *BS*, 9:1177–80, in this regard also. *DHGE*, 13:340–41. Talbert, map 56.

Kümürcü? (in Lydia, to the North of Gecek.) *TAM*, 5.1, #824, is a possibly Christian inscription dating to *ca.*316–17.

Lamounia? (in the province Phrygia I; near modern Bozüyük; see Talbert, map 62.) Ramsay, *Cities*, #401, is the epitaph of Aurelius Zoticus, which Ramsay, 490, hints may be as early at the Third Century. Ramsay suggests that Bozüyük may be ancient Siblia, but the true site of Siblia is still unidentified; see *TIB*, 7:382. Harnack, 772. *Atlas*, 5. Jones, *Cities*, 530.

Lampe? (in Phrygia I, in the region of the Siblianoi, near modern Evjiler; see Ramsay, *Cities*, 227 & 539.) Ramsay, *Cities*, #400, is a Christian inscription, apparently not later than the Fourth Century. Harnack, 772. *TIB*, 7:321–22. *Atlas*, 5.

Lunda? (in the province Phrygia I.) Ramsay, *Cities*, #403, is an inscription with cross and fishes, but no words. On the basis of the artistic motifs, Ramsay dated the inscription not later than the end of the Fourth Century. Harnack, 772. *Atlas*, 5. Jones, *Cities*, 530. *TIB*, 7:329.

Meiros? (in Phrygia II, modern Demirözü; see Jones, *Cities*, 531.) Socrates, 3.15.1–8, mentions martyrs under the Emperor Julian. See also Sozomen, 5.11.1. Ramsay, *Cities*, p. 790 (=*IGRR*, 4: #607), makes mention of a pagan family from here and from Akmoneia who were strongly opposed to Christianity in the early years of the Fourth Century; compare *IGRR*, 4, #607. *TIB*, 7:337–58. Talbert, map 62.

Melos? (island in the Cyclades, administered as part of Asia.) Harnack, 786, dates the catacombs there to the late Third Century. Pallas, 7, more cautiously dates them to before the middle of the Fourth Century. *Atlas*, 5. *EnECh*, 940. *OCD*, 417. Talbert, map 58.

Motella? (Metelloupolis in the province Phrygia I.) *MAMA*, 4: #312 (=Ramsay, *Cities*, #405), is an inscription with cross, from 556 C.E. *MAMA*, 4: #313, is from the Sixth Century. Ramsay, *Cities*, #406, is from the Seventh Century. Based on this evidence, it is difficult to understand why Harnack, 772, included Motella in his list of early Christian sites. *Atlas*, 5. Jones, *Cities*, 71. *TIB*, 7:339. Talbert, map 62.

Pazos/Pazon? Site of a Novatianist synod in the mid or late Fourth Century; see Socrates, 4.28.17, 5.21.7, & 5.21.13–14. Harnack, 772. *TIB*, 7:356–57.

Perdikiai? (presumably the town in Lycia is meant, though the name is also know in relation to one of the demes of Kaunos in Caria; see *SEG* 12 (1955): #463 & #473, and *SEG* 44 (1994): #890.) A Bishop Artemas of Perdikiai is reported in one Greek manuscript and in the Arabic manuscript to have been at the Council of Nicaea; see Gelzer, lxvii, lxx, 73, & possibly 150–151. Harnack, 777. Pauly-Wissowa, 19.1:589–90. Talbert, map 65.

Prymnessos? (in the province Phrygia II; modern Sülün.) *Atlas*, 5. The *Martyrium S. Ariadnes* (*BHG*, #165), set in the time of Hadrian, indicates the possible presence of Christians; see Franchi di Cavalieri, *I martiri*, 123–33, and *Note agiografiche* 1 (Studi e Testi 2): 5–21. Compare *SEC*, 18 September, and *Menologium Sirletianum*, 18 September. *MAMA*, 4: #32, is a Christian inscription from the Fourth Century, found a few kilometers to the Southeast of Prymnessos at Nuri bey. See also *DHGE*, 4:97–99, and *BS*, 2:406–408. Ramsay, *Cities*, 716. Harnack, 772, notes the lateness of the Ariadne legend. *TIB*, 7:364–65. Talbert, map 62.

Themisonium? (in the province Phrygia I; possibly modern Kara-Eyuk-Bazar.) Ramsay, *Cities*, #432, contains the *nomen sacrum* Θ(εό)Σ in a circle. Ramsay does not indicate the date. Harnack, 772. *Atlas*, 5. Jones, *Cities*, 73–74 & 530. *TIB*, 7:403.

Tiberiopolis? (in Phrygia I; exact location unknown, but likely in the modern valley of the Emet Çayi.) Harnack, 772, claims early martyrs there. This is apparently a mistake for Theophylact of Ohrid, *Martyrium SS. Quindecim Illustrium Martyrium*, 17 & 20 (*BHG*, #1199), who mentions martyrs at Tiberiopolis (modern Strumica) in Macedonia on 28 November 360/61 under Julian. It is remarkable that no clearly pre-Constantinian Christian inscriptions have been found at or near Tiberiopolis in Phrygia; see *MAMA*, 10:xxxix.

Socrates, 7.46.9 & 13, mentions the Novatianist presbyter Marcian dwelling at Tiberiopolis in Phrygia before he became bishop in the first half of the Fifth Century.

Fedalto, 1:165, does not mention any bishop before 536. For site information, see *MAMA*, 10:xix–xx. See also, Ramsay, *Cities*, 50, 54, 1–9, 121, 693. Jones, *Cities*, 89–90 & 530. *TIB*, 7:404–405. Talbert, map 62.

Tymandos? (in Pisidia; near Apollonia.) *MAMA*, 4: #264, from the nearby modern village of Pise, contains the Eumeneian formula but is undated. *MAMA*, 4: #236, from the late Third Century, appears to be pagan. *TIB*, 7:408–409. Talbert, map 62.

Zarzela? (in Pisidia.) Fedalto, 1:265, conjectures that the Theodorus of Ouasada listed in Pisidia may belong to Zarzela rather than being a duplicate for Theodore of Ouasada in Isauria; see Gelzer, lxiii. *TIB*, 7:421.

Zemmeana? (modern Çayirbasi/Zemme; in Phrygia I about 10 km Northeast of Appia.) *MAMA*, 10: #198, from *ca.*150–175, has been suggested as Christian on iconographic grounds. *TIB*, 7:420. Talbert, map 52.

Zizima? (in Pisidia; modern Sizma.) Laminger-Pascher, *Beiträge*, #153 (=*SEG* 34 (1984): #1396) records an epitaph of Aurelios Meiros. The script could be as early as the early Third Century, but the A-Ω flanking a Christogram and the two swastikas would better suit the first half of the Fourth Century. *TIB*, 7:421. Talbert, map 63.

DIOECESIS OF PONTICA

Bibliography
AASS
AB
Ameling
Ammianus Marcellinus
Asterius of Amasea
Athanasius, *De synodis*
Atlas
Barhadbešabba
Basil, *Homiliae et Sermones*
Basil, *Letters*
Becker-Bertau
BHG
BHL
BS
Chronicon Paschale
CIL
CPG
Corsten, *Kios*
Corsten, *Prusa*
Cumont, "Sarin"
Cumont, "Zimara"
Cyprian, *Epistulae*
Delehaye, review of Grégoire
Delehaye, *Origines*

DHGE
Dobschütz
pseudo-Dorotheus of Tyre
EnECh
Epiphanius, *Panarion*
Eusebius, *Contra Marcellum*
Eusebius, *Ecclesiastical History*
Eusebius, *Martyrs of Palestine*
Eusebius, *Vita Constantini*
Fedalto
Ferri
Foss
Franchi de' Cavalieri, *I Martirii*
Gelasius of Cyzicus
Gelzer
Grégoire, "Saints jumeaux"
Grégoire, *Saints jumeaux*
Gregory of Nazianzus, *Carmina Historica*
Gregory of Nazianzus, *Epistulae*
Gregory of Nazianzus, *Orationes*
Gregory of Nyssa, *Contra Eunomium*
Gregory of Nyssa, *De vita Gregorii Thaumaturgi*
Gregory of Nyssa, *Encomium in XL martyres, Ia, Ib, & II*
Gregory of Nyssa, *Epistulae*
Halkin
Harnack
Hippolytus, *Commentary on Daniel*
Hippolytus, *Refutatio*
ILCV
Irenaeus, *Adversus haereses*
Itinerarium Burdigalense
Jerome, *Commentarii in Epistolam ad Galatas*
Joannou
Jones, *Cities*
Jones, *Later Roman Empire*
Julian, *Epistles*
Lactantius, *De mortibus persecutorum*
Latyshev, *Menologii*
Le Quien
Lucian, *Satires*

MAMA
Martyrologium Hieronymianum
Martyrologium Romanum
Menologium Basilianum
Menologium Sirletianum
Mercati
Mitchell, *Anatolia*
Mitchell, "Life of Saint Theodotus"
Mitchell, *RECAM*, II
Mommsen, "Zur Lebensgeschichte"
Musurillo
ODCC
Origen, *Letter to Africanus*
Palladius, *Dialogus*
Philostorgius
PL
Pliny the Younger
Praedestinatus
Ramsay, *Church in the Roman Empire*
Ramsay, *Historical Geography*
Ruinart
Schürer
Schwertheim
SEC
SEG
Simeon Metaphrastes, *Certamen Sancti Martyris Callinici*
Simeon Metaphrastes, *Martyrium S. Martyris Christi Autonomi*
Simeon Metaphrastes, *Martyrium S. Thyrsi et Sociorum*
Simeon Metaphrastes, *Martyrum Sanctorum Indae et Domnae*
Socrates
Sozomen
Studia Pontica
Synaxarium Alexandrinum
Tabbernee
Talbert
TAM
Tertullian, *Ad Scapulam*
Tertullian, *Adversus Marcionem*
TIB
Turner

Waelkens
Wilcken
Wordsworth–White
World Atlas

General

Pontica. For the overall list of provinces covered, see Jones, *Later Roman Empire*, 2:1458, and Mitchell, *Anatolia*, 161–63. The province of Pontus Polemoniacus is treated separately below.

Armenia Minor. For the boundaries in the early Fourth Century, see Mitchell, *Anatolia*, 161–63.

Bithynia. (earlier Bithynia et Pontus.) I Peter 1:1 mentions Christians in Bithynia and Pontus. Pliny the Younger, *Letters*, 10.96, gives the Emperor Trajan a vivid description of Christian activity. The prologues to John in two manuscripts of the Latin vulgate indicate, perhaps on the authority of Papias, that the Johannine epistles were addressed to Christian brethren in Pontus, though this may be a surmise on the part of a Latin scribe; for the pertinent texts see Wordsworth–White, 1:490–91, and the comment by Harnack, 736. Lucian, *Satires*, Alexander the False Prophet, 25 (=4:208–209), written in the Second Century, says that Pontus was full of atheists and Christians. Delehaye, *Origines*, 232. Hippolytus, *Commentary on Daniel*, 4.19, records the disturbances caused in Pontus by a Christian visionary. Dionysius of Corinth, recorded in Eusebius, *Ecclesiastical History*, 5.23.4, describes Palmas of Amastris as the eldest of the bishops of Pontus in the late Second Century. Two chorepiscopoi from Bithynia—Theophanes and Eulalius—were at the Council of Nicaea; see Gelzer, lxiv.

Cappadocia. I Peter 1:1 mentions churches in Cappadocia. *Martyrdom of Justin and Companions*, 4, describes the martyrdom at Rome of Euelpistus of Cappadocia; see Musurillo, 44–45 & 50–51. Tertullian, *Ad Scapulam*, 3.4, refers to persecutions in Cappadocia carried out by the governor Claudius Lucius Herminianus because his wife had become a Christian. According to Eusebius, *Ecclesiastical History*, 6.8.7 & 6.11.1–3. Alexander, a bishop in Cappadocia (Caesarea?), was prevailed upon *ca.*211 by the Christians of Jerusalem to become bishop in Jerusalem to assist their Bishop Narcissus in his extreme old age. Later writers place Alexander's home at Flavias in Cilicia, *q.v.* See Eusebius, *Martyrs of Palestine*, 11.25–27, on the soldier Julian of Cappadocia who was martyred in Palestine.

In addition to the several bishops from named sees in Cappadocia who attended the Council of Nicaea, five chorepiscopoi—Gorgonius, Stephanus, Eudromius, Rhodon, and Theophanes—were present in the Cappadocian delegation; see Gelzer, lxii. Eusebius, *Vita Constantini*, 4.43, speaks of the great learning of the bishops from Cappadocia who were present at the dedication of the Church of the Holy Sepulchre in Jerusalem.

The early Arian writer Asterius the Sophist was from Cappadocia; see Athanasius, *De synodis*, 18.2. On the birthplace of Eunomius at Oltiseris in Cappadocia, see Gregory of Nyssa, *Contra Eunomium*, 1.104–105. For further connections of Eunomius, see Philostorgius, 3.20. For the troublesome deacon Glycerius of Venesa in the late Fourth Century, see Basil, *Epistles*, 169–171. Harnack, 745.

Galatia. The mixed linguistic character of Galatia was well known in antiquity; see Jerome, *Commentarii in Epistolam ad Galatas*, 2 (PL 26: 379–80), citing Varro. It is difficult to discern whether Paul's letter to the Galatians was addressed to churches in what was then Southern Galatia (then including part of Phrygia and Isauria) or to Christians in Northern (ethnic) Galatia. The present writer would note that Paul generally uses the names of political entities rather than ethnic groups in the opening of his letters to congregations. It should also be noted that Jewish presence in ethnic Galatia was scanty at best in the Roman period, while the Southern part of the province had several towns with Jewish population; see Schürer, 3.1:34–35. At the same time, Paul's line of reasoning in Galatians seems connected with his thinking in Romans. It may be, then, that Paul was addressing congregations in Southern Galatia, but at the relatively late period in which he composed Romans. I Peter 1:1 mentions churches in Galatia.

The Emperor Julian was greatly concerned to promote paganism in the Diocletianic province Galatia, where many pagan priests had Christian wives, children, and slaves; see Julian, *Epistle* 22 (to Arsacius), in *Works* 3:72–73; compare Sozomen, 5.16.5–15.

Specific Sites

Amaseia. (in Diospontus, later Helenopontus; modern Amasya.) Phaidemus was bishop in the middle of the Third Century; see Gregory of Nyssa, *De vita Gregorii Thaumaturgi*, 26 (908–909M).

On the persecutions at Amaseia under Licinius, see Eusebius, *Ecclesiastical History*, 10.8.15. See also Eusebius, *Vita Constantini*, 2.1, and Gelasius of Cyzicus, 1.11.8. Bishop Basil was at the Council of Ancyra in 314; see Turner, 2:32, 50–51. His name also appears among those who attended the Council of Neocaesarea *ca.*319; see Turner, 2:32, 52–53. Basil was also remembered as a supporter of Arius; see Philostorgius, 1.8 & 1.8a. See *BS*, 2:901–902. For Basil's martyrdom under Licinius, see *Menologium Sirletianum*, 26 April, *AASS*, Aprilis 3:xlii–xliv (*BHG*, #239), and *AASS*, Aprilis 3:xlvii–l (*BHG*, #240). The latter document, xlvii, claims that the first bishop, Nicetas, was installed in office by the apostle Peter. Delehaye, *Origines*, 170.

Bishop Eutychianus represented the city at the Council of Nicaea; see Gelzer, lxii. Asterius of Amaseia was a much younger contemporary of the Emperor Julian; see Asterius of Amaseia, *Homilies*, 3.10.2. Jones, *Cities*, 538. Fedalto, 1:76. *DHGE*, 2:966. *Atlas*, 5. Talbert, map 87.

Amastris. (in Paphlagonia.) Dionysius of Corinth, writing in the late-Second Century, mentions Bishop Palmas; see Eusebius, *Ecclesiastical History*, 4.23.6. *Menologium Basilianum*, 18 July; and *SEC*, 18 July, mention a Bishop Heraclius in the time of the martyr Hyacinthus. See also *Menologium Sirletianum*, 17 July. For more on Hyacinthus, see *AASS*, Julius 4:222–31 (*BHG*, #757). See also *BS*, 6:324–25. Bishop Eupsychius was at the Council of Nicaea; see Gelzer, lxii. *Atlas*, 5. *TIB*, 9:161–70. Talbert, map 86.

Amorion. (in Galatia.) *MAMA*, 7: #297, depicts a fish suspended from a bar and contains the distinctively Christian name Kyriake. *MAMA*, 7: #298, contains a similar fish motif, together with a variation of the Eumeneian formula; see Tabbernee, 144. *MAMA*, 7: xxxix, suggests a Third-Century date for the inscriptions.

Harnack, 772, claims early martyrs but gives no details. *SEC* mentions the following martyrs without specifying a year: Phthasus on 27 September, Agarenous on 5 December, Eudoxius on 8 March, and Blasius on 31 May. *AASS*, Martius 1:880–84 (*BHG*, #1214) lists much later martyrs captured by Saracens and taken to Syria; compare *AASS*, Martius 1:459–65, and *SEC*, 6 March.

The presbyter Tyrannus was at the Council of Constantinople in 381; see Turner, 2:456–57. Jones, *Cities*, 61, 65, 68, 122, 533. *TIB*, 4:122–25. *Atlas*, 5. Talbert, map 62.

Ancyra. (in Galatia.) An early anti-Montanist tract recorded in Eusebius, *Ecclesiastical History*, 5.16.4, mentions disturbances caused by Montanists at Ancyra.

Martyrologium Syriacum lists the martyr Platon on 22 June; compare *SEC*, 18 November. *Martyrologium Syriacum* also lists the confessor Gillas on 30 August, the martyr Marcellus on 4 September, a certain Eusebius on 16 September, and unnamed infants on 23 September.

Martyrdom of Theodotus, 1–36, contains traditions related to the martyr Theodotus and contemporaries under Diocletian; see Franchi de' Cavalieri, *I Martirii*, 61–84 (*BHG*, #1782). For a brief discussion, see Delehaye, *Origines*, 156–57, and also *EnECh*, 829. For fuller analysis, see Mitchell, "Life of Saint Theodotus," 93–113.

SEC, 4 November, mentions a Bishop Theodotus of Ancyra, who is perhaps the same as the martyr. *Menologium Sirletianum*, 3 November, refers to him as Theodorus, bishop and confessor. Le Quien, 1:457. *DHGE*, 2:1540.

SEC, 23 January, records the martyrdom of Bishop Clement during the reign of Diocletian and Maximian. See also *Martyrologium Sirletianum*, 23 January, which, however, does not refer to him as bishop. *BS*, 1:337–38.

The council of Ancyra was held in 314 and hosted by Bishop Marcellus; see Joannou, 1.2.56–73, and Turner, 2:32, 50–51.

Two Latin manuscripts of the signatories at Nicaea list Pancharius as the bishop, as do the Coptic and the Armenian manuscripts; see Gelzer, 31, 88–89 & 200–201. One Latin manuscript lists Marcellus as the bishop, as do Greek, Syriac, and Arabic manuscripts; see Gelzer, 30, 66, 106–107, 130–31. The Armenian manuscript makes Marcellus bishop of Tabia; see Gelzer, 200–201. One Latin manuscript lists both Pancharius and Marc[ell]us as bishops; see Gelzer, 30. Gelzer, lxii, opts for Marcellus as the presiding bishop at Ancyra. Fedalto, 1:55, lists both. Might it not be that Pancharius was the presiding bishop but that Marcellus was his suffragan? Marcellus's writings are known largely through the refutations of them offered in Eusebius, *Contra Marcellum*.

Jerome, *Commentarii in Epistolam ad Galatas*, 2 (PL 26:382) on 3:8–9, speaks of Ancyra as the metropolis of Galatia. Harnack, 768. *TIB*, 4:126–30. *DHGE*, 2:1540. Fedalto, 1:55. *EnECh*, 37. *Atlas*, 5. Talbert, maps 63 & 86.

Apollonia (ad Rhyndacum). (in Bithynia.) The legendary founder of the church was Mark; see *SEC*, 16 June, 21 June, 22 June, 30 June, 20 October. Bishop Gorgonias was at the Council of Nicaea; see Gelzer, lxiv. On connections with Mysia, see Harnack, 764. *Atlas*, 5. Talbert, map 52.

Arabissos. (in Cappadocia.) Philostorgius, 4.4, records that Caesarius, father of Bishop Eudoxius of Germaniceia, was from Arabissos and was martyred there. Philostorgius, 4.8, also notes that Eudoxius was an Armenian. *Atlas*, 5. Talbert, map 64.

Caesarea (Germanice). (in Bithynia; modern Tahtali.) Simeon Metaphrastes, *Martyrium S. Thyrsi et Sociorum*, 10 (PG 116:517) mentions an early bishop Phileas. The Bishop Agricola of Caesarea who attended the Council of Ancyra in 314 may have been from this place; see Turner, 2:32, 50–51. Bishop Rufus of Caesarea in Bithynia was at the Council of Nicaea; see Gelzer, lxiv. *Atlas*, 5. Talbert, map 52.

Caesarea Mazaca. (in Cappadocia.) *AASS*, Martius 2:379–80 (*BHL*, #4965) records the legend of a certain Longinus, said to have been the centurion at the foot of the cross at Jesus' crucifixion and the founder of the church in Caesarea of Cappadocia. Compare *AASS*, Martius 2:927–29 (*BHG*, #988); and *AASS*, Martius 2:930–31 (*BHG*, #990). Gregory of Nyssa, *Epistulae*, 17.15, alludes to the tradition of the centurion from Cappadocia. Some traditions record Longinus's family name as Primianus; see *AASS*, Martius 2:377. For more about the legend, see Le Quien, 1:367–79.

Alexander, mentioned by Eusebius, *Ecclesiastical History*, 6.8.7 & 6.11.1–3, as bishop in Cappadocia, may have been resident in Caesarea. Similarly a certain Theocritus, mentioned by Praedestinatus, 35 (PL 53:598), as bishop in Cappadocia, may also have been resident in Caesarea.

Firmilian was bishop of Caesarea in the middle of the Third Century; see Eusebius, *Ecclesiastical History*, 7.28.1. Compare also Gregory of Nyssa, *De vita Gregorii Thaumaturgi*, 26 (905M). For Firmilian's letter to Cyprian of Carthage, see Cyprian, *Epistulae*, 75.

For the martyr Mamas, killed perhaps under Aurelian; see Basil, *Homiliae et Sermones*, 23, *In sanctum martyrem Mamatem*. Compare Gregory of Nazianzus, *Orationes*, 44.12, and *SEC*, 2 September. See also Sozomen, 5.2.12, for a mention of the tomb. Delehaye, *Origines*, 174–75.

The Bishop Agricola of Caesarea who attended the Council of Ancyra in 314 may have been from this place; see Turner, 2:32, 50–51. Bishop Leontius of Caesarea was possibly at the Council of Neocaesarea in *ca*.319; see Turner, 2:32, 52–53. He was certainly at the Council of Nicaea; see Gelzer, lxii.

On the martyr Eupsychius, killed under Julian, see Basil, *Letters*, 100, 142, 176, & 252. Compare Sozomen, 5.4.7–8 & 5.11.7–8. For further analysis of martyr traditions, see Delehaye, *Origines*, 172–77.

Note the remarkable request from Basil of Caesarea, apparently to Pope Damasus, to send mediators to help resolve the differences within the Eastern church; see Basil, *Letters*, 70.

Eunomius was banished to Caesarea under the Emperor Theodosius; see Philostorgius, 10.6. Fedalto, 1:20. *Atlas*, 5. Talbert, maps 63 & 64.

Chadouthi. Town mentioned in the *Testament of the Forty Martyrs of Sebaste*; see Musurillo, 358–59. Exact location unknown, but perhaps Chadisia is meant; see Talbert, map 87.

Chalcedon. (in Bithynia.) Praedestinatus, 17 (PG 53:592), records a Bishop Theocritus of Chalcedon as opposing the Ophite heresy in the Second or Third Century. One may wonder whether he is identical with the Theocritus of Cappadocia assigned by Le Quien, 1:367–69, to Caesarea.

Martyrologium Hieronymianum records martyrs commemorated on id. Apr.; Euphemia and others on 16 kal. Sept., and 16 & 15 kal. Oct.; Trophimus on 14 kal. Oct.; and Hadrian on 3 id. Oct. *Martyrologium Syriacum*, 17 September lists the martyr Seleucus of Egypt; 13 October lists the martyr Hadrian. *SEC* lists several martyrs. Delehaye, *Origines*, 152–53.

Bishop Maris was at the Council of Nicaea; see Gelzer, lxiv. According to Socrates, 1.8.13 & 31, he was among the few bishops who had reservations about the creed issued by the Council; see also Philostorgius, 1.8a. Sozomen, 5.4.8, shows that Maris, though old and blind, was still active during the reign of Julian. Fedalto, 1:98. *Atlas*, 5. Talbert, map 52.

Charisphone. (exact location unknown.) Mentioned in the *Testament of the Forty Martyrs of Sebaste*; see Musurillo, 358–59.

Colonia/Garsaura. (in Cappadocia; West of Nazianzus.) Bishop Erythrius was at the Council of Nicaea; see Gelzer, lxii. Jones, *Cities*, map facing p. 28. *Atlas*, 5. Talbert, map 63.

Comana. (in Cappadocia according to the list of signatories at Nicaea, but later counted as part of Armenia II; see Jones, *Cities*, 540.) *Martyrologium Romanum*, 21 July, mentions a martyred Bishop Zoticus of Comana in Armenia under the Emperor Severus; compare the mention of Zoticus of Otrous in Eusebius, *Ecclesiastical History*, 5.16.5. *BS*, 12:1505.

Bishop Elpidius of Comana was at the Council of Nicaea; see Gelzer, lxii. *TIB*, 9:241–42. Fedalto, 1:71. *Atlas*, 5. Talbert, map 64.

Comana Pontica. (near modern Tokat; in Diospontus, according to the list of signatories at Nicaea, but later counted in Pontus Polemoniacus; see Jones, *Cities*, 538.) The first bishop, Alexander, was appointed by Gregory Thaumaturgus in the middle of the Third Century; see Gregory of Nyssa, *De vita Gregorii Thaumaturgii*, 62–70 (933–37M).

Basiliscus, Bishop of Comana, was martyred under Maximian, as the biography of John Chrysostom attests; see Palladius, *Dialogus*, 11.96–134. Compare *BHG*, #241–241a. Delehaye, *Origines*, 170–71. *SEC*, 27 January & 22 May, wrongly places Basiliscus in Comana of Cappadocia/Armenia II. For commemoration of John Chrysostom, see *Martyrologium Romanum*, 27 January & 14 September.

Bishop Elpidius of Comana in Diospontus was at the Council of Nicaea; see Gelzer, lxii. Fedalto, 1:45. *Atlas*, 5. Talbert, map 87.

Cybistra. (in Cappadocia.) Bishop Timothy was at the Council of Nicaea; see Gelzer, lxii. *Atlas*, 5. Talbert, map 66.

Drepanon/Helenopolis. (in Bithynia.) Eusebius, *Vita Constantini*, 4.61, mentions that Constantine visited the church dedicated to the martyrs there. Delehaye, *Origines*, 151. Jones, *Cities*, 164 & 537. *Atlas*, 5. Talbert, map 52.

Gdammaua/Ekdaumaua. (in Galatia according to the list of signatories at the Council of Nicaea, but attached to the later province of Lycaonia.) Bishop Erechthius was at the Council of Nicaea; see Gelzer, lxii. Jones, *Cities*, 534. *Atlas*, 5. *TIB*, 4:166. Fedalto, 1:60, makes Erechthios bishop of Lagania. Talbert, map 63.

Hadrianoi. (in Bithynia.) Bishop Euethius was at the Council of Nicaea; see Gelzer, lxiv. Schwertheim does not appear to contain any clearly datable Christian inscriptions from our era. *Atlas*, 5. Talbert, map 62.

Ionopolis/Abonuteichos. (in Paphlagonia.) Lucian, *Satires*, "Alexander the False Prophet," 25 (=4:208–209), writing about Alexander of Abonuteichos in the Second Century, says that Pontus was full of atheists and Christians. This is perhaps an indication that Christians were already present in Alexander's hometown. Bishop Petronius of Ionopolis was at the Council of Nicaea; see Gelzer, lxii. Compare also material related to the Council of Gangra *ca*.340; see Turner, 2:146 & 172–73. *TIB*, 9:219–21. Fedalto, 1:88. *Atlas*, 5. Talbert, map 86.

Iouliopolis. (in Northern Galatia.) Bishop Philadelphus was at the Council of Ancyra in 314; see Turner, 2:32, 50–51. He was also at the Council of Nicaea; see Gelzer, lxii. *TIB*, 4:181–82. *Atlas*, 5. Talbert, map 86.

Kerpişli. (in Galatia, North of Gdammaua.) *MAMA*, 7:xl & #417, is claimed by the editors to be Christian and pre-Nicene. *TIB*, 4:188.

Kinna. (in Galatia.) Bishop Gregorius was at the Council of Neocaesarea *ca.*319; see Turner, 2:32 & 52–53. He may be the same person as the Bishop Gorgonios who was at the Council of Nicaea; see Gelzer, lxii. *TIB*, 4:189. Le Quien, 1:483. Fedalto, 1:60. *Atlas*, 5. Talbert, map 63.

Kios. (in Bithynia; modern Gemlik.) Bishop Cyrillus was at the Council of Nicaea; see Gelzer, lxiv. Corsten, *Kios*, #120 is an inscription for Dionysius and his brothers, perhaps from the Third Century. *Atlas*, 5. Talbert, map 52.

Malos. (about 50 km East-Northeast of Ancyra in Galatia; modern Kalecik.) *Martyrdom of Theodotus*, 10, 12, 21, 32 & 35, mentions the presbyter Fronto of Malos in the time of Diocletian; see Franchi de' Cavalieri, *I Martirii*, 67, 69, 74, 81, & 84. Harnack, 769. Mitchell, "Life of Saint Theodotus," 108–110. Mitchell, *Anatolia*, 65 & 93. *TIB*, 4:201–202. *Atlas*, 5. Talbert, map 86.

Melitene. (in Cappadocia; see Mitchell, 163.) Eusebius, *Ecclesiastical History*, 5.5.1–6, mentions the legend of Christians in the thundering legion in the time of Marcus Aurelius, thus indicating that Christians were known there in Eusebius's own day if not before. Eusebius, 8.6.7–9, also mentions an uprising at Melitene, by persons he does not identify, which resulted in the persecution of Christians. Martyrs from Melitene are commemorated in *Martyrologium Hieronymianum* at 7 id. Jan., 16 kal. Mar., 13 kal. Mai, 5 kal. Mai, 6 non. Mai. Philostorgius, 5.5, records that Bishop Meletius of Antioch was a native of Melitene. *Atlas*, 5. Talbert, map 64.

Nazianzus. (in Cappadocia.) Nona, the mother of Gregory of Nazianzus was from a Christian family. Under her influence, Gregory's father, also named Gregory, was converted from his hypsistarian beliefs to Christianity at the time of the Council of Nicaea. Shortly thereafter he was ordained presbyter by Leontius of Caesarea. For the narrative, see Gregory of Nazianzus, *Orationes*, 18.5–7 & 12, "On the death of his father," which gives the family's religious background. For the names of Gregory's parents, see *Orationes*, 8.4–5, "On his sister Gorgonia." *Atlas*, 5. Talbert, map 63.

Nicaea. (in Bithynia.) *Martyrologium Syriacum* lists martyrs on 19 & 27 January. *SEC*, 9 June, and *Martyrologium Hieronymianum*, 9 June, mention Diomedes. Delehaye, *Origines*, 152.

Bishop Theognius represented his city in the Council held there in 325; see Gelzer, lxiv. According to Socrates, 1.8.13 & 31, Theognius initially declined to accept the creed proposed there; see also Philostorgius, 1.8a. On Novatianists at Nicaea, see Socrates, 4.28.18. Fedalto, 1:108. *Atlas*, 5. Talbert, map 52.

Nicomedia. (Diocletian's capital; in Bithynia; modern Izmit.) *Synaxarium Alexandrinum*, 20 Tubah (15 January), text, 222–23; trans, 359–60, makes Prochorus, one of the seven deacons of Acts 6:5, the first bishop of Nicomedia; see also *BS*, 10:1173–76. Le Quien, 1:581–82.

Praedestinatus, 17 (PG 53:592), mentions a Bishop Evander. The *Martyrum Sanctarum Indae et Domnae*, 1–5, mentions the Bishop Cyril; see Simeon Metaphrastes, PG 116:1039–43 (*BHG*, #823). Le Quien 1:583.

Eusebius, *Ecclesiastical History*, 4.23.4, mentions a letter from Bishop Dionysius of Corinth in the late Second Century to the church at Nicomedia. Origen wrote his letter to Julius Africanus from the house of Ambrose at Nicomedia; see Origen, *Letter to Africanus*, 2, 21 & 24.

Lactantius, *De mortibus persecutorum*, 12.1–5, mentions the destruction of the apparently rather large church building at Nicomedia on 23 February 303, at the beginning of Diocletian's persecutions. At 13.1–3, Lactantius records a martyr, identified by *Martyrologium Syriacum*, 24 February, as Evethius. See also *Martyrologium Hieronymanium*, 6 kal. Martii. Lactantius, 14.1–15.7, describes the persecutions within the imperial household.

Bishop Anthimus was martyred early in Diocletian's persecutions; see Eusebius, *Ecclesiastical History*, 8.5.1–8.6.7 & 8.13.1–2. A letter of Lucian attributed to 303 C.E. also mentions the martyrdom of Bishop Anthimus; see *Chronicon Paschale*, text, 515–516 (PG 92: 683); trans, 5. Compare *BHG*, #134y–135c. An epistle which once circulated under the name of Anthimus is now assigned to Marcellus of Ancyra; see *Anthemi Nicomediensis Episcopi et Martyris de Sanctae Ecclesiae* in Mercati, 95–98, and *CPG*, 2:2802.

The presbyter Lucian of Antioch was also martyred at Nicomedia during the Diocletianic persecutions; see Eusebius, *Ecclesiastical History*,

9.6.3. *Martyrologium Hieronymianum* lists numerous martyrs, as does *Martyrologium Syriacum* and *SEC*. For further discussion of martyrs, see Delehaye, *Origines*, 148–52.

Bishop Eustolus of Nicomedia was at the Synod of Ancyra in 314; see Turner, 2:32 & 50–51.

Bishop Eusebius of Nicomedia was at the Council of Nicaea; see Gelzer, lxiv; also Barhadbešabba 6 (p. 209). Eusebius was one of the bishops who initially refused to accept the creed proposed at Nicaea; see Socrates, 1.8.13 & 31, and Philostorgius, 1.8a. For further information on Eusebius, see Socrates, 1.6.32, 1.27.7, & 1.37.4. Eusebius of Nicomedia survived until the reign of Julian and is claimed as a distant relative of that Emperor; see Ammianus Marcellinus, 22.9.4. On Novatianists at Nicomedia, see Socrates, 4.28.18. Fedalto, 1:94.

TAM, 4.1: #375–76 are possibly early Jewish inscriptions. *SEG* 37(1987): #1081 (=*CIL*, 3: #14188, =*ILCV*, 1: #2180), is the Greco-Latin bilingual Christian epitaph of Oktimos, which may be as early as the Constantinian era. *Atlas*, 5. Talbert, map 52.

Nicopolis. (Northeast of Sebasteia; in Armenia Minor.) *Martyrologium Hieronymianum*, 6 id. Julius and 5 id. Julius, mentions martyrs there. *Menologium Sirletianum*, 10 July, places them in the time of Licinius, as does *SEC*, 10 July. *Atlas*, 5. Talbert, map 87.

Orkistos. (in Galatia Salutaris; modern Alikel.) *MAMA*, 7: #305 (=*CIL*, 3:7000), panels 1–2, is a rescript from Emperor Constantine to Ablabius, *ca*.324–25. In referring to Orkistos at panel 1, lines 39–42, Constantine writes *"quibus omnibus quasi quidam cumulus accedit quod omnes [i]bidem sectatores sanctissimae religionis habitare dicantur."* Evidently someone had told the emperor of the high proportion of Christians in the city in order to help gain his favor. Jones, *Cities*, 67–68 & 533, and map following 28. *TIB*, 4:211. Talbert, maps 62 & 102.

Phargamos/Pharmagos. A village renowned for its early and strong martyr tradition; see Basil of Caesarea, *Letters*, 95. See also Mitchell, "Life," 95.

Phydela. The "venerable Proclianus and his holy church" appear in the *Testament of the Forty Martyrs of Sebaste*; see Musurillo, 358–59. Exact location unknown, though a "Phidalia petra" is known on the Western shore of the Bosporus; see Talbert, map 53. There is also a Phygela in Ionia; see Talbert, map 61.

Pompeiopolis. (in Paphlagonia.) Bishop Philadelphus was at the Council of Nicaea; see Gelzer, lxii. *TIB*, 9:260–62. *Atlas*, 5. Talbert, map 86.

Prusa. (in Bithynia.) *SEC* commemorates three martyred bishops of Prusa: Timotheus on 10 June, Alexander on 9 June, and Patricius on 19 May. Bishop Hesychius was at the Council of Nicaea; see Gelzer, lxiv. Fedalto 1:105. Le Quien 1:615–16.

Corsten, *Prusa*, #115, is the "crypto-Christian" epitaph of Epitherses and Theoktistos from the end of the Second Century and is the earliest epigraphic evidence for Christianity in Bithynia. *Atlas*, 5. Talbert, map 52.

Prusias ad Hypium. (in Bithynia, later counted as part of Honorias.) Bishop Georgius was at the Council of Nicaea; see Gelzer, lxiv. Ameling lists several gravestones, but none appear to record any clearly Christian inscriptions from our era. Jones, *Cities*, 537. *TIB*, 9:264–66. *Atlas*, 5. Talbert, map 86.

Sadagolthina. (in Cappadocia near Parnassos.) The ancestors of Ulfilas, who were already Christian, were deported from there by Goths during the time of Valerian and Gallienus; see Philostorgius, 2.5. *EnECh*, 856. Talbert, map 63.

Sarim/n. (town in the neighborhood of Zela in Diospontus; see Cumont, "Sarim," 241–42.) A presbyter and some deacons are mentioned in the *Testament of the Forty Martyrs of Sebaste*, 1 & 3; see Musurillo, 354–55 & 358–59. Talbert, map 87, notes a region named Saramene/Amisene, which could perhaps be the place intended.

Satala. (in Armenia Minor.) *Menologium Sirletianum*, 24 June, and *SEC*, 24 June, report martyrs connected to the place in the time of Maximian. Bishop Euethius was at the Council of Nicaea; see Gelzer, lxii. *Atlas*, 5. Fedalto, 1:53. Talbert, map 87.

Sebasteia. (in Armenia Minor.) Fedalto, 1:50, tentatively assigns Bishop Meruzanes, who was in fact probably from Armenia Major, to Sebasteia. A certain Bishop Blasius from the early Fourth Century is also doubtfully associated with the city in later sanctoral traditions: see *AASS*, Februarius, 1:334–53; *SEC*, 11 February; and Latyshev, *Menologii*, 1:328–36.

For the *Testament of the Forty Martyrs of Sebaste* during the reign of Licinius, see Musurillo, xlix–l & 354–61. The martyrs are also commemorated in sermons by Basil of Caesarea, *Homiliae et Sermones*, 19, *In Quadraginta martyres Sebastenses* and by Gregory of Nyssa, *Encomium in XL Martyres, Ia, Ib, & II.* The Greek tradition of the works of Ephraem Syrus also includes mention of the forty martyrs, see *CPG*, 2: #3962. See *BS*, 11:768–771, for other recollections of them. The relics of the forty martyrs are mentioned by Sozomen, 9.2.1. Martyrs from Sebasteia are found also in *Martyrologium Hieronymianum*, 8 id. Mar., 7 id. Mar., 7 kal. Apr., and 9 kal. Aug.

Bishop Eulalius was at the Council of Nicaea; see Gelzer, lxii. *Atlas*, 5. Fedalto, 1:50. Talbert, map 64, coordinate E1.

Sebastopolis/Herakleopolis. (Southwest of Comana Pontica.) According to Philostorgius, 1.8 & 1.8a, Bishop Meletius of Sebastopolis was an Arian supporter at the time of the Council of Nicaea. *Atlas*, 5. Fedalto, 1:53. Talbert, map 64, coordinate C1.

Sinope. (in Diospontus.) Irenaeus, *Adversus haereses*, 1.25.1, says that Marcion was a native of Pontus. Hippolytus, *Refutatio*, 7.29.1, indicates the same, as does Tertullian, *Adversus Marcionem*, 1.1.3. Epiphanius, *Panarion*, 42.1.3–5, more specifically says that Marcion was a native of Sinope and that his father had been bishop of the city.

For the well-known martyr Phocas the gardener, see Asterius of Amasea, *Homilies*, 9.5.1–2 & 9.9.3 (*BHG*, #1538). See also Gregory of Nazianzus, *Carmina Historica*, 2.2.3.79 (PG 37:1486). *EnECh*, 685. Harnack, 756. Jones, *Cities*, 538. Fedalto, 1:82–83. *Atlas*, 5. Talbert, map 87.

Spaleia. (in Galatia; later Iustinianopolis; modern Sivrihisar.) Waelkens, #768, is a clearly Christian inscription with mention of "ἀναστά-σεως" from *ca.*225–250. The Coptic manuscript of bishops present at Nicaea lists a certain "Paulus of Spania" in Cappadocia; see Gelzer, 86–87. Gelzer, 247, suggests this may be a mistake for Spaleia in Galatia. Harnack, 743. Jones, *Cities*, 533. *TIB*, 4:227. Talbert, map 62, coordinate G3.

Tabia. (in Galatia.) Bishop Dikasios was at the Council of Nicaea; see Gelzer, lxii. The Armenian tradition makes Bishop Marcellus of Ancyra come from Tabia; see Gelzer, 200–210. *TIB*, 4:229–30. *Atlas*, 5. Talbert, map 86.

Tyana. (in Cappadocia.) Bishop Eutychius was at the Council of Nicaea; see Gelzer, lxii. *Atlas*, 5. Talbert, map 66.

Yurtbeyci/Yurtbeyli. (in Galatia, about 40 km West of Kinna; compare *TIB*, 4: map "topographische grundlage" at end.) Mitchell, *RECAM*, II, #325, is a Christian inscription dating from 247 C.E. and including the words "ἐν τῷ κυ(ρίῳ) ζῶ."

Zela. (modern Zile. In Diospontus according to the list of signatories at Nicaea, but later counted as part of Helenopontus; see Jones, *Cities*, 538.) Mentioned in the *Testament of the Forty Martyrs of Sebaste*, 1; see Musurillo, 354–55. Bishop Heraclius was at the Synod of Ancyra in 314; see Turner, 2:32 & 50–51. He was also at the Council of Nicaea; see Gelzer, lxii. *TIB*, 9:62 & 106. *Atlas*, 5. Talbert, map 87.

Zimara. (in Armenia Minor, on the road between Satala and Melitene.) The family of the martyr Eutychius was from "Ximara" according to the *Testament of the Forty Martyrs of Sebaste*; see Musurillo, 360–61. Cumont, "Zimara," 448. Mitchell, *Anatolia*, 162. *Atlas*, 5. Talbert, map 64.

Possible Sites
Amisus? (in Diospontus.) Pliny the Younger, *Letters*, 10.96–97, contains Pliny's famous letter to Trajan concerning troublesome Christians and Trajan's reply. Pliny mentions some who had given up Christianity more than twenty years earlier. *Letters*, 10.92, mentions benefit societies at Amisus. Mommsen, "Zur Lebensgeschichte," 58–59, suggests that since the letters appear to be in chronological order, Pliny's letter concerning Christians may well have been written from Amisus or nearby. Pliny, *Letters*, 10.110, mentions monies donated more than twenty years earlier at Amisus, though not necessarily by Christians. Ramsay, *Church in the Roman Empire*, 10, 211 & 224–255, points to the excellent road system leading to Amisus, and infers from Mommsen's analysis and from Pliny's mention of some who had given up Christianity long ago that there were Christians in Amisus in the late-First Century. Wilcken, 133–34, correcting points in Ramsay's work, adds further detail to Mommsen's analysis. Harnack, 623 & 737. *TIB*, 9:103–104. Talbert, map 87.

Apameia? (in Bithynia.) *Acta SS. Triphonis et Respicii* reports Tryphon and Respicius (natives of the village of Sansono/Campsade) being martyred at Apameia in Phrygia under Decius; see Ruinart, 208–10, & *AASS*, Novembris 4:368–69 (*BHL*, #8337). Ruinart, 207–08, noting a connection of Tryphon and Respicius with Nicaea, suggests that Apameia in Bithynia is meant. Harnack, 763, accepts this, despite the fact that several traditions related to Tryphon and Respicius affirm that they were from the village of Sampsados near Apamea in Phrygia. For further information on the Tryphon texts, see entry for Apamea Kibotos in Asia.

Similarly, the *Martyrology of Bede* attempts to place the martyrs Victor and Victorinus at Apameia in Bithynia rather than at Appia; see *Martyrologium Hieronymianum*, 2 non. Mar.

More plausibly, *Martyrium Sancti Martyris Codrati*, 12, referring to the time of Decius or Valerian, associates the martyrdom of Quadratus with Apameia near Nicomedia in Bithynia; see *AB* 1(1882): 448–68 (*BHG*, #359). Compare *SEC*, 9 May, and *Martyrologium Sirletianum*, 7 May. *Atlas*, 5. Talbert, map 52.

Borissos? (in Cappadocia.) Philostorgius's maternal grandfather, Anysius, was presbyter there; see Philostorgius, 9.9. His daughter, Eulampia, Philostorgius's mother, was originally orthodox as were her parents. Hence the town must have had a Christian community before the middle of the Fourth Century. Philostorgius's own father, Carterius, was a follower of Eunomius, and drew the rest of the family into the Eunomian fold. *EnECh*, 683–84. Talbert, map 63.

Camulia? (Northwest of Caesarea in Cappadocia.) A later (Sixth Century) sermon circulating under the name of Gregory of Nyssa mentions Christians at Camulia finding an image of Christ in the time of Diocletian; see Dobschütz, 40 & 14**. Harnack, 743.

Claudiopolis? (in Bithynia.) Becker-Bertau, #44, is an inscription from perhaps the latter part of the Third Century mentioning M. Aurelius Demetrianus, "faithful to God." Talbert, map 86.

Gangra? (in Paphlagonia.) A *Life of Hypatius*, 2 (*BHG*, #759a), mentions an early Bishop Athanasius; see Ferri, 76. Compare *DHGE*, 19:1093–94 & 1099.

The martyr Callinicus is associated with Gangra; see *SEC*, 29 July; also Simeon Metaphrastes, *Certamen Sancti Martyris Callinici*, 7 (PG 115:477–88) (=*BHG*, #287). Latyshev, *Menologii*, 2:224–26 (*BHG*, 287a), contains a briefer account. For further information, see Delehaye, *Origines*, 155–56. *BS*, 3:675–76.

The family of Mamas, who was martyred at Caesarea in Cappadocia, is said to have been from Gangra; see *SEC*, 2 September.

Similarly, Philotheus and Eusebia, the parents of the martyrs

Eustathius, Thespesius, and Anatolius are said to have been from Gangra; for the *Passio* of Eustathius and his brothers, see Halkin, 287–311 (*BHG*, #2139); compare also *SEC*, 20 November. *BS*, 5:300.

SEC, 14 November, and *Menologium Sirletianum*, 31 March, claim that Bishop Hypatius was at the Council of Nicaea. The name Hypatius appears among the signatories to the Council of Gangra *ca*.340–41; see Turner, 2:146 & 172–73, and Joannou, 1.2.85. A *Life of Hypatius*, 8 (*BHG*, #759a), indicates that he lived into the reign of Constantius II; see Ferri, 80. The same is recorded in another *Life of Hypatius*, 4 (*BHG*, #759e); see Latyshev, *Menologii*, 1:186–87. For the date of the Council of Gangra, see *EnECh*, 336–37, and *ODCC*, 654–55. Harnack, 754. Jones, *Cities*, 538. *TIB*, 9:196–99. *Atlas*, 5. Talbert, map 86.

Mantineion? (near Claudiopolis in Paphlagonia.) For traditions of the martyr Tatian or Tation, see *SEC*, 24 August. *Menologium Basilianum*, 24 August (PG 117:601), and *Menologium Sirletianum*, 24 August, indicate that he lived and taught at Mantineion. Compare *AASS*, August 4:767a.

Simeon Metaphrastes, *Martyrium S. Martyris Christi Autonomi*, 2, mentions the Bishop Autonomus as passing through the area in the time of Diocletian; see *AASS*, Novembris 4:16–19 and PG 115:693 (*BHG*, #198). *SEC*, 12 September, records an abbreviated version of the same tradition. Foss, 189–91, suggests plausibly that Autonomus was a Novatianist emissary. Compare *BS*, 2:634.

Socrates, 2.38.29–30, indicates the presence of Novatians at Mantineion in the 340s. Harnack, 755. *TIB*, 9:249–51. Talbert, map 86.

Medicones? (near Ancyra in Galatia.) The name appears in *Martyrdom of Theodotus*, 10, as a town associated with the martyr Valens in the time of Diocletian. Franchi de' Cavalieri, *I Martirii*, 67 & 171, however, believes the name to be corrupt. Harnack, 769. *TIB*, 4:178.

Mount Olympus? (Southeast of Prusa in Bithynia.) Socrates, 1.13.1–10, mentions the Novatianist solitary Eutychian[us] in the time of Constantine; compare Sozomen, 1.14.9–11. Harnack, 764. Jones, *Cities*, map following p. 28. Talbert, map 52.

Parnassos? (in Cappadocia.) One Greek manuscript mentions Bishop Eustathius of Parnassos as being present at the Council of Nicaea; see Gelzer, lxx & 74. Harnack, 743. *Atlas*, 5. Talbert, map 63.

Paspasinos? (in Cappadocia near Andabalis; see *TIB*, 2:140–41.) The martyrdom of Speusippus, Elasippus, Melesippus, and their mother is associated with Paspasinos; for the text, see Grégoire, "Saints jumeaux," 462, and Grégoire, *Saints jumeaux*, 10–11 & 55–60 (*BHG*, #1646). The text should probably be dated to the Fifth Century at the earliest; see Delehaye, review of Henri Grégoire, *Saints jumeaux and dieux cavaliers*, in *AB* 24 (1905): 505–507. *SEC*, 16 & 17 January, mentions them as well. For the translation of the martyr relics to the West, see Delehaye, *Origines*, 354. The Bordeaux pilgrim stopped nearby at villa Palmati; see *Itinerarium Burdigalense*, 577.6 (text, 10). Gregory of Nazianzus knew of monastics at Paspasinos; see Gregory of Nazianzus, *Epistulae*, 163.2. Ramsay, *Historical Geography*, 347 & 451. Harnack, 746. Mitchell, *Anatolia*, 116. For the location of Andabalis, see *Atlas*, 5, and also Talbert, map 63.

Pessinous? (in Galatia; modern Ballihisar.) Julian, *Epistles*, 22, to Arsacius (*Works*, 3:72–73), says the town is insufficiently devoted to pagan gods; compare Sozomen, 5.16.15. Hence, Harnack, 769, suggests a substantial Christian presence earlier. *TIB*, 4:214–15. Talbert, map 62.

Pissia? (in Galatia, modern Aşagi Piribeyli.) *MAMA*, 7: #276c, is an early inscription with the "Eumeneian formula." *MAMA*, 7: 277, is a Third- or Fourth-Century inscription with a carving depicting two fish suspended from a tau cross. *MAMA*, 7: #279 has a similar motif. The same motif is suspected of being used by early Christians on signet rings in Dacia Traiana, Georgia, and in the Crimea. *MAMA*, 7: #264 and #278, are also inscriptions with Christian motifs, perhaps from as early as the Third Century. Jones, *Cities*, 533. *TIB*, 4:134. Talbert, map 62.

Sannabolae? (in Diospontus, later Honorias.) Gregory of Nazianzus, *Epistulae*, 238, is addressed to monastics there. Mitchell, *Anatolia*, 116.

Türnük? (ancient name unknown; about 30 km West-Northwest of Amaseia; see *World Atlas*, map 146–47.) An inscription datable to 200/201 contains the names "Kurillos" and "Pistikos," which are suggestive of Christianity; see *Studia Pontica* 3 (1910): #161.

Pontus Polemoniacus, Colchis, and Transcaucasian Iberia

Bibliography
AASS
Agathangelos
Allen
Braund
EEC
Epiphanius Monachus
Eusebius, *Ecclesiastical History*
Gelzer
Gregory of Nyssa, *De vita Gregorii Thaumaturgi*
Harnack
Jerome, *De viris inlustribus*
Jones, *Cities*
Kroushkova
Lordkipanidse
Lordkipanidse & Brakmann
Martyrium Sancti Apostolici Andreae
Menologium Sirletianum
OCD
ODCC
Peeters, "Les débuts"
Peterson
PG
Prieur
Rufinus, *Ecclesiastical History*
Schermann, *Prophetarum*
Schermann, *Propheten und Apostellegenden*
Schneemelcher
SEC
Socrates
Sozomen
Theodoret, *Ecclesiastical History*
Toumanoff, *Studies*
Whittaker

General

Inscriptions and other monuments show that Roman influence, if not always Roman control, extended well into the Caucasus; see Whittaker, 56, 141–43 & 285, n. 41. Christianity was established in many shoreline towns of the Black Sea by 325 as we see from the bishoprics and the martyrdoms. Archaeological work at Mtskheta suggests the possible presence of Christians in the Third Century. Finds at Modinakhe suggest that Christianity was known in the upland regions by the early Fourth Century as well. Yet reports elsewhere of burials of the late Second Century with Christian artifacts would seem to strain credulity; see Braund, 239, and compare other suggestions with regard to the Fayyum in Egypt.

In the early Fourth Century contemporaries of Gregory the Illuminator from Armenia may have been active in spreading the gospel in the region between Klarjeti on the Western border of Iberia, the Darial pass (the "Gates of the Alans") in the North, and the lands of the Massagetae to the East; see Agathangelos, 842, and Harnack, 762. Agathangelos gives no details, though, and refers to this work in general terms as a mission to all areas under Armenian influence.

The traditional account of the bringing of Christianity to the royal house of Iberia by a slavewoman (unnamed in the early accounts, though later called Nino) in the 330s is found in Rufinus, *Ecclesiastical History*, 10.11. Rufinus is followed by Socrates 1.20.1–20; Sozomen 2.7.1–12; and Theodoret, *Ecclesiastical History*, 1.23.1–13. It was not until after this point that a distinctively Christian material culture developed; see Lordkipanidse, 176. The maps in Allen, and in Toumanoff, *Studies*, are helpful in locating early sites.

Specific Sites

Apsaros. (modern Gonio.) Firmus and Firminus died there on the way into exile during the Diocletianic persecutions; see *AASS*, Junius 4: 809–11, *SEC*, 24 June, and *Menologium Sirletianum*, 24 June. Braund, 264–65. Talbert, map 87.

Neocaesarea. (modern Niksar; Northeast of Comana Pontica.) Eusebius, *Ecclesiastical History*, 6.30.1, 7.14.1 & 7.28.1, mentions Gregory and his brother Athenodorus as governing the church in Pontus in the middle of the Third Century. Gregory of Nyssa, *De vita Gregorii Thaumaturgi*, 8–9 (PG 46:897B–900B), 27 (PG 46:909B), & 42–48 (PG 46:920A–924C), indicates that Gregory was the first bishop of

Neocaesarea and that there were only some seventeen Christians in the area when he began. Jerome, *De viris inlustribus*, 65, explicitly identifies Gregory as bishop of Neocaesarea.

Bishop Longinus was at the Council of Nicaea; see Gelzer, lxii. Jones, *Cities*, 170–71 & 538. *Atlas*, 5. Talbert, map 87.

Pityous. (modern Pitsunda.) According to *AASS*, Junius 5: 695, the martyr Longinus and his six companions were condemned to exile at Pityous but never reached the place. Bishop Stratophilus of Pityous was at the Council of Nicaea; see Gelzer, lxii. Remains of an early church and other Christian artifacts have also been found there; see Kroushkova, 2657–86, and Braund, 264. Peeters, "Les débuts," 13–14. Lordkipanidse, 164. *Atlas*, 5. Talbert, map 87.

Trapezus. (modern Trabzon.) Bishop Domnus was at the Council of Nicaea; see Gelzer, lxii. *Atlas*, 5. Talbert, map 87.

Possible Sites

Meschistha? (modern Mtskheta.) Lordkipanidse, 167, 169, & Tafel 43.1. Lordkipanidse & Brakmann, 40–41. Graves of the Second and Third Centuries have been found here and at nearby Samtavro. One grave from the Third Century included a signet ring with fish and anchor motif, perhaps suggestive of Christian presence. Talbert, map 88.

Modinakhe? (ancient name unknown; near Sairkhe. For location, see Braund, 88 & 264.) Burials in evidently Christian style and orientation have been found dating to the reigns of Constantine and Constantius; see Braund, 264. Such finds could well suggest that Christians had been in the region for at least a generation. Talbert, map 88.

Sebastopolis/Dioscurias? (modern Sukhumi; on the coast of the Black Sea.) In the Eighth or Ninth Century, the *Martyrium Sancti Apostolici Andreae*, 4, reports that Andrew the apostle brought Christianity to Sebastopolis/Dioscurias and nearby regions of Colchis; see also Peterson, 18; Prieur, 17, 70 & 121; Schermann, *Propheten und Apostellegenden*, 247–53; and Schneemelcher, 2:101–18 The same basic tradition is found in the Ninth-Century work of Epiphanius Monachus, *Vita S. Andreae*, 43. Sebastopolis is not unlikely as a site for early Christianity, but the reports are all but useless as indicators of Christianity's presence before 325. Talbert, map 87.

ARMENIA MAJOR

Bibliography
Agathangelos
Alexanian
Ananian
Buzandaran Patmut'iwnk'
Ełishe
Eusebius *Ecclesiastical History*
Garsoian "Iranian"
Gelzer
Harnack
Humbach & Skjaervo
Kalantar
Khatchatrian
Koriwn
Moseṣ Khorenats'i
Sahinian
Sebeos
SEG
Sozomen
Talbert
Toumanoff, "Third-Century"
Whittaker

General

On the border between the Roman and Persian Empires, Armenia was influenced by both cultures. As with other parts of the Caucasus, Roman influence, though perhaps not control, extended well into, if not beyond Armenia; see Whittaker, 56, 141 & 285, n. 41, and Kalantar, 53–62. One should also note the temple in Greco-Roman style at Garni; for a royal inscription there *ca*.308, see *SEG* 20 (1964): #110. A Persian influence on Armenian Christianity has been noted in the work of the Fifth-Century writer Agathangelos; see Garsoian, "Iranian," 151–74. Legends associated with the apostle Thaddeus in *Buzandaran Patmut'iwnk'*, 3.1, and Moses Khorenats'i, 2.74, point to Syrian influence; see Harnack, 751. For further references to Syrian influence, see below with reference to Ashtishat.

Eusebius, *Ecclesiastical History*, 6.46.2, notes that Dionysius of Alexandria wrote a letter to the Armenians mentioning their Bishop

Meruzanes. According to Harnack, 747, the name of the bishop is genuinely Armenian and may be connected to the city of Vashpurakan, for the same name can be found in *Buzandaran Patmut'iwnk'*, 4.23. Since Christianity in Armenia Minor was generally Greek in character, by contrast this would seem to suggest that Eusebius is referring to Armenia Major. Eusebius, 9.8.2, refers to a time during the persecutions under Maximinus at which the "exceedingly earnest" Christian population of Armenia was severely persecuted. The list of members present at the Council of Nicaea records Aristakes (son of Gregory the Illuminator) and Akrites as bishops of Armenia Major, but does not record a specific see for them; see Gelzer, lxii, and Agathangelos, 859 & 884–85. Indeed, Gregory himself is said to have been active all over Armenia; see Agathangelos, 842.

Specific Sites

Ashtishat. (site of former pagan shrines in the Province of Taron, Northwest of Lake Van; modern Derik.) Agathangelos, 809–814, says that here Gregory first began to build churches. (For further information on the date of Gregory's work, see the data listed for Valarshapat.) *Buzandaran Patmut'iwnk'*, 3.14, insists that Gregory's see at Ashtishat was the mother church of Armenian Christianity and associates the work of a certain Daniel the Syrian with the site. While the *Buzandaran Patmut'iwnk'* makes Daniel a disciple of Gregory, modern scholars tend to consider him an independent worker; see Garsoian's translation of *Buzandaran Patmut'iwnk'*, pp. 257–58. In any case Syrian influence was strong in the early years of Armenian Christianity, as attested also by Koriwn, 6–8, who indicates that Mashtots looked first to Syrian models in developing the basis for the Armenian script. A corresponding Syrian influence is noted in early Armenian Biblical translations; see Alexanian, 157. *Buzandaran Patmut'iwnk'*, 3.3, notes a shrine to John the Baptist at Ashtishat. Compare also Garsoian's translation of *Buzandaran Patmut'iwnk'*, pp. 449–50. *Atlas*, 5. Talbert, map 89.

Bagawan/Bagaouna. (in the province of Bagrewand, on the headwaters of the Euphrates; modern Üç Kilise.) Site of a former fire temple to Ahura-Mazda according to Moses Khorenats'i, 2.77. Here, according to Agathangelos, 817–18 & 833–36, the recently ordained Bishop Gregory baptized Trdat and built a shrine to John the Baptist. Gregory's role in founding the shrine is confirmed by *Buzandaran*

Patmut'iwnk', 4.15. For the date of Gregory's ordination as bishop, see below under Valarshapat. See also Garsoian's translation of *Buzandran Patmut'iwnk'*. *Atlas*, 5. Talbert, map 89.

Valarshapat/Kainepolis. (the old royal capital, modern Etchmiadzin.) Agathangelos, 137–210 & 731–771, refers to the martyrdoms of the Christian maidens Gayane and Rhipsime there by the king of Armenia, ostensibly at the behest of Diocletian. While the legend is highly developed, the martyrdoms point to the existence of a Christian presence there before the official adoption of Christianity; see Thomson's introduction to Agathangelos, xii. Establishing the date of Christianity's official reception has long occupied scholars. The traditional date is *ca.*303 following a synchronism in Moses Khorenats'i. Yet a date some ten years later is preferable as will be explained below.

According to Agathangelos, 36–47, the royal heir Trdat fled to the Roman empire following the murder of his father Khosrov by Persian agents and remained in exile during an unspecified period. At the same time, a certain Gregory had been exiled to Caesarea Mazaca because of his own father's role in the murder. For Khosrov's death in the fourth year of Diocletian (i.e. 287), see Sebeos, 5 (p. 58), and Toumanoff, "Third-Century," 278.

When Trdat returned from exile, his fellow returnee Gregory was imprisoned for his faith for thirteen or fifteen years; see Agathangelos, 122 & 215. The synchronism in Moses Khorenats'i, 2.82, suggests that Trdat the Great returned from exile and ascended the throne in 287. Yet Sebeos, 5 (p. 58), says that the period of Persian domination lasted for eleven years before Trdat the Great acceded to the throne; see Toumanoff, "Third-Century," 278. Further, Ełishe, text p. 72, trans. p. 123, states that Khosrov had been murdered by his own brothers. Toumanoff, "Third Century," 263–73, following Ananian, 63–73, links the data from Sebeos with a Persian defeat by the Romans in Armenia in 297 and a peace treaty the following year. He thus shows that the Trdat who ascended the throne in 287 and who is mentioned in Nerses's *Inscription of Paikuli*, 92, was not Trdat the Great but a regicide uncle of the same name under Persian domination. (For the data of the *Inscription of Paikuli*, 92, see now Humbach & Skjaervo, 71). Toumanoff builds a cogent case for dating the accession of King Trdat the Great and the beginning of Gregory's imprisonment to 298. For a summary of the evidence, see Thomson's introduction to Agathangelos, xxxv–xxxvi.

Following Gregory's release from prison in the thirteenth or fifteenth year of Trdat's reign, he was able to convert King Trdat; see the legend in Agathangelos, 211–225. Trdat then sent Gregory to Caesarea Mazaca to be ordained by Leontius; see Agathangelos, 794–805. Moses Khorenats'i, 2.91, places Gregory's ordination as bishop for Armenia in year 17 of king Trdat the Great, which according to the dating adopted here would be *ca.*314. Sozomen, 2.8.1, is also aware of Trdat's conversion.

Agathangelos, 733–758, records the foundation legend for the cathedral at Valarshapat/Etchmiadzin, today considered the mother church of Armenian Christianity. Some the foundations of the present church date from the Fourth Century; see Sahinian, 45–51, 64–65, & plate xxix, also Khatchatrian, 67–73. A fire altar discovered in the Eastern apse appears to date from the Persian occupation of the Fifth Century; see Sahinian, 67–68 & fig. 13 (plate xviii). Pagan architectural elements have been found in use in the nearby church dedicated to Hripsime; see Sahinian, 69. Talbert, map 88.

PART TWO

CHRISTIAN COMMUNITIES IN EUROPE BEFORE 325 C.E.

Dioecesis of Thrace

Bibliography
AASS
Atlas
Athanasius, *Apologia contra Arianos*
Athanasius, *Apologia de fuga sua*
Barnea, *Christian Art*
Barnea, "L'épigraphie"
Barnea, *Les Monuments*
Beshevliev
BHG
Cedrenus
EnECh
De Boor
Delehaye, "Saints de Thrace"
Dujčev
Epiphanius, *Panarion*
Epistula ad Mareoticas ecclesias
Eusebius, *Ecclesiastical History*
Eusebius, *Vita Constantini*
Fedalto
Gelzer
Grumel
Harnack
Hefele
Hilary, *Decretum*
Hilary, *Epistula*
Hippolytus, *Refutatio*
Jones, *Cities*
Jones, *Later Roman Empire*
Łajtar
Le Quien
Madjarov
Mansi
Martyrologium Hieronymianum
Martyrologium Syriacum
Menologium Sirletianum

Mikhailov
Nicephorus, *Chronographia*
Papadopoulos-Kerameos
Popescu, *Christianitas*
Popescu, *Inscripţiile*
Radulescu & Lungu
Sayar, *Heracleia—Perinthos*
Schwartz
Simeon Metaphrastes, *Spasaniie*
Sozomen
Stoian
Tacheva-Hitova
Tertullian, *Ad Scapulam*
Theodoret, *Ecclesiastical History*
TIB
TLG
Velkov
Walter
Zeiller, *Provinces Danubiennes*

General

Thrace. The provinces covered are Europa, Haemimontus, Moesia Inferior, Rhodope, Scythia, and Thracia; see Jones, *Later Roman Empire*, 2:1456. For the locations of towns and cities, see *Atlas*, 5 & 20. For towns in Moesia Inferior and Scythia, see Zeiller, *Provinces Danubiennes*, map at end. For towns in Haemimontus, Rhodope, Thracia, and Europa, see Jones, *Cities*. Velkov, map at end, locates many sites. The monuments recorded in Tacheva-Hitova show the continuing strength of paganism in the region. A general survey of Christian developments may be found in Dujčev, 177–205.

According to Athanasius, *Apologia contra Arianos*, 37.1, bishops from Thrace and Rhodope were at the Council of Serdica in 343. Bishop Dioscorus of Thrace (city unidentified) was among them: see Athanasius, *Apologia contra Arianos*, 48.2; also Hilary, *Epistula*, B.II.4.17; and the *Epistula ad Mareoticas ecclesias*. *EnECh*, 837–38.

A decision of the Council of Ephesus in 431 indicates that Europa had sometimes two or three cities under one bishop as an ancient custom; see Mansi, 4:1478, and Schwartz, 355–56. Jones, *Cities*, 25. Hefele, 3:77.

Similarly, Sozomen, 6.21.3, reports that in his day all of Scythia Minor was subject to the Bishop of Tomis. The same is confirmed by Theodoret, *Ecclesiastical History*, 4.35.1.

Specific sites

Anchialus. (in Haemimontus; modern Pomorie.) Eusebius, *Ecclesiastical History*, 5.19.3, records a letter from Bishop Serapion of Antioch (late Second Century) to which the Bishop of Deultum had affixed a note about an attempted exorcism by a certain Sotas at Anchialus. Bishop Timotheus was among those who met at Philippopolis in 343 in opposition to the Council of Serdica; see Hilary, *Decretum*, A.IV.3.72. *Atlas*, 5. Talbert, map 22.

Axiopolis. (in Scythia; modern Hinog hamlet, Cernavoda village, Constanţa county.) *Martyrologium Syriacum*, 12 Iyar (May), records the martyr Cyril and others. *Martyrologium Hieronymianum*, 7 id. Maii records Cyril, Quindei, and Zenon; the same document, 6 id. Maii, records Cyril as a martyr along with Cindis, Dionius, Acacius, Crispionus, and Zenon. Additional martyrs are mentioned in *Martyrologium Hieronymianum*, 6 kal. Maii; and 15 kal. Nov. For a brief study of these and others commemorated at Axiopolis; see Zeiller, 116–17.

An inscription from the late-Third or early-Fourth Century reads: "*Κυρίλλῳ Κυνδαίᾳ Τασείῳ παρατίθομαι Εὐφράσιν;*" see Popescu, *Inscripţiile*, #194. This can be translated as: "close by [the martyrs] Cyril, Kindeas, and Tasios (*i.e.* Dasius) I bury Euphrasi[o]s:" see Barnea, *Christian Art*, plate 4, pp. 9–10 & 44–45; Popescu, *Christianitas*, 107–109; and compare *SEG* 47 (1997): #1117. See also Barnea, *Les Monuments*, #71, pp. 101–104. *Atlas*, 5. Talbert, map 22.

Beroe/Augusta Traiana. (in Thracia; modern Stara Zagora.) The traditions of the forty martyred women and the deacon Ammon from Beroea who were martyred at Heraclea relate to this Beroea. See *Passio SS. mulierum quadraginta martyrum*, in Delehaye, "Saints de Thrace," 194–207 (*BHG*, #2280). Also *Epitome Passionis SS. mulierum quadraginta*, in Delehaye, "Saints de Thrace," 207–209 (*BHG*, #2281). Jones, *Cities*, 24. Velkov, 127–29. Talbert, map 22.

Bizye. (in Europa; modern Vize, see Velkov, 120–21.) Severus and Memnon were among the early martyrs; see *Passio SS. Severi, Memnonis et aliorum*, in Delehaye, "Saints," 192–94 (*BHG*, #2399). Emperor Valens exiled Bishop Eustathius of Antioch there; see Socrates, 4.15.3, and Sozomen, 6.13.4. Jones, *Cities*, 25–26. *DHGE*, 9:44–46. Fedalto, 1:280. *Atlas*, 20. Talbert, map 52.

Byzantium. (in Europa; modern Istanbul.) Tertullian, *Ad Scapulam*, 3.4, records a persecution of Christians in Byzantium by the governor Caecilius Capella. For a brief description of Capella's career, see *SEG*, 41 (1991), #1406.

The heretic Theodotus the cobbler was from Byzantium; see Hippolytus, *Refutatio*, 7.35.1; also Epiphanius, *Panarion*, 54.1.3–54.1.5. Eusebius, *Ecclesiastical History*, 5.28.7–9, dates Theodotus to the time of Pope Victor (*i.e.*, late Second Century).

See Eusebius, *Vita Constantini*, 3.48.1, on martyrs. The martyr Mocius of Amphipolis was put to death in Byzantium under Diocletian; see Delehaye, "Saints de Thrace," 163–76 (*BHG*, #1298c), and *Menologium Sirletianum*, 10 May. Likewise, the martyr Acacius of Cappadocia was killed in Byzantium under Maximian; see *AASS*, Maii 2, xxviii–xli (*BHG*, #13). A certain Lucillianus and companions are said to have been martyred in Byzantium under Aurelian; see *Menologium Sirletianum*, 3 June. The senator Eleutherius of Byzantium is also reported to have been martyred under Maximian; see *Menologium Sirletianum*, 4 August. *Martyrologium Syriacum*, 11 Iyar (May), mentions a martyr Maximus and on 19 Iyar mentions a martyr Heyschius without giving further details.

Nicephorus, *Chronographia*, 112–20, gives a long list of bishops back to the Apostle Andrew and places Metrophanes as the twenty-third bishop. Fedalto, 1:3, apparently doubts the usefulness of this list.

Cedrenus, perhaps on the authority of Simeon Metaphrastes, reports other early bishops who do not appear at all in the list of Nicephorus. For report of a Bishop Philadelphus who served three years during the reign of Caracalla, see Cedrenus, 1:449. For report of a Bishop Eugenius who served for twenty-five years in the mid-Third Century, see Cedrenus, 1:451.

Le Quien, 1:206, apparently citing an earlier edition of Cedrenus, reports a Bishop Rufinus during the reign of Numerian. However, the more recent edition of Cedrenus, 1:464, does not mention a bishop Rufinus at all. Likewise, the Slavonic version of Simeon Metaphrastes, *Spasaniie*, 39, makes no mention of a Rufinus in connection with Numerian. Grumel, 434, and Fedalto, 1:3, give some credence to the bishops listed by Cedrenus and Le Quien.

It is difficult to see anything explicitly Christian in the early grave-stones, but a stone such as Łajtar, #294, from *ca*.294–95, an inscription set up by Aurelia Martha for her son Mamalios, might conceivably be Christian as the names could reflect a Christian context.

The first securely attested bishop is Metrophanes, who was in office *ca*.306–314; see Socrates, 1.37.3.

Bishop Alexander of Byzantium, the immediate successor of Metrophanes, was in office on the eve of the Arian controversy; see Socrates, 1.37.3; also Theodoret, *Ecclesiastical History*, 1.3.3 & 1.19.1.

For the refounding of Byzantium under the name Constantinople, see Philostorgius, 2.9; also Socrates, 1.16.1; and Sozomen, 2.3.1. Jerome, *Chronicle*, dates the dedication of the refounded city to 330. *EEC*, 281–85. *Atlas*, 5. Talbert, map 53.

Deultum. (in Haemimontus; modern Debelt.) Eusebius, *Ecclesiastical History*, 5.19.3, records a letter from Bishop Serapion of Antioch (late Second Century) to which Bishop Aelius Publius Julius of Deultum had affixed his name. *Atlas*, 5. Talbert, map 22.

Dinogetia. (in Scythia; modern Garvăn on the Danube.) The name, much corrupted, seems to appear in *Martyrologium Hieronymianum*, 2 id. Maii; id. Maii; and kal. Oct. See also Barnea, *Christian Art*, 7. Zeiller, 119–120. Popescu, *Inscripţiile*, #241a, records a gnostic "Ἀβρασὰξ Ἰάω" gem of the Third Century. Talbert, map 22.

Dr(o)usipara. (in Europa; see Jones, *Cities*, 24; also *Atlas*, 20. Near modern Kariştiran.) The Roman soldier Alexander was martyred under Maximianus, see *SEC*, 13 May, and *Menologium Sirletianum*, 13 May. See also *AASS*, Maii 3:13*–14* (*BHG*, #48–49). *Martyrologium Romanum*, 27 March, likewise refers to Alexander. *Atlas*, 5. Talbert, map 52.

Durostorum. (in Moesia Inferior, modern Silistra; see Zeiller, *Provinces Danubiennes*, map at end.) For the martyr Dasius under Maximianus and Diocletian, see "Les actes de S. Dasius," in *AB* 16 (1897): 11–16 (*BHG*, #491), and in Musurillo, 272–79; also *Menologium Sirletianum*, 20 November. His cult was commemorated at several nearby towns; see *Martyrologium Hieronymianum*, non. Aug.; 4 non. Oct.; 15 kal. Nov.; and 13 kal. Dec. The account in the "actes" which connects the death of Dasius with the Saturnalia is contradicted in the same document when the date of his martyrdom is given as 20 November.

Nevertheless, the tradition of his death at Durostorum seems secure; see Zeiller, *Provinces Danubiennes*, 110–116.

According to the tradition recorded in *AASS*, Aprilis 2:8*–9* (*BHG*, #1238), the lector Maximus and his companions Dada and Quintillian were martyred under Diocletian in the village of Ozobia near Durostorum. See also *SEC*, 28 April. Durostorum also appears in *Martyrologium Hieronymianum*, 7 kal. Jan.; 8 kal. Jun.; 6 id. Jun.; and 15 kal. Aug.

Similarly, the martyrdom of Julius the veteran seems to have taken place at Durostorum; see Musurillo, 260–65. See also *BHL*, #4555–56.

See also Barnea, *Christian Art*, 7. *Atlas*, 5. Talbert, map 22.

Hadriano(u)polis. (in Haemimontus; likely modern Edirne.) *AASS*, Octobris 9:545–52 (*BHL*, #6834), gives a lengthy account of Bishop Philip of Heraclea martyred at Hadrianopolis, *ca.*304. *Martyrologium Syriacum*, 22 October, records the martyred bishop Philip and others. *Martyrologium Hieronymianum*, 11 & 10 kal. Nov., reports the same tradition, with further martyrs mentioned at 8 id. Nov. Other martyrs commemorated at Hadrianopolis may be found in *SEC*, 22 Jan., 24 Aug., 1 Sept., and 19 Sept.

Athanasius, *Apologia de fuga sua*, 3.3, mentions the orthodox bishops Eutropius and Lucius of Hadrianopolis who were persecuted by the Arian party. See also Theodoret, *Ecclesiastical History*, 2.15.8. *Atlas*, 5. Talbert, map 51.

Halmyris. (in Scythia; modern Zaporzhians [so Barnea, *Christian Art*, 7] or Murighiol [so Talbert, map 23].) Epictetus and Astion, natives of Phrygia, were martyred at Halmyris in the time of Diocletian; see *AASS*, July 2:540–51 (*BHL*, #2568). The account also mentions Evangelicus, Bishop of Scythia, and the presbyter Bonosus. See also Zeiller, *Provinces Danubiennes*, 119.

Heraclea/Perinthus. (in Europa; modern Ereğli.) *Martyrologium Syriacum*, 7 January reports the martyr Candidus, 26 March reports the martyr Marcianus, 29 September reports Eutycius, 13 November reports the presbyter Edistus, and 14 November reports Theodorus and Demetrius. *Martyrologium Hieronymianum*, 7 id Jan. and 16 kal. Mart., report the martyrs Felix and Januarius. The same document reports the martyr Marcianus on 7 kal. April, and further martyrs commemorated on kal. April; 3 kal. Oct.; 18, 15, 14, & 12 kal. Dec.; and 12 kal. Jan. For Marcianus, and/or others, see *BHG*, #2280–81, suppl in t.3.

The martyr Acacius is said to have suffered at Heraclea before being taken to Byzantium; see *AASS*, Maii 2, xxxviii–xli (*BHG*, #13).

The forty women and the deacon Ammonas from Beroea were martyred at Heraclea; see Delehaye, "Saints," 194–207 (*BHG*, #2280). See also *Martyrologium Hieronymianum*, 13 kal. Dec.

Bishop Domitius took charge of the remains of the martyr Glyceria of Traianopolis in the time of "Antonius;" see *AASS*, Maii 3:10*–13* (*BHG*, #699). Bishop Philip of Heraclea was martyred at Hadrianopolis in 304; see *AASS*, Octobris 9:545–52 (*BHL*, #6834); see also Velkov, 16. Bishop Paiderus was at the Council of Nicaea; see Gelzer, lxiv. See also Fedalto, 1:274, and Le Quien, 1:1101–3. *Atlas*, 5. Talbert, map 52.

Marcianopolis. (in Moesia Inferior; modern Reka Devniya. See Jones, *Cities*, 19; also Zeiller, *Provinces Danubiennes*, map at end.) Bishop Pistus was at the Council of Nicaea; see Gelzer, lxiv. Zeiller, *Provinces Danubiennes*, 164–65. *Atlas*, 20. 5 September, martyr Meletina under "Antonius," cf. *BHG*, #2401–2403. *Atlas*, 5. Talbert, map 22.

Nicoliţel. (in Scythia; on the territory of former Noviodunum, about 10km South of that site.) Two important inscriptions from the Fourth Century are known. One on the North wall of a martyrium reads "μάρτυρες Χριστοῦ;" see Popescu, *Inscripţiile*, #267a. Another, on the South wall of the martyrium reads "μάρτυρες Ζώτικος Ἄτταλος Καμάσις Φίλιππος;" see Popescu, *Inscripţiile*, #267b.

Reference is made also to another inscription in a lower chamber "ὧδε κ(αὶ) ὧδε ἰχὼρ μαρτύρων" trans as "here and there [there is] martyr blood;" see Barnea, *Les Monuments*, #63, pp. 91–93; and Barnea, *Christian Art*, plate 3, pp. 8–9 & 42–43. Popescu, *Christianitas*, 100–106. Radulescu & Lungu, 2614–15. Talbert, map 22.

Noviodunum. (in Scythia; modern Isaccea.) *Martyrologium Syriacum*, 25 May & 4 June, reports the martyrs Flavius and Philip. *Martyrologium Hieronymianum*, 13 kal. Feb.; 16 kal. Jun.; 2 non. Jun.; 8 id. Jun.; 2 non. Jul.; and 15 kal. Oct., lists other martyrs commemorated there. For a brief study of the martyrs, see Zeiller, *Provinces Danubiennes*, 119. Barnea, *Christian Art*, 7. *Atlas*, 5. Talbert, map 22.

Philippopolis. (in Thracia; modern Plovdiv.) *Martyrologium Hieronymianum*, 3 kal. Aprilis, contains a reference to Philippopolis that is difficult to interpret.

Philippopolis was capital of Thracia; see Jones, *Cities*, 24. It was also the meeting place of the Eastern bishops who met in opposition to the Council of Serdica in 343; see Socrates, 2.20.9 & 2.22.1; also Sozomen, 3.11.4. Bishop Eutychius of Philippopolis was one of the bishops in opposition; see Hilary, *Decretum*, A.IV.3.70. Harnack, 791, thus supposes the existence of Christianity at Philippopolis before 325. Beshevliev, #207, is a Fourth-Century inscription of possible gnostic character. Beshevliev, #208, is a simple Christian gravestone from the Fourth Century. See also *EnECh*, 838. *Atlas*, 5. Talbert, map 22.

Tomis. (in Scythia Minor; modern Constanţa.) A lamp from a late Third-Century archeological context and with a possible cross monogram has been discovered; see Radulescu and Lungu, 2565–67.

Martyrologium Syriacum, 3 April, records the martyrs Chrestos and Pappos; for Chrestos and others, see also *Martyrologium Hieronymianum*, 3 non. Aprilis. *Martyrologium Hieronymianum*, also lists martyrs commemorated at Tomis on 3 non. Jan.; 6 kal. Junii; 12 kal. Julii; 3 non. Julii; 7 & 6 id. Julii; kal. Aug.; and 6 kal. Sept. Barnea, *Les Monuments*, 7 & 12. For an attempt to sort these out, see Zeiller, 117–19.

A Bishop Evangelicus who had charge of the church of Scythia and the priest Bonosus are mentioned in connection with martyrs of Halmyris in the time of Diocletian; see *AASS*, July 2:546 & 550 (*BHL*, #2568). Sozomen, 6.21.3, records that, "Tomis is the metropolis . . . even now persists there the old tradition of having only one bishop as head of all the churches of the people." See also Sozomen, 7.19.2. Theodoret, *Ecclesiastical History*, 4.35.1, confirms this. Thus it is likely that Evangelicus was bishop of Tomis.

For Bishop Philus or Titus noted respectively in the martyrologies of Bede and Hrabanus, see *AASS*, Januarius 1:133. See also, Fedalto, 1:340, and Le Quien, 1:1211–12.

A cemetery with graves in East-West orientation, hence possibly Christian, has been discovered from the early Fourth Century; see Radulescu & Lungu, 2570–71.

A restored inscription of the Fourth or Fifth Century can be read as "μάρτυ[ς Χριστοῦ] καὶ ἐπί[σκοπος] ἐνταῦ[θα κεῖται]" "here lies . . . martyr unto Christ and bishop;" see Popescu, *Inscripţiile*, #22, and Popescu, *Christianitas*, 214. Barnea, *Les Monuments*, #4, pp. 36–37, and *Christian Art*, plate 4, pp. 10 & 44–45, suggests three possibilities for the person so commemorated:

    1. Titus or Philus martyred under Licinius, *ca.*320–23. See *AASS*, Januarius 1:133.

2. The father of Argeus, Narcissus, and Marcellinus, the bishop's sons martyred under Licinius; *Martyrologium Hieronymianum*, 3 non. Jan. See also *Martyrologium Romanum*, 2 January. Compare Barnea, "L'épigraphie," 635–36.

3. Theogenes, the martyred (son of a) bishop of Parium in Hellespont under Licinius; see *AASS*, Januarius 1:133–35. See *SEC*, 3 January, and *Martyrologium Hieronymianum*, 3 non. Jan.

Popescu, *Inscripţiile*, #21, is the Christian gravestone of Aurelia Januaria from the Fourth Century. See also Barnea, *Les monuments*, #3, pp. 35–36. Barnea, *Christian Art*, plate 9, pp. 54–55.

Popescu, *Inscripţiile*, #27, is the Fourth- or Fifth-Century gravestone of Theodule, daughter of the priest Patricius. See also Barnea, *Les Monuments*, #7, pp. 39–40. Barnea, *Christian Art*, plate 12, pp. 60–61.

Among doubtful inscriptions, the following may be listed: Popescu, *Inscripţiile*, #17 & #18, are possibly Christian inscriptions from between *ca.*300 and the Fifth Century. Similarly possible is the gemstone dated to the Fourth or Fifth Century; see Popescu, *Inscripţiile*, #53 (=*SEG* 40 (1990), #604).

Eusebius, *Vita Constantini*, 3.7.1, mentions a bishop of Scythia at the Council of Nicaea who could well be the Bishop of Tomis; see Le Quien, 1:1213. Popescu, *Christianitas*, 178–86, also suggests that the Bishop of "Gothia" mentioned as being at the Council of Nicaea (see Gelzer, lxiv), could be related to the area North of the Danube.

For further references to bishops of Tomis, see Zeiller, *Provinces Danubiennes*, 169–73, and Barnea, *Christian Art*, 12. On the later Bishop Theotimus, see Sozomen, 7.26.6–9. *Atlas*, 5. Talbert, map 22.

Traianoupolis. (in Rhodope; see Jones, *Cities*, 24.) The martyrs Glyceria and Laodicius are known from the time of "Antonius;" see *AASS*, Maii 3:10*–13* (*BHG*, #699). See also, *SEC*, 13 May, and *Menologium Sirletianum*, 13 May. *Atlas*, 5. Talbert, map 51.

Possible sites

Diocletianopolis? (modern Hisar.) An inscription of the presbyter Florentius may show the early presence of Christians, see Madjarov, 2521–23. However, the editor, Beshevliev, #223, dates the inscription to the Fifth Century. De Boor, 532, #697. Jones, *Cities*, 24. See also *EnECh*, 838. Velkov, 129. Talbert, map 22.

Epibata? (in Europa. *SEC*, 5 May, note, shows that according to Codex Parisiensis 1617, Bishop Euthemius, Bishop of Madytus in the Tenth Century, was a native of the Epibatan countryside. For the location of Madytus, see Velkov, 123. For the date of Euthemius, see *BHG*, #654, and Fedalto, 289. Harnack, 792, places it near Selymbria.) Harnack, 792, suggested a martyrdom at Epibata, but this seems likely to be a confusion between the several saints named Paraskeue. Legends relating to a Paraskeue of Epibata focus on the Tenth Century; see Papadopoulos-Kerameus, k-kb & 438–53 (*BHG*, #1421); compare *BHG*, #1420z. On the artistic traditions related to the several saints named Paraskeue, see Walter, 753–57, who suggests that in artistic works Paraskeue is a personification of Christ's passion. Neither in the topographical indices of *AASS*, nor in *BHG*, nor in *TLG*, do I find any other references to Epibata as a specific place. *TIB*, 6:106. Not in *Atlas*, 5, or in Talbert.

Troesmis? (modern Igliţa.) Popescu, *Inscripţiile*, #236, contains what appears to be a cross dating *ca.*275–325, though this may well be a legionary sign. Talbert, map 22.

NORTH AND NORTHWEST COASTS OF THE BLACK SEA

Bibliography
AASS
BHG
Cyril of Jerusalem
Delehaye, "Saints de Thrace"
Epiphanius, *Panarion*
Gelzer
Glushak
Harnack
Khrshanovskii
Latyshev, "Zhitiia"
Levinskaya
Liber Pontificalis
Martyrion tou Agiou Klementos
Menologium Sirletianum
Metzger
OCD
Philostorgius

Popescu, *Christianitas*
Ruinart
SEG
Simeon Metaphrastes, *Vita S. Clementis Martyris*
Socrates
Sozomen
Struve
Talbert
Zeiller, *Provinces Danubiennes*

General

Goths and the Crimean Region. For Wulfila, a descendant of Cappadocian captives, and his translation of the Bible into Gothic see Socrates, 2.41.23 & 4.33.6–9; Philostorgius, 2.5; and Metzger, 375–77. Sozomen, 2.6.1, refers to Goths and Danubian tribes being converted under Constantine. Epiphanius, *Panarion*, 70.1.1 & 70.14.5, reports the schismatic ascetic Audius being exiled to live and work among the Goths shortly after 325.

See Struve, #994 & #1051, for possibly Christian inscriptions. *SEG* 45 (1995): #982, provides further discussion. Also, Levinskaya, 227–46. Cyril of Jerusalem, 10.19, knows of martyrs among the Goths. Ruinart, 617–20, prints a letter from the Goths concerning the Saint Sabas known from *ca.*370; see also *AASS*, Aprilis, 2:87–90. Delehaye, "Saints de Thrace," 276, publishes a somewhat later fragment of a Gothic sanctoral calendar.

Specific sites

Bosp(h)orus/Pantikapaion. (modern Kerch, on the Bosphorus; see *OCD*, 254 & 1107.) A brief inscription dating to 304 and with a cross in the center has been found; see Struve, addenda, #3. See also Glushak, 34 & 145, for discussion and diagram. Other inscriptions date to the early Fourth Century but may be Jewish in character; see Struve, #64–66. Bishop Cadmus was at the Council of Nicaea; see Gelzer, lxiv. See also Glushak, 50. Talbert, map 87 inset.

Chersonesos. (near modern Sevastapol; see *OCD*, 321.) Later accounts associate some of the legendary travels of Clement of Rome with the region around Chersonesos; see *Martyrion tou Agiou Klementos*, 18–20 (*BHG*, #350), and compare *Liber Pontificalis* (ed. Duchesne), 1:xci, and Simeon Metaphrastes, *Vita S. Clementis Martyris*.

A somewhat more reliable tradition records the martyrs Basilius, Capiton, and others at Chersonesos under Diocletian; see Latyshev, "Zhitiia," 58–62 (*BHG*, #266); and also Latyshev, 63–65 (*BHG*, #267). See also *SEC*, 6 and 7 March, and *Menologium Sirletianum*, 4 March. *Atlas*, 5. Talbert, map 23.

Gothia. Bishop Theophilus of Gothia was at the Council of Nicaea; see Gelzer, lxiv. Gelzer, map at end, places it in the Crimea, as does Zeiller, *Provinces Danubiennes*, 409. Harnack, 797, suggests that the town may be either in the Crimea or identical with Tomi in the province of Scythia. Popescu, *Christianitas*, 178–86, would support a location for Bishop Theophilus somewhere to the North of the Danube.

Possible sites
Hermonassa? (on the Taman peninsula.) A Fourth-Century inscription with a cross in the center and the words "μετὰ τὸν ἄγιον" and "συνθειάσειτ[αι]" (see Struve, #1099) leads Levinskaya, 115, to suggest that the earliest Christians in the area formed associations similar to "thiasoi" known from pagan inscriptions. Talbert, map 87 inset.

Kytai? (modern Kitei on the Crimean peninsula.) A finger ring with a tau-cross flanked by two fish has been found in archaeological strata not later than the end of the Third Century; see Khrshanovskii, 264–65; and Levinskaya, 114. The ring is similar in design to one from Romula in Dacia Traiana; *q.v.* Glushak, 34–35, suggests that Struve, #944, may be a Christian inscription from Kytai. *OCD*, 254. Talbert, map 87 inset.

Phanagor(e)ia? (modern Sennaya.) Struve, #1051, from 307 may be a Christian inscription. Talbert, map 87 inset.

GREECE

Bibliography
AASS
ANRW
Apostolic Constitutions

Aristides
Arnobius
Artemii Passio
Athanasius, *Apologia contra Arianos*
Athanasius, *Epistula ad easdem*
Atlas
Barnea, "L'épigraphie"
Bezae codex
BHG
BHL
BS
Bulletin Épigraphique
CIG
I Clement
II Clement
Clement of Alexandria, *Stromata*
III Corinthians
DACL
De Boor
Delehaye, *Les origines*
Delehaye, "Saints de Thrace"
pseudo-Dionysius, *Corpus*
Doubouniotos
Duchesne, "Anciens"
Ehrhard
EnECh
Epiphanius, *Panarion*
Epistula ad Mareoticas ecclesias
Eusebius, *Chronicle*
Eusebius, *Ecclesiastical History*
Fedalto
Feissel
Ferrua
Gelzer
Gounaris
Gounaris & Velenis
Gounaropolou & Chatzopolou
Gregory of Nazianzus, *Orationes*
Guarducci, *Epigrafia*
Guarducci, *Inscriptiones Creticae*

Harnack
Hilary, *Epistula*
Hoddinott
Honigmann, "L'Évêché"
IG
Jerome, *Chronicle*
Jerome, *De viris inlustribus*
Jones, *Later Roman Empire*
pseudo-Justin
Kitzinger, "Survey"
Lam[p]ros, *Catalogue*
Lampros, *Kerkyraika*
Leake
Le Quien
Liber Pontificalis
Martyrdom of Polycarp
Martyrologium Hieronymianum
Martyrologium Romanum
Martyrologium Syriacum
Mombritius
Murphy-O'Connor
Origen, *Commentarii in Epistolam ad Romanos*
Origen, *Contra Celsum*
Pallas, "Investigations"
Pallas, *Monuments*
PECS
Pelekanidis
Perdrizet
Pilhofer
Philostorgius
Polycarp
Praedestinatus
Quaesten
RBK
Robinson, *Bauer*
SEC
SEG
Socrates
Stikas
Sylloge³

Tertullian, *De virginibus velandis*
Theodoret, *Interpretatio epistolae ad Philippenses*
Theophylact
Turner
Ugolini
Veselý
White
Zeiller, *Provinces Danubiennes*

General

Greece. The sites included in this section are in the Southern part of the Dioecesis of Moesiae as delimited by the *Verona List: i.e.*, Epirus, Thessaly, Macedonia, Achaia, and Crete. For general provincial and diocesan boundaries, see Jones, *Later Roman Empire*, maps following p. 1069. Jones, 1456, indicates that the Southern part of Moesiae was defined as the Dioecesis of Macedonia by the time of the *Notitia Dignitatum*. See further, *Atlas*, 5 & 20.

Tertullian, *De virginibus velandis*, 2.1, knows of the way in which virgins were veiled among the Greeks. According to the editor of the Greek rescension of pseudo-Justin, *Oration to the Greeks*, p. 104, the rescension that survives in Syriac is the *apologia* of a Greek senator Ambrose for his conversion to Christianity early in the Third Century; see pseudo-Justin, Syriac text, 38; English trans., 61. Arnobius, 2.12, comments on the spread of Christianity in Achaia, Macedonia, and Epirus.

Harnack, 787, places some value in the list derived by Duchesne, "Anciens," 378 & 384, from the *Notitiae Episcopatuum* published by De Boor, even though the list relates to the Fifth Century and later. Much closer in time for our purposes are the lists of participants at the Council of Serdica by Hilary of Poitiers and others. Gounaris, 3:2687–2711, provides no additional information for the earliest period.

Achaia. *Sylloge³*, #801, found at Delphi, dates the proconsul Gallio of Acts 18.12 firmly to the year 52 C.E. Delphi itself long continued to be a strongly pagan site; see *Sylloge³*, #901, from *ca.*312–15, and also *Bulletin Épigraphique* (1960), #59. In I Thessalonians 1:7 and in II Corinthians 1:1 Paul makes general reference to Christians in Achaia. Jerome, *De viris inlustribus*, 54, reports that the bishops of Achaia invited Origen to teach among them before he settled in Caesarea; compare Eusebius, *Ecclesiastical History*, 6.23.4. Arnobius,

2.12, comments on the spread of Christianity in Achaia. Athanasius, *Apologia contra Arianos*, 37.1, mentions bishops from Achaia at the Council of Serdica in 343. Philostorgius, 3.2, records that Constantius II brought the relics of Luke and Andrew from Achaia to Constantinople. *EnECh*, 7.

Crete. Acts 2:11 mentions Cretans as part of the crowd on Pentecost day. Acts 27:7–21 records Paul's journey past Crete as a prisoner. Titus 1:5–9 records the tradition of Titus's work in Crete. According to *Apostolic Constitutions*, 7.46, Paul ordained Titus as the first bishop of the place. Eusebius, *Ecclesiastical History*, 4.23.5, mentions a letter from Dionysius of Corinth to "Bishop Philip of Gortyna and to the other Cretan dioceses," so there must have been at least three bishops in Crete by Dionysius' time. Guarducci, *Inscriptiones Creticae*, 1: #188–89, is an imperial edict of *ca*.319 found at Lyttos and related to "*delatores*," ("informers") though it does not specifically mention Christians. It does show, though, that the problem of those who were informants, or who had been informed upon, was of some significance to the residents of Lyttos. Praedestinatus, 1.20, says Bishop Dioscorus of Crete opposed the Archontic heresy. Athanasius, *Apologia contra Arianos*, 37.1, mentions bishops from Crete at the Council of Serdica in 343.

Macedonia. Arnobius, 2.12, comments on the spread of Christianity in Macedonia. Athanasius, *Apologia contra Arianos*, 37.1, mentions bishops from Macedonia at the Council of Serdica in 343. Many of the known early Christian sites in the province stood along the *via Egnatia*; see *ANRW*, II.7.1, map following p. 304.

Thessaly. At Acts 17:15, the *Bezae codex* records that Paul worked in Thessaly. Bishop Claudianus was at the Council of Nicaea; see Gelzer, lxiv. Athanasius, *Apologia contra Arianos*, 37.1 mentions bishops from Thessaly at the Council of Serdica in 343.

Specific sites
Aigina. (in Achaia.) According to *Apostolic Constitutions*, 7.46, Crispus the first bishop, was appointed by Peter. This tradition indicates that Christianity was of long standing in Aegina by the time the *Apostolic Constitutions* was compiled in the Fourth Century. Harnack, 621 & 786. Talbert, map 59.

Amphipolis. (in Macedonia, on the *via Egnatia*.) Acts 17:1 records that Paul and Silas passed through the place. For the martyrdom of the presbyter Mucius of Amphipolis under Licinius and Maximus, see *AASS*, Maii 2:620–22 (*BHL*, #6023–24); also Delehaye, "Saints de Thrace," 163–76. See further *Martyrologium Romanum*, 13 May. Talbert, map 51.

Apollonia. (in Macedonia, on the *via Egnatia*.) Acts 17:1 records that Paul and Silas passed through the place. Talbert, map 51.

Athens. (in Achaia.) Paul's work there is recorded in Acts 17:15–18:1 and in I Thessalonians 3:1. Eusebius, *Ecclesiastical History*, 3.4.10, citing Dionysius of Corinth, claims that Dionysius the Areopagite (see Acts 17:34) was the first bishop of Athens. *Apostolic Constitutions*, 7.46, reports that Dionysius was ordained by Paul. The collection of writings known as pseudo-Dionysius, *Corpus*, is far too late to be of help in establishing the history of the church at Athens; see *EEC*, 335. According to Roman tradition, two of the early popes were natives of Athens; see *Liber Pontificalis*, 5, "Anacletus," & 10, "Hyginus."

Eusebius, *Ecclesiastical History*, 4.3.3, mentions the *Apology* of Aristides as having been written in the time of Hadrian. Eusebius, *Chronicle*, anni Abrahae 2140, places Aristides at Athens, as does Jerome, *Chronicle*, for the year equivalent to 125 C.E., and *De viris inlustribus*, 19. The modern editor of the Syriac version of Aristides argues that Aristides should be dated early in the reign of Antoninus Pius; see Aristides, p. 9.

Eusebius, *Ecclesiastical History*, 4.26.10, records an apology from Melito of Sardis to Marcus Aurelius in which Melito says that Antoninus Pius had forbidden the people of Athens to persecute Christians.

Eusebius, *Ecclesiastical History*, 4.23.2–3, mentions a letter from Bishop Dionysius of Corinth which refers to the earlier martyred Bishop Publius of Athens and his successor Quadratus. Epiphanius, *Panarion*, 32.6.1, seems to indicate that Clement of Alexandria was a native of Athens.

At *Ecclesiastical History*, 6.23.1–4 & 6.32.1–2, Eusebius says that Origen completed his commentary on Ezekiel and began his commentary on the Song of Songs there. Origen, *Contra Celsum*, 3.30, states that the church at Athens was a peaceful one. *AASS*, Maii 3:452, records the martrys Heraclius, Paulinus, and Benedimus at Athens.

Bishop Pistus was at the Council of Nicaea; see Gelzer, lxiv. Gregory of Nazianzus, *Orationes*, 5.23–24, records his experiences at

Athens with the future Emperor Julian, who was busy studying pagan culture. An inscription from the Third Century records that Aurelia Zosima, a native of Athens, died as a Christian at Elis: see Pallas, "Investigations," 3–5; Barnea, "L'épigraphie," 646; and *SEG* 22 (1967), 106, #330. *Atlas*, 5. *DHGE*, 5:12–42. Talbert, map 59.

Ber(r)oia. (in Macedonia; modern Veroia.) Acts 17:10–14 records that Paul and Silas found receptive hearers in the synagogue there. The martyrdom of forty women and the deacon Ammon under Licinius probably refers not to this Beroia, but to Beroia of Thrace; see *EnECh*, 515. *Atlas*, 5. *Apostolic Constitutions*, 7.46, says that Paul ordained Onesimus (mentioned in Philemon, 10) as its first bishop. Gounaropolou & Chatzopolou, #329 (=*SEG* 48 (1998): #736), is the epitaph of a certain "Gregorius" from the Second or Third Century; the name is suggestive of a Christian context. Compare also *SEG* 48 (1998): #733 & #734. Bishop Gerontius was at the Council of Serdica in 343: see Hilary of Poitiers, B.II.4.56; Athanasius, *Apologia contra Arianos*, 48.2; Athanasius, *Epistula ad easdem*; and also *Epistula ad Mareoticas ecclesias*. *Atlas*, 5. Talbert, map 50.

Bouthroton. (in Epirus; modern Butrinti in Albania.) The martyrdom of Therenus of Bouthroton took place under Decius. Greek tradition preserves an encomium on him; see Lam[p]ros, *Catalogue*, #3262.3, for the listing; also Lampros, *Kerkyraïka*, 9–22, (*BHG*, #1799) for the text, with corrections in Doubouniotos, 232. There is also a martyrdom in Greek; see Lam[p]ros, *Catalogue*, #3262.4 (*BHG*, #1798z) for the listing; compare Ehrhard, 902, #6. The Latin martyrdom reports the place-name as "Bosrena;" see Mombritius, 2:598–99 (where the place-name is apparently wrongly understood by *BHL*, #8129, to be a reference to Bostra in Arabia). For a mosiac in the Church of St. George, Thessalonica, depicting Therenus, see Hoddinott, plates 17b & 22h. For further discussion, see Ugolini, 91–93.

   Leake, 1:101, gives an early description of Bouthroton. *RBK*, 2: 232–35, discusses recent finds, including a possible martyrium. *DHGE*, 10:1437–38. *EnECh*, 283. *Atlas*, 5. Talbert, map 54.

Cenchreae. (in Achaia; modern Kechriai.) Acts 18:18 places Paul at Cenchreae, and Romans 16:1 mentions the church there. The Fourth-Century work, *Apostolic Constitutions*, 7.46, says that Paul ordained its first bishop, Lucius. Talbert, map 58.

Corcyra. (off the coast of Epirus and administered as an island; modern Corfu.) Bishop Aletodorus was at the Council of Nicaea; see Gelzer, lxiii. Talbert, map 54.

Corinth. (in Achaia.) Paul's letters to the church at Corinth form an important part of the New Testament canon, detailing his work and the work of Apollos. The church and its members are also mentioned in Acts 18:1, 18:8 & 19:1. Peter may have visited there as well; see *I Clement*. Eusebius, *Ecclesiastical History*, 2.25.8, mentions both Peter and Paul as connected to Corinth. At II Timothy 4:20 Erastus is mentioned at Corinth. *III Corinthians*, purports to be a letter of Paul in response to gnostic theological difficulties at Corinth.

According to *II Clement*, 20.5, the author of the work addressed it to the church at Corinth. The colophon found in *Martyrdom of Polycarp*, 22, records that the narrative about the saint was copied at Corinth by a certain Socrates prior to the time of Pionius. Eusebius, *Ecclesiastical History*, 4.22.1–2, records a fragment by Hegesippus in which Hegesippus tells of his visit with Bishop Primus of Corinth. At 5.23.4, Eusebius mentions Bishop Bacchylus as a contemporary of Pope Victor, *ca.*190, during the Easter controversy. Tertullian, *De virginibus velandis*, 8.4, knows the Corinthian custom of veiling virgins.

At 4.21.1, Eusebius dates Bishop Dionysius of Corinth to the late Second Century. At 4.23.1–13, he discusses Dionysius's writings. Praedestinatus, 1.23, refers to a Bishop Apollonius of Corinth who worked to oppose Cerdo's teaching, and who presumably belongs to this era. Origen, *Contra Celsum*, 3.30, indicates that the church at Corinth was at peace in his own day.

The epitaphs of Agapomene and Agapomenus are Christian and pre-Constantinian; see Pallas, "Investigations," 7. Yet many graves in the cemetery from *ca.*300 do not easily admit of being classed as either pagan or Christian; see Pallas, "Investigations," 9. Also, a basilica was erected in the Fourth or Fifth Century to commemorate the martyrdom of Quadratus under Valerian; see Stikas, 478–79. On Quadratus, see further *AASS*, Martii 2:895–98 (*BHG*, #358).

Martyrologium Syriacum, 16 April, mentions the martyr Leonidas and others at Corinth. The same tradition is recorded in *Martyrologium Hieronymium*, 16 kal. Maii, and 13 kal. Aug. *SEC*, 17 April, wrongly makes Leonidas bishop of Athens. On traditions related to him, see *BS*, 7:1309–10. For a study of texts and archaeology directly relevant to Christianity in the city, see Murphy-O'Connor, 130–76.

Robinson, *Bauer*, 69–77. Fedalto, 1:483. *Atlas*, 5. *EnECh*, 201–202. Talbert, map 58.

Edessa. (in Macedonia.) The epitaphs of Neicandrus and Xanthias appear to be Christian. That of Neicandrus mentions resurrection; see *DACL*, 4:2112. That of Xanthias has a fish and bird motif inscribed upon it; see *DACL*, 4:2111–12, fig. 3975; also Pallas, "Investigations," 6, and Barnea, "L'épigraphie," 646. The dates are not quite certain, but Pallas, 5, takes them to be pre-Constantinian. Edessa is listed at De Boor, #271. Talbert, map 50.

Elis. (in Achaia.) A Third-Century epitaph of a certain Aurelia Zosima, a native of Athens who had died at Elis, mentions "the God of heaven," very possibly a Christian phrase; see *CIG*, 4:9294; also *SEG* 22 (1967): 106, #330. For the date, see Pallas, "Investigations," 3–5.

Bishop Dionysius was at the Council of Serdica in 343: see Hilary, *Epistula*, B.II.4.48; also Athanasius, *Apologia contra Arianos*, 48.2; and *Epistula ad Mareoticas ecclesias*. Talbert, map 58.

Euboea. (an island whose chief city was Chalcis; in Achaia.) Bishop Marcus of [Eu]boea was at the Council of Nicaea; see Gelzer, lxiv. The editors of *Atlas*, 5, seem to question whether Euroea (*q.v. infra*) should be understood as the place name instead. Talbert, map 55. Talbert, map 50, also lists a small town by this name.

Gortyn(a). (in Achaia; on the island of Crete.) Eusebius, *Ecclesiastical History*, 4.23.5, mentions a letter from Dionysius of Corinth to Bishop Philip of Gortyna. For the martyrdom of Bishop Cyril under Diocletian, see *AASS*, Julii 2:684–87 (*BHG*, #467 & 467b). See also *SEC*, 9 July, and *Martyrologium Romanum*, 9 July. For further references to Cyril, see *BS*, 3:1321–22.

For the possible links of Dioscorus of Crete, *q.v.*, with Gortyna, see Fedalto, 1:535. *Atlas*, 5. Talbert, map 60.

Hephaistia. (on the island of Lemnos, geographically in the province of Achaia; modern Kastro Bouni.) Bishop Strategius was at the Council of Nicaea; see Gelzer, lxiv. Bishop Strategius is also listed among the bishops of Asia, the province from which Lemnos was administered; see Gelzer, lxiii. Harnack, 786. *Atlas*, 5 & 20. Talbert, map 56.

Knos(s)os. (in Achaia; capital of the island of Crete.) Eusebius, *Ecclesiastical History*, 4.23.7–8, mentions correspondence between Dionysius of Corinth and Bishop Pinytus of Knossos in the late Second Century. Jerome, *De viris inlustribus*, 28, mentions the letter of Pinytus. *Atlas*, 5. Talbert, map 60.

Lacedaemon. (ancient Sparta; in Achaia.) Eusebius, *Ecclesiastical History*, 4.23.2, mentions a letter from Dionysius of Corinth to the Lacedaemonian church *ca.*190; see also Jerome, *De viris inlustribus*, 27. *Atlas*, 5. Talbert, map 58.

Larissa. (in Thessaly.) Eusebius, *Ecclesiastical History*, 4.26.10, mentions an apology from Melito of Sardis to Marcus Aurelius in which Melito referred to a letter of Antoninus Pius asking the people of Larissa not to persecute Christians. Bishop Claudianus of Thessaly, who attended the Council of Nicaea, had his see at Larissa according to one Greek manuscript; see Gelzer, 70. Bishop Alexander of Larissa was at the Council of Serdica in 343; see Athanasius, *Apologia contra Arianos*, 48.2; Hilary, *Epistula*, B.II.4.26; and *Epistula ad Mareoticas ecclesias*. Barnea, "l'épigraphie," 645–46, and Pallas, "Investigations," 5, list the epitaph of Therinus (*IG* 9.2, #991), which may well be Christian, from the Fourth Century. *Atlas*, 5. Talbert, map 55.

Lasaia. (on the island of Crete.) Acts 27:8, mentions that Paul's ship docked nearby at the harbor called "Fair Havens." There does not, however, appear to be any indication of a continuous Christian community in the area. Talbert, map 60.

Neapolis. (the seaport for Philippi; in Macedonia on the *via Egnatia*; modern Kavalla.) Acts 16:11 records that Paul and his companions landed there on their way to Philippi. No evidence of a continuous community. Talbert, maps 51 & 101.

Nicopolis. (in Epirus; modern Palaio-Preveza.) Titus 3:12 records a tradition of Paul's work there. According to Eusebius, *Ecclesiastical History*, 6.16.2–3, Origen found Greek manuscripts of the Old Testament there. Pope Eleutherius (d. *ca.*185) was a native of the place; see *Liber Pontificalis*, xiv, "Eleutherius." *EnECh*, 283. Bishop Heliodorus was at the Council of Serdica in 343; see Hilary, *Epistula*, B.II.4.39, and Athanasius, *Apologia contra Arianos*, 37.1 & 48.2. *Atlas*, 5. Talbert, map 54.

Philippi. (in Macedonia; on the *via Egnatia*.) Paul's letter to the Philippians is part of the New Testament canon. The church at Philippi is mentioned at Acts 16:12 and 20:6. Paul's sufferings at Philippi are mentioned in I Thessalonians 2:2. Theodoret, *Interpretatio epistolae ad Philippenses*, 1.1–2, indicates that the Epaphroditus mentioned in Philippians 2:25 & 4:18 was the first bishop of Philippi. Polycarp addressed his *Letter to the Philippians* to this congregation.

Pilhofer, 2: #111 & #112 are Latin Christian epitaphs perhaps datable to a time as early as *ca.*300–320. Pilhofer, 2: #360, a memorial tablet by Aurelius Kapiton for his relatives, speaks of him as a "new presbyter of the catholic church" and bears a date of "410." If the year 410 relates to the Macedonian era, this would be 262/63 C.E. If the year 410 relates to the colonial era, it would be *ca.*381 C.E.

Gounaris & Velenis, 3:365–66, identify an early Christian house with coin finds dating to the time of Constantine and Licinius.

Bishop Porphyrus was at the Council of Serdica in 343; see Hilary, *Epistula*, B.II.4.9; and *Epistula ad Mareoticas ecclesias. Atlas*, 5. For the early church at the site with inscriptions dating to the time of Bishop Porphyrus, see White, 2:175–86, and Pilhofer, 2: #328 & #329. Fedalto, 1:448–49. For a general history of the Christian community at Philippi, see Pilhofer, 1:229–58. *Atlas*, 5. Talbert, map 51.

Platea. (in Achaia; in the later eparchy of Hellas.) An inscription from *ca.*300 mentions three presbyters and a reader; see Guarducci, *Epigrafica*, 4:335–36. Bishop Athenodorus was at the Council of Serdica in 343: see Hilary, *Epistula*, B.II.4.24 (compare Turner, 1.2.3: 552–53); also Athanasius, *Apologia Contra Arianos*, 48.2; Athanasius, *Epistula ad easdem*; and *Epistula ad Mareoticas ecclesias*. Pallas, "Investigations," 5 & 7, mentions inscriptions; see also *DACL*, 7:649, and Barnea, "L'épigraphie," 646. See De Boor, #753, for the location also. Fedalto, 1:520.

Pydna. (in Macedonia.) The martyrdom of a certain Alexander took place under Maximian; see *SEC*, 13 March; also *AASS*, Martii II: 339–40 (*BHL*, #280). The site was first described by Leake, 3: 426–32. *PECS*, 745. *RBK*, 5:1097–98, describes remains of an Eighth-Century church built over an early Christian basilica. *Atlas*, 5. Talbert, map 50.

Same. (on the island of Cephallenia, off the coast of Epirus.) Not to be identified with Samos in the Aegean, see Acts 20:15. Same was home to a group of gnostic Christians; see Clement of Alexandria, *Stromata*, 3.2.5.2. *Atlas*, 5. Talbert, map 54.

Samothrace. (island administered as part of Macedonia.) Acts 16:11 mentions that Paul and his companions made a brief stop there. No other indication of an early Christian community. Talbert, maps 51 and 101.

Stobi. (in Macedonia.) Bishop Boudius was at the Council of Nicaea; see Gelzer, lxiv. *Atlas*, 5. Zeiller, *Provinces Danubiennes*, 160–61, notes some confusion in the Nicene lists between the neighboring regions of Macedonia and Dardania, but confirms Boudius as bishop of Stobi. *SEG* 36 (1986): #638, is a mosiac inscription from the first basilica, dating to *ca*.325. For the somewhat later church, see Kitzinger, "Survey," 87–110 & 150–51. *Atlas*, 5. Talbert, map 50.

Thebae. (in Achaia; modern Thivai.) Bishop Cleonicus was at the Council of Nicaea; see Gelzer, lxiv. Bishop Museus was at the Council of Serdica in 343; see Hilary, *Epistula*, B.II.4.13, and Athanasius, *Apologia contra Arianos*, 48.2. The later work *Artemii Passio*, 16, records the tradition that the evangelist Luke worked in Thebes; compare Philostorgius, 3.2. *Atlas*, 5. Fedalto, 1:471. Talbert, map 55.

Thessalonica. (in Macedonia; near the *via Egnatia*; by the Thermaic Gulf.) The letters of Paul to the church at Thessalonica are part of the New Testament canon. In addition, the place and its people are mentioned in Acts 17:1–13, 20:4, 27:2, Philippians 4:16, and II Timothy 4:10. Origen, *Commentarii in Epistolam ad Romanos*, 10.41, states that the Gaius mentioned in Romans 16:23 was the first bishop of Thessalonica. Eusebius, *Ecclesiastical History*, 4.26.10, cites an apology from Melito of Sardis to Marcus Aurelius in which Melito says that Antoninus Pius had forbidden the Thessalonians to persecute Christians.

Tomb paintings of Christian character and dating to perhaps the third quarter of the Third Century have been discovered at Thessalonica; see Pelekanidis, 218–220. Pallas, "Investigations," 14, concurs with the date.

Pallas, "Investigations," 5, identifies two inscriptions with the telltale Christian phrase "until the resurrection" as early: For the Second or Third Century epitaph of Calocerus, see *CIG*, 4:9439 (=*IG* 10.2, #440; =Feissel, #119). For the epitaph of Flavius Callistus, see Perdrizet, 229–33 (=*IG* 10.2, #351; =Feissel, #120), where the editors

date it to the beginning of the Byzantine period. Barnea,"L'épigraphie,"
644–45, identifies *IG* 10.2, #433 & #931 as Christian inscriptions
also.

Bishop Alexander of Thessalonica was at the Council of Nicaea;
see Gelzer, lxiv. *Atlas*, 5. Fedalto, 1:423. Talbert, map 50.

Possible sites

Asopolis? (in Achaia, on the Peloponessus.) Bishop Cocras (*i.e.*
Socrates?) of "Asopofoebiis" was at the Council of Serdica in 343;
see Hilary, *Epistula*, B.II.4.43; compare Turner, 1.2.3: 556–57. Compare
Talbert, map 58.

Chalcis? (in Achaia, on the island of Euboea.) Harnack, 792, pos-
tulates that Jerome, *De viris inlustribus*, 83, has confused Methodius
of Olympus with a martyr of the same name at Chalcis. Duchesne,
378 & 384. *Atlas*, 5, seems to identify the see of Bishop Marcus of
Euboea (see above) with Chalcis. *Atlas*, 5. Talbert, map 55.

Demetrias? (in Thessaly.) *SEG* 28 (1978): #512 lists an inscription
from the late Third or early Fourth Century. If the christogram and
the inscribed fish are contemporaneous with the remainder of the
inscription, it would be an indication of pre-Nicene Christianity.

Diocletianopolis? (in Macedonia; probably classical Argos Orestikon,
modern Chroupista. For the location, see Turner, 1.2.3: 459, and
EnECh, 515.) Bishop Bassus was at the Council of Serdica in 343;
see Hilary, *Epistula*, B.II.4.8; also Athanasius, *Apologia contra Arainos*,
48.2; and *Epistula ad Mareoticas ecclesias*. De Boor, 525, #267. Talbert,
maps 49 & 50, identifies Diocletionopolis with Pella, but as Pella is
mentioned elsewhere in the lists for the Council of Serdica, this seems
unlikely.

Eleutherna? (on the island of Crete.) *SEG* 45 (1995): #1266 is a
graffito with a Christian acclamation reading νείκην τῶι Κυρείωι and
dating possibly to the Third Century.

Euroia? (in Epirus; modern Glyki.) *Atlas*, 5, seems to suggest that
"Euroea," should be read in place of "Euboea," in the list of Bishops
present at the Council of Nicaea, but there is no evidence for this
suggestion in the lists published by Gelzer. Pallas, *Monuments*, 138–40,
does note ruins of an early Christian edifice from the latter part of
the Fourth Century at Euroia. *EnECh*, 283. Talbert, map 54.

Herakleia Linci? (in central Macedonia; on the *via Egnatia*.) Bishop Evagrius was at the Council of Serdica in 343: see Hilary, *Epistula*, B.II.4.21. See also Athanasius, *Epistula ad easdem*, which gives the bishop's name as Eugenius. Fedalto, 1:441. Talbert, map 49.

Hypata? (Nova Patrae; in Thessaly; modern Hypati.) Bishop Hymnaeus was at the Council of Serdica in 343: see Hilary, *Epistula*, B.II.4.18; Athanasius, *Apologia contra Arianos*, 48.2; and Athanasius, *Epistula ad easdem*. Fedalto, 1:467. Talbert, map 55.

Koroneia? (in Hellenopolis, though Harnack, 783, suggests Bithynia.) *SEC*, 28 April, makes Onesiphorus the second bishop of Koroneia, though the traditions regarding Onesiphorus are tangled and of doubtful value in associating him with any locale; see *BS*, 9:1177–80. Talbert, map 55.

Kyparissia? (in the Peloponessus; in Laconia.) Bishop Alexander was at the Council of Serdica in 343: see Hilary, *Epistula*, B.II.4.57; Athanasius, *Apologia contra Arianos*, 48.2; and Athanasius, *Epistula ad easdem* (where the place name is read as "Gyparensis"). For later basilicas, see Pallas, *Monuments*, 196–200. Talbert, map 58.

Lychnidos? (in central Macedonia; on the Eastern edge of the Diocletianic province of Epirus Nova; modern Ohrid.) Bishop Zosimus of "Lignido" was at the Council of Serdica in 343; see Hilary, *Epistula*, B.II.4.23, where he places the site in Macedonia. See also Athanasius, *Apologia contra Arianos*, 48.2; and Athanasius, *Epistula ad easdem*. On the possible association of Saint Erasmus of Illyricum (and/or Formiae) with the place, see Veselý, 680–91. Talbert, map 49.

Makareia? (in Achaia; on the Peloponessus. Turner, 1.2.3: 553, however, suggests "Margo" near Viminacium in Moesia Superior.) Bishop Tryphon was at the Council of Serdica in 343: see Hilary, *Epistula*, B.II.4.30 (where the editor suggests the place name "Macaria" in Arcadia); Athanasius, *Apologia contra Arianos*, 48.2; and Athanasius, *Epistula ad easdem* (where the place name is read "Magara").

Le Quien, 2:203–204, reads the name of the place as "Marathon" and wrongly makes a certain Phelgon of Marathon (who is said to be one of the seventy disciples of the New Testament; see *SEC*, 30 June) the first bishop. *EnECh*, 7, seems to follow this error. Honigmann, "L'Évêché," 289–90, states that the Phlegon mentioned in *SEC* should be placed at Marathon near Edessa in Mesopotamia. See Talbert, map 56 for one possible location.

Megara? (in Achaia; in the later eparchy of Hellados.) Bishop Alypus was at the Council of Serdica in 343: see Hilary, *Epistula*, B.II.4.34; also Athanasius, *Apologia contra Arianos*, 48.2; and *Epistula ad Mareoticas ecclesias*. Le Quien, 2:205–206. Fedalto, 1:508. Talbert, map 58.

Messene? (in Achaia.) Bishop Alexander of "Moremis" was at the Council of Serdica in 343; see Hilary, *Epistula*, B.II.4.60. Le Quien, 2:195–97. Turner, 1.2.3: 558–59. Fedalto, 1:509, conjectures Messene as the name of the site. Talbert, map 58.

Methone/Modon? (in Achaia.) Bishop [Eu]tychius of "Mothona" was at the Council of Serdica in 343; see Athanasius, *Epistula ad easdem*; also Hilary, *Epistula*, B.II.4.58 (following the text of Turner 1.2.3: 558–59). Le Quien, 2:230. Turner, 1.2.3: 558–59, on the basis of Heirocles, conjectures Mantinae as the place name. Fedalto, 1:510, seems correct in identifying the site as Methone. For Christian catacombs on the West coast of the Peloponessus dating from at least as early as the middle of the Fourth Century, see Pallas, "Investigations," 7–8. Talbert, map 58.

Metropolis? (in Thessaly.) One Latin manuscript lists Bishop Marcus of "Metropolitanus" as present at the Council of Nicaea; see Gelzer, 50. Fedalto, 1:467. Talbert, map 55.

Mytilene? (on the island of Lesbos.) Bishop Evagrius of Mytilene was active at the time of the Council of Seleucia *ca.*359; see Socrates, 2.40.43. Talbert, map 56.

Naupactus? (in Achaia; just North of the Gulf of Corinth.) Bishop Martyrius was at the Council of Serdica in 343: see Hilary, *Epistula*, B.II.4.47; and Athanasius, *Epistula ad easdem*. Talbert, map 55.

Opous? (in Achaia; in the later eparchy of Hellados.) Bishop Eucarpus was at the Council of Serdica in 343; see Athanasius, *Apologia contra Arianos*, 48.2, and Athanasius, *Epistula ad easdem*. Talbert, map 55.

Particopolis? (in Macedonia.) Bishop Ionas was at the Council of Serdica in 343; see Hilary, *Epistula*, B.II.4.33; also Athanasius, *Apologia contra Arianos*, 48.2; and *Epistula ad Mareoticas ecclesias*. *Atlas*, 20. Fedalto, 1:448.

Patra(e)? (in Achaia; in the Peloponessus, just South of the Gulf of Corinth.) Bishop Plutarchus was at the Council of Serdica in 343: see Hilary, *Epsitula*, B.II.4.38; Athanasius, *Apologia contra Arianos*, 48.2;

and *Epistula ad Mareoticas ecclesias.* The later work *Artemii Passio,* 16, records the tradition of the Apostle Andrew's activity there; compare Philostorgius 3.2. Delehaye, *Les Origines,* 227. *EnECh,* 7. Talbert, map 58.

Pele? (perhaps in Thessaly.) One Greek manuscript and the Arabic manuscript of participants at the Council of Nicaea list a Bishop Ballachus of Pele; see Gelzer lxx, 72, & 166–67. Harnack, 792.

Pella? (in Macedonia; modern Arkhaia Pella on the *via Egnatia.*) Bishop Antigonus of Pella was at the Council of Serdica in 343: see Athanasius, *Apologia contra Arianos,* 48.2; and Athanasius, *Epistula ad easdem.* Talbert, maps 49 & 50, identifies Pella with Diocletianopolis.

Skyros? (island governed as part of Achaia.) Bishop Irenaeus of "Secoro" was at the Council of Serdica in 343; see Hilary, *Epistula,* B.II.4.46; also Athanasius, *Apologia contra Arianos,* 48.2; and Athanasius, *Epistula ad easdem. Atlas,* 20. Talbert, map 55.

Tenedos? (one of the islands, governed as part of Asia.) Bishop Diodoros was at the Council of Serdica in 342/43; see Athanasius, *Apologia contra Arianos,* 48.2; Hilary, *Epistula,* B.II.4.25; and Athanasius, *Epistula ad easdem.*

Thebes Heptapilos? (in Achaia.) *SEC,* 8 April, claims that Rufus (apparently the one mentioned in Polycarp, *Letter to the Phillipians,* 9.1) was the first Bishop of Phillipi; see also *BS,* 11:489–91. Bishop Juli[an]us was at the Council of Serdica in 343; see Hilary, *Epistula,* B.II.4.22; Athanasius, *Apologia contra Arianos,* 48.2; and Athanasius, *Epistula ad easdem.* Fedalto, 1:523.

Tiberiopolis/Tiberia? (in Macedonia; modern Strumica.) Martyrs are known from the reign of Julian the Apostate; see Theophylact, cols. 152–221 (*BHG,* #1129). Talbert, map 50.

Trikka? (in Thessaly.) Socrates, 5.22.51, mentions that Bishop Heliodorus, of unknown date but taken to be ancient, was the person who introduced the custom of married bishops to Greece. *Atlas,* 5. Talbert, map 55.

PROVINCE DALMATIA

Bibliography
AB
AASS
Atlas
BHL
Brenk
Chevalier
CIL
Delehaye, "Saints d'Istrie et de Dalmatie"
Delehaye, "L'hagiographie"
Duval & Marin
Duval, Marin, & Metzger
Dyggve
EnECh
Gerke
Harnack
Hilary, *Decretum*
Jelić
Jerome, *De viris inlustribus*
Martyrologium Hieronymianum
Martyrologium Syriacum
Talbert
White
Wilkes, *Dalmatia*
Wilkes, *Illyrians*
Wilpert, *I Sarcofagi*
Zeiller, *Dalmatie*

General

Dalmatia. The name for the Roman Province. It is reported in II Timothy 4:10 that Titus had been at work in Dalmatia. *EnECh*, 217–18.

Illyricum. Paul in Romans 15:19, reported that he preached the Gospel as far as Illyricum, by which he most probably means some town on the seacoast. In the First Century the name Illyricum would refer to the region as the geographical entity out of which Augustus had formed the Roman Provinces of Dalmatia and Pannonia. The martyr Erasmus (commemorated at Formiae, *q.v.*, in the Dioecesis of Rome) is sometimes associated with Illyricum, see *Martyrologium Romanum*, 2 June. Wilkes, *Illyrians*, 209–11.

Specific sites

Salona. (modern Solin, just North of Split.) The martyr Anastasius is well attested in the time of Diocletian; see *Martyrologium Hieronymianum*, 7 & 8 kal. Sept. For his *Passio*, see Jelić, 33–36 (=*BHL*, #414). Jelić, 38, records an inscription apparently related to Anastasius. Zeiller, *Dalmatie*, 58, argues strongly for only one martyr of that name in Salona. For other martyrs, see Jelić, 37–41, and Duval, Marin, & Metzger, 124–28.

Bishop Domnio, was executed on 10 April 304, and others were martyred also; see *Martyrologium Hieronymianum*, 3 id. Apr. The deacon Severus and others are listed at *Martyrologium Hieronymianum*, 14 kal. Maii. A shrine grew up around Domnio's grave in the Manasterine cemetery just North of the city wall; see Duval and Marin, 634–38. Dyggve, 23–24, dates the earliest stage of the structure there to the early Fourth Century. An early inscription found at Domnio's martyrium reads *"Domn[io] [. . . di]e III id [Apr . . .]" CIL*, 3:9575, 12870b, and note 9575 on p. 2328.126. See Duval, Marin, & Metzger, 124. See also *Martyrologium Syriacum*, 11 April. *AASS*, Aprilis II, 7–8 (*BHL*, #2268).

A certain Venantius who is depicted on a Seventh-Century mosaic in the Lateran at Rome, and who died perhaps in 312, is claimed as the next bishop by Delehaye and others, see Delehaye, "Saints d'Istrie et de Dalmatie," 393 & 397, and Delehaye, "L'hagiographie," 7; also Harnack, 796. Compare *AASS*, Maii, 4:138–42 (*BHL*, #8523), from which it would appear that the traditions in fact relate to Venantius of Camerinum. Zeiller, 77–82, admits that little is known about Venantius at all, but then attempts to date him to the Third Century. Dyggve, 22, omits Venantius entirely. For more information, see Dyggve, 73, & 79, n. 10.

The next known bishop was Domnio's nephew Primus who flourished *ca.*325; see Dyggve, 22. The inscription at his tomb reads *"depositus episcopus Primus, XI kal. Feb., nepos Domniones martores;"* see *CIL*, 3:14897. See also Zeiller, *Dalmatie*, 99.

The bishop of Salona was one of the recipients of the letter of the Synod of Phillipopolis in 343 against the Synod of Serdica; see

Hilary, *Decretum*, A.IV.1. Zeiller, 100, suggests that the Bishop was named Maximus. Dyggve, 22.

On the church and sarcophagus at Salona, see also White, 434–35. For the sarcophagus, see Wilpert, *I Sarcofagi*, plate 132.1–3; Gerke, 299 & 338; and Deichmann, *Repertorium*, 2: #298. Compare Duval & Marin, 238. Wilkes, *Dalmatia*, 427–30. Dyggve, 80–82, suggests Syrian influence on some of the architecture. Compare, Brenk, 88. *EnECh*, 753. *Atlas*, 5. Talbert, map 20.

Possible sites

Spalatum? (modern Split.) Deichmann, *Repertorium*, 2: #297, is a sarcophagus from the early part of the Fourth Century. See also Duval & Marin, 338–39. Talbert, map 20.

St. Maximus? (modern Majsan.) A memoria of the Fourth Century dedicated to Bishop Maximus of Salona who died in 346 has been found in a villa of the Second-Fourth Centuries. Chevalier, 312–15.

Stridon? (exact location uncertain; North of Salviae and on the border with Pannonia.) Jerome, whose father bore the Christian name Eusebius, was born there; see Jerome, *De viris inlustribus*, 135. If Jerome was born *ca.*340, the town may have had a Christian presence prior to 325, so Harnack, 796. Wilkes, *Dalmatia*, 271, 417 & 419. Talbert, map 20.

MOESIA SUPERIOR

Bibliography
Athanasius, *Apologia contra Arianos*
Athanasius, *Epistula ad easdem*
Atlas
Barnea, "L'épigraphie"
Barnea, *Les Monuments*
Barnea, *Christian Art*
Barton
Beshevliev
Deichmann, *Repertorium*
Delehaye, "Saints de Thrace"
EnECh
Epistula ad Mareoticas ecclesias

Eusebius, *Vita Constantini*
Harnack
Hilary, *Decretum*
Hilary, *Epistula*
Gelzer
Lactantius, *De mortibus persecutorum*
Martyrologium Hieronymianum
Martyrologium Syriacum
Mirkovic & Dusanic
Mócsy, *Pannonia*
Nagy
Nikolajević
Philostorgius
Socrates
Sozomen
Talbert
Velkov
Zeiller, *Provinces Danubiennes*

General

Moesia. For the work of Ulfilas in the general area in the mid-Fourth Century, see Philostorgius, 2.5, and Socrates, 2.41.23 & 4.33.6–7. On Christians in Moesia and Pannonia, see Eusebius, *Vita Constantini*, 4.43.3. Athanasius, *Apologia contra Arianos*, 37.1, mentions bishops from Dardania, both Dacias, and Moesia at the Council of Serdica in 343.

Specific sites

Bononia. (in Dacia Ripense; modern Vidin.) For the martyrs Hermes of Ratiaria, Aggaeus, and Caius of Bononia; see *Martyrologium Hieronymianum*, prid. kal. Jan.; kal. Jan.; and 4 January. *Martyrologium Syriacum*, 30 former Kanun (December). In view of the connection with Ratairia, Zeiller, *Provinces Danubiennes*, 16, 108, and 125, suggests modern Vidin, though Bononia in Cisalpine Gaul might also be meant. Harnack 794. *Atlas*, 5. Talbert, map 21.

Ratiaria. (in Dacia Ripense; modern Archer.) For the martyrs Hermes of Ratiaria, Aggaeus, and Caius of Bononia; see *Martyrologium Hieronymianum*, prid. kal. Jan; kal. Jan.; and 4 January. Talbert, map 21.

Scupi. (in Dardania, in the Diocletianic dioecesis of Moesia Superior; modern Skopje.) Bishop Dacus of "Macedonia in Dardania" was at the Council of Nicaea; see Gelzer, 52–55, 70, 74, etc. But Dardania at that time was counted as part of Moesia; see Mócsy, *Pannonia*, 274–75. Zeiller, *Provinces Danubiennes*, 149 & 160–61, on the basis of some Nicene manuscripts, conjectures that there has been confusion and that the reference is in fact to the town of Scupi. Harnack, 792, seems to follow the same line of reasoning. Bishop Paregorias of Scupi in Dardania was at the Council of Serdica in 343; see Hilary, *Epistula*, B.II.4.29; Athanasius, *Apologia contra Arianos*, 48.2; and *Epistula ad Mareoticas ecclesias*. Talbert, map 49.

Serdica. (originally in Thracia; after the Diocletianic reorganization it was in Dacia Mediterranea; modern Sofia.) Bishop Protogenes was at the Council of Nicaea; see Gelzer, lxiv. Protogenes was still bishop in 343 when the city hosted the Council of Serdica; see Athanasius, *Apologia contra Arianos*, 48.1, and Hilary, *Epistula*, B.II.4.16. *Atlas*, 5. Talbert, map 21.

Singidunum. (in the Northwestern part of Moesia Superior; modern Belgrade.) The martyr Montanus of Singidunum was killed at Sirmium, see *Martyrologium Hieronymianum*, 7 kal. Apr. Mócsy, *Pannonia*, 327 & map following pl. 45. Zeiller, *Provinces Danubiennes*, 105–106. Nagy, 33 & 217. Deichmann, *Repertorium*, 2: #419 is a sarcophagus from *ca.*300. *EnECh*, 565. Barton, 123–24. *Atlas*, 5. Talbert, map 21.

Possible sites

Glava? (in Dacia Ripense; ancient name unknown.) There is an early Fourth-Century Latin inscription suggestive of Christianity; see Barnea, "L'épigraphie," 650, and Beshevliev, #46. Talbert, map 22.

Mezul? (13 km Southwest of Smederovo [ancient Vinceia] between Dobri Dol and Vlaska Dol. In Moesia Superior; ancient name unknown.) Barnea, "L'épigraphie," 247, notes an inscribed Third-Century lamp with a possible Jonah and the whale motif, found in context with coins dating to 247–250. For the original reference, see Mirkovic & Dusanic, 1: #83. Compare Talbert, map 21.

Naissus? (in Dacia Mediterranea; modern Nis.) Sozomen, 3.11.8, notes that Cyriacus preceded Gaudentius as bishop. The opponents of Athanasius who revolted from the Council of Serdica in 343 singled out Cyriacus as having been an ally of Marcellus of Ancyra; see Hilary, *Decretum*, A.IV.1.3.

Bishop Gaudentius of Niassus was at the Council of Serdica; see Hilary, *Epistula*, B.II.4.32; Athanasius, *Apologia contra Arianos*, 48.2; and Athanasius, *Epistula ad easdem*. Talbert, map 21.

Pautalia? (modern Kjustendil. Originally in Thracia; after the Diocletianic reforms it was in Dacia Mediterranea; see *Atlas*, 20, also Velkov, 96.) Beshevliev, #35 & #36, are Christian inscriptions datable to some time in the Fourth Century. See also, *EnECh*, 837. Talbert, map 49.

Romuliana? (modern Gamzigrad. Nikolajević, 2448–51, identifies the place named for Galerius's mother.) Lactantius, *De mortibus persecutorum*, 9 & 11, mentions martyrs at Galerius's palaces during persecutions instigated by his mother. Talbert, map 21.

DACIA TRAIANA

Bibliography
Ardevan
Barnea, *Les Monuments*
Barnea, *Christian*
Harnack
Gelzer
Popescu, *Christianitas*
Popescu, *Inscripţiile*
Radulescu & Lungu
Sanie
SEG
Velkov

General
Dacia Traiana. The Roman legions withdrew from most of Dacia Traiana early in the last quarter of the Third Century, during the reign of Emperor Aurelian, and there is much scholarly debate about the extent of continuing Roman influence after that time. Barnea, *Christian*, 10, notes that no martyrs are recorded for the former province of Dacia Traiana. There does seem to be a continuity of

Christian material culture from the middle of the Fourth Century
onward; for a recent survey of the archaeological evidence, see
Radulescu & Lungu, 3:2561–2615. Yet there is no literary evidence
and at best slim material evidence for Christianity before 325 C.E.
Hence I have listed all the sites below as only possibly showing evidence of a Christian community.

Possible sites

Barboşi? (in modern Galaţi county.) There is a Third- or Fourth-
Century amphora inscribed with the Greek letters "ΒΠ" in red paint
with an accompanying chi-rho monogram. The amphora and the
tombs in the area are ascribed to the Third or perhaps the Fourth
Century. There is some question about whether the chi-rho monogram is of a Christian nature here or is an abbeviation for "χιλίαρχος";
see Barnea, *Christian*, plate 5, pp. 11 & 46–47. See also *SEG* 39
(1989): #688 & 689; and Sanie, 1309–11.

   There is also a Third Century mother of pearl pendentive in the
shape of a rectangle with the sign of the cross in open work at its
center. On the basis of coins found in the same excavation, the ornament can be dated to the reign of Alexander Severus (222–235 A.D.).
As with many such objects there is some question about whether
the object is a Christian symbol or is merely ornamental. Another
Third-Century mother of pearl ornament, though cross-shaped, is
too elaborate to be identified as a Christian symbol. See Barnea,
Christian, plate 6, pp. 11 & 48–49; also Sanie, 1307–309. Talbert,
map 22.

Biertan? Barnea, *Christian*, plate 45, pp. 126–27, records the inscription "*ego Zenovis votum posui*," followed by a chi-rho monogram. See
also Popescu, *Inscripţiile*, #434, where the inscription is dated to the
Fourth or Sixth Century. Popescu, *Christianitas*, 85 & 290.

Dierna? (modern Orşova.) A small gold plate has been found in a
grave of the Third or Fourth Century and bearing the inscription
"ιαω αθωναι"; see Barnea, *Christian*, 12. Popescu, *Christianitas*, 80 &
206. Talbert, map 21.

Gherla? (North of Potaissa and East of Porolissium.) Ardevan, 36,
records a foot of a vase inscribed with a fish motif from the late
Second or early Third Centuries, and also a ceramic plaque with a
partial fish motif from just after 250.

Gornea? Popescu, *Inscripţiile*, #425, is a possibly Christian inscription from *ca*.294–300. Talbert, map 21.

Micia? (modern Veţel, county of Hunedoara.) A Fourth-Century fibula reformed into a ring in *"epais"* inscription reads *"quartine, vivas"*, translated as "Quartinus, live!" Popescu, *Inscripţiile*, #438. Barnea, *Les Monuments*, #84, pp. 114–15. Talbert, map 21.

Orlea? (in modern Olt county.) An "abrasax" gem has been found, perhaps Basilidean gnostic in character; see Barnea, *Christian*, plate 8, pp. 11 & 52–53. Popescu, *Christianitas*, 80 & 205.

Porolissum? (modern Moigrad in Salaj county.) Barnea, *Christian*, 11, notes two gnostic gems otherwise undescribed. For this and later evidence, see Popescu, *Christianitas*, 85 & 210. Talbert, map 21.

Potaissa? (modern Turda in Transylvania.) An onyx gem bearing the inscription "Ἰ(ησοῦς) Χ(ριστὸς) Θ(εοῦ) Υ(ἰὸς) Σ(ωτήρ)," with representations of the Good Shepherd, of Jonah and of the Gospel Tree, dates to the late Third or early Fourth Century. After being recorded, it was lost, presumably during the 1848 revolution. See Popescu, *Inscripţiile*, #435; Barnea, *Les Monuments*, #82, pp. 112–13; and Barnea, *Christian*, plate 6, pp. 11 & 48–49. Popescu, *Christianitas*, 80. Talbert, map 21.

Romula-Malva? (modern Reşca, in Olt county.) A reddish brown cornaline gem with a depiction of two fish hanging head upward on either side of a Tau cross dates to the late Third Century and was recorded as being in private hands; see Barnea, *Les Monuments*, fig. 99.2, p.246; and Barnea, *Christian*, plate 7, pp. 11 & 50–51. Popescu, *Christianitas*, 80 & 205.

Barnea, *Christian*, 11 & 52–53, & plate 8, also records a gem decorated with two peacocks raising their bills to a cross, and two "abraxas" gems. Talbert, map 22.

Transylvania? (exact find site uncertain.) A gem from the Third or Fourth Centuries bears a representation of the Good Shepherd. It is now in the Hungarian National Museum in Budapest; see Barnea, *Les Monuments*, fig. 99.1, pp. 246 & 262; and Barnea, *Christian*, plate 7, pp. 11 & 50–51. Talbert, map 21.

Pannonia

Bibliography
AASS
Acta Concili Aquiliensis
AÉ
Athanasius, *Apologia contra Arianos*
Atlas
Barton
BHL
BS
CIL
EnECh
Fritz
Gelzer
Harnack
ILS
Jerome, *Chronicle*
Jerome, *De viris inlustribus*
Hilary, *Decretum*
Liber Pontificalis
Martyrologium Hieronymianum
Martyrologium Syriacum
Migotti
Mócsy, "Pannonia"
Mócsy, *Pannonia*
Musurillo
Nagy
Paulovics
Póczy
Prudentius
Ruinart
Scheiber
SEG
Simonyi
Socrates
Sulpicius Severus, *Chronicon*
Sulpicius Severus, *Vita Sancti Martini*
Talbert

Thomas, "Frühe Christentum"
Thomas, "Martyres"
Thomas, "Religion"
Thomas, "Villa Settlements"
Ubl
Ulman
Victorinus of Pettau, *Commentarii*
Wilkes, *Illyrians*
Zeiller, *Provinces Danubiennes*

General

Pannonia. (The region of Illyricum was divided into the provinces of Pannonia and Dalmatia under Augustus; see Wilkes, *Illyrians*, 209–210. The present section covers the Northern part of the Diocletianic dioecesis of Pannonia, *i.e.*, Pannonia as it was laid out by Augustus.) Many of the earliest Christians in the region had Greek names; see Mócsy, *Pannonia*, 259. On the persecutions in the region, see Nagy, 53–73. Bishop Domnus from Pannonia was at the Council of Nicaea; see Gelzer, lxiv. Athanasius, *Apologia contra Arianos*, 37.1, mentions bishops from Pannonia at the Council of Serdica in 343. Fritz, 168–69, lists a number of sites with basilical remains from the Fourth Century. Barton, 120–24. For further background, see *EnECh*, 638–39.

Specific sites

Cibalae. (modern Vinkovci.) The *passio* of Pollio (*AASS* Aprilis iii, 572–73; *BHL*, #6869), relating to events under Diocletian, mentions the martyrdom of a certain Eusebius, probably under Valerian. See also, *Martyrologium Hieronymianum*, 4 kal. Maii and 4 kal. Jun., where Eusebius is identified as a bishop. Nagy, 31 & 217.

Migotti, 42–43, records an early sarcophagus in possibly Christian secondary use in the early Fourth Century. For a small and possibly Christian pottery find, see Migotti, 88, and for general information about the site, see Migotti, 21–22. Harnack, 794. Mócsy, "Pannonia," cols. 750–51. Mócsy, *Pannonia*, 325–27. Ulman, 759–60. Zeiller, 73–75. *Atlas*, 5. Talbert, map 20.

Mursa. (modern Osijek.) A Third-Century ring with the name "*Eusebi*" has been found, and also a Fourth-Century gemstone carved with a good-shepherd motif; see Migotti, 70 & 72–73.

Sulpicius Severus, *Chronicon*, 2.38.5, records that in 351, Emperor Magnentius and Bishop Valens took refuge in the *"basilica martyrorum,"* just outside of town. The account thus indicates the likely presence of martyrs at Mursa.

Socrates, 1.27.1, makes mention of Bishop Valens, an Arian, as being active prior to the Council of Tyre in 335. Valens was also one of the Eastern bishops meeting at Philippolis in opposition to the Council of Serdica in 343; see Hilary, *Decretum*, A.IV.3.(73). Harnack, 794, suggests that this episcopal see was established by 325 C.E. See also Nagy, 217, and Fritz, 169. Zeiller, *Provinces Danubiennes*, 138 & 142. *Atlas*, 5. Migotti, 19–21. Talbert, map 20.

Poetovio. (modern Pettau/Pluj.) Victorinus of Pettau, bishop and author, was martyred *ca*.303–04; see Jerome, *De viris inlustribus*, 74. See also *AASS*, Nov. 1:432–37. Victorinus of Pettau, *Commentarii*, 3.1, may reflect the difficulties of the persecutions, and 4.4 shows that he cited the gospel in the order of the "Western" text (*i.e.*, John, Matthew, Luke, Mark); see Nagy, 33 & 42. Zeiller, 63–65, 73, 205–214. *Atlas*, 4. Talbert, map 20.

Savaria. (modern Szombathely.) Christians there witnessed the martyrdom of Quirinius of Siscia on 4 June during the Diocletianic persecutions; see *AASS*, Jun. 1:373–75 (*BHL*, #7035–7038). *Martyrologium Hieronymianum*, prid. non. Jun. Martin of Tours was born at Savaria; see Sulpicius Severus, *Vita Sancti Martini*, 2.1, and Harnack, 794. Nagy, 33. Mócsy, *Pannonia*, 326. Zeiller, 68–73. Thomas, "Frühe Christentum," 266. Póczy, 266, notes a Christian cemetery dating to some time in the Fourth Century. *Atlas*, 4. Talbert, map 20.

Scarbantia. (modern Sopron.) Christian women from the town are mentioned in connection with the martyrdom of Quirinius of Siscia; see *AASS*, Jun. 1:373–75 (*BHL*, #7035–38). Harnack, 794. Nagy, 33. Zeiller, 68–73. *Atlas*, 4. Talbert, map 20.

Sirmium. (modern Mitrovica.) Irenaeus of Sirmium, described as a young man who had been a Christian from his youth, was martyred on 6 April 303/304. *Martyrologium Syriacum*, 6 April. For his *Passio*, see Musurillo, 294–301, also *AASS*, Mar. 3, 554–55. Nagy, 33.

Two inscriptions, *CIL*, 3:10232 & 10233, speak of burials near the shrine of the martyr Synerotas. Numerous others were martyred at about the same time; see Barton, 122–23.

The so-called *Quattuor Corones*, a group of stonecutters at *"Mons Pinguis,"* are often claimed to have been martyred at Alma Mons (modern Frushka Gora) just North of Sirmium *ca.*293 or *ca.*306; see *AASS*, Novembris 3, 765–79 (*BHL*, #1836). Yet the earliest document explicitly to name a place for these martyrs has them commemorated at Monte Caelio in Rome; see *Martyrologium Hieronymianum*, 6 id. Nov; also *Liber Pontificalis*, 72, "Honorius I." See Zeiller, *Provinces Danubiennes*, 88–104, and Nagy, 61–65, for discussions of the problems. Mócsy, *Pannonia*, 326 & map following p. 454. *BS*, 10:1276–86.

There are archaeological remains of an early Christian cemetery at Sirmium; see Mócsy, "Pannonia," cols. 751–52. Mocsy, *Pannonia*, 326–27. Fritz, 170. Zeiller, 79–88, considers Sirmium in general. *Atlas*, 5. Talbert, map 21.

Siscia /Segestica. (modern Sisak/Sissek.) Bishop Quirinius of Siscia was martyred at Sabaria on 4 June; see *AASS* Jun. 1:373–75 (*BHL*, #7035–38). See also Ruinart, 521–25. Jerome, *Chronicle*, dates the martyrdom of Quirinius to 308. See Zeiller, 68–73, for discussion of problems associated with the year 308. Athanasius, *Apologia contra Arianos*, notes the presence of representatives from Siscia at the Council of Serdica in 343. Note also Nagy, 33, 65–68, & 217.

Migotti, 39–41 & 80, records a sarcophagus from the first half of the Fourth Century and a possibly Christian lamp from the early Fourth Century. Migotti, 22–23, provides general information about the site. Harnack, 794. See also Paulovics, 51. Mócsy, "Pannonia," col. 752. *Atlas*, 4. Talbert, map 20.

Possible sites

Alisca? (modern Ocsény.) *SEG* 29 (1979), #1059, records an early Fourth-Century inscription "λεῖβι[ε τῷ π]οιμένι πῖε ζή[σα]ις" on a vase from a Christian sarcophagus. Talbert, map 20.

Aquae Balissae? (modern Daruvar.) *AÉ* 1996, #1222, records an inscription found nearby in connection with a late Third- or early Fourth-Century sarcophagus. The inscription contains apparently Christian vocabulary such as *"obitus," "humanus," "induere,"* and *"aeternum,"* but may be later than the sarcophagus itself. For further information, see Migotti, 43–44 & 47–49. Talbert, map 20.

Aquae Iasae? (modern Varazdinske Toplice; in Upper Pannonia.) *ILS*, #704 (=*CIL*, 3.1: #4121) has been suggested as a possibly

Christian inscription from 316–24, though Harnack, 794, doubts its significance. For general information about the site, see Migotti, 25–27. Talbert, map 20.

Aquincum? (modern Budapest.) There is a Christian cemetery dating back to the Fourth Century. Mócsy, *Pannonia*, 333–34. Fritz, 169. Póczy, 258. Talbert, map 20.

Brigetio? (modern Szony.) There is a fragment of brick inscribed before firing with the words *"hoc die felice[s fratres] sunt persecut[i morie]ntes quorum [anima] non est vict[a et in deo] longius i[ubilabit],"* and then stamped with the mark of Legio I Adiutrix. Thomas argues that the inscription relates to the persecution of 304 C.E. and can be translated as "on this day happy brothers have been persecuted; they will die but their souls will not be overcome and will for long rejoice in God." Thomas suggests that *[s fratres]* may also be restored as *[t . . .]*, so that the translation could then begin "on this day Felice and . . . are being harassed . . ." Thomas, "Martyres," 615–620. Thomas, "Religion," 194–96. Evidently, someone was being persecuted, but is that someone clearly Christian? Note that *"anima," "et in deo,"* and *"iubilabit"* are all restorations. Thomas's interpretation depends heavily on the word *"persecut[i]"* and on the phrase *"non est vict[a]."* Nagy, 78–80. Talbert, map 20.

Carnuntum? (near modern Petronell.) Late Fourth-Century remains of Christian buildings; see Ubl, 302–303. Zeiller, *Provinces Danubiennes*, 141. Talbert, map 13.

Cirtisa? (modern Strbinci.) Migotti, 37–38, records a pair of cross-shaped grave vaults from 320 or later. Their identification as Christian is based on their highly unusual shape. Talbert, map 20.

Donnerskirchen? (between Carnuntum and Scarbantia.) Archaeological remains indicating a church from the first half of the Fourth Century. Fritz, 169. Ubl, 303. Harnack, 794. Compare Talbert, maps 13 & 20.

Intercisa? (modern Dunaújváros.) Small Fourth-Century finds and a small shrine in the cemetery. For Mithraic and Christian finds, see Fritz, 168–69. Thomas, "Frühe Christentum," 266. Scheiber, #3, is a Jewish synagogue inscription from the early Third Century. Zeiller, *Provinces Danubiennes*, 193. Mócsy, "Pannonia," 752. Talbert, map 20.

Iovia? (probably modern Ludbreg; see Talbert, map 20.) Formerly called "Botivo Civitas." Bishop Amantius of "Lotevensium," "Ioviensum," or "Niciensis," was at the Council of Aquileia in 381; see *Acta Concili Aquiliensis*, 64. The name of the bishop's see is unclear in the manuscripts. In any case, the information is far later that the period with which we are concerned. Zeiller, *Provinces Danubiennes*, 138 & 140. Harnack, 795, seems to rule out the possibility of confusion between Iovia and Iuvavum, which would be modern Salzberg. Nagy, 217. Mócsy, *Pannonia*, 329. Migotti, 23–25, gives general information about the site.

Kekkut? Remains of a Fourth-Century basilica. Mócsy, *Pannonia*, 316. Thomas, "Frühe Christentum," 267–68.

Lugio? (modern Dunaszekcso.) Small finds from the Fourth Century; see Fritz, 169. Talbert, map 20.

Sopianae? (modern Pécs.) Simonyi, 174–84, argues that the martyrdom of the so-called *Quattuor Corones*, a group of stonecutters at "Mons Pinguis," took place near Sopiane under Diocletian, and that the name *Quinquae Ecclesiae* recorded for the city of Pécs commemorates them and another martyr. Compare *AASS*, Novembris 3: 765–69 (*BHL*, #1836), and Zeiller, 88–104, & 142. Mócsy, *Pannonia*, map following p. 454. Other scholars locate these martyrs near Sirmium, *q.v.*

See Mócsy, "Pannonia," col. 752. Mócsy, *Pannonia*, 313, 334–35, and plate 40, records a Fourth-Century cemetery and grave chapel there. See also Thomas, "Frühe Christentum," 266. Nagy, 217. Fritz, 172–73. Póczy, 269. Talbert, map 20.

Tricciana? (modern Ságvár.) Mócsy, *Pannonia*, 334. Fritz, 169, mentions a Christian cemetery post-dating the peace of the church. Talbert, map 20.

Ulcisia Castra? (modern Szentendre.) Thomas, "Frühe Christentum," 265–66. There is a Fourth-Century inscription reading *"R[equiescat in Pace. Fl]avios Surus qui officium dedicatum habet vivat per multa secula semper."* Talbert, map 20.

Vindobona? (modern Vienna.) Late Fourth-Century architectural remains. Fritz, 169. Ubl, 302. Talbert, map 13.

DIOECESIS OF THE CITY OF ROME

Bibliography
AASS
AB
Achelis, *Acta*
Acta Pauli
Acta Petri et Pauli
AÉ
Agnello, G.
Agnello, S. L.
Agnellus
Allard
Arnobius
Athanasius, *Apologia contra Arianos*
Pseudo-Athanasius
Atlas
Augustine, *Breviculus*
Augustine, *Sermones*
Augustine, *De unico baptismo contra Petilianum*
Bellucci
BHG
BHL
Cantino Wataghin & Pani Ermini
Cappelletti
Catal. Brux.
Catal. Lat. Rom.
Catalogus Episcoporum Neapolitanorum
Chierici
CIL
I Clement
Clement of Alexandria, *Stromata*
Collectio Avellana
Concilia Galliae
CPG
CPL
Cyprian, *Epistulae*
DACL
Deichmann, *Repertorium*
DHGE

Dufourcq
EEC
EnECh
Epistula ad Mareoticas ecclesias
Eusebius, *Chronicle*
Eusebius, *Ecclesiastical History*
Fasola
Fasola & Testini
Finney
Fiocchi Nicolai, *I Cimiteri*
Fiocchi Nicolai, "Notiziario"
Gaudemet
Gelzer
Gerke
Gesta Episcoporum Neapolitanorum
Gregory the Great, *Dialogues*
Harnack, *Analecta*
Harnack
Hilary, *Epistula*
Hippolytus, *Refutatio*
IG
ILS
Jerome, *Chronicle*
Jerome, *De viris inlustribus*
Koch
Kümmel
Lampe
Lanzoni
Liber Pontificalis
Liberian Catalogue
Martyrologium Hieronymianum
Martyrologium Hieronymianum Cambrense
Mazzoleni
Minucius Felix, *Octavius*
Muratorian Canon
Musurillo
ODCC
Optatus
Papaconstantinou
Passio Sancti Ambrosii Centurionis

Paulinus of Nola, *Carmina*
Paulinus of Nola, *Epistulae*
Pauly-Wissowa
Potter
Praedestinatus
Raspi Serra
Robinson, *Bauer*
Ruinart
Rutgers
Sacco
Saxer, "Pilgerwesen"
Saxer, "L'utilisation"
Schneemelcher
SEC
SEG
Shepherd of Hermas
Snyder
Squarciapino
Suetonius
Surius
Synaxarium Alexandrinum
Tacitus, *Annals*
Talbert
Tertullian, *De praescriptione haereticorum*
Ughelli
Usuard
Veselý
White
Wilpert, *I Sarcofagi*

General

Dioecesis of the City of Rome. In the Diocletianic era, the dioecesis included not only the Central and Southern Italian mainland, but also the islands of Corsica, Sardinia, Sicily, and Malta. Martyr accounts from this and subsequent eras borrowed motifs from each other and so should be used with caution, especially if unconfirmed by other early sources such as *Martyrologium Hieronymianum*. A glance at the map will show that Christian communities were located mainly in three regions: the area around Rome and along the road north to Fanum, Naples and surrounding communities, and the coastal cities of Sicily and Eastern Italy. Athanasius, *Apologia contra Arianos*, 37.1, records bishops from Campania, Calabria, and Apulia. For martyria, see Cantino Wataghin & Pani Ermini, 123–51.

Sardinia. Hippolytus, *Refutatio*, 9.12.9–13, records that Callistus (later pope) was exiled for a time to Sardinia but was released when other martyrs there were freed through the intercession of Marcia, consort of Emperor Commodus. Hippolytus himself, along with Pope Pontianus, was exiled to Sardinia *ca*.235; see *Liber Pontificalis*, 19, "Pontianus." Eusebius of Vercelli was a native of Sardinia; see Jerome, *De viris inlustribus*, 96. *Martyrologium Hieronymianum*, 6 id. Junii and 13 kal. Sept., lists the martyr Salutianus and others. Athanasius, *Apologia contra Arianos*, 37.1, reports bishops from Sardinia at the Council of Serdica in 343. See also *EnECh*, 757. Talbert, map 48.

Sicily. According to an allusion in Clement of Alexandria, *Stromata*, 1.1.10, Pantaenus of Alexandria may have been a native of Sicily; see Eusebius, *Ecclesiastical History*, 5.10.1. Cyprian, *Epistulae* 30.5.2, was sent by presbyters at Rome to Cyprian with a copy going to Sicily. Talbert, map 47.

Specific sites
Abellinum. (in Campania; modern Atripalda near Avellino.) *AASS*, Maii 1:42–43 (*BHL*, #4054–55), lists the martyr Hyppolistus. *CIL* 10.1:1191 is a Christian inscription dating to 357. Talbert, map 44.

Aecae. (in Apulia; modern Troia.) The martyr Bishop Marcus is listed in *Martyrologium Hieronymianum*, non. Nov. Lanzoni, 271–72. Talbert, map 45.

Aeclanum/Eclanum. (on the *Via Appia* in Apulia; modern Mirabella Eclano.) *Martyrologium Hieronymianum*, 8 & 7 kal., Sept., mentions the martyr Mercurius. A Christian cemetery grew up around his grave; see Lanzoni, 264. Talbert, map 45.

Albanum. (in Latium Vetus; modern Albano.) *Martyrologium Hieronymianum*, 6 kal. Octobris, mentions the martyr Senator. *Liber Pontificalis*, 34, "Sylvester," mentions Constantine's gift of a church there dedicated to John the Baptist during the reign of Sylvester (*i.e.* 314–335). *Atlas*, 4. Talbert, map 43.

Amiternum. (modern S. Vittorino in Paese dei Sabini.) *Martyrologium Hieronymianum*, 9 kal. Aug., lists a group of eighty-three soldiers and

Victorinus who were martyred. *Acta martyrii SS. Nerei et Achillei* mentions that Christian people from Amiternum claimed the body of the martyr Victorinus who was killed at nearby Cotylae; see *AASS*, Maii, 3:11–12 (=*BHL*, #6063), and Achelis, *Acta*, 1–23 (*BHG*, #1327). For a study of the pertinent material, see Lanzoni, 359–61. For mention of catacombs, see Fasola & Testini, 129–30. Talbert, map 42.

Ancona. (in Picenum.) *Martyrologium Hieronymianum*, 3 non. Aug., mentions the martyr Stephanus; see also Augustine, *Sermones*, 322–24 (PL 38:1444–46). Lanzoni, 381–82. Talbert, map 42.

Antium. (modern Anzio.) Hippolytus, *Refutatio*, 9.12.13–14, notes that Pope Victor sent Callistus to live at Antium after his release from Sardinia. Hippolytus also records that Zephyrinus, upon accession to the see at Rome, recalled Callistus to the capital. Wilpert, *I Sarcofagi*, plate 118.4, is a sarcophagus of the Constantinian era; see also Gerke, 244, 256, & 342. Talbert, map 43.

Arretium. (modern Arezzo; in Etruria.) Koch, 264, #65 (=Deichmann, *Repertorium*, 2: #15) is a sarcophagus from the first quarter of the Fourth Century. Talbert, map 42.

Atella. (in Campania; modern S. Arpino near Averna.) *Martyrologium Hieronymianum*, 8 kal. Jun., mentions the local martyr Canionis or Anonis. Lanzoni, 204. *Atlas*, 4. Talbert, map 44.

Aureus Mons. (in Picenum.) *Martyrologium Hieronymianum*, 17 kal. Maii, lists the martyrs Marois, Messoris, Proclinus, and Mosinus. Harnack, 812. Compare Talbert, map 42.

Auximum. (in Picenum; modern Osimo.) *Martyrologium Hieronymianum*, 17 kal. Jun., mentions the martyrs Florentius and Diocletianus, as does *Martyrologium Hieronymianum Cambrense* for the same date. Later tradition makes Florentius and Diocletianus bishops; see Lanzoni, 387–88. Deichmann, *Repertorium*, 2: #185 (=Koch, 279, #257; =Wilpert, *I Sarcofagi*, plate 177.2), is a sarcophagus from *ca*.320. See also Gerke, 339 (=Wilpert, *I Sarcofagi*, plate 89.2). Talbert, map 42.

Baccanae. (in Etruria, modern Baccano.) *AASS*, Septembris 6:227–36 (*BHL*, #273), contains an account of Bishop Alexander who was tried and martyred nearby during the time of "Antoninus" (perhaps Caracalla), and whose relics were taken to Baccano in 321. *DACL*, 2:24–27, mentions architectural remains there which may relate to the early shrine. Harnack, 815. Talbert, map 42.

Beneventum. (in Paese degli Hirpini; modern Benevento.) *Martyrologium Hieronymianum*: 7 id. Sept., 15 kal. Nov., 14 kal. Nov., & possibly id. Jan., lists Bishop Januarius. According to local traditions preserved in *AASS*, Septembris 6:866–71 (esp. *BHL*, #4132), he was martyred near Naples under Diocletian. Usuard, 13 kal. Oct., gives the place as Puteoli. Januarius is mentioned also in a letter of Uranius concerning the death of Paulinus of Nola; see *AASS*, Junius 5:170–72 (*BHL*, #6558).

Some manuscripts of *Martyrologium Hieronymianum*, 17 kal. Jul., mention other martyrs at Beneventum also. Bishop Theophilus was at the Synod of Rome in 313; see Optatus, 1.23. Lanzoni, 256–57. *Atlas*, 4. Talbert, map 44.

The bishop Anastasius of Beneventum who was at the Council of Arles in 314 (see *Concilia Galliae*, 15, 17, 19, 20, 22 & 233, and Gaudemet, 62) apparently relates to the Beneventum in Africa Proconsularis, *q.v.*

Brundisium. (in Calabria; modern Brindisi.) *Martyrologium Hieronymianum*, 6 id. Jan., and 3 id. Jan., mentions the martyr Leucius; compare *BHL*, #4894, #4897, & #4898. Bishop Marcus of Calabria was at the Council of Nicaea; see Gelzer, lxiv. Lanzoni, 306, suggests Marcus may have been Bishop of Brundisium. Talbert, map 45.

Capua. (in Campania.) Numerous martyrs appear in *Martyrologium Hieronymianum*; for a study, see Lanzoni, 189–201. Bishop Proterius was at the Council of Rome in 313; see Optatus, 1.23. Bishop Proterius, along with the deacons Agrippa and Pinus, was at the Council of Arles in 314; see *Concilia Galliae*, 14, 16, 17,18, 19, & 21, and Gaudemet, 58. Koch, 262, #25 (=Deichmann, *Repertorium*, 2: #11) is a pre-Constantinian sarcophagus; see also Wilpert, *I Sarcofagi*, plate 9.2, and Gerke, 351). Chierici, 205, suggests that the original construction of the church there may be early Fourth Century. *Atlas*, 4. Talbert, map 44.

Carales. (in Sardinia; modern Cagliari.) For the martyr Saturninus on October 30, see *AASS*, Octobris 13:306–7 (*BHL*, #7490) and 297–98 & 300 (*BHL*, #7491). Catacombs nearby may date to the late Third Century or to the early Fourth Century; see *EnECh*, 425. *AASS*, Januarius 2:280–87, and *AB* 3 (1884): 362–77 (*BHL*, #2567), mention the martyr Ephysius killed under Diocletian.

Bishop Quintasius and the deacon Admonius were at the Council of Arles in 314; see *Concilia Galliae*, 15, 17, 19, 20, 22; and Gaudemet, 62.

Koch, 274, #204 (=Deichmann, *Repertorium*, 2: #23), is a sarcophagus of Constatinian date, but without clear provenance.

Pseudo-Athanasius, *Epistulae II ad Luciferum*, in the second letter supposedly written to Bishop Lucifer, mentions that Lucifer had predecessors. Although spurious and probably written by Lucifer's supporters, the letter is an important indication that Lucifer's followers were aware of those who preceded him in the episcopate; see *CPG*, 2:2232.2, and *CPL*, 117. For Bishop Lucifer himself; see Lanzoni, 2:658 & 663. *Atlas*, 4. Talbert, map 48.

Catina/Katane. (in Sicily; modern Catania.) *Martyrologium Hieronymianum*, non. Feb., and 4 id. Julius, mentions the martyr Agatha. Lanzoni, 626, notes that Agatha's name was later taken up into the Roman liturgy of the mass. The martyr Eupolus is recorded at *Martyrologium Hieronymianum*, prid. id. Aug.; prid. id, Sept. Other martyrs appear at *Martyrologium Hieronymianum*, prid. kal. Jan. See also *CIL*, 10.2:7112, where a Christian infant who died in the Constantinian period at nearby Hybla Maior was interred at Catina. *SEG* 46 (1996): #1261 (=*AÉ* 1996, #792) is a Christian inscription from the first half of the Fourth Century. *Atlas*, 4. Talbert, map 47.

Centum Cellae. (in Etruria; modern Civitavecchia.) Several martyrs are listed in *Martyrologium Hieronymianum*, 5 id. Aug.; compare *AASS*, Junii, 1:34–37 (*BHL*, #7550), where they are dated to the time of Decius. Pope Cornelius was exiled there at the same time; see *Liber Pontificalis*, 22, "Cornelius." Bishop Epictetus was at the Council of Arles in 314; see *Concilia Galliae*, 15, 17, 19, 20, and Gaudemet, 62. Nearby at Tolfa an inscription from the late Third Century or the first half of the Fourth Century has been found with the words "*in pace*," see *AÉ* 1991, #680. *Atlas*, 4. Talbert, map 42.

Clusium. (in Etruria; modern Chiusi.) For a discussion of the catacombs, one of which is named for the Christian matron Mustiola, see *DACL*, 3:1386–1402. For inscriptions from the catacomb named for her, see *CIL*, 11.1:2548–82a. *CIL*, 11.1:2549, mentions Mustiola herself.

Martyrologium Hieronymianum, 9 kal. Dec., also mentions Mustiola. For accounts of the martyrdom of Irenaeus, Mustiola, and others, see *AASS*, Junii 5:389–90 and Surius, 4:76–78 (*BHL*, #4455); see also *AASS*, Julii, 1:560–63 (*BHL*, #4456).

ILCV, #1027 (=*CIL*, 11.1: #2548), mentions Bishop Lucius Petronius Dexter, who died at age 66 on 3 id. December 322. For another possible inscription, see *ILCV*, #3032 (=*CIL*, 11.1: #2573). See also Dufourcq, 3:161–62. Lanzoni, 552–54. *Atlas*, 4. Talbert, map 42.

Cumae. (in Campania; modern Cuma.) Cumae appears in the *Shepherd of Hermas*, if not as a place with a Christian community, at least as a place where Christians regularly ventured; see *Shepherd of Hermas*, vis. 1.1.3 (1.3) & 2.1.1 (5.1). The *Via Campania* also appears at vis. 4.1.2 (22.2). Hermas distinguished his own visions from those of the Cumaean Sybil; see vis. 2.4.1 (8.1). He also describes the church (whether at Cumae or elsewhere is impossible to determine) as being under persecution; see vis. 2.3.4 (7.4) & 3.2.1 (10.1). See Lanzoni, 206–210, for discussion.

Some manuscripts of *Martyrologium Hieronymianum*, 14 kal. Mart., mention the martyr Juliana. *AASS*, Februarius 2:869 suggests that she may have been a native of Cumae, though *AASS*, Februarius 2:875–88 (*BHL*, #4522–27), places her martyrdom at Nicomedia with a later tranfer of relics to Cumae. Talbert, map 44.

Fabrateria vetus. (in Latium Adiectum; modern Ceccano.) *Martyrologium Hieronymianum*, 14 kal. Sept., lists the martyrs Magnus and Leontius. Cappelletti, 6:279–91 (*BHL*, #5168) says that Magnus was originally from Tranum. See also *AASS*, Augustus 3:713–16 (*BHL*, #5170), which places his martyrdom at the time of Decius or Valerian. Other martyr accounts are listed in *BHL*, #5169 & #5171. Harnack, 816. Lanzoni, 300–301. Talbert, map 44.

Fanum Fortunae. (in Umbria Transappennica; modern Fano.) The bishop and confessor Paternianus is known from the time of Diocletian; for the various lives, see *AASS*, Julius 3:283–87, and compare *BHL*, #6472–76. Lanzoni, 497–99. *DHGE*, 16:472–73. Talbert, map 42.

Ferentinum. (in Latium Adiectum; modern Ferentino.) Ambrose the Centurion was said to have been martyred on 16 August under Diocletian; see *Passio Sancti Ambrosii Centurionis*. Under Pope Sylvester (314–335), the Emperor Constantine gave the fundus Barbatianum near Ferentinum to the church; see *Liber Pontificalis*, 34, "Sylvester." Lanzoni, 167–8. Talbert, map 44.

Ferentium. (in Etruria; modern Ferento.) The shrine of the martyr Eutychius at nearby Soriano (ancient Surianum) is mentioned in

Gregory the Great, *Dialogues*, 3.38.1–2, where it is clear that the shrine was part of the territory of the bishop of Ferentum. For the account as placed in the sanctoral calendar, see *AASS*, Aprilis 2:374, and Maius, 3:458–60. Compare *BHL*, #2779–80. *CIL*, 11.1:3054, is a Christian inscription dated to 359 C.E. from the same site. Talbert, map 42.

Firmum. (in Picenum; modern Fermo.) *AASS*, Januarius, 1:675, contains brief mention of the Bishop Alexander, but confirmation is lacking. The name of Alexander also appears in *Martyrologium Romanum*, 11 January. *AÉ* 1992, #514, is an inscription from the late Third or early Fourth Century in the museum there. Talbert, map 42.

Florentia. (in Etruria; modern Florence.) Numerous martyrs are claimed, among them Minias and Crescentius under Decius. For Minias, see *AASS*, Octobris 11:428–30 (*BHL*, #5965), and Usuard, 8 kal. Nov. For Crescentius *et al.*, see *AASS*, Octobris, 10:583–97 (*BHL*, #1987). Bishop Felix was at the Council of Rome in 313; see Optatus, 1.23.

Koch, 266, #89 (=Deichmann, *Repertorium*, 2: #10), is a sarcophagus from the first decade of the Fourth Century; see also Wilpert, *I Sarcofagi*, plate 287.1, and Gerke, 351. Koch 245, #110 (=Deichmann, *Repertorium*, 2: #173), is from a slightly later period; see also Wilpert, *I Sarcofagi*, plate 300.3, and Gerke, 366. Further sarcophagi may be found listed in Wilpert, *I Sarcofagi*, plate 4.1 (=Gerke, 346); Wilpert, *I Sarcofagi*, plate 66.1 (=Gerke, 340); and Gerke, 241 & 338. *Atlas*, 4. Talbert, map 42.

Formiae. (in Latium Adiectum; modern Formia.) *Martyrologium Hieronymianum*, 4 non. Junii, mentions Bishop Erasmus, martyred under Diocletian and Maximian; see also *AASS*, Junii 1:206–14, and *BHL*, #2578–85. *AASS*, Junii 1:212, indicates that Erasmus's relics were later transferred to Caieta. Compare *BHG*, #602, and *Martyrologium Romanum*, 2 June. Lanzoni, 164. Veselý, 682–84, noting that a shrine to Erasmus of Formiae (and/or Illyricum) has also been found at modern Ochrid (ancient Lychnidos), wonders if the martyr should really be attributed to that place. *Atlas*, 4. Talbert, map 44.

Forum Appii. (modern Faiti; in Latium Adiectum; 43 Roman miles Southeast of Rome on the *Via Appia*.) Acts 28:15, mentions that Roman Christians came there to meet Paul, though nothing is said of a continuing community at that place. Talbert, map 43.

Forum Clodii. (in Etruria; modern S. Liberato.) *Passio Sc. Mm. Marciani prbi Macarii Stratoclini et Protogeni* mentions Forum Clodii as site of the martyrdom of Marcianus in the time of Emperor Maximian; see Dufourcq, 3:224–25 (*BHL*, #5265b). Dufourcq, 3:226–27, notes that although the martyrdom itself is quite developed it does seem to preserve an authentic recollection of the martyr Marcianus. It is also possible that the Bishop Alexander who was martyred at Baccanis according to *AASS*, Septembris 6:227–36 (*BHL*, #273) was bishop of Forum Clodii; see *DHGE*, 17:1187. Bishop Donatianus was at the Council of Rome in 313; see Optatus, 1.23. Lanzoni, 528–30. *Atlas*, 4. Talbert, map 42.

Fulginiae. (in Umbria; modern Foligno.) Bishop Felicianus of Fulginum died in the persecutions under Decius; see *AB* 9(1890): 381–92 (*BHL*, #2847), and also *AASS*, Januarius 3:196–97 (*BHL*, #2846). *Martyrologium Romanum* lists his death on 24 January. Lanzoni, 446–51. *DHGE*, 17:756–57. Talbert, map 42.

Fundi. (in Latium Adiectum; modern Fondi.) *Liber Pontificalis*, 13, "Soter," identifies Soter as a native of this place. *Liber Pontificalis*, 20, "Anterus," says that Pope Anterus (235–36) appointed a bishop for Fundi. *AASS*, Augustus 4:402–403, sections 4–7 (*BHL*, #6478), mentions the martyr Paternus under Decius. Lanzoni, 157–63. Talbert, map 44.

Hybla maior/Hybla megara. (near Catina in Sicily; modern Paterno.) *CIL*, 10.2:7112, records the burial of a Christian infant who had died at Hybla during the Constantinian era and was interred at Catina. *Acts of Alphius* and other martyr traditions associated with Hybla are regarded as fables; see *DACL*, 2:216–17 & 15.1:1416. Allard, 2:325. Talbert, map 47.

Interamna Nahars. (in Umbria; modern Terni.) *Martyrologium Hieronymianum*, 16 kal. Martius (*i.e.* 14 February), lists the martyr Valentinus. A tradition concerning his life and teaching may be found in *AASS*, Februarius 2:757–58 (*BHL*, #8460). This Valentinus may or may not be the same as the presbyter Valentinus who is said to have died under Claudius II and for whom a basilica was later named at Rome; see *AASS*, Februarius 2:754–55 (*BHL*, #8465). For various possible solutions to this conundrum see Dufourcq, 3:33; *EnECh*, 859, and *ODCC*, 1675. Other martyrs at Interamna appear at 15 & 12 kal. Mar. The martyr Proculus appears with Valentinus in *Martyrologium Hieronymianum*, 18 kal. Maii, and with others on kal. Maii. Lanzoni, 404–13. For a likely Christian sarcophagus from *ca.*280–132, see Wilpert, *I Sarcofagi*, plate 248.2 (=Gerke, 286, 288, & 346). *Atlas*, 4. Talbert, map 42.

Isola Sacra. (between Ostia and Portus.) Koch, 247, #137 (=Deichmann, *Repertorium*, 2: #163), is a sarcophagus from the end of the Third Century. See also Wilpert, *I Sarcofagi*, plate 250.1, and Gerke 244 & 344. Talbert, map 43.

Labicum Quintianum. (in Latium Vetus; near modern Colonna.) Bishop Zoticus was at the Council of Rome in 313; see Optatus, 1.23. *Atlas*, 4. Talbert, map 43.

Luca. (in Etruria; modern Lucca.) One rescension of the *Liber Pontificalis* says that Pope Lucius (253–54 C.E.) was a native of Luca; see *Liber Pontificalis*, 23, "Lucius." *AASS*, Januarius 3:537–38, mentions the martyr Valeri[an]us of Luca, though there is the likely possibility that he is confused with Valerius of Caesaraugusta.

Koch 241, #33 (=Deichmann, *Repertorium*, 2: #91, =Wilpert, *I Sarcofagi*, plate 166.3, =Gerke, 346–47) is a sarcophagus from the last quarter of the Third Century.

Bishop Maximus was at the Council of Serdica in 343; see Hilary, *Epistula*, B.II.4.7, and Athanasius, *Apologia contra Arianos*, 48.2. Lanzoni, 589–95. *Atlas*, 4. Talbert, map 41.

Melita. (administered as part of the province of Sicily; modern Malta.) According to Acts 28:1–10, Paul was shipwrecked there and gained the respect of several residents. For developments of the orginal account, see Lanzoni, 652–53. Talbert, map 47.

Misenum. (in Campania; modern Miseno.) Lanzoni, 215. The martyred deacon Sosius was said to be from Misenum; see *AASS*, Septembris, 6:870–71 (*BHL*, #4132). *Martyrologium Hieronymianum*, 9 kal. Oct., mentions his commemoration there. Sosius is also commemorated at nearby Baiae; *q.v.* Usuard., 9 kal. Oct., mentions Sosius of Misenum as a martyr in Campania. Talbert, map 44.

Neapolis. (in Campania; modern Naples.) *Gesta Episcoporum Neapolitanorum*, 2–4, and *Catalogus Episcoporum Neapolitanorum* list the first twelve bishops as follows: Aspren, Epithimitus, Maron, Probus, Paulus, Agrippinus, Eustathius, Ephebus, Fortunatus, Maximus, Zosimus, and

Sevrus. Of these, Maximus is said to be a contemporary of the Emperors Diocletian and Maximian, while Zosimus is considered to be a contemporary of Pope Sylvester. If the list can be trusted, then, the bishops of Neapolis are know back to *ca.*200. *Liber Pontificalis*, 34, "Sylvester," mentions a church built at Neapolis with funds from the Emperor Constantine. Bellucci, 494–95, suggests an even earlier dating for the first bishops, with Bishop Aspren dating to the first quarter of the Second Century.

Koch, 279, #256 (=Deichmann, *Repertorium*, 2: #180; =Wilpert, *I Sarcofagi*, plate 185.1), is a sarcophagus from the beginning of the Fourth Century. Wilpert, *I Sarcofagi*, plate 164.5 (=Gerke, 338–59), could perhaps be slightly earlier.

For the catacombs, see *DACL*, 12:701–29. Commemorations of martyrs are listed in *Martyrologium Hieronymianum*: Januarius of Beneventum on 13 kal. Oct.; Sosius of Misenum and others on 14 kal. Nov.; Festus on 12 kal. Nov. For Januarius, see also Usuard, 13 kal. Oct. He may also be the Januarius listed in *Martyrologium Hieronymianum*, id. Jan. *Atlas*, 4. Talbert, map 44.

Nequinum/Narnia. (in Umbria; modern Narni.) *AASS*, Maius 1:387–89 (*BHL*, #4614), mentions the martyred bishop Juvenalis. Gregory the Great, *Dialogues*, 4.13.3, also mentions him as a martyr. He is perhaps the same Juvenalis who appears in *Martyrologium Hieronymianum*, 5 non. Maii. Talbert, map 42.

Nola. (in Campania.) The confessor and presbyter Felix is listed in *Martyrologium Hieronymianum*, 19 kal. Feb., 6 kal. Aug. On Felix, see especially Paulinus of Nola, *Carmina*, 15:1–16:299. Felix appears to date to the era of persecutions under Decius and Valerian; see *EEC*, 426. Again according to Paulinus, *Carmina*, 16.229–43, the bishops Maximus and Quintianus of Nola were contemporaries of Felix. Saxer, "Pilgerwesen," 46, hypothesizes that the frescoes at Nola may date to the first half of the Third Century. For the work of Bishop Paulinus himself in the Fifth Century, see Lanzoni, 238. *Atlas*, 4. Talbert, map 44.

Nuceria (Alfaterna). (in Campania; modern Nocera dei Pagani.) For the martyrs Priscianus, Felix, and Constantius, see *Martyrologium Hieronymianum*, 17–12 kal. Octobris. Paulinus of Nola, *Carmina*, 19:515–23, refers to Prisc(ian)us as bishop. Lanzoni, 242–45. Talbert, map 44.

Olbia. (on Sardinia.) Deichmann, *Repertorium*, 2: #4, is a late Third-Century or possibly Constantinian era sarcophagus originally found at Olbia; see Koch, 242 & 274. Talbert, map 48.

Ostia. (in Latium Vetus.) Ostia was the dramatic setting for Minucius Felix, *Octavius*, 2.3. Numerous martyrs are listed for the city in *Martyrologium Hieronymianum*. Bishop Maximus was at the Council of Rome in 313; see Optatus, 1.23. The presbyters Leontius and Mercurius were at the Council of Arles in the following year; see *Concilia Galliae*, 15, 17, 19, 20, 22, and Gaudemet, 62–63.

There are several early Christian sarcophagi. Koch, 239, #13 (=Deichmann, *Repertorium*, 2: #245) is a sarcophagus of native Ostian work from *ca.*310–320. Koch, 245, #106 (=Deichmann, *Repertorium*, 1: #1037), is from the last quarter of the Third Century. Koch, 245, #113 (=Deichmann, *Repertorium*, 2: #175), is from *ca.*300. Koch, 246, #114 (=Deichmann, *Repertorium*, 2: #178), is from the first third of the Fourth Century. Koch, 248, #160 (=Deichmann, *Repertorium*, 1: #1032), is a pre-Constantinian sarcophagus. Koch, 269, #141 (=Deichmann, *Repertorium*, 1: #1024), is from the first third of the Fourth Century. Deichmann, *Repertorium*, 1: #1022, and 2: #163, #244, & #245 may also be Christian sarcophagi. Deichmann, *Repertorium*, 1: #429–36 come from Ostia or nearby Isola Sacra. For other early Fourth-Century sarcophagi that may be considered Christian; see *DACL*, 13:38–42, and Gerke, 346, 348, 357, 363, & 366.

For the church built with funds from the Emperor Constantine, see *Liber Pontificalis*, 34, "Sylvester." For mention of an early Fourth-Century synagogue; see Squarciapino, 299–315. *Atlas*, 4. Talbert, map 43.

Pisae. (in Etruria; modern Pisa.) Bishop Gaudentius was at the Council of Rome in 313; see Optatus, 1.23. Koch 242, #40 (= Deichmann, *Repertorium*, 2:90), from the last third of the Third Century, and Koch, 273, #88 (=Deichmann, *Repertorium*, 2: #12) from *ca.*310–330 are Christian sarcophagi. For other possibilities, see Gerke, 339–341, 345, 362, & 369. *Atlas*, 4. Talbert, map 41.

Portus. (in Latium Vetus; modern Porto.) Several martyrs appear in *Martyrologium Hieronymianum*. Bishop Gregorius was at the Council of Arles in 314; see *Concilia Galliae*, 15, 17, 19, 20, 22, and Gaudemet, 62. Sacco, #68, 70, & 72, are brief inscriptions of Christian character from the late Third Century. Koch 274, #209 (=Deichmann, *Repertorium*, 2: #5), is a Christian sarcophagus from perhaps the late Third Century. Koch, 248, #161 (=Deichmann, *Repertorium*, 1: #1035), is pre-Consantinian in date. Koch, 245, #105 (=Deichmann, *Repertorium*, 1: #1033), and Koch, 264, #64 (=Deichmann, *Repertorium*, 1: #1028) are sarcophagi from the first quarter of the Fourth Century. For other possible Christian sarcophagi, see Gerke, 338, 340, 348, 363, and 369. *Atlas*, 4. Talbert, map 43.

Potentia. (in Lucania; modern Potenza.) *Martyrologium Hieronymianum*, 7 kal. Sept., and 6 kal., Sept., mentions the martyrs Felix, Arontius, Sabinianus, and Honoratus. For martyrs in the general region of Lucania; see *Martyrologium Hieronymianum*, 14 kal., Sept. Talbert, map 45.

Praeneste. (in Latium Vetus; modern Palestrina.) *Martyrologium Hieronymianum*, 15 kal. Sept. lists Agapitus and 33 soldiers. See also *AASS*, Augustus 3:532–37 (*BHL*, #125), where their martyrdom is dated to the reign of Aurelian. Lanzoni, 132–33, discusses the martyr traditions. Bishop Secundus was at the Council of Rome in 313; see Optatus, 1.23. *Atlas*, 4. Talbert, map 43.

Puteoli/Dikaiarcheia. (in Campania; modern Puzzuoli.) Acts 28:13–14 records that Paul and his companions met believers there. See *Martyrologium Hieronymianum*, 8 & 7 kal. Feb. for the martyr Antimasius; 15 kal., Nov. for Januarius (of Beneventum) and Eutychus; 14 kal. Nov. for Proculus; 13 kal., Nov. for Dasius and others. Usuard lists these martyrs approximately one month earlier, on 13 kal. Oct. *Atlas*, 4. Talbert, map 44.

Rome. Suetonius, 5.25.5, reports that the Emperor Claudius expelled the Jews from Rome because they were creating disturbances "*impulsore Chresto*" (at the instigation of Christ). It may well be that Suetonius is here making a confused reference to the Christian community at Rome. Acts 18:2 reports that Aquila and Priscilla were among those expelled at the time. It is unclear whether they were Christians before being expelled, but such would seem likely in light of the information noted in Suetonius. Paul was aware of Christians at Rome even before visiting the city; see Romans 1:8. If Romans 16:1–16 is taken as a genuine part of the letter, Christians at Rome had wide-ranging contacts early on, and Priscilla and Aquila were then back in the capital.

Philippians 4:22 mentions greetings from Christians who were part of the imperial household, presumably at Rome if the letter was written from there. The narrative of Acts 28:14–31 ends with Paul at Rome. Tacitus, *Annals*, 15.33 & 44, reports that in the year which would correspond to 64 C.E. the Emperor Nero persecuted Christians, blaming them for the fire which devastated Rome.

If the reference to "Babylon" at I Peter 5:13 is taken to mean Rome, then I Peter 1:1 & 5:12–13 preserves the tradition that Peter, Sil[v]a[nu]s, and Mark had come to Rome also; see Kümmel, 422. *I Clement*, 5.1–7 supports the tradition of Peter and Paul as apostles in Rome.

Eusebius, *Ecclesiastical History*; Eusebius, *Chronicle*; *Liberian Catalogue*; Jerome, *Chronicle*; and Optatus, 2.3, are indispensible sources for the succession of bishops (popes), as is *Liber Pontificalis*. The death dates of the popes as listed in *Liber Pontificalis* are tolerably accurate from the death of Victor onward, and those in *Liberian Catalogue* are reasonably accurate from the death of Callistus in 217. For a modern reckoning of the dates, see *EEC*, 864–5.

For the first eighty years of the church at Rome, the sources list the following as bishops after Peter: Linus, Cletus or Anacletus (see *ODCC*, 56), Clement, Evaristus, Alexander I, Sixtus I, Telesphorus, and Hyginus. According to Jerome, *Chronicle*, it was *ca.*140 during the episcopate of Hyginus that the heretics Valentinus, Cerdo, and Marcion, made their way to Rome.

The next pope listed after Hyginus is Pius I, who was the brother of the Hermas who authored the *Shepherd of Hermas*; see *Muratorian Canon*, 73–76. Hermas himself wrote of being sold to a slaveholder at Rome; see *Shepherd of Hermas*, vis. 1.1.1 (1.1). It will be noted from this evidence that low status was apparently no bar to high positions of responsibility in the early days of the Roman congregation. The high percentage of early popes with Greek names is likewise indicative of the cosmopolitan nature of the congregation.

Following Pius I, the above-named sources list Popes Anicetus, Soter, and Eleutherius.

The Christian writer Justin and his companions were martyred at Rome *ca.*163–88 under the prefect Rusticus; for Justin's *Acta*, see Musurillo, 42–61. See also, Jerome, *De viris inlustribus*, 23. Justin's student Tatian was also briefly at Rome, see Eusebius, *Ecclesiastical History*, 4.16.7–9, 4.29.1, and Jerome, *De viris inlustribus*, 29.

A late Second-Century work from Asia Minor, the *Acta Pauli*, Greek text, p. 7; Coptic text, p. 52, makes reference to Paul's preaching at Rome, saying "*κα*[*ì φανερὸν γεν*]*έσθαι ὑπὲρ πάντας τοὺς πιστούς.*" Harnack, *Analecta*, 5–6, takes this as a recognition of the preeminence of Rome by a writer from Asia Minor at the time. Yet Schneemelcher, 258, translates it as referring to Paul's preeminence.

Tertullian, *De praescriptione haereticorum*, 30.2, indicates that Marcion and Valentinus, or their followers, were active in Rome as late as the time of Pope Eleutherius. Hippolytus, *Refutatio*, 9.11.1–9.12.26, records difficulties during the pontificate of Eleutherius's successor Victor when several members of the Christian community looked with sympathy upon gnostic ideas.

On Pope Victor's involvement in the controversy over the date of Easter, see Eusebius, *Ecclesiastical History*, 5.23.1–25.1. *Synaxarium Alexandrinum*, 10 Hatur (6 November), claims that Victor called a council to deal with the Easter controversy and other matters. The Alexandrian date would correspond to 6 November; see Papaconstantinou, 405.

According to the sources for the papal lists, the next three popes were Zephyrinus, Urban, and Callistus (d.217). *Liber Pontificalis*, 17, "Callistus," indicates that Callistus was a native of the "*urbe Ravennactium*" section of Trastavere; see Harnack, 818, 826, & 837. Hippolytus, 9.12.9–13, numbers Zephyrinus and Callistus among the gnostic sympathizers and shows that as a young man Callistus was for a time exiled to Sardinia by the prefect of Rome, though the charge related not to Callistus' alleged gnostic sympathies but to stirring up a dispute with one of the Jewish synagogues. Hippolytus, 9.12.13–14, also notes that Zephyrinus later gave Callistus charge of the Christian cemetery at Rome (hence the famous Catacombs of Callistus). Hippolytus himself, along with Pope Pontianus, was exiled to Sardinia *ca.*235; see *Liber Pontificalis*, 19, "Pontianus."

After Pontianus the sources list Popes Anterus, Fabian, Cornelius, and Lucius I. For events at Rome in the middle of the Third Century, Cyprian's *Epistulae* are often instructive; *e.g. Epistulae*, 30.5.2, sent to Cyprian from Rome. Eusebius, *Ecclesiastical History*, 5.21 & 6.43.11, and elsewhere.

Following the persecutions under Decius until the end of the Diocletianic persecutions, the sources list Popes Stephen, Sixtus II, Dionysius, Felix, Eutychianus, Caius, Marcellinus, Marcellus, Eusebius.

There is a recognized gap of four years from 304 to 308 between Popes Marcellinus and Marcellus, perhaps indicative of the severe stress on the church during the Diocletianic persecutions.

Bishop Miltiades hosted the Council of Rome in 313; see Optatus, 1.23. Arnobius, 2.12, mentions Christians of many nations at Rome. Augustine, *De unico baptismo contra Petilianum*, 16.27–28, mentions Popes Marcellus, Miltiades and Sylvester. Augustine, *Breviculus*, 3.18.34–36, likewise mentions Miltiades. Numerous martyrs are listed in *Martyrologium Hieronymianum*. For a study of some of them, see Dufourcq, 1:1–432. The inscription of Volusian the consul in 314 need not be specifically Christian, and describes him simply as "*religiosissimoque*," see *ILS*, #1213.

During the reign of Pope Sylvester, the church at Rome was the beneficiary of Emperor Constantine's generosity; see *Liber Pontificalis*, 34 "Sylvester." The following three popes were Marcus, Julius, and Liberius, the last of whom took office in 352. Athanasius, *Apologia contra Arianos*, 37.1, mentions representatives from Rome at the Council of Serdica in 343.

For studies of some of the early church buildings at Rome, which date to the first half of the Fourth Century at least, see Snyder, 75–82, and White, 2:209–240. See also Fasola, 509–11, with regard to the possible late Third-Century use of the Basilica of St. Thecla. The earliest literary attestation for one of the *tituli* churches (that of *Titulus Aequitii* = S. Silvestri) is found in *Liber Pontificalis*, 34, "Sylvester;" see Saxer, "L'utilisation," 989. For Christian lamps and catacombs from before *ca.*300, see Finney, 116–274. For sarcophagi at Rome, see Deichmann, *Repertorium*, 1: #3–426 & 2: #139–141. Of these, Deichmann, *Repertorium*, 1: #1019, dates to the third quarter of the Third Century. *SEG* 32 (1982): #1057, is the epitaph of Kornution from the time of Constantine. For another possibly Christian inscription found on the via Tiburtina about 15 km from the center of Rome, see Mazzoleni, 3:2291–93. For detailed prosopological studies of the church at Rome in the Second and Third Centuries, see Lampe, 82–94, 124–300, & 422–25. Rutgers, 42–117 & 153–58, provides a brief introduction to the inscriptional and epigraphic evidence. Robinson, *Bauer*, 77–84. *Atlas*, 4. Talbert, map 43.

Saena. (in Etruria; modern Siena.) For documents related to the martyr Ansanus under Diocletian, see Cappelletti, 17:439–41, and *Catal. Brux.*, 1:129–32 (*BHL*, #515–17). Bishop Florianus was at the Council of Rome in 313; see Optatus, 1.23. For more on Florianus;

see *AASS*, Septembris 4:352 (*BHL*, #1986). *Atlas*, 4. Talbert, map 42.

Salernum. (in Campania; modern Salerno.) *AASS*, Augustus 6:165–66, sections 12–22 (*BHL*, #3086) records the martyr Fortunatus and others under Diocletian. The martyrs Archelaia, Thecla, and Susanna are also believed to have suffered in the time of Diocletian and Maximian, though it is perhaps only their relics that were kept at Salernum; see *AASS*, Jan. 2:555–57 (*BHL*, #660–61). The early Bishops Bonosus (*AASS*, Maii 3:373), Gramatius (*AASS*, Octobris 5:671–74), Verus (*AASS*, Octobris 10:47–48), Eusterius (*AASS*, Octobris 8:436–39), and Valentinianus (*AASS*, Novembris 1:657–58) are also commemorated at Salerno. They are not closely dated, but the editors of *AASS* place them in the middle of the Fourth Century and later. See also Lanzoni, 250–52. For a sarcophagus of *ca.*300, see Gerke, 341 (=Wilpert, *I Sarcofagi*, plate 60.4). Talbert, map 44.

Sipontum/Sipous. (in Apulia; modern S. Maria di Siponto.) Accounts of the martyrs Justinus, Florentius, Felix, and Justa of Sipontum are found in Ughelli, 6:674–78 (*BHL*, #4586); *Catal. Lat. Rom.*, 402 (*BHL*, #4586c); and *AASS*, Augustus 1:42–43 (*BHL*, #4587). Lanzoni, 277–78. *Martyrologium Romanum*, 25 July, also mentions that Florentius and Felix of Sipontum were martyred at Furco. Talbert, map 45.

Spoletium. (in Umbria; modern Spoleto.) A later and somewhat hazy tradition makes Bishop Laurentius of Spoleto a contemporary of Pope Caius (283–86); see Dufourcq, 3:62 (*BHL*, #4748b), and Lanzoni, 443–44.

Martyrologium Hieronymianum, 12 kal. Feb. & 16 kal. Mar., lists the martyr Vitalis. *AASS*, Januarius 2:216 (*BHL*, #6891), lists the martyr Pontianus under Marcus Aurelius. Surius, 6:951–53 (*BHL*, #3677), contains an account of the martyred presbyter Gregory, though Lanzoni, 440, thinks it may actually relate to martyrs elsewhere. For discussion of other martyr traditions, see Lanzoni, 438–42. *Atlas*, 4. Talbert, map 42.

Syracusae. (in Sicily.) Acts 28:12 records a brief stay of Paul at Syracuse. Cyprian of Carthage, letter 30.5. *Martyrologium Hieronymianum*, id. Decembris, records the martyr Lucia. See also *BHL*, #4992–5003. Her name was later taken up into the canon of the Roman mass; see Lanzoni, 632. Several other martyrs appear in *Martyrologium Hieronymianum*. For brief discussions of the catacombs, dating as early as the Third Century; see Lanzoni, 2:635–36; *DACL*, 15.2:1843–55;

and S. L. Agnello, 5–10. Bishop Crispus and the deacon Florentius were at the Council of Arles in 314; see *Concilia Galliae*, 14, 16, 17, 18, 19, & 21, and Gaudemet, 58.

SEG 15 (1958): #582 & 583 are inscriptions of possibly Christian character from *ca*.275–325. *SEG* 46 (1996): #1282–93, are other early inscriptions of possibly Christian character. The earliest clearly Christian inscription dates to 356; see G. Agnello, 309–26. *Atlas*, 4. Talbert, map 47.

Tarracina(e). (in Latium Adiectum; modern Terracina.) The Fourth-Century legend *Acta Petri et Pauli*, 13, mentions a visit by Paul. According to a later legend mentioned in *Acta martyrii SS. Nerei et Achillei*, the virgin Flavia Domitilla was martyred there in the First Century; see *AASS*, Maii, 3:11–12. These legends suggest a Christian community before the beginning of the Fourth Century. Bishop Sabinus was at the Council of Rome in 313; see Optatus, 1.23. Harnack, 813. *Atlas*, 4. Talbert, map 44.

Tauromenium. (in Sicily; modern Taormina.) *Martyrologium Hieronymianum*, 3 non. Aprilis, records the martyr Pancratius. See also *SEC*, February 9 (p. 454), June 6 (p. 733), and July 9 (p. 807).

Harnack, 815, rejects his own earlier suggestion that the *Passio Sancti Felicis Tubzacensis*, 5 (see *AASS*, Octobris 10:627, and more recently Musurillo, 270), may indicate the presence of a Christian community at Tauromenium. Musurillo, xl, has suggested that this appended section of the *Passio* may relate to an otherwise unknown local Italian martyr. *Atlas*, 4. Talbert, map 47.

Teanum Sidicinum. (in Campania; modern Teano.) According to *AASS*, Augustus 2:74–78 (*BHL*, #6466), Bishop Paris, the first bishop of Teanum, was ordained by Pope Sylvester (hence between 314 and 335). *Atlas*, 4. Talbert, map 44.

Tres Tabernae. (in Latium Adiectum; 33 Roman miles Southeast of Rome on the *Via Appia*.) Acts 28:15 records that Christians from Rome came there to meet Paul. Bishop Felix was at the Council of Rome in 313; see Optatus, 1.23. *Atlas*, 4. Talbert, map 43.

Tuder. (in Umbria; modern Todi.) *Martyrologium Hieronymianum*, kal. Sept., mentions the Fourth-Century Bishop Terentianus. *Martyrologium Hieronymianum*, 7 kal. Jun. mentions the martyrs Felicissima, Eraclius, and Paulinus. See also *AASS*, Maii 6:366, for a brief discussion of

other martyrs. Fiocchi Nicolai, "Notiziario," 2228–29, mentions catacombs nearby with pottery from the Third through the Fifth Centuries. Talbert, map 42.

Velitrae. (in Latium Vetus; modern Velletri.) Koch, 241 (=Deichmann,
Repertorium, 2: #242; =Wilpert, *I Sarcofagi*, plate 4.3) is a locally made
Christian sarcophagus from *ca.*300. See also Wilpert, *I Sarcofagi*, plate
173.8 (=Gerke, 369). *DACL*, 15.2:2926–28. Talbert, map 43.

Vindena. (in Umbria, near Terni.) A certain Sabina and Serapia
were martyred there, traditionally under Hadrian; see *AASS*, Augustus
4:500–504 (*BHL*, #7407 & #7586) and *Catal. Brux.*, 2:372 (*BHL*,
#7587). *Martyrologium Romanum*, 23 July, 29 August, and 3 Sept. places
these martyrs at Rome. Yet they are clearly to be associated with
Vindena in Umbria; see Allard, 1:231–34. Compare Pauly-Wissowa,
II.17:41, for the "Vindinates." Compare Talbert, map 42.

Volsinii. (in Etruria; modern Bolsena.) Bishop Evandrus was at the
Council of Rome in 313; see Optatus, 1.23. Lanzoni, 536–44.
Harnack, 813. For the transformation of a civil basilica there into
a funerary chapel in the first half of the Fourth Century, see Fiocchi
Nicolai, "Notiziario," 2232. *Atlas*, 4. Talbert, map 42.

Possible sites

Agrigentum/Akragas? (in Sicily; modern Agrigento.) Harnack, 815,
rejects his own earlier use of one rescension of the *Passio Sancti Felicis
Episcopi Tubzacensis*, 5 (see *AASS*, Octobris, 10:627, and for a recent
edition of the whole work, Musurillo, 266–71) to document Christianity
in Agrigentum. The list of cities appended at the end of that document seems to Harnack to relate to Felix's relics rather than to his
life. Even so, Harnack considers it likely that Agrigentum had a
Christian community early in the Fourth Century.

Lanzoni, 2:639–40, also expresses grave doubts about using the
document to demonstrate the early spread of Christianity in Sicily.
Musurillo, xl, suggests that the appendix may be part of an otherwise lost tradition referring to a local Italian martyr named Felix.
Atlas, map 4, includes Agrigentum. Talbert, map 47.

Aquila? (in modern Abruzzi.) One manuscript of the *Martyrologium
Hieronymianum*, 17 kal. Oct., mentions a martyr, but this appears to
be a confusion with Ancyra in the dioecesis of Pontica. *DHGE*,
3:1105–1108. Compare Talbert, map 42.

Arpi? (in Apulia; near modern Foggia.) According to Ms.C for the Council of Arles in 314, Bishop Pandus and the deacon Crescens represented "*civitate Alpensium provincia Pulia;*" see *Concilia Galliae*, 14, and Gaudemet, 58. Harnack, 814, and Lanzoni, 273–75, take this as meaning Arpi. However, all other manuscripts name the bishop as Pardus and the city as Salpientium or the like, which would be the nearby town of Salapia; see *Concilia Galliae*, 16, 17, 18, 19, 21, and Gaudemet, 59. Lanzoni, 273–75. *Atlas*, 4, identifies the town as Arpi. Talbert, map 45.

Arsoli? (about 5 km South-Southwest of ancient Carsioli.) Koch, 245, #107 (=Deichmann, *Repertorium*, 2: #178), is a sarcophagus from the first third of the Fourth Century. Compare Talbert, map 44.

Asculum Picenum? (in Picenum; modern Ascoli.) A tradition of a supposedly early Bishop Aemygdius is mentioned in medieval documents; see *BHL*, #2535. Harnack, 815, includes Asculum as an early site. Lanzoni, 397–98, doubts the tradition because of the lateness and the fabulous character of the documents. Talbert, map 42.

Asisium? (in Umbria; modern Assisi.) See *AASS*, Junii 3:163–65 (*BHL*, #8597), for traditions connected with the martyr Victorinus *ca.*250. For the medieval sermon of Peter Damian on the martyr Rufinus, see *AASS*, Julii, 7:162–65 (*BHL*, #7369). Lanzoni, 461, points out the late attestation of many martyr traditions associated with Asisium. Koch, 274, #202 (=Deichmann, *Repertorium*, 2: #24) is a sarcophagus from *ca.*320–340, but of uncertain provenance. Talbert, map 42.

Atina? (near Capua.) The martyrs Nicander and Marcian are associated with Atina and Venafrum perhaps *ca.*303; see *AASS*, Jun., 4:217–19 (*BHL*, #6073), *AASS*, Jun. 4:220–22 (*BHL*, #6074), and compare Ruinart, 570–73 (*BHL*, #6070–72). Traditions associated with this site appear to be somewhat contradictory and of doubtful value; see *DHGE*, 5:127–29. Hence one may contrast *BHL*, #5260, where martyrs of similar name are reported for Egypt. Harnack, 816. Talbert, map 44.

Aveia/Aquila? (in the Vestensis region of the Apennines; modern Fossa.) One manuscript of *Martyrologium Hieronymianum*, 17 kal. Oct. contains an uncertain reference to Aquila with regard to a martyred Bishop Paul. Other manuscripts have the reading "Ancyra."

BHL, #5829–36, lists traditions of the martyr Maximus, supposedly under Decius. Usuard, 13 kal. Nov., picks up the tradition from *BHL*, #5834. The traditions are rejected by Lanzoni, 368–69.

The cultus of the martyr Justina of Sipontum and companions was apparently known at Aquila from the late Fourth Century; see the inscription from the nearby crypt of the church of S. Justina datable to 396 C.E. and recorded in *CIL*, 9:3601. For further accounts of Justina, see Ughelli, 6:674–78 (*BHL*, #4586); *Catal. Lat. Rom.*, 402 (*BHL*, #4586c); and *AASS*, Augustus, 1:42–43 (*BHL*, #4587). Talbert, map 42.

Baiae? (in Campania; modern Baia.) According to the Fourth-Century legend *Acta Petri et Pauli*, 13, Paul passed through the town on his journey to Rome. The existence of such a story suggests that a Christian community may have existed at Baiae by the early Fourth Century. *Martyrologium Hieronymianum*, id. Oct. & 17 kal. Nov. mentions the commemoration of the martyr Sosius; see also *AASS*, Septembris 6:870–71, where Sosius is described as a deacon from Misenum. Talbert, map 44.

Caere/Agylla? (in Etruria; modern Cervetri.) Koch, 265, #72 (= Deichmann, *Repertorium*, 2: #17), is a sarcophagus from *ca*.325. Talbert, map 43.

Caieta? (in Campania or Latium Adiectum; modern Gaeta.) According to the Fourth-Century legend *Acta Petri et Pauli*, 13, Paul made a brief visit to Gaeta on his way to Rome. This tradition could reflect the native pride of a Christian community of the Fourth Century. The relics of Bishop Erasmus of Formiae were later translated there; see *AASS*, Junii, 1:212. Ughelli, 1: index & 526–46. Lanzoni, 164. Talbert, map 44.

Cales? (in Campania; modern Calvi.) Bishop Calepodius of Campania was at the Council of Serdica in 343; see Hilary, *Epistula*, B.II.4.45; Athanasius, *Apologia contra Arianos*, 48.2; and *Epistula ad Mareoticas ecclesias*. Later tradition makes Calepodius bishop of Cales, although Hilary, *loc. cit.*, places him at Neapolis; see Cappelletti, 20:184, and Lanzoni, 187. *CIL*, 10.1:4712 is a Christian inscription from 346. Talbert, map 44.

Camerinum? (in Umbria Transappennica; modern Camerino.) Certain *Acta Apocrypha* related to the martyrs Porphyrus, Anastasius, and Venantius in the time of "Rex Antiochus" (perhaps intended to represent a prefect under Decius) are recorded in *AASS*, Maius 4:138–44. *Martyrologium Romanum* lists them thus: 4 May, Porphyrus; 11 May, Anastasius; 18 May, Venantius. Some or all of these traditions may be imported from Salona in Dalmatia; see *BHL*, #414–15 & #8523. Harnack, 815, includes the site. Yet Lanzoni, 487–89, eliminates this site because of the uncertainty of the documents. *Atlas*, 4, does not list. Talbert, map 42.

Campovalano/Campli? (about 12 km South-Southeast of Asculum; ancient name unknown.) Koch, 275, #219 (=Deichmann, *Repertorium*, 2: #101), is a sarcophagus from the first third of the Fourth Century. Talbert, map 42.

Canusium? (in Apulia; modern Canosa.) An inscription mentions the martyred decurion C. Petronius Maginus, thought to have been killed under Decius; see Quacquarelli, 325 & 345. Bishop Stercorius was at the Council of Serdica *ca.*343; see Hilary, *Epistula*, B.II.4.(44), and Athanasius, *Apologia contra Arianos*, 48.2. *CIL*, 9:338, refers to a certain Petronius *ca.*393. Paulinus of Nola, *Carmina*, 17.23, refers to the place, though without indicating anything about Christians there. Early catacombs are also known; see Lanzoni, 1:288–95. Likewise, remains of a church dedicated to the martyr Leucius of Brundisium, *q.v.*, are known. *DHGE*, 11:760–62. Talbert, map 45.

Forum Flaminii? (in Umbria; modern S. Giovanni Profiamma.) *AASS*, Januarius 3:196–97 (*BHL*, #2846), notes that Bishop Felicianus of Fulginum was born at Forum Flamini of Christian parents. *AB* 9 (1890): 381–82 (*BHL*, #2847) supports his birth there, though the date of his birth in the time of the Gordian is to be questioned since he died in the Decianic persecutions. The internal evidence of the document cannot be checked by outside events; see Lanzoni, 451. *DHGE*, 16:852–53 & 17:1188. *Atlas*, 4. Talbert, map 42.

Forum Novum? (near S. Maria in Vescovio and Civita Castellana.) Wilpert, *I Sarcofagi*, plate 70.2, has been suggested as a Christian sarcophagus from *ca.*300; see Gerke, 75, 253, 287, 344, 356, & 397. Koch, 348, classifies the sarcophagus as pagan or neutral in character. Fasola & Testini, mention the martyrs Hyacinthus, Alexander, and Tiburtius; contrast *Martyrologium Hieronymianum*, 5 id. Sept., where they are attributed to Sabinus. Talbert, map 42.

Forum Traiani/Hydata Hypsitana? (modern Fordongianus; in Sardinia.) *AÉ* 1990, #459, is a Sixth Century inscription mentioning the martyr Luxurius; see also *AÉ* 1992, #879a–b. Compare *AASS*, Augustus, 4:416–17 (=*BHL*, #5092). *AÉ* 1990, #460, mentions the bishop Stephen. *AÉ* 1990, #461–463, are other epitaphs. Talbert, map 48.

Galese? (ancient name unknown; half way between ancient Horto and Falerii Veteres.) Koch 274, #206 (=Deichmann, *Repertorium*, 2: #25), is a late Constantinian sarcophagus now kept in the ducal palace. Compare Talbert, map 42.

Hispellum? (in Umbria; modern Spello.) Usuard, 15 kal. Junii, assigns the martyred bishop Felix to Hispellum under Emperor Maximian. The same tradition is reported in *AASS*, May 4:167–68 (*BHL*, #2886). Lanzoni, 459–60, notes that it is unclear whether Hispellum is to be understood as Felix's see or even as the place of his martyrdom. Confusion may have arisen with Spoletium or with Spalatum (Split) in Dalmatia. Talbert, map 42.

Interpromium? Nearby at Torre de' Passeri (S. Clemente de Casauria) a sarcophagus from *ca.*310–330 has been recorded; see Koch 270, #152 (=Deichmann, *Repertorium*, 2: #96); and Wilpert, *I Sarcofagi*, plate 297.1. Talbert, map 42.

Leontini? (in Sicily; modern Lentini.) The *Passio* of Alphius, Philadelphius, and Cyrinus mentions the arrest of martyrs at Leontium, supposedly under Emperor Valerian; see *AASS*, Maii 2:xlvi–lxi (*BHG*, #57), section 13. For reference to parallel accounts, see *BHG*, #58–62. Harnack thinks that the martyr accounts may point to the existence of a church, but according to Lanzoni, 2:629–31, the martyr accounts here are confused both chronologically and topographically. Talbert, map 47.

Lilybaeum? (in Sicily; modern Marsala.) *Praedestinatus*, 1.16, refers to a bishop Eustachius of Lilybaeum, who would date to *ca.*200 when Heracleon, the disciple of Valentinus, was active. Harnack, 816, thinks the story may point to the early existence of Christians there, but Lanzoni, 2:642, points to the lateness of the document and says Harnack's surmise is pure hypothesis. *AÉ* 1996, #810, is a Second- or Third-Century inscription which could perhaps be understood as Christian. *Atlas*, 4. Talbert, map 47.

Luna? (in Northern Etruria.) *Liber Pontificalis*, 28, "Eutychianus," claims Pope Eutychianus as a native of Luna, though it is unclear whether he was a Christian while still settled in his birthplace. Harnack, 819. Talbert, map 41.

Messana? (in Sicily; modern Messina.) Harnack, 815, rejects his earlier use of *Passio Sancti Felicis Episcopi Tubzacensis*, 5 (see *AASS*, Octobris, 10:627, and Musurillo, 270) as evidence for early Christianity at Messana. More recently, Musurillo, xl, has suggested that the pertinent section of the *Passio* may refer to a local Italian martyr.

Harnack, 816, also believes that the tradition in the *Acta Petri et Pauli*, 7, according to which Paul ordained Bacchilus as the first bishop of Messana, points to a Christian community there by the Third Century. More recent attempts to date the *Acta Petri et Pauli* place the document in the Fourth Century; see Schneemelcher, 2:440–42. Lanzoni, 614–16, expresses grave doubts about Harnack's date for the *Acta* and also about the material related to Messana in *Martyrologium Hieronymianum*, 16 kal. Julii, and & 12 kal. Decembris. Talbert, map 47.

Nepet? (in Etruria; modern Nepi.) The martyrs Ptolemaeus and Romanus are associated with Nepet during the time of Claudius, though perhaps the Emperor Claudius II is meant; see *AASS*, Augustus 4:749–50 (*BHL*, #6984–87). The account may indicate an early Christian tradition. For discussion see Lanzoni, 531–32. Talbert, map 42.

Nomentum? (in Sabina; modern Mentana.) Koch, 245, #112 (=Deichmann, *Repertorium*, 2: #165) is a sarcophagus from the last third of the Third Century now kept at Mentana. No exact provenance is stated. Talbert, map 43.

Oriolo Romano? (in Etruria; just North of Forum Clodii.) Fiocchi Nicolai, *I Cimiteri*, 83–85 and Tav. I, records an apparently Christian sarcophagus from the first third of the Fourth Century, but its provenance is unknown; see also Koch, xvi & 270, #168.

Pan(h)ormus? (in Sicily; modern Palermo.) A late document, *Praedestinatus*, 1.16, mentions a Bishop Theodorus of Panormus, who would date to *ca.*200 when Heracleon the disciple of Valentinus was active. Lanzoni, 2:642, doubts the reliability of the tradition. The martyr Olivia was claimed as a native of Panormus; see *AASS*, Junii 2:292–95 (*BHL*, #6329). *IG* 14: #296, confirms Eusebius, *Ecclesiastical*

History, 10.5.23, which relates to Sicily generally. See *DACL*, 13:736–47, for the catacombs. Lanzoni, 2:644–45. Talbert, map 47.

Perusia? (in Etruria; modern Perugia.) The martyr Constantius is of uncertain year, though traditionally dated under Marcus Aurelius; see *Martyrologium Hieronymianum*, 4 kal. Feb., and 3 kal. Maii, also *AASS*, Januarius 3:540–43 (*BHL*, #1938). Lanzoni, 548. Wilpert, *I Sarcofagi*, plate 28.3 (=Gerke, 368), is a Fourth-Century sarcophagus now in secondary use. *Atlas*, 4. Talbert, map 42.

Pisaurum? (Colonia Julia Felix P. in Umbria Transappennica; modern Pésaro.) Athanasius, *Apologia contra Arianos*, 50.1, lists an Italian bishop named Heracleianus as supporting the Council of Serdica in 343. Agnellus, 17, gives the name of Heracleianus's see as Pisaurium and says he was a pupil of Bishop Severus of Ravenna. Lanzoni, 500–502, considers Heracleianus to be the first certain bishop of the place. Talbert, map 42.

Reate? (modern Riete.) A sarcophagus found by stoneworkers nearby dates to the first third of the Fourth Century, see Deichmann, *Repertorium*, 2: #216. Koch, 369. Talbert, map 42.

Sorrina? (near modern Viterbo.) Wilpert, *I Sarcofagi*, plate 19.2 (=Gerke, 74 & 342), is a sarcophagus dating from perhaps the Third Century from Viterbo. Talbert, map 42.

Sulci? (in Sardinia; modern S. Antioco.) An inscription from the Eighth or Ninth Century commemorates the martyr Antiochus; see Lanzoni, 2:669. Yet this inscription almost certainly relates to the cult of an Eastern martyr, and not to a local martyr; see Lanzoni, 2:667–71, and *CIL*, 10:7533 (Sixth Century). For a description of the catacombs, see *DACL*, 15.1:892–93. *Atlas*, 4. Talbert, map 48.

Sutrium? (in Etruria; modern Sutri.) One rescension of the *Passio Mustiola* found in *AASS*, Junii 5:389–90 and Surius, 4:76–78 (*BHL*, #4455), followed by Usuard, 9 kal. Jul., mentions the martyr Felix at Sutrium. Yet another version of the story places his death at Faleriane; see *AASS*, Julius 1:560–63 (*BHL*, #4456). *DACL*, 15.2:1741, mentions catacombs. Raspi Serra, 419, mentions the early cemetery of Geovanelle. Talbert, map 42.

Tarquinii? (in Etruria.) Wilpert, *I Sarcofagi*, plate 81.3 (=Gerke, 61 & 342), is considered by some to be a Christian sarcophagus of Constantinian date. Talbert, map 42.

Tibur? (in Latium Vetus; modern Tivoli.) Bishop Paulus of Tibur ordained the Antipope Ursinus in 366; see *Collectio Avellana*, 1.5, and Jerome, *Chronicle*. Rufinus, 11.10, gives the same account without specifying Paulus. This incident suggests that Tibur was a well-established episcopal see by 366. Talbert, map 43.

Tranum/Turenum? (in Apulia; modern Trani.) Some manuscripts of *Martyrologium Hieronymianum*, 14 kal. Sept., mention the martyr Magnus killed at Fabriteria, who according to some lives (see *BHL*, #5167–71) is associated with Tranum. One manuscript of the *Martyrologium Hieronymianum*, 3 id. Feb., mentions a martyrdom at nearby Volturno. Harnack, 816. Lanzoni, 300–301. Talbert, map 45.

Trea? (modern Treia.) Koch, 270, #166, is a sarcophagus of Constantinian date. Koch, 246, #143 (=Deichmann, *Repertorium*, 2: #55) is a sarcophagus from the first half of the Fourth Century. Talbert, map 42.

Turris Libisonis? (modern Porto Torres; on Sardinia.) Wilpert, *I Sarcofagi*, plate 164.2 (=Gerke, 355) is an early sarcophagus of possibly Christian character. See Koch, 64, 71, & 452, for mention of other fragments. See also *AÉ* 1994, #796, from the first half of the Fourth Century, and *SEG*, 38 (1988), #981. Talbert, map 48.

Venafrum? (modern Venafro; in Campania.) The martyrs Nicander and Marcian are associated with Atina and Venafrum perhaps *ca.*303; see *AASS*, Jun. 4:217–19 (*BHL*, #6073), *AASS*, Jun. 4:220–22 (*BHL*, #6074), and compare Ruinart, 570–73 (*BHL*, #6070–72). Traditions associated with this site are of somewhat doubtful value; see Harnack, 816. Hence one may contrast *BHL*, #5260, which reports martyrs of similar name in Egypt. *Martyrologium Romanum*, 17 June. Talbert, map 44.

Vettona? (in Umbria; modern Bettona.) The *Passio Sancti Crispoliti* is set in the neighborhood of Vettona in the time of Emperor Maximianus; see *AASS*, Maius 3:22–25 (*BHL*, #1800). The document appears to date to the Seventh Century, but may be based on earlier materials; see Dufourcq, 3:138–40. Harnack lists the site, but Lanzoni, 427–34, doubts. Talbert, map 42.

Dioecesis of Italy

Bibliography
AASS
AB
AÉ
Agnellus
Ambrose of Milan, *Epistulae*
Ambrose of Milan, *Expositio evangelii secundum Lucam*
Athanasius, *Apologia contra Arianos*
Athanasius, *Apologia ad Constantium*
Athanasius, *Epistula ad easdem*
Athanasius, *Historia Arianorum*
Atlas
Augustine, *Breviculus*
Augustine, *Contra Cresconium*
BHL
Bovini
Bratož
Cappelletti
Catal. Brux.
Catalogus archiepiscoporum Mediolanensium
CIL
Concilia Galliae
Cuscito, *Martiri*
Cuscito, "Questioni"
Cuscito, "Vescovi"
Datiana Historica Ecclesiae Mediolanensis
Deichmann, *Repertorium*
EnECh
Epistula ad Mareoticas ecclesias
Frend, *Donatist Church*
Gaudentius of Brescia, *Ad benivolum praefatio*
Gaudentius of Brescia, *Tractatus*
Gaudentius of Brescia?, *Ad laudem beati Filastrii Episcopi*
Gerke
Gesta conlationis Carthaginiensis, Capitula Gestorum
Gregori
Harnack
Hilary, *Decretum*

Hilary, *Epistula*
Hilary, *Liber I ad Constantium*
ILCV
Jerome, *Epistulae*
Jerome, *De viris inlustribus*
Joannou
Koch
Kollwitz
Lanzoni
Laudes Veronensis Civitatis (Versus de Verona)
Martyrologium Hieronymianum
Mirabela Roberti
Montini & Valetti
OCD
ODCC
Optatus
Paulinus [the deacon] of Milan, *Vita Ambrosii*
Paulinus of Nola, *Carmina*
Peter Chrysologus, *Collectio Sermonum*
Potter
Prudentius
Rendic-Miocevic
RIS
Savio, "La légende"
Savio, *Gli antichi vescovi, Il Piemonte*
Savio, *Gli antichi vescovi, La Lombardia*
Series Patriarcharum Aquilegiensium
Snyder
Socrates
Sonje, "Il Complesso"
Sonje, "Sarcofagi"
Sulpicius Severus, *Chronicon*
Sulpicius Severus, *Vita Sancti Martini*
Talbert
Testini, *et al.*
Theodore of Mopsuestia, *Commentary on Paul*
Venantius Fortunatus, *Carmina*
Venantius Fortunatus, *Vita Sancti Martini*
Vitricius of Rouen
Wilpert, *I Sarcofagi*

Wilpert, "Die altchristlichen Inschriften Aquileias"
Zenonis Veronensis
Zovatto
Zucca

General
Dioecesis of Italy. The area covered in this section is the Diocletianic
Diocese of Italy, including Corsica, but excluding the Raetian provinces.
Sulpicius Severus, *Chronicon*, 2.32.1, comments on the religious situ-
ation *ca.*200. Harnack, 869, notes Ambrose, *Epistulae*, extra collec-
tionem 14.1, with regard to the organization of Aemilia and Venetia.
This is supported by the more general comment of Theodore of
Mopsuestia, *Commentary On Paul*, on I Timothy 3:8 (2:121–25), that
early bishoprics often covered very large territories. Note also Canon
4 of the Council of Nicaea on the election and elevation of bishops; see Joannou, 1:26. Athanasius, *Apologia contra Arianos*, 37.1, notes
the presence of bishops from Italy at the Council of Serdica in 343.

     Harnack, 870, cautiously suggests that Christianity may have come
into Northern Italy largely from the East—note, *e.g.*, the Eastern
names in the episcopal list for Ravenna. See also *EnECh.*, 419–22.

     There is no clear evidence for Christianity in Corsica before 325;
see Zucca, 195–208. Athanasius, *Historia Arianorum*, 28.2, does mention
bishops from Corsica at a time shortly after the Council of Serdica.

Specific sites
Aquileia. (in Venetia; modern Aquileia.) Three martyrs named
Catianus appear in *Martyrologium Hieronymianum*, 2 kal. Jun. and prid.
kal. Jun. They also appear, along with the martyr Fortunatus, in
Venantius Fortunatus, *Carmina*, 8.3.166. For reference to their martyrium, see Mirabelli Roberti, 631. The martyr Anastasius of Salona,
q.v. is sometimes associated with Aquileia.

     Bishop Theodorus and the deacon Agathon were at the synod of
Arles in 314 (where Aquileia was oddly counted as part of Dalmatia);
see *Concilia Galliae*, 14, 16, 17, 18, 19, 21, and Gaudemet, 58. Bishop
Fortunat(ian)us was at the Council of Serdica in 343; see Hilary,
Epistula, B.II.4.37. According to the episcopal lists, Theodorus is
counted as the fourth or fifth bishop and Fortunat(ian)us is counted
as the eighth bishop; see *Series Patriarcharum Aquilegiensium*. See also
further references to the various rescensions of this document in
Lanzoni, 2:875–85.

For the early church there, see Snyder, 73–75. *CIL* 5.1:1582 & 1617–1757a, and 5.2:8280, 8282, & 8986a. Koch, 264, #67 (=Deichmann, *Repertorium*, 2: #50), is a sarcophagus from the first third of the Fourth Century. *CIL*, 3:10934 (=*ILCV*, 3311) is an inscription from 336. See also, Wilpert, "Die altchristlichen Inschriften Aquleias," 49–58. *Atlas*, 4. Talbert, map 19.

Ariminum. (in Flaminia; modern Rimini.) Lanzoni, 2:706–11. A bishop named Gaudentius, of somewhat uncertain date, may have been active during the persecutions under Diocletian and Maximianus; see *AASS*, Octobris 6:467–72, and *BHL*, #3276. Bishop Stennius/ Stemnius was at the Council of Rome in 313; see Optatus, 1.23. Some clergy from Ariminum were apparently at the Council of Philipopolis in opposition to the Council of Serdica in 343; see Hilary, *Decretum*, A.4.1. *Atlas*, 4. Talbert, map 40.

Bergomum. (in Liguria; modern Bergamo.) The martyrs Firmus and Rusticus of Bergamo were killed at Verona; see *BHL*, #2030–2033. Another martyr, Alexander, is mentioned in a Sixth-Century document; see *BHL*, #275–76. An early Bishop Narnus is mentioned in *AASS*, Augustus 6:8–9. The name Viator, otherwise unidentified, appears in the list of Italian signatories to the council of Serdica; see Athanasius, *Apologia contra Arainos*, 50.1. The shrine of Narnus and Viator is mentioned in *AASS*, Octobris, 12:817. According to Lanzoni, 2:971–73, Viator is counted as the second bishop of Bergomum. Koch, 264 #68 (=Deichmann, *Repertorium*, 2: #21) is a sarcophagus from the first quarter of the Fourth Century. Talbert, map 39.

Bononia. (in Aemilia; modern Bologna.) The martyrs Vitalis and Agricola are mentioned by Vitricius of Rouen, 11, (PL 20:453) and (with Proculus) by Paulinus of Nola, *Carmina*, 21.429. See also *Martyrologium Hieronymianum*, 5 kal. Dec., for Vitalis and Agricola; 3 kal. Maius for Vitalis; and 3 non. Dec., for Agricola. The name Faustinianus, there otherwise unidentified, appears in the list of Italian signatories to the Council of Serdica in 343; see Athanasius, *Apologia contra Arianos*, 50.1. According to a later inscription recorded in Lanzoni, 2:783–85, Faustinianus figures as the second bishop of the place after a certain Bishop Zama. *ODCC*, 221. *Atlas*, 4. Talbert, map 40.

Brixia. (Colonia Civica Augusta Brixia in Venetia; modern Brescia.) Caecilian of Carthage was detained there following the Councils of Rome and Arles; see Optatus, 1.26; also *Gesta conlationis Carthaginiensis, Capitula Gestorum,* 476, 483 & 536. Further discussion in Augustine, *Breviculus,* 3.19.37–3.20.38, and *Contra Cresconium,* 3.69.80–3.71.83. For details, see Frend, *Donatist Church,* 156–57.

The episcopal list for Brixia counts the following early bishops: Anathlon, Clateus, Viator, Latinus, Apollonius, Ursicinus, Faustinus, and Filastrius; for the text, see Cappelletti, 11:546–50. For other references to the list, see *Datiana Historica Ecclesiae Mediolanensis,* p. 16, n. 2. Lanzoni, 2:957–69, notes that the episcopal list counts Filastrius as the eighth bishop, but that *AASS,* Julius 4:389, and Gaudentius of Brescia?, *Ad laudem beati Filastrii Episcopi,* (PL 20:1005) clearly show Filastrius as the seventh bishop. Gaudentius, *Ad benivolum praefatio,* calls Filastrius "*patris nostri.*" Lanzoni therefore removes the name Anathlon from the list and counts Clateus as the first bishop, since the name Anathlon apparently belongs to Milan. See also Savio, "La légende," 46–47. The name Anathlon, may indicate, however, that Brixia was originally eccesiastically dependent upon Milan. Thus bishops would be known at Brixia from *ca.*300 onward.

A commemorative inscription is known for Bishop Latinus; see *CIL,* 5:4846. Bishop Ursacius/Ursicinus was at the Council of Serdica in 343; see Athanasius, *Apologia contra Arianos,* 48.2; Hilary, *Epistula,* B.II.4.50; and Athanasius, *Epistula ad easdem,* 30. On Filastrius, see also Gaudentius of Brescia, *Tractatus,* 16.8 & 21.1–15. For further information on bishops, see Gregori, 92 & 217–49, *passim.* For bibliography on the bishops, see Montini & Valetti. Martyr traditions for Brixia seem to be of a legendary character, see Lanzoni, 2:957–58. Bovini, 133, makes reference to a sarcophagus from the late Third or early Fourth Century. *Atlas,* 4. Talbert, map 39.

Faventia. (in Aemilia; modern Faenza.) Bishop Constantius was at the Synod of Rome in 313; see Optatus, 1.23. Bishop Constantius II was a contemporary of Ambrose; see Ambrose, *Epistulae,* liber 7, ep.36.27. Lanzoni, 2:769. *Atlas,* 4. Talbert, map 40.

Mediolanum. (in Liguria; modern Milan.) The martyr Victor is known from the Diocletianic persecutions; see Ambrose of Milan, *Expositio evangelii secundum Lucam,* 7.178. For the martyrdom of Nabor and Felix during the same persecution, see Ambrose of Milan, *Epistulae,* liber 10, ep.77.2. For further mentions of these martyrs, see Paulinus of Milan, 14.1; and *Martyrologium Hieronymianum*, 4 id. Jul.; prid. non. Maii; and 8 id. Maii. For other references, see *BHL*, #6028–29.

Catalogus archiepiscoporum Mediolanensium lists the first eight bishops as Anatalon, Gagius, Castricianus, Kalimerus, Monas, Mirocles, Maternus, and Protasius. Bishop Mirocles (counted as the sixth bishop) was at the Council of Rome in 313; see Optatus, 1.23. Mirocles was also at the Council of Arles in 314 with the deacon Severus; see *Concilia Galliae*, 14, 16, 17, 18, 19, & 21, also Gaudemet, 58.

Deichmann, *Repertorium*, 2: #247 is a sarcophagus of *ca*.300 from Lambrate near Mediolanum; see also Gerke, 341, and Wilpert, plate 252.2. *CIL*, 5:5592 (=*ILCV*, #1164), is the inscription of a certain Agnellus from 309–322. *ILCV*, #4957, is an early but undated inscription which may be Jewish. For other archaeological remains, see Cuscito, "Vescove," 737–41.

Bishop Protasius was at the Council of Serdica in 343; see Hilary, *Epistula*, B.II.4.51. See also Hilary, *Liber I ad Constantium*, 2.3(8), for references to Mediolanum in the middle of the Fourth Century. Lanzoni, 2:996–1013. For a hagiographic history of the first several bishops, see *Datiana Historica Ecclesiae Mediolanensis. EnECh*, 559. For more information, see Savio, *Gli antichi vescovi, La Lombardia. Atlas*, 4. *EnECh*, 559. Talbert, map 39.

Ravenna. (in Flaminia.) The first bishop was the martyr Apollonaris at Classis, the port of Ravenna; see *Martyrologium Hieronymianum*, 11 kal. Aug., and 10 kal. Aug., and also Peter Chrysologus, *Collectio Sermonum*, 128.1–3. The early names in the episcopal list seem to be basically reliable; see Agnellus, 1–19, for the text, and *EnECh*, 2:729–30, and *ODCC*, 28, for contrasting evaluations. The twelfth bishop in the list, Severus, was at the Council of Serdica in 343, so Christianity may have reached Ravenna by *ca*.200; for documentation, see Athanasius, *Apologia contra Arianos*, 50.1; Hilary, *Epistula*, B.II.4.49, and *Epistula ad Mareoticas ecclesias*. Lanzoni, 2:723–49. *OCD*, 1294. *EEC*, 2:972–73. Gerke, 278–81, plates 51,2, 57, 58.1–2, and Wilpert, plate 2.2, record a pre-Constantinian sarcophagus. For another sarcophagus, see also Kollwitz, 386–87. *Atlas*, 4. Talbert, map 40.

Verona. (in Venetia.) According to the episcopal list, the first bishop is said to have been a certain Euprepius, followed by Bishops Dimidrianus and Simplicius; see *Laudes Veronensis Civitatis (Versus de*

Verona), 14–15. Proculus, supposedly the fourth bishop, was said to have been a confessor; see *ibid.* For the account of the martyrdom of Firmicus and Rusticius of Bergomum at Verona, mentioning Proculus, see *AASS*, Mart., 3:450. For other martyrs at Verona, see *Martyrologium Hieronymianum*, 4 non. Aug. Bishop Luci[ll]us was at the Council of Serdica in 343: see Athanasius, *Apologia contra Arianos*, 48.2; Athanasius, *Epistula ad easdem*; and Hilary, *Epistula*, B.II.4.20. Luci[ll]us is counted as the sixth bishop in the episcopal list, but he is the first one to be known with certainty; see Lanzoni, 2:919–32, and *EnECh*, 2:863. See also Zenonis Veronensis; 1.10.5 & 1.12.1. *Atlas*, 4. Talbert, map 39.

Possible sites

Alba Pompeia? (in Alpes Cottae.) In connection with the synod of Milan in 355, Socrates, 2:32 &36.3, mentions Alba Pompeia as the "metropolis of Italy" and speaks of its Bishop Dionysius. Lanzoni, 2:829. Talbert, map 39.

Caesena? (in Flaminia; modern Cesena.) Some manuscripts of *Martyrologium Hieronymianum*, 12 kal. Aug., mention martyrs, though the manuscript tradition of the place name is uncertain. Accounts of bishops before the Seventh Century are unproven. Lanzoni, 2:714–21. Talbert, map 40.

Comum? (in Liguria; modern Como.) An early medieval document, *BHL*, #2922, mentions a martyr Felix under Maximianus; compare *AASS*, Octobris 12:563–64. Yet the chronology for this martyr Felix would seem to be confused, see Lanzoni, 2:975–78. It is certain, however, that the first known bishop, Felix, is addressed in Ambrose, *Epistulae*, liber 1, ep.5; and liber 7, ep.43. Talbert, map 39.

Cremona? (in Venetia; modern Cremona.) The first certainly known bishops dates to the middle of the Fifth Century, but the episcopal list would start *ca.*320; see Lanzoni, 2:944–56. Talbert, map 39.

Forum Cornelii? (in Aemilia; modern Imola.) The martyr Cassianus is commemorated in Prudentius, *Peristephanon*, 9:1–106. Cassianus also appears at *Martyrologium Hieronymianum*, 3 id. Aug., and id. Aug. The year of his martyrdom is uncertain, though presumably before 325; see Lanzoni, 2:774. Ambrose of Milan, *ca.*378–79, sent Constantius II of Faventia to visit the church at Forum Cornelii; see Ambrose, *Epistulae*, liber 7, ep.36.27. Talbert, map 40.

Forum Livii? (In Aemilia; modern Forli.) The account of Bishop Mercurialis found in *AASS*, Aprilis 3:763–65 (*BHL*, #5932), associates him with Bishop Geminianus of Mutina in the mid-Fourth Century. Lanzoni, 2:767–69. Talbert, map 40.

Forum Popilli? (in Flaminia; modern Forlimpopoli.) The legendary account of Bishop Ruffillus at *AASS*, Julii 4:381, associates him with Bishop Mercurialis of Forum Livii in the mid-Fourth Century. For another account, see *AB* 1 (1882): 112–18. For another mention of the place, see Agnellus, 140. Lanzoni, 2:721–23. Talbert, map 40.

Genua? (in Alpes Cottae; modern Genoa.) Koch, 265, #75 (=Deichmann, *Repertorium*, 2: #52), and Koch, 279, #255 (=Deichmann, *Repertorium*, 2: #181), are Christian sarcophagi from the first third of the Fourth Century. See also Wilpert, plate 267.4 (=Gerke, 346) for another Fourth-Century sarcophagus. Martyrs mentioned in connection with the place are either Roman or African; see Lanzoni, 2:834. Talbert, map 39.

Iulia Concordia? (West of Aquileia; modern Concordia Sagittaria.) Zovatto, 758, records a Fourth-Century martyrium, but there does not appear to be a literary tradition of martyrs from the place. Talbert, map 40.

Laus Pompeia? (in Liguria; modern Lodi.) Martyrdoms here are either unconfirmed or suspect; see Lanzoni, 2:992–93. Talbert, map 39.

Mutina? (in Aemilia; modern Modena.) The Tenth- or Eleventh-Century *Vita Geminianus* (*BHL*, #3296) links Geminianus (the second known bishop) to the time of Emperor Julian, and mentions Geminianus's immediate predecessor and successor; see also *Catal. Brux.*, 1:20. See also *AASS*, Jan. 3:711–15 (*BHL*, #3298). Agnellus, 14, links Geminianus with Severus of Ravenna who attended the Council of Serdica in 343.

Paulinus of Milan, 35.1, links the third known bishop, Theodulus, with Ambrose of Milan. Therefore, it seems unlikely that the first known bishop, Antoni(n)us, would have been active before 325; see Lanzoni, 2:790–93. Talbert, map 39.

Parentium? (in Istria; modern Poreč.) *BHL*, #5786, indicates that a certain Maurus was martyred at Rome under Numerian. His cultus developed early at Parentium; see *AÉ* 1997, #572. For excavations at the church there, see Sonje, "Sarcofagi," 490–93. Sonje, "Il complesso," 805–806, suggests that the present church may rest over a Third-Century *domus ecclesia*. See also Cuscito, "Questioni," 191–92; Cuscito, "Vescove," 741–49; Cuscito, *Martiri*, 111–29; Bratož, 2367 & 2373; and Rendic-Miocevic, 441–49. Testini, *et al.*, 174–77, point out the hypothetical nature of much research devoted to the career of Maurus at Parentium. *EnECh*, 544–45 & 651. Talbert, map 20.

Patavium? (in Venetia; modern Padua.) The martyr Justina is mentioned in Venantius Fortunatus, *Vita Sancti Martini*, 1.4 (vv. 672–73), and in Venantius Fortunatus, *Carmina*, 8.3.169. Bishop Crispinus is mentioned by Athanasius, *Apologia ad Constantium*, 3. Lanzoni, 2:911–12. *OCD*, 1121. Talbert, map 40.

Placentia? (in Aemilia; modern Piacenza.) The martyr Antoni(n)us appears at *Martyrologium Hieronymianum*, prid. kal. Oct. He is also mentioned in Vitricius of Rouen, 11 (PL 20:453). The first known bishop, Victor, appears only after 350; see Lanzoni, 2:813–15. Talbert, map 39.

Pola? (in Istria; modern Pula.) The martyr Germanus is mentioned at the time of Numerian in tradition; see *BHL*, #3482, and Cuscito, "Questioni," 195–98. Sonje, "Sarcofagi," 493–95, mentions a sarcophagus with a cross from the late Third or early Fourth Century. Testini, *et al.*, sound a cautionary note. Bratož, 2364 & 2376, mentions a house chapel in a villa of the first decade of the Fourth Century at Barbariza, some distance up the coast North of Pola. Talbert, map 20.

Ticinum? (in Liguria; modern Pavia.) Martin of Tours, who grew up in Ticinum, fled to the church as the age of ten (i.e. *ca.*326–29) and asked to become a catechumen; see Sulpicius Severus, *Vita Sancti Martini*, 2.1–3. Compare the comments of the anonymous historian of Ticinum as found in *RIS*, 11.1:15 & 22. The first known bishop of Ticinum, Severus, would not have been in place until about the middle of the Fourth Century; see Lanzoni, 2:981–86. *OCD*, 1525. Talbert, map 39.

Vercellae? (in Liguria; modern Vercelli.) Jerome, *Epistulae*, 1.3, and *De viris inlustribus*, 96, relates to Bishop Eusebius (a former lector from Rome) *ca.*355. For further details on Eusebius, see Savio, *Gli antichi vescovi, Il Piemonte*, 412–20. Attestation of the claimed martyr Theonestus is late; see Lanzoni, 2:1036. Talbert, map 39.

Vicetia? (in Venetia; modern Vicenza.) Venantius Fortunatus, *Carmina*, 8.3.165, mentions the martyr Felix, as does *Martyrologium Hieronymianum*, 19 kal. Sept., and *AASS*, Junii 2:456–57 (*BHL*, #2860). Episcopal traditions are vague before the Sixth Century. Lanzoni, 2:917–19. Talbert, map 40.

NORICUM

Bibliography
Alföldy, *Noricum*
Athanasius, *Apologia contra Arianos*
Athanasius, *Historia Arianorum*
Barton
CIL
DACL
Eckhart
Egger, "Bericht," in *Actes du Ve Congrès*
Egger, "Bericht," in *Atti del VI Congresso*
Harnack
Martyrologium Hieronymianum
Noll
Talbert
Ubl

General
Noricum. Athanasius mentioned unnamed bishops from Noricum at the Council of Serdica in 343; see *Apologia contra Arianos*, 37.1, and *Historia Arianorum*, 28.2. See also Noll, 47.

From the Fifth Century, Tiburnia (modern St. Peter in Holz; see Talbert, map 12) has Christian archaeological remains. Both Teurnia and Celeia (see Talbert, map 20) had bishops by the Sixth Century. Ubl, 298, 306–308, and Alföldy, 212. Christianity is not documented at Sabiona before the Sixth Century; see Harnack, 884, and *DACL*, 15.1:238–39.

Specific sites
Cetium. (modern St. Polten.) Florianus resided here before his martyrdom in 304; see *Passio Beatissimi Floriani martyris christi*, 2, in Noll,

27. Ubl, 328–29, notes the existence of small archaeological finds, possibly Christian, from a slightly later era. Barton, 125–29. Talbert, map 12.

Lauriacum. (modern Lorch.) The martyr Florianus suffered persecution there in 304; see *Martyrologium Hieronomianum*, 4 non maii, (Cod. Bern). Also *Passio Beatissimi Floriani martyris christi*, 2; see Noll, 26. Compare Barton, 125–29. Archaeological remains and small finds from the late Fourth Century are noted in Alföldy, *Noricum*, 281; Eckhart, 375–85; and Ubl, 300–301. See also Egger, "Bericht," in *Atti del VI Congresso internazionale*, 36. *Atlas*, 4. Talbert, map 12.

Possible sites

Aguntum? (Dölsach near modern Lienz.) Archaeological remains from the mid Fourth Century and later are noted by Alföldy, *Noricum*, 280, and by Ubl, 309–311. A bishopric existed there by the Sixth Century, see Ubl, 298. Talbert, map 19.

Lavant? (7.5 km from Lienz.) There is a church building with an apse dating perhaps to the first decade of the Fourth Century; see Egger, "Bericht," in *Actes du Vᵉ Congrès international*, 74. Talbert, map 19.

Ovilava? (modern Wels.) There is a funerary inscription from the Fourth Century for a Christian named Ursa, "*Ursa crestiana fidelis*," erected by her husband the soldier Januarius: see *CIL*, 3:13529; Noll, 45–47, Alföldy, *Noricum*, 281; and Ubl, 328. Talbert, map 12.

Virunum? (modern Zollfeld.) A Fourth-Century funerary inscription of Herodiana with the motif of the good shepherd has been noted. There are also archaeological remains of the late Fourth Century: see *CIL*, 3:4921; Noll, 44–45; Alföldy, 279; and Ubl, 304. Talbert, map 20.

Raetia

Bibliography
AASS
Atlas
Barton
BHL

Conversio et Passio Afrae
Dassmann
Gamber
EEC
Harnack
Martyrologium Hieronymianum
Talbert

Specific sites

Augusta Vindelicum. (modern Augsburg.) The martyr Afra died during the Diocletianic persecution. The details of her life are hazy, but the fact of her martyrdom on 5 August 304 seems certain; see *Martyrologium Hieronymianum*, non. Aug., & 7 id. Aug.; also 8 id. Oct.; and 7 id. Oct. See also *AASS*, Aug. II, 55–58, and *BHL*, #108–109. For the developing legend, see *Conversio et Passio Afrae*. Barton, 118–19. *EEC*, 23. Dassmann, 27–40. *Atlas*, 4. Talbert, map 12.

Castra Regina. (modern Regensburg.) A gravestone inscription of the Fourth Century reads "*in* A (chi-rho) Ω *b. m. Sarmann(i)ne quiescenti in pace mart(i)r(i)bus sociatae.*" This can be translated as "Sarmannina rests in peace and is united with the martyrs," thus suggesting that there were earlier martyrs in that place; see Gamber, 14–28. Barton, 118. Dassman, 41–42. *Atlas*, 4. Talbert, map 12.

GERMANIA (SUPERIOR AND INFERIOR)

Bibliography
AÉ
Ammianus Marcellinus
Arnobius
Athanasius, *Apologia contra Arianos*
Athanasius, *Historia Arianorum*
CIL
Concilia Galliae
Dassmann
Drack & Fellmann
Duchesne, *Fastes*
Duval, *et al.*

EnECh
Eusebius, *Ecclesiastical History*
Gaudemet
Gerke
Harnack
Heinemeyer
ILCV
Irenaeus, *Adversus haereses*
King
Martyrologium Hieronymianum
Nesselhauf & Lieb
Neuss
Neuss & Oediger
Nussbaum
Rheinisches Landesmuseum Trier
Schillinger-Häfele
Tertullian, *Adversus Iudaeos*
Wightman

General

Germania. In this section we included both Germania Superior
and Germania Inferior. Irenaeus, *Adversus haereses*, 1.10.2, mentions
churches planted in Germany. Tertullian, *Adversus Iudaeos*, 7.4, mentions the spread of Christianity among the Germans. In the latter
part of the Third Century, Arnobius, 1.16, is aware of Christians in
Germania. *EnECh*, 346–50.

Specific sites

Colonia Aventicum. (modern Avenches; in Germania Superior,
later in Maxima Sequanorum.) Two inscribed glass beakers of Christian
character found in the grave of a young women from the first half
of the Fourth Century read *"vivas in Deo"* and *"[pies] ze[sias]"*, have
a palm branch motif, and suggest an earlier Christian presence; see
Drack & Fellmann, 308 & 337–48. Talbert, map 18.

Colonia Claudia Ara Agrippinensium. (modern Köln/Cologne.)
Capital of Germania Inferior. Codex E of *Martyrologium Hieronymianum*,
commemorates Gereon and some 392 others as martyrs on 8 id.
Oct., presumably during the Diocletianic persecutions. Codices B
and W place the martyrs, somewhat fewer in number, at 7 id. Oct.

Other martyrs are mentioned at id. Oct. Bishop Maternus made a visit to Rome in 313 and was also at the Council of Arles in 314 with his deacon Macrinus: see Optatus, 1.23; Eusebius, *Ecclesiastical History*, 10.5.19; and *Concilia Galliae*, 15, 18, 20, 21.

Pieces of early Fourth-Century gold-glass with Biblical and Christian motifs have been unearthed, as have other objects suggestive of the beginnings of a Christian material culture; see Neuss & Oediger, 100–108. Rheinisches Landesmuseum Trier, #143c, describes one of these. See also *CIL*, 13:10025–216 & 10025–224. For another possible Christian inscription from nearby, see Schillinger-Häfele, #192a.

Athanasius, *Historia Arianorum*, 20.2, indicates that Emperor Constans sent Euphrates to inform the people of Antioch of the work of the Council of Serdica in 342. Euphrates was also ostensibly a subject of discussion at the Council of Cologne in 346; see Gaudemet, 70. Ammianus Marcellinus, 15.5.31, mentions a small chapel at Cologne in the mid-Fourth Century. There was also a Jewish community there in the era of Constantine; see Neuss & Oediger, 38. Dassmann, 108–111 & 176–81. *Atlas*, 4. Talbert, map 11.

Vesontio. (in Germania Superior, later in Maxima Sequanorum; modern Besançon.) *Martyrologium Hieronymianum*, non Sept., mentions martyrs at "Vesontione," but places it in Gaul. *CIL*, 13:5383, inscribed on a sarcophagus from the last quarter of the Third Century, contains a palm branch motif, the word "*virginiae*" and others that have been understood by some as indicative of Christianity; see Harnack, 882. Wightman, 286.

According to Duchesne, *Fastes*, 3:198–200, the first five bishops were Linus, Maximinus Paulinus, Eusebius, and Hylarius, who was a contemporary of the Emperor Constantine. The sixth bishop, Pancharius, was at the Council of Cologne in 346; see Gaudemet, 70. Dassmann, 24. Duval, *et al.*, 3:118, gives a list of bishops. *Atlas*, 4. Talbert, map 18.

Possible sites

Argentorate? (modern Strasbourg; in Germania Superior.) Duval, *et al.*, 3:20–21 records a glass beaker with the Akedah motif from the second half of the Third Century or the early Fourth Century. Bishop Amandus was at the Council of Cologne in 346; see Gaudemet, 70. Talbert, map 11.

Atuatuca? (In Germania Inferior; modern Tongres.) Harnack, 882, notes that Bishop Servatius was at the Council of Rimini in 359 and that Bishop Maternus of Cologne is also listed as the first Bishop of Tongres. From that he concludes that the church at Tongres was perhaps established while Maternus was bishop in Cologne. Dassmann, 109–111. *Atlas*, 4. Talbert, map 11.

Augusta Vaingiorum/Borbetomagus? (modern Worms.) Bishop Victor was at the Council of Cologne in 346; see Gaudemet, 70. Talbert, map 11.

Basilia? (in Germania Superior, later in Maxima Sequanorum; modern Basel.) Bishop Julianus "Rauricorum" was at the Council of Cologne in 346; see Gaudemet, 70–71, who locates Julianus at Basilia. Talbert, map 18.

Bonna? (in Germania Inferior; modern Bonn.) A late Fourth-Century church at Bonna rests on an earlier *"cella memoriae"* that may be as early as the late Third Century. A tradition known from 691–92 C.E. identifies those buried there as the martyrs Cassius and Florentius though it is not clear that Bonn was the place of their martyrdom; see Neuss & Oediger, 62–67. Dassmann, 140–48. Talbert, map 11.

Castrum Rauracense? (modern Kaiseraugst, just Northeast of Col. Augusta Raurica; in Germania Superior, later in Maxima Sequanorum.) There is a gravestone inscription with *"D.M. et memorie aeterne Eusstate . . ."* and an anchor motif, from the first half of the Fourth Century and probably Christian; see Nesselhauf & Lieb, #107, and compare Drack & Fellman, 309–310. There is also a roughly contemporary inscribed plaque with a Chi-Rho monogram, datable to 377 C.E, and remains of a church building from the Fourth Century; see Drack & Fellmann, 309–310 & 411–16. Talbert, map 18.

Colonia Ulpia Traiana? (in Germania Inferior; modern Xanten.) Christian graves dating to between 346 and 388 have been noted; see Dassmann, 150–51. A martyrium is known from not earlier than 348; see Neuss & Oediger, 84–86. Talbert, map 11.

Gelduba? (modern Krefeld-Gellep; in Germania Superior.) *AÉ*, 1966: #266 lists an inscription from the first quarter of the Fourth Century that may be understood as Christian. Talbert, map 11.

Mogontiacum? (Capital of Germania Superior; modern Mainz.) *CIL*, 13:11834, is a Third-Century inscription containing the words "*innocenti spirito*," perhaps indicative of Christianity. Bishop Martin's name is found in the list for the so-called Council of Cologne in 346; see *Concilia Galliae*, 27. He is possibly to be identified with the Gallic bishop Martin who attended the Council of Serdica in 343 but whose see is unidentified; Athanasius, *Apologia contra Arianos*, 49.1. Ammianus Marcellinus, 27.10.1–2, records that Rando, chief of the Alamanni, attacked the city during a Christian festival in 368. Heinemeyer, 7–11. Gerke, 306–307, 338, & plate 47.2, notes some sarcophagus fragments which may date to the first or second decade of the Fourth Century. Dassmann, 24 & 47–49. Talbert, map 11.

Novaesium? (modern Neuss; in Germania Inferior.) Nussbaum, 99–100, notes a cemetery at nearby S. Quirinus dating to the Third or Fourth Century with some apparently Christian graves. Dassmann, 156–57. Talbert, map 11.

Noviomagus/Nemetae? (modern Speyer.) Bishop Iessis was at the Council of Cologne in 346; see Gaudemet, 70. Talbert, map 11.

St. Aldegund? (Kreise Zell on the Mosel.) Nussbaum, 101, notes small finds from the first half of the Fourth Century that may be indicative of Christianity. Compare Talbert, map 11.

Gaul

Bibliography
AASS
Ado of Vienne
AÉ
Athanasius, *Apologia contra Arianos*
Atlas
Beraud Sudreau
BHL
Bromwich
CIL
Comité éditorial
Concilia Galliae

Cyprian of Carthage, *Epistulae*
Deichmann, *Repertorium*
Duchesne, *Fastes*
Duval, *et al.*
Eusebius, *Ecclesiastical History*
Eusebius, *Vita Constantini*
Fevrier, "L'archéologie"
Flodoardus Remensis
Gaudemet
Gauthier
Gauthier & Picard
Gelzer
Gerke
Gregory of Tours, *Gloria Confessorum*
Gregory of Tours, *Gloria Martyrum*
Gregory of Tours, *Historia Francorum*
pseudo-Gregory of Tours, *Passio Sancti Juliani Martyris*
Griffe
Guarducci, *Epigrafia*
Harnack
Hilary, *Epistula*
ICG
ILCV
Jerome, *De viris inlustribus*
Klauser
Koch
Lactantius, *De mortibus persecutorum*
Louis
Marrou
Martyrologium Hieronymianum
Martyrologium Romanum
Musurillo
Noy
Optatus
Paulinus of Nola, *Epistulae*
Peraté
Perpetuus, *De Vigilis*
Prudentius, *Peristephanon*
Rheinisches Landesmuseum Trier
Rivet

Rizzardi
Sulpicius Severus, *Chronicon*
Sulpicius Severus, *Dialogus*
Sulpicius Severus, *Vita Sancti Martini*
Talbert
Thouvenot, "Fouilles"
Van der Straeten
Venantius Fortunatus, *Carmina*
Venantius Fortunatus, *Vita Sancti Martini*
Versus de episcopis Mettensis civitatis Quomodo Sibi ex ordine successerunt
Vita Lupi episcopi Trecensis
Ward Perkins
Weidemann
Wightman
Wilpert, *I Sarcofagi*

General

Gaul. Included in this section are the Alpine Provinces. Corsica is treated with the Dioecesis of Italia. See Bromwich, 6–13, on the vitality of Roman life in Southern Gaul. Wightman, 282–99, notes the continuing strength of pagan influence. Indeed, the prevalence of tribal names alongside Roman names would seem to suggest continuity with the old, pre-Roman, way of life. At the Synod of Turin in 398, Proculus of Marseilles spoke of continuing efforts to organize the church in Gaul; see *Concilia Galliae*, 54–55; also Gaudemet, 138 & 139. The account of the seven missionary bishops recorded by Gregory of Tours, *Historia Francorum*, 1.30, is legendary, but may be useful for the period before 325 when supported by other evidence. Sulpicius Severus, *Chronicon*, 2.32.1–6, discusses the late introduction of Christianity into Gaul. He also mentions the persecutions in Gaul under Marcus Aurelius. Eusebius, *Ecclesiastical History*, 8.13.13, says that Constantius I declined to destroy churches in Gaul, though Lactantius, *De mortibus persecutorum*, 15, says Constantius destroyed churches but did not harm people. Eusebius, *Vita Constantini*, 1.16.17, suggests that Constantius may have leaned toward monotheism. See also Optatus, 1.22; on Constantius. For a listing of martyrs from Gaul, see Griffe, 1:143–44.

The list of bishops for the Council of Cologne in 346 is regarded as genuinely related to that era, though the acts of the council are of dubious authenticity; see Gaudemet, 68–69.

I here treat Gallia Narbonensis as a single entity before its division into Narbonensis I, Narbonensis II, and Viennensis.

Specific sites

Apta Iulia. (in Gallia Narbonensis; modern Apt.) The presbyter Romanus and the exorcist Victor were at the Synod of Arles in 314; see *Concilia Galliae*, 14, and Gaudemet, 60. Duchesne, *Fastes*, 1:281–83. Gauthier & Picard, 2:32. *Atlas*, 4. Talbert, map 15.

Arverni. (in Aquitania; modern Clermont-Ferrand in Auvergne.) Duchesne, *Fastes*, 2:31. Gregory of Tours, *Historia Francorum*, 1.30 & 1:44–46, mentions the evangelist Stremonius and the Bishop Urbicus, who in his reckoning would be contemporary with the Decianic persecutions. *Martyrologium Hieronymianum*, 12 & 8 kal. Feb.; 8 id. Feb.; 11, 10, & 5 kal. Sept.; 8, 7, & 6 kal. Oct.; and 4 id. Dec. lists commemorations of martyrs there. Koch, 262, #26; and 268, #116–117, lists sarcophagi of Constantinian date. *Atlas*, map 4. Talbert, map 17.

Atura/Vicus Iulii. (in Aquitania/Novempopula; modern Aire sur l'Adour.) A sarcophagus dating to *ca*.300 and bearing Christian motifs has been found; see Wilpert, *I Sarcofagi*, plate 65.5; Gerke, 338 & 378; Klauser, 164; and Koch, 240. See also Wilpert, *I Sarcofagi*, plate 175.3 & 4. Talbert, map 25.

Augusta Suessionum. (in Gallia Belgica; modern Soissons.) Flodoardus Remensis, 1.3, indicates that Soissons was originally ecclesiastically dependent upon Reims and names Divitianus as the first independent Bishop of Soissons. According to the episcopal list in Duchesne, *Fastes*, 3:88–92, Mercurianus was the fourth bishop. Bishop Mercurianus is listed among the signatories to the Council of Serdica in 343 and as present at the Council of Cologne in 346; see Athanasius, *Historia contra Arianos*, and Gaudemet, 70. *Martyrologium Hieronymianum*, 6 id. Jun.; 18 kal. Jul.; and 8 kal. Nov. lists commemorations of martyrs. Wightman, 287, rejects the martyr traditions. The *Life of Onesimus*, the fifth bishop, mentions bishops Rufinus, Filanus, and Mercurianus; see *AASS*, Maii, 3:204. *Atlas*, 4. Talbert, map 11.

Augustodunum. (in Gallia Lugdunensis; modern Autun.) Artifacts are known from the latter part of the Third Century; see Graillot; 47–56. Especially interesting is the metrical inscription of Pectorius: see *DACL*, 2:3194–98; Guarducci, *Epigrafia*, 487–94, #1; and Gauthier

& Picard 4:43. See also Griffe, 1:80–82. According to a tradition recorded in *AASS*, Augusti, 4:496–97, the youth Symphorianus was martyred in the late Third Century under Aurelian, though the fact of a persecution under Aurelian is doubtful; see Van der Straeten, 117–18 & 124–25. For other martyr reports, see *Martyrologium Hieronymianum*, kal. Jan.; non Maii; & id. Maii.

Bishop Reticius was summoned to the Synod of Rome in 313; see Eusebius, *Ecclesiastical History*, 10.5.19; Optatus, 1.23; and Jerome, *De viris inlustribus*, 82. In the following year he was at the Council of Arles with his presbyter and deacon; see *Concilia Galliae*, 14, 16, 18, 20, & 21, and Gaudemet, 60. Bishop Simplicius is listed among the signatories in support of the Council of Serdica in 343 and as present at the Council of Cologne in 346; see Athanasius, *Apologia contra Arianos*, 49.1, and Gaudemet, 70. See also Gauthier & Picard, 4:41. Duval, *et al.*, 3:69, suggests that a mausoleum there may date to the early Fourth Century. *Atlas*, 4. Talbert, map 18.

Autessiodurum. (in Gallia Lugdunensis; modern Auxerre.) According to *Martyrologium Hieronymianum*, 3 non. Maii, the lector Iuvenianus suffered martyrdom. Bishop Valerianus is mentioned in the list of signatories to the Council of Serdica in 343, and in the list of bishops at the Council of Cologne in 346; see Athanasius, *Apologia contra Arianos*, 49.1, and Gaudemet, 70. Later episcopal lists name Marcellianus as the predecessor of Valerianus; see Duchesne, *Fastes*, 2:430–52. Louis, 12, would date Marcellianus to *ca*.306–335. Peregrinus, Marcellianus, and Valerianus are respectively commemorated in *Martyrologium Hieronymianum* at 17 kal Jun.; 3 id. Maii; and prid. non. Maii. By the time the Seventh-Century *Vita* of Peregrinus was composed, Peregrinus was said to have been an envoy of Pope Sixtus II (*ca*.257–58) and also the first bishop of Auxerre; see *AASS*, Maii, 3:560–61 (*BHL*, #6623). See also Gauthier & Picard, 8:53. *Atlas*, 4. Talbert, map 14.

Burdigala. (in Aquitania; modern Bordeaux.) Bishop Orientalis and the deacon Flavius were at the Council of Arles in 314; see *Concilia Galliae*, 15, 16, 18, 20, & 21, and Gaudemet, 60. *CIL*, #13.633 (=*ILCV*, #4445a), is a possible Christian inscription from 258; see Gauthier, 24–25. Beraud Sudreau, 375, mentions a First-Century Arretine ware vase with the word Chrystus apparently inscribed later. *Atlas*, 4. Talbert, map 14.

Cemenelum. (in Alpes Maritimae; modern Cimiez, about 3 km from the center of Nice.) A certain Pontius is said to have been martyred on 14 May under Valerian; see *BHL*, #6896–97. The shrine of Pontius at Cimiez has been dated to the late Fourth Century; see Gauthier & Picard, 84–85. For the list of bishops, see Duchesne, *Fastes*, 1:295–96. For later episcopal buildings, see Duval, *et al.*, 1:103–108. Talbert, map 16.

Civitas Gabalum/Anderitum. (in Aquitania, the Gevaudan region; modern Javols.) The deacon Genialis represented the city at the Synod of Arles in 314; see *Concilia Galliae*, 15, 16, 18, 20 & 21, and Gaudemet, 60. Also; Gauthier & Picard, 6: 82–83. Duchesne, *Fastes*, 2:54–55. *Atlas*, 4. Talbert, map 17.

Colonia Arausio. (in Gallia Narbonensis; modern Orange.) The presbyter Faustinus was at the Synod of Arles in 314; see *Concilia Galliae*, 14, 16, 18, 19, & 21, & Gaudemet, 58. Bishop Diclopetus was at the Council of Cologne; see Gaudemet, 70. Also Gauthier & Picard, 3:96. Duchesne, *Fastes*, 1:265–66. Duval, *et al.*, 2:79. *Atlas*, 4. Talbert, map 15.

Colonia Arelate. (in Gallia Narbonensis; modern Arles.) Bishop Marcianus was accused by Cyprian of Carthage, *Epistulae*, 68, of having Novatianist sympathies. Prudentius, *Peristephanon*, 4.35–36, mentions the martyr Genesius. See also Griffe, 1:84–86. Gregory of Tours, *Historia Francorum*, 1.30, records the legend of the Bishop Trophimus at the time of Decius. The Bishop Marinus was summoned to the Synod of Rome in 313; see Eusebius, *Ecclesiastical History*, 10.5.19, and Optatus, 1.23. In the following year, Marinus, the presbyter Salamas, and several deacons represented the church at the Council held at Arles in 314; see *Concilia Galliae*, 14, 16 18, 19, & 21, and Gaudemet, 58. Bishop Valentinus was a signatory to documents in support of Athanasius at the time of the Council of Serdica in 343; see Athanasius, *Apologia contra Arianos*, 49.1. Bishop Valentinus also represented the city at the Council of Cologne in 346; see Gaudemet, 70. *CIL*, 12:831, 833, 834, 850, 878, & 964, are possibly, but not necessarily, Christian inscriptions from before the Constantinian era. Koch, 262, #24; 266, #88; 268, #110–13; 272, #184–86; 277, #236; and 279, #252, are all Christian sarcophagi from at least as early as the Constantinian era. Compare Deichmann, *Repertorium*, 2: #36–37. Gerke, 346, 351, 357, & 368, notes other possibly early Christian sarcophagi. Gauthier & Picard, 3:79. Duchesne, *Fastes*, 1:249–62. Duval, *et al.*, 1:118–20. *Atlas*, 4. Talbert, map 15.

Colonia Augusta Treverorum. (in Gallia Belgica; modern Trier.) Bishop Agricius and the exorcist Felix were at the Synod of Arles in 314; see *Concilia Galliae*, 15, 16, 18, 20 & 21, & Gaudemet, 60. Agricius is fourth (after Eucherius, Maternus, and Maternus) in the episcopal list for Trier published by Duchesne and regarded by him as having some value; see Duchesne, *Fastes*, 3:30–32, & Gauthier, 457. Bishop Maximinus was a signatory in support of the Council of Serdica in 343; see Athanasius, *Apologia contra Arianos*, 49.1. He was also present at the Council of Cologne in 346; see Gaudemet, 70.

   Coin finds in conjunction with the Southern basilica suggest a foundation date of *ca.*321; see Gauthier & Picard, 1:21–22. Noy, #1.226, is an inscription which has been classed as Jewish or Christian, though without certain evidence. Deichmann, *Repertorium*, 2: #420–21, are locally made sarcophagi from *ca.*300. Gerke, 300–306, 338, & plate 47.1, lists other possible Christian sarcophagi. Rheinisches Landesmuseum Trier, #33b, found at Ruwer near Trier, is a probably Christian ring from the first half of the Fourth Century. Wightman, 290. *Atlas*, 4. Talbert, map 11.

Colonia Dea Vocontiorum. (in Gallia Narbonensis; modern Die.) Bishop Nicasius was at the Council of Nicaea; see Gelzer, lxiv. Also Gauthier & Picard, 3:66. Koch, 274, #205, records a sarcophagus of Constantinian date. Duchesne, *Fastes*, 1:233–35. *Atlas*, 4. Talbert, map 17.

Colonia Lugdunum. (in Gallia Lugdunensis; modern Lyon.) Eusebius, *Ecclesiastical History*, 5.1, mentions the first Bishop Potheinus, as does Irenaeus who wrote his *Adversus haereses* from Lyon. The *Martyrs of Lyon* is an important source for local martyrdoms *ca.*170; see Eusebius, *Ecclesiastical History*, 5.1.3–5.2.8; also Musurillo, 62–85. Guarducci, *Epigrafia*, 494, #2, records the epitaph of the missionary Euteknios, a native of Laodicea in Syria, from this era. Cyprian of Carthage, *Epistulae*, 63.1, mentions Bishop Faustinus *ca.*254. The city was represented at the Council of Arles in 314 by Bishop Vosius and the exorcist Petulianus; see *Concilia Galliae*, 15, 16, 18, 20 & 21, and Gaudemet, 60. Also Gauthier & Picard, 4:22. The earliest dated Christian inscription is claimed to be *CIL* 13:2351 (=*ICG*, 62 =*ILCV*,

3029), which dates to 334. Hilary, *Epistula*, B.II.4, records Bishop Verissimus of Lyon as present at the Council of Serdica in 343. Gregory of Tours, *Gloria Confessorum*, 61, mentions Bishop Helius. Duchesne, *Fastes*, 2:157–74. *EnECh*, 280. *Atlas*, 4. Talbert, 17.

Colonia Narbo Martius. (in Gallia Narbonensis; modern Narbonne.) Prudentius, *Peristephanon*, 4.34, mentions the martyr Paul. Gregory of Tours, *Historia Francorum*, 1.30, dates him to the reign of Decius. See also *Martyrologium Hieronymianum*, 11 kal. Aprilis. Paul is variously identified as founder, bishop, or confessor of the church there; see Gauthier & Picard, 7:20. For the church built later in Paul's memory, see Duval, 1:39–42. For the list of bishops, see Duchesne, *Fastes*, 1:302–306. Koch, 268, #121, lists a sarcophagus of Constantinian date. Duval, *et al.*, 1:42. *Atlas*, 4. Talbert, map 25.

Colonia Valentia. (in Gallia Narbonensis [Viennois]; modern Valence.) *Martyrologium Hieronymianum*, 9 kal. Maii, lists as martyrs the presbyter Felix and the deacon Fortunatus. The same document, at 3 non. Oct., lists the Bishop Apollonaris. For the list of bishops, see Duchesne, *Fastes*, 1:215–25. *Atlas*, 4. Talbert, map 17.

Colonia Vienna. (in Gallia Narbonensis; modern Vienne.) The *Martyrs of Lyon* in which the deacon Sanctus of Vienne is mentioned, is one of the earlier martyrological documents, dating from *ca.*170; see Eusebius, *Ecclesiastical History*, 5.1.3 & 17; also Musurillo, 62–85. The later chronicler Ado of Vienne, col. 83, also mentions the incident. In the early years, the church at Vienne was probably dependent upon Lyon; see Gauthier & Picard, 3:24–25. *Martyrologium Hieronymianum*, 14 & 13 kal. Oct.; also 7 id. Oct. Bishop Verus and the exorcist Beclas were at the Synod of Arles in 314; see *Concilia Galliae*, 14, 16, 19 & 21, and Gaudemet, 58. According to the episcopal list published by Duchesne, *Fastes*, 1:148, Verus was the fourth bishop after Crescens, Zacharias, and Martinus. *Atlas*, 4. Talbert, map 17.

Durocatalaunum. (in Gallia Belgica; modern Châlons-sur-Marne.) Duchesne, 3:92–99. *Martyrologium Hieronymianum*, non. Aug., mentions the martyred Bishop Mimius and others. The Bishop Domitianus also appears in *Martyrologium Romanum*, 7 & 9 Aug. The first clearly datable bishops, Alpinus and Amandinus, appear in the Fifth Century; see Duchesne, *Fastes*, 3:92–99. *Atlas*, map 4. Talbert, map 11.

Durocortorum Remorum. (in Gallia Belgica; modern Reims.) Bishop Inbetausius and the deacon Primigenius were at the Synod of Arles in 314; see *Concilia Galliae*, 14, 16, 18, 20 & 21, and Gaudemet, 60. Inbetausius appears fourth on the list of bishops of Remorum; see Duchesne, *Fastes*, 3:77–81. Bishop Discolius was a signatory to the Council of Serdica in 343 and was present at the Council of Cologne in 346; see Athanasius, *Apologia contra Arianos*, 49.1, and Gaudemet, 70. Duval, *et al.*, 3:96. *Atlas*, 4. Talbert, 11.

Elusa. (in Aquitania; modern Eauze.) Bishop Mamertinus and the deacon Leontius were at the Synod of Arles in 314; see *Concilia Galliae*, 15, and Gaudemet, 60, where the reading "Elusa" of ms. C is to be preferred to the "Tolosa" of the other manuscripts. *Atlas*, 4. Talbert, map 25.

Limonum Pictavis. (in Aquitania; modern Poitiers.) Martyrs are noted in *Martyrologium Hieronymianum*, 18 kal. Feb, and 6 non. Oct. The first historically attested bishop is Hilary, who was deposed at the Council of Beziers in 356 for his anti-Arian activity; see *Concilia Galliae*, 31, & Gaudemet, 86. Duchesne, *Fastes*, 2:75–87. For Third- or Fourth-Century mosaics at nearby Locoteiacus (modern Ligugé), see Thouvenot, "Fouilles," 740. *Atlas*, 4. Talbert, map 14.

Lugdunum Convenarum. (in Novem Populi/Aquitania; modern St. Bertrand de Comminges.) At Valcabrère, only 0.6 km away, sarcophagus fragments with Christian motifs have been found dating to the first quarter of the Fourth Century; see Duval, *et al.*, 2:201. Koch, 265–66, #84, classifies the sarcophagus as Roman work. Yet scientific tests show that the marble came from a local quarry; see Comité éditorial, 123–24.

An inscription on another monument reads "*Val. Severa egit annos xxx recessit iii non Iul. Rufino et Eusebio conss. Pac. Patroculus praesbyter sibi in pace*" and bears a chi-rho symbol; see *ICG*, #596; and *CIL* 13: 299 (=*ILCV*, 272). Rufinus and Eusebius were consuls in 347, so, if the inscription was all carved at the same time, this could be the earliest use of the chi-rho in Gaul. See also Peraté, 165. Talbert, map 25.

Lutetia Parisiorum. (in Gallia Lugdunensis; modern Paris.) The martyrdom of Dionysius which Gregory of Tours, *Historia Francorum*, 1.30, attributes to the era of Decius is rather doubtful, though Harnack, 875 & 877, seems to give the tradition some credence.

Martyrologium Hieronymianum, 7 id. Oct., lists Dionysius as martyred along with a presbyter and a deacon. Commemorations of other martyrs are reported as well. Bishop Victurinus was a signatory to the Council of Serdica in 343 and was present at the Council of Cologne in 346; see Athanasis, *Apologia contra Arianos*, 49.1, and Gaudemet, 70. The list presented by Duchesne, *Fastes*, 2:464–69, counts Victurinus as the sixth bishop. Also Gauthier & Picard, 8:108. The relatively early attestation of bishops together with the martyr accounts may well suggest a founding date before 325 for the local Christian congregation. *Atlas*, map 4. Talbert, map 11.

Massalia. (in Gallia Narbonenesis; modern Marseille.) *CIL*, 12:489, with an anchor motif and the word "*refrigeret*," perhaps from as early as the Second Century, has been taken as Christian by some. Venantius Fortunatus, *Carmina*, 8.3.156, mentions the martyr Victor. Victor is also listed in *Martyrologium Hieronymianum*, 12 kal. Aug. Likewise by Gregory of Tours, *Gloria Martyrum*, 76. At *Historia Francorum*, 9.22, Gregory mentions the church built in Victor's memory. Duval, *et al.* 1:125–41, who suggest a date in the middle of the Third Century for Victor, also note the church, now known as the Abbaye Saint-Victor. Yet epitaphs claimed to be those of martyrs or other early Christians are uncertain; see Gauthier & Picard, 3:128; also Griffe, 1:76. Bishop Oresius and the deacon Nazareus were at the Synod of Arles in 314; see *Concilia Galliae*, 14, 16, 18, 19 & 21, and Gaudemet, 58. Duchesne, *Fastes*, 1:274–77. Koch, 270, #148, records a sarcophagus of Constantinian date. Duval, *et al.*, 1:138–39. *Atlas*, 4. Talbert, map 15.

Mettis/Mediomatricum/Divodurum. (in Gallia Belgica; modern Metz.) Bishop Victor is listed as a signatory to the Council of Serdica in 343 and among the attendees at the Council of Cologne in 346; see Athanasius, *Apologia contra Arianos*, 49.1, and Gaudemet, 70. According to the Eighth-Century *Versus de episcopis Mettensis*, 60–61, the name Victor was carried by the fifth and sixth bishops of Metz. Gauthier & Picard, 1:42, thus cautiously conclude that a Christian community was established at Metz prior to the peace of the church. Duchesne, 3:44–58. See also Griffe, 1:128. Duval, *et al.*, 3:239 & 250. *Atlas*, 4. Talbert, map 11.

Nicaea. (in Alpes Maritimae; modern Nice.) The deacon Innocentius and the exorcist Agapitus were at the Synod of Arles in 314; see

Concilia Galliae, 14, 16, 18, 19 & 21, and Gaudemet, 60. According to Athanasius, *Apologia contra Arianos*, 49.1, Bishop Nicasius of Nicaea was a signatory to the Council of Serdica in 343. See also Gauthier & Picard, 2:84–85. *Atlas*, 4. Talbert, map 16.

Rotomagus. (in Gallia Lugdunenis; modern Rouen.) Bishop Ausanius/ Avitianus and the deacon Nicetius were at the Synod of Arles in 314; see *Concilia Galliae*, 14, 16, 18, 20 & 21, and Gaudemet, 60. Bishop Eusebius was a signatory to the Council of Serdica in 343 and was present at the Council of Cologne in 346; see Athanasius, *Apologia contra Arianos*, 49.1, and Gaudemet, 70. According to Septimius Severus, *Dialogus*, 3.2, Bishop Vitricius was a contemporary of Martin of Tours. Paulinus of Nola, *Epistles*, 18 & 37, are addressed to Vitricius. Duchesne, *Fastes*, 2:201–212. See also Gauthier & Picard, 9:29–30. Duval, *et al.*, 3:325, mentions artifacts from *ca.*337–350. *Atlas*, 4. Talbert, map 11.

Vasio Vocontiorum. (in Gallia Narbonensis; modern Vaison.) Bishop Dafnus and the exorcist Victor were at the Synod of Arles in 314; see *Concilia Galliae*, 14, 16, 18 & 19, and Gaudemet, 58. Also Gauthier & Picard, 3:92. For the list of bishops, see Duchesne, *Fastes*, 1:262–63. *Atlas*, 4. Talbert, map 15.

Possible sites

Agedincum/Senonum? (in Gallia Lugdunensis; modern Sens.) Bishop Severinus was a signatory to the Council of Serdica in 343 and was at the Council of Cologne in 346; see Athanasius, *Apologia contra Arianos*, 49.1, and Gaudemet, 70. He appears on the episcopal list after Savinianus, Potentianus, and Leuntius. Neither the episcopal list for Sens nor the tradition of the tombs of Savinianus and Potentianus can be dated earlier than the Ninth Century; see Duchesne, *Fastes*, 2:395–415, and compare *BHL*, #7413–37. *Martyrologium Hieronymianum*, prid. kal. Jan.; 13 kal. Apr.; kal. Maii; 12 kal. Jun.; and 7 id. Sept., does list several martyr commemorations. *Atlas*, 4. Talbert, map 11.

Aginnum? (in Aquitania; modern Agen.) *Martyrologium Hieronymianum*, 5 id. Jun.; 2 non. Oct.; and 13 kal. Nov., respectively lists the martyrs Vincentius, Fi/edis, and Caprasius. See also Gregory of Tours, *Gloria Martyrum*, 104. There is reason to question each one of these martyr traditions; see Duchesne, *Fastes*, 2:144–46. Talbert, map 14.

Alba Helviorum? (in Gallia Narbonensis; modern Aps/Alba la Romaine.) The first bishop on the episcopal list is a certain Januarius; see Duchesne, *Fastes*, 1:235–39. After five bishops, the see was moved to Vivarium (modern Viviers). Since the second bishop of Viviers, Lucianus, was active in the late Fifth Century, it may be that Januarius was active before the middle of the Fourth Century. Talbert, map 17.

Apollinaris Reiorum? (in Narbonensis; modern Riez.) Just to the North, at Puimoisson, a possibly Christian inscription from the Third or beginning of the Fourth Century was found with the words "*Dis manibus Neroni civi Batavo memoriam et aeternalem vivus fecit;*" see *AÉ* 1976, #380, & 1986, #483. Talbert, map 16.

Articlavorum/Virodunum? (in Gallia Belgica; modern Verdun.) Bishop Sanctinus was at the Council of Cologne in 346; see Gaudemet, 70. He is named first on the episcopal list, which dates from the Ninth Century; see Duchesne, *Fastes*, 3:66–69. Gauthier, 460. Talbert, map 11.

Augusta Viromanduorum? (in Gallia Belgica; modern St. Quentin; the see was later moved to Noviomagus [Noyon].) The twelfth bishop in the episcopal list is Suffronius, whom Duchesne, *Fastes*, 3:99–100, dates to 511. Since, according to Duchesne, the first four names on the list are likely to be legendary, it is difficult to see how St. Quentin could have been an episcopal see before 325. Talbert, map 11.

Augustomagus/Castrum de Silvanectis? (in Gallia Belgica; modern Senlis.) The episcopal list is preserved on a Ninth-Century sacramentary. According to the episcopal list, the first bishop is said to have been Regulus; see Duchesne, *Fastes*, 3: 117& 147. He is said to have been a contemporary of Fuscianus and Victoricus of Ambianorum during the Diocletianic persecutions; see the *Vita Reguli* in *AASS*, Martius, 3:813–21 (*BHL*, #7106) and especially the extract from the *Passio* of Fuscianus and Victoricus at *AASS*, Martius, 3:814. Yet the first datable bishop is the ninth, Libanius, *ca.*511, so it seems unlikely that the see was established before 325; see Duchesne, *Fastes*, 3:115–17 & 147. Wightman, 287, also notes the difficulties with the episcopal list for Senlis. Talbert, map 11.

Autricum/Carnutes? (in Gallia Lugdunensis; modern Chartres.) Martyrs and confessors are mentioned by some witnesses to the tradition represented by the Epternacht Codex of *Martyrologium Hierony-mianum*, 7 id. Maii & 17 kal. Oct. The name Adventius appears first and fourteenth in the episcopal lists. The first name is followed by Optatus and Valentinus. Duchesne, *Fastes*, 2:422–24, dates Valentinus to *ca.*395, so if Adventius was indeed the first bishop, he would prob-ably have come to the episcopal office at some time after 325. See also Sulpicius Severus, *Dialogus*, 3.2, for an additional mention of Valentinus. Gauthier & Picard, 8:38. *Atlas*, map 4. Talbert, map 11.

Avaricum/Biturgae? (in Aquitania; modern Bourges.) Gregory of Tours, *Historia Francorum*, 1.31, records the tradition of an evange-list, said to have been one of the disciples of the seven bishops from the time of Diocletian. At *Gloria Confessorum*, 79, he identifies the evangelist as Ursicinus. The Ursicinus tradition lacks further confir-mation. Duchesne, *Fastes*, 2:21–22 & 26. *Atlas*, map 4. Talbert, map 14.

Baiocensium/Augustodurum? (in Gallia Belgica; modern Bayeux.) According to the episcopal lists, the first bishop was Exuperius, but the date is unknown; see Duchesne, *Fastes*, 2:212–22. This is confirmed by Wightman, 287. Talbert, map 11.

Bellovacorum/Caesaromagus? (in Gallia Belgica; modern Beauvais.) Duchesne, *Fastes*, 3:119–120, dates the thirteenth bishop, Maurinus, to *ca.*632, so it is just possible that Beauvais was an organized epis-copal see by 325. Talbert, map 11.

Brivas? (modern Brioude.) According to pseudo-Gregory of Tours, *Passio Sancti Juliani Martyris*, 4, the martyr Julian, connected with the late Second-Century martyrdoms at Colonia Vienna, was interred at Brivas, perhaps his hometown. See also *Martyrologium Hieronymianum*, 13 kal. Oct. Talbert, map 17.

Cabilonnum? (in Gallia Lugdunensis; modern Châlons-sur-Saône.) Bishop Donatianus was a signatory to the Council of Serdica in 343 and was present at the Council of Cologne in 346; see Athanasius, *Apologia contra Arianos*, 49.1, and Gaudemet, 70. Also, Gauthier & Picard, 4:70. Talbert, map 18.

Civitas Andecavorum/Iuliomagus? (in Gallia Lugdunensis; mod-ern Angers.) According to Sulpicius Severus, *Vita Sancti Martini*, 9.4–7, the first known bishop of Andecavorum was Bishop Defensor, who was present at Martin's consecration in 371. For the list of bishops, see Duchesne, *Fastes*, 2:347–56. Talbert, map 14.

Civitas Aurelianorum/Cenabum? (in Gallia Lugdunensis; modern Orleans.) Bishop Diclopetus was a signatory to the Council of Serdica in 343 and was present at the Council of Cologne in 346; see Athanasius, *Apologia contra Arianos*, 49.1, and Gaudemet, 70. See also Gauthier & Picard, 8:88. Talbert, map 14.

Civitas Lingonum/Andematunnum? (in Gallia Lugdunensis; modern Langres.) Bishop Desiderius was a signatory to the Council of Serdica in 343 and was at the Council of Cologne in 346; see Athanasius, *Apologia contra Arianos*, 49.1, and Gaudemet, 70. Also, Gauthier & Picard, 4:4:52. *Atlas*, 4. Talbert, map 18.

Civitas Namnetum? (in Gallia Lugdunensis; modern Nantes.) Duchesne, 2:360–71. The first bishop on the episcopal list, Clarus, is undatable, as is his successor Emius. The third bishop, Similianus, is mentioned by Gregory of Tours, *Gloria Martyrum*, 59. Compare also *Martyrologium Hieronymianum*, 16 June. The fourth bishop, Eumelius, may be the Eumerius of the Council of Valence in 374; see Duchesne, *Fastes*, 2:360–71. Talbert, map 14.

Civitas Turonorum/Caesarodunum? (in Gallia Lugdunensis; modern Tours.) Martin was consecrated as Bishop of Tours in 371 by an already established Christian community; see Sulpicius Severus, *Vita Sancti Martini*, 9.1. According to *Vita Sancti Martini*, 11.2, Martin had more than one predecessor as bishop. Perpetuus, *De Vigiliis*, mentions the three bishops Litorius, Martin, and Bricius. Gregory of Tours, *Historia Francorum*, 1.30 & 10.31.2–5, dates the beginning of their episcopates to 337, 371, and 397 respectively. At 10.31.1, Gregory prefixes to Perpetuus's list a Bishop Gatianus, whom he links with Saturninus and dates to the era of the Diocletianic persecutions. The existence of Gatianus is, however, suspect; see Gauthier & Picard, 5:27–28. See also Duchesne, *Fastes*, 2:283–312. Paganism was still lively in Martin's day; see Sulpicius Severus, *Vita Sancti Martini*, 13.1–9. See also Venantius Fortunatus, *Vita S. Martini. Atlas*, 4. Talbert, map 14.

Dinia? (in Narbonensis; modern Digne.) The *Vita Marcellinus*, 6, mentions the two evangelists Domninus and Vincentius, who would probably fall in the mid-Fourth Century; see *AASS*, Aprilis 2:749. Duchesne, *Fastes*, 1:290. Talbert, map 16.

Eburodunum? (in Alpes Cottae; modern Embrun.) The first known bishop is Marcellinus, who would have been consecrated by Eusebius of Vercelli around the middle of the Fourth Century; see the *Vita Marcellinus*, 5, in *AASS*, Aprilis 2:749. See also Duchesne, *Fastes*, 1:292. Talbert, map 17.

Exidualum? (modern Civaux, Southeast of Poitiers.) Possible Fourth-Century remains; see Duval, *et al.*, 2:276. Talbert, map 14.

Gratianopolis/Cularo? (in Gallia Narbonensis; modern Grenoble.) Bishop Domninus is mentioned *ca.*381 in *Vita Marcellinus*; see *AASS*, Aprilis 2:751. See also Duchesne, *Fastes*, 1:230–33. Talbert, map 17.

La Gayole? (in Narbonensis; near Brignoles.) Gerke, 265–71 & 337, identifies Wilpert, *I Sarcofagi*, plate 1.3, as a possibly Christian sarcophagus from just after 250 C.E. Koch, 20, 22, & 475, identifies it as pagan rather than Christian. See also Ward Perkins, 650, and Griffe, 1:75. Fevrier, "L'archéologie," 83. Talbert, map 16.

Lemovicum/Augustoritum? (in Aquitania; modern Limoges.) For the list of bishops, see Duchesne, *Fastes*, 2:47. Bishop Martialis was supposedly the first in the list of bishops and is mentioned by Gregory of Tours, *Historia Francorum*, 1:30, as being active about the time of Decius. The next bishop mentioned comes in the late Fourth Century. Talbert, map 14.

Martres-Tolosanes? (Just North of and across the river from villa Chiragan.) Duval, *et al.*, 2:175, makes reference to an early Christian necropolis with sarcophagi from the first third of the Fourth Century. Talbert, map 25, villa #94.

Mimatensis vicus/Mimas. (modern Mende.) *Martyrologium Hieronymianum*, 12 kal. Sept., mentions the martyr Privatius; see also Gregory of Tours, *Historia Francorum*, 1.34. Gauthier & Picard, 6:82–83, express doubt about the martyr tradition. The see of Gabalum was moved to Mende at a later date. Talbert, map 17.

Montpellier? (Southwest of Arles.) Koch, 268, #120 (=Wilpert, *I Sarcofagi*, plate 99.5), is a sarcophagus of Constantinian date. Compare Talbert, map 15.

Nemausus? (in Gallia Narbonensis; modern Nîmes.) A Christian sarcophagus originally from Nîmes and now at Avignon dates to *ca.*320–330: see Wilpert, *I Sarcofagi*, plate 209.2; Rizzardi, 59–61, #10; and Koch, 279, #253. Talbert, map 15.

Nerviorum? (in Gallia Belgica; territory of a tribe living just Northeast of Cameracum [modern Cambrai].) Superiorus of Nerviorum is mentioned by Athanasius, *Apologia contra Arianos*, 49.1, as a signatory to the Council of Serdica in 343, and also in the list of those present at the Council of Cologne in 346; see Gaudemet, 70. He had no known successor. Duchesne, *Fastes*, 3:110. Wightman, 287. Talbert, map 11.

Psalmodi? (about 30 km West-Southwest of Arelate.) Koch, 270, #149, lists a sarcophagus of Constantinian date manufactured at Rome. Talbert, map 15.

Samarobriva Ambianorum/Eumeianorum? (in Gallia Belgica; modern Amiens.) Eulogius of Ambianorum/Eumeinanorum was a signatory to the Council of Serdica in 343 and was present at the Council of Cologne in 346; see Athanasius, *Apologia contra Arianos*, 49.1, and Gaudemet, 70. For the episcopal list, see Duchesne, *Fastes*, 3:122–30. *Martyrologium Hieronymianum*, 3 id. Dec., speaks of the martyrs Fuscianus and Victoricus; for the later accounts pertaining to them, see *BHL*, #3224–29. See *AASS*, Mar. 3:814, for the tradition of their connection with Regulus of Augustomagus/Silvanectum. For their relics, see *AASS*, Januarii 1:704, n. 6. Talbert, map 11.

Santones/Mediolanum? (in Aquitania; modern Saintes.) *Martyrologium Hieronymianum*, 4 id. Feb., 8 id. Maii, 3 id. Maii, 5 kal. Sept., 8 kal. Nov., reports martyrs. Duchesne, *Fastes*, 2:72–75. *Atlas*, map 4. Talbert, map 14.

Sidoloucum? (Described as a vicus near Augustodunum; in Gallia Lugdunensis; modern Saulieu.) *Martyrologium Hieronymianum*, 8 kal. Oct., reports martyrs. Talbert, map 18.

Tarusco? (modern Tarascon; in Gallia Narbonensis.) Koch, 268, #123, lists a sarcophagus of the Constantinian era. Talbert, map 15.

Tolosa? (in Gallia Narbonensis; modern Toulouse.) Harnack, 877. The martyr traditions associated with the Bishop Saturninus and claimed by Gregory of Tours, *Historia Francorum*, 1.30, for the middle of the Third Century are not quite certain; see *Martyrologium Hieronymianum*, 3 kal. Nov., & 3 kal. Dec. Similarly, the martyrdom of Bishop Orontius listed at *Martyrologium Hieronymianum*, kal. Maii, is suspect. For an assessment of the reliability of these martyr traditions, see Duchesne, *Fastes*, 1:306–309. Many manuscripts of the lists of cities represented at the Synod of Arles in 314 read the name "Tolosa" in place of "Elusa;" *q.v. Atlas*, 4. Talbert, map 25.

Tournissan? (ancient name unknown; a few km Southeast of Carcaso [modern Carcassonne]; in Gallia Narbonensis.) Koch, 273, #187, records a sarcophagus of the Constantinian era found at Tournissan and now kept at Carcassonne; see also Rizzardi, 68–69, #13. Talbert, map 25.

Tricassium/Augustobona? (in Gallia Lugdunensis; modern Troyes.) Bishop Optatianus was a signatory to the Council of Serdica in 343 and was also at the Council of Cologne in 346; see Athanasius, *Apologia contra Arianos*, 49.1, and Gaudemet, 70. See also Gauthier & Picard, 8:74. *Atlas*, 4. Talbert, map 11.

Tullum? (in Gallia Belgica; modern Toul.) The fifth bishop on the episcopal list is dated to *ca.*472; see Duchesne *Fastes*, 3:58–66. It is thus hardly likely that a bishopric was established at Toul before 325. A Christian family, that of the later bishop Lupe of Troyes, is known from Tullum (Leuchorum) at about this time, see *Vita Lupi episcopi Trecensis*, 293 & 295. See also Gauthier, 103 & 461. Talbert, map 11.

Vintium? (in Alpes Maritimae; modern Vence.) Rivet, 342, notes the presence of early Christian funerary items. Talbert, map 16.

Vivarium? (in Gallia Narbonensis; modern Viviers.) Duval, *et al.*, 1:216–17, notes part of a sarcophagus found under the cathedral and datable to *ca.*325–350. Koch, 274, #213, dates it to the Constantinian era. Viviers had no bishop of its own until the middle of the Fifth Century, when the see was moved from Alba Helviorum; see Duchesne, *Fastes*, 1:235–39. Talbert, map 17.

BRITANNIA

Bibliography
Atlas
Bede
Collingwood & Wright
Concilia Galliae

Constantius of Lyon, *Vita Germani Episcopi Autissiodorensis*
Delehaye, *'In Britannia'*
EEC
EnECh
Ellison
Eusebius, *Demonstratio Evangelica*
Frend, *Archaeology*
Gaudemet
Gildas
Green
Harnack
Hassall & Tomlin, "Roman Britain in 1981"
Hassall & Tomlin, "Roman Britain in 1992"
Jones, Michael
Liber Pontificalis
Martyrologium Hieronymianum
Mawer
ODCC
Origen, *Homilies on Ezekiel*
Painter, "Fourth-Century"
Painter, "Recent"
Painter, "Villas"
Sulpicius Severus, *Chronicon*
Sozomen
Talbert
Tertullian, *Adversus Iudaeos*
Thomas, *Christianity*
Thomas, "Churches"
Turner, Robin
Watts
White

General
Britain. Tertullian, *Adversus Iudaeos*, 7.4, makes reference to Christianity in Britain. Origen, *Homilies on Ezekiel*, 4.1, refers to Christianity in Britain and among the Mauri. Eusebius, *Demonstratio Evangelica*, 3.5, also make mention of Britain. Sozomen, 2.6.1, mentions Christianity among the Celts, though he does not specify Britain. The somewhat dubious account of the conversion of Lucius is mentioned by *Liber Pontificalis*, 14, "Eleutherius," followed by Bede, 1.4. For other possible

martyrs, see *Martyrologium Hieronymianum*, 14 kal. Mart., 12, 7, & 5 kal. Jun., 5 kal. Aug., and 15 kal. Oct. For a critique of some of these, see Harnack, 680 & 685. Thomas, *Christianity*, 197, indicates the possibility that the list of signatories to the Council of Arles might conceal a bishop from an additional, unnamed, see. Sulpicius Severus, *Chronicon*, 2.1, says that at the Council of Ariminum in 359 three British bishops requested funds to cover their expenses at the council.

A variety of inscriptions have been found indicative of Christianity in the Roman period, but none of these can be dated securely before 325; among the more recent publications, see Hassall & Tomlin, "Roman Britain in 1992," 317–18. Mawer, 42–55, lists a number of spoons with Christian graffito from the late Fourth Century. Frend, *Archaeology*, 252–53, notes that Patrick's grandfather, who would have been living in the second half of the Fourth Century, was a Christian. Thomas, *Christianity*, 300–301, suggests that Christianity could have reached Ireland as early as *ca.*360. *EnECh*, 129–34. Delehaye, 'In Britannia,' 21, notes that none of the martyrs listed in *Martyrologium Hieronymianum* can be shown to go back to the earliest form of that document. Even Albanus of Verulamium, *q.v.*, is mentioned only in the Gallican rescension.

Specific sites

Colonia Lindum. (modern Lincoln.) Bishop Adelfius was at the Council of Arles in 314 along with the priest Sacerdos and the deacon Arminius; see *Concilia Galliae*, 15, 16, 18, 20, 22, and Gaudemet, 60. The list of signatories to the council reads "*Colonia londenensium*," which some have suggested should be emended to "*Camulodunum*," *i.e.* Colchester, rather than to "*Colonia Lindum*." Frend, 252, apparently favors Colchester, but Thomas, *Christianity*, 197, finds it unconvincing. A church with possible Fourth-Century elements has been excavated at Lincoln; see Watts, 119–22, and *EnECh*, 129. Yet note the later date suggested by Frend, *Archaeology*, 375. See also Thomas, "Churches," 142. Talbert, map 8.

Eburacum. (modern York.) Bishop Eborius was at the Council of Arles in 314; see *Concilia Galliae*, 15, 16, 18, 20, 22, and Gaudemet, 60. For some possibly Christian small finds, see Mawer, 77 & 86–87. *Atlas*, 4. Talbert, map 9.

Isca/Urbis Legionis. (modern Caerleon.) Gildas, 9.1 & 10.2, mentions the martyrdoms of Aaron and Julius, perhaps (as he says) during the era of Diocletian. Bede, 1.7, also mentions them. For the martyr tradition and for excavations there, see Thomas, *Christianity*, 48–50 & 168–69. Painter, "Villas," 149–50 suggests Chester or Carlisle as alternative sites for the martyrdoms. *Atlas*, 4. Talbert, map 8.

Londinium. (modern London.) Bishop Restitutus was at the Council of Arles in 314; see *Concilia Galliae*, 15, 16, 18, 20, 22, and Gaudemet, 60. *Atlas*, 4. Talbert, map 8.

Verulamium. (modern St. Albans.) Constantius of Lyon, *Vita Germani episcopi Autissiodorensis*, 16 & 18; Gidas, 9.1 & 10.2; and Bede, 7, all mention the martyr Albanus. Gildas tentatively dates him to the time of Diocletian, but he may have been martyred toward the middle of the Third Century; see Thomas, *Christianity*, 48–50, and *EEC*, 28–29. Note also the reference in *Martyrologium Hieronymianum*, 10 kal. Jul., but see Delehaye, '*In Britannia*,' 21. Thomas, "Churches," 142–43 & 147. Painter, "Recent," 2037. *Atlas*, 4. Talbert, map 8.

Possible sites

Appleshaw? (in Hampshire. No ancient name known.) Mawer 23 & 25, notes a pewter bowl with a chi-rho apparently abandoned before 350.

Aquae Sulis? (modern Bath.) An inscribed curse tablet with Latin cursive script of the Fourth Century discovered in the temple of Minerva Sulis brings imprecations against a thief "whether pagan or Christian," see Hassall & Tomlin, "Roman Britain in 1981," 404–406, #7; also Painter, "Recent," 2049–51; and Frend, *Archaeology*, 377. Mawer, 85, suggests a date in the late Fourth Century.

Collingwood & Wright, 1: #152, may also be pertinent as reflecting efforts to rebuild a pagan altar after attacks by Christian zealots; see Thomas, *Christianity*, 136. A presumed inscription mentioned in Harnack, 887, has proven to be nonsensical; see Collingwood & Wright, 1: #2349. Talbert, map 8.

Calleva Atrebatum? (modern Silchester.) Thomas, *Christianity*, 169 & 214–17, notes remains of a mid to late Fourth-Century church, perhaps with baptistry. See also Watts, 123, 129–30, & 144, and Thomas, "Churches," 142. For possibly Christian small finds, see Mawer, 70–71. Frend, *Archaeology*, 86. Talbert, map 8.

Cironium/Korinion? (modern Cirencester.) Thomas, *Christianity*, 101–102, 133, 182, 192, 197, 252, and 262, conjectures that the text for the Council of Arles in 314 should have Sacerdotus as presbyter, and Arminius as deacon; see also Gaudemet, 60–61. Watts, 144. *Atlas*, 4. Talbert, map 8.

Colonia Camulodunum? (modern Colchester.) Thomas, *Christianity*, 168 & 174–75, suggests the presence of Christian buildings of the late Fourth Century. Watts, 104 & 116, 122–23, & 144. Indeed, Michael Jones, 397 & 415, notes the presence of an extra-mural church with what may be a martyrium from *ca.*320–340. Thomas, "Churches," 141 & 145. Mawer, 37. *Atlas*, 4, takes Colchester rather than Lincoln (*q.v.*) as the city referred to in the list of signatories to the Council of Nicaea. Talbert, map 8.

Durnovaria? (Dorchester.) At nearby Poundbury, Painter, "Recent," 2048, reports a large cemetery with several apparently Christian burials going back to the Fourth Century. See also Green, 2073–75. Thomas, "Churches," 146. Mawer, 93–94, discusses some small finds. Talbert, map 8.

Durobrivae? (modern Water Newton.) A hoard of church plate buried *ca.*350, consisting of items dating to the late Third and early Fourth Centuries, was discovered in 1975. The history of its users, and whether the hoard may have been brought from elsewhere, is unknown, though it is suspected that the hoard may have been used locally. For further information, see Painter "Fourth-Century," 333–45; Thomas, *Christianity*, 113–22; and Painter "Recent," 2058. Mawer, 18 & 87–89, suggests caution with regard to the earliest dating. Talbert, map 8.

Durovernum Cantiacorum? (modern Canterbury.) Thomas, *Christianity*, 168 & 170–74, argues that the Cathedral, and also the nearby Church of St. Pancras, rest over Christian buildings of the late Fourth Century. See also Thomas, "Churches," 141 & 143–45; and Watts, 111–112, & 144. Bede, 1.26, refers to a late Roman church dedicated to St. Martin. Talbert, map 8.

Eccles? (in Kent; no ancient name known.) Painter, "Recent," 2051 & 2054, lists a curse tablet from the Fourth Century that may be Christian. Mawer, 85–86, identifies it as a pagan inscription. Thomas, "Churches," 157, records the discussion about whether the name

Eccles might be a holdover from a Roman place-name involving the latin word "Ecclesia." Talbert, map 8.

Frampton? (near Dorchester; no ancient name known.) A mosaic, of the mid-Fourth Century and probably Christian, was found in what was presumably a villa. The mosaic is now lost, but is reported in Thomas, *Christianity*, 181–83. See also Watts, 127–28; Thomas, "Churches," 148; and Frend, 351. Talbert, map 8.

Hinton St. Mary? (in Dorset; no ancient name known.) A mosaic floor, dating *ca.*340, with a head of Christ and chi-rho monogram has been discovered in a Roman villa; see Thomas, 181–83; Watts, 128; and Frend, 351. Talbert, map 8.

Icklingham? (in Suffolk, East of Mildenhall; no ancient name known.) Thomas, *Christianity*, 175 & 217–18, records a church and baptistry of the late Fourth Century. See also Watts, 116 & 144. Thomas, "Churches," 146. Mawer, 26. Talbert, map 8.

Littlecote (Park)? (ancient name unknown.) Thomas, "Churches," 148–49, notes a late Fourth-Century building with a possibly Christian plan. Talbert, map 8.

Lullingstone? (no ancient name known.) Mosaics and frescoes of a villa in use by Christians just after the middle of the Fourth Century; see Thomas, *Christianity*, 180–81; Thomas, "Churches," 147–48; White, 2:243–57; and Frend, 350–51. For small finds, see Mawer, 33–34. Talbert, map 8.

Rutupiae? (modern Richborough.) Thomas, *Christianity*, 1, 169, & 216–17, records a church and baptistry from *ca.*400. Watts, 103 & 144, indicates the presence of small finds. See also Mawer, 40 & 94, and Thomas, "Churches," 142. Frend, *Archaeology*, 86. Talbert, map 8.

Uley? (no ancient name known; in Southwest Gloucesterchire.) Thomas, 136, notes the possibility of a pagan shrine destroyed in the Fourth Century. For further information on the apparently Christian buildings that succeeded it, see Ellison, 310–14, and Watts, 105, 110–111, 124, 130–31, 141 & 144. Not included in the list of Frend, *Archaeology*, 376. Talbert, map 8.

Venta Belgarum? (modern Winchester.) A Fourth-Century tile inscribed with a chi-rho monogram has been found; see Hassall &

Tomlin, "Roman Britain in 1992," 316–17, #8. See also Painter, "Recent," 2031–34. Talbert, map 8.

Wells? (in Somerset, Southwest of Bath.) Painter, "Recent," 2034–35, notes a mausoleum of the Fourth Century that may in fact be a martyrium.

Witham? (in Essex, Southwest of Colchester.) Remains of a baptistry have been found nearby in succession to what appears to be a pagan shrine destroyed in the Fourth Century; see Thomas, *Christianity*, 104 & 219, and Robin Turner, 51–55 & 247–53. Also Watts, 106, 110, 124, 130–31, 140, & 143–144. Not included in the list of Frend, *Archaeology*, 376.

Hispania

Bibliography
AASS
Alföldy, *Die Römischen Inschriften*
Arnobius
Athanasius, *Apologia contra Arianos*
Athanasius, *Epistula ad easdem*
Atlas
Atlas de España
Augustine, *Sermones*
BHL
BS
I Clement
Concilia Galliae
Cyprian, *Epistulae*
DACL
EEC
EnECh
Epistula ad Mareoticas ecclesias
Gaudemet
Gelzer
Gomez
Harnack
Hauschild

Hilary, *Epistula*
Irenaeus, *Adversus haereses*
Keay
Koch
Lipsius & Bonnet
Martinez Diez
Martyrologium Hieronymianum
Martyrologium Romanum
Muratorian Canon
Musurillo
Paulinus of Nola, *Carmina*
Pliny the Elder
Prudentius
Soriano Sanchez
Sotomayor [y Muro], *Datos*
Sotomayor [y Muro], "Dos Fragmentos"
Sotomayor y Muro, "La Iglesia"
Sotomayor [y Muro], "Leyenda"
Sotomayor [y Muro], "Sarcofagos paleocristianos"
Sotomayor [y Muro], "Sarcofagos"
Sotomayor [y Muro], *Sarcofagos*
Talbert
Tertullian, *Ad Scapulam*
Tertullian, *Adversus Iudaeos*
Thouvenot, *Essai*
Viletta Masana
Villoslada

General

Hispania. With regard to Paul's proposed journey to Spain mentioned in Romans 15:23–29, we have an uncertain reference to the "limits of the West" in *I Clement*, 5.7. The *Muratorian Canon*, 38–39, more clearly attests the belief that Paul reached his goal in Spain. The earliest clear reference to Paul actually having accomplished the journey comes in the Third-Century *Acta Petri et Pauli*, 1; see Lipsius & Bonnet, 1:118. Sotomayor y Muro, "La Iglesia," 160–65.

Irenaeus, *Adversus haereses*, 1.3, writing *ca.*180–88, mentions Christians in Iberia. In the early Third Century, Tertullian, *Adversus Iudaeos*, 7.4–5, mentions Christians having reached all the borders of the Hispanic provinces, *"Hispaniarum omnes termini."* Arnobius, 1.16, mentions

Christians in Hispania. Sotomayor y Muro, "La Iglesia," 40–41. For locations of churches represented at the Council of Elvira (Iliberri) in the first decade of the Fourth Century, see Sotomayor y Mura, "La Iglesia," 90–92. For the date of the Council, see *EnECh*, 270, and *EEC*, 370. Athanasius, *Apologia contra Arianos*, 37.1, notes the presence of bishops from Hispania at the Council of Serdica in 343.

According to Sotomayor y Muro, "La Iglesia," 136–142, the most ancient Christian artifacts known from Hispania are sarcophagi, 32 of which date from Constantinian or pre-Constantinian times (*i.e.* *ca.*300–340) and show signs of having been imported from Roman workshops. He does not note any church building from before the mid-Fourth Century.

Viletta Masana, 1256–58, lists Christian correspondence to and from Spain between *ca.*300 and 408. Sotomayor y Muro, "La Iglesia," 158, notes that an episcopal list for Iliberri, Hispalis, and Toletum (codex Emilianensis) was drawn up in 962. The tradition of Santiago is of no use for the history of our period; see Sotomayor y Muro, "La Iglesia," 150–51.

Specific sites

Acci. (Colonia Julia Gemella Acci in Carthaginiensis; modern Gaudix in Granada.) The local Christian community was represented at the Council of Elvira by Bishop Felix; see Martinez Diez, 239. *Atlas*, 4. Talbert, map 27.

Acinippo. (in Baetica; modern Ronda la Vieja.) The presbyter Leo represented the local Christians at the Council of Elvira; see Martinez Diez, 240. *Atlas*, 4. Talbert, map 26.

Aiune/Iune. (in Baetica; ancient Urgao/Vircao; modern Arjona near Jaén; see Sotomayor y Muro, "La Iglesia," 92.) Represented at the Council of Elvira by presbyter Titus; see Martinez Diez, 241. *Atlas*, 4. Talbert, map 27.

Alauro. (in Baetica; possibly Iluro, which would be modern Alora; see Sotomayor y Muro, "La Iglesia," 91, and Talbert, map 26, coordinate F5. Talbert, map 26, coordinate F4 also lists a Lauro [modern Cerro de Hachillo].) The presbyter Ianuarius of Alauro represented the local Christians at the Council of Elvira; see Martinez Diez, 240.

Astigi/Advingi. (Colonia Astigi Augusta Firma in Baetica; present Écija.) Represented at the Council of Elvira by presbyter Barbatus; see Martinez Diez, 240. *Atlas*, 4. Talbert, map 26.

Asturica Augusta. (in Galaecia; modern Astorga.) Cyprian, *Epistulae*, 67, wrote *ca.*250 "to the people of Asturica" and others to give instructions for dealing with Basilides and Martialis, who had apostasized in the Decianic persecution. At the time of the Council of Elvira, Legio and Asturica may have formed a single episcopal see; see Sotomayor y Muro, "La Iglesia," 42, 70–72, 90–91, 203. There is a sarcophagus from *ca.*305–312 with motifs of the resurrection of Lazarus, arrest of Peter, Adam and Eve, multiplication of loaves and fishes, and the sacrifice of Isaac; see Sotomayor y Muro, *Sarcofagos*, 11, 47–54. Represented at the Council of Serdica in 343 by Bishop Domitianus; see Athanasius; *Apologia contra Arianos*, 48.2; Hilary, *Epistula*, B.II.4.4; and *Epistula ad Mareoticas ecclesias*. *Atlas*, 4. Talbert, map 24.

Ategua. (in Baetica; modern Cortijo de Teba la Vieja.) Represented at the Council of Elvira by presbyter Felicissimus; see Martinez Diez, 240. *Atlas*, 4. Talbert, map 27.

Baecula. (in Baetica; probably modern Bailén.) A presbyter Sabinus of "civitas Betica" was at the Council of Arles in 314; see *Concilia Galliae*, 15, 18, 20, 22 & 233; and Gaudemet, 62–63. *Atlas*, 4, apparently takes this as a reference to the city of Baecula. According to *Concilia Galliae*, 16, one manuscript identifies Sabinus as a bishop; if such is the case he could well have been the same person as the bishop of Hispalis, *q.v.* Talbert, map 27.

Barba. (in Baetica; evidently Singilia Barba; modern Cortijo del Castillón.) Represented at the Council of Elvira by presbyter Ianuarianus; see Martinez Diez, 240. *Atlas*, 4. Talbert, map 26.

Baria. (in Carthaginiensis, formerly Baetica; modern Villaricos near Vera.) Represented at the Council of Elvira by presbyter Emeritus; see Martinez Diez, 241. *Atlas*, 4. Talbert, map 27.

Basti(gensium). (in Carthaginiensis, formerly Tarraconensis and Baetica; modern Baza.) Represented at the Council of Elvira by Bishop Euticianus; see Martinez Diez, 240. Represented at the Council of Arles in 314 by presbyter Getnesius and lector Victor; see *Concilia Galliae*, 15, 17, 19, 20, & 22; and Gaudemet, 62–63. Sotomaytor y Muro, "La Iglesia," 195. *Atlas*, 4. Talbert, map 27.

Calagurris (Nassica) Iulia. (modern Calahorra.) For the martyrs Emeterius and Chelidonius, see Prudentius, *Peristephanon*, 1. They possibly belonged to a detachment of the Legio VII Gemina stationed in Calagurris; see Sotomayor y Muro, "La Iglesia," 70–71. *Atlas*, 4. Talbert, map 25.

Carbula/Carula. (in Baetica; probably modern Almodóvar del Rio.) Represented at the Council of Elvira by presbyter Lamponianus; see Martinez Diez, 240. *Atlas*, 4. Talbert, map 26.

Carthago Nova. (Colonia Urbs Iulia Nova Carthago, capital of Carthaginiensis; modern Cartagena.) Represented at the Council of Elvira by presbyter Eutices; see Martinez Diez, 241. *Atlas*, 4. Talbert, map 27.

Castulo. (in Carthaginiensis; modern Cortijos de S. Eufemia y de Yangues, about 7 km South of modern Linares in Cazalona.) Represented at the Council of Elvira by Bishop Secundinus and presbyter Turrinus; see Martinez Diez, 239 & 241. Represented at the Council of Serdica in 343 by Bishop Anianus; see Athanasius, *Apologia contra Arianos*, 48.2; Athanasius, *Epistula ad easdem*; and Hilary, *Epistula*, B.II.4.2. Sotomayor y Muro, "La Iglesia," 203. *Atlas*, 4. Talbert, map 27.

Colonia Barcino. (modern Barcelona.) For the martyr Cucufas, see Prudentius, *Peristephanon*, 4.33–34. There are one sarcophagus and two fragments from *ca.*315–335 with motifs of the resurrection of Lazarus, arrest of Peter, healing of the blind, an orante, Peter and the cock, changing water into wine; see Sotomayor y Muro, *Sarcofagos*, 11, 93–96, 99. Represented at Council of Serdica in 343 by Bishop Praetextatus; see Athanasius, *Apologia contra Arianos*, 48.2; Athanasius, *Epistula ad easdem*; and Hilary, *Epistula*, B.II.4.6. Sotomayor y Muro, "La Iglesia," 72–74, 203. *Atlas*, 4. Talbert, map 25.

Colonia Caesaraugusta. (in Tarraconensis; modern Saragossa;) Cyprian, *Epistulae*, 67, writing to Caesaraugusta and other churches *ca.*250 to give instructions for dealing with Bisilides and Marcialis who had apostasized in the Decianic persecution, mentions "Felix of Caesaraugusta, man of faith and defender of the truth," who was presumably bishop of the place. Cyprian likewise mentions the presbyter Felix of Legio VII Gemina, and perhaps another Felix as well.

Eighteen martyrs (at least fourteen known by name) are commemorated in a basilica of the late Fourth Century, named as Optatus, Lupercus, Sucessus, Martialis, Urbanus, Quintilian, Iulia, Publius, Fronto, Felix, Caecilianus, Evotius, Primitivus, and Apodemius, (possibly also Cassianus, Ianuarius, Mutatinus, and Faustus according to Eugenius of Toledo). Note also the confessors Caius and Crementius. For the martyrs and confessors, see Prudentius, *Peristephanon*, 4. Augustine, *Sermones*, 274–77, is an extended treatment of the martyr Vincent of Caesaraugusta, who was martyred at Valentia, *q.v.* Compare *Martyrologium Romanum*, 16 April, and *DACL*, 15.1:761.

The Christians of the city were represented at the Council of Elvira by Bishop Valerius; see Martinez Diez, 240. Represented at Council of Arles in 314 by presbyter Clementius and exorcist Rufinus; see *Concilia Galliae*, 15, 17, 19, 20 & 22; and Gaudemet, 62–63. There is a sarcophagus of *ca.*330–340 with motifs of Adam and Eve, an orante, changing of water into wine, and an inscription; see Sotomay y Muro, *Sarcofagos*, 12, 159–69. Represented at Council of Serdica in 343 by Bishop Castus; see Athanasius, *Apologia contra Arianos*, 48.2; Athanasius, *Epistula ad easdem*; and Hilary, *Epistula*, B.II.4.5. Sotomayor y Muro, "La Iglesia," 44, 65–70, 90, 195, 203. *Atlas*, 4. Talbert, map 25.

Colonia Tarraco. (modern Tarragona.) An inscription with the words "*memoriae*" and "*anima sancta*" from *ca.*200 has been understood by some as Christian; see Alföldy, *Die Römischen Inschriften*, #236. Bishop Fructuosus and the deacons Aurgurius and Eulogius were arrested in Valerian's persecution on 16 January 259 and later martyred; see Prudentius, *Peristephanon*, 6, and Musurillo, xxxii, 176–85.

Alföldy, *Die Römischen Inschriften*, #961, is a possibly Christian inscription from the Third or Fourth Century, and #93 dates to *ca.*300. The presbyter Probatius and the deacon Castorius were at the Council of Arles in 314; see *Concilia Galliae*, 15, 16, 18, 20, & 22; also Gaudemet, 62–63. Koch, 246, lists a sarcophagus of possibly pre-Constantinian date. Alföldy, *Die Römischen Inschriften*, #95, #, 96, & #97 from 324–26, describe the Emperor Constantine as "*semper devotissimus.*" Koch, 246, notes a pre-Constantinian sarcophagus. There is also a Fourth-Century mausoleum nearby at Centcelles; see Keay, 195–97. Sotomayor y Muro, "La Iglesia," 51–53, 142–43, 195. *EnECh*, 813–14. *Atlas*, 4. Talbert, map 25.

Complutum. (modern Alcalá de Henares.) Unnamed martyrs are mentioned by Paulinus of Nola, *Carmina*, 31:605–14. Possibly the same as Justus and Pastor mentioned in Prudentius, *Peristephanon*, 4.41–44. Sotomayor y Muro, "La Iglesia," 76–77, 90. *Atlas*, 4. Talbert, map 25.

Corduba. (Colonia Patricia Corduba, capital of Baetica; modern Cordoba.) Prudentius, *Peristephanon*, 4,19–20, and *Martyrologium Hieronomianum*, 5 kal. Julii & 14 kal. Dec., mention the martyrs Acisclus and Zoellus. Corduba was represented by Bishop Hosius and by presbyter Iulianus at the Council of Elvira; see Martinez Diez, 239.

There is a sarcophagus fragment from *ca.*305–312 showing a motif of Daniel among the lions. Four sarcophagi or fragments dating from *ca.*315–335 have motifs of an orantes, Peter and the cock, Adam and Eve, multiplications of loaves and fishes, and the arrest of Peter. See Sotomayor y Muro, *Sarcofagos*, 11, 67–70, 113–28, 133–34.

Corduba was represented at the Council of Nicaea by Bishop Hosius, who presided; see Gelzer, lx. Sotomayor y Muro, "La Iglesia," 74–76, 90. *Atlas*, 4. Talbert, map 26.

Drona. (Desconocida; possibly Brona or Brana, which would be near modern Cadiz; see Sotomayor y Muro, "La Iglesia," 92.) The local Christians were represented at the Council of Elvira by the presbyter Luxurius; see Martinez Diez, 241. Compare Talbert, map 26.

Ebora. (Municipium Liberalitas Julia Ebora in Lusitania; modern Evora in Southeastern Portugal. Harnack, 923, suggests Ebura, South of Seville, as an alternative.) Represented at the Council of Elvira by Bishop Quintianus; see Martinez Diez, 240. *Atlas*, 4. Talbert, map 26.

Eliocroca. (in Carthaginiensis, formerly Tarraconense; near modern Lorca.) Represented at the Council of Elvira by Bishop Successus; see Martinez Diez, 240. *Atlas*, 4. Talbert, map 27.

Emerita Augusta. (Capital of Lusitania; modern Mérida.) Cyprian, *Episulae*, 67, wrote to the churches at Emerita and elsewhere *ca.*250 to give instructions for dealing with Basilides and Martialis who had apostasized in the Decianic persecution. Prudentius, *Peristephanon*, 3; 4.37–40; and 11.238, mentions the martyred girl Eulalia.

Represented at the Council of Elvira by Bishop Liberius; see Martinez Diez, 240. Represented at the Council of Arles in 314 by Bishop Liberius and the deacon Florentius; see *Concilia Galliae*, 15, 16, 18, 20, & 22; also Gaudemet, 60–61. Represented at the Council of Serdica in 343 by Bishop Florentius (apparently the same as the deacon of 314); see Athanasius, *Apologia contra Arianos*, 48.2; Athanasius, *Epistula ad easdem*; and Hilary, *Epistula*, B.II.4.3. Sotomayor y Muro, "La Iglesia," 42, 78–80, 90, 195, 203. *Atlas*, 4. Talbert, map 26.

Epora. (in Baetica; modern Montoro.) The local Christians were represented at the Council of Elvira by presbyter Restutus; see Martinez Diez, 240. *Atlas*, 4. Talbert, map 27.

Fiblaria/Fibularia. (in Tarraconensis, probably Calagurris Fibularia [modern Loarre near Huesca]; see Pliny the Elder, *Natural History*, 3.3.24.) Represented at the Council of Elvira by Bishop Ianuarius; see Martinez Diez, 240. *Atlas*, 4. Talbert, map 25.

Gerunda. (modern Girona.) For the martyr Felix, see Prudentius, *Peristephanon*, 4.29–30. There are four sarcophagi or fragments from *ca.*305–312 with motifs of the good shepherd, an orantes, arrest of Peter, healing of the blind man, healing of the paralytic, multiplication of loaves and fishes, a scene of resurrection, Christ treading on the lion and the serpent, and the sacrifice of Isaac. There are two sarcophagi from *ca.*315–335 with motifs of the arrest of Peter, a fountain, healing of the paralytic, Peter and the cock, changing water into wine, healing of the blind, multiplication of loaves and fishes, and the resurrection of Lazarus; see Sotomayor y Muro, *Sarcofagos*, 11, 19–46, 83–92. Sotomayor y Muro, "La Iglesia," 71–72. *Atlas*, 4. Talbert, map 25.

Hispalis. (Colonia Iulia Romula Hispalis in Baetica; modern Seville.) Justa and Rufina, martyrs during the Diocletianic persecution; see *BHL*, #4566–69. Represented by Bishop Sabinus at the Council of Elvira; see Martinez Diez, 239. Sabinus was possibly also at Arles in 314 if "*de civitate Baetica*" refers to the capital Hispalis; see *Concilia Galliae*, 15, 16, 18, 20, 22; also Gaudemet, 62–63. Alternatively, "*Baetica*" here has been suggested on the basis of later tradition as a mistake for Beteca (modern Boticas in what would have been Galaecia). Sotomayor y Muro, "La Iglesia," 63–64, 90, 195. *Atlas*, 4. Talbert, map 26.

Igabrum/Egabrum. (in Baetica; modern Cabra.) Represented at the Council of Elvira by presbyter Victorinus; see Martinez Diez, 241. *Atlas*, 4. Talbert, map 27.

Iliberri. (Municipium Florentinum Iliberritanum in Baetica, also known as Elvira, modern City of Granada.) Represented at the Council of Elvira by Bishop Flavianus and presbyter Eucharius; see Martinez Diez, 240–41. *EnECh*, 270. *EEC*, 370. *Atlas*, 4. Talbert, map 27.

Iliturgi. (In Baetica; probably modern Cerro Máquiz, East of Mengibar.) Represented at the Council of Elvira by presbyter Maurus; see Martinez Diez, 240. *Atlas*, 4. Talbert, map 27.

Ipagrum/Epagra. (probably Cerro del Castillo in modern Aguilar de la Frontera.) Represented by at the Council of Elvira by Bishop Sinagius; see Martinez Diez, 239. *Atlas*, 4. Talbert, map 26.

Layos. (in Cartagenensis; about 10 km South-Southwest of modern Toledo.) Two sarcophagi from *ca.*312–320 have been found with motifs of Adam and Eve, resurrection of Lazarus, multiplication of loaves and fishes, an orante, sacrifice of Isaac, healing of the paralytic, and adoration of the magi; see Sotomayor y Muro, *Sarcofagos*, 11, 59–66, 71–75. *Atlas de España*, 1:83. Compare Talbert, map 27.

Legio VII Gemina. (in Galaecia, formerly Tarraconensis; modern Leon.) Cyprian wrote from Carthage to the presbyter Felix and to the people of Legio VII and to Elio the deacon *ca.*250 to give instructions for dealing with Basilides and Martialis who had apostasized in the Decianic persecution; see Cyprian, *Epistulae*, 67. Tertullian, *Ad Scapulam*, 4.8, mentions persecutions by the governor. The martyr Marcellus, executed at Tingi in 298, may have been a soldier of the Legio VII Gemina, see Musurillo, xxxvii–xxxix. Legio was represented at the Council of Elvira by Bishop Decentius; see Martinez Diez, 240. Note the martyrium of the mid-Fourth Century at Marialba, 7 km South of Leon; see Sotomayor y Muro, "La Iglesia," 42, 70–72, 90–91, 144, 203. Talbert, map 24.

Malaca. (Municipium Flavium Malacitanum in Baetica; modern Málaga.) Represented at the Council of Elvira by Bishop Patricius; see Martinez Diez, 240. *Atlas*, 4. Talbert, map 27.

Mentesa Bastia. (in Carthaginiensis; in modern La Guardia de Jaén.) Represented at the Council of Elvira by Bishop Pardus; see Martinez Diez, 239. *Atlas*, 4. Talbert, map 27.

Municipio. (probably Iliberri [Elvira] itself; see Sotomayor y Muro, "La Iglesia," 90.) Represented at the Council of Elvira by presbyter Eucarius; see Martinez Diez, 241. Talbert, map 27.

Ossigi. (in Baetica; possibly modern Cerro Alcal.) Represented at the Council of Elvira by presbyter Clementianus; see Martinez Diez, 241. *Atlas*, 4. Talbert, map 27.

Ossonoba. (in Lusitania; modern Estoi, near Faro in Southern Portugal.) Represented at the Council of Elvira by Bishop Vincentius; see Martinez Diez, 240. *Atlas*, 4. Talbert, map 26.

R(h)oda. (in Tarraconensis; modern Ciutadella de Roses.) A sarcophagus fragment from *ca.*312–320 has been found; see Sotomayor y Muro, *Sarcofagos*, 11, 57–58. Talbert, map 25.

Segalbinia/Selambina. (in Baetica; possibly modern Salobreña.) Represented at the Council of Elvira by presbyter Silvanus; see Martinez Diez, 241. *Atlas*, 4. Talbert, map 27.

Solia. (in Baetica; possibly modern Alcaracejos to the North of Cordoba.) Represented at the Council of Elvira by presbyter Cumancius; see Martinez Diez, 241. *Atlas*, 4. Talbert, map 26.

Temes. (in Galaecia; about 65 km South-Southwest of Lugo [ancient Lucus Augusti].) There is a large sarcophagus lid dating from *ca.*312–25 with motifs of adoration of the magi, Adam and Eve, and Jonah; see Gomez, 322, who notes that the lid is presently in secondary use. Sotomayor y Mura, "La Iglesia," 136. Talbert, map 24.

Toletum. (in Carthaginiensis, formerly Tarraconense; modern Toledo.) Represented at the Council of Elvira by Bishop Melantius; see Martinez Diez, 240. There is also a small fragment of a sarcophagus of *ca.*315–335; see Sotomayor y Muro, *Sarcofagos*, 11, 137. *Atlas*, 4. Talbert, map 27.

Tucci. (Colonia Augusta Gemella Tucci in Baetica; modern Martos; see Sotomayor y Muro, "La Iglesia," 90.) Tucci was represented at the Council of Elvira by Bishop Camerinnus and presbyter Leo; see Martinez Diez, 239 & 241. The presbyter Leo may, however, represent Ad Gemellas; see *Atlas*, 4. There is also a sarcophagus from *ca.*330–340 with motifs of Jonah, resurrection of the widow's son, healing of the blind, Peter and the cock, healing of the paralytic, multiplication of loaves and fishes, changing water into wine; see Sotomayor y Muro, *Sarcofagos*, 12 & 147–56. Talbert, map 27.

Ulia. (Municipium Ulia Fidentia in Baetica; modern Montemayor.) Represented at the Council of Elvira by presbyter Victor; see Martinez Diez, 241. *Atlas*, 4. Talbert, map 26.

Ursi/Urci. (in Baetica near the border with Carthaginiensis; probably modern Chuche/Pechina.) Represented at the Council of Elvira by Bishop Cantonius and presbyter Ianuarius; see Martinez Diez, 240–41. *Atlas*, 4. Talbert, map 27.

Urso. (Colonia Genetiva Iulia Urbanorum Urso in Baetica; modern Osuna.) Represented at the Council of Elvira by the presbyter Natalis; see Martinez Diez, 240. Natalis was also at the Council of Arles in 314 with the deacon Citerius; see *Concilia Galliae*, 15, 16, 18, 20, & 22; also Gaudemet, 62–63. Sotomayor y Muro, "La Iglesia," 195. *Atlas*, 4. Talbert, map 26.

Valentia. (modern Valencia.) A martyr named Vincent was from Colonia Caesaraugusta, *q.v.*, but was killed at nearby Valentia (modern Valencia); see *BHL*, #8630–33; Prudentius, *Peristephanon*, 4.77–108 & 5; and *AASS*, Januarius 3:7–10. See also Soriano Sanchez, 1193–1201; *BS*, 12:1149–55; and Sotomayor y Muro, "La Iglesia," 66–70. Talbert, map 27.

Possible sites

Ad Ello? (modern Elda/El Monastil.) Sotomayor [y Muro], "Sarcofagos paleocristianas," 175–79, notes a sarcophagus fragment now in secondary use but datable to the first third of the Fourth Century. Koch, 245, #109, classifies it a pre-Constantinian. Talbert, map 27.

Ad Gemellas? (probably modern Benameji.) If the deacon Leo assigned to Gemellas in the list for the Council of Elvira was not from Tucci (Colonia Augusta Gemella Tucci), then he would probably have represented Ad Gemellas; see Martinez Diez, 241, and Sotomayor y Muro, "La Iglesia," 90. *Atlas*, 4. Talbert, map 27.

Baetulo? (in Tarraconensis; modern Badalona.) There is a sarcophagus fragment from *ca.*315–335; Sotomayor y Muro, *Sarcofagos*, 11, 97–98. Talbert, map 25.

Berja? (West of Almería [ancient Portus Magnus]; in Baetica.) There is a sarcophagus of *ca.*315–335 with motifs of resurrrection of Lazarus, and the entry into Jerusalem; see Sotomayor y Muro, *Sarcofagos*, 11, 101–107. Compare Talbert, map 27.

Castiliscar? Koch, 268, #115, classifies Sotomayor [y Muro], *Sarcofagos*, 181–87, as a sarcophagus of Constantinian date. *Atlas de España*, 1:169. Compare Talbert, map 25.

Dianium? (in Carthaginiensis; modern Denia.) There is a sarcophagus fragment of *ca*.330–340; see Sotomayor y Muro, *Sarcofagos*, 12, 157–58. Talbert, map 27.

El Sotillo Nuevo? (a farm 25 km East of Jérez de la Frontera [Roman Colonia Hasta Regia] in Baetica.) Two sarcophagus fragments dating *ca*.330–340 have been found; see Sotomayor [y Muro], "Dos Fragmentos," 399–406. Sotomayor y Muro, "La Iglesia," 136. Talbert, map 26.

Erustes? (in Carthaginiensis; about 20 km East of ancient Caesarobriga.) There is a sarcophagus fragment of *ca*.330–340; see Sotomayor y Muro, *Sarcofagos*, 12, 143–45. *Atlas de España*, 1:83. Compare Talbert, map 27.

Italica? (in Baetica; modern Santiponce.) There is a sarcophagus fragment of *ca*.315–335 with motif of arrest of Peter; see Sotomayor y Muro, *Sarcofagos*, 11, 13. Keay, 188–89. *Atlas*, 4. Talbert, map 26.

Los Palacios? (in Baetica; about 25 km South of Seville.) There is a sarcophagus fragment of *ca*.315–335 with motif of Peter and the cock; see Sotomayor y Muro, *Sarcofagos*, 11, 129–30. Compare Talbert, map 26.

Marialba de la Ribera? (about 7 km South-Southeast of Leon.) Hauschild, 322–29, records a mortuary chapel near a cemetery that dates back to the Fourth Century. *Alas de España*, 1:50. Talbert, map 24.

Murcia? Koch, 274, #206, records of sarcophagus of Constantinian date. See Sotomayor [y Muro], *Sarcofagos*, 179ff. Talbert, map 27.

Saguntum? *Martyrologium Hieronymianum*, 11 kal. Feb., lists the martyr Vincent and others. This is unconfirmed; see Harnack, 922. Talbert, map 27.

Sosontigi? (in Baetica; modern Alcaudete in the Province of Jaén.) There is a sarcophagus fragment of *ca*.315–335 with motif of Daniel among the lions; see Sotomayor y Muro, *Sarcofagos*, 11, 109–112. Talbert, map 27.

PART THREE

CHRISTIAN COMMUNITIES IN AFRICA BEFORE 325 C.E.

EGYPT

Bibliography
AASS
AB
Abu Salih
Acta Sancti Menae
Acts of the Pagan Martyrs
Alexander of Alexandria, *Deposition of Arius*
Apophthegmata Patrum, alphabetical series
Athanasius, *Apologia contra Arianos*
Athanasius, *Epistula ad easdem*
Athanasius, *Festal Letters*
Athanasius, *Historia Arianorum*
Athanasius, *Letter to Dracontius*
Athanasius, *Life of Antony*
Athanasius, *Tomus ad Antiochenos*
Autori vari
Bagnall, "Conversion"
Bagnall, *Egypt*
Bagnall, *et al.*
Balestri & Hyvernat
Ball
Barns & Chadwick
Bauer
Baumeister
Bell
Besa
Bezae codex
BHG
BHL
BHO
BKT
Bowen
Bowman
Breydy
Calderini
Chitty

Clement of Alexandria, *Letter to Theodore*
Clement of Alexandria, *Stromata*
Constantine?
DACL
De Cosson
Delehaye, "Les martyrs d'Egypte"
Epiphanius, *Panarion*
Eusebius, *Chronicle*
Eusebius, *Ecclesiastical History*
Eutychius of Alexandria
Evelyn-White
Fedalto
Finney
Frankfurter
Gallazzi
Gelzer
Graf
Griggs
Griggs, *et al.*
Haelst
Harnack
Hatch
Historia Acephala
Historia monachorum in Aegypto
Hope
Horn
Irenaeus, *Adversus haereses*
Jerome, *Chronicle*
Jerome, *Epistulae*
Jerome, *Vita S. Hilarionis*
Jerome, *Vita S. Pauli*
Judge
Judge & Pickering
Justin Martyr, *Apology I*
Klijn, "Jewish"
Lefebvre
Lefort, *Les vies*
Martin, *Athanase*
Martin, "L'église"
Martin, "Aux origines"

Martin, "Topographie"
Martyrologium Hieronymianum
Menologium Basilianum
Menologium Sirletianum
Metzger, *Text*
Michael the Syrian
Mina
Muratorian Canon
Munier
Musurillo
Naldini
Nautin
New Documents
OCD
O'Leary
Orlandi
P. Achm.
P. Amh.
P. Ant.
P. Berl. Bork
P. Coll. Youtie
P. Edgerton
P. Fay.
P. Genova
P. Giss. Univ.
P. Kell.
P. Köln.
P. Lond. VI
P. Mich.
P. Oxy.
P. Ryl.
P. Wurzb.
Palladius, *Lausiac History*
Papaconstantinou
Pauly-Wissowa
Pearson, "Earliest"
PG
PGM
Photius, *Interrogationes decem*
Plasburg

PSI
Reymond & Barns
Roberts
Robinson, *Nag Hammadi*
Robinson, *Bauer*
Römer, (1997)
Römer, (1998)
Römer, (2000)
Ropes
Rossi
Rufinus
Sammelbuch
S. Pachomii Vita
SEC
SEG
Severus of al-Ashmunein
Synaxarium Alexandrinum
Talbert
Timm
Treu
Van der Meer & Mohrman
Van Minnen, "Earliest"
Van Minnen, "Roots"
Veilleux
Vivian
Walters
Wessely
ZPE

General

Egypt. Due to the fullness of evidence for Egypt, it is possible to break this section into four parts: general, specific sites, possible sites, and sites certainly attested only after 325.

Colin H. Roberts, 45 & 49–60, on the basis of nomina sacra and other characteristics of early papyri, believes that there is evidence for Christianity with a strong Jewish influence in Egypt by *ca.*100, which was brought to a halt by the revolt of the Jews under Trajan *ca.*115. The oldest known manuscript of the New Testament, P[52] [P. Ryl. III (1938) 457] dates to the first half of the Second Century and was discovered in Egypt; see Metzger, *Text*, 38–39. It is also the earliest known Christian artifact anywhere. The *Fragment of an Unknown Gospel* (P. Edgerton 2) and the related P. Köln. no. 255 are from Egypt before *ca.*200; see Schneemelcher, 96–99. Also, the *Gospel of the Hebrews*, and the *Gospel of the Egyptians* are usually associated with Egypt at about the same time period; see Schneemelcher, 172–78, & 209–15. The dating of Gregory-Aland P^{40} from Qarara is uncertain; see Haelst, #492.

Because of what he saw as the paucity of early evidence for "orthodox" Christianity in Egypt, the activity of the gnostic Valentinus, and the presumed provenance of the *Gospel of the Egyptians* and other peculiar works, Walter Bauer, 44–60, believed that earliest Christianity in Egypt was "heretical." More recently, the papyrus discoveries have suggested to Roberts, 45 & 49–60; Pearson, "Earliest," 154–56; Klijn, "Jewish," 161–62; Robinson, *Bauer*, 59–69; and Griggs, 32 & 45, that earliest Christianity in Egypt was influenced by Judaism and that much of Christianity in Egypt was doctrinally undifferentiated until the late Second Century. The sheer variety of early Christian documentary and literary papyri from one single city, Oxyrhynchus, would seem to bear out the more recent scholarly trend; see, for example, early papyri listed in Haelst, 409–13.

As with many other provinces, the principal ecclesiastical see dominates the records of church life in the country. Athanasius, *Apologia contra Arianos*, 71.4, claims that in the 330s there were nearly one hundred bishops in Egypt, Libya, and Pentapolis. Bishop Paphnutius, the renowned ascetic and confessor, was from the region of Thebes, though his see is not located with certainty; see Gelzer, lxix, 5, & 62, and Sozomen, 1.10.1–2. Athanasius, *Apologia contra Arianos*, 37.1, records the general note that bishops from Egypt were at the Council of Serdica in 343. Details of later bishops can be found in Munier.

The martyrological literature of Coptic Egypt stands in large measure beyond the realm of confirmability because of the late date of many manuscripts. Delehaye, "Les martyrs," 148, believes that some topographical details may be recoverable if there is evidence for a continuous veneration, thus his reliance on Abu Salih and Makrizi. I would add that the commemoration should be demonstrable at the site of martyrdom or in the martyr's hometown. Some early and relatively unornate acta would seem to have historical value of their own, e.g., Coluthus, Dioscorus, Isaac, Herais, Phileas, Psote, Victor of Lycopolis. Similarly, if Christian communities are otherwise known to exist by *ca.*325 or shortly thereafter in a given city, the possibility that martyrdoms associated with those localities are historical is increased. The several Egyptian martyrdoms found in Eusebius, *Ecclesiastical History* and *Martyrs of Palestine*, and listed in Delehaye, "Les martyrs," 30–31, are in large measure not localizable. It is difficult to assess the reliability of later martyr accounts such as those of Isaac of Tiphre and Julius of Kbehs (modern Aqfahs), the latter of whom may well have been a literary fiction; see Baumeister, 115–17. As a counterbalance to the Christian martyrological literature, one should also note the *Acts of the Pagan Martyrs*. For the continuity and change of religious practices in Roman Egypt, see Frankfurter, 257–64.

Harnack, 714, notes the survival of several papyri containing *libelli* of those (whether suspected Christians or not) who swore by the emperor at the time of the Diocletianic persecutions, though these *libelli* ("certificates") do not in and of themselves prove the presence of Christians. Harnack's mention, 717, of "Porphyritis," seems to be of a personal name rather than a place name; compare Eusebius, *Martyrs of Palestine*, 11.1, 11.7, & 11.15. Yet an Egyptian place named "Porphyritis" is known, see Calderini, 4:182. Papaconstantinou, 405, provides a table to convert from the Coptic calendar to the Julian calendar.

Specific sites

Alexandria. According to Acts 18:24–25, the teacher Apollos was from Alexandria, but it is uncertain whether he was a Christian while still in his native city. Only the *Bezae codex* indicates unequivocally that he was a Christian while still there. *Muratorian Canon*, line 64, mentions a spurious *Letter of Paul to the Alexandrians*.

The traditional account credits Mark with the founding of Christianity in Alexandria; see Eusebius, *Ecclesiastical History*, 2.16.1–3, who perhaps attributes his information to Clement and Papias; see Griggs, 26, following Morton Smith. In fact, Clement of Alexandria, *Letter to Theodore*, if indeed authentic, would indicate some knowledge of the Mark tradition in Alexandria *ca.*200. The traditional account lacks any earlier verification.

The list of bishops provided by Eusebius is sketchy before *ca.*190. At *Ecclesiastical History*, 3.21.1, he names Annianus, Abilius (who served for thirteen years and died in 98), and Cerdo, as the first three bishops in order. He says, 4.1.1, that Cerdo was succeeded by Primus about the twelfth year of the Emperor Trajan (i.e. *ca.*109). Primus then served until *ca.*121 when he was succeeded by Justus (see Eusebius, *Ecclesiastical History*, 4.4.1, although Eusebius, *Chronicle*, would give Primus ten years). The gnostic teacher Basilides was active at Alexandria in the first half of the Second Century; see Irenaeus, *Adversus haereses*, 1.24.1, and Clement of Alexandria, *Stromata*, 7.106.4. Epiphanius, *Panarion*, 24.1.1, expands the list of cities associated with Basilides.

Epiphanius, *Panarion*, 31.2.2–3, records the tradition that Valentinus was a native of Phrebonitis/Phragonitis or Paralia (either place would be in the Delta near the Sebennitic mouth of the Nile; see Calderini, 5:98 and 4:52 respectively), educated in Alexandria. Valentinus would have journeyed to Rome *ca.*140 when Hyginus was bishop; see Irenaeus, *Adversus haereses*, 3.4.3, and Eusebius, *Chronicle*. Brief reference to Valentinus, as well as to Basilides, may be found in *Muratorian Canon*, lines 81–85. Justin Martyr, *Apology I*, 29.1–4, mentions "one of ours" at Alexandria who wished to castrate himself *ca.*150. Heracleon would have been active in Egypt about a generation later.

Eusebius informs us that after serving for some eleven years, Justus was succeeded by the sixth bishop, Eumenes; see Eusebius, *Ecclesiastical History*, 4.5.5. According to Eusebius, Eumenes served for thirteen years, and Marcus for ten years, before Celadion became bishop; see *Ecclesiastical History*, 4.11.6. After fourteen years, about 168 C.E., Celadion was followed by Agrippinus; see *Ecclesiastical History*, 4.19.1–4.20.1.

Twelve years later, in 180 C.E., Julian succeeded Agrippinus as bishop in Alexandria. At that time Pantaenus was the leader of the catechetical school there. When Pantaenus journeyed to "India" (in reality probably South Arabia), Clement of Alexandria succeeded him as head of the school; see Eusebius, *Ecclesiastical History*, 5.9.1.–5.10.2. For Clement's attitude toward Christian art, see Finney, 111–16.

About 189/90, Julian was succeeded as bishop by Demetrius; see Eusebius, *Ecclesiastical History*, 5.22.1. Later tradition records that Demetrius had correspondence with Victor of Rome, Maximinus of Antioch, and Gaius of Jerusalem concerning the Easter controversy; see Eutychius of Alexandria, text 1:127, lines 10–14; translation in PG 111:989. For analysis, see Breydy, 97. See also *DHGE*, 14:198–99.

In 202, during the reign of Septimius Severus, Leonides, father of Origen, suffered martyrdom when Origen himself was only seventeen; see Eusebius, *Ecclesiastical History*, 6.1.1 & 6.2.12, and *Chronicle*.

For other martyrs of the time, see Eusebius, *Ecclesiastical History*, 6.2.2–6.3.2, 6.4.1–3, and 6.5.1–7. Origen became head of the catechetical school the following year and taught at Alexandria from time to time until 232; see Eusebius, *Ecclesiastical History*, 6.3.3. & 6.26.1. At that point, after some years of apparently strained relations with Demetrius, Origen relocated to Caesarea Maritima; see Eusebius, *Ecclesiastical History*, 6.26.1.

In 233, Origen's student Heraclas succeeded Demetrius as bishop and Dionysius took up leadership of the catechetical school; see Eusebius, *Ecclesiastical History*, 6.26.1 & 6.29.4. About 247, Dionysius himself became bishop; see Eusebius, *Ecclesiastical History*, 6.35.1. Dionysius is the earliest witness to the practice of referring to the bishops of Alexandria as "papa" (i.e. "pope"), a term which he used of his predecessor; see Eusebius, *Ecclesiastical History*, 7.7.4. Jerome, *Epistulae*, 146.1, notes that, until the time of Dionysius, the Bishop of Alexandria was chosen by the local presbyters from among themselves. Perhaps this fact would account in part for the paucity of information on individual bishops of Alexandria before *ca.*180.

At *Ecclesiastical History*, 6.41.12–18, Eusebius touches on the Decianic persecutions. Shortly after the persecutions of Valerian, Maximas succeeded Dionysius as bishop; see Eusebius, *Ecclesisastical History*, 7.11.26. P. Amh. I (1900) 3a, dating to 264–282, mentions Bishop Maximas; see Judge & Pickering, #8 (=Naldini #6). After eighteen years, Maximas was succeeded by Theonas, see Eusebius, *Ecclesiastical History*, 7.32.30. After serving for nineteen years, Maximus was followed by Bishop Peter. Peter himself was martyred after serving for twelve years, in what Eusebius calls the ninth year of the persecutions (i.e. 311); see Eusebius, *Ecclesiastical History*, 7.32.31. Further sources for Peter's life are discussed in Vivian, 64–84. For the catacombs at Karmouz on the outskirts of Alexandria, see *DACL*, 1:1125–54. Martin, "Topographie," 1:1133–44, with reference to Epipanius, *Panarion*, 69.1.2–3 & 69.2.2, and *Historia Acephala*, 2, 5, & 7, discusses the location of early churches in Alexandria.

The *Synaxarium Alexandrinum* attributes several martyrs to Alexandria during the persecutions; see Delehaye, "Les martyrs," 93–110 passim. At least one apostate, Peireus, is known from the persecutions; see *Acta Phileae* in Musurillo, 330–31. Peter was succeeded for a brief period by Achillas; see Athanasius, *Apologia contra Arianos*, 59.2; *Epistula ad easdem*; and *Historia Arianorum*, 77.4. For the possible memorial of Achillas, see *DACL*, 1:1150, and Lefebvre, #39. Likewise, Lefebvre,

#22, is an apparently Christian inscription from the first quarter of the Fourth Century.

Bishop Alexander deposed Arius from the presbyterate and was at the Council of Nicaea; see Socrates, 1.6, and Gelzer, lx. Bishop Agathammon was one of several Melitian clergy in Alexandria at the time; see the letter of Melitius in Athanasius, *Apologia contra Arianos*, 59.3 & 71.5–6. Antony visited Alexandria *ca.*338; see Athanasius, *Life of Antony*, 69, and *Festal Letters*, index. Athanasius, *Apologia contra Arianos*, 37.1, records the presence of representatives from Alexandria at the Council of Serdica in 343. *Atlas*, 5. Papaconstantinou, 282. Fedalto, 2:581–82. Talbert, map 74.

Antaiopolis. (Coptic Tkoou; modern Qaw.) *Synaxarium Alexandrinum*, 15 Choiak (11 December) records the tradition that Amsah of Koptos was martyred at Antaiopolis during the great persecution; see also Abu Salih, fol. 103a. Gelzer, 80–81, giving the Coptic list of those present at the Council of Nicaea, names Dius as Bishop of Antaiopolis. Timm, 5:2120–32. Papaconstantinou, 295. Talbert, map 77.

Antinoe/Antinoopolis. (in the Thebaid.) Bishop Alexander of Jerusalem wrote a letter to the Christians at Antinoe early in the Third Century; see Eusebius, *Ecclesiastical History*, 6.9.3. P. Ant. 1.12 & 2.54 are fragments of the New Testament from the Third Century, and P. Ant. 3.112 & 3.149 are theological fragments from the same era. Colluthus was martyred at Antinoe *ca.*304–06; see his *Passio* in Reymond & Barns, text 25–29, trans. 145–50. The *Martyrologium Hieronymianum* and *SEC* attribute further martyrs to Antinoe; see Delehaye, "Les martyrs," 66, 69, & 86. Likewise, *Synaxarium Alexandrinum* attributes numerous martyrs of the great persecution to Antinoe; see Delehaye, "Les martyrs," 66, 69, & 93–110 passim. Bishop Tyrannus was at the Council of Nicaea; see Gelzer, lx. The Melitian bishop at the time was Lucius; see Athanasius, *Apologia contra Arianos*, 59.3 & 71.5–6. Athanasius, *Festal Letter* 19 (of 347), notes that Bishop Arion succeeded Ammonius and Tyrannus. Timm, 1:111–128. Papaconstantinou, 289. *Atlas*, 5. Talbert, map 77.

Apollonopolis Magna/Apollonopolis Ano. (modern Edfou; see Calderini, 1.2:161–9.) Papyrus fragments of Irenaeus, *Adversus haereses*, probably from Apollonopolis Magna and dating from the late Third Century or perhaps the early Fourth Century, have been found; see the SC edition of Irenaeus, *Adverus haereses*, vol. 5, pt. 1:

119–57 & 355–77. For other references, see Haelst, #672. The date at which the fragments were discarded is unstated. Regarding new interpretations of the Christian polemic on the reverse of the fragments, see Römer (2000), 304. A martyr account of Banina and Naou, with several anachronisms, is found in *Synaxarium Alexandrinum*, 7 Choiak (3 December). Timm, 3:1148–57. Papaconstantinou, 304. Talbert, map 80.

Apollonopolis Kato. (Coptic "Sbeht", modern Kom Isfaht just upriver from Asyut; see Calderini, 1.2:170–2.) Bishop Plutarch apostasized during the Diocletianic persecutions; see the *Martyrdom of S. Coluthus*, 90Vi, in Reymond & Barns, text 27 & trans. 147. It would seem that Athanasius, *Festal Letter* "12, to Serapion" (of 340), mentioning Serapion succeeding Plution as bishop of "lower Apollonopolis" in 339 pertains to this place rather than to another Apollonopolis (modern Qus; see Calderini 1.2:169–70). Timm, 3:1433–38. Papaconstantinou, 295. Talbert, map 77.

Arsinoe/Krokodilopolis. (capital of the Arsinoite nome; modern Madinat al-Fayyum.) A fragment of the *Shepherd of Hermas* (P. Mich. 130) from the Fayyum is written in a hand of *ca.*200 on the back of a late Second-Century document; see P. Mich. 130, and Roberts, 22 & 29. Another papyrus of the *Shepherd of Hermas*, reported in *BKT*, 6.21.1, comes from the Third Century. P. Vindob. Inv. Nr. G32016, from the first half of the Third Century mentions Antonius Dioscorus "Christian" as candidate for a local office; see Van Minnen, "Roots," 74, and *Sammelbuch*, 16:12497. Bishop Dionysius of Alexandria journeyed to Arsinoe to oppose chiliastic tendencies promoted by Bishop Nepos among local Christians; see Eusebius, *Ecclesiastical History*, 7.24.1. P. Amh. I (1900) 3a, of the Third Century, was sent from Rome to "brethren" in the Arsenoite nome in the days of Bishop Maximus of Alexandria; see Wessely, #7 (=Judge & Pickering, #8, =Naldini, #6).

P. Kiseleff 3, of the late-Third or early-Fourth Century, is a hymn in Greek and Fayyumic Coptic; see Römer (1997), 127–28. *Synaxarium Alexandrinum* associates several martyrdoms with the Fayyum region; see Delehaye, "Les martyrs," 93–110 *passim*, and compare Papaconstantinou, 283–85. Haelst, #s 378, 485, 536, 605, 636, & 1139, are other early papyri from the Fayyum. At the time of the Council of Nicaea, Melas was the Melitian bishop; see Athanasius, *Apologia contra Arianos*, 59.3 & 71.5–6. Athanasius, *Festal Letter* "12, to Serapion" (of 339), indicates that Silvanus succeeded Calosiris as bishop. *Festal Letter* 19 (of 347) then indicates that Andreas succeeded Silvanus. Griggs, *et al.*, 82–87, would seem to be off base in attributing graves from the late-First and early-Second Centuries to Christians. Timm, 4:1506–25. *Atlas*, 5. Talbert, map 75.

Athribis. (modern Hathribi in the Delta.) *Martyrdom of S. Shenoufe and His Brethren*, 105Vii, mentions a Bishop Plasse who was in the neighborhood of Alexandria during the great persecution and who may thus be related to this Athribis; see Reymond & Barns, 86 & 188. *Synaxarium Alexandrinum*, 13 Mechir (7 February), attributes the martyr Sergius to Athribis; see also Delehaye, "Les martyrs," 101.

At the time of the Council of Nicaea, Ision was the Melitian bishop of Athribis; see Athanasius, *Apologia contra Arianos*, 59.3 & 71.5–6. Ision appears in Athanasius, *Festal Letter* 4 (of 332), in the company of the Melitian bishops of Tanis and Pelusium, so he would seem to relate to Athribis in the Delta. *Atlas*, 5. Talbert, map 74.

Boubastis. (modern Tell Basta.) The *Synaxarium Alexandrinum* associates the martyr tradition of Apoli with this place on 1 Mesore (25 July); see also Delehaye, "Les martyrs," 109. At the time of the Council of Nicaea, Harpocration was the Melitian bishop; see Athanasius, *Apologia contra Arianos*, 59.3 & 71.5–6. Timm, 1:362–65. *Atlas*, 5. Talbert, map 74.

Bousiris. (modern Abusir in the Delta, see Calderini, 2:66, #3.) At the time of the Council of Nicaea, Hermaeon was the Melitian bishop of Kunopolis and Bousiris; see Athanasius, *Apologia contra Arianos*, 59.3 & 71.5–6. *Atlas*, 5. Talbert, map 74.

Bousiris. (near Hermopolis Magna in the Thebaid; modern Hod Abusir; see Calderini 2:67, #4.) The *Martyrdom of SS. Paese and Thecla* would relate to this place; see Reymond & Barns, 31–79 & 151–84. See also *Synaxarium Alexandrinum*, 8 Choiak (4 December). Talbert, map 77.

Chenoboskion. (Coptic Sheneset, modern Kasr-es-Sayad; see Lefort, *Les vies*, 80.) Pachomius was baptized there *ca.*313 and remained in the town for three years; see *S. Pachomii Vita*, Bohairic p. 5 & Greek p. 4. The Nag Hammadi gnostic texts containing Fourth-Century copies of the *Gospel of Philip* and other documents were found nearby; see Robinson, *Nag Hammadi*, 16–17. Timm, 5:2113–18. Talbert, map 77.

Chortasa. (modern Qartasa; just North of Hermopolis Parva.) Martyrs from there are mentioned in the *Martyrdom of Shenoufe and His Brethren*, 105Vi; see Reymond & Barnes, 86 & 188. Pauly-Wissowa, 3:2444. Timm, 5:2107. Calderini, 5:128, in an apparent misprint, puts it in the Herakleopolite nome. Compare Talbert, map 74.

Chusis. (in the Oxyrhynchite nome; modern Shusha.) P. Oxy. 2673 is a report of confiscation of church property in Chusis in 304. Calderini, 5:130–31. Timm 5:2414–16. Talbert, map 75.

Der Boulos. Retreat of the hermit Paul, which Jerome, *Vita S. Pauli*, 1–7, suggests was established slightly earlier than Antony's abode at Der Mar Antonios. Evelyn-White, 12 & plate 1. Walters, 239. Griggs, 275. Timm, 3:1359–78.

Der Mar Antonios/Der al-Qaddis Antun. The "Inner Mountain" of the hermit Antony, three days journey into the inner desert from his original settlement at Pispir. Antony took up residence there shortly after the death of Bishop Peter of Alexandria in 311; see Athanasius, *Life of Antony*, 47.1–3 & 49.1–50.9. Jerome, *Vita S. Hilarionis*, 30–31, describes a later visit by Hilarion to the same place. Evelyn-White, 15–16 & plate 1. The modern monastery is not exactly on the original site; see Walters, 238–39. Griggs, 104–105 & 275. Martin, *Athanase*, 751. *ODCC*, 80–81. Timm, 3:1287–1330.

Diospolis Mikra. (modern Huw.) At the time of the Council of Nicaea, Ammonius was the Melitian bishop of Diospolis. Since the Melitian bishop of Diospolis Magna (Thebes) is otherwise mentioned, Ammonius must, by process of elimination, relate to Diospolis Parva; see the letter of Melitius in Athanasius, *Apologia contra Arianos*, 59.3 & 71.5–6. Timm, 3:1120–25. *Atlas*, 5. Talbert, map 77.

Great Oasis. (in general.) Judge & Pickering, #1 (=Naldini, #4), is a letter from the early Third Century ending with the phrase "ἐν κυρίῳ." Judge & Pickering, #11 (=Naldini, #43) also from the Third Century, appears to be Christian in character. Timm, 6:2956–77. Talbert, map 79.

Heliopolis. (ancient On.) The Letter of Melitius in Athanasius, *Apologia contra Arianos*, 59.3 & 71.5–6, mentions, but does not name, the bishop of Heliopolis, as being of the Melitian party at the time of the Council of Nicaea. Harnack, 721. Martin, *Athanase*, 58 & 94. Timm, 2:910–14. Talbert, map 74.

Herakleopolis Magna. (modern Ihnasya el-Medina.) The so-called "Fayyum fragment," (P. Vindob. Inv. Nr. G 2325) is a fragment of an unknown gospel from the Third Century generally associated with Herakleopolis Magna; see Wessely, #14; Haelst, #589; and Schnee-melcher, 102. At the time of the Council of Nicaea, Peter was listed as the Melitian bishop; see the letter of Melitius in Athanasius, *Apologia contra Arianos*, 59.3 & 71.5–6. Some versions of the list of bishops present at the Council of Nicaea indicate that Peter was present there; see Gelzer, 70–71, 80–81, 146–147; Michael the Syrian, 7.2 (Syriac text 4:124; French trans. 1:248); and Severus of al-Ashmunein, 2.4 (p. 489). Martin, *Athanase*, 34–35, 42, 316–17, 362, & 366, takes this as an indication that Peter was reconciled to the great church at or shortly before the Council of Nicaea. Timm, 3:1161–72. Papaconstantinou, 286. *Atlas*, 5. Talbert, map 75.

Herakleopolis Mikra/Herakleopolis Parva. (Coptic Sethroitis.) Bishop Potamon was at the Council of Nicaea; see Gelzer, lx, 6–7, 60–61, 78–79, 96–97, 120–121, 178–79, 186–87, and Michael the Syrian, 7.2 (Syriac text 4:124; French trans. 1:248). Athanasius, *Festal Letter* 19 (of 347), indicates that Orion succeeded Potamon as bishop. Martin, *Athanase*, 102. Timm, 6:2960–85. Talbert, map 74.

Hermonthis. (modern Armant.) The parents of the martyred Bishop Bidaba of Koptos are said to have been Christians from Hermonthis; see *Synaxarium Alexandrinum*, 19 Epip (13 July). At the time of the Council of Nicaea, Cales was the Melitian bishop; see the letter of Melitius in Athanasius, *Apologia contra Arianos*, 59.3 & 71.5–6. Papaconstantinou, 300–304. *Atlas*, 5. Talbert, map 80.

Hermopolis Magna. (modern al-Ashmunein.) Eusebius, *Ecclesiastical History*, 6.46.2, notes a letter from Dionysius of Alexandria to Bishop Colon of Hermopolis. Three Christian literary works from *ca.*300 are associated with Hermopolis Magna: P. Berlin inv. 11863 (=Gregory-Aland, 0171) is a fragment of Matthew; P. Giss. Univ. Bibl. 2.17 is a fragment in the style of Origen; and P. Wurzb. 3 is a liturgical prayer of intercession. For further information, see Haelst, #s 356, 694, & 1036.

Synaxarium Alexandrinum indicates that Bishop Callanicus was martyred on 2 Tobi (28 December) during the Diocletianic persecutions; see also Delehaye, "Les martyrs," 98. P. Ryl. IV (1952) 616–51, the papyrus archive of Theophanes from *ca.*317–323, may also be relevant here; see Judge & Pickering, #7. Papaconstantinou, 289–94.

Historia Monachorum in Aegypto, 8.1, mentions the holy man Apollos of Hermopolis, who spent some forty years as an anchorite before emerging from the desert to found his community during the reign of Julian (i.e. *ca*.361–63), so Apollos would have taken up his ascetic life in the early 320s. The same source also mentions Hermopolis Magna as a place visited by Joseph, Mary, and the infant Jesus; a similar tradition is reported in Sozomen, 5.21.8–9. For Apollos's community at Bawit, see Walters, 243.

At the time of the Council of Nicaea, Phasilius was the Melitian bishop of Hermopolis Magna; see the letter of Melitius in Athanasius, *Apologia contra Arianos*, 59.3 & 71.5–6. Timm, 1:198–220. *Atlas*, 5. Talbert, map 77.

Hermopolis Mikra/Hermopolis Parva. (modern Damanhur, in the Delta near Alexandria.) The martyrs Cyril, John, and others are mentioned from the Diocletianic persecutions, Paoni 14 (8 June): see *Synaxarium Alexandrinum*, 14 Paoni (8 June); Delehaye, "Les martyrs," 106; *BHL*, #2077–2080; and *BHO*, #239 (*AB* 25: 236–40). For the translation of John's relics, see Abu Salih, fol. 45b.

Harnack, 721, hints that the Alexandrian chorepiscopos Agathammon mentioned in the letter of Melitius recorded in Athanasius, *Apologia contra Arianos*, 59.3 & 71.5–6, may relate to this place.

Athanasius, *Letter to Dracontius*, 1–10, and *Historia Arianorum*, 72, indicate that Bishop Dracontius was banished to Clysma by the Arian party *ca*.354. Athanasius, *Tomus ad Antiochenos*, 10, gives the name of his and several other sees. Timm, 2:508. Talbert, map 74.

Karanis. (modern Kom Awshuim; on the Northern edge of the Fayyum.) P. Fay. 2 is a Naassene gnostic psalm from the Second Century; see also Haelst, #1066. P. Coll. Youtie 77, a petition of Isidorus in which he calls Antoninus "diakonos" and Isaac "monachos" as witnesses on 6? June 324, is the earliest known direct attestation of a monk; see Judge, 72–89, also Judge & Pickering, #24. Timm, 3:1222–24. Talbert, map 75.

Kellis. (modern Esment el-Kharab in the Dakhleh Oasis.) Bowen, 1:152–54, suggests onomastic evidence for Christians there in the late Third Century based on securely dated documents from the Fourth Century. *PUG* 1.20 + P. Med. Inv., 68,82, from 319 mentions an Aurelius Timotheus as party to a contract and uses the phrase "σὺν θεῷ;" for a study of the document, see Autori vari,

138–39, and for the complete text of it, see P. Genova II, appendix I (pp. 73–75). According to Bowen, the name Timotheos can be taken as Christian, so Aurelios Timotheos would likely have been born of Christian parents before 300. The phrase "σὺν θεῷ" might strengthen the case for his Christian beliefs.

Similarly, P. Kell. 1.24, dated 352, mentions the probably Christian names Psenpnouthes, Aurelius Timotheus son of Loudon, Aurelius Timotheus son of Timotheus, Psenouphis son of Psenouphis, alias Besas. If one assumes an average age of 33 years per generation, as Bowen does, then the fathers Timotheus and Psenouphis would have been born *ca.*286.

P. Kell. 1.8, from 362, lists as a witness one Aurelius Horion son of Timotheos. If one follows Bowen's reasoning, then the father Timotheus could have been born *ca.*296.

P. Kell. 1.23, from 353, mentions a Psekes son of Psennouphis. Again following Bowen's reasoning, Psennouphis could have been born *ca.*287. Even if one assumes a lower average length of generations for the men in each of these documents, there is still a substantial case for Christianity at Kellis well before 325.

Two small church buildings were erected before Kellis was abandoned in the late Fourth Century; see Hope, 222–26. The site also had a strong Manichean community and a pagan temple. Talbert, map 79.

Kephro. Dionysius of Alexandria was exiled there during the Decianic persecutions and was joined by a large following; see Eusebius, *Ecclesiastical History*, 7.11.12–17. Calderini, 3:116, puts the town in Libya. Atlas, 5, seems to locate it in the Northwest Nile Delta. Dionysius himself described the town as Libya-like but in the neighborhood of the Mareotis; see Eusebius, *Ecclesiastical History*, 7.11.10–14. Perhaps it is to be identified with Chabriou koma, an unlocated site to the Northwest of the Nile delta; compare Talbert, map 74.

Kleopatris. (in the Hermopolite nome.) P. Duk. inv. 438, a Coptic document from the late-Fourth Century, records the martyr acts of Stephanus, presbyter of Lenaios, who was tried at Kleopatris in the Hermopolite nome in 305; see Van Minnen, "Earliest," 13–38. At the time of the Council of Nicaea, Isaac was the Melitian bishop of Kleopatris; see Athanasius, *Apologia contra Arianos*, 59.3 & 71.5–6. Timm, 3:1273–78. Talbert, map 77. *Atlas,* 5, identifies a site of this name in Lower Egypt, so it is possible that Isaac was bishop of the

Kleopatris in Lower Egypt, though the strength of the Melitians seems to have been in Upper Egypt; compare Talbert, map 74.

Kolluthion. (apparently to the West of Alexandria.) Dionysius of Alexandria was moved there from Kephro during his exile and was delighted to discover that the town was near enough to Alexandria for him to receive regular visitors; see Eusebius, *Ecclesiastical History*, 7.11.15. Calderini, 3:132–33. *Atlas*, 5.

Koma. (in the Herakleopolite nome; modern Qiman al-Arus; Calderini, 3:137.) Birthplace of Antony to Christian parents *ca.*251; see Athanasius, *Life of Antony*, 1; Jerome, *Chronicle*, year corresponding to 251; and Sozomen, 1.13.2. Talbert, map 75.

Koptos. (modern Qift.) *Synaxarium Alexandrinum* lists two martyrs from Koptos: Amsah on 15 Choiak (11 December) and Bishop Bidaba— whose parents were said to be from Hermonthis—on 19 Epip (13 July). For the memorial of Bidaba, see Abu Salih, fol. 103a. At the time of the Council of Nicaea, Theodorus was the Meletian bishop; see Athanasius, *Apologia contra Arianos*, 59.3 & 71.5–6. Athanasius, *Festal Letter* 19 (of 347), indicates that Psenosiris succeeded Theodorus as bishop, so Theodorus must have been reconciled by that date. Timm, 5:2140–54. Papaconstantinou, 299. *Atlas*, 5. Talbert, map 80.

Kunopolis Inferior. (modern Bana.) Bishop Adamantius was at the Council of Nicaea; see Gelzer, lx. At the time of the Council of Nicaea, Hermaeon was the Melitian bishop of Kunopolis and Busiris; see the letter of Melitius in Athanasius, *Apologia contra Arianos*, 59.3 & 71.5–6. Timm, 1:318–24. *Atlas*, 5. Talbert, map 74.

Kunopolis Superior. (Southeast of Oxyrhynchus.) The martyrdom of Dioscorus apparently relates to this Kunopolis since a Fourth-Century manuscript of it was found not far away at Oxyrhynchus; see P. Oxy. 3529, and further references cited there. Delehaye, "Les martyrs," 325, suggests that the place name "Anacipoli" found for Discorus in *Martyrologium Hieronymianum*, 15 kal. Jun., may be a corruption for "Ano Kunopolis," which would strengthen the case for placing Dioscorus at Kunopolis superior. At the time of the Council of Nicaea, Coluthus was the Melitian bishop; see the letter of Melitius in Athanasius, *Apologia contra Arianos*, 59.3 & 71.5–6. Timm, 5:2132–40. Papaconstantinou, 288–89. *Atlas*, 5. Talbert, map 75.

Kusae/Koussai. (modern Qusiya; see Talbert, map 77.) At the time of the Council of Nicaea, Achilles was the Melitian bishop; see Athanasius, *Apologia contra Arianos*, 59.3 & 71.5–6. Timm, 5:2180–91. *Atlas*, 5, seems to identify it with Chusis, as does Harnack, map V.

Kusis. (in the Khargeh Oasis; modern Douch.) P. Grenf. II (1897) 73, a papyrus found at Kusis and addressed to the presbyter Apollon by the presbyter Psenosiris of Toeto, concerns the custody of a certain lady Politike and dates to the late-Third or early-Fourth Century (comparable to handwriting from 242–310); see Wessely #6 (=Judge & Pickering, #9, =Naldini, #21). Timm, 3:1480–81. Talbert, map 79.

Lenaios. (In the Antinoite nome; see Calderini, 3: 105.) P. Duk. inv. 438, a Coptic document from the late-Fourth Century, records the martyr acts of Stephanus, presbyter of Lenaios, who was tried at Kleopatris in 305; see Van Minnen, "Earliest," 13–38.

Leontopolis. (Coptic Natho; modern Natu.) According to the *Martyrdom of S. Shenoufe and His Brethren*, 105Vii, a certain Antony was bishop during the time of the Diocletianic persecutions; see Reymond & Barns, 86 & 188. At this time the heretic Hieracas lived nearby; see Epiphanius, *Panarion*, 67.1.1–4 & 68.1.2–3. By 325, Amos was the Melitian bishop, see the letter of Melitius in Athanasius, *Apologia contra Arianos*, 59.3 & 71.5–6. Timm, 4:1743–48. *Atlas*, 5. Talbert, map 74.

Letopolis. (Coptic Ausim; modern Wasim.) The martyrdom of Phiobamon (Bagham) of Letopis is mentioned by Makrizi on 2 Choiak (28 November); see Delehaye, "Les martyrs," 98, and Abu Salih, 316. For an analysis of the Phiobamon traditions and for Phiobamon's later shrine at narby Tima, see Horn, 145, with reference to *Synaxarium Alexandrinum*, 27 Tobi (22 June). At the time of the Council of Nicaea, Isaac was the Melitian bishop; see Athanasius, *Apologia contra Arianos*, 59.3 & 71.5–6. Timm, 6:2986–93. *Atlas*, 5. Talbert, map 74.

Lykopolis. (Coptic Siout; modern Asyut in the Thebaid.) Bishop Apollonius apostasized during the Diocletianic persecutions; see the letter attributed to Peter of Alexandria in Barns & Chadwick, 450–55. The apostasy of Apollonius is confirmed by the *Martyrdom of S. Coluthus*, 90Rii, in Reymond & Barns, text 26, trans., 147. *Synaxarium Alexandrinum* associates three martyrs with Lykopolis: Victor of Lykopolis on 5 Choiak (1 December), Phiobamon the soldier on 1 Paoni (26 May), and Ischyron of Qillin on 7 Paoni (1 June); see Delehaye, "Les martyrs,"

99 & 105, and compare Papaconstantinou, 295. On Victor's martyrdom at the garrison of Shu near Lykopolis, see Horn, 2:137–40, and Makrizi, 310, in Abu Salih. On Phiobamon, see Horn, 2:142–46.

The schismatic Bishop Melitius held the see in succession to Apollonius and following the Diocletianic persecutions. His hard line toward the lapsed was apparently in part the result of the apostasy of Apollonius; see Barns and Chadwick, 449. Melitius was deposed by Peter of Alexandria but readmitted at the Council of Nicaea; see Athanasius, *Apologia contra Arianos*, 59.1–3 & 71.5–6, and Epiphanius, *Panarion*, 68.1.1–68.5.1. The documents cited by Athanasius with reference to Melitius are the first to use the style "archbishop." Bishop Plousianus represented Lykopolis at the Council of Nicaea; see Gelzer, lx. Athanasius, *Festal Letter* 19 (of 347) indicates that Eudaemon succeeded Plousianus as bishop. Timm, 1:235–51. *Atlas*, 5. Talbert, map 77.

Mareotis region. (lake region South of Alexandria and ecclesiastically dependent upon it.) *Martyrdom of S. Shenoufe and His Brethren*, 106Ri, indicates that the martyr Shenoufe came from a village named Empaiat, which was apparently in the Mareotis; see Reymond & Barnes, 86 & 189. The shrine of the Egyptian martyr Menas was at Karm Abu Mina in the Mareotis; for the difficulties and details of his cult, see *DACL*, 11:324–97. For the Greek traditional account of his martyrdom on Athor 15 (11 November), see *Acta Sancti Menae*. Alexander of Alexandria, *Deposition of Arius*, intro, written *ca*.319, mentions the clergy of Mareotis. Athanasius, *Apologia contra Arianos*, 64.3, mentions several presbyters *ca*.335. De Cosson, 36–58 & 106–56. Timm, 4:1593–1603. Talbert, map 74.

Maximianopolis. (modern Qena; ancient Kaine.) The letter of Melitius in Athanasius, *Apologia contra Arianos*, 59.3 & 71.5–6, mentions, but does not name, the Melitian bishop at the time of the Council of Nicaea. Athanasius, *Festal Letter* "12 to Serapion" (of 339), indicates that Herminus succeeded Atras as bishop. Timm, 4:1624–27. Talbert, map 80.

Memphis. (modern Manf.) The *Synaxarium Alexandrinum* mentions the martyred soldier Timothy of Memphis on 21 Paoni (15 May); also see Delehaye, "Les martyrs," 106. A monastery in his honor near the pyramids is noted by Abu Salih, fol. 65a. Bishop Antiochus represented the city at the Council of Nicaea; see Gelzer, lx. At the time of the Council of Nicaea, John was the Melitian bishop; see the letter of Melitius in Athanasius, *Apologia contra Arianos*, 59.3 & 71.5–6. Timm, 1549–48. Papaconstantinou, 283. *Atlas*, 5. Talbert, map 75.

Metelis. (modern Masil.) *Synaxarium Alexandrinum*, 9 Tut (6 September), mentions the martyr Bishop Pisoura. At the time of the Council of Nicaea, Cronius was the Melitian bishop; see the letter of Melitius in Athanasius, *Apologia contra Arianos*, 59.3 & 71.5–6. Harnack, 718. Timm, 4:1604–10. *Atlas*, 5. Talbert, map 74.

Neiloupolis. Bishop Chaeremon of Neilopolis and his wife fled to Arabia during the Decianic persecutions according to Dionysius of Alexandria; see Eusebius, *Ecclesiastical History*, 6.42.3. At the time of the Council of Nicaea, Theon was the Melitian bishop; see the letter of Melitius in Athanasius, *Apologia contra Arianos*, 59.3 & 71.5–6. Athanasius, *Festal Letter* 19 (of 347), indicates that Amatus and Isaac succeeded Theon as bishop. Talbert, map 75, identifies two cities—one in the Fayyum and one near Hermopolis Magna—with this name. Timm, 2:498–501, does not state a preference for one town or the other as the home of Chaermon and Theon. Harnack, map V., and *Atlas*, 5, opt for the location in the Fayyum.

Nikiou/Nikiopolis. (Coptic Pshat, modern Ibshadi, about midway up the Rosetta branch of the Nile; not to be confused with Nikopolis, which was on the outskirts of Alexandria.) According to the *Synaxarium Alexandrinum*, 28 Hathor (24 November), Bishop Sarapamon was martyred during the great persecution; see also Delehaye, "Les martyrs," 96. At the time of the Council of Nicaea, Heraclides was the Melitian bishop of Nikiou; see the letter of Melitius in Athanasius, *Apologia contra Arianos*, 59.3 & 71.5–6. For the location, see Abu Salih, fol. 29b. Timm, 3:1132–40. *Atlas*, 5. Talbert, map 74.

Nitria. Palladius, *Lausiac History*, 8.3 & 5, says that Ammoun and his wife lived as celibates for eighteen years (apparently near Nitria) before Ammoun moved to Nitria for the next twenty-two years before his death. Since Jerome, *Chronicle*, says that Antony died in 356, and Athanasius, *Life of Antony*, 60, says that Antony had a vision of Ammoun's death, it follows that Ammoun would have taken up residence at Nitria at some time before *ca.*334. Further precision is difficult to obtain, although the general consensus of the evidence would place Ammoun at Nitria before 325.

Sozomen, who in 1.13.13 says that he is working in chronological order, mentions Ammoun as a disciple of Antony at 1.14.1 and the Council of Nicaea in 1.15.1. *Menologium Basilianum*, 1.94 (cols. 89–92), says that Ammoun retired to Nitria in the days of Maximian. (Maximian's first reign began in 286, and his last reign, as usurper, was in 310.)

Historia monachorum in Aegypto, 22.1–3, preserves a slightly different tradition indicating that Ammoun was the first ascetic at Nitria, having moved there in celibacy with his wife shortly after their marriage. This is followed by Socrates, 4.23.1–8.

Since the *Menologium Sirletianum*, 4 October (compare *AASS*, Octobris 2: 413–14), says that Ammoun married in the reign of Maximian, Evelyn-White, 46–47, would date Ammoun's residence at Nitria from *ca.*315. In fact, following this tradition in conjunction with Palladius, Ammoun could have moved to Nitria as late as *ca.*328.

Walters, 244–45, opts for the general date of *ca.*320–330 for Ammoun's establishment at Nitria. The settlement furnished a bishop in 359; see Martin, *Athanase*, 79. Chitty, 11–13. Timm, 3:978–84. Talbert, map 74.

Oxyrhynchus. (modern Behnesa.) Numerous papyri, some of them Christian from before 325, have been found. Judge & Pickering, 2, 3, 4, and 6 (respectively Naldini #18; 13; *PSI* 14 [1957] 1412; and Naldini, #35) are personal letters dating from the early-Third to the early-Fourth Centuries and containing Christian formulae such as "ἐν κυρίῳ" or Christian cryptograms. Judge & Pickering, #15 (P. Oxy. 3035) is an order to arrest Petosorapis, "χρησιανόν" dating to 256. Judge & Pickering, #16, 17, 18 are also official inquiries mentioning Christians. Judge & Pickering, #20 (P. Oxy. 43 verso), mentions a Northern and a Southern "ἐκκλησία" which may be a reference to Christian buildings *ca.*295. Judge & Pickering #31 and 32 (respectively P. Oxy. 2474 and P. Oxy. 907) are Third-Century wills written by persons likely to have been Christians. P. Oxy. 2665 from 305/306 relates to the confiscation of the assets of a certain Paul, whose name may be indicative of Christianity; see Judge & Pickering, #18.

Papyrologists have discovered several works of Christian literature whose date of writing can be determined, though naturally the date at which they were discarded will be later. P. Oxy. 3523 (=Gregory-Aland P[90]) is a fragment of John 18:36–19:1, 2–7 from the Second

Century. P. Oxy. 4009 may be a fragment of the *Gospel of Peter* from the Second Century. P. Oxy. 2949 is apparently a fragment of an apocryphal gospel from the late-Second or early-Third Century. P. Oxy. 1786, from the Third Century, is the earliest Christian hymn with musical notation. P. Oxy. 3525 and P. Ryl. III (1938) 463 are fragments of the *Gospel of Mary* from the Third Century. From the same era, P. Oxy. 412 contains part of the *Kestoi* of Julius Africanus. Several fragments of the *Shepherd of Hermas* have been found, for example P. Oxy. 3528 from the late-Second or early-Third Century and P. Oxy. 3527 from the Third Century. P. Oxy. 2384 (=Gregory-Aland, P[70]) is from the Third Century. The fragments of Matthew found in P. Oxy. 2683 (=Gregory-Aland, P[77]) are from *ca.*300.

PSI 10.1165 (=Gregory Aland P[48]) is a manuscript of Acts from the end of the Third Century. P. Oxy. 2684 (=Gregory-Aland, P[78]) is a manuscript of Jude from the late Third or early Fourth century. P. Oxy. 4010 is a copy of the Our Father from the Fourth Century. P. Oxy. 1224 is a Fourth-Century text from a noncanonical gospel. Gregory-Aland P[13] (=*PSI* 12.1292 + P. Oxy. 657) is a copy of Hebrews on a scroll from the Third or Fourth Century. Numerous other early Christian papyri have been found; see the lists in Haelst, 409–13, in Treu (1969–91), and in Römer (1997, 1998, & 2000).

Synaxarium Alexandrinum attributes several martyrs of the great persecution to Oxyrhynchus: Ibehada on 24 Tobi (19 January), Elias on 28 Tobi (23 January), Sinouthius on 14 Phamenoth (10 March), and Bima on Epip 8 (2 July); see Delehaye, "Les martyrs," 93–110 *passim*. Compare Papaconstantinou, 286–88.

At the time of the Council of Nicaea, Pelagius was the Melitian bishop; see the letter of Melitius in Athanasius, *Apologia contra Arianos*, 59.3 & 71.5–6. Athanasius, *Festal Letter* 19 (of 347), indicates that Theodorus succeeded Pelagius, so Pelagius must have been reconciled before 347. Timm, 1:283–300. *Atlas*, 5. Talbert, map 75.

Panephusis. (in the Nesut Nome; modern el-Manza.) The martyr Serapion was said to be from there; see his *Martyrdom* in Balestri & Hyvernat, text CSCO 43, Scriptores Coptici 3:63–68; trans. CSCO 44, Scriptores Coptici 4:47–60. See also *Synaxarium Alexandrinum*, 27 Tubah (22 January). Bishop Philip was at the Council of Nicaea; see Gelzer, lx. Timm, 1:186–88 & 324–27. *Atlas*, 5. Talbert, map 74.

Panopolis. (modern Akhmim.) P. Strasb. inv.1017 is a late Third- or early Fourth-Century text containing sentences attributed to the apostles; see Plasburg, 217–24, and Haelst, #1178. P. Berl. Bork., a document dating from *ca.*315–320, mentions numerous individuals, among them six deacons at I.29, IX.29, XI.7, XI.32, XIV.30, and A.IV.10, as well as two women named Maria at II.29 and XIII.32. Bagnall, "Conversion," 246, takes the name Maria to be distinctively Christian. P. Gen. inv. 108, a list of buildings dating from between 298 and 341, mentions a house that is somehow connected to an "ἐκκλησία" and property at two other places owned by persons titled "διάκονος"; see Judge & Pickering, #21, and *Sammelbuch* 8 (1967): 9902. Two ascetic martyrs of Akhmim are commemorated in the *Synaxarium Alexandrinum* on 29 Choiak (25 December) or 1 Tubah (27 December). According to the Coptic list of signatories, Bishop Gaius of Panopolis was at the Council of Nicaea; see Gelzer, 79. Athanasius, *Festal Letter* 19 (of 347), states that because of old age and infirmity Bishop Artemidorus had requested that a certain Arius be appointed as his coadjutor. P. Achm. 1, dated in Wessely #20 to the Third Century, in reality dates no earlier than the end of the Fourth Century; see Haelst, #693. Timm, 1:80–96. Papaconstantinou, 298. *Atlas*, 5. Talbert, map 77.

Parembole. (near Nikopolis, to the East of Alexandria; see Martin, *Athanase*, 58, citing P. Lond. VI., 1914, lines 13–15.) *Martyrdom of S. Shenoufe and His Brethren*, 105Vii, makes passing reference to a certain Bishop Eisidimus of Parembole near the Alexandrian nome; see Reymond & Barns, 86 & 189. At the time of the Council of Nicaea, Macarius was a Melitian presbyter at Parembole; see the letter of Melitius in Athanasius, *Apologia contra Arianos*, 59.3 & 71.5–6. Socrates, 4.23.54–55, says that a gnostic monk from Parembole lived by Lake Maerotis.

Pelusium. (modern Farama.) *SEC*, 5 Oct., attributes the martyr Epimachus to Pelusium; compare *BHG*, #593. *Synaxarium Alexandrinum* attributes the following martyrs to Pelusium during the great persecution: Isidorus and Sina on 18 Phamenoth (14 March) and 24 Pharmouthi (19 April), Pirou and Athom on 8 Epip (2 July); see also Delehaye, "Les martyrs," 102–3 & 106, also *BHO*, #994. Bishop Dorotheus was at the Council of Nicaea; see Gelzer, lx. At the same time, Callinicus was the Melitian bishop; see the letter of Melitius in Athanasius, *Apologia contra Arianos*, 59.3 & 71.5–6. Callinicus also appears in Athanasius, *Festal Letter* 4 (of 332). Timm, 2:926–35. *Atlas*, 5. Talbert, map 74.

Phakoussa. (modern Faqus.) At the time of the Council of Nicaea, Moses was the Melitian bishop; see the letter of Melitius in Athanasius, *Apologia contra Arianos*, 59.3 & 71.5–6. Timm, 2:923–26. *Atlas*, 5. Talbert, map 74.

Pharbaithos. (modern Farbet.) Bishop Arbetius was at the Council of Nicaea; see Gelzer, lx. The letter of Melitius in Athanasius, *Apologia contra Arianos*, 59.3 & 71.5–6, mentions, but does not name, the Melitian bishop at the time. Calderini, 5:62. Timm, 2:936–39. *Atlas*, 5. Talbert, map 74.

Phragonis. (modern Horbeit.) Martin, *Athanase*, 32–39, suggests that this place name should be read from Michael the Syrian's list of Nicene bishops; see Michael the Syrian, *Chronicle*, 7.2 (Syriac text 4: 124; French trans. 1:248). This would replace the corrupt "Alphokranon" in the other lists; see Gelzer, lx & 80–81. Bishop Harpocrates was at the Council of Nicaea. It is perhaps Phragonis that Epiphanius had in mind when he mentioned the home town of Valentinus; see Epiphanius, *Panarion*, 31.2.2–3. Calderini, 5:97–98. Timm, 1:73–75 & 2:940–44. Talbert, map 74.

Phthenegys. At the time of the Council of Nicaea, Pininuthes was the Melitian bishop; see the letter of Melitius in Athanasius, *Apologia contra Arianos*, 59.3 & 71.5–6. *Atlas*, 5. Compare Talbert, map 74.

Pispir. (modern Der Anba Antonios/Der al-Memun, across the Nile from Koma.) The "Outer Mountain" of Antony. Jerome, *Chronicle*, dates Antony's birth to *ca.*251. Athanasius, *Life of Antony*, 10.1–13.7, says that Antony took up residence on the mountain beginning at about age 35 and remained there for 20 years, so *ca.*285–305. *Historia monachorum in Aegypto*, 15.1, alludes to the place. Palladius, *Lausiac History*, 21.1, gives the name of the place and mentions some of Antony's disciples. Rufinus, *Ecclesiastical History*, 2.7–8, mentions his own visit to the place. Evelyn-White, 13–14 & plate 1. Timm, 2:742–49. Griggs, 104–105 & 275.

Ptolemais Hermiou. (Coptic Psoi; modern el-Menshyah.) The *Passio Psote* places the martyrdom of Psote during the Diocletianic persecutions on 7 Choiak (3 December); see Orlandi, 24–41. *Synaxarium Alexandrinum* calls the martyr Absadi/Ibehada and dates the martyrdom to 27 Choiak (23 December); see also Delehaye, "Les martyrs," 98. The letter of Melitius in Athanasius, *Apologia contra Arianos*, 59.3

& 71.5–6, mentions, but does not name the Melitian bishop of Ptolemais at the time of the Council of Nicaea. Timm, 3:1140–47. Papaconstantinou, 299. Not to be confused with the Ptolemais in Cyrene, see Fedalto, 2:648. Talbert, map 77.

Sais. *Synaxarium Alexandrinum* attributes the following martyrs to Sais during the great persecution: Theoclia on 10 Mechir (4 February), Sophia and her daughters on 10 Paoni (4 June), and Warasanuphius and others on 29 Epip (23 July); see also Delehaye, "Les martyrs," 101, 105, & 108. The letter of Melitius in Athanasius, *Apologia contra Arianos*, 59.3 & 71.5–6, mentions, but does not name, the Melitian bishop of Sais at the time of the Council of Nicaea. Athanasius, *Festal Letter* 19 (of 347), indicates that Paphnutious succeeded Nemesion as bishop. *Atlas*, 5. Talbert, map 74.

Sebennytos. (modern Sammanud.) At the time of the Council of Nicaea, Soterichus was the Melitian bishop; see the letter of Melitius in Athanasius, *Apologia contra Arianos*, 59.3 & 71.5–6. Timm, 5:2254–62. *Atlas*, 5. Talbert, map 74.

Sinary. (modern Shinara; near Oxyrhynchus.) The little-known martyr Maximus of Shinara continued to be commemorated there as late as the time of Abu Salih; see Horn, 2:114–15, and Abu-Salih, fol. 91b. Graf, 1:536, mentions an Arabic manuscript (Cairo 712, fol. 273r–275v) with record of this martyr tradition. Maximus is mentioned incidentally in a Ninth-Century Sahidic manuscript of the *Martyrdom of Epima*, fol. 26b, in Mina, text 7, trans. 48. Timm, 5:2351–53. Talbert, map 75.

Skedias/Schedia. Bishop Atthas was at the Council of Nicaea; see Gelzer, lx. *Atlas*, 5. Talbert, map 74.

Tabennesis. (modern Tabanisin.) Pachomius was discharged from the army *ca*.313; see Veilleux, 267. He then spent about three years in Chenoboskion and seven years with the ascetic Palamon before founding the monastery at Tabennesis, so Tabennesis was founded *ca*.323; see *S. Pachomii Vita*, Bohairic pp. 7 & 18. Martin, *Athanase*, 126–27. Timm, 6:2438–51. Talbert, map 77.

Tanis. (modern San.) Delehaye, "Les martyrs," 67–68, 86, & 122, mentions a very dubious martyr tradition associated in Latin martyrdoms with Tanis. At the time of the Council of Nicaea, Eudaemon was the Melitian bishop; see the letter of Melitius in Athanasius,

Apologia contra Arianos, 59.3 & 71.5–6. Eudaemon also appears in Athanasius, *Festal Letter* 4 (of 332). Athanasius, *Festal Letter* "12, to Serapion" (of 339), indicates that Theodorus succeeded Elias as bishop. Timm, 5:2264–70. *Atlas*, 5. Talbert, map 74.

Taposiris Megale. (just to the West of Alexandria; see Timm, 6:2515–19.) Dionysius of Alexandria had sympathizers in the place who freed him when he was held under arrest there; see Eusebius, *Ecclesiastical History*, 6.40.4–9. Athanasius, *Apologia contra Arianos*, 64.3 mentions the presbyter Didymus *ca.*335. De Cosson, 109–115. *Atlas*, 4. Talbert, map 74.

Tauthites. (perhaps the otherwise unlocated Tantathoites and the related town of Taya in the Phthemphoutite nome of the Delta, compare Talbert, map 74.) Bishop Tiberius was at the Council of Nicaea; see Gelzer, lx. Calderini, 4:355 & 368.

Tentyra. (Dendara in the Ptolemaite nome.) *Synaxarium Alexandrinum* attributes the following martyrs to Tentyrae during the Diocletianic persecutions: Ptolemy on 11 Choiak (7 December), Paphnutius/Babnudah on 20 Pharmouthi or 6 Pachon (15 April or 1 May); see Delehaye, "Les martyrs," 97 & 103–4. For the *Martyrdom of Paphnutius*, see Delehaye, "Les martyrs," 328–43. At the time of the Council of Nicaea, Pachumes was the Miletian bishop; see the letter of Melitius in Athanasius, *Apologia contra Arianos*, 59.3 & 71.5–6. Athanasius, *Festal Letter* "12, to Serapion" (of 339), records that Andronicus succeeded his father Saprion as bishop. Timm, 2:543–48. *Atlas*, 5. Talbert, map 80.

Thebes. (Diospolis Magna; Coptic Ne; ancient Karnak and Luxor; modern al-Uqsur; see Lefort, *Les vies*, 82.) Jerome, *Vita S. Pauli*, 1–2, asserts that Paul of Thebes, who is said to have taken up the ascetic life in the time of the persecutions under Decius and Valerian, was the first hermit. *Synaxarium Alexandrinum*, 20 Hathur (16 November), mentions martyrs Sophronius and Sanazum. *S. Pachomii Vita*, Sahidic p. 212 & Greek p. 3, indicates that when Pachomius was a conscript *ca.*312 he was ministered to in Thebes by a group of Christians. *S. Pachomii Vita*, Bohairic p. 4, calls the place Sne, "Latopis," but this was probably a copyist's mistake since the manuscripts describe the place as the capital of the ancient empire, which would have been Thebes; see Lefort, *Les vies*, 82. The letter of Melitius in Athanasius, *Apologia contra Arianos*, 59.3 & 71.5–6, mentions, but does not name, the Melitian bishop of Thebes at the time of the Council of Nicaea. Athanasius, *Festal Letter* "12, to Serapion" of 339, records that Philon succeeded Philon as bishop. P. Lugd. Bat. II W (=*PGM* 2.XIII) is as apocryphon of Moses from the late Third or early Fourth Century mentioning "the Christ" in line 290; see also Haelst, #1071. P. Bib. Nat. Supp. Gr. inv. 574 (=*PGM* 1.IV) is a magical papyrus of the same era invoking among others "the God of the Hebrews, Jesus" at lines 3019–20; see also Haelst, #1074. See Timm, 6:2904–19 and compare 4:1762–63. Papaconstantinou, 300. *Atlas*, 5. Talbert, map 80.

Thmouis. (modern Timay.) Photius, *Interrogationes decem*, 9, probably on the authority of Pamphilus's now lost *Apology for Origen*, records a tradition indicating that Heraclas of Alexandria had difficult relations with Bishop Ammonius of Thmuis, even replacing him with a certain Philip because Ammonius had earlier shown hospitality to Origen when Origen was banished in 232; see the analysis in Nautin, 167–68.

Bishop Phileas of Thmuis was martyred in the Diocletianic persecutions; see Eusebius, *Ecclesiastical History*, 8.9.7–8.10.12, and *Acta Philae* in Musurillo, 328–45. Bishop Gaius represented the city at the Council of Nicaea; see Gelzer, lx. By contrast, the Coptic list of participants makes Gaius the bishop of Panopolis and a certain Tiberius bishop of Thmuis; see Gelzer, 78–79.

At the time of the Council of Nicaea, Ephraim was the Melitian bishop; see the letter of Melitius in Athanasius, *Apologia contra Arianos*, 59.3 & 71.5–6. Athanasius, *Festal Letter* "12" (of 339), is addressed to Bishop Serapion. Timm, 6:2670–78. *Atlas*, 5. Talbert, map 74.

Toeto. (modern Tahta, in the Panopolite nome.) P. Grenf. II (1897) 73, a papyrus from the late-Third or early-Fourth Century, records a letter from the presbyter Psenosiris of Toeto to his fellow presbyter Apollon at Kusis in the Great Oasis regarding the lady Politike; see Judge & Pickering, #9 (=Naldini, #21). For the location, see Calderini, 5:18. Timm, 6:2467–69. Talbert, map 77.

Possible sites

Athribis? (Atripe, in the Thebaid.) The "White Monastery" founded by Shenoute's uncle Pjol was nearby; see Besa, *Sinuthii Archimandrite vita*, 5–7, and Abu Salih, fol. 82b. Walters, 241–42, noting that the monastery was founded on the model of Tabenessi, places the founding of the White Monastery *ca.*320–330. If, however, Tabenessi was

not established until *ca*.323 as indicated above, the foundation date
of the White Monastery would most probably fall after 325. Bell,
94, n. 11, would place the date of the White Monastery's foundation further toward the middle of the century. *Synaxarium Alexandrinum*,
8 Tut (5 September), mentions commemoration of the martyr
Timotheus there. Talbert, map 77.

Babylon? (the Roman fortress near modern Fustat in Old Cairo.)
A parchment fragment of Romans (Gregory-Aland, 0220) dating to
the late Third or possibly the Fourth Century is said to have been
found in Fustat; see Hatch, 81–85.

Harnack, 722 & map V, is mistaken in indicating that there may
be literary evidence for Christianity at the Roman fortress Babylon
before 325. The evidence he cites from Constantine?, *To the Assembly
of the Saints*, 16, refers to Babylon in Assyria and in any case does
not state that Christians were present there. Talbert, map 74.

Bagawat? (in the Khargeh Oasis.) *SEG* 38 (1988): #1716, one of
numerous inscriptions found at the church there, contains the word
"εἰρήνη" and a cross, and is dated by the editors to *ca*.300. Talbert,
map 79.

Ch(e)imo/Chi? (modern el-Bordan at the Western end of the Mareotis;
see De Cosson, 115–16.) Van der Meer & Mohrman, map 4, lists
"Chino," as a place represented at the Council of Nicaea. This is
apparently followed in part by *Atlas*, 5. Indeed, the Arabic list of
cities represented at Nicaea does mention a "Cino," but this is evidently a corruption of "Cuno" for Kunopolis inferior, where the
Nicene bishop was Adamantius; see Gelzer, 160–61. If Adamantius
of "Cuno" is to be distinguished from the Meletian bishop Hermaeon
of Kunopolis and Busiris, however, it might be possible to assign
Adamantius to Cheimo. Timm does not appear to mention the place.
Pauly-Wissowa, 3.2:2205 & 2274. Ball, 104, 131, & 136. Calderini,
5:123. Talbert, maps 73 & 74.

Hanipiar? (in the Herakleopolite nome.) The *Martyrdom of SS. Apaioule
and Pteleme*, 171Ri, mentions the holy man Apaioule of Hanipar at
the beginning of the Fourth Century; see Reymond & Barnes, 134
& 226. Calderini, 1.2:46. Timm, 3:1088.

Hipponon? (modern Esbet Qarara.) Haelst, #492, notes that Gregory-
Aland P[40], dating perhaps as early as the Third Century, may well
have come from Qarara. Talbert, map 75.

Kellia? (about 12 roman miles from Nitria.) The Kellia ("Cells") seem to have been established by monastics under the guidance of Ammoun of Nitria, see *Apophthegmata Patrum, alphabetical series*, Antony, 34. Presumably they were established before settlements were founded at Sketis *ca*.330. *Historia monachorum in Aegypto*, 20.5–8, gives a general description. Palladius settled near there *ca*.391; see his *Lausiac History*, 7.1. Evelyn-White, 49–50. Walters, 244–45. Timm, 1691–1712. Talbert, map 74.

Latopolis? (Coptic Sne, modern Isna, in the Thebaid.) *Synaxarium Alexandrinum* preserves elaborate but uncertain traditions of a Bishop Ammonius of Latopis (who is said to have been installed by Peter of Alexandria) and his whole church being martyred there by the governor Arrianus on 13 Choiak (9 December) and of a large number of martyrs on 19 Tobi (14 January) during the great persecution; see also Delehaye, "Les martyrs," 97 & 99. Graf, 1:536, cites two Arabic manuscripts, Paris ar.153, fol. 438r–445r, and 780, fol. 24v–115v, for the latter tradition. One is led to suspect that the martyred Ammonius has been confused with the later bishop of the same name.

The reference to Christians at Latopis (Coptic "Sne") *ca*.313 in *S. Pachomii Vita*, Bohairic p. 4, is probably a copyist's error for Thebes (Coptic "Ne."). Athanasius, *Festal Letter* 19 (of 347), notes that Masis succeeded Ammonius as bishop of Latopolis. Timm, 3:1181–93. Talbert, map 80.

Narmouthis? (modern Medinet Madi in the Fayyum.) P. Narmuthis 69.29a + 229a (=Gregory-Aland P[92]), a fragment of the New Testament containing Ephesians 1:11–13, 19–21 and II Thessalonians 1:4–5, 11–12, dates to the Third or Fourth Century and was found in a grave at Narmuthis; see Gallazzi, 117–22, and Treu (1984), 123. The question remains open as to the date at which the text was placed in the grave. Talbert, map 75.

Pboou? (modern Faw Qibli.) *S. Pachomii Vita*, Bohairic p. 18 & Greek p. 8, indicates that Pboou was founded a few years after Tabennesi. Veilleux, 71, dates the founding of Pboou to *ca*.329. Chitty, 23–5. Martin, *Athanase*, 126–27. Timm, 2:947–57. Talbert, map 77.

Philadelphia? Harnack, 714, suggests that *libelli* issued to those who sacrificed under Diocletian may indicate the presence of Christians or suspected Christians, yet Judge & Pickering, 70, rightly point out that there is no way to know whether the persons who received the certificates were Christians. Some of the documents listed at Judge & Pickering, #5 (=Naldini, #14–17), however, from *ca*.297, may be Christian in nature. *Atlas*, 5. Talbert, map 75.

Sketis? (Wadi al-Natrun.) Palladius, 17.2 & 13, indicates that Macarius the Egyptian took up the ascetic life at Sketis at the age of about thirty and lived there for some sixty years, dying only about a year before Palladius himself went out into the desert monasteries. At 1.1 & 7.1, Palladius says that he himself had arrived in Egypt during the second consulate of the Emperor Theodosius (i.e., 388) and entered the desert monasteries about three years later, so it follows that Macarius arrived at Scetis *ca*.330. For the year 388, see Bagnall, *et al.*, 310–11. See also Evelyn-White, 65; Walters, 237; and Chitty, 13. The traditions about Macarius the Egyptian are confused with those of Macarius of Alexandria in *Historia monachorum in Aegypto*, 21.1–17 & 23.1–4. Talbert, map 74.

Syene? (modern Aswan.) According to the *Martyrdom of Apa Epima*, Diocletian gave the order to destroy churches as far upriver as Syene; see Balestri and Hyvernat, text CSCO 43, Scriptores Coptici 3:124; trans. CSCO 44, Scriptores Coptici 4:80. *S. Pachomii Vita*, Bohairic sect. 28, & Greek p. 20, indicates that *ca*.329–30 Athanasius intended to visit the churches as far upriver as Syene. Athanasius, *Festal Letter* 19 (of 347), says that Nilamon succeeded Nilamon of the same name as bishop. Athanasius, *Historia Arianorum*, 72.4, says that the presbyters Hierakas and Dioscorus were banished there *ca*.354. Timm, 1:222–35. Papaconstantinou, 304. Talbert, map 80, inset.

Talmis? (modern Kalabsha in the Dodekaschoinos region above Syene.) The words "πιέ ζησης διὰ [π]αντὸ[ς ἀε] ἴ" with a Christogram, dating *ca*.300–330, have been found on a glass plate excavated in the Wadi Qitna cemetery there; see *SEG* 34 (1984): #1632. Talbert, map 81.

Tama? *SEC*, 5 Sept. and 23 Sept., lists the martyr Herais; compare also *Menologium Sirletianum*, 5 September. An early account on papyrus of her martyrdom may be found in Rossi, text 262–71 and trans. 293–97; see *BHO*, #376. The later tradition recorded in *Synaxarium Alexandrinum* places the martyrdom of Herais and her supposed brother Apater at Tout 28 (25 September); see Delehaye, "Les martyrs," 94, and *BHO*, #73–74. Eusebius, *Ecclesiastical History*, 6.4.3,

records her martyrdom without mentioning the place. For an evaluation of the martyrdom of Herais, see Baumeister, 102–103. Timm,
6:2476–77, suggests that the name "Tama" is a corruption of the
name Ansina. For the shrine of Apater and Herais at modern Amshul
(ancient Seneilais), see Horn 2:42 & 87–94. Talbert, map 75, includes
a town named Tamais.

Tepot? (perhaps on the Canopic branch of the Nile.) According to
the *Martyrdom of Paese and Thecla*, 86Vi–86Vii, Paese and his companions were tried there; see Reymond & Barnes, 77 & 182–83
Timm, 6:2587–88.

Tsimise nt-Parembole? (near Nikopolis.) Bishop Eisidemos of
Tsimise is mentioned in connection with the *Martyrdom of Shenoufe
and His Brethren*, 105Vii; see Reymond & Barnes, 86 & 109. Timm,
6:2857–59.

Turranion? P. Oxy. 1773 (=Naldini, #10), a letter from the Third
Century, contains a message from Eytychis to his mother Ametrion
with wording that is possibly Christian. Timm, 6:2900. Calderini,
5:38–39.

Sites for which the earliest evidence is clearly post 325

Aphroditopolis? Athanasius, *Festal Letter* "12, to Serapion" (of 339),
indicates that Serenus succeeded Theodorus as bishop of Aphroditopolis.
Timm, 1:251–56. Talbert, maps 75, 77, & 80, all contain towns with
the name "Aphroditon." Athanasius's letter does not give sufficient
context to determine which town he was writing about. For one possible site (Kom Išqaw), compare Timm 3:1438–61 & Papaconstantinou,
296–98.

Bomotheus? Athanasius, *Apologia contra Arianos*, 64.3, mentions the
presbyter Justus *ca*.335.

Boukolia? Athanasius, *Festal Letter* "12, to Serapion" (of 339) indicates that Heraclius was the new bishop.

Chenebri? Athanasius, *Apologia contra Arianos*, 64.3, mentions the
presbyter Boccon *ca*.335.

Dicella? Athanasius, *Apologia contra Arianos*, 64.3, mentions the presbyter Ammonas *ca*.335.

Diosphacos? Athanasius, *Festal Letter* 19 (of 347), indicates that Theodorus succeeded Serapammon as bishop. Timm, 6:2904–19, apparently tries to read the name as Diospolis [Magna], which would be Thebes, but this would seem to be an impossibility since the unnamed bishop of Thebes is otherwise mentioned in the letter of Athanasius.

Hypsele? (modern Shutb.) Athanasius, *Festal Letter* 19 (of 347), indicates that Bishop Arsenius had been reconciled. Timm, 5:2416–24. *Atlas*, 5. Talbert, map 77.

Klysma? (modern Qulzum.) Athanasius, *Festal Letter* 19 (of 347), indicates that Tithonas and Paul succeeded Jacob as bishop. At *Historia Arianorum*, 72.4, Athanasius says that bishop Dracontius of Hermopolis Parva was banished there *ca.*354. Compare Athanasius, *Letter to Dracontius*, 1–10, and *Tomus ad Antiochenos*, 10. Timm, 5:2164–71.

Myrsine? Athanasius, *Apologia contra Arianos*, 64.3, mentions the presbyter Achillas *ca.*335.

Paralos? Athanasius, *Festal Letter* "12, to Serapion" (of 339) indicates that Nemesion succeeded Nonnos as bishop. Timm, 1:450–55.

Phascos? Athanasius, *Apologia contra Arianos*, 64.3, mentions the presbyter Heraclius *ca.*335.

Prosopites? Athanasius, *Festal Letter* 19 (of 347), indicates that Triadelphus succeeded Serapammon as bishop. Talbert, map 74.

Rhinocolura? Athanasius, *Festal Letter* "12, to Serapion" (of 339), notes that Salomon became bishop. Timm, 1:147–52. Talbert, map 70.

Tmou n-Pahom? P. Lond. VI., 1920, line 1, from 335, mentions Meletian Christians at the place. Timm, 6:2711–12.

Tmounakon? P. Lond. VI., 1914, line 6, from 335, mentions a certain Christian named Hor of Tmounakon. Timm, 6:2836.

Tohe? P. Lond. VI., 1920, line 61, from 335, mentions Meletian Christians at the place. Timm, 6:2723–24.

Xois? (modern Saha.) Athanasius, *Festal Letter* 19 (of 347), notes that Theodorus and Isidorus succeeded Anubion as bishop. Timm, 5:2231–37. Talbert, map 74.

CYRENAICA AND LIBYA

Bibliography
Alon
Athanasius, *Festal Letters*
Basil, *Letters*
BHG
BS
Calderini
DACL
Eusebius, *Ecclesiastical History*
Fedalto
Gelzer
Harnack
Irenaeus, *Adversus haereses*
Joannou
Leynaud
Martyrologium Hieronymianum
Martyrologium Romanum
Menologium Sirletianum
OCD
Philostorgius
Reynolds
Romanelli, *Cirenaica*
Roques
Rowe
SEC
Socrates
Synesius of Cyrene
Theodoret, *Correspondance*

General

Cyrenaica and Libya. The region was known to have a large Jewish population right up until the revolt of Quietus, *ca.*117; see Alon, 376–90. Persons from Cyrene played significant parts in the narratives of the gospels and Acts. Simon from Cyrene is mentioned in the gospels as present at Jesus' crucifixion; Matthew 27:32, Mark 15:21, Luke 23:26. On the evidence of Mark, two of Simon's sons, Alexander and Rufus, were apparently part of the Christian community in the First Century. Jews from Cyrene were also said to be present at Pentecost and at the stoning of Stephen; Acts 2:10 & 6:9. Lucius of Cyrene was connected with the church at Antioch *ca.*44 or 45; see Acts 13:1. Later tradition counts Lucius as Bishop of Cyrene: see *SEC*, 22 August; *BHG*, #2243; *Martyrologium Romanum*, 6 May; *BS*, 8:281; and Fedalto, 2:659. Irenaeus, *Adversus haereses*, I.10.2, from *ca.*180, mentions the presence of Christians in Libya, but provides no further details. Likewise, Sabellius, who was active in Rome at the time of Zephyrinus (*ca.*217–222) was considered by later writers to have been a native of Libya, perhaps of the Pentapolis; see Basil *Letters*, 207, and Theodoret, *Correspondance*, 4:4.196–97. Sabellius may or may not have been from Cyrenaica, but it is clear that beliefs similar to Sabellianism were known in Cyrenaica *ca.*257–260; see Eusebius, *Ecclesiastical History*, 7.6.1 & 7.26.1–3; also Roques, 324. Dionysius of Alexandria addressed a treatise on the beginning of Ecclesiates to Basilides, Bishop of the communities of the Pentapolis at this time; see Eusebius, *Ecclesiastical History*, 7.26.3.

Canon 6 of the Council of Nicaea states that Libya and the Pentapolis are under the jurisdiction of the Bishop of Alexandria; see Joannou, 29. There are no clearly Christian inscriptions from before the late Fourth Century; see Reynolds, 284. *DACL*, 3.2:3220–27.

Specific sites

Antipyrgos/Antiphra. (modern Tobruk.) Bishop Serapion was at the Council of Nicaea; see Gelzer, lx. *Atlas*, 5. Fedalto, 2:662. Talbert, map 73.

Barke. (modern el-Merg.) Bishop Zopyrus was at the Council of Nicaea; see Gelzer, lx. *Atlas*, 5. Fedalto, 2:658. Talbert, map 38.

Berenike. (modern Benghazi.) Dionysius of Alexandria wrote to Bishop Ammon at the time of the Sabellian disturbance *ca.*257–260; see Eusebius, *Ecclesiastical History*, 7.26.1. Bishop Dakes was at the Council of Nicaea; see Gelzer, lx. He was described by Philostorgius, I.8a, as a supporter of Arius. *Atlas*, 5. Fedalto, 2:658. Talbert, map 38.

Boreum/Boreion. (modern Bu Grada.) Bishop Sentianus, was a supporter of Arius at the Council of Nicaea; see Philostorgius, I.8a. *Atlas*, 5. Fedalto, 2:659. Talbert, map 37.

Cyrene. (modern Ain Shahat.) The bishop at the time of the Sabellian disturbance *ca.*257–260 may have been Basilides since Cyrene was the metropolis of the province at the time; see Romanelli, *Cirenaica*, 231, and Roques, 325.

Bishop Theodorus and others were martyred under Diocletian *ca.*303–305; see *SEC*, 4 July and 22 August. Likewise, *Martyrologium Hieronymianum*, 7 kal. Aprilis, mentions Bishop Theodorus and others as martyrs in the Pentapolis. See also *Menologium Sirletianum*, 4 July.

From *ca.*365 an inscription for the Christian lady Demetria and her son Gaius has been found in the Northern necropolis; see Rowe, 10–11, and Reynolds, #6. *Atlas*, 5. Fedalto, 2:659. Talbert, map 38.

Marmarica. (region in Libya.) Bishop Theonas was a supporter of Arius at the Council of Nicaea; see Philostorgius, 1.8a, and Socrates, 1.8.13 & 31. Athanasius, *Festal Letter*, 12 (of 339), mentions Arabion, who was also bishop of Stathma. *OCD*, 926. Fedalto, 2:663, dates Arabion too early. Talbert, maps 38 & 73.

Paraetonium. (in Libya Inferior.) In the middle of the Third Century, Dionysius of Alexandria spent a part of his exile in an isolated and unnamed spot three day's journey from Paraetonium; see Eusebius, *Ecclesiastical History*, 7.11.23. Bishop Titus of Paraetonium was at the Council of Nicaea; see Gelzer, lx. *Atlas*, 5. Fedalto, 2:663. Talbert, map 73.

Ptolemais. (modern Tolmeta.) Dionysius of Alexandria mentioned Ptolemais as one of the cities disturbed by Sabellianism *ca.*257–260; see Eusebius, *Ecclesiastical History*, 7.6.1. The bishop at the time may have been Telesphorus; see Roques, 325, commenting on Eusebius, *Ecclesiastical History*, 7.26.1. Similarly, Fedalto, 2:661, seems to assign Bishop Basilides of the Pentapolis region to Ptolemais; compare Eusebius, *Ecclesiastical History*, 7.26.2. Bishop Secundus seems to have had an ambiguous position at the Council of Nicaea; Philostorgius, I.8a, and Socrates, 1.8.13 & 31, list him as a supporter of Arius. Yet Secundus is found with bishops from Egypt (not Libya) in the lists of those present at the Council; see Gelzer, lx. *Atlas*, 5. Talbert, map 38.

Taucheira/Arsinoe. (modern Tocra.) Bishop Secundus was at the Council of Nicaea; see Gelzer, lx. *Atlas*, 5. Fedalto, 2:661. Talbert, map 38.

Possible sites

Dar(da)nis? (modern Derna.) Seat of the metropolitan for Libya II by 367; see Athanasius, *Festal Letter* 39 (of 367). Fedalto, 2:662. Talbert, map 38.

Eastern Gareathis? (a region either East of Darnis or West of Catabathmus maior; see Talbert, maps 38 & 73.) Athanasius, *Festal Letter*, 12 (of 339), mentions that Andragathius had succeeded Hierax as bishop. Fedalto, 2:662.

Hydrax? (possibly modern Ain Mara.) Synesius of Cyrene, *Epistle* 66 [67], mentions a Bishop Siderius of Palaebisca promoted by Athanasius to become bishop of Ptolemais and later retiring to the villages of Palaebisca and Hydrax again. Siderius may relate to Ptolemais Hermiou in Egypt, though the bishops of Alexandria also had oversight of Libya and the Pentapolis; see Canon 6 of the Council of Nicaea in Joannou, 1:29. It is easier to see why Synesius would have mentioned an incident connected with his native region. Fedalto, 2:660, puts the site in Libya. Talbert, map 38.

Palaebisca? (possibly modern Beit Tamer or el-Marazig.) Synesius of Cyrene, *Epistle* 66 [67], mentions a Bishop Siderius of Palaebisca promoted by Athanasius to become bishop of Ptolemais and later retiring to the villages of Palaebisca and Hydrax again. Siderius may relate to Ptolemais Hermiou in Egypt, though the bishops of Alexandria also had oversight of Libya and the Pentapolis; see Canon 6 of the Council of Nicaea in Joannou, 1:29. It is easier to see why Synesius would have mentioned an incident connected with his native region. Fedalto, 2:660, puts the site in Libya. Compare Talbert, map 38.

Southern Gareathis? (a region either South of Darnis or West of Catabathmus maior; see Talbert, maps 38 & 73.) Athanasius, *Festal Letter* "12, to Serapion" (of 339), mentions that Quintus had succeeded Nikon as bishop. Fedalto, 2:663.

Stathma? Athanasius, *Festal Letter* "12, to Serapion" (of 339), mentions Bishop Arabion, who was also bishop of Marmarica. Fedalto, 2:663.

AFRICA PROCONSULARIS

Bibliography
AB
Acta purgationis Felicis
Akakpo
Athanasius, *Apologia contra Arianos*
Atlas
Augustine, *Ad Donatistas post collationem*
Augustine, *Contra Cresconium*
Augustine, *De baptismo contra Donatistas*
Augustine, *De Civitate Dei*
Augustine, *Enarrationes in Psalmos*
Augustine, *Epistulae*
Augustine, *Sermones*
BHL
CIL
Concilia Africae
Concilia Galliae
Cyprian, *Epistulae*
Cyprian, *De lapsis*
DACL
DHGE
DiVita
Duval, Yvette, *Chrétiens*
Duval, Yvette, *Loca*
Ennabli
Evodius of Uzalis
Floriani Squarciapino
Frend, *Donatist Church*
Gerke
Harnack
ILCV
Jerome, *De viris inlustribus*
Kalendarium Carthaginense
Koch
Leynaud
Mai
Maier
Mandouze

Martyrologium Hieronymianum
Mattingly
M'charek
Mesnage
Monceaux
Musurillo
Optatus
PL
Poinssot & Lantier
Prudentius
Raven
Rives
Romanelli, "Le sedi"
Saxer. *Vie liturgique et quotidienne*
Sent. Episcop. 87
Tabbernee
Talbert
Tertullian, *Ad nationes*
Tertullian, *Ad Scapulam*
Tertullian, *Apologeticum*
Tertullian, *De fuga in persecutione*
Tertullian, *De monogamia*
Tertullian, *De pallio*
Tertullian, *Scorpiace*
Tilley
Van der Meer & Mohrmann
Vita Caecilii Cypriani
Wilpert, *I Sarcofagi*

General
Africa. During much of the Roman era, part of historic Numidia, the District of Hippo, was administered as part of Africa Proconsularis. I here treat the District of Hippo in light of its historic connections with the rest of Numidia and exclude it from Africa Proconsularis.

Athanasius, *Apologia contra Arianos*, 37.1, notes the presence of bishops from Africa at the Council of Serdica in 343.

Specific sites
Abbir Germanicus. Location uncertain; for general information, see *CIL*, 8:814, p.102. Bishop Successus of "Abbir Germaniciana"

was at the Council of Carthage in 256; see *Sent. Episcop. 87*.16. Locating Abbir Germanicus (Abbir Minus) near Germaniciana between Aquae Regiae and Aeliae would agree with the manuscripts of the document and is the choice favored by Harnack, 905–06; compare Talbert, map 33. *Martyrologium Hieronymianum*, 14 kal. Feb., suggests that Harnack is right, yet Saxer, *Vie liturgique*, 449, believes that Abbir Germanicus is Henchir en Naam.

Mesnage, 122 & 175, notes that Henchir en-Naam could be ancient Abbir Cellae or perhaps ancient Abbir Maius. Talbert, map 32, likewise distinguishes Abbir Cellae (identified now as modern Henchir en-Naam) from Abbir Maius, which was Southwest of Thimida in Zeugitana.

In any case, Bishop Successus may be the one who is mentioned as a martyr under Valerian in the *Mart. Montanus et Lucius*, 21; see Musurillo, xxxiv–xxxvi & 214–239. *Atlas*, 4.

Abitina(e). (possibly modern Chahoud el-Batin; West of Membressa in Zeugitana.) Bishop Saturninus was at the Council of Carthage in 256; see *Sent. Episcop. 87*.64. He is also mentioned in Augustine, *De Baptismo contra Donatistas*, 7:28. Bishop Fundanus was a *traditor* under Diocletian in 304; see *Passio Sanctorum Dativi, Saturnini presbyteri, et aliorum* in Maier, 64. Translated in Tilley, 27–49. Mesnage, 42. Saxer, 449. Talbert, map 32.

Abthugni/Aptugni. (modern Henchir es-Souar; on the Southern border of Zeugitana.) Bishop Felix of Abthungi ordained Caecilian as Bishop of Carthage; see Optatus, 1.18. Felix was later accused by the Donatists of being a *traditor* under Diocletian, but was absolved in 315; see *Acta Purgationis Felicis*. For a study of the episode, see Yvette Duval, *Chrétiens*, 213–346. Mesnage, 144. *Atlas*, 4. Talbert, map 32.

Aggya. (Acbia/Agbia, modern Ain Hedja; in Zeugitana.) Bishop Quintus was at the Council of Carthage in 256; see *Sent. Episcop. 87*.65. Mesnage, 84. Saxer, 449. *Atlas*, 4.

Ausvaga/Uzaae. (modern Msaken; to the North[west] of Beja.) Bishop Ahymnus was at the Council of Carthage in 256; see *Sent. Episcop. 87*.50. Mesnage, 181, refers to this place as Ausvaga I. Augustine, *Epistulae*, 93,(8).24, notes that the tribe of the "Arzuges" heard Christian preaching, though no indication of date is given. Saxer, 450. Talbert, map 33.

Avioccala/Abiocatense. (modern Henchir Sidi Amara; near Henchir el Khima in Byzacene.) See *Acta SS. Donati et Advocati* (more correctly named *Acta S. Donati ep. Abiocal(ensis)* in Maier, 198–211, with respect to events of 317. Translated in Tilley, 52–60. Mesnage, 30. *Atlas*, 4. Talbert, map 32.

Beneventum. A Bishop Anastasius was at the Council of Arles in 314; see *Concilia Galliae*, 14, 15, 17, 19, 20, 22. Mandouze, 68, locates Beneventum generally in Africa Proconsularis. *DHGE*, 7:1290.

Biltha. (Henchir Salah el Balti; North of Bulla Regia.) Bishop Caecilius was at the Council of Carthage in 256; *Sent. Episcop. 87.*1. Mesnage, 137. Saxer, 449.

Bol/Vol. (near Carthage.) Augustine, *Sermones*, 156 (PL 38:849), was delivered in memory of the martyrs there; compare *Kalendarium Carthaginense*, 16 kal. Nov. Mesnage, 236–37.

Buslacenae. (either Bisica Lucana [modern Henchir Bichga] in Zeugitania or Lacene to the North of Gabes.) Bishop Felix was at the Council of Carthage in 256; see *Sent. Episcop. 87.*63. Mesnage, 186. Talbert, map 32.

Capsa. (modern Gafsa; in Byzacene. Yet Harnack, 907, also suggests a Capsus [Ain Guigba] in Numidia.) Cyprian, *Epistulae*, 56.title, mentions Bishop Donatulus. Donatulus was also at the Council of Carthage in 256; *Sent. Episcop. 87.*69. Mesnage, 69. Saxer, 449. *Atlas*, 4. Talbert, map 33.

Carpi(s). (modern Mraissa; in Zeugitana.) Bishop Secundinus was at the Council of Carthage in 256: *Sent. Episcop. 87.*24. Mesnage, 121. Saxer, 449. *Atlas*, 4. Talbert, map 32.

Carthage. Tertullian refers to Carthage explicitly in *Apologeticum*, 25.9; *Ad nationes* 2.14.6 & 2.17.7; *Scorpiace*, 6.2; and *De pallio*, 1.1–3. See also Jerome, *De viris inlustribus*, 53. A certain Optatus was bishop of Carthage or Thuburo in 202 when Perpetua and her maid suffered martyrdom; see *Mart. Perpetua et Felicitas*, 13, in Musurillo, 120–23. Castus and Aemelius were martyred at about this time; see Cyprian, *De lapsis*, 13, and *Kalendarium Carthaginense*, 11 kal. Jun. See also Augustine, *Sermones*, 285.4 (PL 38:1295). Monceaux, 1:45 & 3:537, gives the year of their martyrdom as 203.

Bishops Agrippinus and Donatus were active before Cyprian; see Cyprian, *Epistulae*, 80.1. For Cyprian at the Council of Carthage in 256, see *Sent. Episcop. 87*, preface and 87. *Vita Caecilii Cypriani*, 19. For a study of church life in Third-Century Carthage, see Saxer. For the martyrs Montanus and Lucius under Valerian; see *Passio Sanctorum Montani et Lucii* in *AASS*, Februarius 3, 461–64, and in Musurillo, xxxiv–xxxvi & 214–239. For Caecilian as deacon under Bishop Mensurius when food was withheld from martyrs during the Diocletianic persecution, see *Passio Sanctorum Dativi, Saturnini presbyteri, et aliorum*, 20, in Maier, 85–87. Caecilian became bishop shortly after the persecutions of 303–305; see Optatus, 1.18. He and the deacon Sperantius were at the Council of Arles in 314; *Concilia Galliae*, 15, 17, 19, 20, & 22. Caecilian was also at the Council of Nicaea; Gelzer, lxiv. Tabbernee, #14.1–#15, are early inscriptions in memory of Perpetua. Poinssot & Lantier, 388, refer to an inscription with DMS and an anchor motif that is possibly anterior to Constantine. Wilpert, *I Sarcofagi*, plates 288.1 and 288.4–9, are Christian sarcophagi from perhaps as early as the early Fourth Century; see Gerke, 348–49. Ennabli, 1087–1101. For a fuller study of Christianity at Carthage, see Rives, 223–310. *Atlas*, 4. Talbert, map 32.

Cephalitana possessio. (near Thuburo, just North of Uzalis. "Cepahalitana" would be the Greek translation of the Punic "*rus*" = "*cape*" or "*point of land.*") Maximilla, Domatilla, and Secunda were arrested there; see *Passio SS. Maximae, Secundae, et Donatillae*, 1.7, in Maier 92–105, translated in Tilley, 17–24. Evodius of Uzalis, *De miraculis S. Stephani Protomartyris*, 1.7 (col. 838), mentions the place as "*promontoriensi ecclesia.*" Monceaux 3:149. Mesnage, 189–90.

Chullabi. (in Byzacene.) Perhaps modern Kasrine (ancient Cillium) or modern Ain Djeloula (ancient Cululi); see Mesnage, 91 & 53–54; *Atlas*, 4; and Talbert, map 33. A less likely candidate would be modern Chullu (ancient Collo in Numidia); see Mesnage 274–75, and Talbert, map 31. From the Council of Carthage in 256, the name of Bishop Aurelius appears with the bishops of Byzacene in the *Sent. Episcop. 87.81*.

Cibalia(na). (probably modern Henchir Kelbia in Africa Proconsularis.) Bishop Donatus was at the Council of Carthage in 256; *Sent. Episcop. 87.55*. Mesnage, 190. Saxer, 449. Talbert, map 32.

Curubis. (in Zeugitana; modern Korba.) Cyprian went into exile there. See *Acta Cypriani*, in Musurillo, xxx–xxxi & 168–75. *Atlas*, 4. Talbert, map 32.

Dionysiana. (in Byzacene.) Possibly near the modern villages of Sousse and Monastir close to the city of Hadrumetum where there was a promontory called "Dionysios." Bishop Pomponius was at the Council of Carthage in 256; see *Sent. Episcop. 87*.48. He is mentioned in the titles of Cyprian, *Epistulae*, 4, 57, 67, & 70. He may also be the Pomponius mentioned in *Martyrologium Hieronymianum*, 15 kal. Jan. Mesnage, 194. *Atlas*, 4. Compare Talbert, map 33.

Furnae. (Furnos Maius; in Southern Zeugitana.) Harnack, 908 & 914. According to *Acta Purgationis Felicis*, 4, a Christian basilica was destroyed there *ca*.304. See Mesnage, 67. *Atlas*, 4. Talbert, map 32.

Furni. (Furnos Minus = Municipium Aurelium Antonianum, modern Henchir Msaadine in Zeugitania.) Bishop Geminus was at the Council of Carthage in 256; see *Sent. Episcop. 87*.59. Mesnage, 122. *Atlas*, 4. Talbert, map 32.

Gemellae. Probably modern Sidi Aich since the name of Bishop Litteus appears between bishops from Byzacene and Tripolitana in the *Sent. Episcop. 87*.82 from 256; so Mesnage, 23, and Saxer, 450. Less likely would be the Numidian sites Biar Ouled Athman or Mlili (site of the "limes Gemellensis"); see Mesnage, 250 & 336. Talbert, map 33.

Germaniciana. (modern Hadjeb el Aioun; in Byzacene.) Bishop Iambus was at the Council of Carthage in 256; see *Sent. Episcop. 87*.42. Mesnage, 200. Compare Talbert, map 33.

Girba. (modern Djerba/Houmt-Souk; in Tripolitania.) Bishop Monnulus was at the Council of Carthage in 256; see *Sent. Episcop. 87*.10. Mesnage, 55–56. Saxer, 449. Mattingly, 210. *Atlas*, 4. Talbert, map 35.

Gori(tana). (modern Henchir Draa el Gamra; in Zeugitana.) Bishop Victor was at the Council of Carthage in 256; see *Sent. Episcop. 87*.40. Mesnage, 62. Saxer, 449. *Atlas*, 4. Talbert, map 32.

Gurgaita. (in Byzacene.) Bishop Felix was at the Council of Carthage in 256; see *Sent. Episcop. 87*.74. Mesnage, 202. Compare Talbert, maps 32 & 33.

Hadrumetum. (modern Sousse; in Byzacene.) Tertullian, *De fuga in persecutione*, 5.3, mentions the early martyr Rutilius. Tertullian, *Ad Scapulam*, 3.5, mentions the martyr Malvius. Bishop Polycarpus is mentioned in Cyprian, *Epistulae*, 48.1, 57.title, 67.title, 70.title. According to the *Sent. Episcop. 87.3*, Polycarp was at the Council of Carthage in 256. Leynaud, 133–244, surveys catacomb inscriptions and other artifacts, many of them of Christian character and apparently of Third-Century date. Bishop Innocentius was martyred under Diocletian; see *AASS*, Maii 1:138. Mesnage, 146–49. *Atlas*, 4. Talbert, map 33.

Hippo Diarrhytus. (modern Bizerte; in Zeugitana.) Bishop Petrus was at the Council of Carthage in 256; see *Sent. Episcop. 87.72*. Mesnage, 39. Saxer, 449. *Atlas*, 4. Talbert, map 32.

Horrea Caelia. (modern Hergla; in Byzacene.) Bishop Tenax was at the Council of Carthage in 256; see *Sent. Episcop. 87.67*. Mesnage, 86. Saxer 449. *Atlas*, 4. Talbert, map 32.

Lepcis Maior/Lepcis Magna. (modern Lebda; in Tripolitania.) Lepcis Maior may have had a bishop as early as *ca*.200 when a Bishop Archaeus, apparently a contemporary of Pope Victor, composed a work on the dating of Easter; see Mai, 3:707, Monceaux, 1:54, and Romanelli, "Le sedi," 156–57. Bishop Dioga was at the Council of Carthage in 256; see *Sent. Episcop. 87.85*. Mesnage, 101. Saxer, 449. Mattingly, 210. Floriani Squarciapino, 55. Talbert, map 35.

Lepcis Minor. (modern Lamta; in Byzacene.) Bishop Demetrius was at the Council of Carthage in 256; see *Sent. Episcop. 87.36*. Mesnage, 101–102. Saxer, 449. *Atlas*, 4. Talbert, map 33.

Luperciana. (possibly Afsa Luperci; West of Djerba and South of Gabes.) Bishop Pelagianus was at the Council of Carthage in 256; see *Sent. Episcop. 87.44*. Mesnage, 206.

Mactaris. (modern Mactar; in Byzacene.) Bishop Marcus was at the Council of Carthage in 256; see *Sent. Episcop. 87.38*. Mesnage 103. For the pagan background, see M'charek, 213–23. Saxer, 450. *Atlas*, 4. Talbert, map 33.

Marazanae. (in Byzacene.) Bishop Felix was at the Council of Carthage in 256; see *Sent. Episcop. 87.46*. Mesnage, 208. Exact location unknown; compare Talbert, map 33.

Marcelliana. (Exact location unknown; somewhere in Africa Proconsularis.) Bishop Julianus was at the Council of Carthage in 256; see *Sent. Episcop. 87*.66. Mesnage, 208–9.

Maxula Prates/Massila. (modern Radès; just South of Carthage.) Martyrs are recorded in Augustine, *Sermon* 283 (PL 38:1286). *Martyrologium Hieronymianum*, 11 kal. Aug. Also in *Kalendarium Carthaginense*, 11 kal. Aug. Mesnage, 131. Lepelley, 2:140–41. Yvette Duval, *Loca*, 672–73 & 724. *Atlas*, 4. Talbert, map 32.

Membressa. (modern Medjez el Bab; in Zeugitania.) Bishop Lucius was at the Council of Carthage in 256; see *Sent. Episcop. 87*.62. Mesnage, 113. Saxer, 450. *Atlas*, 4. Talbert, map 32.

Midili/Medele. (probably modern modern Henchir Menkoub or Henchir Bou Rebia, which would be in Zeugitana: see Mesnage, 115; Saxer, 450; *Atlas*, 4; and possibly Talbert, map 33. Less likely would be the modern Mdila, Northwest of Negrine in Numidia; see Mesnage, 327, Harnack, 910, and Talbert, map 34.) Bishop Iader was at the Council of Carthage in 256 according to *Sent. Episcop. 87*.45.

Mi(s)girpa. (exact location unknown; evidently near Carthage.) Bishop Primus was at the Council of Carthage in 256; see *Sent. Episcop. 87*.2. Mesnage, 211. Compare Talbert, map 32.

Muzuc/Muzula. (perhaps modern Henchir Ka[ra]choum in Zeugitana; less likely modern Henchir Besra in Byzacene.) Bishop Januarius was at the Council of Carthage in 256; see *Sent. Episcop. 87*.34. Mesnage, 96 & 38. *Atlas*, 4. Talbert, map 32.

Neapolis. (probably the city of Neapolis [modern Nabeul Kedim] in Zeugitania; less likely would be the view that the Neapolis mentioned is a quarter of Leptis Magna.) Bishop Junius was at the Council of Carthage in 256; see *Sent. Episcop. 87*.86. Mesnage, 123–24. Saxer, 450. *Atlas*, 4. Talbert, map 32.

Nova. (possibly in Zeugitania; less likely would be Nova Sparsa [modern Henchir ben Khelifi] North of Diana in Numidia or Nova Petra [modern Henchir el Atech], for which see Talbert, map 34.) Bishop Rogatianus is named among other Bishops of Africa Proconsularis at the Council of Carthage in 256; see *Sent. Episcop. 87*.60. See also Cyprian, *Epistulae*, 3.title. Mesnage 213 & 497. Saxer, 450, opts for one of the Numidian sites.

Oea. (modern Tripoli; in Tripolitania.) Bishop Natalis was at the Council of Carthage in 256; see *Sent. Episcop. 87.83*. Christian artifacts have been found from perhaps as early as the second quarter of the Fourth Century; see DiVita, 243–44. Mesnage, 164. Mattingly, 210. Talbert, map 35.

Pocofelta/Cocofelta. Bishop Surgentius was at the Council of Arles in 314; see *Concilia Galliae*, 15, 17, 19, 20, 22. Mesnage, 216, following Toulotte, tentatively places the site in Africa Proconsularis. Mandouze, 1097.

Rucuma. The prefix "*ru(s)*" would mean "*cape*" or "*point of land*" in Punic, so the site is somewhere near the seashore in Africa Proconsularis. Saxer, 450, suggests Henchir Rekoub, followed by Talbert, map 32. Yvette Duval, *Loca*, 30, identifies the site as Henchir Djalta. Bishop Lucianus was at the Council of Carthage in 256; see *Sent. Episcop. 87.43*. Mesnage, 130 & 218. *Atlas*, 4.

Sabratha. (modern Henchir Sabrat; in Tripolitania.) Bishop Pompeius was at the Council of Carthage in 256; see *Sent. Episcop. 87.84*. Mesnage. 135–36. Mattingly, 210. Talbert, map 35.

Segermes. (modern Henchir Harat; in Zeugitana.) Bishop Nicomedes was at the Council of Carthage in 256; see *Sent. Episcop. 87.9*. Mesnage, 82. Saxer, 450. *Atlas*, 4. Talbert, map 32.

Sicilibba. (modern Bordj Alouine; in Zeugitana.) Bishop Sattius was at the Council of Carthage in 256; see *Sent. Episcop. 87.39*. Mesnage, 24. Saxer, 450. *Atlas*, 4. Talbert, map 32.

Sufes. (modern Henchir Sbiba; in Byzacene.) Bishop Privatus was at the Council of Carthage in 256; see *Sent. Episcop. 87.20*. Mesnage, 141. Saxer, 450. *Atlas*, 4. Talbert, map 33.

Sufetula. (modern Sbeitla; in Byzacene.) Bishop Privatianus was at the Council of Carthage in 256; see *Sent. Episcop. 87.19*. See also *Martyrologium Hieronymianum*, non. Maii. Mesnage, 138–39. Saxer, 450. *Atlas*, 4. Talbert, map 33.

Sutunurca. (Ain el Askeur; 7 km North of old Giufi.) According to Cyprian, *Epistulae*, 59.10.3, Bishop Repositus was a collaborator during the persecution under Decius. Mesnage, 23. *Atlas*, 4. Talbert, map 32.

Thambae. (Tambeae; in Byzacene but not otherwise identified.) Bishop Secundianus was at the Council of Carthage in 256; see *Sent. Episcop. 87.*80. Mesnage, 225.

Tharassa. (possibly Taraqua in Byzacene rather than Tarsa to the Southwest of Cirta in Numidia.) At the Council of Carthage in 256, the name of Bishop Zosimus appears with names of bishops from Byzacene; see *Sent. Episcop. 87.*56. Mesnage 226 & 432.

Thasualthe/Thasarte. (modern Segui; in the Southern part of Byzacene.) Bishop Adelfius was at the Council of Carthage in 256; see *Sent. Episcop. 87.*35. Mesnage, 142. Saxer, 450.

Thelepte. (modern Medinet el Khedima; in Byzacene.) Bishop Julianus was at the Council of Carthage in 256; see *Sent. Episcop. 87.*57. See also *Martyrologium Hieronymianum.* 5–7 kal. Feb. Mesnage, 110–13. Yvette Duval, *Loca,* 85. *Atlas,* 4. Talbert, map 33.

Thenae. (modern Henchir Thina; in Byzacene.) Bishop Eucratius was at the Council of Carthage in 256; *Sent. Episcop. 87.*29. See also *Martyrologium Hieronymianum,* 19 kal. Feb. Mesnage, 160. *Atlas,* 4. Tlabert, map 33.

Thibari. (modern Thibar; in Zeugitania.) Bishop Vincentius was at the Council of Carthage in 256; see *Sent. Episcop. 87.*37. See also Cyprian, *Epistulae,* 58. Mesnage, 159. *Atlas,* 4. Talbert, map 32.

Thibiuca. (Henchir Zouitina or Henchir el-Gassa; in Zeugitana; possibly near Thuburo minus, on the right bank of the Medjerda. For another possible identification, see Tilley, 7–9.) Bishop Felix was martyred on 15 July 303; see *Acta S. Felicis* in *AASS,* Oct. 10, 625–28, in Musurillo, xl & 266–71, and in Maier, 46–57. Translated in Tilley, 8–11. Mesnage, 172. Delehaye, *AB* 39 (1921): 241–79. Yvette Duval, *Loca,* 28–30. *Atlas,* 4. Talbert, map 32.

Thimida (Regia). (modern Sidi Ali es Sedfini; in Zeugitana.) Bishop Faustus was at the Council of Carthage in 256; see *Sent. Episcop. 87.*58. Mesnage, 28. Saxer, 450. Yvette Duval, *Chrétiens,* 391–93. *Atlas,* 4. Talbert, map 32.

Thinisa. (or Thunisa, modern Ras el Djebel; in Zeugitana.) Bishop Venantius was at the Council of Carthage in 256; see *Sent. Episcop. 87.*49. Mesnage, 132. Saxer, 450. *Atlas,* 4. Talbert, map 32.

Thizika. (modern Techga; in Zeugitania; Northwest of Thuburo minus.) Augustine, *Ad Donatistas post collationem*, 22.38, mentions Bishop Novellus at the Donatist synod in 307/8 or 311/12; see Mesnage, 156. Talbert, map 32.

Thubur(b)o. (Thuburbo Maius would be modern Henchir el Kasbat in the Southern part of Africa Proconsularis, but Thuburbo Minus would be modern Teboura in Zeugitana.) A certain Optatus was Bishop of Thuburo or Carthage when Perpetua and Felicitas of Thuburo were martyred in 202/203; see *Mart. Perpetua et Felicitas*, 13, in Musurillo, 120–23. Bishop Sedatus was at the Council of Carthage in 256; see *Sent. Episcop.* 87.18. According to *Martyrologium Hieronymianum*, non Mar., Maximilla, Domitilla, and Secunda were martyred there between 303 and 305; see also *Passio SS. Maximae, Secundae, et Donatillae*, in Maier, 92–105. Augustine, *Ad Donatistas post collationem*, 22.38, mentions a Bishop Faust[in]us at the Donatist Council of 307/8 or 311/12. Bishop Faustus was at the Council of Arles in 314; see *Concilia Galliae*, 15, 17, 19, 20, 22. Mesnage, 90, 155. Harnack, map XI, shows both possible locations. Saxer, 450. *Atlas*, 4, opts for Thuburbo maius. Talbert, map 32.

Thysdrus. (modern El Djem; in Byzacene.) Tertullian, *Ad Scapulam*, 4.3, mentions Christians being questioned there. Mesnage, 54. Saxer, 450. *Atlas*, 4. Talbert, map 33.

Tuccabor. (modern Toukabeur; in Zeugitana.) Bishop Fortunatus was at the Council of Carthage in 256; see *Sent. Episcop.* 87.17. Mesnage, 161–62. Saxer, 450. *Atlas*, 4. Talbert, map 32.

Ucres/Verum. (probably modern Bordj bou Djadi to the West-Northwest of Carthage rather than Henchir el Hatba, which would be the ancient fundus Ver[ona] between Ammaedara and Thucca Terebinthis.) Bishop Vitalis was at the Council of Arles in 314; see *Concilia Galliae*, 15, 17, 19, 20, & 22. *CIL* 8:11735, p. 1215. Mesnage, 51 & 83. *Atlas*, 4. Talbert, map 32.

Urusi/Buruc. (modern Henchir Sougda in Africa Proconsularis; if the "a Buruc" read by the editor Hartel should really be "ab Uruc.") Bishop Quietus was at the Council of Carthage in 256; see *Sent. Episcop.* 87.27. Mesnage, 145. Talbert, map 33.

Ululi. (Mesnage, 63 & 232, suggests that Ululi may be Ellez, but Saxer, 450, seems to think that "Ululos" is a misreading of Sululos, which would be Mesnage, 87. Lepelley, 2:165, makes no comment on whether Ululos may be Sululos.) Bishop Irenaeus was at the Council of Carthage in 256; see *Sent. Episcop. 87*.54. For Sululos, see Talbert, map 32.

Uthina. (modern Oudna; in Zeugitana.) Tertullian, *De monogamia*, 12.3, mentions, but does not name, the Bishop of Uthina. For Bishop Felix at the Council of Carthage in 256, see *Sent. Episcop. 87*.26. Bishop Lampadius was at the Council of Arles in 314; see *Concilia Galliae*, 15, 17, 19, 20, & 22. Mesnage, 127. *Atlas*, 4. Talbert, map 32.

Utica. (modern Henchir Bou Chateur; in Zeugitana.) Tertullian, *De pallio*, 1.2, mentions Utica as the sister-city of Carthage. Bishop Aurelius was at the Council of Carthage in 256; see *Sent. Episcop. 87*,17. Three hundred martyrs are said to have been killed in the region called Massa Candida near Utica in 258; see Prudentius, *Peristephanon*, 13:76-8, and Augustine *Enarrationes in Psalmos*, 144. Maurus was bishop in 303; see *Acta purgationis Felicis*, 10. Bishop Victor was at the Council of Arles in 314; see *Concilia Galliae*, 15, 17, 19, 20, & 22. Monceaux 2: 142-44. *Atlas*, 4. Talbert, map 32.

Uzalis. (modern El Alia; near Utica. Harnack, map XI, notes a possible Uzelis in Numidia as well.) Felix and Gennadius were martyred on 16 May 304; see Evodius of Uzalis, *De miraculis S. Stephani Protomartyris*, I.2 (col. 835). See also, *AASS*, Maii 3:570; Monceaux, 3:541; and *BHL*, 7860-61. Saturninus was Bishop *ca.*338; see Augustine, *De Civitate Dei*, 22.8.3, line 98. Mesnage, 25. Talbert, map 32.

Uzappa. (or Uzafa/Ausafa; modern Ksour Abed el Melek; in Byzacene.) Bishop Lucius was at the Council of Carthage in 256; see *Sent. Episcop. 87*.73. Mesnage, 20-21. Talbert, map 33.

Vaga. (modern Beja; near the coast in Zeugitana.) *Kalendarium Carthaginense*, 29 Oct./kal. Nov. lists martyrs. Bishop Libosus was at the Council of Carthage in 256; see *Sent. Episcop. 87*.30. Mesnage, 36. Saxer, 450. *Atlas*, 4. Talbert, map 32.

Vallis/Vallita. (modern Sidi Mediene; in Zeugitana, East of Abitinae.) According to Optatus, 2.4, Bonifacius would have been the Donatist bishop *ca.*330. Mesnage, 110. Talbert, map 32.

Victoriana. (in Byzacene.) Bishop Saturninus was at the Council of Carthage in 256; *Sent. Episcop. 87*.51. Mesnage, 234-35.

Zama. (most likely Zama Regia [modern Jama Biar] in Zeugitana; see Mesnage, 30; Saxer, 450; *Atlas*, 4; and Talbert, map 32. For Zama minor [Colonia Zama, modern Djama], see Mesnage 52. For a third Zama, see Mesnage, 167.) Bishop Marcellus represented Zama at the Council of Carthage in 256; see *Sent. Episcop. 87*.53. There is reference to a Christian basilica destroyed at Zama *ca*.303 in *Acta Purgationis Felicis*, 4.

Zigga/Ziqua. (modern Zaghouan; near Thubur(b)o in Zeugitania.) *Acta purgationis Felicis*, 6–10, mentions a Christian decurion named Ingentius from there at the time of the persecutions. See also Augustine, *Epistulae* 88, and *Contra Cresconium*, 3.70.81. Mesnage, 167, 237. *Atlas*, 4. Talbert, map 32.

Possible sites

Sullecthum? (modern Salakta; in Byzacene.) Leynaud, 439–45, records badly preserved catacomb inscriptions which appear to be comparable in date to those at Hadrumetum and which could be Christian in character. No bishops are known before 394; see Mesnage, 138, and Mandouze, 1284. Talbert, map 33.

Thapsus? (near Leptis Minor.) Harnack, map XI, lists Thapsus as a possible early Christian site but does not refer to it in his text. Van der Meer & Mohrmann, map 22, note it as a city represented at the Council of Carthage in 256. This is almost certainly a mistake. Although several cities, for example Capsa or Thenae, in *Sent. Episcop. 87* could be misreadings of "Thapsus," there is no evidence for such a misreading in the manuscripts cited.

Tunes? (modern Tunis.) Wilpert, *I Sarcofagi*, plates, 290.1, 290.4–5, 288.10, 290.3, and 290.6 are all early Christian sarcophagi. Wilpert, *I Sarcofagi*, 290.1 may be early Constantinian; see Gerke, 340, 348, 353, and 357. See Koch, 536–37, for a discussion of possible evidence for pre-Nicene sarcophagi. Talbert, map 32.

Numidia

Bibliography
AASS
AÉ
Akakpo
Atlas
Augustine, *Contra Cresconium*
Augustine, *Contra epistulam Parmeniani*
Augustine, *De Civitate Dei*
Augustine, *De mendacio*
Augustine, *Epistulae*
Augustine, *Retractationum, Libri II*
Augustine, *Sermones*
Berthier
CIL
Concilia Africae
Concilia Galliae
Cyprian, *Epistulae*
Cyprian, *De lapsis*
Duval, Yvette, *Chrétiens*
Duval, Yvette, *Loca*
EnECh
Frend, *Donatist Church*
Gaudemet
Gesta apud Zenophilum
Gui
Harnack
ILCV
Jerome, *De viris inlustribus*
Kalendarium Carthaginense
Lepelley
Maier
Mandouze
Marec & Marrou
Martyrologium Hieronymianum
Mesnage
Metzger, *The Early Versions*
Minucius Felix, *Octavius*
Mommsen, *Provinces*

Monceaux
Musurillo
OCD
Optatus
Pauly-Wissowa
PL
Pliny the Elder, *Natural History*
Raven
Ruinart
Salama
Saxer, *Vie liturgique*
Sent. Episcop. 87
Tabbernee
Talbert
Tertullian, *Ad Scapulam*
Tilley

General

Numidia. Historically, the province of Numidia was created in 197/98 C.E. when the old province Africa Proconsularis (which had incorporated the Numidian region) was divided. The heart of the ancient Numidian kingdom became what modern historians call the District of Hippo in Africa Proconsularis, while the outlying territories became the Province of Numidia with its capital at Lambaesis; see Berthier 139–42. The Province of Numidia was subdivided by Diocletian in 303, but was reunited by 314 when the capital was moved to Cirta; see Berthier, 182–84. In the following survey, I treat the District of Hippo ("Numidia proconsularis") as part of historical Numidia. Identifications of cities are largely from Saxer, 449–450.

Specific sites

Ammaedara. (modern Haidra; near the border between the District of Hippo and the region of Byzacene in Africa Proconsularis.) Bishop Eugenius was at the Council of Carthage in 256; see *Sent. Episcop. 87.32*. Marcellus and 34 others were martyred in the time of Diocletian and Maximian; see Yvette Duval, *Loca*, 105–23, where pertinent inscriptions may also be found. Mesnage, 77–78. Saxer, 449. For later Christian inscriptions, see *CIL*, 8:449–464. Lepelley, 2:64–68. *Atlas*, 4. Talbert, map 33.

Aquae (Thibilitanae). (near modern Hammam Meskhoutine and Announa). Bishop Marinus was active *ca*.305; see Optatus, 1.13–14; Augustine, *Contra Cresconium*, 3.27.30; and Augustine *De Civitate Dei*, 22.8.line 265. For the location, see Mesnage, 306, and the translation of Optatus by Edwards, 13. *Atlas*, 4. Talbert, map 31.

Assuras. (modern Zanfour, which would be on the border between the District of Hippo and Byzacene.) Cyprian, *Epistulae*, 65, mentions Bishop Fortunatianus as being deposed for apostasy during the repression under Decius and replaced by Bishop Epictetus. Bishop Victor was at the Council of Carthage in 256; see *Sent. Episcop. 87*.68. Harnack, 906. Mesnage, 168. Saxer, 449. *Atlas*, 4. Talbert, map 33.

Badias/Vadis. (modern Badès.) Bishop Dativus was at the Council of Carthage in 256; see *Sent. Episcop. 87*.15. Mesnage, 253. *Atlas*, 4. Talbert, map 34.

Bagai. (modern Ksar Bahgai.) Bishop Felix was at the Council of Carthage in 256; see *Sent. Episcop. 87*.12. Later the site of a Donatist uprising; Optatus, 3.1 & 4. Mesnage, 253. Saxer, 449. *Atlas*, 4. Talbert, map 34.

Bamacorra. (The site apparently took its name from tribe of the Vamacures, who were located near Thamugadi; see Pliny, *Natural History*, 5.4.) Bishop Felix was at the Council of Carthage in 256; see *Sent. Episcop. 87*.33. Mesnage, 404. Compare Talbert, map 34.

Bulla (Regia). (evidently modern Hamman Darradji; in the District of Hippo. Harnack, 906, also notes a Bulla minor.) Bishop Therapius of Bulla was at the Council of Carthage in 256; see *Sent. Episcop. 87*.61. Mesnage, 50. Lepelley, 2:87–90. *Atlas*, 4. Talbert, map 32.

Caesariana. (possibly Kessaria[na] between Cirta and Sitifis. See *CIL*, 8:6041; Harnack, map XI, and compare Talbert, map 31.) *Gesta apud Zenophilum*, 5, mentions a certain Eutychius *ca*.305. Mesnage, 312.

Calama. (modern Guelma; in the District of Hippo.) Bishop Donatus was active *ca*.305; see Optatus, 1.13, and Augustine, *Contra Cresconium*, 3.27.30. Mesnage, 296–98. Lepelley, 2:90–103. *Atlas*, 4. Talbert, map 31.

Casae Nigrae. (probably the Oasis Négrine. For a general description, see *CIL*, 8: pp. 276 & 953.) Bishop Donatus, whose name was later given to the Donatist controversy, is mentioned as active *ca.*305; see Augustine, *Retractationum, Libri II*, 1.21, and *Contra Cresconium*, 2.12.14. Mesnage, 342–43. Talbert, map 34.

Castra Galbae. (in Numidia.) Bishop Lucius was at the Council of Carthage in 256; see *Sent. Episcop. 87*.7. Mesnage, 410.

Cedias. (modern Henchir Ounkif.) Bishop Secondinus was at the Council of Carthage in 256; see *Sent. Episcop. 87*.11. Perhaps this is the same Bishop Secundinus who is mentioned in the *Passio Sanctorum Mariani et Jacobi*, as being present at Muguas in the time of Valerian's persecution; see Musurillo, 196–97. Leynaud, 451, reports the presence of poorly explored catacombs. For general information on the site, see *CIL*, 8, p.256. Mesnage, 346. Saxer, 449. Gui, 290–91. *Atlas*, 4. Talbert, map 34.

Centuriones. (possibly El Kentour; North of Cirta.) Against, Mesnage, 311–12, and Harnack, 914, reference to a *"magistratus Centurionum et Cirtensium"* ("magistrate of Centuriones and Cirtensium") in the *Passio Sanctorum Mariani et Jacobi* is incorrect. The correct reading is "*centurione et Cirtensium magistratibus,*" i.e. "centurion and magistrates of Cirta;" see Musurillo, 198–201. Optatus, 1.14, mentions the Donatist Bishop Nabor of Centuriones *ca.*305. *Atlas*, 4.

Cirta. (modern Constantine, capital of the Province of Numidia after 314; see Berthier, 182–84.) The Caecilius mentioned in Minucius Felix seems to have been a native of Cirta as he mentions his fellow countryman Fronto; see Minucius Felix, *Octavius*, 9.6 & 31.2. Even so it seems that Caecilius became a Christian only at Rome. For an M. Caecilius at Cirta, see *CIL*, 8:7094–7098. Bishop Crescens of Cirta was at the Council of Carthage in 256; see *Sent. Episcop. 87*.8. The Agapius who suffered in Valerian's repression was possibly the next bishop; see *Passio Sanctorum Mariani et Jacobi* in Musurillo, 196–97 & 206–07. Paulus was bishop *ca.*303; see *Gesta apud Zenophilum*, 3, and Augustine, *Epistulae*, 53.4. For Bishop Silvanus *ca.*305, see Optatus, 1.14. *CIL*, 8:7094–7098. Mesnage, 275–78. Saxer, 449. On the persecutions and their aftermath, see Yvette Duval, *Chrétiens*, 65–209. For remains of a church building from the Fourth Century; see Gui, 205–208. *Atlas*, 4. Talbert, map 31.

Cuicul. (modern Djemila.) Bishop Pudentianus was at the Council of Carthage in 256; see *Sent. Episcop. 87*.71. *CIL*, 8:8296 (=*ILCV*, #3631A) from 212 has been interpreted by some as a possibly

Christian inscription. For the probably local martyrs Claudius and Pascentius, see Yvette Duval, *Loca*, 293–95. An inscription found on a milepost nearby and datable to 319/320 has perhaps the earliest use of the chi-rho monogram in Africa; see Salama, 537–43, and *AÉ* 1992, #1885. Mesnage, 283–84. Saxer, 449. For possible late Fourth-Century churches; see Gui 92–103. *Atlas*, 4. Talbert, map 31.

Garba. (possibly Ain Garb, East-Southeast of Cuicul. Yet Talbert, map 31, opts for Ain Tamda.) Optatus, 1.14 & 2.4, and Augustine, *Contra Cresconium*, 3.27.30, mention the Donatist Bishop Victor *ca*.305, who later may have become the Donatist Bishop of Rome. Mesnage, 292.

Gazaufala/Gadiaufala. (modern Ksar Sbai, see Gui, 325–26.) Bishop Salvianus was at the Council of Carthage in 356; see *Sent. Episcop 87*.76. Mesnage, 364. Saxer, 449. For a possible, but undated, Christian inscription, see *CIL*, 8:4807. *Atlas*, 4. Talbert, map 31.

Hippo Regius. (modern Annaba/Bône; in the District of Hippo.) Bishop Theogenes was at the Council of Carthage in 256; see *Sent. Episcop. 87*.14. He was apparently martyred under Valerian; see Ruinart, 224–25, and Augustine, *Sermones*, 273.7 (PL 38:1251). Marec & Marrou, 165–76, describe a Greek inscription from the Third Century set up by Aurelius Barlaas in memory of his wife Flavia Kosmopolis. Bishops Leontius and Fidentius were martyred under Diocletian; see *AASS*, Martii 2: 341. For Leontius, see also Augustine, *Sermones*, 260 (PL 38:1201–1202); 262 (PL 38:1207–1209); and *Epistulae* 29, title. For the "twenty martyrs" of Hippo, see *De Civitate Dei*, 22.8.lines 243–64; and also *Sermones*, 148 (PL 38:799–800); 325.1 (PL 38:1447–48); and 326.2 (PL 38:1449–50). Martyrs are also listed at *Martyrologium Hieronymianum*, 17 kal. Dec. See also Mesnage, 263, Monceaux, 3:152–53, and Saxer, 449. For the catholic martyr Nabor, see Yvette Duval, *Loca*, 182–83 & 717. Gui, 346–49, notes possible Fourth-Century mosaics. Lepelley, 2:113–25. *Atlas*, 4. Talbert, map 31.

Lamasba. (modern Henchir Merouana/Cornielle.) Bishop Pusillus was at the Council of Carthage in 256; see *Sent. Episcop. 87*.75. Mesnage, 279. Saxer, 449–50. *Atlas*, 4. Talbert, map 34.

Lambaesis. (ancient Legio, the first capital of the Province Numidia; modern Lambèse.) Persecutions there are mentioned by Tertullian, *Ad Scapulam*, 4.8. Cyprian, *Epistulae*, 59.10, mentions a heretic named

Privatus from *ca*.240. Januarius was bishop in 256 according to the *Sent. Episcop. 87*.6. See also the *Passio Sanctorum Mariani et Jacobi* in Musurillo, 206–9. For the Sixth-Century church building, see Gui, 145–47. *Talbert*, 4. Talbert, map 34.

Lares/Laribus. (modern Henchir Lorbeus.) Bishop Hortensianus was at the Council of Carthage in 256; see *Sent. Episcop. 87*.21. Since the name "Hortinsus" is listed in the *Martyrologium Hieronymianum* at 3 id. Jan., he may have been martyred under Valerian. Mesnage, 102. Saxer, 449. *Atlas*, 4. Talbert, map 32.

Legisvolumni. Bishop Victor was at the Synod of Arles in 314; see *Concilia Galliae*, 15, 17, 19, 20, & 22. Also Gaudemet, 62. Mesnage, 419.

Limata/Liniata. (near Milev, but location uncertain; compare Talbert, map 31.) See of the apostate Bishop Purpurus in the Diocletianic persecutions; see Optatus, 1.13, and Augustine, *Contra Cresconium*, 3.27.30. Mesnage, 419. Yvette Duval, *Chrétiens*, 175–80.

Macomades. (probably modern Mrikeb Thala/Canrobert; see Mesnage, 331 & 420, and Talbert, map 34.) Bishop Cassius was at the Council of Carthage in 256; see *Sent. Episcop. 87*.22. If Macomades minor (modern Henchir Ghorib/Bordj Yonca) is meant, it would be in Africa Proconsularis near the coast of Byzacene; see Mesnage, 71; *Atlas*, 4; and Saxer 449.

Madauros. (modern Madaurouch; in the District of Hippo.) According to Augustine, the first martyr in Africa was Namphamo *ca*.180, closely followed by Lucitas, Miggin, and Sanamo; see Augustine, *Epistulae*, 16.2 & 17.2. For general information, see *CIL*, 8:p.472. For an early church building, see Gui, 327–32. Lepelley, 2:127–39. *Atlas*, 4. Talbert, map 32.

Mascula. (modern Khenchela.) Bishop Clarus was at the Council of Carthage in 256; *Sent. Episcop. 87*.79. Whether the inscriptions about *"Domini Muntani"* refer to Montanus or to a martyr is an unresolved question; see Yvette Duval, *Loca*, 167–71, and Tabbernee, #71. See Augustine, *Epistulae*, 53.4. Mesnage, 314. Saxer, 449. Leynaud, 449–50, notes the presence of some poorly reported catacombs. *Atlas*, 4. Talbert, map 34.

Milev. (modern Mila; sister city of Cirta.) Bishop Polianus was at the Council of Carthage in 256; see *Sent. Episcop. 87*.13. For inscriptions relating to martyrs, see *CIL*, 8:6700 & 8:19353. Optatus was bishop in the late Fourth Century. Mesnage, 335–36. Saxer, 450. Note also Yvette Duval, *Loca*, 245–47. *Atlas*, 4. Talbert, map 31.

Muguas. (near Cirta.) Bishops Agapius and Secundinus were held under arrest there in 259; see *Passio Sanctorum Mariani et Jacobi* in Musurillo, xxxiii–xxxiv & 194–213. *DACL*, 12:505–8. Compare Talbert, map 31.

Obba. (modern Ebba; in the District of Hippo.) Bishop Paul was at the Council of Carthage in 256; see *Sent. Episcop. 87*.47. He was apparently the same Paul who was martyred in 259 under Valerian; see *Passio Sanctorum Montani et Lucii*, 21, in *AASS*, Februarius 3: 464, and in Musurillo 234–35. Also *Martyrologium Hieronymianum*, 19 kal. Feb. Monceaux, 2:167. Mesnage, 63. *Atlas*, 4. Talbert, map 33.

Octava. The name of Bishop Victor appears among the names of other Numidian bishops at the Council of Carthage in 256; see *Sent. Episcop. 87*.78. Optatus, 3.14, notes later activities of Circumcellions there. Mesnage, 426.

Rotaria. Optatus 1.14, and Augustine, *Contra Cresconium*, 3.27.30, mention a Donatist Bishop Felix *ca.*305. Mesnage, 356.

Rusic(c)ade. (modern Ras Skikda/Philippeville; sister city of Cirta.) Bishop Verulus was at the Council of Carthage in 256; see *Sent. Episcop. 87*.70. Bishop Victor was active *ca.*305; see Optatus, 1.13, and Augustine, *Contra Cresconium*, 3.27.30. A basilica was established in honor of the local martyr Digna; see *CIL*, 8:19913, and Yvette Duval, *Loca*, 184–86 & 716. Mesnage, 350–52. Saxer, 450. *Atlas*, 4. Talbert, map 31.

Scillium. (unlocated site in Numidia.) *Acts of the Scillitan Martyrs*, the first document of Christianity from North Africa, refers to events of *ca.*180. When questioned, one of the martyrs named Speratus said that they had in their possession "*libri et epistulae Pauli viri iusti.*" That is, "books and letters of Paul, a just man;" see Musurillo, xxii–xxiii & 86–89. Presumably the books would have been translations into Latin; see Metzger, *Early Versions*, 289. The *Passio Sancti Felicis Episcopi*, in Musurillo, 270–71, contains reference to a "*via Scillitanorum,*" which may be a reference to these famous martyrs, see Tilley, 8–11. Yet Harnack, 902, says the *Acts of the Scillitan Martyrs* places them clearly in Numidia.

Sicca Veneria. (modern El Khef; in the District of Hippo.) Bishop Castus of Sicca Veneria, perhaps a namesake of the Carthaginian martyr, was at the Council of Carthage in 256; see *Sent Episcop. 87.*28. Arnobius, the teacher of Lactantius, was a native of Sicca; see Jerome, *De viris inlustribus*, 79–80. *CIL*, 8:16255 may be the reliquary of a martyr. *CIL*, 8:27690 & 27691, may also be pertinent. Note also *CIL*, 8:16249 (=*ILCV*, #869). *CIL*, 8:16396, is a somewhat later non-local list of martyrs found about 20 km South at Aubuzza (modern Henchir Djezza/Ain Djezza). Mesnage, 92–93. Saxer, 450. Yvette Duval, *Loca*, 96–99. Lepelley, 2:156–61. *EnECh*, 2:778. *Atlas*, 4. Talbert, map 32.

Thabraca. (modern Tabarca; in the District of Hippo.) Bishop Victorius was at the Council of Carthage in 256; see *Sent. Episcop. 87.*25. Mesnage, 150. Saxer, 450. Lepelley, 2:170–72. *Atlas*, 4. Talbert, map 32.

Thagaste. (modern Souk Ahras; in the District of Hippo.) Bishop Firmus is know to have been active prior to the era of Constantine; see Augustine, *De mendacio*, 13. Augustine, *Epistulae*, 126.7, says that he himself was born in the town. Mesnage, 371. Lepelley, 2:165–84. *Atlas*, 4. Talbert, map 32.

Thagura. (modern Taoura; in the District of Hippo.) Crispina, martyred at Tebessa on 5 December 304, came from the village of Thagura; see Musurillo, 302–3, and Maier, 107. *Kalendarium Carthaginense*, non. Dec. Mesnage, 376. Lepelley, 2:184–85. *Atlas*, 4. Talbert, map 32.

Thamugadi. (modern Timgad). Bishop Novatus was at the Council of Carthage in 256; see *Sent. Episcop 87.*4. A certain Faustinus was martyred on 10 June 259, see *Acta Mammarii*, 3 &11 in *AASS*, Jun. 2: 264–68. Monceaux 2:150 & 3:540. Mesnage, 386–88. Saxer, 450. Eleven ancient churches are known. Churches 2 and 7 may date from the Fourth Century; see Gui, 265–67 and 274–78. *Atlas*, 4. Talbert, map 34.

Theveste. (modern Tébessa; in the District of Hippo.) Bishop Lucius was at the Council of Carthage in 256; see *Sent. Episcop. 87.*31. For the martyr Maximilian on 12 March 295, see Musurillo, xxxvii & 244–49. For the martyr Crispina on 5 December 304, see Musurillo, xliv & 302–9, and Maier, 107–12. See also the *Kalendarium Carthaginense*, non. Dec. For a church dedicated to the martyr Crispina, see Gui, 311–16. Yvette Duval, *Loca*, 123–29. Optatus, 2.18, records a Donatist Council there in the mid-Fourth Century. Mesnage, 379. Saxer, 450. Lepelley, 2:185–89. *Atlas*, 4. Talbert, map 33.

Thubunae. (modern Tobna.) Bishop Nemesianus was at the Council of Carthage in 256; see *Sent. Episcop. 87*.5. He is mentioned in Cyprian, *Epistulae*, 62, 72, 76, & 77. Nemesianus was martyred under Valerian; see *Kalendarium Carthaginense*, 10 kal. Jan. Mesnage, 388. *Atlas*, 4. Talbert, map 34.

Tigisi(s) Numid. (modern Ain el-Bordj.) Optatus, 1:14 & 19, and Augustine *Contra Cresconium*, 3.26.27 & 3.29.30, mention Bishop Secundus *ca*.305 as one of the accusers of Caecilian of Carthage. See also Augustine, *Epistulae*, 43.2; 43.5; 43.14; 53.4; 58.3; and 88.3. Also Augustine, *Contra epistulam Parmeniani*, 1.3.5. Mesnage, 267–68. *Atlas*, 4. Talbert, map 31.

Possible sites

Astora? (modern Stora; not far from Rusic(c)ade.) See the undated inscription of one Marinian, possibly dating to the Third Century; *CIL*, 8:8191. Monceaux, 2:125. Mesnage, 373. Saxer, 22 & 450. Akakpo, map at end. Talbert, map 31.

Diana Veteranorum? (modern Zana.) Cyprian, *Epistulae*, 34.1, makes mention of a certain presbyter *"Gaio Didensii"* and his deacon. Harnack, 908, suggests that Gaius may have been from Diana Veteranorum. Compare Mesnage, 394. Pauly-Wissowa, 5:339. Talbert, map 34.

Thamallae? (Thamallula; modern Tocqueville/Ras el-Oued.) *CIL*, 8:20587 (=*ILCV*, #4156c) is a possibly Christian inscription from *ca*.240. Pauly-Wisssowa, II, 9:1231. Yvette Duval, *Loca*, 339–41. Compare Talbert, map 31.

MAURETANIA SITIFENSIS

Bibliography
AASS
Akakpo

Atlas
Augustine, *De baptismo contra Donatistas*
Augustine, *Epistulae*
CIL
Concilia Africae
Cyprian, *Epistulae*
Duval, Yvette, *Loca*
Fevrier, "Aux origines"
Frend, *Donatist Church*
Gui
Harnack
ILCV
Mesnage
Monceaux
OCD
Origen, *Homilies on Ezekiel*
Raven
Talbert
Tertullian, *Adversus Iudaeos*
Wilken

General

Mauretania Sitifensis. Tertullian, *Adversus Iudaeos*, 7.8, mentions Christians in Mauretania generally. Origen, *Homilies on Ezekiel*, 4.1, mentions the presence of Christianity among the Mauri. Until the era of Diocletian, Mauretania Sitifensis was part of the larger province of Mauretania Caesarea, but the cities are listed separately here. No sees in the *Sent. Episcop. 87* can be localized in Mauretania Sitifensis or Caesariensis; see Fevrier, "Aux origines," 796.

Specific sites

Novaricia. (modern Beni Fouda; South of Satafi.) Bishop Jubaianus mentioned by Cyprian, *Epistulae*, 73, might be from here if the reference to Jubianus in Augustine, *De baptismo contra Donatistas*, 11.16, could be read as "*Novaliciensis;*" see Harnack, 914–15. Fevrier, "Aux origines," 796, doubts the reference, and indeed the text at that point reads "*Novatianenses.*" Mesnage, 369.

    CIL, 8:10930 = 20478 from 324 reads in part "*mensa eterna Ianuarii, v(ixit) a(nnis) LXXV . . . d.m.s. eterna . . . a.p. CCLXXV.*" Here the "*d.m.s.*" coupled with the "*eterna*" seems to indicate a Christian presence. See also *CIL*, 8:20474 from 331. Duval, *Loca*, 299–301 also notes later depositories of relics. *Atlas*, 4. Talbert, map 31.

Satafis. (modern Ain Kébira/Perigotville.) *CIL*, 8:20277 (=*ILCV*, #1570), from 299, expresses sentiments which could be, but are not necessarily, Christian. *CIL*, 8:20305 (=*ILCV*, #3615), with the word "*memoria*" from 322 likewise is possibly Christian. *CIL*, 8:20302 (=*ILCV*, #3247), which mentions an "*ancilla Christi*" from 324, is clearly Christian; see Fevrier, "Aux origines," 781. See also *CIL*, 8:20277 (=*ILCV*, #1570) from *ca*.299. Yvette Duval, *Loca*, 302–304. For an early church, see Gui, 90–91. *Atlas*, 4. Talbert, map 31.

Sitifis. (modern Sétif.) *CIL*, 8:8501a & b are inscriptions from 225 & 226, but nothing in them need be specifically Christian. *CIL*, 8:8430 (=*ILCV*, #3665), with the phrase "*domus aeternalis*" could be Christian. *CIL*, 8:8608, is from 321 and reads "*d.m.s. l.S.C. Antius Faustus vixit annis xxv, decessit a. pr. CCLXXXII.*" On the ambiguity of the d.m.s. inscriptions, see Wilken, 78. *CIL*, 8:10930 (=*ILCV*, 3715), with the words "*mensa eterna*" from 324 is likely to be Christian. *CIL*, 8:10919 & 20475 (=*ILCV*, #3617), from 327 may just possibly be a Christian inscription.

A slightly later tablet commemorates the martyrs Justus and Decurius; see *CIL*, 8: p. 1920 (=*ILCV*, 1911). Decurius, at least, seems to have been a local martyr as his name is unknown elsewhere. Yvette Duval, *Loca*, 312–15. See also Harnack, 903. Augustine, *Epistulae*, 108.14 & 209.3, mentions the need for interpretation and instruction of Christians in the Punic language even in his day. *Atlas*, 4. Talbert, map 31.

MAURETANIA CAESARIENSIS

Bibliography
AASS
AB
Akakpo
Atlas
CIL
Concilia Africae
Concilia Galliae

Cyprian. *Epistulae*
DACL
Duval, Paul-Marie
Duval, Yvette, *Loca*
Fevrier, "Aux origines"
Frend, *Donatist Church*
Gerke
Gui
Harnack
ILCV
Martyrologium Hieronymianum
Monceaux
OCD
Raven
Sent. Episcop. 87
Talbert
Tertullian, *Adversus Iudaeos*
Tertullian, *Ad Scapulam*
White
Wilken
Wilpert, *I Sarcofagi*
Zenonis Veronensis

General

Mauretania Caesariensis. Aside from two doubtfully Christian inscriptions from Tipasa and Auzia, all our evidence for specific Christian locales in Mauretania Caesariensis comes from the period after the Council of Carthage in 256. In Mauretania Caesariensis, martyr documents may refer to Diocletianic and earlier martyrs, or to those killed in Donatist uprisings, or to those martyred under the Vandals, or to relics of martyrs moved from elsewhere; see Yvette Duval, *Loca*, 476–92.

In the context of the broader Mauretanian provinces, Tertullian: *Adversus Iudaeos*, 7.8, mentions Christians in a general way. *Ad Scapulam*, 4.8, mentions persecutions by the governor. Cyprian, *Epistulae*, 71, is addressed to Quintus, a bishop in Mauretania. The prologue to *Sent. Episcop. 87* also indicates that some bishops from Mauretania were known in 256.

Specific sites

Altava. (modern Ouled Mimoun.) Harnack, 916, notes *CIL*, 8:9862 (=*ILCV*, #2853 from 302. Also *CIL*, 8:21734 (=*ILCV*, #2854) from 310, and *CIL*, 8:9855 (=*ILCV*, #2854a) from 333. See also *CIL*, 8:9890, add. p. 2059 (=*ILCV*, #2855a). All of these could be Christian, but none is certainly so; compare White, 2:240. There is, however, a reasonably straightforward inscription relating to the martyrdom of Januarius and reading "*mesa Ianuari marturis, pie, zeses;*" see Yvette Duval, *Loca*, 412–17, compare *Martyrologium Hieronymianum*, 16 kal. Nov. and 4 non. Dec. Fevrier, "Aux origines," 775 & 787. *Atlas*, 4. Talbert, map 29.

Auzia. (modern Sour-Ghazlan.) Two early inscriptions are known. *CIL*, 8:9162 dates to 227, and 8:20780 (=*ILCV*, #1571) dates to 318. Harnack (1924), 903, took both of these to be Christian, apparently mistaking a defective spelling of "*maritus*" in 8:9162 for the word "*martus*". Yet 8:20780 from 318 seems to me to be clearly Christian. See also Fevrier, "Aux origines," 769–70 & 780. *Atlas*, 4. Talbert, map 30.

Caesarea Mauretania. (ancient Iol; modern Cherchel.) For the martyrs Severianus and Aquila; see *AASS*, Januarius 3, 68, and also *Martyrlogium Hieronymianum*, 10 kal. Feb. For the martyr Arcadius, see Zenonis Veronensis, *Tractatus*, 1.39. For the martyrdom of Fabius *vexillifer* on prid. ides Aug. in the consular year of Diocletian and Maximian (i.e. probably 303 or 304), see "*Passio S. Fabii vexiliferi,*" in *AB* 9 (1890): 123–34. For the martyr Marciana, see *AASS*, Januarius 1, 569–70. The martyr Theodota appears in *Martyrologium Hieronymianum*, 4 non. Aug., and in *AASS*, Aug. I, 147. Bishop Fortunatus and deacon Deuterius attended the Council of Arles in 314; see *Concilia Galliae*, 15 & 17. Note also *CIL*, 8: 9585, with a palm branch motif & 8:20958. A chapel is known from the Fifth Century, see Gui, 16–17. Fevrier, "Aux origines" 789. Paul-Marie Duval, 69–163. *Atlas*, 4. Talbert, map 30.

Castellum Tingitanum. (modern El Asnam/Orleansville.) *ILCV*, #2855, from 314, has been understood as Christian by some. An inscription from 324 reads as follows "*anno provinciae CCLXXX et V XII kal. Dec. eius basilicae fundamenta posita sunt et fa[. . .]ma anno prov. CCLXX[X . . .], in mente habeas [////]m servum dei [et? i]n deo vivas*"; see *CIL*, 8:9708 (=*ILCV*, #1821). Harnack, 917. For the ruins of a basilica, see Gui, 11–14. For possible early martyrs, see Yvette Duval, *Loca*, 392–400. *Atlas*, 4. Talbert, map 30.

Médiouna. (formerly known as Renault.) The martyrs Rogatus, Maientus, Nasseus, and Maxima from 21 October 329 were commemorated in *CIL*, 8:21517 (=*ILCV*, #2071), a monument erected by their parents; see Yvette Duval, *Loca*, 402–405, and Fevrier, "Aux origines," 787. The date and number of the martyrs suggest that there were Christians in Médiouna before 325, but were these martyrs the victims of a pagan uprising or of an altercation between Donatists and Catholics? Compare *Martyrologium Hieronymianum*, 12 kal. Nov. Talbert, map 30.

Rusucurru. (modern Dellys.) The martyr Marciana, executed at Caesarea Mauretania *ca.*304–305, was from the region of Rusucurru; see *AASS*, Januarius 1:569–70. For identification of the two ancillary villages Rusippisir (modern Taksebt) and Iomnium (modern Tigzirt), see *CIL*, 8, p. 766, and Gui, 57–69. *DACL*, 15.2, cols. 1966–1969 relates to Taksebt, and 15.2, cols. 2300–2313 relates to Tigzirt. Yvette Duval, *Loca*, 350–51, cites an inscription from Tigzirt referring to the relics of a certain Eusebius, but it it not clear who this Eusebius was or whether the relics originated there or were brought from elsewhere. Likewise, the epitaph of M. Junius Bassus of 299 seems to my mind doubtfully Christian; but see Monceaux, 2:123, & Harnack, 916. See Fevrier, "Aux origines," 789–90. *Atlas*, 4. Talbert, map 30.

Sufasar. (modern Amoura.) An inscription reading in part "*bona memoria Emmartis et filiae eius . . .*" dates to 318 and may be Christian; see *CIL*, 8:21479 =*ILCV*, 2791. The "*puer*" Maximus and also Dativus were martyred in 322; see Yvette Duval, *Loca*, 386–87 & 722. Fevrier, "Aux origines," 787. Talbert, map 30.

Tigava. (modern Bel-Abbès/el-Kherba.) Tipasius the veteran was martyred in 298; see "*Passio S. Typasii Veterani*," in *AB* 9 (1890): 116–123. See Gui, 14–15, for remains of a church from as early as the Fifth Century. *Atlas*, 4. Talbert, map 30.

Tipasa. An inscription from 238 reads as follows: "*Rasinia Secunda redd(idit). XVI kal. Novem p. CLXXXXVIIII.*" On the evidence of the word "*reddidit*," it may be Christian; see *CIL*, 8:9289, 8:20856, and *ILCV*, #3319. Harnack, 903, took the inscription to be so, yet Fevrier, "Aux origines," 771 & 787, expresses grave doubts. For later inscriptions, see also *CIL*, 8:20892 with an anchor motif, and *CIL*, 8:20903. Another inscription records that Victorinus was martyred on 8 May of 315 or 320; see Yvette Duval, *Loca*, 367–71. Salsa was martyred there *ca*.320, and a church in her memory soon followed; see *CIL*, 8:20914; Yvette Duval, *Loca*, 358–62; and Gui, 38–44. The martyrs Rogatus and Vitalis are also known from an inscription; see Yvette Duval, *Loca*, 371–72. On the site, see Paul-Marie Duval, 21–67. Gerke, 340 & 353, lists two sarcophagi which can be understood as Christian: Wilpert, *I Sarcofagi*, plate 67.5, which may date to the Third Century, and Wilpert, *I Sarcofagi*, plate 290.2, from the early Fourth Century. Talbert, map 30.

Possible sites

(Ad) Regiae? (modern Arbal.) A possibly Christian inscription from 295 reads "*d.m.s. Aurelia Saturina benemoria, qui vixt ans p. m. LX provinciae CCLc. Mallius Fidensus una cum filios fecit*;" see *CIL*, 8:21638 (= *ILCV*, #3952). On the ambiguity of "*d.m.s.*" inscriptions, see Wilken, 78. A certainly Christian inscription reading "*memoria Maeci Rust[ici] qui precessit in pace . . .*" dates to 345; see *CIL*, 8:9793 (=*ILCV*, #3265). Fevrier, "Aux origines," 774 & 782. Gui, 1. Talbert, map 29.

Bourkika? (ancient name unknown; 6km East of Hadjout in the plain of Mitidja.) For the possible Fourth-Century martyrium of Renatus and Optata, perhaps victims of an early Fourth-Century persecution or of an altercation between Catholics and Donatists; see Yvette Duval, *Loca*, 384–86.

Cartenna? (modern Ténès.) *CIL*, 8:9692 (=*ILCV*, 2044), mentions names of martyrs and other faithful, but the circumstances of the inscription are not clear. The martyrs could have been from Cartennae or they could have been martyred elsewhere and their relics deposited there; see Yvette Duval, *Loca*, 401–402, and Fevrier, "Aux origines," 772. A particularly striking inscription, *CIL*, 8:9693 (=*ILCV*, #614), dates probably to 357, has palm branch and fish motifs, and reads "*bone memoriae Rozoni medici vixit annis LXX, dies XX, precessit nos in pace . . .*" Talbert, map 30.

Numerus Syrorum? (modern Lalla Maghnia/Marnia.) *CIL*, 8:9968 (=*ILCV*, #3682), dates to 344/47. *CIL*, 8:21805, would date to 359. The first certainly Christian inscription, *CIL*, 8:21806 (=*ILCV*, #3686), dates to 389. Fevrier, "Aux origines," 776 & 782. Talbert, map 29.

Obori? (modern Bou Ismail/Castiglione?) An undated inscription from Tipasa reads *"memoria mart[uro]rum perigri[nor(um)] qui passi sunt a[d C. Ar.?]bores . . ."*. The last lacuna may also be restored as *"a[d O]bores."* Centum Arbores would be in Mauretania Sitifensis or Numidia. Yet if Obores/Obori is the correct reading, the place would be just East of Tipasa; see Yvette Duval, *Loca*, 375–77 & 702. Talbert, map 30, tentatively identifies the site of Obori as modern Sidi Ferruch. Remains of a church, possibly from as early as the Fourth Century are known at Obori; see Gui, 44–46.

Oppidum Novum? (modern Ain Defla.) At least some of the martyrs named on the inscription cited by Duval are from elsewhere; see Yvette Duval, *Loca*, 387–89. Talbert, map 30.

MAURETANIA TINGITANA

Bibliography
Carcopino
Delehaye, "Les Actes"
Euzennat
Euzennat & Marion
Galand, Fevrier, & Vajda
Harnack
Lactantius, *De mortibus persecutorum*
Martyrologium Hieronymianum
Musurillo
Prudentius
Talbert
Thouvenot, "Les origines"
Thouvenot, "Statuette"
Tertullian, *Ad Scapulam*
Tertullian, *Adversus Iudaeos*

General
Mauretania Tingitana. Mauritania Tingitana was administered from Spain. At *Ad Scapulam*, 4.8, Tertullian mentions persecutions taking place in Legio and in Mauretania, so perhaps the governor's residences at Legio in Hispania and Tingi in Mauretania are meant here.

Tertullian, *Adversus Iudaeos*, 7.8, makes reference to Christians in Mauretania generally, but does not further define the area. The reference could just as easily be to Mauretania Caesariensis or to Mauretania Sitifensis.

Specific sites

Tingi. (modern Tangier). For the martyrdom of Marcellus in 298; see Musurillo, xxxvii–xxxix & 250–59. One should probably also note the martyrdom of Cassian, the detailed account of which is doubted by Delehaye, "Les Actes," 277–78, but the fact of which would seem to be confirmed by Prudentius, *Peristephanon*, 4:45–48, and by *Martyrologium Heronymianum*, December 3. See also Thouvenot "Les origines," 359–60. An inscription from Tingi and datable to 345 reads "*Aurelia Sabina, ancilla Cresti, vixsit pl(us) mi(nus)* [Chi-Rho symbol] *annis XXIII, me(nsibus) V, di(ebus) XII, or(is) VIIII. Fe(delis?) in pace requet?, Amantio et Albino consolibus;*" see Euzennat & Marion, pp. 28–29, #16. Talbert, map 28.

Possible sites

Souk-el-Arba (de Rharb)? (about 15 km Northeast of Banasa.) A small bowl inscribed with an anchor, was found in the baths of a settlement destroyed *ca.*280. The inscribed anchor was believed by Thouvenot, "Statuette," 143–44, and Carcopino, 288, to be indicative of Christianity; see also Thouvenot, "Les origines," 355. Unfortunately, Euzennat, 109 & 117, notes that a similar motif has been found on objects of the First Century B.C.E., so it cannot be an exclusive indicator of Christianity. Talbert, map 28.

Volubilis? (modern Ksar Pharoun.) An ivory statuette, 6cm high and representing a good shepherd with crossed arms, was found near the Tangier gate on the same level with Roman era remains, chiefly of the Third Century. Thouvenot suggests that the crossed arms may represent an apotropaic use of the Chi-Rho symbol. If the statuette is indeed Christian, Lactantius, *De mortibus persecutorum*, 10, would be early Fourth-Century evidence for the apotropaic function of crossing oneself. See Thouvenot, "Statuette," 137–46; Carcopino, 288; and Thouvenot "Les origines," 372–73. Talbert, map 28.

Unlocatable Christian Communities in North Africa

Bibliography
AASS
Akakpo
Atlas
BHL
CIL
Duval, Yvette, *Loca*
Harnack
Mandouze
Mesnage
Musurillo
Ruinart
Saxer
Sent. Episcop. 87
Talbert

General

A few places in North Africa that are known to have contained early Christian communities have proved impossible to locate within any single province. Those sites are listed here with as much geographical and historical information as possible in the hope that further study may be able to place them more specifically.

Specific sites

Tucca/Thucca. Two places, neither of which is clearly locatable, are known by this name. *Sent. Episcop. 87*.52, records Saturninus as bishop of a place called Tucca or Thucca. At the same time *Sent. Episcop. 87*.77, records Honoratius as bishop of another place called Thucca. Mesnage, 49, suggests that Saturninus could be from the Thugga that is now modern Dougga (Talbert, map 32). Yet Mesnage, 61, and Saxer, 450, also note the place name Thugga Terebinthina, which would be modern Henchir Dougga, as a possibility (Talbert, map 33). The modern Henchir el Abiod (Talbert, map 31) in Numidia could also fit the description of Tucca; see Mesnage, 241. Likewise, modern Henchir el Merdja in Mauretania could be a possibility for a place called Thucca; see Mesnage, 331. Harnack, 912–13, points out the difficulties. *Atlas*, 4, records both bishoprics, placing Tucca at Henchir el Abiod and Thucca at Henchir Dougga.

Fuscianum. The martyrs Montanus and Lucius, killed under the Emperor Valerian, asked for greetings to be given to the brethren at Fuscianum; see *Passio Sanctorum Montani et Lucii* in Musurillo, xxxiv–xxxvi, 232–33, & 236–37. Fuscianum was either a region near Milev in Numidia or a region in Byzacene with estates possibly connected with the family of the Roman Christian Fusciana who died in the early Fourth Century. Mesnage, 198.

Vicus Caesaris. The exact site is unknown. There are three ancient sites with the name "Vicus Augusti:" modern Kahila/Bou Seba (Talbert, map 32) which would be in Africa Proconsularis; modern Sidi el Hani (Talbert, map 33) which would be in Byzacene, and modern Bir bou Saadia (Talbert, map 31) in Numidia. There are also two sites with the name "Caesaris." The site of ancient Aquae Caesaris would be at modern Youks les Bains (Talbert, map 34) near Theveste in Numidia. The site of Turris Caesaris would be in Numidia near modern Sigus; compare Talbert, map 34. Bishop Januarius of Vicus Caesaris was at the Council of Carthage in 256; see *Sent. Episcop. 87*.23. Mesnage 88 & 392–93.

Sites for which the name itself is uncertain

Ambiensis/Ambia? Regarding the name itself as problematic, Mesnage, 488, does note that *CIL*, 8:9745, can be read as containing a gentilic for this place. Harnack, 916, notes one manuscript of the *Acta Sancti Maximi Martyris*, which identifies Maximus as being from Ambiensis; see *AASS*, Aprilis 3: 740–41 (*BHL*, #5829); also Ruinart, 202–204 (=*AASS*, Octobris 8: 420–21). Mandouze, 423, 1248, & 1269, with respect to a certain Bishop Felix in 411, indicates that "*Ambiensis*" is a misreading of "*Lambiensis*," which would be modern Lambèse. Mesnage, 319 & 460, also notes a "Lambia" (modern Medea) in Mauretania.

Centum Arbores? The place-name is a generic one. The name of the site could be a misreading for Obori, *q.v.*, in Mauretania Caesarensis. Yet if Centum Arbores is to be read, the site could be in Numidia or in Mauretania Sitifensis. Martyrs from "[. . .]*bores*" were killed at Tipasa at an uncertain, but perhaps early, date and are recorded in inscriptions; see Yvette Duval, *Loca*, [#149] 341–42, 375–77, 477–78, 706–7, & 721.

ETHIOPIA (AKSUM) TO THE MID-FOURTH CENTURY

Bibliography
Anfray, Caquot, & Nautin
Athanasius, *Apologia ad Constantium*
Budge, *Book*
Budge, *History*
EnECh
Epiphanius, *De XII Gemmis*
Harnack
Kaplan
Kobishchanov
Munro-Hay
Munro-Hay & Juel-Jensen
New Documents
ODCC
Origen, *Commentary on Matthew*
Periplus Maris Erythraei
Phillipson
Philostorgius
Rufinus, *Ecclesiastical History*
Schneider, "L'Inscription Chrétienne"
Schneider, "Trois nouvelles inscriptions"
Sergew
Socrates
Talbert

General
Ethiopia. Information on Christianity before the middle of the Fourth Century is vague, though certainly Christians were present from the middle of the Third Century. Acts 8:26–39 records the story of Philip preaching to the Ethiopian eunuch, servant of the Candace of Ethiopia. According to the story, the eunuch was baptized and went on his way back to Ethiopia rejoicing. Unfortunately we have no more reliable information about him. *Periplus Maris Erythraei*, 50–53, shows that travelers would have had easy access to the Ethiopian port at Adulis and the capital at Aksum from the First Century.

Writing in the first half of the Third Century, Origen, *Commentary on Matthew*, *commentariorum series* 39, says "*non ergo fertur praedicatum esse evangelium apud omnes Aethiopas, maxime apud eos qui sunt ultra flumen.*" "It is not reported that the gospel has been preached to all the Ethiopians, especially to those who are beyond the river." He thus clearly implies that *some* Ethiopians had been reached by Christian teaching. At *Commentary on Matthew, commentariorum series* 134, Origen plainly distinguishes between Ethiopia and India.

Rufinus, *Ecclesiastical History*, 10.9–10, records the account of Aedesius and Frumentius, nephews of the Phoenician trader Meropius, who were kidnapped on the coast of "further India" in the time of Constantine and later raised at the royal court. Rufinus, who claims to have the account from Aedesius himself, notes that the two were successful in converting the crown prince. He also tells how Frumetius went on to become the first bishop of the place early in the episcopate of Athanasius of Alexandria, thus dating the incident to *ca.*330. Compare Socrates, 1.19.1–14. See also Philostorgius, 3.6, who notes the close connection between South Arabia and Aksum, but mistakenly attributes the ordering of the churches in Ethiopia to a certain "Theophilus the Indian" in the middle of the Fourth Century. Epiphanius, *De XII Gemmis*, 4 (text, 39; trans., 132), also mentions the development of Christianity among the Ethiopians of Africa.

In his account, Rufinus has fallen prey to the common confusion between India and Ethiopia. Athanasius, *Apologia ad Constantium*, 31, in telling how Constantius II tried by letter to convince the Ethiopians to depose Frumentius, clearly identifies the crown prince and his brother as Ezana and Sazana of Aksum.

After the crown prince Ezana became king, he erected a number of inscriptions. Early inscriptions of King Ezana in Ge'ez show a pagan mindset; see Budge, *History*, text 247–48, trans. 248–49 (= Littmann, #10). Later inscriptions appear to be monotheistic; see Budge, *History*, text 252–55, trans. 255–58 (= Littmann, #11). Finally, the latest inscription in Greek is clearly Christian; see Anfray, Caquot, & Nautin, text 264–65, trans., 266. Its fragmentary counterpart in South Arabic, however, seems to retain the earlier simple monotheistic language; see Schneider, "Trois nouvelles inscriptions," text 1:768, analysis 769–70; and also Schneider, "L'Inscription Chrétienne," text 110, analysis 112–116.

Criticisms of the dating and interpretation of the inscriptions have been raised by Kobishchanov, 63–90, and *New Documents*, 1:143–44 & 2:209–11. However, the evidence of the coinage confirms the inscriptional evidence of Ezana's conversion, making it virtually certain that there was only one King Ezana who began his coinage with a disc and crescent motif and then changed to a cross motif; see Munro-Hay & Juel-Jensen, 41–47 & 119–39. See also Munro-Hay, 25–26, where Ousanas, the father of Ezana, is identified as the Ella Amida of Ethiopian tradition; compare Budge, *Book*, 4:1164–65, for the tradition recounted on 26 Hamle. Harnack, 729. Sergew, 92–110. *EnECh*, 19, 289–91, 314, & 331. Kaplan, 101–109. *ODCC*, 565–66 & 644–45. Phillipson, 2:475–76. Talbert, map 4.

MAPS

Unplaced Sites

The following sites are listed in the text but could not be placed certainly on the maps because of insufficient geographical information.

Map 1:

Alassos
Arbokadama
Beretane
Margarita

Map 3:

Ardabau
Charisphone
Kalytos
Marcianopolis
Phargamos
Phydela

Map 5:

Halmyris

Map 6:

Aureus Mons
Vindena

Map 8:

Drona

Map 9:

Kephro
Kolluthion
Neiloupolis
Parembole

Map 11:

In Africa Proconsularis:

Abbir Germanicus
Beneventum
Bol
Gurgaita
Marazanae
Marcelliana
Midili
Mi(s)girpa
Nova
Pocofelta
Thambae
Tharassa
Ululi
Victoriana

In Numidia:

Bamacorra
Castra Galbae
Legisvolumni
Limata
Muguas
Octava
Scillium

Uncertain:

Tucca/Thucca
Fuscianum
Vicus Caesaris

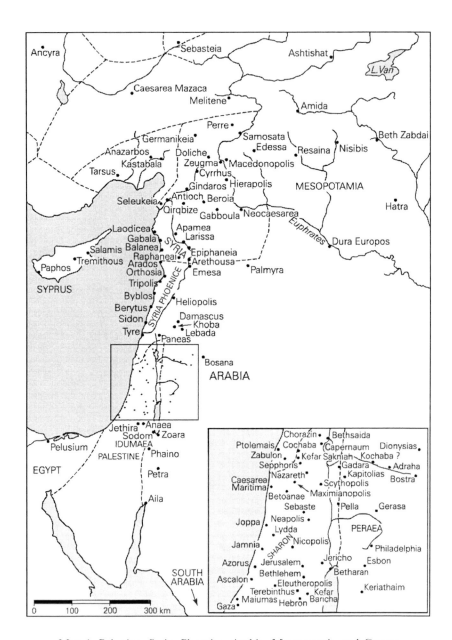

Map 1. Palestine, Syria, Phoenice, Arabia, Mesopotamia and Cyprus

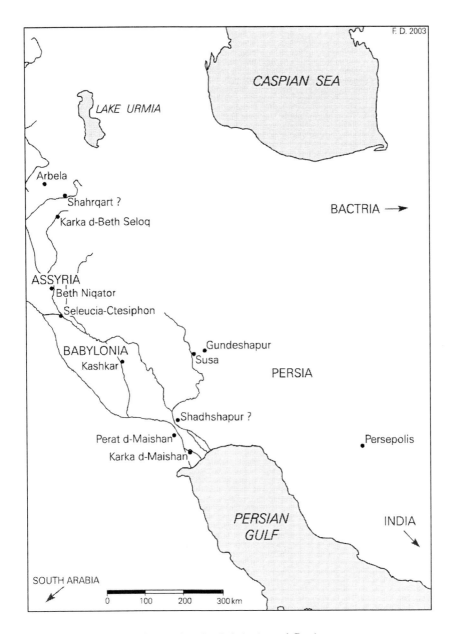

Map 2. Assyria, Babylonia and Persia

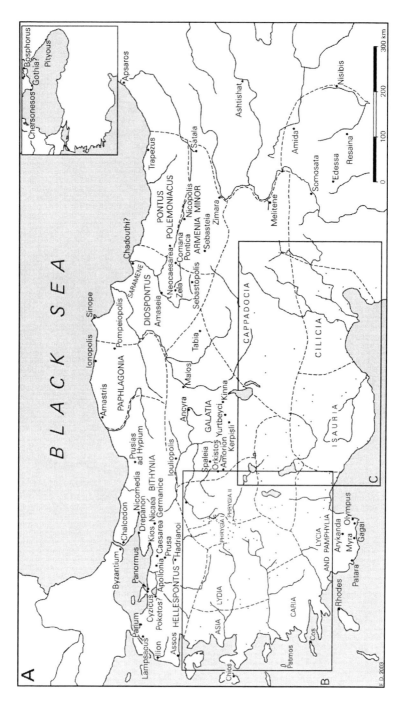

Map 3A. Asia, Pontica, Isauria and Cilicia

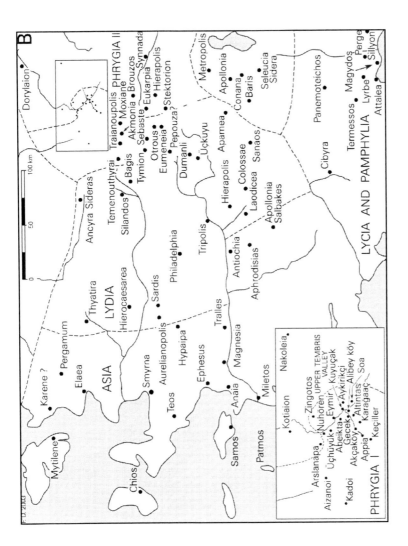

Map 3B. Asia

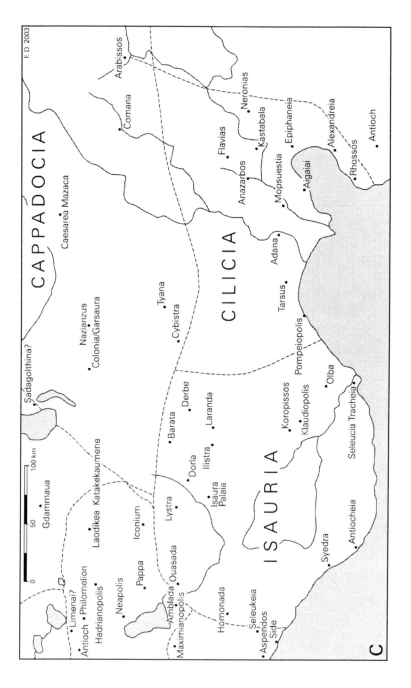

Map 3C. Asia, Pontica, Isauria and Cilicia

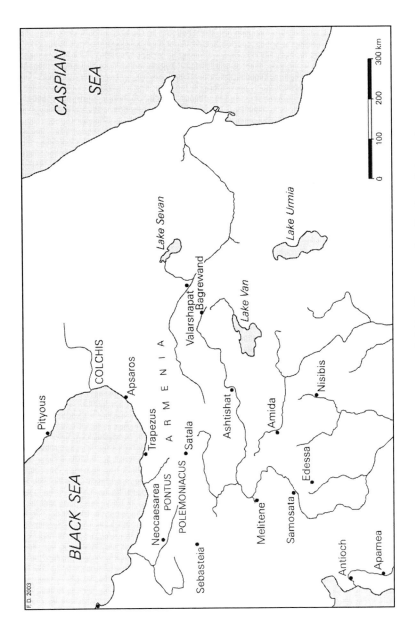

Map 4. Pontus Polemoniacus, Colchis, Transcaucasian Iberia and Armenia

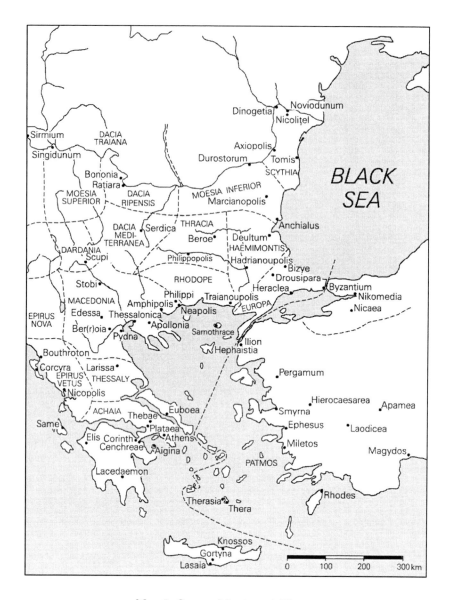

Map 5. Greece, Moesia and Thrace

Map 6. Italy, Raetia, Noricum, Dalmatia and Pannonia

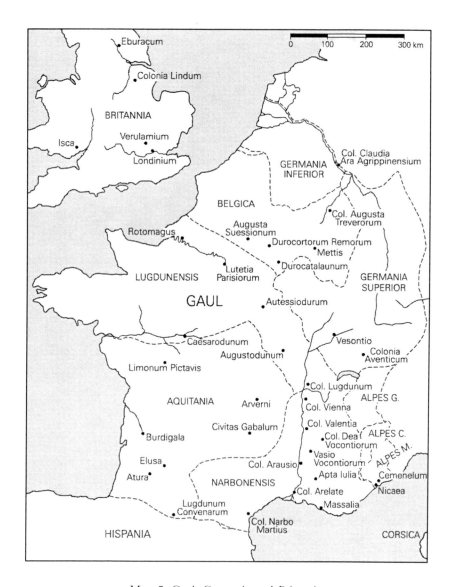

Map 7. Gaul, Germania and Britannia

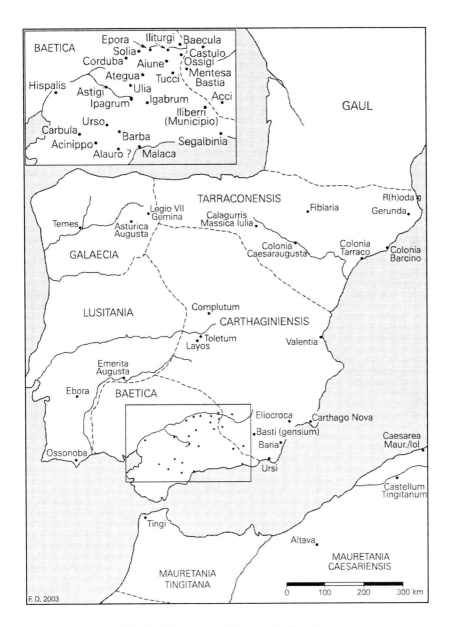

Map 8. Hispania and Mauritania Tingitana

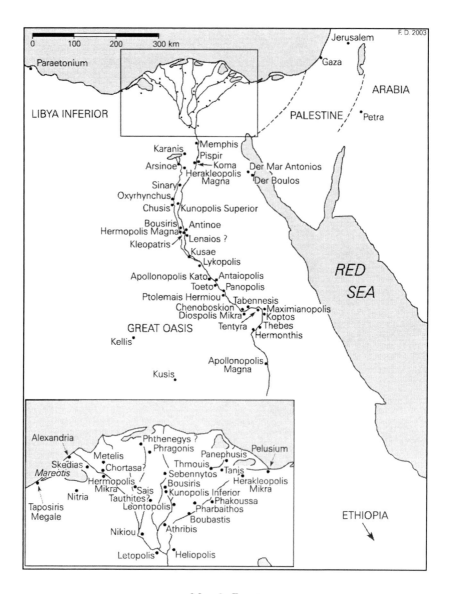

Map 9. Egypt

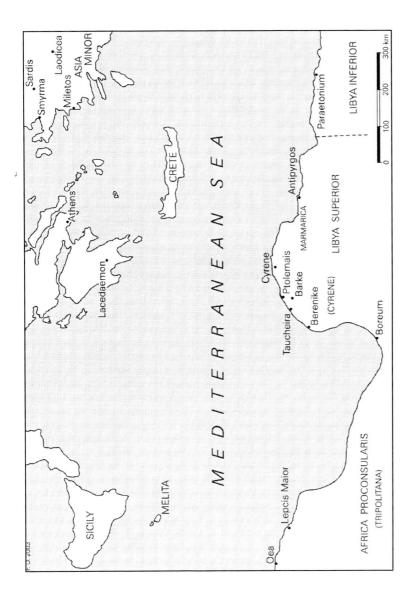

Map 10. Libya and Cyrene

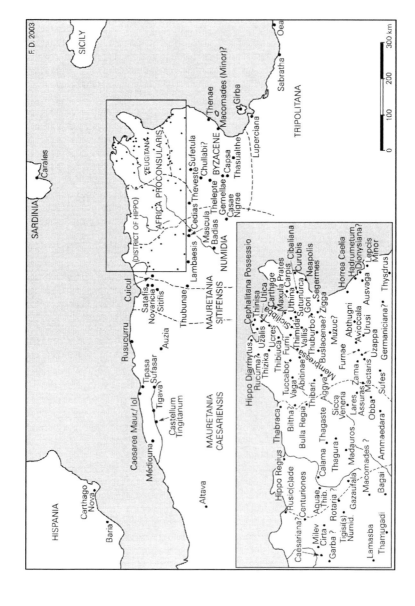

Map 11. Mauretania Caesariensis, Mauretania Sitifensis, Numidia and Africa Proconsularis

BIBLIOGRAPHY AND ABBREVIATIONS

AASS. Acta Sanctorum. 3rd Edition. Multiple vols. Paris: V. Palme, 1863–.

AB. Analecta Bollandiana.

ABD. Anchor Bible Dictionary. Freedman, David Noel, ed. 6 vols. New York: Doubleday, 1992.

Abicht, Dr., and Dr. Reichelt. "Quellennachweise zum Codex Suprasliensis." In *Archiv für Slavische Philologie*, 20 (1898): 181–200.

Abu 'l-Fath. *Kitāb al-Tarikh*. Text edited by Stenhouse, Paul. "The Kitab al-Tarikh of Abu 'l-Fath, a New Edition with Notes." Ph.D. dissertation. University of Sydney, 1980. Translated by Stenhouse, Paul. *The Kitab al-Tarikh of Abu'l-Fath, Translated into English with Notes*. Mandelbaum Judaica Series, 1. Sydney: Mandelbaum Trust, University of Sydney, 1985.

Abu Salih. *Churches and Monasteries of Egypt*. Evetts, B. T. A., ed. and trans. Oxford: Clarendon, 1895.

Abul-Faraj al-Isbahani. *Kitāb al-Aghānī*. New Edition. Vol. 2. Cairo: al-Hay'a al-Misriya al-ʿĀmma lil-Taʾlīf wa al-Nashr, 1970.

Achelis, Hans. *Das Christentum in den ersten drei Jahrhunderten*. 2nd Edition. Leipzig: Quelle & Meyer, 1925; reprint Aalen: Scientia Verlag, 1975.

Achelis, Hans, ed. *Acta SS. Nerei et Achillei*. [*BHG*, #1327.] TU 11.2. Leipzig: Hinrichs, 1893.

Acta XIII Congressus Internationalis Archaeologiae Christianae, Split—Porec (25.9–1.10. 1994). 3 vols. Studi di antichità cristiana 54. Vatican City: Pontificio Istituto di archeologia cristiana, 1998.

Acta Concili Aquiliensis. [=Ambrose of Milan, *Epistula* 2(10).] Faller, Otto, and Michaela Zelzer, eds. In *Sancti Ambrosi opera, Pars decima, Epistulae et Acta*, 3:316–68. CSEL 82.3. Vienna: Hoelder-Pilcher-Tempsky, 1968–96.

Acta Pauli. Lipsius and Bonnet, 1:23–44, 104–17, & 235–72. Schmidt, Carl, ed. *Acta Pauli aus der Heidelberger Koptischen Papyrushandschrift Nr. 1*. 2 vols. Leipzig: Hinrichs, 1904–04; reprint Hildesheim: Olms, 1965. Schmidt, Carl, ed. *Acta Pauli nach dem Papyrus der Hamburger Staats und Universitäts-Bibliothek*. Glückstadt & Hamburg: J. J. Augustin, 1936. (For analysis and translation, see Schneemelcher, 2:213–70, whose divisions I use.)

Acta Petri et Pauli, see Lipsius and Bonnet, 178–222.

Acta Primi Congressus Internationalis Archaeologiae Christianae. Marin, Aemilius, [and Victor Saxer], eds. Studi di Antichità Cristiana 50. Jadera: apud Lucam Vitaliani et filios, 1894; reprint with continuous pagination, Vatican City and Split: Pontificio Istituto di Archeologia Cristiana and Arheolos'ki Muzej, 1993.

Acta purgationis Felicis. Ziwsa, Carolus, ed. In *S. Optati Milevitani Libri VII*, 197–204. CSEL 26. Prague, Vienna, and Leipzig: F. Tempsky and G. Freytag, 1893. More recently in Maier, 171–87. Translated in Optatus, *Against the Donatists*. Edwards, Mark, trans. and ed., 170–80. Liverpool: Liverpool University Press, 1997.

Acta Sancti Menae. In *AB*, 3 (1884): 258–70.

Actas del VIII Congreso Internacional de Arqueologia Cristiana, Barcelona, 5–11 Octubre 1969. 2 vols. Studi di Antichità Cristiana 30. Vatican City: Pontificio Istituto di Archeologia Cristiana, 1972.

Actes du Vᵉ Congrès international d'archéologie chrétienne, Aix-en-Provence, 13–19 Septembre 1954. Studi di Antichità Cristiana 22. Vatican City: Pontificio Istituto di Archeologia Cristiana, 1957.

Actes du X *Congrès international d'archéologie chrétienne, Thessalonique, 28 Septembre–4 Octobre 1980.* 2 vols. Studi di Antichità Cristiana 37. Vatican City: Pontificio Istituto di Archeologia Cristiana, 1984.

Actes du XI *Congrès international d'archéologie chrétienne: Lyon, Vienne, Grenoble, Genève, et Aoste (21–28 Septembre 1986).* 3 vols. Studi di Antichità Cristiana 41. Collection de L'École Française de Rome 123. Vatican City: Pontificio Istituto di Archeologia Cristiana, 1989.

Acts of the Pagan Martyrs. Musurillo, Herbert, ed. Oxford: Clarendon, 1954; reprint [Oxford]: Sandpiper Books, 2000.

Ado of Vienne. *Chronicon.* Migne, J.-P., ed. PL 123:23–138. Paris: Garnier Fratres, 1879.

AÉ. L'Année épigraphique.

Agathangelos. *Patmut'iwn Hayots'.* [History of the Armenians]. Thomson, R. W., ed. and trans. Albany: State University of New York Press, 1976.

Agnello, G. "Recenti scoperte di monumenti paleocristiani nel Syracusano." In *Akten des VII Internationalen Kongresses,* 309–26.

Agnello, S. L. "Nuova planimetria dell' area cimiteriale dell' ex Vigna Cassia in Siracusa." In *Atti del IX Congresso Internazionale,* 2:5–10.

Agnellus, Andreas. *Liber Pontificalis Ecclesiae Ravennatis.* Holder-Egger, O., ed. *MGH,* SRLI, 265–391. Hannover: Hahn, 1878. Also see Nauerth, Claudia, ed. *Liber Pontificalis/Bischofsbuch.* Fontes Christiani 21. Freiburg: Herder, 1996–.

Akakpo, Amouzouvi. *Afrique Romaine, les persécutions contre les chrétiennes au III* *siècle d'après les relations de martyre.* Abidjan: Nouvelles Éditions africaines, 1980.

Akten des VII Internationalen Kongresses für Christliche Archäologie, Trier, 5–11 September 1965. 2 vols. Studi di Antichità Cristiana 27. Vatican City: Pontificio Istituto di Archeologia Cristiana, [1969].

Akten des XII Internationalen Kongresses für Christliche Archäologie, Bonn, 22–28 September 1991. 2 vols. Jahrbuch für Antike und Christentum, Ergänzungsband 20.1–2. Münster: Aschendorffsche Verlagsbuchhandlung, 1995.

Albertini, Eugène. *L'Afrique Romaine.* Leschi, Louis, rev. Algiers: Imprimerie Officielle, 1955.

Alexander of Alexandria. *Deposition of Arius.* Opitz, Hans-Georg, ed. In *Athanasius Werke,* 3: 6–11. Berlin: Walter de Gruyter, 1934–.

Alexanian, Joseph M. "The Armenian Version of the New Testament." In Ehrman, Bart D., and Michael W. Holmes, eds. *The Text of the New Testament in Contemporary Research,* 157–72. S&D 46. Grand Rapids: Eerdmans, 1995.

Alföldy, Géza. *Noricum.* Birley, Anthony, trans. London and Boston: Routledge and Kegan Paul, 1974.

——. *Die Römischen Inschriften von Tarraco.* 2 vols. Madrider Forschungen 10. Berlin: Walter de Gruyter, 1975.

Allard, Paul. *Histoire des persécutions.* 4 vols. in 5 parts. Studia Historica, 98–101. Paris: Lecoffre, 1903–08; reprint Rome: Bretschneider, 1971.

Allen, W. E. D. *History of the Georgian People.* London: Kegan Paul, Trench, Trubner, & Co., 1932.

Alon, Gedaliah. *The Jews in Their Land in the Talmudic Age.* Cambridge: Harvard University Press, 1989.

Ambrose of Milan. *Epistulae.* Faller, Otto and Michaela Zelzer, eds. 4 vols. CSEL 82.1–4. Vienna: Hoelder-Pilcher-Tempsky, 1968–96.

——. *Expositio evangelii secundum Lucam.* Adriaen, M., ed. In *Sancti Ambrosi opera, Pars quarta,* 1–400. CCSL 14. Turnhout: Brepols, 1957.

Ameling, Walter, ed. *Die Inschriften von Prusias ad Hypium.* Inschriften griechischer Städte aus Kleinasien 27. Österreichische Akademie der Wissenschaften/Nordrhein-Westfälische Akademie der Wissenchaften. Bonn: Dr. Rudolf Habelt Gmbh., 1985.

Ammianus Marcellinus. *Rerum gestarum libri.* Rolfe, John C., ed. 3 vols. LCL. Cambridge: Harvard University Press, 1950–52.

Ananian, Paolo. "La data e le circonstanze della consecrazione de S. Gregorio Illuminatore." *Muséon* 74 (1961): 43–73 & 317–60.

Anderson, J. C. G. "Paganism and Christianity in the Upper Tembris Valley." In Ramsay, William M., ed. *Studies in the History and Art of the Eastern Provinces*, 181–227. Aberdeen: Aberdeen University Press, 1906.

Anfray, Francis, André Caquot, and Pierre Nautin. "Une nouvelle inscription grecque d'Ezana roi d'Axoum." *Journal des Savants* 72 (1970): 260–73.

ANRW. Aufstieg und Niedergang der römischen Welt.

Aphrahat. *Demonstrationes.* Parisot, Ioannes, ed. PS 1.1:1–1.2:489. Paris: Firmin-Didot et socii, 1894–1907.

Apophthegmata Patrum, alphabetical series. Migne, J.-P., ed. PG 65:7–442. Paris: Migne, 1864.

Apostolic Constitutions. Metzger, Marcel, ed. *Les constitutions apostoliques.* SC 320, 329, & 336. Paris: Cerf, 1985–87.

Apostolic Fathers. Lake, Kirsopp, ed. and trans. LCL. 2 vols. Cambridge: Harvard University Press, 1912–13; reprint 1976–77. For the same collection with updated references, see *Apostolic Fathers.* Lightfoot, J. B., and J. R. Harmer, eds. Holmes, Michael W., rev. 2nd Edition. Grand Rapids: Baker, 1992.

Appold, Mark. "The Mighty Works of Bethsaida: Witness of the New Testament and Related Traditions." In Arav, Rami and Richard A. Freund, eds. *Bethsaida, a City by the North Shore of the Sea of Galilee. Volume One, Bethsaida Excavations Project*, 229–42. Kirkville, MO: Thomas Jefferson University Press, 1995.

Archiv für Papyrusforschung.

Ardevan, Radu. "Autour de deux pièces paléochrétiennes de Gherla." In *Acta XIII Congressus Internationalis*, 3:29–36.

Aristides. *The Apology of Aristides on Behalf of the Christians.* Harris, J. Rendel, ed. TS 1.1. Cambridge: Cambridge University Press, 1893; reprint Nendeln/Liechtenstein: Kraus Reprint, 1967.

Arnobius. *Adversus nationes.* Reifferscheid, Augustus, ed. CSEL, 4. Vienna: C. Geroldi, 1875.

Artemii Passio. [*BHG*, 160.] *AASS*, October, 8:856–85. Partially edited by Bidez, Joseph. In Philostorgius. *Kirchengeschichte*, 26–27, 29–32, 49–59, & 151–57. GCS 21. Leipzig: Hinrichs, 1913.

Assemani, Joseph Simonis. *Bibliotheca Orientalis Clementino-Vaticana.* 3 vols. in 4 parts. Rome: Typis Sacrae Congregationis de Propaganda Fide, 1719–28; reprint Hildesheim: Olms, 2000.

Assemani, Stephanus Evodius, ed. *Acta sanctorum martyrum orientalium et occidentalium.* Vol. 1. Rome: J. Collini, 1748; reprint Westmead: Gregg International Publishers Limited, 1970.

Asterius of Amasea. *Homilies I–XIV: Text, Introduction, and Notes.* Datema, C., ed. Leiden: Brill, 1970.

Athanasius. *Apologia ad Constantium.* Opitz, Hans-Georg, ed. In *Athanasius: Werke*, 2:279–80. Berlin: Walter de Gruyter, 1934–. Also see Szymusiak, Jan M., ed. *Deux apologies. À l'Empereur Constance, pour sa fuite*, 86–175. SC 56bis. Paris: Cerf, 1987.

———. *Apologia contra Arianos.* Opitz, Hans-Georg, ed. In *Athanasius: Werke*, 2:87–168. Berlin: Walter de Gruyter, 1934–.

———. *Apologia de fuga sua.* Opitz, Hans-Georg, ed. In *Athanasius: Werke*, 1:68–86. Berlin: Walter de Gruyter, 1934–. Also see Szymusiak, Jan M., ed. *Deux apologies. À l'Empereur Constance, pour sa fuite*, 176–245. SC 56bis. Paris: Cerf, 1987.

———. *De synodis Arimini in Italia et Seleuciae in Isauria.* Opitz, Hans-Georg, ed. In *Athanasius Werke*, 2:231–78. Berlin: Walter de Gruyter, 1934–.

———. *Epistula ad easdem apud Mareotam ecclesias.* [*CPG*, 2:2112]. In Turner, 1.2.3:659–62.

———. *Festal Letters.* Syriac text: Cureton, William, ed. *The Festal Letters of Athanasius.* London: Society for the Publication of Oriental Texts, 1848. Coptic text: Lefort,

L. Th., ed. *S. Athanase, lettres festales et pastorales en Copte.* CSCO 150–51, Scriptores Coptici 19–20. Louvain: Peeters, 1965. Robinson, Archibald, trans. "Letters of Athanasius." *Nicene and Post-Nicene Fathers,* Series 2, vol. 8, 495–581. Reprint: Grand Rapids, Eerdmans, 1978.

———. *Historia Arianorum.* Opitz, Hans-Georg, ed. In *Athanasius Werke,* 2:183–230. Berlin: Walter de Gruyter, 1934–.

———. *Letter to Dracontius.* ed. Migne, J. P. PG 25:524–33. Paris Garnier Fratres, 1884.

———. *Life of Antony.* Bartelink, G. J. M., ed. *Vie d'Antoine.* SC 400. Paris: Cerf, 1994.

———. *Tomus ad Antiochenos.* Migne, J.-P. ed. PG 26:796–809. Paris: Garnier Fratres, 1887.

pseudo-Athanasius. *Epistulae II ad Luciferum.* Hartel, Guilelmus, ed. In *Luciferi Calaritani Opuscula,* 322–27. CSEL 14. Vienna: G Geroldi, 1886.

Atiya, Aziz S. *History of Eastern Christianity.* Notre Dame: University of Notre Dame Press, 1968.

Atlas. Atlas zur Kirchengeschichte. Jedin, Herbert, Kenneth Scott Latourette, and Jochen Martin, eds. 3rd Edition. Freiburg: Herder, 1987.

Atlas de España. 2 vols. Madrid: El Pais/Aguilar, 1992.

Atti del II° Congresso Internazionale di Archeologia Cristiana tenuto in Roma nell' Aprile 1900. Rome: Libreria Spithöver, 1902.

Atti del III Congresso Internazionale di Archeologia Cristiania, Ravenna, 25–30 Settembre 1932. Studi di Antichità Cristiana 8. Rome: Pontificio Istituto di Archeologia Cristiana, 1934.

Atti del IV Congresso Internazionale di Archeologia Cristiana, Città del Vaticano, 16–22 Ottobre 1938. 2 vols. Studi di Antichità Cristiana 16 & 19. Rome: Pontificio Istituto di Archeologia Cristiana, 1940–48.

Atti del VI Congresso Internazionale di Archeologia Cristiana, Ravenna, 23–30 Settembre, 1962. Studi di Antichità Cristiana 26. Vatican City: Pontificio Istituto di Archeologia Cristiana, 1965.

Atti del IX Congresso Internazionale di Archeologia Cristiana, Roma, 21–27 Settembre, 1975. 2 vols. Studi di Antichità Cristiana 32. Rome: Pontificio Istituto di Archeologia Cristiana, 1978.

Augustine. *Ad Donatistas post collationem.* Petschenig, M., ed. In *Sancti Aureli Augustini Scripta contra donatistas,* 3:95–162. CSEL 53. Vienna & Leipzig: F. Tempsky & G. Freytag, 1910.

———. *Breviculus conlationis cum Donatistis.* Lancel, S., ed. In *Gesta conlationis Carthaginiensis, anno 411. Accedit Sancti Augustini breviculus conlationis cum Donatistis,* 259–306. CCSL 149a. Turnhout: Brepols, 1974.

———. *Contra Cresconium.* Petschenig, M., ed. In *Sancti Aureli Augustini Scripta contra donatistas,* 2:325–582. CSEL 52. Vienna & Leipzig: F. Tempsky & G. Freytag, 1909.

———. *Contra epistulam Parmeniani.* Petschenig, M., ed. In *Sancti Aureli Augustini Scripta contra donatistas,* 1:17–142. CSEL 51. Vienna & Leipzig: F. Tempsky & G. Freytag, 1980.

———. *De baptismo contra Donatistas.* Petschenig, M., ed. In *Sancti Aureli Augustini Scripta contra donatistas,* 1:143–376. CSEL 51. Vienna & Leipzig: F. Tempsky & G. Freytag, 1908.

———. *De Civitate Dei.* Dombart, Bernardus, and Alphonsus Kalb, eds. 2 vols. CCSL 47–48. Turnhout: Brepols, 1955.

———. *De mendacio.* Zycha, J., ed. In *Sancti Aureli Augustini de fide et symbolo,* 411–66. CSEL 41. Vienna & Leipzig: F. Tempsky & G. Freytag, 1900.

———. *De unico baptismo contra Petilianum.* Petschenig, M., ed. In *Sancti Aureli Augustini Scripta contra donastistas,* 3:1–34. CSEL 53. Vienna & Leipzig: F. Tempsky & G. Freytag, 1910.

———. *Enarrationes in Psalmos.* Dekkers, Eligius, and Iohannes Fraipont, eds. 3 vols. CCSL 38–40. Turnhout: Brepols, 1956.

——. *Epistulae*. Goldbacher, Al., *et al.*, eds. 5 vols. CSEL 34, 44, 57, 58, 88. Vienna & Leipzig: F. Tempsky & G. Freytag, 1895–1981.

——. *Retractationum, Libri II*. Mutzenbecher, Almut, ed. CCSL 57. Turnhout: Brepols, 1984.

——. *Sermones ad Populum*. Migne, J.-P., ed. PL 38–39. Paris, 1865.

Autori vari. "Papiri documentari dell' Università Cattolica di Milano." In *Aegyptus* 54 (1974): 1–140.

Avi-Yonah, Michael. *Gazetteer of Roman Palestine*. Qedem 5. Jerusalem: Institute of Archaeology, The Hebrew University of Jerusalem and CARTA, 1976.

——. *The Holy Land from the Persian to the Arab Conquest (536 B.C.–A.D. 640)*. Revised Edition. Grand Rapids: Baker, 1977.

——. *The Jews under Roman and Byzantine Rule: a Political History of Palestine from the Bar Kochba War to the Arab Conquest*. Jerusalem: Magnes Press, 1984.

Baarda, Tjitze. *The Gospel Quotations of Aphrahat the Persian Sage, vol. 1 and appendix, Aphrahat's Text of the Fourth Gospel*. Amsterdam: Vrije Universiteit, 1975.

Babylonian Talmud. Hebrew—English Edition of the Babylonian Talmud. Epstein, I., ed. London: Soncino Press, 1988.

Baccache, E. *Églises de village de la Syrie du Nord*. BAH 105.1–2. Paris: Paul Geunthner, 1979–80.

Back, Michael. *Die Sassanidischen Staatsinschriften*. Acta Iranica 18 [Troisième Serie, Textes et Mémoires, 8]. Leiden/Teheran and Liège: Brill/Bibliothèque Pahlavi, 1978.

Bagatti, Bellarmino. *The Church from The Circumcision*. Hoade, Eugene, trans. Studium Biblicum Franciscanum, Collectio Minor, 2. Jerusalem: Franciscan Printing Press, 1971; reprint 1984.

——. *The Church from the Gentiles in Palestine*. Hoade, Eugene, trans. Studium Biblicum Franciscanum, Collectio Minor, 4. Jerusalem: Franciscan Printing Press, 1971; reprint 1984.

Bagnall, Roger S. "Conversion and Onomastics: a Reply." *ZPE* 69 (1987): 243–50.

——. *Egypt in Late Antiquity*. Princeton: Princeton University Press, 1993.

Bagnall, Roger S., *et al. Consuls of the Later Roman Empire*. Philological Monographs of the American Philological Association 36. Atlanta: Scholars Press, 1987.

BAH. Bibliothèque archéologique et historique.

Balestri, I., and H. Hyvernat. *Acta Martyrum*. 4 vols. Text, CSCO 43 & 86, Scriptores Coptici 3 & 6. Louvain: Imprimerie Orientaliste L. Durbecq, 1950–55. Translation, CSCO 44 & 125, Scriptores Coptici 4 & 15. Louvain: Imprimerie Orientaliste L. Durbecq, 1950–55.

Ball, John. *Egypt in the Classical Geographers*. Ministry of Finance, Egypt, Survey of Egypt. Cairo: Government Press, Bulâq, 1942.

Bardaisan. *Book of the Laws of Countries*. Drijvers, H. J. W., ed. and trans. Assen: Van Gorcum, 1965. See also the earlier edition *Liber Legum Regnorum*. Nau, F., *et al.*, eds. PS 1.2:490–658. Paris: Firmin-Didot et socii, 1907.

Barhadbešabba. *Histoire Ecclésiastique (Ire Partie)*. Nau, F., ed. PO 23.2. Paris: Firmin-Didot, 1932; reprint Turnhout: Brepols, 1994.

Bar-Hebraeus, Gregory. *Gregorii Barhebraei chronicon ecclesiasticum*. Abbeloos, Joannes Baptista, and Thomas Josephus Lamy, eds. 3 vols. Louvain: Excudebat Car. Peeters, 1872–77.

Barnard, Leslie W. *The Council of Serdica, 343 A.D.* Sofia: Synodal Publishing House, 1983.

Barnea, I[on]. *Christian Art in Romania*. I. *3rd–6th Centuries*. Bantas, Andrei, trans. Bucharest: Bible and Mission Institute of the Romanian Orthodox Church, 1979.

——. "L'épigraphie chrétienne de l'Illyricum Oriental." In *Actes du Xe Congrès international*, 1:631–78.

——. *Les monuments paléochrétiens de Roumanie*. Sussidi allo studio delle antichità cristane, 6. Vatican City: Pontificio Istituto di Archeologia Cristiana, 1977.

Barns, John, and Henry Chadwick. "A Letter Ascribed to Peter of Alexandria." In *JTS*, n.s. 24 (1973): 443–455.

Barton, Peter F. *Geschichte des Christentums in Österreich und Südmitteleuropa, Band 1, Frühes Christentum in Österreich und Südmitteleuropa*. Vienna: Böhlau Verlag, 1992.

Basil of Caesarea. *Homiliae et Sermones*. Migne, J. P., ed. In *Opera Omnia quae extant*, 3:163–618. PG 31:163–618. Paris: Garnier Fratres, 1885.

——. *In Quadraginta Martyres Sebastenses*. Migne, J.-P., ed. In *Opera Omnia quae extant*, 3: 508–25. PG 31:508–25. Paris: Garnier Fratres, 1885.

——. *Letters*. Deferrari, Roy J., ed. LCL, 190, 215, 243, 270. Cambridge: Harvard University Press, 1926–34.

Bauckham, Richard. *Jude and the Relatives of Jesus in the Early Church*. Edinburgh: T & T Clark, 1990.

Bauer, Walter. *Orthodoxy and Heresy in Earliest Christianity*. Kraft, Robert A., et al., trans. Philadelphia: Fortress, 1971.

Baum, Wilhelm, and Dietmar W. Winkler. *The Church of the East, a Concise History*. Henry, Miranda G., trans. London and New York: Routledge Curzon, 2003.

Baumeister, Theofried. *Martyr Invictus*. Münster: Verlag Regensberg, 1972.

BCH. Bulletin de Correspondance Hellénique.

Becker-Bertau, Friedrich. *Die Inschriften von Klaudiu Polis*. Inschriften griechischer Städte aus Kleinasien 31. Österreichische Akademie der Wissenschaften/Nordrhein-Westfälische Akademie der Wissenchaften. Bonn: Dr. Rudolf Habelt Gmbh., 1980.

Bede. *Historia ecclesiastica gentis Anglorum*. King, J. E., ed. *Bede, Historical Works*. 2 vols. LCL. Cambridge: Harvard University Press, 1930.

Bedjan, Paulus. *Acta martyrum et sanctorum Syriace*. 7 vols. Leipzig: Harrasowitz, 1890–97; reprint Hildesheim: Olms, 1968.

Bell, David N. *The Life of Shenoute, by Besa*. Cistercian Studies 73. Kalamazoo: Cistercian Publications, 1983.

Bellucci, P. A. "Le origini della chiesa di Napoli e nuovi ritrovamenti nel cimiterio di San Gennaro extra moenia." In *Actes du Ve Congrès international*, 487–504.

Beraud Sudreau, J. "Documents d'archéologie chrétienne, à l'époque Constantinienne, provenant de l'Aquitania Secunda, dont Burdigala était la métropole." In *Akten des VII Internationalen Kongresses*, 1:373–78.

Berthier, André. *La Numidie, Rome et le Maghreb*. Paris: Picard, 1981.

Besa. *Sinuthii Archimandritae vita*. In Leipoldt, I., and W. Crum, eds. *Sinuthii Archimandritae vita et opera omnia. I. Sinuthi vita bohairice*, 7–76. CSCO 41, Scriptores Coptici 1. Louvain: L. Durbecq, 1951. For English trans., see Bell.

Beshevliev, Veselin. *Spätgriechische und spätlateinische Inschriften aus Bulgarien*. Berliner Byzantinische Arbeiten 30. Berlin: Akademie Verlag, 1964.

Bezae codex cantabrigiensis. Scrivener, Frederick, H., ed. Pittsburgh Reprint Series 5. Cambridge: Deighton, Bell, and Co., 1864; reprint Pittsburgh, Pickwick Press, 1978.

BHG. Bibliotheca hagiographica graeca. Halkin, François, ed. 3rd Edition. 2 vols. Subsidia hagiographica 8A. Brussels: Socii Bollandiniani, 1957. *Bibliotheca hagiographica graeca auctarium*. Halkin, François, ed. Subsidia hagiographica 47. Brussels: Société des Bollandistes, 1969. *Novum auctarium bibliothecae hagiographicae graecae*. Halkin, François, ed. Subsidia hagiographica 65. Brussels: Société des Bollandistes, 1984.

BHL. Bibliotheca hagiographica latina. Subsidia hagiographica 5–6 & 13.3 vols. Brussels: Socii Bollandiniani, 1898–1911. *Bibliotheca hagiographica latina, novum supplementum*. Fros, Henricus, ed. Subsidia hagiographica 70. Brussels: Société des Bollandistes, 1986.

BHO. Bibliotheca hagiographica orientalis. Subsidia hagiographica 10. Brussels: Socii Bollandiniani, 1910.

BKT. Berliner Klassikertexte, VI, Altchristliche Texte. Schmidt, C., and W. Schubart, eds. Berlin: Weidmann, 1910.

Bovini, G. "Le ultime scoperte d'antichità Cristiane nell' Italia centro-settentrionale." In *Actes du Ve Congrès international*, 125–46.

Bowen, Gillian. "The Spread of Christianity in Egypt in light of Recent Discoveries from Ancient Kellis." 2 vols. Ph.D. thesis. Monash University, 1998.

Bowersock, G. L. *Roman Arabia*. Cambridge: Harvard University Press, 1983.

Bowman, Alan K. *Egypt after the Pharaohs*. Berkeley: University of California Press, 1989.

Bratke, Eduard. *Das Sogenannte Religionsgespräch am Hof der Sasaniden*. TU 19.3. Leipzig: Hinrichs, 1899.

Bratož, Rajko. "The Development of the Early Christian Research in Slovenia and Istria between 1976 and 1986." In *Actes du XIe Congrès international*, 3:2345–88.

Braun, Oskar. *Ausgewählte Akten persischer Märtyrer*. Bibliothek der Kirchenvater. Kempten & Munich: Kösel, 1915.

———. "Die Briefwechsel des Katholikos Pappa von Seleucia." In *Zeitschrift für Katholische Theologie* 18 (1894): 163–82.

Braund, David. *Georgia in Antiquity*. Oxford: Clarendon, 1994.

Brenk, Beat. "Der Kultort, seine Zugänglichkeit und seine Besucher." In *Akten des XII Internationalen Kongresses*, 1:69–122.

Breydy, Michael. *Études sur Sa'id ibn Batriq et ses sources*. CSCO 450, Subsidia 69. Louvain: Peeters, 1983.

Brightman, F. E., ed. *Liturgies Eastern and Western*. Vol. 1. Oxford: Clarendon, 1896.

Brock, Sebastian. "A Martyr at the Sasanid Court under Vahran II: Candida." In *AB* 96 (1978): 167–81. Reprint in Brock, Sebastian. *Syriac Perspectives on Late Antiquity*. Aldershot: Variorum, 1997, IX:167–81.

———. Review of Wiessner, Gernot. *Untersuchungen zur syrischen Literaturgeschichte*, 1. In *JTS* NS.19 (1968): 300–309.

Brock, Sebastian, and Susan Ashbrook Harvey. *Holy Women of the Syrian Orient*. Berkeley: University of California Press, 1987.

Bromwich, James. *The Roman Remains of Southern France: a Guidebook*. London and New York: Routledge, 1993.

Brown, Raymond, E. and John P. Meier. *Antioch & Rome, New Testament Cradles of Catholic Christianity*. New York: Paulist Press, 1983.

Brunnow, Rudolf Ernst and Alfred v. Domaszewski. *Die Provincia Arabia*. Vol. 1. Strassburg: Trubner, 1904.

BS. Bibliotheca Sanctorum. 12 vols. with index and appendix. Rome: Istituto Giovanni XXIII nella Pontificia Università Laterenense, 1961–70.

Budge, E. A. Wallis. *Book of the Saints of the Ethiopian Church*. 4 vols. Cambridge: Cambridge University Press, 1928.

———. *History of Ethiopia, Nubia, and Abyssinia*. 2 vols. London: Methuen & Co., 1928; reprint as one volume, Oosterhout: Anthropological Publications, 1970.

Bulletin Épigraphique. Section in *Revue des études grecques*.

Burkitt, F. C. *Euphemia and the Goth, with the Acts of Martyrdom of the Confessors of Edessa*. London: Williams and Norgate, 1913; reprint, Amsterdam: Philo Press, 1981.

Buzandaran Patmut'iwnk'. P[atkanyan], K[erovbe], ed. St. Petersburg: i Tparani Kayserakan Chemaranin Gitut'yants', 1883; reprint, Delmar, NY: Caravan Books, 1984. Garsoian, Nina G, trans. *The Epic Histories (Buzandaran Patmut'iwnk')*. Harvard Armenian Texts and Studies, 8. Cambridge: Harvard University Press, 1989.

Calder, William M. "Early Christian Epitaphs from Phrygia." In *Anatolian Studies*, 5 (1955): 25–38.

———. "Some Monuments of the Great Persecution." In *Bulletin of the John Rylands Library* 8 (1924): 345–64.

Calderini, Aristide. *Dizionario dei nomi geografici e topografici dell' Egitto greco-romano*. Milan: Cisalpino-Goliardico, 1966–.

Canivert, P. and M. T. Canivert. *Huarte, Sanctuaire chrétien d'Apamène*. BAH 122. Paris: Paul Guenthner, 1987.

Cantino Wataghin, Gisela, and Letizia Pani Ermini. "Sanctuari martiriali e centri di pellegrinaggio in Italia fra tardo antichità e alto medioevo." In *Akten des XII Internationalen Kongresses*, 1:123–51.

Cappelletti, Giuseppe. *Le Chiese d'Italia*. 21 vols. Venice: Giuseppe Antonelli, 1844–70.

Carcopino, Jerome. *Le Maroc Antique*. 6th Edition. Paris: Gallimard, 1943.

Catal. Brux. Hagiographici Bollandiniani. *Catalogus codicum hagiographicorum bibliothecae regiae Bruxellensis*. 2 vols. Subsidia hagiographica 1. Louvain: Socii Bollandiniani, 1886–89.

Catal. Lat. Rom. Poncelot, A., ed. *Catalogus codicum hagiographicorum latinorum bibliothecarum Romanarum praeter quam Vaticanae*. Subsidia hagiographica 9. Louvain: [Socii Bollandiniani], 1909; reprint 1981.

Catalogue. *Catalogue of the Greek Coins in the British Museum*, 25, *Catalogue of the Greek Coins of Phrygia*. Head, Barclay V., ed. London: Trustees of the British Museum, 1906.

Catalogus archiepiscoporum Mediolanensium. Bethman, L. C., and W. Wattenbach, eds. *MGH*, Scriptores, 8:102–110. Hannover: Hahn, 1848; reprint Leipzig: Hiersmann, 1925.

Catalogus episcoporum Neapolitanorum. Waitz, G., ed. *MGH*, SRLI, 436–39. Hannover: Hahn, 1878.

CCSL. Corpus Christianorum Series Latina.

Cedrenus, George. [*Compendium Historiarum.*] Bekker, Immanuel, ed. 2 vols. Corpus Scriptorum Historiae Byzantinae, 34–35. Bonn: Weber, 1838–39. Reprint edition in Migne, J.-P., ed. PG 121:1–122:368. Paris: Garnier Fratres, 1889–94.

Chabot, J. B. *Synodicon Orientale, ou recueil de synodes Nestoriens*. Paris: Imprimerie Nationale, 1902.

Chaumont, M.-L. *La Christianisation de l'Empire Iranien*. CSCO 499, Subsidia 80. Louvain: Peeters, 1988.

Chehab, M. "Découvertes archéologiques au Liban d'époque paléo-chrétiennes." In *Akten des VII Internationalen Kongresses*, 1:405–406.

———. "Une nécropole paléochrétienne à Tyr." In *Atti del IX Congresso internazionale*, 2: 157–61.

Chevalier, Pascale. *Salona II,1–2, Ecclesiae Dalmatiae*. Collection de l'École Française de Rome, 194.1. Rome and Split: École Française de Rome and Musée Archéologique de Split, 1996.

Chierici, Gino. "Contributo allo studio dell' architettura paleocristiana nella Campania." In *Atti del III Congresso internazionale*, 203–16.

Chitty, Derwas J. *The Desert a City*. Oxford: Basil Blackwell, 1966.

Chronicle of Arbela. Kawerau, Peter, ed. and trans. *Die Chronik von Arbela*. CSCO 467–68, Scriptores Syri 199–200. Louvain: Peeters, 1985.

Chronicle of Edessa. Hallier, Ludwig, ed. *Untersuchungen über die Edessenische Chronik*. TU 9.1. Leipzig: Hinrichs, 1892.

Chronicle of Seert. Scher, Addai, and J. Perier, eds. *Histoire Nestorienne Inédite (Chronique de Séert), première partie (1)*. PO 4:214–312. Paris: Firmin Didot, 1908.

Chronicon Paschale. Dindorf, Guilelmus, ed. Corpus Scriptorum Historiae Byzantinae, 16–17. Bonn: impensis E. Weberi, 1832. Reprint edition in Migne, J.-P. PG 92:9–1160. Paris: Migne, 1865. Whitby, Michael, and Mary Whitby, trans. *Chronicon Paschale*. Translated Texts for Historians 7. Liverpool: Liverpool University Press, 1989.

CIG. *Corpus Inscriptionum Graecarum*. Boeckhius, Augustus, *et al.*, eds. 4 vols. Berlin: Officina Academia, 1828–77.

CIJ. *Corpus Inscriptionum Iudaicarum*. Frey, Jean-Baptiste, ed. Sussidi allo studio delle antichità cristane 1 & 3. Vatican City: Pontificio Istituto di Archeologia Cristiana, 1936–52; partial reprint New York: KTAV, 1975.

CIL. *Corpus Inscriptionum Latinarum*. Multiple vols. Berlin: Akademie der Wissenschaften, 1862–.

I Clement. See *Apostolic Fathers*.

II Clement. See *Apostolic Fathers*.

Clement of Alexandria. *Letter to Theodore*. Morton Smith, ed. In *Clement of Alexandria and a Secret Gospel of Mark*, 448–450. Cambridge: Harvard University Press, 1971.
——. *Stromata*. Books 1–6 in Stählin, Otto; Ludwig Fruchtel; and Ursula Treu., eds. *Clemens Alexandrinus*. Vol. 2. 4th Edition. GCS. Berlin: Akademie Verlag, 1985. Books 7–8 in Stählin, Otto, and Ursula Treu, eds. *Clemens Alexandrinus*. Vol. 3. 3rd Edition. GCS [12], 15, 17. Berlin: Akademie-Verlag, 1970.
pseudo-Clement. *Epistula II ad Virgines*. Migne, J.-P. ed. *Duae epistolae Sancti Clementis*. Villecourt, Clemente, trans. PG 1:379–452. Paris: Garnier Fratres, 1886.
——. *Homilies*. Rehm, Bernhard, and Georg Strecker, eds. *Homilien*. GCS [42]. 3rd Edition. Berlin: Akademie Verlag, 1992.
——. *Recognitiones*. Rehm, Bernhard, and Franz Paschke, eds. *Rekognitionen*. GCS 51. Berlin: Akademie Verlag, 1951.
Collectio Avellana. Guenther, Otto, ed. CSEL 35. Prague, Vienna, & Leipzig: F. Tempsky & G. Freytag, 1895–98.
Collingwood, R. G., and R. P. Wright. *Roman Inscriptions of Britain*. Multiple vols. Oxford & Gloucester: Clarendon Press & Haverford Bequest, 1965–.
Comité éditorial. "Appendice, les analyses de marbres." In Duval, Noël, *et al. Les Sarcophages d'Aquitaine*, 123–24. Antiquité Tardive 1. Turnhout: Brepols, 1993.
Concilia Africae. Munier, C., ed. CCSL 259. Turnhout: Brepols, 1974.
Concilia Galliae. Munier, C., ed. CCSL 148. Turnhout: Brepols, 1963.
Constantine? *To the Assembly of the Saints*. Heikel, Ivar A., ed. In Eusebius. *Vita Constantini*. *Eusebius Werke*, 1: 149–92. GCS 7. Leipzig: Hinrichs, 1902.
Constantius of Lyon. *Vita Germani episcopi Autissiodorensis*. In Krusch, B., and W. Levison, eds. *Passiones vitaeque sanctorum aevi Merovingici*. *MGH*, SRM 7.1: 247–83. Hannover & Leipzig: Hahn, 1919.
Conversio et Passio Afrae. Krusch, Bruno, ed. MGH, SRM 3: 41–64. Hannover: Hahn, 1896.
III Corinthians. In Testuz, Michel, ed. *Papyrus Bodmer X–XII, x: Correspondance apocryphe des Corinthiens et de l'apôtre Paul, xi: Onzième Ode de Salomon, xii: Fragment d'un hymne liturgique*, 32–44. Cologny-Geneva: Bibliotheca Bodmeriana, 1959. See also, Hovhanessian, Vahan. *Third Corinthians, Reclaiming Paul for Orthodoxy*, 147–51. Studies in Biblical Literature 18. New York: Peter Lang, 2000.
Corsten, Thomas. *Die Inschriften von Kios*. Inschriften griechischer Städte aus Kleinasien 29. Österreichische Akademie der Wissenschaften/Nordrhein-Westfälische Akademie der Wissenschaften. Bonn: Dr. Rudolf Habelt Gmbh., 1985.
——. *Die Inschriften von Prusa ad Olympium*. 2 vols. Inschriften griechischer Städte aus Kleinasien 39–40. Österreichische Akademie der Wissenschaften/Nordrhein-Westfälische Akademie der Wissenschaften. Bonn: Dr. Rudolf Habelt Gmbh., 1991–93.
CPG. Clavis Patrum Graecorum. 5 vols. and supplement, Geerard, Maritius, *et al.*, eds. Turnhout: Brepols, 1974–98.
CPL. Clavis Patrum Latinorum. Dekkers, Elegius, and Aemilius Garr, eds. 3rd Edition. Turnhout: Brepols, 1995.
Crouzel, Henri. *Origen*. Worrall, A. S., trans. Edinburgh: T & T Clark, 1989.
CSCO. Corpus scriptorum Christianorum Orientalium.
CSEL. Corpus scriptorum Ecclesiasticorum Latinorum.
Cumont, Franz. "Les inscriptions chrétiennes de l'Asie Mineure." In *MEFRA* 15 (1895): 245–99.
——. "Sarin dans le Testament des Martyrs de Sébaste." In *AB* 25 (1906): 241–42.
——. "Zimara dans le Testament des Martyrs de Sébaste." In *AB* 23 (1904): 448.
Cureton, William. *Ancient Syriac Documents*. London: Williams and Norgate, 1864; reprint Amsterdam: Oriental Press, 1967.
——. *Spicilegium Syriacum*. London: Rivingtons, 1855; reprint Lexington, KY: American Theological Library Association, 1965.

Cuscito, Giuseppe. *Martiri Cristiani ad Aquileia e in Istria.* Università degli Studi di Trieste, Facoltà di Magistero, III, 25. Udine: del Bianco Editore, 1992.

——. "Questioni agiografiche di Aquileia e dell' Istria. Contributo alla conoscenza del Cristianesimo Preconstantino." In *Atti del IX Congresso internazionale,* 2:167–98.

——. "Vescove e cattedrale nella documentazione epigrafica in Occidente (Italia e Dalmazia)." In *Actes du XIe Congrès international,* 1:735–76.

Cyprian. *De lapsis.* Bévenot, M., ed. In *Sancti Cypriani episcopi opera,* 1:223–242. CCSL 3. (Turnhout: Brepols, 1972).

——. *Epistulae.* Diercks, G. F., ed. In *Sancti Cypriani episcopi opera,* 3.1–2. CCSL 3b–3c. Turnhout: Brepols, 1994–96.

Cyril of Jerusalem. *Catechetical Lectures.* Reischel, Wilhelm Karl, and Joseph Rupp, eds. *Cyrilli Hierosolymorum archiepiscopi opera quae supersunt omnia.* 2 vols. Munich: Sumptibus Librariae Lentnerianae, 1848–60; reprint Hildesheim: Olms, 1967.

Cyril of Scythopolis. *Bios tou hosiou patros hemon Saba.* In Schwartz, Eduard, ed. *Kyrillos von Skythopolis,* 85–200. TU 49.2. Leipzig: Hinrichs, 1939. Translated in Cyril of Scythopolis. *Lives of the Monks of Palestine,* 93–219. Price, R. M., trans. Cistercian Studies 114. Kalamazoo: Cistercian Publications, 1991.

DACL. Dictionnaire d'archéologie chrétienne et de liturgie. Cabrol, F. and H. LeClercq, eds. Paris: Letouzy et Ane, 1907–53.

Dagron, Gilbert, ed. *Vie et miracles de Sainte Thècle.* Subsidia hagiographica 62. Brussels: Société des Bollandistes, 1978.

Dassmann, Ernst. *Die Anfänge der Kirche in Deutschland.* Stuttgart: Verlag W. Kolhammer, 1993.

Datiana historia ecclesiae Mediolanensis. Biraghi (Biragus), Aloysius, ed. Milan: Ex typographia Boniardo-Polianea, 1848.

De Bhaldraithe, Eoin. "Early Christian Features Preserved in Western Monasticism." In Kreider, Alan, ed. *Origins of Christendom in the West,* 153–78. Edinburgh and New York: T & T Clark, 2001.

De Boor, Carl. "Nachträge zu den *Notitiae Episcopatuum.*" *Zeitschrift für Kirchengeschichte* 12 (1890–1): 303–22, 519–34, & 14 (1893–4): 573–99.

De Cosson, Anthony. *Mareotis.* London: Country Life Ltd., 1935.

Deichmann, Friedrich Wilhelm, *et al.,* eds. *Repertorium der Christlich-Antiken Sarkophage.* Multiple vols. Wiesbaden: Franz Steiner Verlag Gmbh., 1967–.

Déléage, André. *La Capitation du Bas-Empire.* Macon: Imprimerie Protat Frères, 1945.

Delehaye, Hippolyte. "Les Actes de S. Marcel le Centurion." In *AB* 41 (1923): 257–87.

——. "Contributions récentes à l'hagiographie de Rome et d'Afrique." In *AB* 54 (1936): 265–313.

——. "L'hagiographie de Salone d'après les dernières découvertes archéologiques." In *AB* 23 (1907): 5–18.

——. "Hagiographie Napolitaine." In *AB* 57 (1939): 5–64.

——. '*In Britannia*' dans le *Martyrologie Hiéronymien.* From the Proceedings of the British Academy, vol. 17. London: Humphrey Milford, [1933].

——. "Les martyrs d'Égypte." In *AB* 40 (1922): 1–154 & 299–364.

——. *Les origines du culte des martyrs.* 2nd Edition. Subsidia hagiographica 20. Brussels: Société des Bollandistes, 1933.

——. Review of Grégoire, Henri. *Saints jumeaux et dieux cavaliers.* In *AB* 24(1905): 505–07.

——. "Saints d'Istrie et de Dalmatie." In *AB* 18 (1899): 369–411.

——. "Saints de Thrace et de Mésie." In *AB* 31 (1912): 161–300.

DHGE. Dictionnaire d'histoire et de géographie ecclésiastiques. Baudrillart, Alfred, *et al.,* eds. Paris: Librare Letouzy et Ané, 1912–.

Didascalia Apostolorum. Vööbus, Arthur, ed. CSCO 401 & 407, Scriptores Syri 175 & 179. Translated in CSCO 402 & 408, Scriptores Syri 176 & 180. Louvain: Secrétariat du CSCO, 1979.

Dihle, A. "Early Christianity in India." In Hilliard, T. W., *et al.* eds. *Ancient History in a Modern University*, 2:305–316. Grand Rapids: Wm. B. Eerdmans and The Ancient History Documentary Research Centre, Macquarrie University, 1998.

pseudo-Dionysius. *Corpus Dionysiacum*. 2 vols. Suchla, Beate Regina, Günter Heil, and Adolf M. Ritter, eds. PTS 33 & 36. Berlin: Walter de Gruyter, 1990–91.

pseudo-Dionysius of Tell Mahre. [*Incerti auctoris*] *Chronicon Anonymum pseudo-Dionysianum vulgo dictum*. Chabot, I.-B., ed. 2 vols. CSCO 91 & 104, Scriptores Syri 43 & 53. Louvain: Imprimerie Orientaliste L. Durbecq, 1927–33. Chabot, I.-B., & Robert Hespel, trans. *Chronicon Anonymum Pseudo-Dionysianum vulgo dictum*. 2 vols. CSCO 121 & 507, Scriptores Syri 66 & 213. Louvain: Peeters, 1949–89.

Di Vita, A. "L'Ipogeo di Adamo ed Eva a Gargaresc." In *Atti del IX Congresso internazionale*, 2:199–256.

Dobschütz, Ernst von. *Christusbilder, Untersuchungen zur christlichen Legenden*. TU, 18. Leipzig: Hinrichs, 1899.

Dodds, E. R. *Pagan and Christian in an Age of Anxiety*. Cambridge: Cambridge University Press, 1968; reprint, 1990.

pseudo-Dorotheus of Tyre. *De septuaginta Domini discipulis*. Migne, J.-P., ed. PG 92: 1059–86. Paris: Migne, 1865.

Doubouniotos, K. I. "Kerkyraïka Anekdota." In *Neos Hellenomnemon* 16 (1922): 231–35.

Downey, Glanville. *A History of Antioch in Syria, from Seleucus to the Arab Conquest*. Princeton: Princeton University Press, 1961.

Drack, Walter, and Rudolf Fellmann. *Die Römer in der Schweiz*. Stuttgart and Jona SG: Konrad Theiss Verlag and Raggi Verlag, 1988.

Drew-Bear, Thomas. *Nouvelles inscriptions de Phrygie*. Zutphen: Terra, 1978.

Drew-Bear, Thomas, and Christian Naour. "Divinités de Phrygie." In *ANRW*, II.18.3: 1907–2004. Berlin: Walter de Gruyter, 1990.

Drijvers, H[an] J. W. *Bardaisan of Edessa*. Assen: Van Gorcum, 1966.

——. "Facts and Problems in Early Syriac Speaking Christianity." In *Second Century* 2 (1982): 157–75. Reprint in Ferguson, Everett, ed. *Studies in Early Christianity*, 12, *Missions and Regional Characteristics of the Early Church*, 251–96. New York and London: Garland, 1993.

——. "Jews and Christians at Edessa." In *Journal of Jewish Studies* 36 (1985): 88–102. Reprinted in Ferguson, Everett, ed. *Studies in Early Christianity*, 6, *Early Christianity and Judaism*, 350–64. New York and London: Garland, 1993.

Duchesne, L. "Les anciens évêchés de la Grèce." In *MEFRA* 15 (1895): 375–85.

——. *Fastes épiscopaux de l'ancienne Gaule*. 2nd Edition. 3 vols. Paris: Fontemoing, 1907–15.

Dufourcq, Albert. *Étude sur les Gesta Martyrum Romaines*. 6 vols. Paris: Fontemoing, 1900–.

Dujčev, Ivan. "Testimonianze archeologiche ed epigrafiche sul Cristianesimo primitivo in Bulgaria (I–VII Sec.)" *Atti della Pontificia Accademia Romana di archeologia (Serie III), Rendiconti* 53–54 (1984): 177–205.

Dussaud, René. *Topographie Historique de la Syrie Antique et Médiévale*. BAH 4. Paris: Librairie Orientaliste Paul Geuthner, 1927.

Duval, N[oël], and E. Marin, eds. *Salona III, Manastirine*. Collection de l'École Française de Rome 194.3. Rome and Split: École Française de Rome and Musée Archéologique de Split, 2000.

——, E. Marin, and C. Metzger. *Salona I, Catalogue de la sculpture architecturale paléochrétienne de Salone*. Collection de l'École Française de Rome 194.1. Rome and Split: École Française de Rome and Musée Archéologique de Split, 1994.

——, *et al.* eds. *Les premiers monuments chrétiens de la France*. 3 vols. Paris: Picard & Ministère de la culture et de la Francophonie, 1995–98.

Duval, Paul-Marie. *Cherchel et Tipasa*. BAH 43. Paris: Librairie Orientaliste Paul Guenthner, 1946.

Duval, Yvette. *Chrétiens d'Afrique à l'aube de la paix constantinienne*. Collection des Études Augustiniennes, Série Antiquité 164. Paris: Institut d'Études Augustiniennes, 2000.

——. *Loca Sanctorum Africae, le culte des martyrs en Afrique du IVe au VIIe siècle*. 2 vols.

Collection de la École Française de Rome 58. Rome: École Française de Rome, 1982.

Dyggve, Ejnar. *History of Salonitan Christianity.* Instituttet for Sammenlignende Kultur-forskning, Serie A, 21. Oslo: H. Aschehoug & Co., 1951.

Ecclesiastes Rabbah. Text in *Midrash Rabbah.* 2 vols. Vilnius: Romm, 1884; reprint, No place: No publisher, 1970, volume 2, last part. Translated by Cohen, A. in Freedman, H., and Maurice Simon, eds. *Midrash Rabbah.* 3rd Edition. London and New York: Soncino Press, 1983, vol. 8, part 2.

Eckhart, Lothar. "Die archaeologischen Ausgrabungen 1960 bis 1966 in der St.-Laurentius Basilica von Enns-Lorch-Lauriacum." In *Severin, zwischen Römerzeit und Volkerwanderung,* 375–85. Linz: Land Oberösterreich, Amt der Oö. Landesregierung, Abt. Kultur, 1982.

EEC. Encyclopedia of Early Christianity. Ferguson, Everett, ed. 2 vols. New York & London: Garland, 1997.

Egeria. *Itinerarium.* Franceschini, Aetius, and R. Weber, eds. In *Itineraria et alia geographica,* 27–103. CCSL 175. Turnhout: Brepols, 1965. John Wilkinson, trans. *Egeria's Travels to the Holy Land.* Revised Edition. Jerusalem: Ariel Publishing House, 1981.

Egger, Rudolf. "Bericht ueber die altchristlichen Funde in Oesterreich, ab 1938." In *Actes du Ve Congrès international,* 73–81.

———. "Bericht über die altchristlichen Funde in Österreich." In *Atti del VI Congresso internazionale,* 35–42.

Ehrhard, Albert. *Überlieferung und Bestand der hagiographischen und homiletischen Literatur der griechischen Kirche.* Teil 1, Band 3. TU 52. Leipzig: Hinrichs, 1952; reprint Osnabrück: Otto Zeller, 1965.

Elias of Nisibis. *Opus Chronologicum.* Brooks, E. W., ed. CSCO 62*–62**, Scriptores Syri 21 & 22. Chabot, I.-B., trans. CSCO 63*–63**, Scriptores Syri 23 & 24. Reprint Louvain: Imprimerie Orientaliste L. Durbecq, 1954.

Elishe. *Ełishei vasn Vardanants'ew Hayots' Paterazmin.* Ter-Minasyan, E., ed. Erevan: Haykstan S.S.R. Gitut'yunneri Akademiahi Hratarakzut'yun, 1957; reprint, Delmar, NY: Caravan Books, 1993. Thomson, Robert W., trans. *History of Vardan and the Armenian War.* Harvard Armenian Texts and Studies 5. Cambridge: Harvard University Press, 1982.

Ellison, Ann. "Natives, Romans, and Christians on West Hill, Uley." In Warwick, Rodwell, ed. *Temples, Churches, and Religion in Roman Britain,* 1:305–320. BAR British Series 77. Oxford: B.A.R., 1980.

EnECh. Encyclopedia of the Early Church. Di Berardino, Angelo, ed. Walford, Adrian, trans. 2 vols. Oxford: Oxford University Press, 1992.

Ennabli, L. "Topographie chrétienne de Carthage: les régions ecclésiastiques." In *Actes du XIe Congrès international,* 2: 1087–1101.

Epiphanius. [*Ancoratus und*] *Panarion.* 3 vols. Vol. 1. Holl, Karl, ed. GCS, 25. Leipzig: Hinrichs, 1915. Vols. 2–3. Dummer, Jurgen, ed. GCS, 31bis & 37bis. Berlin: Akademie-Verlag, 1980–85. Williams, Frank, trans. *The Panarion of Epiphanius of Salamis.* Nag Hammadi (and Manichean) Studies 35–36. Leiden: Brill, 1987–94.

———. *De XII Gemmis.* Blake, Robert P. and Henri de Vis, ed. and trans. *Epiphanius' "De Gemmis."* S&D, 2. London: Christophers, 1934.

———. *De Mensuris et Ponderibus.* Georgian version: Esbroeck, Michel-Jean van, ed. and trans. *Les versions géorgiennes d'Épiphane de Chypre, Traité des poids et des mesures.* CSCO 460–61, Scriptores Iberici, 19–20. Louvain: Peeters, 1984. Syriac version: Dean, James Elmer, ed. *Epiphanius' Treatise on Weights and Measures, the Syriac Version.* Oriental Institute of the University of Chicago, Studies in Ancient Oriental Civilization 11. Chicago: University of Chicago Press, 1935.

Epiphanius Monachus. *Vita S. Andreae.* Migne, J.-P. ed. PG 120:215–60. Paris: Garnier Fratres, 1880.

Epistula ad Mareoticas ecclesias. [*CPG,* 4: 8565.] In Turner, 1.2.3:657–58.

Erbetta, Mario. *Gli Apocrifi del Nuovo Testamento*. 3 vols. Casale: Marietti, 1966–81.

Eusebius. *Chronicle*. Aucher, John Baptistae, ed. *Chronicon Bipartitum*. 2 vols. Venice: Typis Coenobii PP. Armenorum in Insula S. Lazaro, 1818. [Armenian version with recent Latin translation]. For the older Latin version, see Jerome, *Chronicle*. Annotated German translation of the Armenian version in Karst, Josef, ed. *Die Chronik. Eusebius Werke*, 5. GCS 20. Leipzig: Hinrichs, 1911.

——. *Contra Marcellum*. Hansen, Günther Christian, ed. In *Eusebius Werke*, 4:1–58. 2nd Edition. GCS. Berlin: Akademie-Verlag, 1972.

——. *Commentary on Isaiah*. Ziegler, Joseph, ed. In *Eusebius Werke*, 9. GCS. Berlin: Akademie-Verlag, 1975.

——. *Ecclesiastical History*. Lake, Kirsopp, and J. E. L. Oulton, eds. 2 vols. LCL. Cambridge: Harvard University Press, 1926–32.

——. *Martyrs of Palestine*. Schwartz, Eduard, ed. In *Eusebius Werke*, 2.2. GCS 9.2. Leipzig: Hinrichs, 1908. For the second and longer recension preserved in Syriac, see Cureton, William, ed. *History of the Martyrs in Palestine*. London: Williams and Norgate, 1861.

——. *Onomasticon*. Klostermann, Erich, ed. *Das Onomastikon der Biblischen Ortsnamen*. In *Eusebius Werke*, 3.1. GCS 11,1. Leipzig: Hinrichs, 1904; reprint Hildesheim: Olms, 1966.

——. *Praeparatio evangelica*. Mras, Karl, ed. In *Eusebius Werke*, 8. GCS 43. Berlin: Akademie-Verlag, 1956. Gifford, Edwin Hamilton, trans. *Preparation for the Gospel*. 2 vols. Oxford: Clarendon, 1903; reprint Grand Rapids: Baker, 1981.

——. *Vita Constantini*. Winkelmann, Friedhelm, ed. In *Eusebius Werke*, 1.1 GCS [8]. 2nd Edition. Berlin: Akademie-Verlag, 1991.

Eutychius of Alexandria. *Annales*. Cheicko, L., B. Carra de Vaux, and H. Zayat, eds. 2 vols. CSCO 50 & 51, Scriptores Arabici 6 & 7. Louvain: Peeters, 1954. Latin translation in Eutychius of Alexandria, *Summa Gemmarum, sive Eutychii Patriarchae Alexandrini Annales*. Selden, John, ed. Pocock, Edward, trans. Oxford: Excudebat H. Hall, 1654–56; reprint PG 111:889–1156. Paris: Migne, 1863.

Euzennat, Maurice. *Le limes de Tingitane*. Paris: CNRS, 1989.

Euzennat, Maurice, and Jean Marion. *Inscriptions antiques de Maroc, II, Inscriptions latines*. Paris: CNRS, 1982.

Evelyn-White, Hugh G. *The Monasteries of the Wadi 'n Natrun, 2, The History of the Monasteries of Nitria and Scetis*. Hauser, Walter, ed. New York: Metropolitan Museum of Art, 1932, reprint [New York]: Arno Press, 1973.

Evodius of Uzalis. *De miraculis S. Stephani Protomartyris*. Migne, J.-P., ed. PG 41: 833–54. Paris: Migne, 1845.

Falla Castelfranchi, Marina. "Le sepolture di vescovi e monaci in Mesopotamia (IV–VIII Secolo)." In *Actes du XIe Congrès international*, 2:1267–79.

Fasola, U. M. "La Basilica sotterranea di S. Tecla sulla Via Laurentiana." In *Akten des VII Internationalen Kongresses*, 1:509–510.

Fasola, U. M., and P. Testini. "I cimiteri Cristiani." In *Atti del IX Congresso internazionale*, 1:103–39.

Fedalto, Giorgio, ed. *Hierarchia ecclesiastica orientalis*. 2 vols. Padua: Edizioni Messagero, 1988.

Feissel, Denis. *Recueil des inscriptions chrétiennes de Macédonie du IIIe au VIe siècle*. BCH, Supplément 8. Paris École Française d'Athènes, 1983.

Ferri, Silvio. "Il *bios* e il *martyrion* di Hypatios di Gangrai." In *Studi bizantini et neoellenici* 3 (1931): 69–103.

Ferrua, Antonio. "Gli angeli di Tera." [*Miscellanea Guillaume de Jerphanion*.] *OCP* 13 (1947): 149–67.

Février, Paul Albert. "L'archéologie chrétienne en France de 1954 à 1962." In *Atti del VI Congresso internazionale*, 57–93.

——. "Aux origines du christianisme en Maurétanie Césarienne." In *MEFRA* 98(1986): 767–809.

Fiey, J[ean]-M[aurice]. *Assyrie Chrétienne*. 3 vols. Beirut: Imprimerie Catholique & Dar el-Machreq, 1965–68.

———. "Diptyques Nestoriens du XIVe Siècle." *AB* 81 (1963): 371–413.

———. "L'Élam, la première des métropoles ecclésiastiques syriennes orientales." IIIa in Fiey, Jean Maurice. *Communautés syriaques en Iran et Irak des origines à 1552*. London: Variorum, 1979.

———. *Jalons pour une histoire de l'église en Iraq*. CSCO 310, Subsidia 36. Louvain: Secrétariat du Corpus SCO, 1970.

———. *Nisibe, métropole syriaque orientale et ses suffragants des origines à nos jours*. CSCO 388, Subsidia 54. Louvain: Secrétariat du Corpus SCO, 1977.

———. *Pour un Oriens Christianus Novus, Répertoire des diocèses Syriaques Orientaux et Occidentaux*. Beiruter Texte und Studien 49. Beirut: in Kommission bei Franz Steiner Verlag Stuttgart, 1993.

———. "Vers la réhabilitation de l'Histoire de Karka de Beth Seloq." *AB* 82 (1964): 189–222.

Finegan, Jack. *New Testament Archaeology*. Revised Edition. Princeton: Princeton University Press, 1992.

Finney, Paul Corby. *The Invisible God, the Earliest Christians on Art*. New York: Oxford University Press, 1994.

Fiocchi Nicolai, Vincenzo. *I cimiteri paleocristiani del Lazio, I, Etruria meridionale*. Monumenti di Antichità Cristiana, II Serie, X. Vatican City: Pontificio Istituto di Archeologia Cristiana, 1988.

———. "Notiziario delle scoperte avvenute in Italia nel campo dell' Archeologia Cristiana negli anni 1981–86." In *Actes du XIe Congrès international*, 3:2221–44.

Flodoardus Remensis. *Historia Remensis ecclesiae*. Stratmann, Martina, ed. MGH, Scriptores 36. Hannover: Hahn, 1998.

Floriani Squarciapino, Maria. *Leptis Magna*. Basel: Raggi Verlag, 1966.

Foss, Clive. "St. Autonomus and his Church in Bithynia." *Dumbarton Oaks Papers* 41 (1987): 187–98.

Fox, Robin Lane. *Pagans and Christians*. San Francisco: Harper & Row, 1986; reprint Harmondsworth: Penguin, 1988.

Franchi de' Cavalieri, Pio. *I Martirii di S. Theodoto e di S. Ariadne*. Studi e Testi 6. Rome: Tipografica Vaticana, 1901.

———. *Note agiografiche*. 9 vols. Studi e Testi (Biblioteca Apostolica Vaticana) 8, 9, 22, 24, 27, 33, 49, 65, 175. Rome: Tipografica Vaticana, 1902–53.

Frankfurter, David. *Religion in Roman Egypt, Assimilation and Resistance*. Princeton: Princeton University Press, 1998.

Frend, William H. C. *The Archaeology of the Early Church, a History*. Minneapolis: Fortress, 1996.

———. *The Donatist Church*. Oxford: Clarendon, 1952.

Freyne, Sean. "Christianity in Sepphoris and Galilee." In Nagy, Rebecca Martin, ed. *Sepphoris in Galilee, Crosscurrents of Culture*, 67–73. Raleigh and Winona Lake: North Carolina Museum of Art and Eisenbrauns, 1996.

Fritz, Jeno. "The Way of Life." In Lengyel and Radan, 161–75.

Fuller, Michael, and Neathery Fuller. "Archaeological Discoveries at Tell Tuneinir, Syria." In *Journal of Assyrian Academic Studies* 12.2 (1998): 69–82.

Gabrieli, F. "Adi b. Zayd." In *Encyclopaedia of Islam*, 1:196. 2nd Edition. Leiden: Brill, 1960.

Galand, Lionel, James Fevrier, and Georges Vadja. *Inscriptions antiques du Maroc, I, Inscriptions libyques, Inscriptions puniques et néopuniques, Inscriptions hébraïques*. Paris: CNRS, 1966.

Gallazzi, Claudio. "Frammenti di un codice con le Epistole di Paolo." In *ZPE* 46 (1982): 117–22.

Gamber, Klaus. *Sarmannina*. Studia Patristica et Liturgica 11. Regensburg: Kommissionsverlag Friedrich Pustet, 1982.

Garsoian, Nina G. "The Iranian Substratum of the 'Agat'angelos' Cycle." In *East of Byzantium: Syria and Armenia in the Formative Period*, 151–74. Garsoian, Nina G., Thomas F. Matthews, and Robert W. Thomson, eds. Dumbarton Oaks Symposium, 1980. Washington: Dumbarton Oaks, 1982.

Gaudemet, Jean, ed., *Conciles Gaulois du IVe siècle*. SC 241. Paris: Cerf, 1977.

Gaudentius of Brescia. *Ad benivolum praefatio*. Glueck, Ambrosius, ed. In *S. Gaudentii episcopi Brixiensis tractatus*, 3:15. CSEL 68. Vienna & Leipzig: Holder-Pilcher-Tempsky & Akademische Verlagsgesellschaft, 1936.

———. *Tractatus XXI*. Glueck, Ambrosius, ed. In *S. Gaudentii episcopi Brixiensis tractatus*, 16–189. CSEL 68. Vienna & Leipzig: Holder-Pilcher-Tempsky & Akademische Verlags-gesellschaft, 1936.

Gaudentius of Brescia? *Ad laudem beati Filastrii episcopi*. Migne, J.-P., ed. PL 20: 1003–1006. Paris: Migne, 1845.

Gauthier, Nancy. *L'évangélisation des pays de la Moselle*. Paris: Boccard, 1980.

Gauthier, Nancy, and J.-Ch. Picard. *Topographie chrétienne des cités de la Gaul des origines au milieu du VIIIe siècle*. Paris: Boccard, 1986–.

GCS. Die Griechischen Christlichen Schriftsteller.

Gelasius of Cyzicus. *Ecclesiastical History. Kirchengeschichte*. Loeschke, Gerhard, and Margaret Heinemann, eds. GCS 28. Leipzig: Hinrichs, 1918.

Gelzer, Henricus. *Patrum Nicaenorum nomina Latine, Graece, Coptice, Syriace, Arabice, Armeniace*. Leipzig: Teubner, 1898; reprinted with afterword by Christoph Markschies, Stuttgart and Leipzig: Teubner, 1995.

Gerke, Friedrich. *Die christlichen Sarkophage der vorkonstantinischen Zeit*. Berlin: Walter de Gruyter, 1940; reprint 1978.

Gesta apud Zenophilum. Ziwsa, Carolus, ed. In *S. Optati Milevitani Libri VII*, 185–97. CSEL 26. Prague, Vienna, and Leipzig: F. Tempsky and G. Freytag, 1893. More recently in Maier, *Le Dossier du Donatisme, Tome 1*, 214–39. Translated in Optatus, *Against the Donatists*, 150–69. Edwards, Mark, ed. and trans. Liverpool: Liverpool University Press, 1997.

Gesta conlationis Carthaginiensis, Capitula Gestorum. Lancel, S., ed. In *Gesta conlationis Carthaginiensis, anno 411*, 6–52. CCSL 149a. Turnhout: Brepols, 1974.

Gesta episcoporum Neapolitanorum. Waitz, G., ed. *MGH*, SRLI, 402–36. Hannover: Hahn, 1878.

Giamil, Samuelis. *Genuinae Relationes inter Sedem Apostolicam et Assyriorum Orientalium seu Chaldaeorum Ecclesiam*. Rome: Ermanno Loescher, 1902.

Gibson, Elsa. *The "Christians for Christians" Inscriptions of Phrygia*. HTS 32. Missoula: Scholars Press, 1978.

Gildas. *The Ruin of Britain and Other Works*. Winterbottom, Michael, ed. London & Totowa, NJ: Phillimore & Rowman and Littlefield, 1978.

Girshman, R. *Iran*. Harmondsworth: Penguin, 1954.

Glushak, A. S., *et al.* eds. *Krym Khristianskiia*. Sevastopol, 1996.

Goldstein, Morris. *Jesus in the Jewish Tradition*. New York: Macmillan Company, 1950.

Gomez, Jaime Delgado. "Tapa de Sarcofago Paleocristiano en Santa Maria de Temes-Carballedo Lugo (Espana)." In *Rivista di Archeologia Cristiana* 52 (1976): 303–24.

Goodchild, Richard George. *Kyrene und Apollonia*. Zurich: Raggi Verlag, 1971.

Goodman, Martin. *Mission and Conversion, Proselytizing in the Religious History of the Roman Empire*. Oxford: Clarendon Press, 1994.

Goranson, Stephen. "Joseph of Tiberias Revisited, Orthodoxies and Heresies in Fourth-Century Galilee." In Meyers, Eric, M., ed. *Galilee Through the Centuries, Confluence of Cultures*, 335–43. Winona Lake: Eisenbrauns, 1999.

Gounaris, Georgios. "L'archéologie chrétienne en Grèce de 1974 à 1985." In *Actes du XIe Congrès international*, 3:2687–2711.

Gounaris, Georgios, and Georgios Velenis. "Casa paleocristiana di Philippi." In *Actas XIII Congressus*, 3:355–66.

Gounaropoulou, Lukretias, and M. V. Chatzopoulou. *Epigraphes kato Makedonias*, 1, *Epigraphes Veroias*. Athens & Paris: Diffusion de Boccard, 1998.

Graf, Georg. *Geschichte der christlichen arabischen Literatur*. Studi e Testi 118. Vol. 1. Vatican City: Biblioteca Apostolica Vaticana, 1944.

Graillot, Henri. "Objets d'archéologie chrétienne trouvés à Autun." In *Mémoires de la société éduenne*, new series, 27 (1899): 47–56.

Green, Christopher Sparey. "The Early Christian Cemetery at Poundbury." In *Actes du XIᵉ Congrès international*, 3:2073–75.

Grégoire, Henri. "Notes Épigraphiques." In *Byzantion* 8 (1933): 49–91.

——. *Recueil des inscriptions grecques-chrétiennes d'Asie Mineure, fasc. 1*. Paris: Leroux, 1922; reprint, Amsterdam: Adolf M. Hakkert, 1968.

——. "Saints jumeaux et dieux cavaliers." In *Revue de l'Orient chrétien* 9 (1904): 453–90.

——. *Saints jumeaux et dieux cavaliers*. Paris: Libraire A. Picard et Fils, 1905.

Gregori, Gian Luca. *Brescia romana, ricerche di prosopografia e storia sociale*. 1.1. *I documenti*. Rome: Casa Editrice Quasar, 1990.

Gregory of Nazianzus. *Carmina Historica*. Migne, J.-P., ed. PG 37:969–1600. Paris: Migne, 1862.

——. *De vita Gregorii Thaumaturgi*. Heil, Gunterus, ed. In Gregory of Nyssa. *Sermones*, Pars II. Heil, Gunterus, *et al.*, eds. *Gregorii Nysseni Opera*. Vol. 10.1:1–57. Jaeger, Werner, *et al.*, eds. Leiden: Brill, 1990. Slusser, Michael, trans. *St. Gegory Thaumaturgus, Life and Works*, 41–87. Fathers of the Church, 98. Washington: CUA Press, 1998.

——. *Epistulae*. Gallay, Paul, ed. *Saint Grégoire de Nazianze, Lettres*. 2 vols. Paris: Les Belles lettres, 1964–67.

——. *Orationes*. Clémencet, C. and A. B. Caillau, eds. Paris, 1774–1840. Reedited by Migne, J.-P. PG 35:396–1252 & 36:12–664. Paris: Garnier Fratres, 1886.

Gregory of Nyssa. *Contra Eunomium*. Jaeger, Werner, ed. In *Gregorii Nysseni Opera*. Vols. 1–2. Jaeger, Werner, ed. Berlin: Weidmann, 1921.

——. *Encomium in XL martyres [Ia, Ib, & II]*. Lendle, Otto, ed. In Gregory of Nyssa. *Sermones*, Pars II. Heil, Gunterus, *et al.*, eds. *Gregorii Nysseni Opera*. Vol. 10.1:135–69. Jaeger, Werner, *et al.*, eds. Leiden: Brill, 1990.

——. *Epistulae*. Pasquali, Georgius, ed. In *Gregorii Nysseni Opera*. Vol. 8.2. Jaeger, Werner, ed. Editio altera. Leiden: Brill, 1959.

Gregory of Tours. *Gloria Confessorum*. Krusch, Bruno, ed. *MGH*, SRM, 1.2: 294–370. New Edition. Hannover: Hahn, 1969.

——. *Gloria Martyrum*. Krusch, Bruno, ed. *MGH*, SRM, 1.2:34–111. New Edition. Hannover: Hahn, 1969.

——. *Historia Francorum*. Arndt, W., and Bruno Krusch, eds. *MGH*, SRM, 1.1. New Edition. Hannover: Hahn, 1961.

pseudo-Gregory of Tours. *Passio Sancti Juliani martyris*. Arndt, W., and Bruno Krusch, eds. *Gregorii Turonensis Opera*. *MGH*, SRM, 1.2:879–81. Hannover: Hahn, 1885.

Gregory the Great (Pope Gregory I). *Dialogues*. De Vogüé, Adalbert, ed. SC 251, 260, 265. Paris: Cerf, 1978–80.

Griffe, Élie. *La Gaule chrétienne à l'époque romain*. New Edition. 3 vols. Paris: Letouzy et Ané, 1964–66.

Griggs, C. Wilfred. *Early Egyptian Christianity, from its Origins to 451 C.E.* 2nd Edition. Leiden: Brill, 1991.

Griggs, C. Wilfred, *et al.* "Identities Revealed, Archaeological and Biological Evidences for a Christian Population in the Egyptian Fayum." In Hilliard, T. W., *et al.*, eds. *Ancient History in a Modern University*, 1:82–87. Grand Rapids: Eerdmans, 1988.

Grumel, V. *La Chronologie*. Traité d'études Byzantines, 1. Paris: Presses Universitaires de France, 1958.

Guarducci, Margherita. *Epigrafia Greca*. Vol. 4. Rome: Istituto Poligrafico dello Stato, 1978.

——. *Inscriptiones Creticae*. Vol. 1. Rome: La Libreria dello Stato, 1935.

Gui, Isabelle, Noël Duval, and Jean-Pierre Caillet. *Basiliques chrétiennes d'Afrique du Nord, I, Inventaire de l'Algérie*. 2 vols. Collection des Études Augustiniennes, Série Antiquité 129–30. Paris: Institut d'Études Augustiniennes, 1992.

Guralnick, Eleanor, ed. *Sardis, Twenty-Seven Years of Discovery*. Chicago: Chicago Society of the Archaeological Institute of America, 1987.

Haelst, Joseph van. *Catalogue des Papyrus littéraires juifs et chrétiens*. Paris: Publications de la Sorbonne, 1976.

Hagel, Stefan, and Kurt Tomaschitz. *Repertorium der Westkilikischen Inschriften*. Österreichische Akademie der Wissenschaften, Philosophisch-Historische Klasse, Denkschriften 265. Vienna: Österreichische Akademie der Wissenschaften, 1998.

Halkin, François. "Le passion inédite des saints Eustathe, Thespésius, et Anatole." In *AB* 93 (1975): 277–311.

Harnack, Adolf (von). *Analecta zur ältesten Geschichte des Christentums in Rom*. TU 28.2. Leipzig: Hinrichs, 1905.

——. *Die Chronologie*. In Harnack, Adolf (von). *Geschichte der Altchristlichen Literatur bis Eusebius*. Teil 2, bd. 1–2. 2nd Edition. Leipzig: Hinrichs, 1958.

——. *Marcion, Das Evangelium vom Fremden Gott*. 2nd Edition. TU 45. Leipzig: Hinrichs, 1924.

——. *The Mission and Expansion of Christianity in the First Three Centuries of the Christian Era*. Moffatt, James, trans. 2 vols. London and New York: Williams and Norgate and G. P. Putnam's Sons, 1908.

——. *Die Mission und Ausbreitung des Christentums in den ersten drei Jahrhunderten*. 4th Edition. 2 vols. Leipzig: Hinrichs, 1924; reprint Leipzig: Zentral-Antiquariat der Deutschen Demokratischen Republik, 1965; reprint Wiesbaden: VMA-Verlag, n.d.

Hasluck, F. W. *Cyzicus*. Cambridge Archaeological and Ethnological Series. Cambridge: Cambridge University Press, 1910.

Haspels, C. H. Emilie. *The Highlands of Phrygia, Sites and Monuments*. 2 vols. Princeton: Princeton University Press, 1971.

Hassall, W. C., and R. S. O. Tomlin. "Roman Britain in 1981, II, Inscriptions." In *Britannia* 13 (1982): 396–422.

——. "Roman Britain in 1992, II Inscriptions." In *Britannia* 24 (1993): 310–22.

Hatch, William H. P. "A Recently Discovered Fragment of the Epistle to the Romans." In *Harvard Theological Review* 45 (1952): 81–85.

Hauschild, Theodor. "Untersuchungen in der Märtyrkirche von Marialba (Prov. Leon) und im Mausoleum von Las Vegas de Pueblanueva (Prov. Toledo)." In *Actas del VIII Congreso Internacional*, 327–32.

Hefele, Charles Joseph. *A History of the Councils of the Church from the Original Documents*. Vol. 3. Edinburgh: T & T Clark, 1883.

Hegemonius. *Acta Archelai*. Beeson, Charles Henry, ed. GCS 16. Leipzig: Hinrichs, 1906.

Heinemeyer, Karl. *Das Erzbistum Mainz in römischer und fränkischer Zeit. I. Die Anfänge der Diözese Mainz*. Veröffentlichungen der Historischen Kommission fur Hessen, 39. Marburg: N. G. Elwert Verlag, 1979.

Herrmann, Peter, ed. *Inschriften von Milet. Milet*, 6. 2 vols. Berlin: Walter de Gruyter, 1997–98.

Higgins, Martin J., "Chronology of the Fourth-Century Metropolitans of Seleucia-Ctesiphon." In *Traditio* 9 (1953): 45–99.

Hilary. *Decretum synodi Orientalium apud Serdicam episcoporum*. Feder, Alfredus, ed. In *S. Hilarii episcopi Pictaviensis opera, Pars quarta*, 48–78. CSEL 65. Vienna and Leipzig: F. Tempsky and G. Freytag, 1916.

——. *Epistula synodi Sardicensis ad Iuliam papam*. Feder, Alfredus, ed. In *S. Hilarii episcopi Pictaviensis opera, Pars quarta*, 126–140. CSEL 65. Vienna & Leipzig: F. Tempsky & G. Freytag, 1916.

——. *Liber I ad Constantium (Oratio Synodi Sardicensis ad Constantium Imperatorem)*. Feder, Alfredus, ed. In *S. Hilarii episcopi Pictaviensis opera, Pars quarta*, 181–87. CSEL 65. Vienna & Leipzig: Tempsky & Freytag, 1916.

——. *De synodis*. Migne, J.-P., ed. PL 10:479–546. Paris: Excudebat Vrayet, 1844.

Hippolytus. *Commentary on Daniel. Kommentar zu Daniel*. Bonwetsch, Georg Nathaniel, and Marcel Richard, eds. 2nd Edition. GCS, n.f., 7. Berlin: Akademie Verlag, 2000.

——. *Refutatio omnium haeresium*. Marcovich, Miroslav, ed. PTS 25. Berlin: de Gruyter, 1986.

Historia Acephala. See Turner, 1:663–71.

Historia monachorum in Aegypto. Festugière, André-Jean, ed. *Historia monachorum in Aegypto: Édition critique du texte grec et traduction annotée*. Subsidia hagiographica 53. Brussels: Société des Bollandistes, 1971.

Hoddinott, R. F. *Early Byzantine Churches in Macedonia and Southern Serbia*. London: Macmillan & Co., 1963.

Hoffmann, Georg. *Auszüge aus Syrischen Akten Persischer Märtyrer*. Abhandlungen fur die Kunde des Morgenlandes, 7.3. Leipzig: Deutsche Morgenlandische Gesellschaft, 1880; reprint Nedeln: Kraus Reprint, 1966.

Hoglund, Kenneth G., and Eric M. Meyers. "The Residential Quarter on the Western Summit." In Nagy, Rebecca Martin, ed. *Sepphoris in Galilee, Crosscurrents of Culture*, 39–43. Raleigh and Winona Lake: North Carolina Museum of Art and Eisenbrauns, 1996.

Honigmann, Ernest. "L'Évêché de Carphia ou Pentapolis en Grèce." In *AB* 67 (1949): 287–99.

——. "La Liste Originale des Pères de Nicée." In *Byzantion* 14 (1939): 17–76.

——. "The Original Lists of the Members of the Council of Nicaea, the Robber-Synod, and the Council of Chalcedon." In *Byzantion* 16 (1942–43): 20–80.

Hope, Colin A. "Dakhla Oasis, Ismant el Kharab." In Bard, Kathryn A., ed. *Encyclopedia of the Archaeology of Ancient Egypt*, 222–26. London and New York: Routledge, 1999.

Horn, Jürgen. *Studien zu den Märtyrern des nördlichen Oberägypten*. 2 vols. Göttinger Orientforschungen, IV Reihe: Ägypten, bd. 15. Wiesbaden: Otto Harrassowitz, 1986.

Horovitz, Josef. "Adi b. Zeyd, the Poet of Hira." In *Islamic Culture* 4 (1930), 31–69.

Horsley, G. R. H. "The Inscriptions of Ephesos and the New Testament." In *Novum Testamentum* 34 (1992): 105–168.

Howard, George, ed. *The Teaching of Addai*. SBL Texts and Translations 16, Early Christian Literature Series 4. Atlanta: Scholars Press, 1981.

HTS. Harvard Theological Studies.

Humbach, Helmut, and Prods O. Skjaervo, eds. *The Sassanian Inscription of Paikuli*, 3.1, *Restored Text and Translation*. Wiesbaden: Dr. Ludwig Reichert Verlag, 1983.

'Ibn Ishaq. *Kitāb sīrat Rasūl 'Allāh*. Wüstenfeld, Heinrich Ferdinand, ed. 2 volumes in 3 parts. Göttingen: Dieterichsche Universitats-Buchhandlung, 1858–60; reprint Leipzig: Dieterich'sche Verlagsbuchhandlung, 1900. Guillaume, A., trans. *The Life of Muhammad*. Oxford: Oxford University Press, 1955.

ICE. *Inscriptions of the Christian Empire*. Mansfield, John M., ed. CD-ROM, #7. Los Altos, CA: Packard Humanities Institute, 1996.

ICG. *Inscriptions chrétiennes de la Gaule antérieures au VIII siècle*. Le Blant, Edmond Frédéric, ed. 2 vols. Paris: Imprimerie impériale, 1852–65.

IG. *Inscriptiones Graecae*. Multiple vols. Berlin: apud Georgium Reimerum, 1873–.

IGLS. *Recueil des inscriptions grecques et latines de la Syrie*. Jalabert, Louis *et al.*, eds. Multiple vols. BAH 12, 32, 46, 51, 61, 66, 78, 89, 104, 113, 114, 115, etc. Paris: Librairie Orientaliste Paul Geuthner, 1929–.

Ignatius of Antioch. See *Apostolic Fathers*.

IGRR. *Inscriptiones Graecae ad res Romanas pertinentes*. Lafaye, G., ed. Vol. 4. Paris: Leroux, 1927; reprint Rome: "L'Erma di Bretschneider", 1964.

ILCV. Inscriptiones Latinae christianae veteres. Diehl, Ernst, ed. 3 vols. Berlin: Weidmann, 1925–31.

ILS. Inscriptiones Latinae selectae. Dessau, Hermann, ed. 3 vols. in 5 parts. Berlin: Weidmann, 1892–1916.

Irenaeus. *Adversus haereses.* Harvey, W. Wigan, ed. *Sancti Irenaei episcopi Lugdunensis, libros quinque adversus haereses.* 2 vols. Cambridge: Cambridge University Press, 1857. See also Rousseau, Adelin, and Louis Doutreleau, eds. *Irenée de Lyon, Contre les hérésies.* SC 100.1–2, 152–53, 210–11, 263–64, 293–94. Paris: Cerf, 1965–82. I have given references according to the divisions of Harvey's text.

Isidore of Charax. *Parthian Stations.* Schoff, Wilfred H., ed. and trans. Philadelphia: Commercial Museum, 1914; reprint Chicago: Ares, 1989.

Itinerarium Burdigalense. Geyer, P., and O. Cuntz, eds. In *Itineraria et alia geographica,* 1–26. CCSL, 175. Turnhout: Brepols, 1965.

Jelić, L[ucas]. "I monumenti scritti e figurati dei martiri Salonitani del cimiterio della Lex sancta christiana." In *Acta Primi Congressus Internationalis Archaeologiae Christianae,* 33–44 & t. IV–V.

Jerome. *Chronicle.* Helm, Rudolf & Ursula Treu, eds. *Die Chronik des Hieronymus.* In *Eusebius Werke,* 7. GCS. 2nd Ed. Berlin: Akademie-Verlag, 1984.

——. *Commentarii in Epistolam ad Galatas.* Migne, J.-P., ed. PL 26:331–468. Paris: Garnier Fratres, 1884.

——. *Commentarii in Esaiam.* Adriaen, Marci, ed. 2 vols. CCSL 73–73a. Turnhout: Brepols, 1963.

——. *Epistulae.* Hilberg, Isidorus Hilberg, ed. Index, Margit Kemptner. Editio altera. 3 vols. CSEL 54–56. Vienna: Österreichische Akademie der Wissenschaften, 1996.

——. *In Hieremiam prophetam.* Reiter, Sigefredus, ed. CCSL 74. Turnhout: Brepols, 1960.

——. *Onomasticon.* Klostermann, Erich, ed. *Das Onomastikon der Biblischen Ortsnamen.* In *Eusebius Werke,* 3.1. GCS 11.1. Leipzig: Hinrichs, 1904, reprint Hildesheim: Olms, 1966.

——. *De viris inlustribus.* Richardson, Ernest Cushing, ed. TU 14.1. Leipzig: Hinrichs, 1896.

——. *Vita Malchi.* Migne, J.-P., ed. PL 23: 55–62. Paris: Migne, 1883.

——. *Vita S. Hilarionis.* Migne, J.-P., ed. PL 23:29–54. Paris: Migne, 1883. See also *AASS,* Octobris IX, 43–69.

——. *Vita S. Pauli.* Migne, J.-P., ed. PL 23:17–28. Paris: Migne, 1883.

JHS. Journal of Hellenic Studies.

Jidejian, Nina. *Byblos through the Ages.* Beirut: Dar el-Machreq, 1968.

——. *Sidon through the Ages.* Beirut: Dar el-Machreq, 1971.

——. *Tyre through the Ages.* Beirut: Dar el-Mashreq, 1969.

Joannou, Périclès-Pierre, ed. *Fonti. Fasciculo IX. Discipline générale antique. Tome I.* Rome: Typographica Italo-Orientale, 1962.

Johnson, Gary T. *Early Christian Epitaphs from Anatolia.* Atlanta: Scholars Press, 1995.

Jones, A. H. M. *Cities of the Eastern Roman Provinces.* 2nd Edition. Oxford: Clarendon, 1971.

——. *The Later Roman Empire, 284–602: A Social and Economic Survey.* 2 Vols. Baltimore: Johns Hopkins University Press, 1986.

Jones, Michael J. "Recent Discoveries in Britain and Ireland." In *Acta XIII Congressus Internationalis.* 3:395–411.

Josephus. *Antiquities.* Thackeray, H. St. J., Ralph Marcus, Allen Wikgren, and Louis H. Feldman., eds. In *Josephus,* 4–9. LCL. Cambridge: Harvard University Press, 1926–1965.

——. *Vita.* Thackeray, H. St. J., ed. In *Josephus,* 1:1–159. LCL. London: Heinemann, 1926.

JTS. Journal of Theological Studies.

Judge, E. A. "The Earliest Use of Monachos for >Monk< (P. Coll. Youtie 77) and the Origins of Monasticism." In *Jahrbuch für Antike und Christentum* 20 (1977): 72–89.

Judge, E. A., and S. R. Pickering, "Papyrus Documentation of Church and Community in Egypt to the Mid-Fourth Century." In *Jahrbuch für Antike und Christentum* 20 (1977): 47–71. Reprint in Ferguson, Everett, ed. *Studies in Early Christianity*, 12, *Missions and Regional Characteristics of the Early Church*, 37–61. New York and London: Garland, 1993.

Julian. *Epistulae*. Wright, Wilmer Cave, ed. In *The Works of the Emperor Julian*, 3:2–303. LCL. Cambridge: Harvard University Press; reprint 1961.

Julius Africanus. *Kestoi*. Vieillefond, Jean-René, ed. *Les "Cestes" de Julius Africanus*. Florence and Paris: Edizioni Sansoni Antiquariato & Libraire Marcel Didier, 1970.

Juster, Jean. *Les Juifs dans l'empire romain*. Paris: Paul Geunthner, 1914.

Justin Martyr. *Apology I*. Marcovich, Miroslav, ed. In *Apologia pro Christianis*, 31–133. PTS 38. Berlin Walter de Gruyter, 1994.

———. *Dialogue with Trypho*. Marcovich, Miroslav, ed. *Dialogus cum Tryphone*. PTS 47. Berlin: Walter de Gruyter, 1997.

pseudo-Justin. *Oration to the Greeks*. Syriac recension ed., Cureton, William. In *Spicilegium Syriacum*; Syriac text, 38–42; English trans., 61–69 & 99–100. London: Rivingtons, 1855; reprint Lexington, KY: American Theological Library Association, 1965. Greek recension ed., Marcovich, Miroslav. In *Cohortatio ad Graecos/De Monarchia/Oratio ad Graecos*, 109–119. PTS 32. Berlin: Walter de Gruyter, 1990.

Kalantar, Ashkharbek. *Armenia from the Stone Age to the Middle Ages*. Karakhanian, G., ed. Gurzadyan, V. G., trans. Civilisations du Proche-Orient, Série I, Archéologie et Environnement 2. Neuchâtel-Paris: Recherches et Publications, 1994.

Kalendarium Carthaginense. In *AASS*, Novembris, 2.1, lxx–lxxi.

Kaplan, Steven. "Ezana's Conversion Reconsidered." In *Journal of Religion in Africa* 13.2 (1982): 101–109.

Kartir Inscription. Parallel versions along with a German translation may be found in Back, 384–489. English translation in Sprengling, 49–53.

Keay, S. J. *Roman Spain*. Berkeley: University of California Press, 1988.

Khatchatrian, A. *L'architecture arménienne du IVe au VIe siècle*. Bibliothèque des Cahiers Archéologiques 7. Paris: Klincksieck, 1971.

Khrshanovskii, V. A. "Raskopkia Nekropolia Keteia/Excavations of Kitei Necropolis." In *Arkheologicheskie Issledovaniia v Krymu/Archaeological Researches in the Crimea, 1993*, 262–66. Simferopol: "Tavriia," 1994.

King, Anthony. *Roman Gaul and Germany*. Berkeley: University of California Press, 1990.

Kirsch, G. P. "I primordi: gli edifici sacri cristiani nei primi tre secoli della Chiesa." In *Atti del IV Congresso Internazionale*, 1:113–26.

Kitzinger, Ernst. "The Cleveland Marbles." In *Atti del IX Congresso internazionale*, 653–75. Reprint in Finney, Paul Corbey, ed. *Studies in Early Christianity*, 18, *Art, Archaeology, and Architecture of Early Christianity*, 117–39. New York: Garland, 1993.

Kitzinger, Ernst. "A Survey of the Early Christian Town of Stobi." In *Dumbarton Oaks Papers* 3 (1946): 81–162.

Klauser, Theodor. "Studien zur Entstehungsgeschichte der Christlichen Kunst VIII." In *Jahrbuch für Antike und Christentum* 8/9 (1965/66): 126–70.

Klijn, A. F. J. *Acts of Thomas*. NovTSupp. 5. Leiden: Brill, 1962.

———. "Jewish Christianity in Egypt." In Pearson and Goehring, 161–75.

Klijn, A. F. J., and G. J. Reinink. *Patristic Evidence for Early Christian Sects*. Novum Testamentum Supp. 36. Leiden: Brill, 1973.

Klostermann, Erich. *Apocrypha, II, Evangelien*. Kleine Texte für Vorlesungen und Übungen 8. 3rd Ed. Berlin: Walter de Gruyter, 1929.

Knopf, Rudolf, and Gustav Krueger. *Ausgewählte Märtyrerakten*. 3rd edition. Tübingen: Mohr, 1929.

Kobishchanov, Yuri M. *Axum*. Kapitanoff, Lorraine T., ed. University Park: Pennsylvania State University Press, 1979.

Koch, Guntram. *Frühchristliche Sarkophage*. Munich: C. H. Beck, 2000.

Koester, Helmut. "Ephesus in Early Christian Literature." In Koester, Helmut, ed. *Ephesos, Metropolis of Asia*, 119–40. HTS, 41. Valley Forge: Trinity Press International, 1995.

Kollwitz, Johannes. "Ravenna zwischen Orient und Occident." In *Atti del VI Congresso Internazionale*, 383–402.

Koriwn. *Varkʿ Mashtotsʿi*. Abelyan, M., ed. Erevan: Haypethrat, 1941. Norehad, Bedros, trans. *Koriun, the Life of Mashtots*. New York: Armenian General Benevolent Union, 1964. Both reprinted with introduction by Maksoudian, Krikor H. *Varkʿ Mastotsʿi*. Classical Armenian Texts Reprint Series. Delmar, NY: Caravan Books, 1985.

Kraeling, Carl H. *The Excavations at Dura-Europos, Final Report VIII, Part II, The Christian Building*. Welles, C. Bradford, ed. New Haven, CT and Locust Valley, NY: Dura-Europos Publications and J. J. Augustin, 1967.

Kreider, Alan. "Changing Patterns of Conversion in the West." In Kreider, Alan, ed. *Origins of Christendom in the West*, 3–46. Edinburgh and New York: T & T Clark, 2001.

Kroushkova, Lioudmila-Georgievna. "Pitiunt et le littoral oriental de la Mer Noire à l'époque paléochrétienne." In *Actes du XIᵉ Congrès international*, 3: 2657–86.

Kümmel, Werner Georg. *Introduction to the New Testament*. Kee, Howard Clark, trans. Nashville: Abingdon Press, 1975.

Labourt, J. *Le Christianisme dans l'empire perse*. Paris: Libraire Victor Lecoffre, 1904.

Labriolle, Pierre de. *La réaction païenne: étude sur la polémique antichrétienne du Iᵉʳ au VIᵉ siècle*. Paris: L'Artisan du Livre, 1934.

Lactantius. *De mortibus persecutorum*. Creed, J. L., ed. Oxford Early Christian Texts. (Oxford: Clarendon, 1984).

Lactantius. *Divinae Institutiones*. Brandt, Samuel, and Georg Laubmann, eds. In *L. Caeli Firminiani Lactanti Opera omnia*, 1:1–672. CSEL 19. Prague, Vienna, & Leipzig: F. Tempsky & G. Freytag, 1890.

LaGrange, F. *Les Actes des martyrs d'Orient*. Nouvelle Édition. Tours: Alfred Mame et Fils, Éditeurs, 1871.

Łajtar, Adam. *Die Inschriften von Byzantion*. Inschriften griechischer Städte aus Kleinasien 58. Österreichische Akademie der Wissenschaften/Nordrhein-Westfälische Akademie der Wissenschaften. Bonn: Dr. Rudolf Habelt Gmbh., 2000.

Laminger-Pascher, Gertrud. *Beiträge zu den griechischen Inschriften Lycaoniens*. Österreichische Akademie der Wissenschaften, Philosophisch-Historische Klasse, Denkschriften 173. Vienna: Österreichische Akademie der Wissenschaften, 1984.

———. *Die Kaiserzeitlichen Inschriften Lykaoniens, Faszikel 1: der Süden*. Österreichische Akademie der Wissenschaften, Philosophisch-Historische Klasse, Denkschriften 232. Ergänzungsbände zu der Tituli Asiae Minoris 15. Vienna: Österreichische Akademie der Wissenschaften, 1992.

Lampe, Peter. *Die stadtrömischen Christen in den ersten beiden Jahrhunderten: Untersuchungen zur Sozialgeschichte*. Wissenschaftliche Untersuchungen zum Neuen Testament, 2 Reihe, 18. 2nd Edition. Tübingen: J. B. Mohr (Paul Siebeck), 1989. Revised English translation forthcoming from Fortress Press.

Lam[p]ros, Spyridon P. *Catalogue of the Greek Manuscripts on Mount Athos*. 2 vols. Cambridge: Cambridge University Press, 1895–1900.

———. *Kerkyraika Anekdota*. Athens: ek tou Typographeiou Parnassou, 1882. For emendations see Doubouniotos, 231–35.

Land, J. P. N. *Anecdota Syriaca*. 4 vols. in 2. Leiden: Brill, 1862–75; reprint; Osnabruck: Biblio Verlag, 1989.

Lanzoni, Francesco. *Le diocesi d'Italia, dalle origini al principio del secolo VII (an. 604)*. 2 vols. Studi e Testi 35. Faenza: Stabilimento Grafico F. Lega, 1927.

Lassus, Jean. *Sanctuaires chrétiens de Syrie*. BAH 42. Paris: Paul Geunthner, 1947.

Latyshev, Vasilij Vasil'evich, ed. *Menologii Anonymi Byzantini Saeculi X quae Supersunt*.

2 vols. St. Petersburg, 1911–12; reprint in 1 vol., Leipzig: Zentralantiquariat der Deutschen Demokratischen Republik, 1970.

——. "Zhitiia Sv. Episkopov Khersonskikh," in *Zapiski Imperatorskoi akademii nauk, po Istoriko-filologicheskomu otdieleniiu (Mémoires de l'Académie impériale des sciences de St.-Pétersbourg, Classe historico-philologique).* 8th Series. 8.3 (1906): 1–81.

Laudes Veronensis Civitatis (Versus de Verona). Duemmler, Ernestus, ed. *MGH,* Poeti Latini 1:118–22. Berlin: Weidmann, 1880.

LCL. Loeb Classical Library.

Leake, William Martin. *Travels in Northern Greece.* 4 vols. London: J. Rodwell, 1835; reprint Amsterdam: Adolf M. Hakkert, 1967.

Le Bas, Philippe, and William Henry Waddington. *Inscriptions grecques et latines recueillies en Grèce et en Asie Mineure.* 2 vols. Paris: Didot Frères, Fils, et Cie., 1870; reprint Hildesheim: Olms, 1972.

Leclercq, H. "Alexandrie, archéologie." In *DACL,* 1:1098–1182.

Lefebvre, Gustave. *Inscriptiones Christianae Aegypti: recueil des inscriptions grecques-chrétiennes d'Égypt.* Inscriptiones Graecae Aegypti, 5. Cairo: Imprimerie de l'Institut Français d'archéologie orientale, 1907; reprint Chicago: Ares, 1978.

Lefort, L. Th., "Les premiers monastères Pachomiens." In *Muséon* 52 (1939): 379–407.

——. *Les vies coptes de Saint Pachôme et de ses premiers successeurs.* Bibliothèque du *Muséon* 16. Louvain: Bureaux du *Muséon,* 1943.

Lehmann, Clayton Miles, and Kenneth G. Holum. *The Greek and Latin Inscriptions of Caesarea Maritima.* The Joint Expedition to Caesarea Maritima Excavation Reports, 5. Boston: American Schools of Oriental Research, 2000.

Lengyel, A., and G. T. B. Radan, eds. *The Archaeology of Roman Pannonia.* Lexington and Budapest: University Press of Kentucky and Akadémiai Kaidó, 1980.

Leontius Scholasticus. *De sectis.* Migne, J.-P., ed. PG 86.1:1193–1268. Paris: Migne, 1865. [See *CPG,* 6823.]

Lepelley, Claude. *Les cités de l'Afrique romaine au Bas-Empire.* 2 vols. Paris: Études Augustiniennes, 1979–81.

Le Quien, Michaelis. *Oriens Christianus.* 3 vols. Paris: Typographia Regia, 1740; reprint Graz: Akademische Druck, 1958.

Levinskaya, Irina A. *The Book of Acts in its Diaspora Setting.* The Book of Acts in its First Century Setting 5. Grand Rapids: Eerdmans, 1996.

Leynaud, A. F. *Les catacombes africaines, Sousse-Hadrumtète.* 2nd Edition. Algiers: Jules Carbonel, 1922.

Liber Pontificalis. Mommsen, Theodor, ed. *Libri Pontificalis pars prior.* MGH, Gestorum Pontificum Romanorum. Berlin: Weidmann, 1898. Duchesne, L, and Cyrille Vogel, eds. *Liber Pontificalis.* Bibliothèque des Écoles Françaises d'Athènes et de Rome, 2ᵉ Série, 3. Paris: Ernest Thorin, & E. de Boccard, 1886–1957.

Liberian Catalogue. Mommsen, Theodor, ed. *Chronographus anni 354.* In *Chronica minora saec. IV, V, VI, VII (1).* MGH, Auctores Antiquissimi 9.1:73–76. Berlin: Weidmann, 1891.

Liebeschuetz, Wolfgang. "Epigraphic Evidence for the Christianization of Syria." In Fitz, J., ed. *Limes. Akten des XL internationalen Limeskongresses,* 485–508. Budapest: Akadémiai Kaidó, 1977.

Lightfoot, J. B. *Apostolic Fathers.* 2 vols. in 5 parts. 2nd Revised Edition. London: MacMillan & Co., 1889–90.

——. *Saint Paul's Epistles to the Colossians and to Philemon.* Revised Edition. London: Macmillan & Company, 1879; reprint Grand Rapids: Zondervan, 1959.

Lipsius, Ricardus Adelbertus, and Maximilianus Bonnet. *Acta Apostolorum Apocrypha.* 2 vols. in 3 parts. Leipzig: Mendelsson, 1891–1903; reprint Hildesheim: Olms, 1990.

Lordkipanidse, Otar. *Archäologie in Georgien von der Altsteinzeit zum Mittelalter.* Weinheim: VCH-Acta Humaniora, 1991.

Lordkipanidse, Otar, and Heinzgerd Brakmann. "Iberia II (Georgien)." In *RAC* 17 (1996): 12–106.

Louis, Réné. *Autessiodurum Christianum, Les églises d'Auxerre des origines au XIme siècle.* Paris: Clavreuil, 1952.

Lucian. *Satires.* Harmon, A. M., K. Kilburn, and M. D. MacLeod, ed. and trans. 8 vols. LCL. Cambridge: Harvard University Press, 1913–67.

Lüdemann, Gerd. "The Successors of Pre-70 Jerusalem Christianity: A Critical Evaluation of the Pella-Tradition." In Sanders, E. P., ed. *Jewish and Christian Self-Definition, Volume 1, the Shaping of Christianity in the Second and Third Centuries,* 161–73. Philadephia: Fortress, 1980.

MacMullen, Ramsay. *Christianizing the Roman Empire (A.D. 100–400).* New Haven: Yale University Press, 1984.

Madjarov, Mitco. "*Diocletianopolis,* ville paléochrétienne de Thrace." In *Actes du XIe Congrès international,* 3:2521–37.

Mai, Angelo. *Spicilegium Romanum.* Vol. 3. Rome: Typis Collegi Urbani, 1840.

Maier, Jean-Louis. *Le Dossier du Donatisme, Tome 1.* TU 134. Berlin: Akademie-Verlag, 1987.

MAMA. Monumenta Asiae Minoris Antiqua. William Moir Calder, *et al.,* eds. Multiple vols. Manchester & London: Manchester University Press and [later] Society for the Promotion of Roman Studies, 1928–.

Mandouze, André. *Prosopographie chrétienne du Bas-Empire.* Paris: CNRS, 1982.

Mansi, Joannes Domenicus. *Sacrorum conciliorum nova, et amplissima collectio.* Multiple vols. Florence: Expensis Antonii Zatta Veneti, 1759–; reprint Paris & Leipzig: H. Welter, 1901; reprint, Graz: Akademische Druck-U. Verlagsanstalt, 1960–61.

Marec, E., and H. I. Marrou. "Une inscription grecque chrétienne d'Hippone." In *Rivista di Archeologia Cristiana* 43 (1967): 165–76.

Mark the Deacon. *Marc le Diacre: Vie de Porphyre, évêque de Gaza.* Grégoire, Henri, and M.-A. Kugener, eds. Paris: Les Belles lettres, 1930.

Marrou, H., *et al.,* eds. *Recueil des inscriptions chrétiennes de la Gaul.* Paris: CNRS, 1975–.

Martin, Annick. *Athanase d'Alexandrie et l'Église d'Égypte au IVe siècle (328–73).* Collection de l'École Française de Rome 216. Rome: École Française de Rome, 1996.

———. "L'église et le khôra égyptienne au IVe siècle." In *Revue des études Augustiniennes* 25 (1979): 3–26.

———. "Aux origines de l'église copte: l'implantation et le développement du Christianisme en Égypte (I^e–IVe siècles)." In *Revue des études anciennes* 83 (1981): 35–56.

———. "Topographie et liturgie: le problème des 'Paroisses' d'Alexandrie." In *Actes du XIe Congrès international,* 1:1133–44.

Martinez Diez, Gonzalo, and Felix Rodriguez, eds. "Concilium Eliberritanum." In *La Coleccion Canonica Hispana, 4, Concilios Galos, Concilios Hispanas: Primera Parte,* 233–69. Monumenta Hispanae Sacrae, Serie Canonica 4. Madrid: Consejo Superior de Investigaciones Cientificas, 1984.

Martyrdom of Polycarp. See *Apostolic Fathers.*

Martyrion tou Agiou Klementos. Cotlier, J.-B., ed. PG 2:617–32. Paris: Migne, 1886.

Martyrium Sancti Apostolici Andreae. Bonnet, Max, ed. In *AB* 13 (1894): 353–71.

Martyrologium Hieronymianum. De Rossi, Iohannes Baptista and Ludovico Duchesne, eds. In *AASS,* Novembris 2.1 (1894). Also see Quentin, H[enri], and H[ippolyte] Delehaye, eds. In *AASS,* Novembris 2.2 (1931).

Martyrologium Hieronymianum Cambrense. Delehaye, Hippolyte, ed. *AB* 32 (1913): 369–407.

Martyrologium Romanum. Johnson, Cuthbert, and Anthony Ward, eds. Bibliotheca 'Ephemerides Liturgicae,' Subsidia 97. Rome: Sacrae Rituum Congregationis, 1956, reprint Rome: CLV-Edizioni Liturgiche, 1998. O'Connell, J. B., trans. *Roman Martyrology.* London: Burns and Oates, 1962.

Martyrologium Syriacum. Wright, W., ed. "An Ancient Syrian Martyrology." In *Journal of Sacred Literature* new series, 8 (1866): 45–56 & 423–32. Also see De Rossi, Iohanne Baptista, *et al.,* eds. "Breviarium Syriacum," in *AASS,* Novembris 2.1, lii–lxv. Also see Nau., F., ed. "Martyrologies et Ménologes Orientaux, I–XIII." PO 10:11–26. Paris: Firmin Didot, 1915.

Mattingly, David J. *Tripolitania*. London: B. T. Batsford, 1995.

Mawer, C. F. *Evidence for Christianity in Roman Britain, the small finds*. BAR, British Series, 243. London: Tempus Reparatum, 1995.

Mazzoleni, D. "Le ricerche di epigrafia cristiana in Italia (esclusa Roma)." In *Actes du XIe Congrès international*, 3:2273–2299.

M'charek, Ahmed. "Documentation épigraphique et croissance urbaine: l'example de *Mactaris* aux trois premiers siècles de l'ère chrétienne." *L'Africa romana*, 5, *Atti del II Convegno di Studio Sassari, 14–16 dicembre 1984*. (Rome: Gallizi, 1985).

Meeks, Wayne A. *The First Urban Christians*. New Haven: Yale University Press, 1983.

Meeks, Wayne A., and Robert L. Wilken. *Jews and Christians in Antioch in the First Four Centuries of the Common Era*. SBL Sources for Biblical Study 13. Missoula, MT: Scholars Press, 1978.

MEFRA. Mélanges de L'École Française de Rome, Antiquité.

Melito. *On Pascha and Fragments*. Hall, Stuart George, ed. Oxford Early Christian Texts. Oxford: Clarendon, 1979.

Mendel, Gustave. "Catalogue des monuments grecs romains et byzantins du Musée Impérial Ottoman de Brousse." In *BCH* 33 (1909): 245–435.

Menologium Basilianum. Migne, J.-P., ed. PG 117:9–614. Paris: Garnier Fratres, 1894.

Menologium Sirletianum. Canisius, Henricus, ed. "Martyrologium Graecorum." In Basnage, Jacobus, ed. *Thesaurus monumentorum ecclesiasticorum et historicorum*, 3.1: 409–520. Amsterdam: Rudolphum & Gerhardum Wetstenios, 1725.

Mercati, Giovanni. *Note de letteratura biblica e cristiana antica*. Studi e Testi 5. Rome: Typografia Vaticana, 1901.

Mesnage, J. *L'Afrique chrétienne: Évêchés & ruines antiques*. Paris: Ernest Leroux, 1913.

Methodius of Olympus. *De Resurrectione*. Bonwetsch, G. Nathanael, ed. *Methodius von Olympus, I, Schriften*, 70–289. Erlangen & Leipzig: Andr. Diechert'sche Verlagsbuchhandlung Nachf. (Georg Böhme), 1891. Later edition: Bonwetsch, G. Nathanael, ed. *Methodius*, 217–424. GCS 27. Leipzig: Hinrichs, 1917.

Metzger, Bruce M. *The Canon of the New Testament: Its Origin, Development, and Significance*. Oxford: Clarendon, 1987.

——. *The Early Versions of the New Testament: their Origin, Transmission, and Limitations*. Oxford: Clarendon, 1977.

——. *The Text of the New Testament: Its Transmission, Corruption, and Restoration*. 3rd Edition. New York: Oxford University Press, 1992.

Meyers, Eric M., and James F. Strange. *Archaeology, the Rabbis, and Early Christianity*. Nashville: Abingdon, 1981.

MGH, Auctores Antiquissimi. *Monumenta Germaniae Historica*, Auctores Antiquissimi.

MGH, Gesta Pontificum Romanorum. *Monumenta Germaniae Historica*, Gesta Pontificum Romanorum.

MGH, Poetae Latini. *Monumenta Germaniae Historica*, Poetae Latini Aevi Carolini.

MGH, Scriptores. *Monumenta Germaniae Historica*, Scriptores.

MGH, SRLI. *Monumenta Germaniae Historica*, Scriptores Rerum Langobardicarum et Italicarum, Saec. VI–IX.

MGH, SRM. *Monumenta Germaniae Historica*, Scriptores Rerum Merovingicarum.

Michael the Syrian. *Chronique de Michel le Syrien*. Chabot, J. B., ed. 4 vols. Paris: E. Leroux, 1899–1910, reprint Brussels: Culture et Civilisation, 1963.

Migotti, Branka. *Evidence for Christianity in Roman Southern Pannonia (Northern Croatia), a catalogue of finds and sites*. BAR International Series 684. Oxford: Archaeopress, 1997.

Mikhailov, Georgius. *Inscriptiones graecae in Bulgaria repertae*. Academia litterarum Bulgarica, Institutum archaeologicum, Series epigraphica 10. Sofia: in aedibus Typographicis Academiae litterarum Bulgaricae, 1958–1970.

Millar, Fergus. *The Roman Near East, 31 B.C.–A.D. 337*. Cambridge: Harvard University Press, 1993.

Mina, Togo. *Le Martyre d'Apa Epima*. Cairo: Imprimerie Nationale, Bulâq, 1937.

Mingana, A[lphonse]. "The Early Spread of Christianity in India." In *Bulletin of the John Rylands Library* 10 (1926): 535–510. Reprint in Ferguson, Everett, ed. *Studies in Early Christianity*, 12, *Missions and Regional Characteristics of the Early Church*, 289–364. New York and London: Garland, 1993.

Minucius Felix. *Octavius*. Kytzler, Bernhard, ed. Leipzig: Teubner, 1982.

Mirabella Roberti, M. "Memoriae paleocristiane nell' area aquileiense." In *Akten des VII Internationalen Kongresses*, 1:629–35.

Mirkovic, M., and Sloboden Dusanic. *Inscriptions de la Mésie Supérieure*. Vol. 1. Belgrade: Centre d'études épigraphiques et numismatiques, 1976.

Mitchell, Stephen. *Anatolia, Volume II, the Rise of the Church*. Oxford: Clarendon, 1993.

——. "The Life of Saint Theodotus of Ancyra." In *Anatolian Studies* 32 (1982): 93–113.

Mitchell, *RECAM*, II. Mitchell, Stephen, *et al.*, eds. *Regional Epigraphic Catalogues of Asia Minor*, II, *the Ankara District, the Inscriptions of North Galatia*. BAR International Series 135. Oxford: B.A.R., 1982.

Mitchell, Stephen, and Marc Waelkens. *Pisidian Antioch*. London: Duckworth and the Classical Press of Wales, 1998.

Mócsy, András. "Pannonia." In Pauly-Wissowa, Supplementband 9 (1962): cols. 516–776.

——. *Pannonia and Upper Moesia, a History of the Middle Danube Provinces of the Roman Empire*. London and Boston: Routledge and Kegan Paul, 1974.

Moffett, Samuel Hugh. *A History of Christianity in Asia*, I, *Beginnings to 1500*. San Francisco: Harper Collins, 1992.

Mombritius, Boninus. *Sanctuarium, seu Vitae sanctorum*. "duo monachi Solesmenses," eds. New Edition. 2 vols. Paris: Fontemoing et socios, 1910.

Mommsen, Theodor. *The Provinces of the Roman Empire*. Dickson, William P., trans. New York: Charles Scribner's Sons, 1909; reprint Barnes and Noble, 1996.

——. "Zur Lebensgeschichte des jüngeren Plinius." In *Hermes, Zeitschrift für klassische Philologie* 3 (1869): 31–139.

Monceaux, Paul. *Histoire littéraire de l'Afrique chrétienne*. 7 vols. Paris: Ernest Leroux, 1901–23; reprint Brussels: Culture et Civilisation, 1963.

Montina, Chiara, and Ornello Valetti. *I vescovi di Brescia, ricerca bibliografica*. Commentari dell' Ateneo di Brescia, Supplemento. Brescia: Ateneo di Brescia, Accademia di Scienze, Lettere ed Arti, 1987.

Moreau, J. *Dictionnaire de géographie historique de la Gaule et de la France*. Paris: Picard, 1972.

Moses Khorenats'i. *Patmut'iwn Hayots'*. Abelyan, M., and S. Yarut'iwnyan, eds. Tiflis: Hratarakchakan Masnazhoghov, 1913. Thomson, Robert W., trans. *Moses Khorenats'i, History of the Armenians*. Harvard Armenian Texts and Studies 4. Cambridge: Harvard University Press, 1978.

Munier, H. *Recueil des listes épiscopales de l'église Copte*. Cairo: Imprimerie de l'Institut Français d'archéologie orientale, 1943.

Munro-Hay, S[tuart] C. *Excavations at Aksum: an account of research at the ancient Ethiopian capital directed in 1972–4 by the late Dr. Neville Chittick*. London: British Institute in Eastern Africa, 1989.

——, and Bent Juel Jensen. *Aksumite Coinage*. London: Spink, 1995.

Muratorian Canon. Text in Hahneman, Geoffrey Mark. *The Muratorian Fragment and the Development of the Canon*, 6–7 & 9–10. Oxford: Clarendon, 1992. Translation in Metzger, *Canon*, 305–7.

Murphy-O'Connor, Jerome. *St. Paul's Corinth*. Good News Studies 6. Collegeville: Liturgical Press, 1983.

Musurillo, Herbert. *Acts of the Christian Martyrs*. Oxford: Clarendon, 1972; reprint [Oxford]: Sandpiper Books, 2000.

Nagy, Tibor. *A Pannoniai Kereszténység Története a Római Védorendszer Összeomlásáig*. Dissertationes Pannonicae, 2.12. Budapest: A Királyi Magyar Pázmány Péter Tudományegyetem Érem- És Régiségtani Intézete, 1939.

Naldini, Mario. *Il cristianesimo in Egitto*. New Edition. Fiesole: Nardini Editore, 1998.

Nau, F. "Analyse de la seconde partie inédite de l'Histoire Ecclésiastique de Jean d'Asie." In *Revue de l'Orient chrétien* 2 (1897): 453–93.

——. "Deux notices relatives au Malabar." In *Revue de l'Orient chrétien* 17 (1912): 74–99.

——. "Étude sur les parties inédites de la Chronique Ecclésiastique attribuée à Denys de Tellmahré." In *Revue de l'Orient chrétien* 2 (1897): 41–61.

Nautin, Pierre. *Origène, sa vie et ses oeuvres*. Paris: Beauchesne, 1979.

NEAEHL. New Encyclopedia of Archaeological Excavations in the Holy Land. Stern, Ephraim, ed. 2nd Edition. 4 vols. New York: Simon & Schuster, 1993.

Nesbitt, John W. "A Geographical and Chronological Guide to Greek Saints Lives." In *OCP* 35.2 (1969): 443–89.

Nesselhauf, Herbert, and Hans Lieb. "Dritter Nachtrag zu CIL XIII." In *Bericht der Römisch-Germanischen Kommission des Deutschen Archäologischen Instituts*, 40 (1959): 120–230.

Neusner, Jacob. *A History of the Jews of Babylonia, I. The Parthian Period*. Brown Judaic Studies 62. Leiden: Brill, 1969, reprint Chico, CA: Scholars Press, 1984.

Neuss, Wilhelm. *Die Anfänge des Christentums im Rheinlande*. 2nd Edition. Bonn: L. Rohrscheid, 1933.

Neuss, Wilhelm, and Friedrich Wilhelm Oediger. *Geschichte des Erzbistums Köln. 1. Das Bistum Köln von den Anfängen bis zum Ende des 12 Jahrhunderts*. Cologne: J. P. Bachem, 1964.

New Documents. New Documents Illustrating Early Christianity.

Nicephorus. *Chronographia syntomos*. De Boor, Carolus, ed. In *Opuscula Historica*, 79–135. Leipzig: Teubner, 1880.

Nicephorus Callistus. *Ecclesiastical History*. Ducaeus, Fronto, ed. PG 145: 559–147: 448. Paris, Sumptibus Sebastiani et Gabrielis Cramoisy, 1630; reprint, Paris: Migne, 1865–1904.

Nicetas Paphlagon. *Oratio IX, In laudem S. Philippi apost*. Migne, J.-P., ed. PL 105: 163–96. Paris: Migne, 1862.

Nikolajević, Ivanka. "Recherches nouvelles sur les monuments chrétiens de Serbie et du Monténégro." In *Actes du XIe Congrès international*, 3:2441–62.

Nock, A. D. *Conversion*. Oxford: Clarendon, 1933; reprint, Baltimore: Johns Hopkins University Press, 1998.

Nöldeke, Theodor. *Die von Guidi herausgegebene syrische Chronik*. Sitzungsberichte der Kaiserlichen Akademie der Wissenschaften, Philosophisch-Historische Classe, 128 Band, IX Abhandlung. Vienna: F. Tempsky, 1893.

Noll, Rudolf. *Frühes Christentum in Österreich*. Vienna: Franz Deuticke, 1954.

Nollé, Johannes. *Side im Altertum*. 2 vols. Inschriften griechischer Städte aus Kleinasien 43–44. Österreichische Akademie der Wissenschaften/Nordrhein-Westfälische Akademie der Wissenschaften. Bonn: Dr. Rudolf Habelt Gmbh., 1993–2001.

Noy, David. *Jewish Inscriptions of Western Europe*. 2 vols. Cambridge: Cambridge University Press, 1993–95.

Nussbaum, Otto. "Frühchristliche Funde in Deutschland." In *Atti del VI Congresso internazionale*, 95–108.

OCD. Oxford Classical Dictionary. Hornblower, Simon and Antony Spawforth, eds. 3rd Edition. Oxford and New York: Oxford University Press, 1996.

OCP. Orientalia Christiana Periodica.

ODCC. Oxford Dictionary of the Christian Church. Livingstone, E. A., ed. 3rd Edition. Oxford: Oxford University Press, 1997.

OEANE. Oxford Encyclopedia of Archaeology in the Near East. Meyers, Eric M., ed. 5 vols. New York and Oxford: Oxford University Press, 1997.

OGIS. Orientis Graeci inscriptiones selectae. Supplementum Sylloges inscriptionum graecarum. Dittenberger, Wilhelm, ed. 2 vols. Leipzig: S. Hirzel, 1903–05.

O'Leary, DeLacy. *The Saints of Egypt in the Coptic Calendar*. London: Church Historical Society, 1937; reprint Amsterdam: Philo Press, 1974.

Optatus. *S. Optati Milevitani Libri VII.* Ziwsa, Carolus, ed. CSEL 26. Prague, Vienna, and Leipzig: F. Tempsky & G. Freytag, 1893. Optat de Milève. *Traité contre les Donatistes.* Labrousse, Mirielle, ed. SC 412 & 413. 2 vols. Paris: Cerf, 1995–96. Optatus. *Against the Donatists.* Edwards, Mark, trans. and ed. Liverpool: Liverpool University Press, 1997.

Origen. *Commentarii in Epistolam ad Romanos.* Delarue, Carolus, and Carolus Vincentius Delarue, eds. In *Origenis Opera omnia,* 4. PG 14:833–1292. Paris: Migne, 1862.

———. *Commentary on John.* Blanc, Cécile, ed. *Commentaire sur Saint Jean.* 5 vols. SC 120, 157, 222, 290, 385. Paris: Cerf, 1966–92.

———. *Commentary on Matthew.* Klostermann, Erich, ed. *Origenes Werke,* 11, *Matthäuserklärung II, die Lateinische Übersetzung der Commentariorum series.* GCS 38. Leipzig: Hinrichs, 1933.

———. *Contra Celsum.* Borret, Marcel, ed. SC 132, 136, 147, 150, 227. Paris: Cerf, 1967–76.

———. *Homilies on Ezekiel.* Baehrens, W. A., ed. In *Origenes Werke,* 8:319–454. GCS 33. Leipzig: Hinrichs, 1925.

———. *Homilies on Luke.* Rauer, Max, ed. *Die Homilien zu Lukas. Origenes Werke,* 9. GCS 35. Leipzig: Hinrichs, 1930. Lienhard, Joseph T., trans. Fathers of the Church 94. Washington: Catholic University of America Press, 1996.

———. *Letter to Africanus.* De Lange, Nicholas, ed. In Harl, Marguerite, and Nicholas de Lange, eds. *Origène, Philocalie, 1–20, sur les Écritures et la Lettre à Africanus sur l'Histoire de Suzanne,* 514–73. SC 302. Paris: Cerf, 1983.

Orlandi, Tito. *Il dossier Copto del martire Psote.* Testi e documenti per lo studio dell' antichità 61. Milan: Cisalpino-Goliardica, 1978.

Ortiz de Urbina, Ignatius. *Patrologia Syriaca.* 2nd Edition. Rome: Pont. Institutum Orientalium Studiorum, 1965.

P. Achm. Collart, Paul, ed. *Les Papyrus grecs d'Achmîm à la Bibliothèque Nationale de Paris.* Bulletin de l'Institut français d'archéologie orientale, 31. Cairo: Imprimerie de l'Institut français d'archéologie orientale, 1930.

P. Amh. Grenfell, Bernard P., and Arthur S. Hunt, eds. *The Amherst papyri; being an account of the Greek papyri in the collection of the Right Hon. Lord Amherst of Hackney, F.S.A., at Didlington Hall, Norfolk.* 2 vols. London: Henry Frowde, 1900–1901.

P. Ant. Roberts, C. H., et al., eds. *The Antinopolis Papyri.* 3 vols. London: Egypt Exploration Society, 1950–67.

P. Berl. Bork. Borkowski, Zbigniew, ed. *Une description topographique des immeubles à Panopolis.* Warsaw: Panstwowe Wydawn Naukowe, 1975.

P. Coll. Youtie. Hanson, Ann Ellis, et al., eds. *Collectanea Papyrologica: Texts Published in Honor of H. C. Youtie.* Papyrologische Texte und Abhandlungen, 19–20. 2 vols. Bonn: Dr. Rudolf Habelt Gmbh., 1976.

P. Edgerton. Bell, H. Idris, and T. C. Skeat, eds. *Fragments of an Unknown Gospel and Other Early Christian Papyri.* London: Trustees of the British Museum, 1935.

P. Fay. Grenfell, Bernard P., Arthur S. Hunt, and David G. Hogarth. *Fayum Towns and their Papyri.* London: Egypt Exploration Society, 1900.

P. Genova. Zingale, Livia Migliardi, ed. *Papiri dell' Università di Genova (PUG II).* Papyrologica Florentina 6. Florence: Edizioni Gonelli, 1980.

P. Giss. Univ. Glaue, Paul, ed. *Mitteilungen aus der Papyrussammlung der Giessner Universitätsbibliothek.* Vol. 2. Giessen: Alfred Töpelmann, 1928.

P. Kell. Worp, K. A., ed. *Greek Papyri from Kellis, I.* Dakhleh Oasis Project, Monograph 3. Oxford: Oxbow Books, 1995.

P. Köln. Gronewald, Michael, et al., eds. *Kölner Papyri,* 6. Papyrologica Coloniensia 7. Opladen: Westdeutscher Verlag, 1987.

P. Lond. VI. Bell, H. Idris, ed. *Jews and Christians in Egypt.* London: British Museum, 1924.

P. Mich. Bonner, Campbell, ed. *A Papyrus Codex of the* Shepherd of Hermas *(Similitudes 2–9): with a Fragment of the* Book of Mandates. Ann Arbor: University of Michigan

Press, 1934. Also see Bonner, Campbell. "A New Fragment of the *Shepherd of Hermas* (Michigan Papyrus 44–H)." In *Harvard Theological Review*, 20 (1927): 105–116.

P. Oxy. Grenfell, Bernard P., and Arthur S. Hunt, *et al.*, eds. *Oxyrhynchus Papyri.* Vols. 1–. London: Egypt Exploration Fund, 1898–.

P. Ryl. Hunt, Arthur S., *et al. Catalogue of the Greek and Roman Papyri in the John Rylands Library at Manchester.* 4 vols. Manchester: Manchester University Press, 1911–52.

P. Wurzb. Wilcken, Ulrich. *Mitteilungen aus der Würzburger Papyrus-sammlung.* Berlin: Akademie der Wissenschaften, 1934.

Painter, K[enneth] S. "A Fourth-Century Christian Silver Treasure Found at Water Newton, England, in 1975." In *Rivista di Archeologia Cristiana* 51(1975): 333–45. Reprint in Finney, Paul Corbey, ed. *Studies in Early Christianity*, 18, *Art, Archaeology, and Architecture of Early Christianity*, 259–71. New York: Garland, 1993.

——. "Recent Discoveries in Britain." In *Actes du XIᵉ Congrès international*, 3:2031–71.

——. "Villas and Christianity in Roman Britain, Recent Finds 1962–69." In *Actas del VIII Congreso Internacional.* 1:149–66.

Palladius. *Dialogus de Vita S. Joannis Chrysostomi.* Malingrey, Anne-Marie, and Philippe LeClercq, eds. *Dialogue sur la vie de Jean Chrysostome.* SC 241–42. Paris: Cerf, 1988.

——. *Lausiac History of Palladius.* Butler, Cuthbert, ed. TS 6.1–2. Cambridge: Cambridge University Press, 1898–1004, reprint Nendeln/Liechtenstein: Kraus Reprint, 1967. Meyer, Robert T., trans. *Palladius: the Lausiac History.* Ancient Christian Writers 34. Westminster, MD: Newman Press, 1965.

Pallas, D. I. "Investigations sur les monuments chrétiens de Grèce avant Constantin." *Cahiers Archéologiques* 24 (1975): 1–19.

——. *Les monuments paléochrétiens de Grèce découverts de 1959 à 1973.* Sussidi allo studio delle antichità cristiane 5. Vatican City: Pontificio Instituto di Archeologia Cristiana, 1977.

Papaconstantinou, Arietta. *Le culte des saints en Égypte des Byzantins aux Abbasides, L'apport des inscriptions et des papyrus grecs et coptes.* Paris: CNRS Éditions, 2001.

Papadopoulis-Kerameos, A. *Analekta Ierosolymitikes Stakhyologias.* Vol. 1. Petroulei: ek tou typographeiou V. Kirsbaoum, 1891; reprint, Brussels: Culture et Civilisation, 1963.

Paris, Pierre. "Inscriptions d'Eumenia." *BCH* 8 (1884): 233–54.

Parker, S. Thomas. "The Roman Aqaba Project, The Economy of Aila on the Red Sea." In *Biblical Archaeologist* 59.3 (1996): 182.

Passio Sancti Ambrosii Centurionis. The work exists in two recensions. For recension one (*BHL*, 375), see *Catalogus codicum hagiographicorum latinorum antiquiorum saeculo xvii qui asservantur in Bibliotheca Nationali Parisiensi*, 3:546–48. Subsidia hagiographica 2. Brussels: Hagiographi Bollandiani, 1889–93. For recension two (*BHL*, 376), see Cappelletti, 6:392–95.

Paulinus of Milan. *Vita Ambrosii.* Bastiaensen, A. A. R., ed. In *Vite dei Santi*, 3:50–125. Mohrmann, Christine, ed. Fondazione Lorenzo Valla: Arnoldo Mondadori Editore, 1975.

Paulinus of Nola. *Carmina.* Hartel, Guilelmus de, and Margit Kemptner, eds. 2nd Edition. CSEL 30. Vienna: Österreichische Akademie der Wissenschaften, 1999.

——. *Epistulae.* Hartel, Guilelmus de, and Margit Kemptner, eds. CSEL 29. 2nd Edition. Vienna: Österreichische Akademie der Wissenschaften, 1999.

Paulovics, Stefano. "'Basilica ad scarabetensem portam' di S. Quirino in Savaria." In *Atti del IV Congresso Internazionale*, 2:49–63.

Pauly-Wissowa. *Paulys Real-Encyclopädie der Classischen Altertumswissenschaft.* Wissowa, Georg, and Wilhelm Kroll, *et al.*, eds. Stuttgart: J. B. Metzlersche Verlagsbuchhandlung, 1914–.

Pearson, Birger A. "Earliest Christianity in Egypt: Some Observations." In Pearson and Goehring (1986), 132–59.

——. *Gnosticism, Judaism, and Egyptian Christianity.* Philadelphia: Fortress Press, 1990.

Pearson, Birger A., and James E. Goehring. *The Roots of Egyptian Christianity.* Philadelphia: Fortress, 1986.

PECS. Princeton Encyclopedia of Classical Sites. MacDonald, William L., ed. Princeton: Princeton University Press, 1976.

Peek, Werner. *Griechische Vers-Inschriften, Band I, Grab-Epigramme.* Berlin: Akademie-Verlag, 1955.

Peeters, Paul. "Les débuts du Christianisme en Géorgie d'après les sources hagiographiques." In *AB* 50 (1932): 5–58.

——. "S. Demetrianus." In *AB* 42 (1924): 288–314.

Pelekanidis, S. "Die Malerei der Konstantinischen Zeit." In *Akten des VII Internationalen Kongresses,* 1:215–35.

Peraté, Andre. "Les Travaux récents d'archéologie chrétienne en France." In *Atti del III Congresso Internazionale,* 159–67.

Perdrizet, Paul. "Inscriptions de Thessalonique." *MEFRA* 20 (1900): 223–33.

Periplus Maris Erythraei. Casson, Lionel, ed. Princeton: Princeton University Press, 1989.

Perpetuus. *De Vigiliis.* In Gregory of Tours. *Historia Francorum,* 10.31.6.

Petrus Chrysologus. *Collectio Sermonum, Pars II.* Olivar, Alexandri, ed. CCSL, 24b. Turnhout: Brepols, 1982.

Peterson, Peter Megill. *Andrew, Brother of Simon Peter: His History and His Legends.* NovTSupp. 1. Leiden: Brill, 1958.

Petzl, Georg. *Die Inschriften von Smyrna.* 2 vols. Inschriften griechischer Städte aus Kleinasien 23–24. Österreichische Akademie der Wissenschaften/Nordrhein-Westfälische Akademie der Wissenschaften. Bonn: Dr. Rudolf Habelt Gmbh., 1982–1990.

Pfister, Friedrich. *Kleine Schriften zum Alexanderroman.* Beiträge zur Klassischen Philologie 61. Meisenheim am Glan: Verlag Anton Hain, 1976.

PG. Patrologiae Cursus Completus, Series Graeca.

PGM. Preisendanz, Karl, ed. *Papyri Graecae Magicae.* 3 vols. Leipzig: Teubner, 1928–41. Betz, H. Dieter, ed. and trans. *The Greek Magical Papyri in Translation, including the Demotic Spells.* Chicago: University of Chicago Press, 1986.

Phillipson, David W. *Archaeology at Aksum, Ethiopia (1993–7).* 2 vols. Memoirs of the British Institute in Eastern Africa, 17. Research Committee of the Society of Antiquaries of London, report 65. London: British Institute in Eastern Africa and the Society of Antiquaires of London, 2000.

Philostorgius. *Kirchengeschichte.* Bidez, Joseph, and Friedhelm Winkelmann, eds. GCS. 3rd Edition. Berlin: Akademie-Verlag, 1981. Walford, Edward, ed. and trans. In *The Ecclesiastical History of Sozomen,* 425–528. London: Henry G. Bohn, 1855.

Photius. *Bibliotheca.* Henry, René, ed. *Bibliothèque.* 9 vols. Paris: Les Belles lettres, 1959–91.

——. *Interrogationes decem.* Migne, J.-P., ed. PG 104:1219–32. Paris: Garnier Fratres, 1896.

Pilhofer, Peter. *Philippi.* 2 vols. Wissenschaftliche Untersuchungen zum Neuen Testament 87 & 119. Tübingen: Mohr Siebeck, 1995–2000.

Pitra, Joannes Baptista. *Analecta sacra spicilegio Solesmensi parata.* Venice: Mechitaristarum Sancti Lazari, 1883; reprint Farnborough: Gregg Press Limited, 1966.

PL. Patrologiae Cursus Completus, Series Latina.

Plasburg, O. "Strassburger Anekdota." In *Archiv für Papyrusforschung,* 2 (1903): 185–228.

Pliny the Elder. *Natural History.* Rackham, H., W. H. S. Jones, and D. E. Eichholz, ed. and trans. LCL. 10 vols. Cambridge: Harvard University Press, 1938–63.

Pliny the Younger. *Letters and Panegyricus.* Radice, Betty, ed. and trans. 2 Vols. LCL. Cambridge: Harvard University Press, 1969–75.

PO. Patrologia Orientalis.

Póczy, Klára. "Pannonian Cities." In Lengyel and Radan, 239–74.

Poinssot, L. and R. Lantier. "L'Archéologie chrétienne en Tunésie." In *Atti del III Congresso internazionale,* 387–410.

Poljakov, Fjodor B, ed. *Die Inschriften von Tralleis und Nysa, I, Die Inschriften von Tralleis.* Inschriften griechischer Städte aus Kleinasien 36.1. Österreichische Akademie der Wissenschaften/Nordrhein-Westfälische Akademie der Wissenschaften. Bonn: Dr. Rudolf Habelt Gmbh., 1989.

Polycarp. See *Apostolic Fathers*.

Popescu, Emilian. *Christianitas daco-romana: florilegium studiorum*. Bucharest: Editura Academiei Române, 1994.

———. *Inscripţiile greceşti şi latine din secolele IV–XIII descoperite în România*. Bucharest: Editura Academiei Republicii Socialiste România, 1976.

Potter, T. W. *Roman Italy*. Berkeley: University of California Press, 1987.

Praedestinatus. Sirmond, Jacobus, ed. PL 53:587–672. Paris: Migne, 1865.

Prieur, Jean Marc, ed. *Acta Andreae*. Corpus Christianorum, Series Apocryphorum 5–6. Turnhout: Brepols, 1989.

Pritz, Ray A. *Nazarene Jewish Christianity*. Jerusalem: Magnes Press, 1992.

Protevangelium Jacobi. Strycker, Émile de, ed. *La Forme la plus ancienne du Protévangile de Jacques*, 64–191. Subsidia hagiographica 33. Brussels: Société des Bollandistes, 1961.

Prudentius Clemens, Aurelius. *Peristephanon*. Thompson, H. J., ed. and trans. LCL. Cambridge: Harvard University Press, 1979.

PS. Patrologia Syriaca.

PSI. Pubblicazioni della Società Italiana per la ricerca dei papiri greci e latini.

PTS. Patristische Texte und Studien.

Quacquarelli, Antonio. "Note sulle origini di Canosa di Puglia, S. Leucio, e la catacomba inedita di S. Sofia." In *Atti del VI Congresso internazionale*, 321–47.

Quaesten, Johannes. *Patrology*. 3 vols. Utrecht: Spectrum, 1950; reprint, Westminster, Md.: Christian Classics, 1983. Vol. 4., Berardino, Angelo di, ed. Rome: Augustinian Patristic Institute, 1978; reprint Westminster, MD: Christian Classics, 1988.

RAC. Reallexikon für Antike und Christentum.

Radulescu, Adrian, and Virgil Lungu, "Le Christianisme en Scythie Mineure à la lumière des dernières découvertes archéologiques." In *Actes du XIe Congrès international*, 3:2561–2615.

Ramsay, A. Margaret. "Isaurian and East Phrygian Art in the Third and Fourth Centuries after Christ." In Ramsay, W. M., ed. *Studies in the History and Art of the Eastern Provinces of the Roman Empire*, 4–92. University of Aberdeen Studies 20. Aberdeen: Aberdeen University Press, 1906.

Ramsay, W. M. *The Church in the Roman Empire before A.D. 170*. Mansfield College Lectures, 1892. London: Hodder and Staughton, 1893.

———. "Cities and Bishoprics of Phrygia." In *JHS* 4(1883): 370–436.

———. *Cities and Bishoprics of Phrygia*. 2 parts. Oxford: Clarendon, 1895–97; reprint New York: Arno Press, 1975.

———. *Historical Geography of Asia Minor*. Royal Geographical Society, Supplementary Papers 4. London: John Murray, 1890; reprint, Amsterdam: Adolf M. Hakkert, 1962.

Raspi Serra, J. "Abitati e cimiteri Cristiani nella Tuscia." In *Atti del IX Congresso internazionale*, 2:417–23.

Raven, Susan. *Rome in Africa*. 3rd Edition. London and New York: Routledge, 1993.

RBK. Reallexikon zur byzantinischen Kunst. Wesel, Klaus, *et al.*, eds. Stuttgart: Anton Hiersmann, 1966–.

Rehm, Albert, ed. *Didyma, zweiter Teil, die Inschriften*. Berlin: Verlag Gbr. Mann, 1958.

———. *Milet, Ergebnisse der Ausgrabungen und Untersuchungen seit dem Jahre 1899*, I.9, *Thermen und Palaestren*. Berlin: Verlag von Hans Schoetz und Co., 1928.

Rendic-Miocevic, D. "Per una nuova interpretazione dell' epigrafe sepolcrale del Vescovo e 'Confessor' Parentino Mauro." In *Atti del IX Congresso internazionale*, 2:441–49.

Res Gestae Divi Saporis. Parallel Middle Persian, Parthian, and Greek versions may be found along with a German translation in Back, 284–371. For English translation, see Sprengling, 14–20.

Reymond, E. A. E., and J. W. B. Barns. *Four Martyrdoms from the Pierpont Morgan Coptic Codices*. Oxford: Clarendon, 1973.

Reynolds, Joyce. "The Christian Inscriptions of Cyrenaica." In *JTS*, n.s. 11 (1960): 284–94.

Rheinisches Landesmuseum Trier. *Trier, Kaiserresidenz und Bischofssitz: die Stadt in spätantiker und frühchristlicher Zeit.* Mainz am Rhein: Verlag Philip von Zabern, 1984.
RIS. Rerum Italicarum Scriptores. Vol. 11.1. Carducci, Giosue, and Vittorio Fiorini, eds. New Edition. Città di Castello: Coi tipi dell'editore S. Lupi, 1903.
Rives, J. B. *Religion and Authority in Roman Carthage from Augustus to Constantine.* Oxford: Clarendon, 1995.
Rivet, A. L. F. *Gallia Narbonensis.* London: B. T. Batsford, 1988.
Rizzardi, Clementina. *I sarcofagi paleocristiani con rappresentazione del passagio del Mar Rosso.* Saggi d'arte e d'archeologia 2. Faenza: Fratelli Lega Editori, 1970.
Robert, Louis. *Hellenica, Recueil d'épigraphie de numismatique et d'antiquités grecques.* Volume 4. Paris: Libraire d'Amérique et d'Orient, 1948.
Roberts, Colin H. *Manuscript, Society, and Belief in Early Christian Egypt.* Schweich Lectures, 1977. London: Oxford University Press for the British Academy, 1979.
Robinson, James A. *The Nag Hammadi Library in English.* 3rd Edition. San Francisco: Harper Collins, 1988.
Robinson, Thomas A. *The Bauer Thesis Examined.* Lewiston/Queenston: Edward Mellen Press, 1988.
Romanelli, Pietro. *La Cirenaica romana.* Verbania: A. Airoldi, 1943.
——. "Le sedi episcopali della Tripolitania antica." In *Atti della Pontificia Accademia romana di archeologia (Serie III), Rendiconti,* 4 (1926): 155–66.
Römer, Cornelia. "Christliche Texte (1989–August 1996)." In *Archiv für Papyrusforschung,* 43.1 (1997): 107–45.
——. "Christliche Texte II (1996–97)." In *Archiv für Papyrusforschung,* 44.1 (1998): 129–39.
——. "Christliche Texte (1998–99) mit einem Nachtrag aus dem Jahr 1992." In *Archiv für Papyrusforschung* 46.2 (2000): 302–308.
Roques, Denis. *Synésios de Cyrène et la Cyrénaïque du Bas-Empire.* Paris: CNRS, 1987.
Ross, Steven K. *Roman Edessa.* London and New York: Routledge, 2001.
Rossi, Francesco. "I martirii di Gioore, Heraei, Epimaco e Ptolomeo con altri frammenti, trascriti e tradotti dai papiri copti del museo Egizio de Torino." *Memorie della Reale Accademia delle Scienze di Torino.* Ser. 2. [Scienze morali, storichi, e filologici]. 38 (1888), 233–308.
Rowe, Alan. *Cyrenaican Expeditions of the University of Manchester, 1952, 1956, and 1957.* Manchester: Manchester University Press, 1959.
Rubenson, Samuel. *The Letters of St. Antony.* Minneapolis: Fortress, 1995.
Rufinus. *Ecclesiastical History.* Schwartz, Eduard and Theodor Mommsen, eds. In *Eusebius Werke,* 2.1–2.3. GCS 9.1–9.3. Leipzig: Hinrichs, 1903–1909. Amidon, Philip R., partial trans. *The Church History of Rufinus of Aquileia, Books 10 and 11.* Oxford: Oxford University Press, 1997.
Ruinart, Theodoricus. *Acta martyrum.* 5th Edition. Regensburg: G. Josephi Manz, 1859.
Rutgers, Leonard V. *Subterranean Rome.* Louvain: Peeters, 2000.
S. Pachomii Vita. Lefort, L. Th, ed. In *S. Pachomii vita, Bohairice scripta.* CSCO 89, Scriptores Coptici 7. Reprint Louvain: Imprimerie Orientaliste L. Durbecq, 1953. Lefort, L. Th, ed. *S. Pachomii vitae, Sahidice scriptae.* CSCO 99–100, Scriptores Coptici 9–10. Reprint Louvain: Imprimerie Orientaliste L. Durbecq, 1952. Halkin, François. *Sancti Pachomii vitae Graecae.* Subsidia hagiographica 19. Brussels: Société des Bollandistes, 1932). For English translation, see Veilleux. For French translation, see Lefort.
S&D. Studies and Documents.
Sacco, Giulia. *Iscrizioni Greche d'Italia, Porto.* Rome: Edizioni di Storia e Letteratura, 1984.
Şahin, Sencer. *Die Inschriften von Arykanda.* Inschriften griechischer Städte aus Kleinasien 48. Österreichische Akademie der Wissenschaften/Nordrhein-Westfälische Akademie der Wissenschaften. Bonn: Dr. Rudolf Habelt Gmbh., 1994.
——. *Die Inschriften von Perge,* I. Inschriften griechischer Städte aus Kleinasien 54. Österreichische Akademie der Wissenschaften/Nordrhein-Westfälische Akademie der Wissenschaften. Bonn: Dr. Rudolf Habelt Gmbh., 1999.

Sahinian, Alexandre. "Recherches Scientifiques sous les voûtes de la cathédrale d'Étchmiadzine." *Revue des études arméniennes*, New Series, 3 (1966): 39–71.

Salama, Pierre. "Le plus ancien chrisme officiel de l'Afrique Romaine." In *Atti del VI Congresso internazionale*, 537–43.

Sammelbuch. Sammelbuch Griechischer Urkunden aus Ägypten.

Sanie, Silviu. "Kulte und Glauben im römischen Süden der Moldau (Ostrumänien)." In *ANRW*, II.18.2:1272–1316.

Sartre, Maurice. *Bostra, des origines à l'Islam.* BAH 117. (Paris: Libraire Orientaliste de Paul Geuthner, 1985).

Savio, Fedele. *Gli antichi vescovi d'Italia dalle origini al 1300 descritti per regioni. Il Piemonte.* Biblioteca istorica della antica e nuova Italia 139. Turin: Fratelli Bocca, 1899; reprint Bologna: Forni Editore, 1971.

———. *Gli antichi vescovi d'Italia dalle origini al 1300 descritti per regioni. La Lombardia, parte 1, Milano.* Biblioteca istorica della antica e nuova Italia 111. Florence: Libreria Editrice Fiorentina, 1913; reprint Bologna: Forni Editore, 1971.

———. "La légende des SS. Faustin et Jovite." *AB* 15 (1896): 5–72, 113–159, & 377–99.

Saxer, Victor *Vie liturgique et quotidienne à Carthage vers le milieu du IIIe siècle.* Studi di Antichità Cristiana 29. Vatican City: Pontificio Instituto di Archeologia Cristiana, 1969.

———. "Pilgerwesen in Italien un Rom in Späten Altertum und Fruhmittelalter." In *Akten des XII Internationalen Kongresses*, 1:36–57.

———. "L'utilisation par la liturgie dans l'espace urbain et suburbain: l'exemple de Rome dans l'antiquité et le haut moyen-âge." In *Actes du XIe Congrès international*, 2:917–1033.

Sayar, Mustafa Hamdi. *Die Inschriften von Anazarbos und Umgebung*, 1. Inschriften griechischer Städte aus Kleinasien 56. Österreichische Akademie der Wissenschaften/ Nordrhein-Westfälische Akademie der Wissenschaften. Bonn: Dr. Rudolf Habelt Gmbh., 2000.

———. *Perinthos—Herakleia (Marmara Ereğlesi) und Umgebung.* Österreichische Akademie der Wissenschaften, Philosophisch-Historische Klasse, Denkschriften 269. Veröffentlichungen der Kleinasiatischen Kommission, nr. 9. Vienna: Österreichische Akademie der Wissenschaften, 1998.

SC. Sources Chrétiennes.

Scheiber, Sándor. *Jewish Inscriptions in Hungary. Corpus inscriptionum Hungariae Judaicarum.* Budapest & Leiden: Akadémiai Kaidó & Brill, 1983.

Schermann, Theodor. *Propheten und Apostellegenden, nebst Jüngerkatalogen des Dorotheus und Verwandter Texte.* TU 3rd Series 1.3 (*i.e.*, 31.3 of the full set). Leipzig: Hinrichs, 1907.

———. *Prophetarum vitae fabulosae; Indices apostolorum discipulorumque Domini, Dorotheo, Epiphanio, Hippolyto aliisque vindicata.* Leipzig: Teubner, 1907.

Schillinger-Häfele, Ute. "Vierter Nachtrag zu CIL XIII." In *Bericht der Römisch-germanischen Kommission des Deutschen Archäologischen Instituts*, 58 (1977): 447–603.

Schneemelcher, Wilhelm. *New Testament Apocrypha.* Wilson, R. McL., trans. Revised Edition. 2 vols. Cambridge & Louisville: James Clarke & Co., and Westminster/John Knox, 1991–92.

Schneider, Roger. "L'Inscription Chrétienne d'Ezana en écriture Sudarabe." *Annales d'Éthiopie* 10 (1976): 109–117.

———. "Trois nouvelles inscriptions royales d'Axoum." In *IV Congresso internazionale di studi etiopici (Roma, 10–15 aprile 1972)*, 1:767–86 & plates. Rome: Accademia Nazionale dei Lincei, 1974.

Schoedel, William R. *Ignatius of Antioch.* Hermeneia. Philadelphia: Fortress, 1985.

Schürer, Emil. *History of the Jewish People in the Age of Jesus Christ.* Vol. 3.1. Vermes, Geza, Fergus Millar, and Martin Goodman, rev. and ed. Edinburgh: T & T Clark, 1986.

Schwartz, Edvardus. *Acta Conciliorum Oecomenicorum*, 1.5, *Concilium Universale Ephesenum.* Berlin: Walter de Gruyter, 1924–26.

Schwertheim, Elmar. *Die Inschriften von Hadrianoi und Hadrianeia.* Inschriften griechischer Städte aus Kleinasien 33. Österreichische Akademie der Wissenschaften/Nordrhein-Westfälische Akademie der Wissenschaften. Bonn: Dr. Rudolf Habelt Gmbh., 1987.

Scriptores historiae Augustae. Magie, David, trans. LCL 139, 140, 263. Cambridge: Harvard University Press, 1921–32.

Sebeos. *Patmut'iwn Sebeosi.* Abgaryan, G. V., ed. Erevan: Haykakan SSH Gitut'yunneri Akademiayi Hratarakch'ut'yun, 1979. "Primary History," trans. in Robert W. Thomson. *Moses Khorenat'si: History of the Armenians,* 357–68. Harvard Armenian Texts and Studies 4. Cambridge: Harvard University Press, 1978. "Chronology," partially summarized in Toumanoff, "Third-Century," 76–79. "History of Herakleos," trans. in Robert W. Thomson, James Howard-Johnston, and Tim Greenwood. *The Armenian History attributed to Sebeos.* 2 vols. Translated Texts for Historians 31. Liverpool: Liverpool University Press, 1999.

SEC. Synaxarium ecclesiae Constantinopolitanae. Delehaye, H., ed. In *AASS,* Novembris, propylaeum. Brussels: Socii Bollandiniani, 1902.

SEG. Supplementum epigraphicum graecum.

Segal, J. B. *Edessa, the Blessed City.* Oxford: Clarendon, 1970.

Sent. Episcop. 87. Sententiae Episcoporum numero 87. Hartel, Wilhelm, ed. In *S. Thasci Caecili Cypriani Opera omnia,* 435–461. CSEL 3.1. Vienna: C. Geroldi, 1868.

Sergew Hable Selassie. *Ancient and Medieval Ethiopian History to 1270.* Addis Ababa: United Printers, 1972.

Series Patriarcharum Aquilegiensium. O. Holder-Egger, ed. In *MGH,* Scriptores 13:367–68. Hannover: Hahn, 1881.

Severus of al-Ashmunein. *Histoire des conciles (Second livre).* Leroy, L. and S. Grebaut, eds. PO 6:465–640. Paris: Firmin-Didot, 1911.

Shahid, Irfan. *Rome and the Arabs: a Prolegomenon to the Study of Byzantium and the Arabs.* Washington: Dumbarton Oaks, 1984.

Shepherd of Hermas. See *Apostolic Fathers.*

Simeon Metaphrastes. *Certamen Sancti Martyris Callinici.* In *Vitae sanctorum.* Migne, J.-P., ed. PG 115:477–88. Paris: Garnier Fratres, 1899.

———. *Martyrium S. Martyris Christi Autonomi.* In *Vitae sanctorum.* Migne, J.-P., ed. PG 115:692–97. Paris: Garnier Fratres, 1899.

———. *Martyrium S. Thyrsi et sociorum.* In *Vitae sanctorum.* Migne, J.-P., ed. PG 116: 508–560. Paris: Garnier Fratres, 1891.

———. *Martyrium SS. Martyrum Leonis et Paregorii.* In *Vitae sanctorum.* Migne, J.-P., ed. PG 114: 1452–62. Paris: Garnier Fratres, 1903.

———. *Martyrum sanctorum martyrum Indae et Domnae.* In *Vitae sanctorum.* Migne, J.-P., ed. PG 116:1037–81. Paris: Garnier Fratres, 1891.

———. *Spasaniie mira ot bytiia I lietovnik.* Sreznevskij, V. I., ed. St. Petersburg: Izdanie Imperatorskoe Akademia Nauk, 1905; reprint with introduction by Robert Zett, Munich: Wilhelm Fink Verlag, 1971.

———. *Vita S. Clementis Martyris.* In *Vitae sanctorum.* Migne, J.-P., ed. PG 116:179–190. Paris: Garnier Fratres, 1891.

Simon, Marcel. *Verus Israel.* MacKeating, H., trans. Oxford: The Littman Library and Oxford University Press, 1986.

Simonyi, D. "Sul origine del toponimo 'Quinque Ecclesiae' de Pecs." In *Acta antiqua Academiae Scientiarum Hungaricae* 8 (1960): 165–184.

Snyder, Gradon F. *Ante Pacem: Archaeological Evidence of Church Life before Constantine.* Macon, GA: Mercer University Press, 1985.

Socrates. *Kirchengeschichte.* Hansen, Günther Christian, ed. GCS, N.F. 1. Berlin: Akademie-Verlag, 1995.

Sonje, Ante. "Il complesso della prima basilica nella zona della Basilica Eufrasina di Parenzo." In *Atti del VI Congresso internazionale,* 799–806.

Sonje, Ante. "Sarcofagi paleocristiani dell' Istria." In *Actas del VIII Congreso Internacional,* 485–99.

Soriano Sanchez, Ráfaella. "L'édifice cultique de la prison de Saint Vincent à Valence/Espagne." In *Akten des XII Internationalen Kongresses*, 2:1193–1201.

Sotomayor [y Muro], Manuel. *Datos historicos sobre los sarcofagos Romano-Cristianos de España*. Granada: University of Granada, 1973.

——. "Dos Fragmentos Ineditos de un Sarcofago Paleocristiano en Jerez de la Frontera." In *Habis* 8 (1977): 399–406 & plates 35–36.

——. "La Iglesia en la España Romana." In Villoslada, Ricardo Garcia, ed. *Historia de la Iglesia en España, I, La Iglesia en la España romana y visigoda (siglos I–VIII)*, 1–400. Biblioteca de Autores Cristianos, maior 16. Madrid: EDICA, 1979.

——. "Leyenda y realidad en los origenes del cristianismo hispano." In *Proyección* 36, no. 154 (1989), 179–98.

——. "Sarcofagos paleocristianos en Murcia y zonas limitrofes." In González Blanco, Antonio, ed. *Arte Poblamiento en el SE Penensular durante los ultimos siglos de Civilizacion Romana*, 165–84. Antigüedad y Cristianismo 5. Murcia: Universidad de Murcia, 1988.

——. *Sarcofagos Romano-Cristianos de España, Estudio Iconográfico*. Granada: Facultad de Teologia, 1975.

——. "Sarcofagos Romano-Cristianos de España, Notas de Cronologia." In *Actas del VIII Congreso Internacional*, 501–509.

Sourdel, Dominique. *Les cultes du Hauran à l'époque romaine*. BAH 53. Paris: Imprimerie Nationale & Paul Guenthner, 1952.

Sozomen. *Kirchengeschichte*. Bidez, Joseph, and Günther Christian Hansen, eds. 2nd Edition. GCS, N.F., 4. Berlin: Akademie-Verlag, 1995.

Sprengling, Martin. *Third Century Iran: Sapor and Kartir*. Chicago: University of Chicago Oriental Institute, 1953.

Squarciapino, Maria Floriani. "La Sinagoga di Ostia." In *Atti del VI Congresso internazionale*, 299–315.

Stark, Rodney. *The Rise of Christianity, a Sociologist Reconsiders History*. Princeton: Princeton University Press, 1996.

Stikas, Elias. "La basilique cémétériale récemment découverte à Corinth." In *Atti del VI Congresso Internazionale*, 471–79.

Stoian, Iorgu. *Inscripţiile din Scythia Minor Greceşti şi Latini, 2, Tomis şi Teritoriul Său*. Bucharest: Editura Academiei Republicii Socialiste România, 1987.

Stoneman, Richard. *Palmyra and its Empire: Zenobia's Revolt against Rome*. Ann Arbor: University of Michigan Press, 1992.

Strack, H. L., and G. Stemberger. *Introduction to the Talmud and Midrash*. Bockmuehl, Marcus, trans. Edinburgh: T & T Clark, 1991.

Strange, James F., Dennis E. Groh, and Thomas R. W. Longstaff. "Excavations at Sepphoris: The Location and Identification of Shikhin." In *IEJ* 44 (1994): 216–27, and 45 (1995): 171–87.

Struve, Vasilii Vasil'evich. *Korpus bosporskikh nadpisei/Corpus Inscriptionum Regni Bosporani*. Moscow and Leningrad: "Nauka," 1965.

Studia Pontica. Anderson, John George Clark, *et al.*, eds. Vol. 3. *Recueil des inscriptions grecques et latines du Pont et de l'Arménie*. Brussels: H. Lamertin, 1910.

Suetonius. *De vita Caesarum*. Rolfe, J. C., ed. and trans. 2 vols. LCL. Cambridge: Harvard University Press, 1913–14; reprint 1989–92.

Sulpicius Severus. *Chronicon*. Halm, Carolus, ed. In *Sulpicii Severi libri qui supersunt*, 1–105. CSEL 1. Vienna: C Geroldi, 1866.

——. *Dialogus*. Halm, Carolus, ed. In *Sulpicii Severi opera qui supersunt*, 152–216. CSEL 1. Vienna: C. Geroldi, 1866. Also edited by Augello, Giuseppe. Palermo: Manfredi, [1969].

——. *Vita Sancti Martini*. Halm, Carolus, ed. In *Sulpicii Severi opera qui supersunt*, 107–137. CSEL 1. Vienna: C. Geroldi, 1866. Also edited by Smit, Jan W., in *Vite Dei Sancti, 4, Vita di Martino, Vita di Ilarione, in Memoria di Paolo*, 4: 1–67. Mohrmann, Christine, ed. [Milan]: Fondazione Lorenzo Valla, 1975.

Surius, Laurentius. *De probatis sanctorum historiis.* 7 vols. Coloniae Agrippinae: apud Geruinum Calenium & haeredes Quintelios, 1570–81.

Syll.³ Sylloge inscriptionum graecarum. Dittenberger, Wilhelm, ed. 3rd Edition. 4 vols. Leipzig: apud S. Hirzelium, 1915–1924.

Synaxarium Alexandrinum. Text edited by Forget, I[acobus]. CSCO 47–49 & 67, Scriptores Arabici 3–5 & 11. Trans., Forget, I[acobus]. CSCO 78 & 90, Scriptores Arabici 12–13. Louvain: Peeters, 1905–32. English abstracts in O'Leary.

Synesius of Cyrene. *Epistles.* Garzya, Antonio, ed. In *Synésios de Cyrène,* 2–3, *Correspondance.* 2 vols. Collection des universités de France. Paris: Les Belles lettres, 2000.

Tabbernee, William. *Montanist Inscriptions and Testimonia.* Patristic Monograph Series 16. Macon, GA: Mercer University Press, 1997.

———. "Portals of the Montanist New Jerusalem: The Discovery of Pepouza and Tymion." In *Journal of Early Christian Studies* 11 (2003): 87–93.

Tacheva-Hitova, Margarita. *Eastern Cults in Moesia Inferior and Thracia.* Leiden: Brill, 1983.

Tacitus. *Annals.* Jackson, John, ed. and trans. 2 vols. LCL. Cambridge: Harvard University Press, 1937; reprint 1986–91.

Talbert, Richard J. A., ed. *Barrington Atlas of the Greek and Roman World.* One volume atlas and two-volume map-by-map directory. Princeton and Oxford: Princeton University Press, 2000.

TAM. Tituli Asiae Minoris. Kalinka, Ernestus, *et al.,* eds. Multiple vols. Vienna: Alfredi Hoelder & Academia Scientiarum Austriaca, 1920–.

Tchalenko, Georges. *Églises syriennes à bêma.* BAH 105.3. Paris: Paul Geunthner, 1990.

———. *Villages antiques de la Syrie du Nord.* 3 vols. BAH 50. Paris: Paul Geunthner, 1953–58.

Tertullian. *Ad nationes.* Borleffs, J. G. Ph., ed. In *Tertulliani opera,* 1:9–76. CCSL 1–2. Turnhout: Brepols, 1954.

———. *Ad Scapulam.* Dekkers, E., ed. In *Tertulliani opera,* 2:1125–32. CCSL 1–2. Turnhout: Brepols, 1954.

———. *Adversus Iudaeos.* Kroymann, Aem., ed. In *Tertulliani opera,* 2:1337–96. CCSL 1–2. Turnhout: Brepols, 1954.

———. *Adversus Marcionem.* Kroymann, Aem., ed. In *Tertulliani opera,* 1:437–730. CCSL 1–2. Turnhout: Brepols, 1954.

———. *Apologeticum.* Dekkers, E., ed. In *Tertulliani opera,* 1:77–172. CCSL 1–2. Turnout: Brepols, 1954.

———. *De fuga in persecutione.* Thierry, J. J., ed. In *Tertulliani opera,* 2:1133–56. CCSL 1–2. Turnhout: Brepols, 1954.

———. *De monogamia.* Dekkers, E., ed. In *Tertulliani opera,* 2:1227–53. CCSL 1–2. Turnhout: Brepols, 1954.

———. *De pallio.* Gerlo, A., ed. In *Tertulliani opera,* 2:731–50. CCSL 1–2. Turnout: Brepols, 1954.

———. *De praescriptione haereticorum.* Refoulé, R. F., ed. In *Tertulliani opera,* 1:185–224. CCSL 1–2. Turnhout: Brepols, 1954.

———. *Scorpiace.* Reifferscheid, A. and G. Wissowa., eds. In *Tertulliani opera,* 2:1067–98. CCSL 1–2. Turnhout: Brepols, 1954.

———. *De virginibus velandis.* Dekkers, E., ed. In *Tertulliani opera,* 2:1207–26. CCSL 1–2. Turnhout: Brepols, 1954.

Testini, P., *et al.* "La Cattedrale in Italia." In *Actes du XIᵉ Congrès international,* 1:5–229.

Thee, Francis C. R. *Julius Africanus and the Early Christian View of Magic.* Tübingen: Mohr, 1974.

Theissen, Gerd. *Social Reality and the Early Christians.* Kohl, Margaret, trans. Minneapolis: Fortress Press, 1992.

Theodore of Mopsuestia. *Commentary on Paul.* Swete, H. B., ed. *In epistolas B. Pauli commentarii.* 2 vols. Cambridge: Cambridge University Press, 1880–82.

Theodoret. *Correspondance.* Schwartz, E. and Yvan Azéma, eds. 4 vols. SC 40, 98, 111, 429. Paris: Cerf, 1955–98.

———. *Ecclesiastical History.* Parmentier, Leon, ed. Hansen, Günther Christian, rev. *Kirchengeschichte.* 3rd Edition. GCS, N.F. 5. Berlin: Akademie Verlag, 1998.

———. *Interpretatio epistolae ad Philippenses.* [Marriott, Charles, and E. B. Pusey], eds. In *Theodoreti episc. Cyri, Commentarius in omnes B. Pauli Epistolas,* 2:43–67. 2 vols. Bibliotheca Patrum Ecclesiae Catholicae. Oxford: J. H. Parker, 1852–70.

Theophylact of Ohrid. *Martyrium SS. Quindecim Illustrium Martyrum.* Migne, J.-P., ed. PG 126: 152–221. Paris: Garnier Fratres, [1902].

Thomas, Charles. *Christianity in Roman Britain to A.D. 500.* Berkeley: University of California Press, 1981.

———. "Churches in Late Roman Britain." In Rodwell, Warwick, ed. *Temples, Churches, and Religion in Roman Britain,* 1:125–64. BAR British Series 77. Oxford: B.A.R., 1980.

Thomas, Edit B. "Das frühe Christentum in Pannonien im Lichte der archäologischen Funde." In *Severin, zwischen Römerzeit und Volkerwanderung,* 255–93. Linz: Land Oberösterreich, Amt der Oö. Landesregierung, Abt. Kultur, 1982.

———. "Martyres Pannoniae." In *Atti del IX Congresso internazionale,* 615–20.

———. "Religion." In Lengyel and Radan, 177–206.

———. "Villa Settlements." In Lengyel and Radan, 275–321.

Thomsen, Peter. *Loca Sancta.* Halle: Rudolf Haupt, 1907; reprint Hildesheim: Olms, 1966.

Thouvenot, Raymond. *Essai sur la province romaine de Bétique.* Bibliothèque des Écoles Françaises d'Athènes et de Rome 149. Paris: Boccard, 1940.

———. "Fouilles à Ligugé (Vienne-France)." In *Akten des VII Internationalen Kongresses,* 1:739–44.

———. "Les origines chrétiennes en Maurétanie Tingitane." In *Revue des études anciennes* 71 (1969): 354–78.

———. "Statuette d'ivoire trouvée à Volubilis (Maroc)." In *Société de Géographie et d'Archéologie [de la province] d'Oran, Bulletin* 60 (1939): 137–44.

TIB. Tabula Imperii Byzantini. Hunger, Hubert, *et al.,* eds. Multiple vols. Österreichische Akademie der Wissenschaften, Philosophisch-Historische Klasse, Denkschriften. (Vienna: Österreichische Akademie der Wissenschaften, 1976–).

Tilley, Maureen A. *Donatist Martyr Stories.* Translated Texts for Historians 24. Liverpool: Liverpool University Press, 1996.

Timm, Stefan. *Das christlich-koptische Ägypten in arabischer Zeit.* 6 vols. Wiesbaden: Dr. Ludwig Reichert Verlag, 1984–92.

TIRJP. Tabula Imperii Romani/Iudaea-Palaestina. Tsafrir, Yoram, Leah DiSegni, and Judith Green, eds. Jerusalem: Israel Academy of Sciences and Humanities, 1994.

Tisserant, Eugene. *Eastern Christianity in India.* Hambye, E. R., trans. London: Longmans, Green and Co., 1957.

TLG. Thesaurus Linguae Graecae. CD ROM #E. Irvine, CA: University of California, 1999.

Tomaschitz, Kurt. *Unpublizierte Inschriften Westkilikiens aus dem Nachlass Terrence B. Mitfords.* Ergänzungsbände zu den Tituli Asiae Minoris, nr. 21. Österreichische Akademie der Wissenschaften, Philosophisch-Historische Klasse, Denkschriften 264. Vienna: Österreichische Akademie der Wissenschaften, 1998.

Tosefta. Zuckermandel, Moshe Shmuel, ed. Pasewalk: bi-Defus Yissakhar Yitshak Meir, 1880/81; reprint, Jerusalem: Sifrei Wahrman, 1970. Neusner, Jacob, *et al.,* trans. *Tosefta.* 6 vols. New York: KTAV, 1977–86.

Toumanoff, Cyril. *Studies in Christian Caucasian History.* Washington: Georgetown University Press, 1963.

———. "The Third-Century Armenian Arsacids, a Chronological and Genealogical Commentary." *Revue des études arméniennes* 6 (1969): 233–81.

Treu, Kurt. "Christliche Papyri [I–XVI]." In *Archiv für Papyrusforschung* 19–37 (1978–91), *passim.*

Trimingham, J. Spencer. *Christianity among the Arabs in Pre-Islamic Times*. London and Beirut: Longman Group and Libraire du Liban, 1979; reprint Beirut: Libraire du Liban, 1990.

TS. Texts and Studies.

TU. Texte und Untersuchungen.

Turner, C. H. *Ecclesiae occidentalis monumenta iuris antiquissima*. 2 volumes in 7 parts. Oxford: Clarendon, 1899–1939.

Turner, Robin. *Excavation of an Iron Age Settlement and Roman Religious Complex at Ivy Chimneys, Witham, Essex 1978–83*. East Anglian Archaeology 88. Chelmsford: Essex County Council, Heritage Conservation, 1999.

Ubl, Hannsjörg, "Frühchristliches Österreich." In *Severin, zwischen Römerzeit und Völkerwanderung*, 295–336. Linz: Land Oberösterreich, Amt der Oö. Landesregierung, Abt. Kultur, 1982.

Ughelli, Ferdinand. *Italia sacra sive de episcopis Italiae*. Coleti, Nicolai, ed. 2nd Edition. 10 vols. in 9. Venice: apud Sebastianum Coleti, 1717–22; reprint Nendeln: Kraus reprint, 1970.

Ugolini, Luigi M. *Butrinto, il mito d'Enea gli scavi*. Rome: Istituto Grafico Tiberino, 1937.

Ulman, Alojzija. "Le Christianisme à Cibalae (Vinkovci)." In *Acta XIII Congressus Internationalis*, 3:759–60.

Usuard. *Le martyrologe d'Usuard, texte et commentaire*. DuBois, Jacques, ed. Subsidia hagiographica 40. Brussels: Société des Bollandistes, 1965.

Van der Meer, F., and Christine Mohrmann. *Atlas of the Early Christian World*. Hedlund, Mary F., and H. H. Rowley, ed. London: Thomas Nelson and Sons Ltd., 1958.

Van der Straeten, Joseph. "Les actes des martyrs d'Aurelien en Bourgogne." *AB* 79 (1961): 115–44.

Van Minnen, Peter. "The Earliest Account of a Martyrdom in Coptic." In *AB* 113 (1995), 13–38.

———. "The Roots of Egyptian Christianity." In *Archiv für Papyrusforschungen* (1994): 71–85.

Veilleux, Armand. *Pachomian Koinonia, 1, The Life of Saint Pachomius*. Cistercian Studies 45. Kalamazoo: Cistercian Publications, 1980.

Velkov, Velizar. *Cities in Thrace and Dacia in Late Antiquity (Studies and Materials)*. Amsterdam: Adolf M. Hakkert, 1977.

Venantius Fortunatus. *Carmina*. Leo, Fridericus, ed. *MGH*, Auctores Antiquissii 4.1: 1–292. Berlin: Weidmann, 1881.

———. *Vita Sancti Martini*. Leo, Fridericus, ed. *MGH*, Auctores Antiquissimi 4.1: 293–370. Berlin: Weidmann, 1881.

Versus de episcopis Mettensis civitatis Quomodo Sibi ex ordine successerunt. Duemmler, Ernestus, ed. *MGH*, Poetae Latini 1:60–61. Berlin: Weidmann, 1881.

Veselý, J. M. "Saint' Erasmo di Formia o di Ochrida?" In *Actes du Xᵉ Congrès international*, 680–91.

Victorinus, episcopi Petavionensis. *Commentarii in Apocalypsin*. Haussleiter, Iohannes, ed. In *Victorini episcopi Petavionensis Opera*, 11–154. CSEL 49. Vienna & Leipzig: F. Tempsky & G. Freytag, 1916; reprint, New York: Johnson Reprint Corporation, 1965.

Viletta Masana, Josep. "Les Voyages et les correspondances à caractère religieux entre l'Hispanie et l'extérieur selon la prosopographie chrétienne (300–589)." In *Akten des XII Internationalen Kongresses*, 2:1125–61.

Villoslada, Ricardo Garcia, ed. *Historia de la Iglesia en España, I, La Iglesia en la España romana y visigoda (siglos I–VIII)*. Biblioteca de Autores Cristianos, maior 16. Madrid: EDICA, 1979.

Vita Caecilii Cypriani. Hartel, G., ed. In *S. Thasci Caecili Cypriani opera omnia*, cx–cx. CSEL 3.3. Vienna: C. Geroldi, 1871.

Vita Lupi episcopi Trecensis. Krusch, Bruno, and W. Levison, eds. *MGH*, SRM 7: 284–302. Hannover and Leipzig: Hahn, 1920.

Vita Sancti Epiphanii. Migne, J.-P., ed. PG 41:23–114. Paris: Migne, 1863.

Vitricius of Rouen. *De laude sanctorum.* J. P. Migne, ed. PL 20:443–58. Paris: Migne, 1845.

Vives, Jose. *Inscripciones Cristianas de la España Romana y Visigoda.* 2nd Edition. Monumenta Hispaña Sacra, Series Patristica 2. Barcelona: Consejo Superior de Investigaciones Cientificas-Instituto Enrique Florez, 1969.

Vivian, Tim. *Saint Peter of Alexandria, Bishop and Martyr.* Studies in Antiquity and Christianity. Philadelphia: Fortress, 1988.

Waddington, W. H., [and Philippe LeBas]. *Inscriptions grecques et latines de la Syrie.* Paris: F. Didot, 1870; reprint Rome: Bretschneider, 1968.

Waelkens, Marc. *Die kleinasiatischen Türsteine.* Mainz: Philipp von Zabern, 1986.

Wallace-Hadrill. D. S. *Christian Antioch, a Study of Early Christian Thought in the East.* Cambridge: Cambridge University Press, 1982.

Wallis Budge, E. A. *The Book of the Saints of the Ethiopian Church.* 4 vols. Cambridge: Cambridge University Press, 1928.

Walter, Christopher. "The Portrait of Saint Paraskeve." In *Byzantinoslavica* 56 (1995): 753–57 & plates xxv–xliv.

Walters, C. C. *Monastic Archaeology in Egypt.* Warminster: Aris & Phillips, 1974.

Ward Perkins, J. B. "The Role of the Craftsmanship in the Formation of Early Christian Art." In *Atti del IX Congresso internazionale,* 1:637–52.

Warmington, E. H. *The Commerce between the Roman Empire and India.* 2nd Edition. Cambridge: Cambridge University Press, 1974; reprint New Delhi: Mushiram Manoharlal Publishers, 1995.

Watts, Dorothy. *Christians and Pagans in Roman Britain.* New York: Routledge, 1991.

Weidemann, Margarete. "Itinerare des Westlichen Raumes." In *Akten des XII Internationalen Kongresses,* 1: 389–451.

Wellesz, Egon. *Eastern Elements in Byzantine Chant.* Monumenta musicae Byzantinae, subsidia 2. Oxford: Oxford University Press for the Byzantine Institute, 1947.

Wessely, Charles. *Les plus anciens monuments du Christianisme écrits sur papyrus.* PO 4.2: 95–210. Paris: Firmin Didot, 1908.

Wheeler, Robert Eric Mortimer. *Rome Beyond the Imperial Frontiers.* London: Bell, 1954.

White, L. Michael. *The Social Origins of Christian Architecture.* 2 vols. HTS 42. Valley Forge: Trinity Press International, 1996–97.

Whittaker, C. R. *Frontiers of the Roman Empire, a Social and Economic Study.* Baltimore and London: Johns Hopkins University Press, 1994.

Wiessner, Gernot. *Untersuchungen zur syrischen Literaturgeschichte, I, Zur Märtyrerüberlieferung aus der Christenverfolgung Schapurs II.* Abhandlungen der Akademie der Wissenschaften in Göttingen, Philologisch-Historische Klasse, Dritte Folge, Nr. 67. Göttingen: Vandenhoeck & Ruprecht, 1967.

Wightman, Edith Mary. *Gallia Belgica.* London: B. T. Batsford, 1985.

Wigram, W. A. *An Introduction to the History of the Assyrian Church.* London: SPCK, 1910.

Wilcken, Ulrich. "Plinius' Reisen in Bithynien und Pontus." In *Hermes, Zeitschrift für klassische Philologie* 49 (1914): 120–36.

Wilken, Robert L. *The Christians as the Romans Saw Them.* New Haven: Yale University Press, 1984.

Wilkes, J[ohn] J. *Dalmatia.* Cambridge: Harvard University Press, 1969.

——. *The Illyrians.* Oxford and Cambridge, Blackwell, 1992.

Wilpert, Giuseppe. *I Sarcofagi Cristiani Antichi.* 3 vols. in 5 parts. Rome: Pontificio Istituto di Archeologia Cristiana, 1929–36.

Wilpert, Joseph. "Die altchristlichen Inschriften Aquileias." In *Acta Primi Congressus,* 49–58.

Wischmeyer, Wolfgang. "The Sociology of pre-Constantine Christianity: Approach from the Visible." In Kreider, Alan, ed. *Origins of Christendom in the West,* 121–52. Edinburgh & New York: T & T Clark, 2001.

Wolff, H. J. "Römisches Provinzialrecht in der Provinz Arabia." *ANRW* II.13: 763–806.

Wordsworth, Johannes, Henrico Juliano White, *et al.*, eds. *Novum Testamentum Domini Nostri Iesu Christi Latine secundum editionem Sancti Hieronymi.* 3 vols. Oxford: Clarendon, 1889–1954.

World Atlas. 2nd Edition. Moscow: Chief Administration of Geodesy and Cartography under the Council of Ministers of the USSR, 1967.

Wright, W. *Apocryphal Acts of the Apostles.* 2 vols. London and Edinburgh: Williams and Norgate, 1871; reprint Amsterdam: Philo Press, 1968; reprint Hildesheim: Olms, 1990. Syriac text is volume 1; translation is volume 2.

Wright, W. *Catalogue of the Syriac Manuscripts in the British Museum.* Vol. 3. London: The British Museum, 1872.

Yamauchi, Edwin M. *New Testament Cities in Western Asia Minor.* Grand Rapids: Baker, 1980.

Zeiller, Jacques. *Les origines chrétiennes dans la province romaine de Dalmatie.* Studia Historica 47. Paris: Bibliothèque de l'École des Hautes Études, 1906; reprint, Rome: Bretschneider, 1967.

Zeiller, Jacques. *Les origines chrétiennes dans les provinces danubiennes de l'Empire Romaine.* Studia Historica 48. Paris: Boccard, 1918; reprint, Rome: Bretschneider, 1967.

Zeno Veronensis. *Tractatus.* Löfstedt, B., ed. CCSL 22. Turnhout: Brepols, 1971.

ZPE. Zeitschrift für Papyrologie und Epigraphik.

Zovatto, P. L. "Un incunabulo dell' architettura tardoantica, la trichora de Concordia." In *Akten des VII Internationalen Kongresses,* 753–80.

Zucca, Raimondo. *La Corsica romana.* Oristano: Editrice S'Alvure, 1996.

GEOGRAPHICAL INDEX OF ANCIENT
AND MODERN NAMES

SUPPLEMENTS TO VIGILIAE CHRISTIANAE

1. Tertullianus. *De idololatria*. Critical Text, Translation and Commentary by J.H. Waszink and J.C.M. van Winden. Partly based on a Manuscript left behind by P.G. van der Nat. 1987. ISBN 90 04 08105 4

2. Springer, C.P.E. *The Gospel as Epic in Late Antiquity*. The *Paschale Carmen* of Sedulius. 1988. ISBN 90 04 08691 9

3. Hoek, A. van den. *Clement of Alexandria and His Use of Philo in the* Stromateis. An Early Christian Reshaping of a Jewish Model. 1988.
   ISBN 90 04 08756 7

4. Neymeyr, U. *Die christlichen Lehrer im zweiten Jahrhundert.* Ihre Lehrtätigkeit, ihr Selbstverständnis und ihre Geschichte. 1989.
   ISBN 90 04 08773 7

5. Hellemo, G. *Adventus Domini.* Eschatological Thought in 4th-century Apses and Catecheses. 1989. ISBN 90 04 08836 9

6. Rufin von Aquileia. *De ieiunio* I, II. Zwei Predigten über das Fasten nach Basileios von Kaisareia. Ausgabe mit Einleitung, Übersetzung und Anmerkungen von H. Marti. 1989. ISBN 90 04 08897 0

7. Rouwhorst, G.A.M. *Les hymnes pascales d'Éphrem de Nisibe.* Analyse théologique et recherche sur l'évolution de la fête pascale chrétienne à Nisibe et à Édesse et dans quelques Églises voisines au quatrième siècle.
   2 vols: I. Étude; II. Textes. 1989. ISBN 90 04 08839 3

8. Radice, R. and D.T. Runia. *Philo of Alexandria.* An Annotated Bibliography 1937–1986. In Collaboration with R.A. Bitter, N.G. Cohen, M. Mach, A.P. Runia, D. Satran and D.R. Schwartz. 1988. repr. 1992.
   ISBN 90 04 08986 1

9. Gordon, B. *The Economic Problem in Biblical and Patristic Thought.* 1989.
   ISBN 90 04 09048 7

10. Prosper of Aquitaine. *De Providentia Dei.* Text, Translation and Commentary by M. Marcovich. 1989. ISBN 90 04 09090 8

11. Jefford, C.N. *The Sayings of Jesus in the Teaching of the Twelve Apostles.* 1989.
    ISBN 90 04 09127 0

12. Drobner, H.R. and Klock, Ch. *Studien zu Gregor von Nyssa und der christlichen Spätantike.* 1990. ISBN 90 04 09222 6

13. Norris, F.W. *Faith Gives Fullness to Reasoning.* The Five Theological Orations of Gregory Nazianzen. Introduction and Commentary by F.W. Norris and Translation by Lionel Wickham and Frederick Williams. 1990.
    ISBN 90 04 09253 6

14. Oort, J. van. *Jerusalem and Babylon.* A Study into Augustine's *City of God* and the Sources of his Doctrine of the Two Cities. 1991.
    ISBN 90 04 09323 0

15. Lardet, P. *L'Apologie de Jérôme contre Rufin.* Un Commentaire. 1993.
    ISBN 90 04 09457 1

16. Risch, F.X. *Pseudo-Basilius: Adversus Eunomium IV-V.* Einleitung, Übersetzung und Kommentar. 1992. ISBN 90 04 09558 6

17. Klijn, A.F.J. *Jewish-Christian Gospel Tradition.* 1992. ISBN 90 04 09453 9

18. Elanskaya, A.I. *The Literary Coptic Manuscripts in the A.S. Pushkin State Fine Arts Museum in Moscow.* ISBN 90 04 09528 4

19. Wickham, L.R. and Bammel, C.P. (eds.). *Christian Faith and Greek Philosophy in Late Antiquity.* Essays in Tribute to George Christopher Stead. 1993. ISBN 90 04 09605 1

20. Asterius von Kappadokien. *Die theologischen Fragmente.* Einleitung, kritischer Text, Übersetzung und Kommentar von Markus Vinzent. 1993. ISBN 90 04 09841 0

21. Hennings, R. *Der Briefwechsel zwischen Augustinus und Hieronymus und ihr Streit um den Kanon des Alten Testaments und die Auslegung von Gal. 2,11-14.* 1994. ISBN 90 04 09840 2

22. Boeft, J. den & Hilhorst, A. (eds.). *Early Christian Poetry.* A Collection of Essays. 1993. ISBN 90 04 09939 5

23. McGuckin, J.A. *St. Cyril of Alexandria: The Christological Controversy.* Its History, Theology, and Texts. 1994. ISBN 90 04 09990 5

24. Reynolds, Ph.L. *Marriage in the Western Church.* The Christianization of Marriage during the Patristic and Early Medieval Periods. 1994. ISBN 90 04 10022 9

25. Petersen, W.L. *Tatian's Diatessaron.* Its Creation, Dissemination, Significance, and History in Scholarship. 1994. ISBN 90 04 09469 5

26. Grünbeck, E. *Christologische Schriftargumentation und Bildersprache.* Zum Konflikt zwischen Metapherninterpretation und dogmatischen Schrift-beweistraditionen in der patristischen Auslegung des 44. (45.) Psalms. 1994. ISBN 90 04 10021 0

27. Haykin, M.A.G. *The Spirit of God.* The Exegesis of 1 and 2 Corinthians in the Pneumatomachian Controversy of the Fourth Century. 1994. ISBN 90 04 09947 6

28. Benjamins, H.S. *Eingeordnete Freiheit.* Freiheit und Vorsehung bei Origenes. 1994. ISBN 90 04 10117 9

29. Smulders s.j., P. (tr. & comm.). *Hilary of Poitiers' Preface to his* Opus historicum. 1995. ISBN 90 04 10191 8

30. Kees, R.J. *Die Lehre von der* Oikonomia *Gottes in der* Oratio catechetica *Gregors von Nyssa.* 1995. ISBN 90 04 10200 0

31. Brent, A. *Hippolytus and the Roman Church in the Third Century.* Communities in Tension before the Emergence of a Monarch-Bishop. 1995. ISBN 90 04 10245 0

32. Runia, D.T. *Philo and the Church Fathers.* A Collection of Papers. 1995. ISBN 90 04 10355 4

33. De Coninck, A.D. *Seek to See Him.* Ascent and Vision Mysticism in the Gospel of Thomas. 1996. ISBN 90 04 10401 1

34. Clemens Alexandrinus. *Protrepticus.* Edidit M. Marcovich. 1995. ISBN 90 04 10449 6

35. Böhm, T. *Theoria – Unendlichkeit – Aufstieg.* Philosophische Implikationen zu *De vita Moysis* von Gregor von Nyssa. 1996. ISBN 90 04 10560 3

36. Vinzent, M. *Pseudo-Athanasius, Contra Arianos IV.* Eine Schrift gegen Asterius von Kappadokien, Eusebius von Cäsarea, Markell von Ankyra und Photin von Sirmium. 1996. ISBN 90 04 10686 3

37. Knipp, P.D.E. *'Christus Medicus' in der frühchristlichen Sarkophagskulptur.* Ikonographische Studien zur Sepulkralkunst des späten vierten Jahrhunderts. 1998. ISBN 90 04 10862 9

38. Lössl, J. *Intellectus gratiae.* Die erkenntnistheoretische und hermeneutische Dimension der Gnadenlehre Augustins von Hippo. 1997.
ISBN 90 04 10849 1

39. Markell von Ankyra. *Die Fragmente. Der Brief an Julius von Rom.* Herausgegeben, eingeleitet und übersetzt von Markus Vinzent. 1997.
ISBN 90 04 10907 2

40. Merkt, A. *Maximus I. von Turin.* Die Verkündigung eines Bischofs der frühen Reichskirche im zeitgeschichtlichen, gesellschaftlichen und liturgischen Kontext. 1997. ISBN 90 04 10864 5

41. Winden, J.C.M. van. *Archè.* A Collection of Patristic Studies by J.C.M. van Winden. Edited by J. den Boeft and D.T. Runia. 1997.
ISBN 90 04 10834 3

42. Stewart-Sykes, A. *The Lamb's High Feast.* Melito, *Peri Pascha* and the Quartodeciman Paschal Liturgy at Sardis. 1998. ISBN 90 04 11236 7

43. Karavites, P. *Evil, Freedom and the Road to Perfection in Clement of Alexandria.* 1999.
ISBN 90 04 11238 3

44. Boeft, J. den and M.L. van Poll-van de Lisdonk (eds.). *The Impact of Scripture in Early Christianity.* 1999. ISBN 90 04 11143 3

45. Brent, A. *The Imperial Cult and the Development of Church Order.* Concepts and Images of Authority in Paganism and Early Christianity before the Age of Cyprian. 1999. ISBN 90 04 11420 3

46. Zachhuber, J. *Human Nature in Gregory of Nyssa.* Philosophical Background and Theological Significance. 1999. ISBN 90 04 11530 7

47. Lechner, Th. *Ignatius adversus Valentinianos?* Chronologische und theologiegeschichtliche Studien zu den Briefen des Ignatius von Antiochien. 1999.
ISBN 90 04 11505 6

48. Greschat, K. *Apelles und Hermogenes.* Zwei theologische Lehrer des zweiten Jahrhunderts. 1999. ISBN 90 04 11549 8

49. Drobner, H.R. *Augustinus von Hippo:* Sermones ad populum. Überlieferung und Bestand – Bibliographie – Indices. 1999. ISBN 90 04 11451 3

50. Hübner, R.M. *Der paradox Eine.* Antignostischer Monarchianismus im zweiten Jahrhundert. Mit einen Beitrag von Markus Vinzent. 1999.
ISBN 90 04 11576 5

51. Gerber, S. *Theodor von Mopsuestia und das Nicänum.* Studien zu den katechetischen Homilien. 2000. ISBN 90 04 11521 8

52. Drobner, H.R. and A. Viciano (eds.). *Gregory of Nyssa: Homilies on the Beatitudes.* An English Version with Commentary and Supporting Studies. Proceedings of the Eighth International Colloquium on Gregory of Nyssa (Paderborn, 14-18 September 1998) 2000 ISBN 90 04 11621 4

53. Marcovich, M. (ed.). *Athenagorae qui fertur* De resurrectione mortuorum. 2000. ISBN 90 04 11896 9

54. Marcovich, M. (ed.). *Origenis: Contra Celsum Libri VIII.* 2001.
ISBN 90 04 11976 0

55. McKinion, S. *Words, Imagery, and the Mystery of Christ*. A Reconstruction of Cyril of Alexandria's Christology. 2001. ISBN 90 04 11987 6

56. Beatrice, P.F. *Anonymi Monophysitae* Theosophia, *An Attempt at Reconstruction*. 2001. ISBN 90 04 11798 9

57. Runia, D.T. *Philo of Alexandria:* An Annotated Bibliography 1987-1996. 2001. ISBN 90 04 11682 6

58. Merkt, A. *Das Patristische Prinzip*. Eine Studie zur Theologischen Bedeutung der Kirchenväter. 2001. ISBN 90 04 12221 4

59. Stewart-Sykes, A. *From Prophecy to Preaching*. A Search for the Origins of the Christian Homily. 2001. ISBN 90 04 11689 3

60. Lössl, J. *Julian von Aeclanum*. Studien zu seinem Leben, seinem Werk, seiner Lehre und ihrer Überlieferung. 2001. ISBN 90 04 12180 3

61. Marcovich, M. (ed.), adiuvante J.C.M. van Winden, *Clementis Alexandrini* Paedagogus. 2002. ISBN 90 04 12470 5

62. Berding, K. *Polycarp and Paul*. An Analysis of Their Literary and Theological Relationship in Light of Polycarp's Use of Biblical and Extra-Biblical Literature. 2002. ISBN 90 04 12670 8

63. Kattan, A.E. *Verleiblichung und Synergie*. Grundzüge der Bibelhermeneutik bei Maximus Confessor. 2002. ISBN 90 04 12669 4

64. Allert, C.D. *Revelation, Truth, Canon, and Interpretation*. Studies in Justin Martyr's Dialogue with Trypho. 2002. ISBN 90 04 12619 8

65. Volp, U. *Tod und Ritual in den christlichen Gemeinden der Antike*. 2002. ISBN 90 04 12671 6

66. Constas, N. *Proclus of Constantinople and the Cult of the Virgin in Late Antiquity*. Homilies 1-5, Texts and Translations. 2003. ISBN 90 04 12612 0

67. Carriker, A. *The Library of Eusebius of Caesarea*. 2003. ISBN 90 04 13132 9

68. Lilla, S.R.C. *Neuplatonisches Gedankengut in den 'Homilien über die Seligpreisungen' Gregore von Nyssa*. 2004. ISBN 90 04 13684 3

69. Mullen, R.L. *The Expansion of Christianity*. A Gazetteer of its First Three Centuries. 2004. ISBN 90 04 13135 3

70. Hilhorst , A. *The Apostolic Age in Patristic Thought*. 2004. ISBN 90 04 12611 2

Distribution

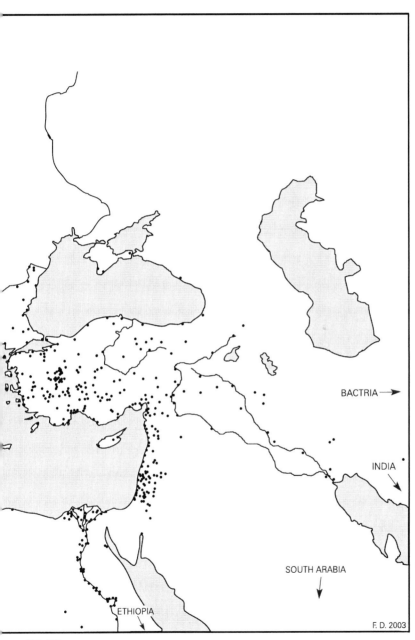

BACTRIA⟶

INDIA

SOUTH ARABIA

ETHIOPIA

F. D. 2003

es to 325 C.E.